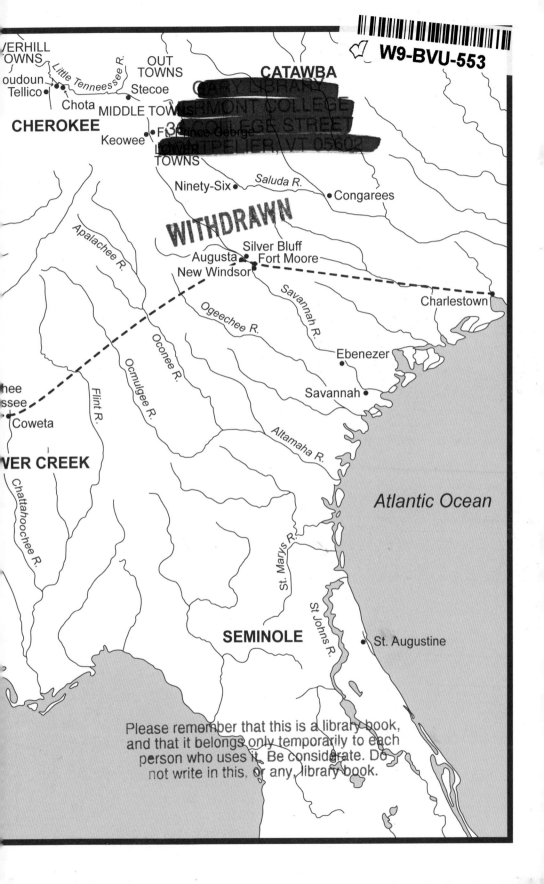

OVERHILL TOWNS
oudoun
Tellico
Little Tenneessee R.
Chota
OUT TOWNS
Stecoe
CATAWBA

CHEROKEE
MIDDLE TOWNS
Keowee
Fort Prince George
LOWER TOWNS

Ninety-Six
Saluda R.
Congarees

WITHDRAWN

Augusta
New Windsor
Silver Bluff
Fort Moore

Charlestown

Apalachee R.
Ogeechee R.
Savannah R.
Oconee R.
Ocmulgee R.
Ebenezer

Savannah

Flint R.
Altamaha R.

hee ssee
Coweta

VER CREEK

Chattahoochee R.

Atlantic Ocean

St. Marys R.

St Johns R.
SEMINOLE
St. Augustine

GARY LIBRARY
VERMONT COLLEGE
36 COLLEGE STREET
MONTPELIER, VT 05602

W9-BVU-553

Please remember that this is a library book,
and that it belongs only temporarily to each
person who uses it. Be considerate. Do
not write in this, or any, library book.

THE HISTORY OF THE AMERICAN INDIANS

THE HISTORY OF THE AMERICAN INDIANS

by JAMES ADAIR

Edited and with an Introduction and Annotations
by KATHRYN E. HOLLAND BRAUND

THE UNIVERSITY OF ALABAMA PRESS
Tuscaloosa

973.25
A191h
2005

65.00

Copyright © 2005
The University of Alabama Press
Tuscaloosa, Alabama 35487-0380
All rights reserved
Manufactured in the United States of America

Typeface: Bembo

∞

The paper on which this book is printed meets the minimum requirements of American National Standard for Information Science–Permanence of Paper for Printed Library Materials, ANSI Z39.48–1984.

Library of Congress Cataloging-in-Publication Data

Adair, James, ca. 1709–1783.
    The history of the American Indians / by James Adair ; edited and with an introduction and annotations by Kathryn E. Holland Braund.
        p. cm.
    Originally published: London : Edward and Charles Dilly, 1775.
    Includes bibliographical references and index.
    ISBN 0-8173-1393-1 (cloth : alk. paper)
    1. Indians of North America—Southern States. 2. Indians of North America—Origin. I. Braund, Kathryn E. Holland, 1955– II. Title.
    E78.S65A65 2005
    973.2′5—dc22

                                                                    2004009056

Contents

Illustrations and Maps

Acknowledgments

Special appreciation is extended to the following manuscript repositories and libraries that provided documents and information from their collections: American Philosophical Society, Philadelphia, Pennsylvania; South Caroliniana Library, University of South Carolina, Columbia; South Carolina Department of Archives and History, Columbia; Charleston Library Society, Charleston, South Carolina; William L. Clements Library, University of Michigan, Ann Arbor; Georgia Historical Society, Savannah; Library of Congress, Washington, D.C.; Public Record Office, Kew, England; Birmingham Public Library, Birmingham, Alabama; Alabama Department of Archives and History, Montgomery; and the American Antiquarian Society, Worcester, Massachusetts.

The following people graciously responded to written request for information on Adair-related materials at their repositories: Charles Lesser and Robert Mackintosh, of the South Carolina Department of Archives and History; Henry G. Fulmer and Robin Copp of the South Caroliniana Library; Jerry Wager, Rare Book and Special Collections Division of the Library of Congress; Edward C. Shoemaker, Director, Library Resources Division, Oklahoma Historical Society; Norwood Kerr, Alabama Department of Archives and History; Kayla Barrett, Georgia Department of Archives and History; Catherine Sadler, Librarian of the Charleston Library Society; and Yvonne Crumpler of the Birmingham Public Library. Special thanks to Ellen Garrison and Special Collections of the University of Alabama Library for permission to use their copy of Adair's book for editorial purposes. I am indebted to each for their prompt responses and cheerful expert assistance. I am also grateful to Dana Franklin of the Horseshoe Bend Regional Library who helped me obtain microfilm via interlibrary loan, and to that same end, I thank Dennis McNew and Ernest J. Emrich of the Library of Congress for helping me locate microfilm in their collections. I also thank the staff of Auburn University's Ralph Brown Draughon Library for their assistance in procuring rare books via interlibrary loan. A special note of appreciation is due to Sarah Mattics, who produced the map.

Greg O'Brien, James Atkinson, Gregory A. Waselkov, James Taylor Carson, Ed Cashin, Josh Piker, Jason Baird Jackson, John Hall, and Tim Atkins were the recipients of questions relating to obscure details that defied safe answers, and I thank them for their thoughtful replies.

Leon Weinberger graciously provided information on Adair's Hebrew. Special thanks to Steven L. Jacobs for assistance in proofreading the Hebrew. Kyle G. Braund and Kirk Summers of the University of Alabama provided translations for the many Latin phrases used by Adair, as did Margaret Sanke and Mary Kuntz of Auburn University. Patricia B. Kwachka provided insights on Adair's Chickasaw and Choctaw. A Marguerite Scharnagel Award from the Auburn University Department of History provided partial funding for research in South Carolina.

I would also like to thank Judith Knight, of the University of Alabama Press, for her assistance in technical aspects of transforming eighteenth-century pages into modern word processing format by the magic of scanning, and I especially thank her for her unending patience.

Patricia Galloway, Ed Cashin, and Gregory A. Waselkov provided helpful comments on an earlier draft of the manuscript. Kyle G. Braund provided assistance at every stage of the endeavor, including accompanying me to distant libraries and reading and proofing many versions of the manuscript. Any errors and omissions in the background research and the final transcription are all my own.

I would especially like to thank Professor Robin F. A. Fabel, who long ago introduced me to James Adair and set me on the path toward the eighteenth-century backcountry.

Kathryn E. Holland Braund
Dadeville, Alabama

James Adair's *History of the American Indians*
A Note on This Edition

In the spring of 1775, James Adair's *History of the American Indians* was re-leased by publishers Edward and Charles Dilly of London. The book was actually a study of the major tribes residing adjacent to Britain's southern colonies, particularly the Cherokee, Chickasaw, Creek, and Choctaw Indians. In addition to providing a survey of southern Indian history from the 1740s through the 1760s, a review of the book in the May 1775 issue of *London Magazine* promised "an Account of their Origin, Manners, Religious and Civil Customs, and other Particulars sufficient to render it a complete Indian System." Central to that goal was a carefully formulated thesis, consisting of twenty-three arguments, proposing to prove that the Indians of America were of Hebrew descent. Specific chapters devoted to the history of each major southern tribe followed. The book concluded with an appendix bearing advice to British policy makers regarding the southern backcountry.

From the start, the author's elaborate origin thesis proved controversial. As the reviewer for *Scots Magazine* (June 1775) observed, once Adair's "fancy" had been taken with the notion of Hebrew descent, he had attempted "to evince it by every consideration which his ingenuity could suggest . . . his imagination being strongly impressed with the preconceived opinion." But debates were then raging over the subject, and others found themselves agreeing that there was "indeed an amazing similarity between their rites and customs." Adair's supporters pointed to the author's long years among the Indians and his stated high regard for the truth. The *London Magazine* review of May 1775 recommended the work to the public for "information, entertainment, and solid instruction."

Today, historians, ethnohistorians, and anthropologists regard Adair's *History of the American Indians* as one of the most valuable primary accounts of the southeastern Indians. It has been, as the first reviewer promised, a source of "information, entertainment, and solid instruction" about the southeast-ern Indians for over two centuries. Adair's long tenure among the southern tribes as a deerskin trader presented many opportunities for intimate obser-vation of Indian culture, and his broad education and literary skill provided him with the tools to build an incredibly detailed and singular account of life among the eighteenth-century southern Indians. His unique and per-ceptive work offers a telling glimpse of backcountry life absent from offi-cial reports and narratives left by those whose lives were spent as colonials rather than cultural brokers. This new edition of Adair's *History* is designed to introduce general readers to Adair and his famous work, as well as make it more accessible to scholars. To that end, this edition carries an introduc-tory essay as well as annotations and a bibliography.

The introductory essay includes a summary of Adair's career and at-tempts to place his history in perspective so that the nonspecialist reader may better appraise the text. Annotations to the work itself vary in charac-ter from entries designed to provide readers with general introductory in-formation on the topic under consideration to more detailed discussion of sources for those who wish to do further reading on a topic. Where possible, people, places, and events mentioned by Adair are identified, as are obscure terms and foreign phrases. Comparative evidence by Adair's near contem-poraries is also included where appropriate. These comparative notes are not intended to be definitive but rather to illustrate the kind of material avail-able to support Adair's work and expand upon details provided by him. The nature of this endeavor, as well as the rambling quality of *A History of the American Indians* itself, has necessarily led to some minor repetition in a few cases, but was judged appropriate in light of the convenience this affords the reader.

The book shares a number of peculiarities common to books of the pe-riod. The most striking to the eyes of modern readers was the use of the old style ſ. In *The History of the American Indians,* like other eighteenth-century texts, *s* was rendered ſ, except at the conclusion of a word. In this ver-sion, the modern *s* has been substituted for the old style ſ. To aid the reader, eighteenth-century books usually printed the first word of a following page immediately below the last word on every page. *The History of the American Indians* followed this practice, which, of necessity, was not retained in a modern version.

There are numerous inconsistencies and nonstandardized spellings in the book, particularly of place and proper names. Adair's original spellings have been retained. In a few instances when an error or obsolete spelling might confuse the reader, a correction, in square brackets, has been included. Extraneous space preceding or following marks of punctuation has been closed up. Certain type features, including setting of leading section words

As the Hebrews carefully buried their dead, fo on any accident, they gathered their bones and laid them in the tombs of their fore-fathers: Thus, all the numerous nations of Indians perform the like friendly office to every deceafed perfon of their refpective tribe; infomuch, that thofe who

them conftantly in their holy of holies, without touching them in the leaft, only in the time of their compounded firft-fruit-offering, and annual expiation of fins; at which feafon, their magus carries one under his arm, a-head of the people, dancing round the facred arbour; next to him their head-warrior carries another; and thofe warriors who chufe it, carry the reft after the manner of the high-prieft; all the others carry white canes with fwan-feathers at the top. Hearing accidentally of thefe important monuments of antiquity, and en-quiring pretty much about them, I was certified of the truth of the report by four of the fouthern traders, at the moft eminent Indian-trading houfe of all Englifh America. One of the gentlemen informed me, that at my requeft he endeavoured to get a liberty of viewing the aforefaid tables, but it could not poffibly be obtained, only in the time of the yearly grand facrifice, for fear of polluting their holy things, at which time gentlemen of curiofity may fee them. *Old Bracket,* an Indian of perhaps 100 years old, lives in that old beloved town, who gave the following defcription of them:

Old Bracket's account of the *five copper* and *two brafs plates* under the beloved cabbin in Tuccabatchey-fquare.

The fhape of the five copper plates; one is a foot and half long and feven inches wide, the other four are fhorter and narrower.

The largeft ftamped thus (ÆЕ) The fhape of the two brafs plates,—about a foot and a half in diameter.

He faid—he was told by his forefathers that thofe plates were given to them by the man we call God; that there had been many more of other fhapes, fome as long as he could ftretch with both his arms, and fome had writing upon them which were buried with parti-cular men; and that they had inftructions given with them, viz, they muft only be handled by particular people, and thofe fafting; and no unclean woman muft be fuffered to come near them or the place where they are depofited. He faid, none but this town's people had any fuch plates given them, and that they were a different people from the Creeks. He only remembered three more, which were buried with three of his family, and he was the only man of the family now left. He faid, there were two copper plates under the king's cabbin, which had lain there from the firft fettling of the town

This account was taken in the Tuccabatchey-fquare, 27th July, 1759, per *Will. Bolfover.*

Page 179 of the 1775 edition of *The History of the American Indians* (courtesy of Tutwiler Collection of Southern History and Literature, Birmingham Public Library, Birmingham, Alabama).

in all capital letters has not been retained. A few obvious printer or typesetting errors were silently corrected. Original page numbers are placed in brackets in the text at the beginning of the page. In the event a page break occurs in the middle of a word, the bracketed number is placed at the end of the word. Adair's original Dedication, Preface, and Contents pages were unnumbered. Readers should note that the original edition contained no page numbered 101 but carried two pages labeled 102. Original pages numbered 374 and 376 are blank and have been omitted from the current edition.

In the case of Adair's original footnotes, set at the bottom on the page, readers may derive the original page number by referring to the page number of the symbol used to indicate the footnote. In the event the footnote carried to a second page in the original book, a bracketed number is included to indicate the page break. In the event of multiple notes on a single page, the 1775 edition generally employed an asterisk to mark the first and a dagger for the second. In the modern version, this system was impossible to maintain as in some instances footnotes from two original pages have been set on a single page. Thus, in certain cases, the reference symbols have been changed from the original mark to avoid confusion.

The most frequently cited modern edition of Adair's work was edited by Samuel Cole Williams and published under the auspices of the National Society of the Colonial Dames of America, in Tennessee, in 1930. Williams's edition has had numerous reprintings. In 1968, a facsimile edition with an introduction by Robert K. Berkhofer, Jr., was published by Johnson Reprint Company.

A xerographic reprint of the 1775 edition of Adair's *History* prepared by UMI Books on Demand served as the basis for the text reproduced here. In addition, copies of the 1775 edition housed at the Birmingham Public Library, Birmingham, Alabama, and the Charleston Library Society, Charleston, South Carolina, were also consulted. An on-line version of the text, including transcriptions and textual images of the original edition, is now available at the Library of Congress website and was also consulted. The volume owned by the Charleston Library Society belonged to the dedicatee, George Galphin, and contains a number of handwritten corrections made by James Adair. Most of the corrections concern matters of punctuation or have little or no bearing on content. Several are significant. They are identified at the appropriate locations in the text by footnotes. Readers can locate all the notations from that edition deemed worthy of mention by consulting the index under Charleston Library Society.

James Adair: His Life and *History*

> I told him, with that vehemence of speech, which is always requisite
> on such an occasion, that I was an English Chikkasah.
>
> —James Adair, *History of the American Indians*

James Adair hardly seems to exist outside the confines of his monumental history of southern backcountry. Shadowy rumors of his existence else-where abound: born the youngest son of Irish gentry;[1] later, the head of a family by a Cherokee woman in North Carolina on the eve of the Ameri-can Revolution.[2] Yet not a shred of hard evidence is offered to support these claims. James Adair deserves better—for his larger-than-life existence among the southeastern Indians is far more interesting than genealogical conjec-ture.[3] Adair was, in fact, a self-proclaimed "English Chickasaw," and most of what we know of him begins and ends with the southeastern Indians, among whom he made his home for the meatier part of forty years.[4] His life story, interwoven with his historical account and ethnological musing on the southeastern Indians, is an amazing one indeed.

Virtually nothing is known of Adair's family, early life, or education, al-though his work makes clear that he "had the advantages of a liberal edu-cation in the early part of life."[5] And, as advertisements for his book would later tout, he was furnished with "a Genius naturally formed for curious Enquiries."[6] By 1735, the inquisitive Adair entered the Indian country to trade with the Catawba Indians.[7] The Catawba, an amalgam of remnant tribes struggling on the margins of colonial South Carolina society, were beset by numerous problems, notably encroachments, constant harassment from enemy northern tribes, and growing problems with alcohol misuse.[8] Opportunities for advancement through the dying Catawba trade were slim, and almost immediately Adair ventured farther west, testing his for-tunes among the Cherokee Indians. He was in their towns by 1736, trading for a time at Kanootare (Conutory or Connutra), one of the Cherokee Out Towns along the Tuckaseigee River. There are almost no clues to Adair's business partners, but his mention of George Haig and Thomas Brown suggest that he was in some loose association or alliance with them in both the Catawba and Cherokee trade.[9]

Almost at once upon his arrival among the Cherokee, Adair encountered Christian Gottlieb Priber, a German intellectual also newly arrived in the Cherokee country, whom Adair described as "a gentleman of a curious and speculative temper."[10] Settling in Tellico, Priber adopted the dress and mode of living of the Cherokee, and by "smooth deluding art" he began an attempt at reorganizing Cherokee society and making plans for a utopian refuge among the Indians.[11] South Carolina envisioned only trouble in Priber's odd schemes and plotted his arrest. But before that could be effected, Priber and Adair corresponded for a time, until the Cherokee grew suspicious of the letters passing between them. According to Adair, Priber was composing a Cherokee dictionary and "set down a great deal that would have been very acceptable to the curious."[12] Perhaps it was Priber's efforts that inspired Adair to begin setting down his own observations and thoughts on the southeastern Indians, for Adair's account of Priber and his capture and his relation of Cherokee reaction to a lunar eclipse that occurred in 1736 are the earliest datable occurrences found in his *History*.[13]

The year 1736 was a momentous year for the Chickasaw Indians as well. Long allies of the English, with whom they had traded since the later part of the seventeenth century, the Chickasaw found themselves embroiled in war with France by virtue of the aid and comfort they afforded fleeing Natchez Indians, who were involved with a bitter struggle with the French from 1729 until 1733. Sandwiched between Francophile Choctaw and France's more northern Indian allies, the small but stalwart Chickasaw nation had embarked on its own campaign against the French, repeatedly harassing French supply boats traveling the Mississippi River from atop the renowned Chickasaw Bluffs, near modern Memphis, Tennessee. They also stalked French settlers in Louisiana. In early 1736, entrenched in fortified towns and very accurately dispensing English bullets, they managed to rebuff a massive French attack on their towns led by Jean-Baptiste Le Moyne, sieur de Bienville, the governor of French Louisiana.

News of the great Chickasaw victory was met with jubilation in Charleston, for until that point, French Louisiana had seemingly garnered the upper hand in the southern backcountry. First, they had established an alliance with the Alabama Indians of the Creek confederacy, a feat made palpable by the establishment of Fort Toulouse in 1717. With the destruction of the Natchez and a Choctaw alliance, the French seemed on the verge of not only destroying Carolina's commerce but endangering her security. With Christian Priber machinating among the Cherokee and French-speaking Shawnee attacking neighboring Catawba Indians with impunity, South Carolina and her neighbor Georgia seemed exposed indeed. Meanwhile,

Spanish forces, ensconced in Florida, lent more immediacy to Carolina's fears.

As South Carolina's fears translated into action, James Adair quickly became an actor. His early association with the Chickasaw seems to indicate that he had already begun trading with them by the late 1730s. Adair recorded in his history, without providing any details, that he was directed by South Carolina's governor to "decoy" the Chickasaw Indians to settle near New Windsor. Although he failed to make clear the exact date of his involvement, Adair was perhaps referring to South Carolina's 1738 effort to entice a band of Chickasaw to resettle at New Windsor, near Fort Moore, on the Savannah River.[14] A band of Chickasaw Indians had lived near the garrison since the end of the Yamasee War, but after the establishment of Augusta, Georgia, many of them had abandoned the more exposed northern bank of the Savannah River for the more convenient Georgia side of the river. To entice the Chickasaw to return to their province, South Carolina offered them a grant of more than 21,000 acres of land. The government hoped the Indians would provide a first line of defense against attacks by French-allied Indians as well as a buffer against Spanish Florida. The ploy failed, and the Chickasaw Indian community on the Georgia side of the river just below Augusta soon came to be known as New Savannah.[15] To further counter the perceived threat of the Spanish in Florida, Georgia's governor, General James Oglethorpe, marched against St. Augustine in 1740, during the War of Jenkins' Ear.[16] Oglethorpe's army included many South Carolina volunteers, among them James Adair. In addition, several hundred Indian warriors participated in the campaign, including the New Windsor Chickasaw as well as Creek and Cherokee warriors.[17]

Oglethorpe's assault was a disaster, and on the farthest edge of English influence the turbulent times grew even more uncertain and violent. In 1738, Soulouche Oumastabé or Red Shoe of Couëchitto and eight other Choctaw chiefs had visited Governor William Bull in Charleston and formally ratified a peace between the Choctaw and English, but the skirmishes between factions of the Choctaw and Chickasaw continued and the promised English trade failed to materialize.[18] The Chickasaw, tired of constant attacks and hoping for better relations with the French, made peace overtures to the newly arrived governor of French Louisiana, Pierre François Rigault, marquis de Cavagnal et Vaudreuil, in August 1743.[19] Vaudreuil's terms proved unacceptable, for he demanded the ouster of the English traders as the price of peace.[20] Hopes for a Chickasaw-French rapprochement were further dashed when, in November 1743, three English traders and two Chickasaw Indians were killed on the trade path by Choctaw Indians, acts presumed by Charlestonians to have been engineered by the French.[21] The repeated attacks on English traders by the Choctaw, some of which occurred during times of peace, turned mere merchants into hard-core Francophobes. While such attacks were costly in terms of lost time and merchandise, it was the murder and capture of English subjects that forged irreversible animosity. In some cases, those killed were more quickly forgotten than those captured, for the result of capture by French-allied Choctaw was certain imprisonment in Mobile or New Orleans and, on occasion, shipment to France, where further imprisonment and an uncertain future awaited.[22]

When in mid-March of 1744 France and Britain resumed formal warfare, an epic struggle for control of the backcountry began, and French attitudes toward the Chickasaw began to soften. The French concluded that if peace could be made with the Chickasaw, a similar pact might be made with the Cherokee.[23] The French challenge was met by James Glen, South Carolina's new governor, who arrived in Charleston in late 1743. Both Vaudreuil and Glen recognized that success among the various tribes depended on a plentiful and dependable supply of trade goods to their Indian allies. For South Carolina, deerskin traders would play a key role in the conflict. By June of 1744, Glen began proceeding with countermeasures against the French that ultimately included efforts to strengthen South Carolina's frontier fortifications, to build an English fort among the Creeks as a counter to French influence emanating from Fort Toulouse and to "seduce" the Choctaw Indians from the French influence.[24] It should come as no surprise that James Adair—an extremely well educated man, a man of experience among the Indians as both a trader and a war veteran—should have been immediately drawn into Glen's orbit.[25]

"On His Majesty's Service": James Adair as Agent Provocateur

> I watch'd Opportunities, and so brib'd Red Shoes, the Head Warriour
> of the Chactaws, that I created a great many murmurings, and so im-
> prov'd it as to cause an intire Revolution.
> —James Adair to James Glen, February 12, 1747

Into this hostile environment of constant conflict and omnipresent danger, James Adair sallied forth to trade with the western Chickasaw in 1744.[26] On his way, he paid a visit to James Glen's country house, ostensibly to inquire if the governor had any "Comands" for the Chickasaw traders. During the course of their conversation, Glen inquired how the Chickasaw might be profitably used in the war against the French. Adair, noting that there were few Chickasaw Indians, pointed out that a Choctaw alliance would be more useful in hindering the French and held the promise of untold profits to be made from eager Choctaw consumers. According to Glen, Adair suggested that given "proper Encouragement," he and his partner might be able to swing the Choctaw nation to the English side.[27] In another document, Glen took credit for the idea himself and noted that he recommended the course of action to "one of the Chickasaw traders. . . . I instructed him in every step he was to take, and in every word he was to speak."[28]

A subsequent letter by Glen, published in *American Magazine and Monthly Chronicle for the British Colonies* in 1758, provides a unique look at just how precise Glen's instructions to his messengers could be as well as revealing the governor's systematic curiosity concerning the American Indians. In addition to very detailed instructions on the contents of a speech to be delivered to the Choctaw headmen, Glen instructed his unnamed emissary to keep a journal, even providing an example of the kind of "short notes by way of memorandum, without studying connection, or how to make it read well" that he desired. Moreover, he provided an extensive list of queries on Indian history, government, marriage, funerals, religion, war, hunting, language, and customs among the Indians.[29] The published letter, probably dating from 1749, provides a rare glimpse of Glen the curious scholar. Whether Glen's curiosity and queries were inspired by Adair or inspired Adair to keep his own journals is lost. But the two men were most certainly of a like mind, and their analytical approach to Indian affairs and culture must have drawn them together instantly.

Although all the facts concerning Glen and Adair's earliest communication are not known, it is clear from surviving records that, together, they devised a scheme that would rend the backcountry and precipitate internecine warfare among the Choctaw Indians.[30] Adair's mission: "to use the best ways and means to bring the Chactaw Nation of Indians to the British Interest." The best way to achieve this goal, everyone agreed, was to open a reliable English trade. In return for his best efforts, Glen promised Adair ample reward.[31] Adair's mission would prove to be the most difficult, dangerous, and controversial episode of his career. For Glen, the Choctaw project was the first in a series of bold moves made without the advice or the consent of his council or the assembly.

By the time Adair reached the Chickasaw towns, the Chickasaw and Choctaw were still engaged in hot war, although covert peace efforts were under way. Moreover, there was considerable division among the Choctaw over the French alliance. Soulouche Oumastabé (Red Shoe) of Couëchitto in particular pointed to the desirability of a trade with the English and an end to the Chickasaw war. He and his confederates in the western division of the Choctaw confederation were virtually alone in their desire for better relations, for the other Choctaw divisions remained firm friends of France.[32]

Already, the growing European war had resulted in trouble for the French, whose warehouses stood empty. Even the annual distribution of presents from the French governor to allied Indian tribes was delayed. With French goods in short supply, Choctaw had ventured into the Creek towns to trade and, in January 1745, freshly licensed Creek trader Lachlan McGillivray sent a report back to Charleston detailing the "Most miserable starving Condition for want of cloathing" that the Choctaw faced.[33]

Severe though the lack of goods was, another matter provided the straw that buckled Choctaw solidarity and produced the crack needed for an agent provocateur to break the southeastern backcountry wide open. Lust was the straw and James Adair the agent. As Adair so nicely put it, "one of the French of Tumbikpe-fort, being guided by Venus instead of Apollo, was detected in violating the law of marriage with the favourite wife of the warlike chieftain of Quansheto, *Shulashummashtabe,* who by his several transcendant qualities, had arrived to the highest pitch of the red glory."[34] Red Shoe, through intermediaries, let the English know of his outrage.[35] English anger at "Monsieur," as Adair and the other English traders derisively called the French, had likewise reached a fever pitch, for just two months earlier, in October 1745, two English traders, Adair's partner and one of his employees, had been killed on the Chickasaw trading path by a war party of twenty Choctaw Indians.[36]

Already in the fray, actively inveigling the "defection" of the Choctaw, was longtime trader John Campbell, a man fluent in the Choctaw language and perhaps the most experienced Choctaw hand among the Carolinians. Adair related Glen's proposal to Campbell, and the two began concerted activities to accomplish the mission.[37] Adair and Campbell, acting in concert with leading Chickasaw, sent sympathetic peace overtures and a massive shipment of presents to Red Shoe's village.[38] As Adair later reported to Governor Glen, he had "watch'd Opportunities, and so brib'd Red Shoes . . . [and] created a great many murmurings, and so improv'd it as to cause an intire Revolution."[39]

The messengers and presents arrived among the disaffected towns in late March 1746 while leading Choctaw loyal to the French were in Mobile receiving their annual present of trade goods.[40] At some point in the negotiations, French Choctaw, attempting to thwart the peace talks, fired on one of the Chickasaw delegations, killing three, including John Campbell's Chickasaw wife and two of the "most famous partisans of these Chickasaws." Campbell, although shot in the arm, escaped and was escorted to safety by Red Shoe.[41] To forestall English and Chickasaw retaliation for the attack, Red Shoe sent "swans-wings, white beads, pipes and tobacco . . . a strong confirmation of our treaty of peace" to the English traders living in the Chickasaw towns.[42] And, according to Adair, he asked for reassurances that English traders "would live, and deal among them," as they did among the Chickasaw. Implicit in Red Shoe's formalization of a peace with the

Chickasaw and an English trade alliance was a declaration of war against the French. The bargain struck, Adair and Campbell provided "arms, ammunition . . . a French scalping knife which had been used against us, and even vermilion" war paint. In return, Red Shoe promised French scalps to revenge the "crying blood" of the English dead.[43] Within a month, Red Shoe and his partisans had killed three Frenchmen, and, as Adair recorded, "the flame speedily raged very high."[44] In Charleston, the governor received letters from traders in the Creek towns with news of the "rupture" as well as the "Red shoes King having sent the scalps of three French Men to the Chickasaws in order to be sent down to this government as satisfaction for our traders that were killed in the chickasaw Path." When the scalps arrived in the Chickasaw towns, the traders there (Adair and Campbell) sent as payment to Red Shoe "four pieces of Strouds."[45]

The secret machinations, captured by Adair's reminiscences, engendered shock waves that traveled from New Orleans to Charleston. Morbid attention focused on the reason why the three Frenchmen were killed and who could thus claim "credit" (or be blamed) for the "revolt" of the Choctaw from the French interest. The French reported that three murders were in retaliation for the attack on the Chickasaw peace delegation.[46] In Charleston, the chairman of a committee later appointed to investigate the "revolt" of the Choctaw from the French alliance eventually decided it was long-delayed atonement for the three British traders killed in 1743, conveniently forgetting the deaths of two traders in 1745 and the attack on Campbell.[47] But James Adair, whose firsthand testimony was challenged and then rebuffed by Charleston bureaucrats, asserted that he was the one who demanded French blood for English. Adair claimed that he asked for only one French scalp, in vengeance for that of his partner.[48] Contemporary French records also relate that the English traders had demanded only one death "for an Englishman who had been killed by the Choctaw of the village of Blue Wood," meaning Adair's partner. But Red Shoe's warriors, the French were told, "exceeded" orders, killing the others in the heat of the moment. Ironically, Henri de Verbois, the man accused of the rape and one of the three Frenchmen killed, had earlier reported the attack on the English caravan by the warriors of Blue Wood.[49] Adair's claim is further supported by a report passed along by deerskin trader Charles McNaire to the South Carolina Council, when he related that the Choctaw asserted that by the end of 1747, "for one White Man that was killed they had lost six."[50] Doubtless, the truth lies jumbled amid the mixed resentments of all those involved, for different parties to the fray viewed actions from varying angles and no simple answer seems possible. But clearly, the immediate revenge and larger goals of both Adair and Red Shoe converged as they cooperated against the French to build an Anglo-Choctaw trade alliance.[51]

But for the Choctaw, the deaths held a far greater significance than a simple conception of *lex talionis*. Proper retaliation for the English and Chickasaw dead, according to Choctaw law, would have demanded the lives of an equal number of Choctaw. Red Shoe's decision to kill three French-men was politically calculated to avoid killing his own people. He was well aware that the immediate consequence of his actions would be war with French Louisiana and almost certainly a cataclysmic division within his own nation unless artful political management and English trade goods could silence opposition in his own nation to an English alliance. His strategy dovetailed nicely with that of the English and Chickasaw, for they preferred to blame the French for past misdeeds of the Choctaw as the means to achieve peace and welcome the entire Choctaw nation into their trading fold. In fact, both the English and the Chickasaw realized the im-possibility of securing a true satisfaction and found the French both con-venient and tempting targets.[52] For their part, the French, who under the Choctaw law of *lex talionis* would have been required to seek their own blood revenge for the death of their three people, demanded that the Choc-taw carry out the executions, even naming those who were to die: Red Shoe and the leaders of the two villages where the dead traders had lived. The demand carried with it the implication that fellow clansmen of those named would have to cooperate and execute the men, since only clan mem-bers would be exempt from murder under clan laws of blood revenge. As an alternative to killing their own people, some Choctaw would eventually take the easier course and kill English traders to satisfy French demands.[53]

Adair, having set "this retaliating scheme" in motion, set out for Ooeasah, better known as the Breed Camp, in the Creek nation, to obtain supplies for South Carolina's new Choctaw allies. While there, Red Shoe's men ar-rived with the French scalps, which Adair had requested as proof of their "revolt" from the French. Creek headmen and traders alike were horrified at the implications of French scalps passing through their country and, to Adair's chagrin, refused to allow the grisly trophies to be taken in tri-umph to Charleston. In the end, Adair was forced to turn the scalps over to the Creeks, who forwarded them to the French at Fort Toulouse for burial.[54] The Choctaw delegation that had carried the scalps continued on to Charleston without them.

Adair, having obtained goods from the supply stores at the Breed Camp, then returned to the Chickasaw towns. On November 12, 1746, Red Shoe himself arrived in the Chickasaw nation with "a great many head-men and warriors" to confirm the peace between the English and his people.[55] Ac-cording to Adair's *History,* the Choctaw were eager to "be relieved in their poverty, and to concert to best measures of still annoying the common enemy."[56] While at the Breed Camp, Adair had arranged for letters to be sent to Governor Glen in South Carolina.[57] As Adair bitterly noted in his *History*, the Creek traders opened his parcel, destroyed some of the papers contained in the "large packet," and delayed its delivery so as to give them ample time to proceed to the Choctaw villages with their own dearly valued trade goods.[58]

Among the letters by Adair that eventually did reach the governor was one dated February 12, 1747, a petition from Adair, John Campbell, and William Newbury seeking a monopoly of the Choctaw trade for "two or three Years" to allow them to be able to recoup the losses they had incurred in supplying the Chickasaw against the French as well as their having "bribed and managed the Chactaw as to compleat a firm Peace between them and the English." The petition, along with Adair's letter, a talk from Red Shoe, and a letter from Creek merchants John Rae and Isaac Barksdale, was presented by Governor Glen to the South Carolina assembly in early April of 1747.[59] The assembly promptly turned the papers over to the Committee of Indian Affairs for examination. Meanwhile, the fifty-five Choctaw who had accompanied the packet of documents, led by Imataha Pouscouche or Little King, Red Shoe's brother, fervently expounded on their desperate need for weapons with which to fight their new French war.[60]

The Choctaw leader, desperate for trade goods, quickly agreed to South Carolina's terms: prosecute the war against the French "with Vigour; and without Loss of Time," expel all French traders from Choctaw towns, provide guards for English trade caravans, assist in an assault against Fort Tombecbé and the capture of its commander, build a fort for English traders if requested, aid the Creeks in "demolishing" Fort Toulouse, and consider the possibility of moving some of their towns closer to South Carolina for the convenience of trade.[61] Meanwhile, Adair waited at his fortified store on the Chickasaw-Choctaw frontier for a massive shipment of presents and trade goods from South Carolina. What he got instead was the news that the contract for the lucrative Choctaw trade had been awarded to Charles McNaire, who also delivered additional instructions from Governor Glen directing Adair to act as South Carolina's representative.

Charles McNaire was, according to Edmond Atkin, the chairman of the South Carolina Council's committee on Indian affairs, "a more sober decent sort of man than commonly goes to trade in the Indian nations."[62] While that might have been true, he was completely inexperienced in frontier matters and had never been in the Indian country, being "a Stranger lately come to Carolina . . . [who] having met with Misfortunes at sea . . . was willing to try his Luck on shore."[63] His real advantage was powerful friends and relations, including Charleston merchant Mathew Roche, who promised to fit him out on credit and provide horses and goods for immediate dispatch to the Choctaw country. Roche also promised to find him an interpreter. Other partners in Charles McNaire and Company—derisively dubbed the Sphynx Company by Adair—included Jordan Roche, who was experienced in the trade, James Maxwell, Thomas Maxwell, Arthur Harvey, John Vann, and, ultimately, Doctor Thomas Glen, the governor's brother.[64] The partners of the hastily formed company were certainly hoping for substantial return.

Governor James Glen has been criticized for his role in securing a monopoly for the company as well as profit for his family. But higher motives moved him as well. As Glen noted in an address to the Assembly, "the Affairs of Carolina were so closely connected & interwoven with those of the Indians, he had given his Attention for some years to what might not only strengthen the Alliances we had, but procure new ones with Nations with whom we had little or no Intercourse; in order to baffle the Designs of the French." McNaire's investors promised to deliver the goods and do it more quickly than any other company could manage. And they promised to deliver South Carolina's presents to the Choctaw, some nine horse-loads of goods, at no cost. As Edmond Atkin would later observe, "dispatch was what appeared most needful," and so McNaire and Company received the contract.[65]

But McNaire's company, inexperienced and delayed by the magnitude of their cargo, didn't deliver quickly. It took the company nearly two months to make ready, and McNaire did not set out for the Choctaw country until early June with a massive caravan of over two hundred horses. He did not arrive in the Chickasaw towns until September 25, 1747—somehow managing to double the normal travel time between Charleston and the Choctaw country.[66] By the time he arrived, Red Shoe had been assassinated, and the alliance begun so hopefully was quickly falling to pieces.[67] The assassination of Red Shoe, who was killed by one of his own people while escorting a pack train of English goods from the Chickasaw nation, was engineered by Pierre Annibal Develle, the French commander at Fort Tombecbé, and Red Shoe's murderer, having perpetrated the deed, quickly sought shelter there.[68]

Once in the Chickasaw towns, McNaire called the Chickasaw traders together and produced not only a trading license for his company but a proclamation from Governor Glen prohibiting unlicensed trade with the Choctaw.[69] Since only McNaire's people had licenses to trade with the Choctaw, he was in fact, as Adair reported, attempting to effect a monopoly, by "frighten[ing] every other trader from dealing with the Choktah, at their peril."[70] The result was a continued shortage of goods among the Choctaw, for McNaire had lodged most of his goods at a warehouse in the Creek town of Weoka, where they were presumably safe.[71]

Adair was openly contemptuous of McNaire's officially sanctioned "sheep-skin" license bearing the governor's official beeswax seals and dismissed them as mere "scare-crows." Though in his book Adair wrote that he told McNaire that he would "not by any means oppose their aim in grasping the whole Choktah trade," McNaire claimed otherwise.[72] In a letter to Glen, McNaire enumerated the "Expence Mr. Adaire led us into," noting that the Choctaw demanded "all our Guns . . . [and then] they demanded Powder, Bullets, paint, Knives, &c. and as the weather was now grown cold they said they must have Blankets for their Old Warriors." McNaire, it seems, blamed Adair for the message, for the Choctaw, according to McNaire, pointed out that they had gone to war for the English and they must be supplied by the English. McNaire saw only conspiracy and "schemes" by his rivals.[73] But, after all, it was true that he was supposed to be delivering the English present. South Carolina had authorized only arms and ammunition, but, as the Choctaw pointed out, warriors also needed and expected war paint, knives, and blankets. As a result of Choctaw insistence, McNaire was forced to pass out most of his first consignment of goods gratis. Adair, according to McNaire, also presented the Indians with an oversized yardstick with which to measure McNaire's dry goods, as well as a price tariff barely above the prime cost of goods.[74] If Adair did provide a yardstick that was a quarter longer than usual, it was an unusual twist on the usual trader trick of measuring with a short yard. Whatever actually happened, McNaire sent a letter to South Carolina complaining bitterly of Adair's actions and denouncing him as a marplot.[75] But McNaire's claims tended to contradict each other. Even James Glen found it puzzling that McNaire should charge that Adair demanded he dispense all his goods as presents and also pass out false measures. As Glen observed, "but if the goods were for presents as he seems to insinuate Adair made them believe, what had they to do with prices, or weights, or measures."[76]

McNaire, out of goods and finding the English Choctaw unable to make winter hunts due to the rising war within their tribe, soon came to embrace the view of his fellow Indian countrymen. In late October, he sent desperate accounts of the situation among the Choctaw, reporting an attack on a convoy of his goods and the resultant death of his employee John Elsley. He advised Glen that instead of selling goods, he had fallen in with Adair's scheme of "purchasing" the Choctaw with presents. In a letter to Glen, he wrote that the expenditure was "absolutely necessary."[77] In fact, the Little King, Red Shoe's successor, had found his own situation almost untenable, and he refused to allow McNaire to leave the Choctaw nation until the trader produced "presents" to supply the English-allied Choctaw sufficiently in their time of need. For the Choctaw, though they desired trade, also saw their relationship with South Carolina as a reciprocal alliance in which the exchange of goods had nothing to do with profit and everything to do with loyalty. For their French war, they needed and expected—and had been promised—Carolina's aid.[78] In any case, trading was a moot endeavor, for the Choctaw had nothing to trade to the English, hunting having been completely stopped by the raging war.

McNaire's letter home warned the governor that "he had already been at the Expence of £1300 Currency (or about £185 Sterling) with the Choctaws, besides what they expected or would take, if they went to war again, *he would not venture to go to the further Expence without some Certainty of being reimbursed by the Publick.*"[79] When the governor read McNaire's advice to the council in mid-December, not unexpectedly it "created great Astonishment & Uneasiness."[80] Glen impressed upon the hastily convened council that "that was the time to lose or Secure the Chactaw Nation" and that the only way to secure the Indians was with presents. Since the situation seemed to demand immediate action, the council promptly authorized sending further presents of arms and ammunition to the Choctaw, as well as armaments for the Chickasaw and the Creeks, without waiting for the assembly to be called to approve the measure.[81]

Meanwhile, Adair turned his attention to the letter from Glen delivered by McNaire, in which Glen had recalled Adair to Charleston "on his majesty's service."[82] The "service" was instructions for Adair "to stir up the Chactaws against the French, & to take Tambekke Fort." The taking of Tombecbé was especially important, for this bastion of French influence not only sat astride the major trade artery into the Choctaw country but was the distribution point for goods to French-allied Choctaw towns.[83] Though Glen's letter assured him of the governor's continued "contenance and friendship," Adair's view of the governor had soured. Glen, obviously aware that explanations were in order, plainly wrote, "the sooner you come down, [to Charleston] the better." Glen guaranteed Adair protection from his creditors, thereby eliminating the usual excuse deerskin traders fell back on when they wished to avoid Charleston. Adair was convinced the governor was simply attempting to lure him from the profits of the Choctaw trade, but nonetheless he proceeded to Charleston as requested.[84]

Adair arrived in Charleston to find himself the center of a brewing storm. For the South Carolina Council, upon receiving McNaire's hastily written letter of early October complaining of Adair's actions, had recommended "that a Proclamation should be issued, warning all Persons that they would be prosecuted for any Breach of the Indian Trading Act; And that the Commissioner for regulating that Trade should have Notice to take great care to whom he granted Licenses." According to council member Edmond Atkin, "Much was said by some of the Members of Adair's Proceedings as deserving Punishment."[85]

Thus caught between the council's condemnation and what he perceived as the governor's betrayal, Adair promptly aired his resentments to Glen before abruptly leaving town. Upon learning Adair had taken off without leave, Glen sent fellow trader George Galphin after Adair, who agreed to accompany Galphin back to Glen's residence. There, according to Adair, Glen "earnestly pressed [Adair] to forget and forgive all that was past" and assured him of "full redress" from his own pocket if South Carolina did not reimburse him for his expenses.[86] In fact, Glen would later report to the Board of Trade that Adair and Campbell never received compensation for their services other than "small sums that I have from time to time given them out of my own Pocket."[87] Moreover, Glen stood by his man publicly. He compelled the commissioner of Indian affairs to issue a Choctaw trading license to Adair (and one for Campbell also) despite the doubts the commissioner expressed about Adair's "character" in the wake of McNaire's letter. Moreover, the governor declared to the council he would recommend to the home government that Adair be rewarded for services to the colony for his efforts in seducing the Choctaw from the French interest.[88]

With that, Adair turned westward in late November and returned to the Chickasaw towns "in the severity of winter."[89] As he was returning to the Chickasaw towns, he crossed paths with a Chickasaw headman, Paya Mataha, and Imataha Pouscouche, leader of the English-allied Choctaw, who were traveling to Charleston with "one of the beaus of the Sphynx-company," Charles McNaire.[90] The trio arrived in Charleston on December 29 and stayed a fortnight before departing. There were no public ceremonies for the two great Indian leaders, only private meetings with Glen and the leading investors of McNaire's company.[91] While Imataha Pouscouche continued to stress the need for a steady stream of arms and ammunition, the main topic of conversation among the McNaire company investors was how to scotch competition. Jordan Roche had apparently reached an understanding with the officials in both South Carolina and Georgia and was astounded to learn from Glen that William Pinckney, South Carolina's Indian commissioner, had indeed granted two new licenses—to Adair and Campbell. To assuage Roche and McNaire, Glen then promised an "*Expedient* of a Proclamation forbidding all Persons whatever to enter the Choctaw Country 'till Mcnaire's Return." The proclamation, carrying the provincial seal, prohibited traders from entering the Choctaw country in McNaire's absence upon penalty of one year's imprisonment. The edict was thus geared to thwart not only unlicensed traders but licensed ones as well.[92]

Clearly, the parties were working at cross-purposes, but for Glen and Adair—and the other staunchly anti-French English deerskin traders—the larger aim was inveigling the Choctaw to continue their campaign against the French. Safely ensconced in comfortable quarters in South Carolina's leading port, the gentlemen merchants and bureaucrats, mulling affairs over their "sparkling bowls and decanters,"[93] could look with disdain at Adair and his hard-nosed approach to diplomacy. But Glen, for all his many faults, shared the view of those who lived on the English edge: the French must be opposed at every opportunity, and public money would be required to win the battle. McNaire would later recall that Glen had accused him of being "too sparing of his goods That the bringing over the Choctaw Nation was a matter of Such Importance to this Province and to the British Interest that if he the said NcNair had made presents of all his goods he the governor himself would have become his paymaster."[94]

Adair, meanwhile, had arrived to find the Choctaw nation completely devoid of English goods, for the Chickasaw and Creek traders had withdrawn under threat of penalty from South Carolina. McNaire's company, though they had distributed the public present, had lost most of their goods through bad management and attacks by French-armed Choctaw.[95] From their fortified posts in the Chickasaw towns, James Adair and other Chickasaw traders sent a missive to William Pinckney, bemoaning the ineptitude of McNaire and his traders. Most specifically, they condemned the company, tongue in cheek, as "bold Sons of Mars for leaving that Nation, in a cowardly Manner, when there was not the least appearance of danger." Their point was that the Choctaw, although they had "detained" the McNaire company traders, had no malicious intent but rather had held the traders to ensure that further goods would be sent to them.[96]

For their part, the English-allied Choctaw had, as promised, launched an assault on French farms and settlements around Mobile in late 1747, killing at least seven people and capturing others. But the raid quickly expended the limited supplies they had received from McNaire and Company. Meanwhile, the French sphere of influence was waxing, largely as a result of diplomacy and presents of goods distributed from captured English convoys. Seeking their own retaliation for the murder of their traders and settlers, the French began offering rewards for English scalps and horsetails.[97] Among the first victims of the new French offensive was Henry Elsley, who, as McNaire reported, had been killed in late October 1747 while leading a caravan of four packhorsemen and sixty horses along the treacherous Tombecbé path. Experienced Indian traders blamed Elsley's foolishness for his death, for he had taken the shortest yet most dangerous path and was killed only ten miles from the French post.[98]

Quickly following Adair's return to the Chickasaw towns was the arrival of McNaire from Charleston, who delivered "a friendly and polite letter" from Glen to Adair.[99] Glen's aim in writing to Adair was twofold: to assist McNaire in recouping his losses and to deliver further directions to incite the Choctaw to war against the French with Fort Tombecbé the primary target.[100] Glen also, according to Adair, provided more "artful promises," reporting that Mathew Roche, one of those who stood to lose the most by McNaire's failure to profit, would guarantee Adair's "obligation" to his own creditors. Glen added that Roche looked upon Adair's public service in strengthening the Choctaw alliance as a service to his business interests as well as those of the public. To McNaire, Glen also had advice: do not put private profit in the way of public service and "leave no stone unturned" in winning the Choctaw.[101] Glen also recommended Adair as a man "upon whose Integrity and Activity on this matter I can very well rely."[102]

Adair, so he recorded in his *History,* then furnished McNaire with his own goods, "the necessity of the times requiring a liberal distribution."[103] Imataha Pouscouche, according to Adair, had returned from Charleston "freighted with plenty of courtly promises, and for his own security he was not backward in relating them to his brethren; otherwise, they would have killed both him and me; which would have reconciled them to the French."[104] Carolina goods being distributed, Imataha Pouscouche, Adair, McNaire and other English traders undertook a tour of the Choctaw country and distributed more goods, but they could not persuade the Choctaw to storm Fort Tombecbé.[105] But, as Adair observed, though "they declined a French war, their own civil war became bitter beyond expression."[106]

Among Adair's other public duties during this difficult period was a trip with a Chickasaw delegation to the camp of Peter Chartier's Shawnee Indians, which lay some fifty miles northeast of the Chickasaw towns. According to Adair, Chartier was actively working with the French to "subvert" the Creek Indians from the British fold. Adair and the Chickasaw warriors, though they carried emblems of peace, intended to "apprehend" Chartier and send him to South Carolina—or so Adair reported in his *History.*[107] Adair's mission, according to James Glen's reports to the Board of Trade, was supposedly more conciliatory than predatory. According to Glen, his aim was to invite Chartier to visit Charleston under the protection of the provincial seal. Glen hoped to persuade him to settle his Shawnee warriors on South Carolina's western border, among the Catawba nation, to bolster their strength and help provide protection from the raids of northern tribes—a faint hope at best. According to Glen, "he did not care to come down."[108] The governor of Louisiana, apprised of the English mission by their allied Alabama Indians, vowed to "spare nothing to keep watch" over the proceedings of the English delegation.[109] Vaudreuil need not have worried, for Chartier's people settled among the Upper Creeks and continued to menace South Carolina's interests from afar.

Back in Charleston, Glen, as promised, had written to the Duke of Newcastle, head of the Board of Trade, praising the efforts of Adair and Campbell, "masters of that [Choctaw] Language and very enterprizing," and recommending a reward of one hundred guineas each.[110] Shortly afterward, the

South Carolina Commons House of Assembly received a claim from Adair for £755 as reimbursement for ammunition and other goods he had provided to the Choctaw. The parsimonious committee assigned to look over expense claims decreed it an "extraordinary one, and ought not to be allowed, as it may be an Inlett for other Persons to make such extravagant Accounts." Thus, as Adair asserted, his claim for compensation was denied not on the basis of merit but on contingency.[111]

Just when Adair learned of this rejection is unclear, for at the time, he was among the Chickasaw and Choctaw. There, bad times had grown even worse, for smallpox had reached the backcountry, carrying off more souls than warfare, the number of dead exceeding one thousand.[112] McNaire's company, though aided by Adair, Campbell, and other more experienced traders, continued to meet with repeated misfortunes, many the result of poor planning and mismanagement, even losing track of the public present of arms and ammunition. And as the war widened, casualties on all sides rose. French-armed Choctaw ventured into the Chickasaw towns, attacking English trading houses, including Adair's.[113] Caravans were attacked on the trade paths, their merchandise plundered, and their horses killed. On one occasion, a wounded English trader was sent as a prisoner to Mobile.[114] British-armed Choctaw ranged almost to New Orleans, leaving smoldering ruins and taking scalps and captives.[115] In the Choctaw towns, fortifications were erected by Anglophile Choctaw, while French-supplied war parties from the opposite side sought the scalps and heads of the "rebels."[116] As summer fighting intensified, the lack of adequate ammunition became a disaster for the English-allied Choctaw. Adair reported that in the most infamous engagement, the Choctaw factions met "in the open fields: when our friends had fired away all their ammunition, they took to their hiccory-bows and barbed arrows, and rushed on the opposite party, with their bare tomohawks, like the most desperate veterans, regardless of life."[117] Some even began firing glass beads, small pebbles, and acorns from their British muskets.[118] James Glen, in reporting the carnage to the home government, related that the "pitched Battle . . . was the only one that I ever heard of amongst Indians." The battle, which lasted "from morning till night," left thirty-five French-allied Choctaw dead, according to reports received in South Carolina. After noting that their allies were forced to withdraw for lack of adequate ammunition, Glen purposely failed to relate the number of English-allied Choctaw who died in the melee, but the toll was high.[119] Adair, echoing the sentiments not only of deerskin traders but of the politicians in Charleston, blamed the bloodbath on the ineptitude of the "Sphynx-Company."

Adair, fearing for the lives of the English, convened yet another Choctaw delegation and sent them to Charleston, thinking they would serve as secu-

rity for the lives of the traders. For should the English be killed, the Choctaw knew that their friends and relations would not return from South
Carolina. The twenty Choctaw Indians reached Charleston in early January.
South Carolina's policy makers, thinking only of the expense of entertaining and providing for their guests, noted with alarm there were only two
headmen of distinction in the group. The Choctaw response to this concern
was blunt, their spokesman relating that "all the headmen of his Place were
killed, and they should all be soon destroyed by the French, if the Gov'r
did not supply them with Arms and Ammunition to fight the French and
their Indians." Destitute and desperate, the party was reduced to begging.
Edmond Atkin, the council's leading light on Indian affairs, was "quite
ashamed of this Audience," and sullenly noted the "contrivance" that Adair
had thrust upon them.[120]

For his part, the governor continued to praise Adair as well as John
Campbell, who had ushered the Choctaw into town and served as their
interpreter. However, with the cost skyrocketing, Glen, the investors in
McNaire's company, and the South Carolina assembly were rapidly becoming embittered antagonists over the entire Choctaw war, particularly over
questions about the seemingly "lost" or undelivered public presents. As Atkin wrote, the "Affair of McNaire's became a *Party Matter*."[121] With war on
the frontier and political infighting in South Carolina, Adair received another letter from Glen (dated September 17, 1749), asking him to escort a
Chickasaw delegation to South Carolina. Glen's aim was to produce Adair
as an expert witness concerning McNaire's mismanagement, and no doubt
he thought that Adair would be amenable to fighting for him on the coast
just as he had done in the backcountry.

Controversy and Disgrace

> The World thinks it strange that I should be punishable both by the
> English and French, for that in Effect that was done for the one, and
> against the other in Time of a hot War. But so it happens in Time of
> Iron-Age.
>
> —James Adair to William Pinckney, May 7, 1751

Adair thus prepared for a triumphal return to South Carolina. His traveling
party included Paya Mataha, twenty Chickasaw warriors and a number of
Chickasaw women, and three French prisoners taken by the Chickasaw, plus
other packhorsemen and traders, including a "corpulent member of the
Sphynx-company."[122] The caravan was attacked by Choctaw on their way
through the treacherous *Book'pharaah,* the Long Swamp, where one of the
English traders was killed and scalped.[123] Then smallpox broke out among

the travelers. Leaving the ailing Chickasaw behind at the Breed Camp, Adair continued on to Charlestown.[124] The Chickasaw delegation, after recovering, finally reached New Windsor three months after leaving their own country. But they were without their French captives, for once again Muskogee politics had intervened, and the Creeks had insisted that the French prisoners be released. They were sent to Fort Toulouse.[125]

In Charleston, Adair and the Chickasaw delegation met with a "cold reception." Glen was particularly displeased.[126] And so was everyone else, for the Carolinians feared that the Chickasaw were carrying smallpox.[127] Glen's particular pique was the inclusion of a letter from Adair to McNaire in a vitriolic pamphlet then circulating in Charleston. The pamphlet, "A Modest Reply to His Excellency the Governor's Written Answer to the Affidavit of Charles McNaire & Matthew Roche, concerning the Late Revolt of the Choctaw Nation of Indians from the French to the British Interest," had been written by Matthew Roche and printed for the anti-Glen forces by printer Peter Timothy, a man who wholeheartedly shared their sentiments.[128] Roche's pamphlet seems not to have survived the ravages of time, so the exact contents of Adair's letter remain a mystery, but there is no doubt that in his letter Adair had aired his grievances against the governor. Not surprisingly, the inclusion of the letter immediately cost Adair the governor's support. As R. Nicholas Olsberg, the historian of the South Carolina assembly, has observed, the McNaire affair now became "a raging, public controversy."[129]

Under such circumstances, Adair's Chickasaw friends received a cold reception, and Adair claimed that most of their expenses came from his own pocket. According to Adair, Glen accosted the Indians and accused them of coming only for presents. Adair, chiding the governor for his penury, noted "my words seemed to lie pretty sharp upon him, and I suppose contributed not a little to the uncourtly leave he took of our gallant, and faithful old friends."[130] The rift between trader and governor was now complete.

The political firestorm then raging over what Carolinians styled the "Choctaw Revolt" had begun in May 1749 when Charles McNaire appealed to the South Carolina assembly for compensation for his massive losses—some £11,000. In addition to well-wishers in the assembly, two of his partners and seven of his creditors held seats in the lower house while three creditors sat on the council, which also served as the upper house of the assembly. Naturally, he expected a sympathetic hearing.[131] The reception to McNaire's petition was mixed, but he was granted £1000 to offset his expenses in pursuing his claims in London, for among other things, he claimed he had been acting in an official capacity. With that, McNaire almost immediately set out for London to pursue his claim.[132] This left James Glen in a troubling dilemma, for McNaire's testimony in London would

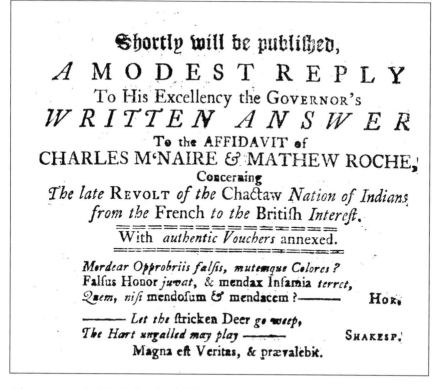

Advertisement for "A Modest Reply" from the *South Carolina Gazette,* February 26–March 5, 1750 (courtesy of Charleston Library Society, Charleston, South Carolina).

reveal not only his role in the company but also his attempts to thwart provincial laws by attempting to effect a monopoly. Thus, Glen embarked on a campaign to undermine McNaire's effort and denied that the trader had ever been empowered to act on behalf of the government.[133] His recall of Adair had been part of the plan to discredit McNaire.

The solidarity of the McNaire company partners and conspirators thus broken, and with Glen's forces in nominal control of the assembly, McNaire's partner Mathew Roche decided to appeal "to the Public without doors."[134] The publicity that preceded the actual publication of the "Modest Reply" had embroiled the entire colony in the dispute. Glen, enraged by the pre-publication announcements and then the widespread circulation of the "Modest Reply," demanded that the Commons conduct an inquiry into McNaire and Company's failures, particularly the delay and supposed "loss" of the public presents to the Choctaw.[135]

Clearly, the inclusion of Adair's letter condemning the governor's duplicity in Roche's pamphlet had cost Adair the support and friendship of Glen. Seething over his abandonment and realizing no further support would come from Glen, Adair composed a petition directed to the assembly asking for compensation for his losses. Further, he let it be known that he was more than willing to assist the assembly in its investigation of the Choctaw matter, and for two weeks running he placed an advertisement in the *South Carolina Gazette* giving "notice, that he is ready and willing to attend on the Public Service until the first Day of *April* next, to make Answer to all such Questions as may be demanded of him, with regard to the Knowledge he may have concerning the *Chactaw* Affairs, &c." The advertisement concluded with an impertinent *nota bene:* "*I am at my old Lodgings, where his Excellency the Governor knows.*"[136]

Glen, forgetting he had once supported Adair for reimbursement, now turned his full fury on the trader, reporting to his council that the advertisements were insulting and deserving of punishment. According to the governor, if "such obscure Fellows were permitted to insult Gov. or Government without punishment there would be an End to all Order, Distinction and Authority." He also sought to prevent Adair from returning to the Indian country "as it might be attended with bad Consequences he being a Man of a General bad Character and so Notorious that it required no Proof." Glen suggested a charge of libel. The council agreed that the wording was "very Sawcy and Insolent" and turned the advertisement over to the attorney general.[137] The attorney general found the note at the bottom of Adair's notice particularly alarming "as it insinuates an improper or too great intimacy or Familiarity between" Adair and the governor. The implication was that such intimacy could "scandalize the Govt." But the libel was a stretch, even by the loose standards the council seemed ready to employ, and the attorney general further noted that Adair "can not be restrained or prosecuted till some offense is actually committed contrary" to the trade act and the license he held under it.[138]

Adair's declaration that he would leave Charleston carried practical as well as political overtones, for he was in Charleston under the provincial seal, with protection from his creditors. The night before he was set to leave, Glen sent a written summons to him and Adair complied "with respect to both time and place."[139] Adair met with Glen as well as the committee investigating the entire Choctaw debacle. The meetings did not go well, and before he left Charleston, Adair placed yet another advertisement in the *South-Carolina Gazette,* advising that he would shortly publish "A Treatise" on Choctaw affairs which would include a "*genuine* Account" of the affair. His tartly worded notice warned that it would contain "some Scenes of a FARCE, as the same was some time ago first rehearsed in private, and afterwards acted publickly; in which are contained, some comical and instructive

𝕿𝖍𝖊 Subfcriber intending to fet out upon a long Journey, gives Notice, that he is ready and willing to attend on the Public Service until the firft Day of *April* next, to make Anfwer to all fuch Queftions as may be demanded of him, with regard to the Knowledge he may have concerning the *Chaᴙaw* Affairs, &c.   JAMES ADAIR.

N.B. *I am at my old Lodgings, where His Excellency the Governor knows.*

James Adair's "very Sawcy and Insolent" notice to Governor James Glen, *South Carolina Gazette,* March 12–19, 1750 (courtesy of Charleston Library Society, Charleston, South Carolina).

Dialogues between the several modest Pretenders to the Merit of a certain Revolt." A thorough chronicler, Adair closed the notice promising the work would be "supported by Records, original Letters, and living Witnesses."[140] The advertisement, by insinuating that Glen had met with Adair in an attempt to influence his testimony before the committee, did not ease tensions between the parties.

The committee members, now thoroughly prejudiced against Adair and deftly manipulated by Glen to protect his own self-interest, found it convenient to hear only what they wanted to hear. They accused Adair of prevarication, largely because he had at first bad-mouthed McNaire and then two years later refused to lay the entire blame for the "loss" of the Choctaw on McNaire's company. Whatever drove Adair—hope for compensation, anger at Glen, pique at politicians who regarded connection more than ability—it made him even more plainspoken. He refused to become entangled in the political endgame, and though he was accused of prevarication, he would not bow to political pressure and "assist the prime magistrate in a bad cause."[141]

Instead, he threw more fuel on the fire, sending a letter to William Pinckney in late April urging him to assert his authority as Indian commissioner, blasting the governor's management of the Indian affairs, and accusing Pinckney of neglecting his duty. In Adair's words, Glen "seems to me to punish Virtue as far as he can and not Vice." In addition to relating news of the murder of a packhorseman, Adair repeated his charges against Creek traders who opened letters bound for Charleston and destroyed contents at their pleasure with no rebuke from the authorities. Since Glen had snubbed the Chickasaw when they were in Charleston and they were denied assistance by the governor and council, Adair asked Pinckney to apply

Shortly will be publifhed,

A TREATISE

Upon the Importance and Means of fecuring

The *CHACTAW* Nation of INDIANS

in the *Britifh* Intereft.

In which are interfperfed many curious REMARKS
Concerning the *Hiftory*, *Policy*, and *Intereft* of that Nation.
With

Several inconteftable Reafons, and chronological
Obfervations, to prove, that the Year of our Lord 1738
was feveral Years antecedent to the Year 1747.

To which is added,

A *genuine* ACCOUNT
Of the moft remarkable OCCURRENCES
fince that Period of Time.

Concluding with

Some SCENES *of a* FARCE, *as the fame was fome time
ago firft rehearfed in private, and afterwards acted
publickly; in which are contained, fome comical and
inftructive* Dialogues *between* the feveral modeft
Pretenders *to the Merit of a certain Revolt, faid by
them to be lately projected and effected.*

The whole fupported by Records,
original Letters, and living Witneffes.

What fhould be *grave*, you turn to *Farce.*
I wifh the ———— —— —— ————.   PRIOR.

O Magnus pofthac inimicis Rifus ! ————   HOR.
         Quod magis ad nos
Pertinet, & nefcire Malum eft, agitemus ————   Id.

Treatise advertisement. *South Carolina Gazette,* April 2–8, 1750 (courtesy of Charleston Library Society, Charleston, South Carolina).

to the legislature for the six swivel guns requested by the Chickasaw, noting that they feared French retaliation for the Choctaw war. He railed against those who ignored trade laws while those who assisted the government with intelligence and conformed to the trade laws were vilified. Such unequal treatment meant that "the disorderly trader Lived and triumphed in our Ruins without any evident Punishment." In Adair's view "the Laws of Nature and general Reason Supercede the Municipall and possitive Laws of Nations [so that] we possibly could not be fetter'd by such Unequal Laws." His injunction to Pinckney: "correct every Vice and encourage every Virtue which is the true design of Ruling."[142] Pinckney may have been sympathetic, but in the superheated atmosphere, Glen's partisans on the council decreed the letter had taken "very Scurilous and Scandalous Libertys with his Excellencys Character."[143] This time, the attorney general found ample cause to recommend that Adair be charged with "Seditious libel" at the next session of the assembly, and the attorney general was ordered to issue a "Warrant for apprehending the said Adair."[144]

Adair's petition, devoid of emotional language, fared no better. In it, he claimed to have acted only on "Orders and Directions from the Governor to use the best ways and means to bring the Choctaw Nation to the British Interest." Glen, he attested, has "assured" him of reward. Acting on Glen's orders, Adair claimed that he had "first opened the way" to a English-Choctaw alliance. Further, he later assisted McNaire, as requested by the governor. In short, Adair's petition pleaded "That in these Actions and Endeavours . . . he had been at great Expences, undergone the greatest Hardships and Fatigues, taken many long Journeys, often risqued his Life, spent his Time, and his *All*. That he has not yet received any Reward for his services, tho by *Them* he is reduced to want, and unable (without Relief) further to serve the Public or support himself."[145] The petition, which included a copy of one of Glen's letters supporting his contentions, was, as Adair wryly observed, "traduced."[146] William Pinckney, called by the committee to comment on Adair's various letters, was obliged to agree that the two letters concerning McNaire, written two years apart, did contradict one another, one "greatly in praise of Mr. McNaire's Conduct, among the Choctaws, and the other very much blamed it." The committee refused to consider the circumstances under which letters had been written and decided that Adair and McNaire were in cahoots and that Adair's second letter had been contrived "for purpose." When the committee asked Pinckney "what Credit he thought ought to be given to the Testimony of a Man who has so manifestly prevaricated and contradicted himself," Pinckney fell in line with the consensus and opined that "Adair was a great Villain, and that not much credit ought to be given to him."[147]

With that, Adair's petition, though factually correct and supported by numerous letters and documents available to the committee, was rejected. McNaire and his partners were deemed to have been guilty of "Misconduct, Misrepresentation and Negligence," and McNaire's claim was likewise dismissed.[148] Matthew Roche's "Modest Reply" was denounced as "a false and malicious Paper." He was ultimately charged with libel and imprisoned for his huge debts.[149] But at least Adair and McNaire had survived: numerous English traders lost their lives in the backcountry war, including John Campbell, who was killed by a Choctaw war party near the end of November 1750.[150]

The Choctaw fared even worse, being repeatedly deceived and then deserted by their new English allies. The leaders of the English faction had by this time been killed or discredited and their towns destroyed. In a despicable act of abandonment, the South Carolina assembly decided it was not even necessary to inform their rapidly diminishing allies that the war with France had ended and that peace could be made. The French, freshly supplied with goods many believed had been shipped directly from Charleston, ultimately regained the allegiance of the Choctaw towns. By 1750, the Choctaw seemed permanently lost to English favor and trade, while the Chickasaw were under constant attack by French-allied Indians.[151]

Adair left Charleston and, so it was reported, "went over to the French."[152] Adair's "defection" to the French at Fort Toulouse provides the most intriguing episode in his career. Because he was an inveterate enemy of the French, it seems unlikely that Adair, even destitute and disgraced, would have seriously considered becoming a French agent. Nor is there any indication that the French would have trusted him. What is clear is that for three weeks in the summer of 1750, James Adair was a "guest" at Fort Toulouse. Adair would later explain that he had traveled to Fort Toulouse and that "Monsieur endeavoured to tempt me" with 32,000 French livre. When he refused, he was promptly made a prisoner. He claimed that the French intended to ship him to Mobile to put him on trial "for all the Consequences of the Chactaw War." But Adair, ever resourceful, "behaved like a Desperado against their Garrison," escaped, and eluded not only the French but parties of allied Alabama Indians set on his trail. He mused in a later letter to William Pinckney, "The World thinks it strange that I should be punishable both by the English and French, for that in Effect that was done for the one, and against the other in Time of a hot War. But so it happens in Time of Iron-Age."[153]

Suspicion that English traders dealt secretly with the French was not new, and even Lachlan McGillivray, who sent two contradictory letters regarding Creek affairs to South Carolina in 1746, was suspected of having illicit dealings with the French at Fort Toulouse.[154] But McGillivray's two letters, like Adair's, were the practical devices of a man who understood the power structure and sent one letter to inform and the other to please. Another motive comes to mind in Adair's bizarre visit to Fort Toulouse. It involves the report that the missing goods McNaire and Company had failed to deliver had somehow been shipped out of Charleston and ultimately reached Mobile during wartime, thereby greatly enriching those who sent the cargo and allowing the French to send goods to their Choctaw friends at a time the English-allied Choctaw had none. Edmond Atkin, in particular, mulled over the possibility, and thought he saw Governor Glen's hand in the incident.[155] It is entirely possible that Adair was attempting to garner evidence of some sort on the contraband trade during the war with which to discredit his political enemies—hence his trip to Fort Toulouse. As he would note years later, "In the last war, they [the French] had a plentiful supply by our Carolina vessels, if we can credit Chocktaws, or the french of Louisa; for the Chickasaw took prisoners and saw the goods."[156]

Redemption: "The goose-quill" and the Sword

He will throw away the goose-quill, and cheerfully take up the sword, without believing there is any real danger in serving God and his country, as soon as honour sounds the trumpet.

—"Lauglin McGilvery" [James Adair] to
William H. Lyttelton, July 14, 1758

Adair's encounter with the French at the Fort Toulouse adventure rendered him even more destitute, as he lost his horse and sidearms to the French. Following the misadventure, Adair returned to live with friends in the Carolina backcountry and worked for a time in the Cherokee trade.[157] In early February 1751, he became the center of an inquiry into the theft of three hundred deerskins stolen from a party of Cherokee Indians. Adair was found in possession of a pipe belonging to the Indians, which they said had been packed with the skins. Adair had no part in the theft, and the incident soon passed, for even his political enemies did not seriously believe the charges. But troubles were brewing among the Cherokee. Adair, noting warlike activities and growing unease among the Cherokee over encroachments as well as movements by Shawnee and Iroquois Indians, sent intelligence reports to Charleston. His assessment of Cherokee attitudes was essentially correct, and some whites were killed by the Cherokee. Adair encouraged South Carolina to take the offensive and offered to lead Chickasaw and "brave Woods-men" against the Cherokee on Carolina's behalf, noting "if I'm not mistaken in myself, with such brave wanton Fellows, I should be somewhat remarkable." His offer was ignored.[158] When Governor Glen later sent messengers to the backcountry making inquiries as to Adair's whereabouts, word went back to Charleston that the trader "was going to quit the Country and gett a Passage from the Northward to Jamaica."[159] But, as far as the record relates, that journey never materialized. Instead, as promised in the "Treatise" advertisement, Adair took up the "goose-quill" and began crafting a history of his view of the Choctaw revolt—a story that he would eventually shape into his *History*.[160]

For the next decade, Adair lived a shadowy backcountry existence as a trader and storekeeper. Like most of the other traders, he maintained a residence and store in the Indian country, but he also spent at least part of the year around New Windsor, South Carolina, the settlement which lay across the river from Augusta, Georgia.[161] A good deal of Adair's time was spent around the settlements of the "Lower" Chickasaw in South Carolina and at New Savannah.[162] Another fleeting reference places him at the Breed Camp, the Chickasaw settlement of the Upper Creeks, in 1754.[163] His name is absent from extant lists of those licensed to trade with either the Cherokee or Chickasaw Indians in the 1750s—but there are few extant lists. He is also noticeably absent from a list of Chickasaw traders who were the subjects of a censure by Edmond Atkin in 1759.[164] It seems that Adair lived quietly, employed in trade and study.

While Creek traders grew rich on the proceeds of their lucrative trade with the most powerful southeastern tribe, Chickasaw traders did not fare well. The Chickasaw, bombarded by assault after assault, were barely able to hunt or purchase ammunition.[165] Their traders suffered in kind. Although a political outcast and a man of little wealth, Adair was still a valued source of advice on backcountry matters, and his reputation as a scholar grew. Adair's associates—men like Lachlan McGillivray and George Galphin—stood by him, and in time his reputation was rehabilitated as old enemies faded away and backcountry residents rallied around one of their own.

As the years passed, Adair's "Choctaw treatise," now styled "A Treatise of the Indian Americans," began to take final form. By August 1758, Adair began collecting subscriptions for the work, declaring it "no Fiction, but drawn from the very Life of the *Indian* after 14 Years Observation and Experience."[166] The advertisement promised "a long Chain of Arguments" examining the "original Descent" of the Indians as well as an account of Indian customs and culture. Although his advertisement declared the work was "now ready" and would go to press as soon as subscriptions were raised to defray the cost of printing, the book was not published. No doubt, the attention of both the author and his potential subscribers was diverted from the project by yet another war with France—the Seven Years' War.

As Anglo-French hostilities escalated, so too did South Carolina's frontier machinations. In June 1758, South Carolina's new governor, William Henry Lyttelton, had visited Fort Moore, ostensibly to inspect the facility but more likely to chat with the deerskin traders and merchants, especially Lachlan McGillivray, whom his predecessor, Glen, had recommended as "a man of sense and substance."[167] Lyttelton's purpose in meeting McGillivray was to obtain advice on the backcountry and to sound out those knowledgeable on Indian affairs as to the feasibility of an overland attack on French Louisiana. McGillivray, whose trading store in the Creek nation was only a few miles from Fort Toulouse, was the obvious man to give such advice. James Adair, one of the few Englishmen to have seen the interior of the French fort, also possessed the widely advertised skill of warmongering in the backcountry as well as good intelligence on Fort Tombecbé and the western tribes.

Lyttelton's mission was part of a broader intelligence-gathering effort that had been under way for some time. The previous year, South Carolinian William Bonar, in disguise as a packhorseman, had been captured while reconnoitering Fort Toulouse. He was later released at the insistence of Anglo-allied Creeks. It is instructive that his ill-fated mission had begun at Lachlan McGillivray's trading store, which lay only five miles from the fort.[168] In addition, Carolina agents had been questioning Indians, deerskin traders, and their employees for several years about French fortifications and troop deployments.[169]

After talking with the traders, Lyttelton asked McGillivray for his thoughts "in writing." Following Lyttelton's short visit, Lachlan McGillivray dispatched a twelve-page document, dated July 14, 1758, to Lyttelton together with a shorter letter dated July 13, noting that the longer document contained "Mr. Adair's opinion in regard to the situation of Mobile."[170] The two letters were delivered to Lyttelton by James Adair. Although the longer, three-part letter is signed "Lauglin McGilvery," it is not in McGillivray's handwriting, and, as McGillivray's biographer Edward J. Cashin notes, the "emotional, exaggerated style is that of James Adair."[171] Cashin attributes the ideas contained in the document to McGillivray, but internal evidence strongly suggests that the thoughts as well as the penmanship belonged to James Adair. In any case, both men were of the same opinion: British possession of Mobile or New Orleans "would certainly be attended with the most advantageous consequences to the British Interest in America."[172] In fact, the writer of the long letter noted that it contained "our humble opinion" before laying out thoughts on land and sea advances against French Louisiana. Presumably, Adair concealed his identify due to his tarnished reputation and the fact that Lyttelton had approached McGillivray. Under the more respectable pseudonym, Adair did not hesitate to dispense advice and recommend himself for service.

Adair's written discourse recounted the danger of "Monsieur's [France's] sly insinuations" among the leading southeastern tribes, pointing out it was "dangerous to the british interest, that so cunning an enemy shou'd have the ear of so continguous, fickle, numerous, and martial a nation [the Creek nation]." At the same time, he pointed out the "almost unsurmountable and needless difficulties" and expenses that an overland campaign against French Louisiana would involve. He suggested that an army of six thousand men, at least "one half of them to be daring, hardy, active, and good gun-men; such as cou'd run and ambushcade, after the manner of the Indians" would be required. Further, it advised that generous shipments of presents—"harden'd sugar plumbs"—should be doled out to the Creeks as well as the Choctaw and Chickasaw. Adair was named as the proper man to "warm the hearts of our brave, friendly Chickesaws." Concerning the Choctaw: "what can be effected with the Choctaws, he can do: (for he, in the last french war, sett them on Monsieur)." The writer (Adair) declared that there could be no "real danger in serving God and his country, as soon as honour sounds the trumpet" and "that the only reward he shall take, under the exigencies of his Country, is what he will carry with himself, a consciousness of intending well for the country."[173]

The improbable recommendation that thousands of men would be required for the campaign was obviously designed to make an alternative to an overland march more desirable, with an approach by sea the obvious tactic. A seaborne assault, Adair pointed out, might avoid a repetition of "Xerxes . . . against the Greeks." In conjunction with the naval assault, Adair could have Indian "spies" in place to meet the British troopships when they arrived at Mobile—ships that could also carry well-supplied Chickasaw and Choctaw allies. The combined forces could then march north and "reduce Tumbigby hog-pen to dust." Adair compared the Anglo-French rivalry to that epic contest between Rome and Carthage and recalled the Roman leader Cato the Elder's injunction: "*Delenda est Carthago*" (Carthage must be utterly destroyed).

Adair noted that the possession of Tombecbé and Toulouse would "prove an over-balance against all the northern nations of Indians, beget a very great extent of territory, enough for several fine provinces, tho great part as fit for hemp, wine, indicoe &c as any such climate under the sun; woud enable us to supply those nations, by water-carriage; bring great profits to our Mother Country."[174] These were themes Adair would continue in his growing history, under the heading "Advice to Statesmen." McGillivray described the long letter as "Mr. Adair's opinion," and in the cover letter he forwarded to Lyttelton he pointed out that Adair could answer "all the necessary questions" the governor might have concerning the plan. McGillivray closed his own letter by noting that Adair "may be usefull in his way: he is a person I have no connection with. I pity his misfortunes."[175]

Lyttelton, musing on the difficulties outlined in the letter, pointed out ways to overcome them in the position paper on the proposed assault he provided to William Pitt, and he enclosed extracts of Adair's letter, as well as referring to them as the opinions of two Augusta traders. In the end, Lyttelton's overland scheme was rejected, but Adair's reputation as a man of intelligence and influence had been restored.[176] And he would soon find that many shared his views on the value of French Louisiana.

But events elsewhere were soon to force attention from the French forts on the Alabama and Tombigbee rivers, for by 1759 Cherokee warriors had murdered and scalped a number of Carolina backsettlers in retaliation for the prior murders of some of their own people at the hands of settlers on the Virginia frontier. At the time of their deaths, the Cherokee warriors were on their way home, having assisted the British against the French at Fort Stanwick. The situation teetered from bad to worse, and diplomacy failed completely to assuage the growing crisis. And there were other insults— some recounted by James Adair in his history, including the rape of Chero- kee women by British soldiers—and encroachments on Cherokee land. The Carolinians, led by Governor Lyttelton, engaged in a series of bungled ini- tiatives that included making hostages of a Cherokee peace delegation sent to Charleston and issuing hard-line demands that left no room for the Cherokee to salvage the situation. From the Creek country, rumors that the Cherokee were talking to the French failed to ameliorate tensions. Taken together, all these events had the unsurprising effect of igniting an Anglo- Cherokee war in 1759.[177] By mid-February 1760, the hostages, imprisoned at Fort Prince George, had been murdered, and Cherokee raiding parties had devastated the Carolina backcountry. Residents took shelter at Fort Moore and the Augusta garrison, as well as in heavily fortified private com- pounds. South Carolina appealed for help, and soon two regiments of Brit- ish regulars, commanded by Colonel Archibald Montgomery, arrived to supplement Carolina's paltry militia forces.

South Carolina called on her Indian allies to join her against the Chero- kee. In a message to the Assembly, Lieutenant Governor William Bull laid out the plan in April. The "far" or "upper" Chickasaw were to attack the Cherokee on the western frontier, while Upper and Lower Creek warriors, all led by "bold Englishmen," were to attack the Cherokee from the south at different places. The New Savannah Chickasaw were specifically enlisted to "act as an advanced or Scouting Party, to gain daily Intelligence for Colonel Montgomery, when he approaches the Enemy."[178]

In his message to the Assembly, the lieutenant governor recommended lieutenants' commissions for those leading the Upper Chickasaw, the Upper Creeks, and Lower Creeks but recommending the rank of captain in the case of the commissions "disposed of already . . . which being of higher Rank may inspire the officers with more Ambition to distinguish themselves." Presumably, this was Adair, who, Bull specifically noted, had already agreed to lead the "Lower" Chickasaw. In the end, the Assembly awarded captain's commissions to all four men, with the pay of £50 per month.[179] It is significant that Adair was the leader of the "Savannah or Lower Chicke-saws" and seems to confirm his primary place of residence around New Windsor. John Brown was selected to lead the "Upper Chickesaws." The total force of Chickasaw Indians was estimated at forty to fifty.[180]

In his *History,* Adair expressed contradictory sentiments regarding the Cherokee War. While he generally praised Lyttelton, he condemned the policies espoused by the governor that ultimately led to war, including the taking of hostages and what he termed "our uniform misconduct" of Indian diplomacy. Adair's truncated account of the Cherokee war contains an apt summation of the situation: "we forced the Cheerake to become our bitter enemies, by a long train of wrong measures."[181]

As Adair's *History* indicates, the fighting was bitter as British armies and parties of allied Indians stalked Cherokee warriors, burned towns, and de-stroyed horses and corncribs with impunity. As the spring of 1760 pro-gressed, Adair and Brown and the Chickasaw were active, and reports placed them on raids at Estatoe, Keowee, and Toxoway. Adair and his Savannah River Chickasaw seem to have confined their efforts largely to the Lower Cherokee Towns.[182] The devastated Cherokee soon sued for peace.

Adair, hoping to capitalize on the resuscitation of his reputation by his service to the colony in the war, submitted a revised memorial to the South Carolina Assembly seeking compensation for his losses in the decade-old Choctaw revolt in early 1761. But enemies still sat in the assembly, and, as Adair related, though he had the support of Lyttelton, now the governor of Jamaica, and the country members, "the infected air which had prevailed in that house for fourteen years" lingered still.[183] In addition to pointing out the age of the claim, after "long and warm debate" the politicians "seized on a couple of unfortunate monosyllables," and at Adair's mention of "*fine* promises" and Glen's "*smooth* artful letter" they took offense. According to the Commons House Journal, Adair's memorial contained "very improper and indecent Language [and] was Rejected without being read thro'."[184]

The Chickasaw Trader and West Florida

> . . . the only OLD Trader left alive . . .
>
> —*Georgia Gazette,* October 11, 1769

The end of the Seven Years' War promised as well an end to the ceaseless backcountry warfare. But even the ouster of France from territory east of the Mississippi River did not end the turmoil. Adair and his colleagues among the Chickasaw—Alexander McIntosh, John Brown, James High-rider, James Colbert, Robert Hannah, James Bubbie—had persisted rather than prospered through the tumultuous war years.[185] Under the new British hegemony, they hoped to prosper at last, but a new series of challenges awaited. The new troubles began with the issuance of the Proclamation of 1763 by the government of George III. The proclamation established new colonies in East and West Florida, but, more important from the traders' point of view, it destroyed the decades-old limit on the number of traders who could legally enter the Indian country. In effect, anyone who could post a small bond could obtain a general license giving them the right to trade freely anywhere in the Indian country. In the past, colonial governors had only issued a limited number of licenses to specific towns, thereby controlling competition and insuring a rough semblance of order in the back-country. The new licenses required traders to abide by all British trade regulations but neglected to state what the regulations were.[186]

In the wake of the proclamation, many novice traders headed for the Indian country for the first time, hoping to make a quick fortune. Their disregard for established practices and lawless behavior brought cries of foul from the old-line traders who had weathered the lean years. The first hint of trouble in the Chickasaw towns came in August 1764, when the old traders there received word that new traders were believed to be on their way to the Chickasaw country with goods "at a very great under rate." The intent of these men, it was reported, was to trade rum for the famous Chickasaw horses "in the woods," away from the stores of respectable traders.[187] The established traders quickly reported the rumors to West Florida officials, and although they realized the problem was real and took steps to thwart the "new" traders, the efforts provided fruitless. Rum, easy to transport and easier to "water down" to increase one's profit margin, also created disturbances and impoverished the Indians, for if they traded their deerskins for rum, they had nothing with which to obtain needed clothing and arms.

At a series of congresses beginning in 1765, the British superintendent of Indian affairs, John Stuart, attempted to establish a standardized tariff for traders and establish trade regulations for the Choctaw, Chickasaw, and Creek nations.[188] Following the congress in Mobile with the Choctaw and Chickasaw, Adair obtained a West Florida trading license from Governor George Johnstone, who stood bond for him. Adair praised Johnstone in his book and submitted intelligence reports and advice to Johnstone on Chickasaw affairs.[189] The prices established in 1765 were substantially lower than those set by the French and also lowered the legal price of goods sold by Chickasaw traders. Because of the long distances they traveled, the overhead of the Chickasaw traders was higher. The new tariff provided a double blow to law-abiding traders like Adair who not only saw their profit margin shaved dramatically but also had to compete with the new generation of itinerant traders that Adair condemned for their "Arabian-like method of plundering the Indians."[190] Many of these new traders, who had no established contacts with Indian towns, did not settle among the Indians and participate in regular town life but moved from place to place peddling rum, bargained for unprocessed deerskins, and overextended credit—or even worse, took deerskins rightfully owed to the hunter's established town trader who had outfitted the hunter on credit. In his *History*, Adair would claim that he lost "in the space of a year, to the amount of two and twenty hundred dollars-worth of goods at prime costs."[191] But monetary loss was not Adair's sole motive in denouncing use of "maddening rum, & lying fair speeches" to cheat and abuse the trust of the Chickasaw, for the new traders, by their own account, threatened to "make a New Hell of this Place."[192]

To compete, many of Adair's long-time colleagues succumbed to the pressure and were among those mentioned in Adair's complaints. Lawlessness reigned as such unscrupulous traders openly challenged the authority of both the Chickasaw leading men and John McIntosh, the British commissary who was responsible for enforcing British trade laws. Adair at first allied with McIntosh and, on at least one occasion, accompanied him on an investigation of illegal trading practices.[193] But even the commissary broke the law and became involved in a scheme to obtain land for private purposes among the Chickasaw. Factional disputes arose among the Chickasaw, as traders competed for customers and sought to undermine the authority of the commissary. Paya Mataha, in disgust, resigned his newly awarded position as Chickasaw Great Medal Chief.[194] The outbreak of war between the Creek and Choctaw Indians imposed additional risks and hardships, and by the fall of 1766 war parties of Creek and Choctaw Indians made the most direct trade path from the Chickasaw towns to Mobile unsafe. Adair was forced to take the long path that led through the western Choctaw towns when he traveled to Mobile.[195] The times, as Adair's reminiscences show, were just as dangerous without the French—and just as unprofitable. By 1766, there were seven licensed traders among the Chickasaw. Since there were only 350 Chickasaw hunters, John Stuart estimated that they needed only three traders. Under such conditions, it was impossible to prosper through legal trade.[196]

Adair's postwar tenure among the western Chickasaw towns was remembered decades later by Malcom McGee. Interviewed in the 1840s, McGee recorded that Adair was not in the towns when he arrived in the 1760s but arrived "soon after," stayed "two or three years and then went to the Cherokees." McGee was mistaken about Adair's date of arrival, which he placed in 1769, as well as his ultimate destination, but was perhaps reliable in his memory that all the traders at that time, including Adair, had Chickasaw wives.[197] More important, McGee remembered that Adair had departed soon after his arrival. And it does seem that James Adair made his last journey from the western Chickasaw towns to Charleston in late 1768.

And what of Adair's life among the Chickasaw? The peripatetic scholar reckoned that he was intimately acquainted with "near two thousand miles" of trading paths twisting through "remote woods" and Indian towns from his decades of travel among the southeastern Indians.[198] His usual route before the war led from New Windsor, South Carolina, across the Savannah River to Augusta, Georgia, and from there along the major trade artery to the Tallapoosa towns of the Creeks. From there, for most of his career, he opted for the "longest yet the safest path,"[199] which turned northward, toward the Creek town of Coosa and the nearby Chickasaw Breed Camp, established as a transshipment point for English Chickasaw traders. There, the path veered to the northwest, across the mountainous passes that rise along the northwestern limit of the Coosa River. From there, the Chickasaw Path cut through *Book'pharaah,* the Long Swamp, before ultimately reaching the fortified towns of the Chickasaw.[200]

Part of Adair's success was no doubt due to the quality of his mounts. A particular favorite, Eagle, was the "swiftest of any in the Chikkasah country," and Chickasaw horses were renowned for their gallop.[201] Traveling through this landscape constructed of swirling rapids, clear springs, waterfalls, cane swamps, and heaps of stone that marked where those who had died on the path were killed or buried, Adair ranged from the Great Smoky Mountains to the palmetto swamps around St. Augustine, through abandoned Indian villages, ancient camping sites, and the well-ordered towns of every major southeastern Indian tribe.[202]

Travel was hard; there were few comforts. Parched corn flour and freshly killed game satisfied hunger, while a hollow cane, conveniently corked, carried water to quench one's thirst.[203] Rum relieved the tedium, for Adair was often alone.[204] And there is no doubt that a "hearty draught of punch" could engender courage as well, especially when danger threatened.[205] Adair, like all the traders, traveled well-armed, carrying a musket, two pistols stashed in a belt, scalping knives, and hatchets. When in the company of other traders, the journey was less monotonous, with rowdy and like-minded companions providing idle conversation as well as "noisy bacchanalian" scenes and such diversions as wrestling or horse racing.[206]

Once at his fortified trading post, Adair settled in to town life, and by 1747 he already considered the Chickasaw country "home."[207] Only the merest hint of his domestic arrangements emerge from the pages of his history. While Adair recorded that his bed was "always hung round with various arms of defence," he failed to mention with whom he shared that bed, noting offhandedly that in 1748 his household included "women and children." He also owned mastiffs who stood guard and assisted in the hunt.[208] In more peaceful times, Adair had the "pleasure of writing" his recollections and shaping his theories on Indian origins in the company of a Chickasaw woman, whom he declared "as great a princess as ever lived among the ancient Peruvians, or Mexicans." It is the only hint of affection for his companion to be found in his writings. No doubt, she was a teacher of incalculable value and perhaps the reason he remained so long among her people. Her identity remains a mystery. His one mention of her reveals an intimate domestic scene of writer and informant at work—Adair recording the Indian method of preparing corn as his wife chides him to avoid errors lest it "spoil the making of good bread, or hommony, and of course beget the ill-will of our white women." [209]

Adair mentions no offspring, but in describing to his readers the "young-rising prolific family" of traders, one cannot help but imagine that Adair was surrounded by his own.[210] Unrecorded also are the disappointments, difficulties, and sorrows of his domestic life, including the fate of his wife and any children. He described the trader's life as one of "greatest plenty," and his fondly recalled accounts of daily life in the Indian country, one would hope, surely spring from happy memories.[211] By his own account, Indian countrymen "possessed all the needful things to make a reasonable life easy." And for Adair, the fact that "through all the Indian countries, every person lives at his own choice, not being forced in the least degree to any thing contrary to his own inclination" must have been part of the appeal of his chosen profession.[212]

As an Indian countryman, trader, and sometime diplomat, Adair credited his success to the fact that he refused to keep the Indians "at a proper distance," as he denounced others for doing. Rather, Adair "sat and smoked with the head-men on bear-skins, set the young people to their various diversions and then viewed them with pleasure."[213] He told them about English women, engaged them in complex philosophical discussions over religion and politics, told tall tales, played practical jokes, got drunk and sang Irish melodies, joined Indian men on hunting and fishing expeditions, and argued with them about everything from the true size of the sun to the efficacy of rainmaking.[214] Then he retired to the privacy of his fortified trading house, to study and to write.

Writing his *History* proved to be a tedious and extended exercise. He wrote in isolation, save for the company of his Chickasaw wife. Frequently, he was forced to hide his papers from the prying eyes of the Indians around him, who were suspicious of traders' correspondence. Denied "the conversation of the learned" and distant from libraries, he imported his own books and taught himself rudimentary Hebrew. Business concerns hampered his effort, as did the "secrecy and closeness of the Indians as to their own affairs." Yet, in addition to his keen powers of observation, Adair held a sublime advantage over every previous historian of the southern tribes. As he noted in his preface, "I sat down to draw the Indians on the spot—had them many years standing before me,—and lived with them as a friend and brother."[215]

Adair, although he described himself as an "English Chickasaw," was an anomaly rather than a hybrid. Like others of his kind, he was a man who wafted tenuously between two very different worlds and was not completely of one or the other. He lived among the Indians for nearly forty years but was never a full member of Indian society. He was excluded from many ceremonies, barred from observing "sacred employment" of Indian religious leaders,[216] not allowed to attend the funerals of friends, and required to sleep apart when he accompanied Chickasaw men on the warpath.[217] He was rarely invited into the private households of his most intimate Indian friends, who were all community leaders and met him in public places where men gathered.[218] Yet, as a trader of long standing among them, a brave and honest man possessing esoteric knowledge about other worlds, he was a "friend and brother."[219] He was also a husband and no doubt a father.

But he was still an outsider. "*Nothings* is the most favourable name they give us," he wrote. A chagrined Natchez warrior, his eyes stinging from one of Adair's more energetic practical jokes, perhaps spoke the true view from the other side: Adair was an "impure accursed nothing, who lied, drank, ate hog's flesh, and sung *Tarooa Ookproo'sto,* 'the devil's tune,' or song of the evil ones."[220] If the old Natchez warrior had his doubts about Adair, so too the trader expressed conflicting views and dashed hopes regarding Indians among whom he lived. Adair's ambivalence toward them is clearly perceptible in his work. At times they are honest, true, brave and uncorrupted—equals and allies. Pages later, the mood shifts, and Adair's Indians are unenlightened and simple, "wolfish," superstitious, untrustworthy. In sum, Adair reveals shifting and conflicting points of view acquired over a hard lifetime in the backcountry.

From the British perspective, where a trader's success was measured by how soon he acquired enough wealth to leave the Indian country and establish himself in a respectable occupation, such as storekeeping and planting, Adair was an abject failure. Unlike his fellow traders George Galphin and Lachlan McGillivray, he built no extensive estate in South Carolina or Georgia. Frequently in debt, what he earned through the trade he seemingly exchanged for books and paper.[221] He held no offices, nor did he acquire the approbation of colonial assemblies, governors, or the British Indian department. He rarely seems to have served as an official interpreter. And yet, by the standards of those who had lived the bitter and dangerous years on the English edge, men like George Galphin, Lachlan McGillivray, and Paya Mataha, Adair was a valued friend and respected chronicler of times hardly recorded—much less commemorated—in the more powerful parts of the empire.

James Adair, Esquire, Author

Mr. James Adair is well recommended to me from America, as a Person of Credit and Veracity, whose Accounts of what he has seen among the Indians of various Nations with whom he traded and resided many Years, may be relied on.

—Benjamin Franklin to Charles and
Edward Dilly, March 25, 1774

By 1768, his massive tome on the southeastern Indians finished, Adair headed north, seeking support for the publication of his book. In late 1768, he visited Sir William Johnson, superintendent of Indian affairs for the Northern District. In pointed contrast, no record survives of any attempt to solicit help from John Stuart, the southern superintendent of Indian affairs, who would have seemed the logical choice.[222] Johnston entertained Adair at Johnson Hall and introduced him to a kindred spirit in his deputy George Crogan. Though he subscribed to the proposed work, he offered little in the way of encouragement. He did provide a lackluster letter of introduction to General Thomas Gage, noting that Adair's "appearance may not be much in his favor and his voluminous work may rather be deemed Curious than entertaining, but he is certainly well acquainted with the Southern Indians, and a man of Learning tho Rusticated by 30 years residence in a Wild Country."[223] General Gage refused to see him, and Adair supposed it was due to his outspoken condemnation of the Indian trade policies then in effect and supported by Gage and John Stuart. Adair informed Johnson of the rebuff and reported he viewed the snub "with a philosophic eye . . . as a most imaginary trifle; Especially, if what I said to a curious inquisitive Son of Caledonia [presumably John Stuart], concerning ye well-known mis-management, & ill situation, of our Indian affairs, westwardly, should have occasioned it; For truth will prevail, when painted with its genuine honest colours."[224]

While Gage refused to see him, others did not. He may have been "rusticated" by his time in the wilderness and blunt to the point of rudeness, but it was clear to other learned men that James Adair was an intelligent and educated man, well-versed in classical literature, history, and religion. As a London writer would observe, "he appears to be a scholar."[225] Among those who received Adair was John Ogilvie, an Anglican missionary with years of experience among the Mohawk Indians.[226] At King's College (now Columbia), the college president, Dr. Myles Cooper, pronounced Adair's work fit and offered his support, as did Professor Charles Inglis and Samuel Auchmuty, the rector of Trinity Church. More important, it was through their encouragement that Sir Henry Moore, governor of New York, lent his assistance in publicizing the book both in his colony and in the West Indies, although he had not met Adair. Moore's assistance was particularly valuable, and Adair claimed that Moore persuaded the members of his council to subscribe to his work and recommended it to assembly members as well. Adair was so grateful for the superintendent's and governor's assistance in continuing to solicit subscriptions for the work that he planned to dedicate the volume to Moore and Johnson.[227]

In conversations with Johnson, Adair had informed him that he wished to take a Chickasaw delegation with him to England—a group that would have almost certainly included Adair's friend Paya Mataha. He also suggested missionaries be sent to the Chickasaw territory.[228] A jaded eye might see in Adair's plan an attempt merely to secure the patronage of influential American churchmen and the Society for the Propagation of the Gospel in Foreign Parts. But for Adair, who had observed "the familiar easy way in which our traders live with them, begetting imperceptibly an emulous spirit of imitation," the situation seemed self-evident. If only lawless, unprincipled traders who plied their customers with liquor and "ignorant and wicked clergymen" were settled among "the uncorrupt part of the Indians, in general, and of the Chikkasah, in particular," disaster would result. And Adair supplied a description of the developing disaster, not only in his manuscript but in a memorial to West Florida officials, condemning the liquor trade and the resultant degradation of native culture. He noted further in his *History* the dissolute state of the New Windsor Chickasaw who had been corrupted by excessive drink. Adair's call for praiseworthy examples no doubt had strong appeal to his New York audience, who, through the example of the Mohawk Indians, had indeed seen that proper missionary work could make "a great advance toward their being civilized."[229] From New York, Adair proceeded to Philadelphia.[230] By late 1769, the *Georgia Gazette* noted that Adair's "Essays on the American Aborigines" had been "perused and patronized by most of the great and learned in our Northern colonies, and have in print the sanction of all the Professors of the celebrated rising Academies of New-York and Philadelphia." [231]

Adair's accomplishments in successfully promoting his book cannot be overstated. The transformation of a manuscript to a published production was no small feat for any American, much less an eccentric man who still reeked of backcountry leather. But Adair's resources, though limited, proved substantial. It seems clear that he enjoyed the support of members of the small yet influential community of rising planter and business elites in South Carolina and Georgia who valued knowledge and had proprietary pride in their own short history, as well as interest in Indian culture. He was also supported in his efforts by the printers of the two primary southern newspapers, the *South Carolina Gazette* and the *Georgia Gazette.* Both papers printed and distributed proposals and took subscriptions for the work. And leading citizens supplied Adair with letters of introduction that advanced his cause and opened influential doors as he traveled to Philadelphia, New York, and New Jersey—and ultimately London—in pursuit of subscribers and patrons.[232] Proposals promised a book to be published in two octavo volumes, printed on "a good Paper, with Letter entirely new." Priced at two Spanish dollars, one-half the price was due at the time of subscription and one-half upon delivery of the completed work.[233] Adair did not collect the money personally; rather the money was held by agents—various merchants and printers or attorneys—acting on his behalf in London, Charleston, and Savannah.[234]

While in Philadelphia, Adair had met with Joseph Galloway, the speaker of the Pennsylvania assembly. Galloway, from his perusal of the manuscript, believed Adair to be "very capable of Executing his Design" but "in Need of the Assistance and Judgment of Men of Letters." Galloway noted that Adair believed that "he can better execute his Design in England than in this Country" and provided a letter of introduction for Adair to present to Benjamin Franklin, then in London.[235] By September 1769, the *South Carolina Gazette* announced that Adair intended to embark for London soon, and Adair wrote patrons advising them he planned to sail for England in the summer of 1770.[236] Meanwhile, current events gave Adair an opportunity to ruminate on British Indian policy, particularly the 1769 effort of John Stuart to negotiate a peace between the Choctaw and Creek Indians, and he wrote to Sir William Johnson, noting that it was the "universal opinion of all us, who have gain'd sufficient skill in Indian affairs" that once the peace was made the Creeks would attack Georgia.[237] Adair's warning proved prophetic, and in late December 1773 Creek warriors descended on the Georgia frontier. By that time, Adair had left America for London.

Along the way, he called on Elias Boudinot, of Elizabethtown, New Jersey, who would later serve as president of the Continental Congress. Boudinot's neighbor was William Livingston, "a correct scholar, well known for his literary abilities and knowledge of the belle-lettres." According to Boudinot, Adair brought "ample recommendations and gave a good account of himself" and hoped to have the two New Jersey scholars examine his work. But the men advised Adair not to delay his trip to England, owing to the "political troubles then increasing." As a result, Adair "accordingly took passage in the first vessel that was bound to England."[238] The troubles to which Boudinout referred were the growing rift between the colonies and Great Britain.

Years later, Boudinot recalled that his meeting with Adair was "sometime about the year 1774, or 1775."[239] It would seem that Boudinot erred in his remembrance, for by early 1772, Adair was in London, and surviving accounts reveal that misadventure continued to plague Adair. According to Francis H. Tuckey, who published a history of Cork, Ireland in 1837, Adair arrived in Cork on June 4, 1772:

> in consequence of the following circumstances; being in London a few weeks before he arrived here, he was persuaded by a sharper, who went by the name of captain Redmond Magra, to let him have his manuscripts to shew lord Camden, Mr. Burke, Mr. Wilkes and others, and promised faithfully to deliver them afterwards to a printer for publication; but instead of doing so, he eloped to Dublin and from thence to this city, whither he was pursued by the author, and secured on the 8th of June at his lodgings near the old drawbridge; and the production of many years laborious study was thus recovered by the owner.[240]

Tuckey's "sharper" or confidence man who absconded with Adair's manuscript was no doubt Dr. Raymond Magra, an acquaintance of Sir William Johnson. By March of 1774, Adair and his manuscript were back in London.

Adair's time in London was evidently brief, and to date virtually no information concerning his time there has been recovered. As Adair was arriving, Benjamin Franklin, the best-known American of the age, was still smarting from his grilling before the Privy Council.[241] Word of the Boston Tea Party had infuriated many Englishmen, and it is not too much of a stretch to imagine that a "rusticated" American woodsman would not have fared well in light of the political climate. In the preface to his book, Adair noted that "the whole empire is discontented and America in strong convulsions," and he inserted passing negative references to the Tea Act and Quebec Act in his study.[242] There is no doubt that James Adair's sentiments were firmly with the Americans.

Once in London, Adair carried letters of introduction and recommendation to Benjamin Franklin, seeking advice on the best publishing house for his manuscript.[243] Franklin, whose meteoric career had begun as a printer and publisher in Philadelphia, knew the business well, and he recommended publishers Charles and Edward Dilly. In a letter to them on Adair's behalf, Franklin noted that Adair was "well recommended to me from America, as a Person of Credit and Veracity, whose Accounts of what he has seen among the Indians of various Nations with whom he traded and resided many Years, may be relied on." He also thought that a "judicious Abridgment" of Adair's voluminous manuscript "might be entertaining and of course saleable." [244] Franklin noted that the Dillys could pay Adair "as much for it [the manuscript] as any of the Trade," and he recommended them as "honourable Dealers." Adair had indicated to Franklin that he "would take perhaps the greatest Part of what it [the manuscript] may be thought worth in the printed Copies of it."[245] Apparently, Adair intended to make his profits from filling the subscriptions already on record in America.[246]

The Dillys were not only among the most highly respected London printers and booksellers but were also friends of the American cause. Edward Dilly's home and bookshop at "the Poultry" was a gathering spot for such literary giants as Samuel Johnson and James Boswell, as well as political radicals, who were welcomed at Dilly's table and frequently boarded in his establishment.[247] The Philadelphia physician Benjamin Rush dubbed the Dillys' bookstore "a kind of Coffee house for authors." Rush was only one of the many Americans whose business interests and sensibilities took them to the Poultry, where the Dillys were always on the lookout for fresh work from America.[248] At the Poultry, Adair continued to refine his manuscript under his publisher's supervision, and the latest dated comment in the book concerns the "late Quebec act," which was signed June 22, 1774.[249] His *History* bears a publication date of 1775. Adair evidently left London before the book was published, for by late autumn of 1774 he was back in Georgia, a party to one of the most bizarre land schemes in southern colonial history—Jonathan Bryan's attempt to lease from the Creek Indians nearly five million acres of land in the old Apalache territory.

Bryan, born in South Carolina in 1708, had participated, like Adair, in General Oglethorpe's attack on St. Augustine in 1740. In later years, he amassed a considerable estate and in the 1750s moved to Georgia, where he became a member of the Georgia Council. Throughout his career, he remained active in Indian affairs. It seems highly probable that Bryan and Adair were old acquaintances, but details of their relationship are lacking. James Adair is listed as one of three white men who witnessed the second of Bryan's controversial leases for valuable land in East Florida. The only evidence recovered concerning the transaction is Adair's name on a copy of a lease agreement dated October 28, 1774. Since the signatures on the document were copied by a clerk, there is no way to ascertain if the signer was James Adair the author, but, because of his associations, historians have regarded the signer to be the James Adair under consideration here.[250] The lease, which went against the spirit if not the letter of royal decrees, was denounced by the governors of Georgia and East Florida as well as by John Stuart. No doubt the Creeks who signed the lease and were promised a

THE

H I S T O R Y

OF THE

AMERICAN INDIANS;

PARTICULARLY

Thofe NATIONS adjoining to the MISSISIPPI, EAST AND
WEST FLORIDA, GEORGIA, SOUTH AND
NORTH CAROLINA, AND VIRGINIA:

CONTAINING

An ACCOUNT of their ORIGIN, LANGUAGE, MANNERS, RELIGIOUS and
CIVIL CUSTOMS, LAWS, FORM of GOVERNMENT, PUNISHMENTS, CONDUCT in
WAR and DOMESTIC LIFE, their HABITS, DIET, AGRICULTURE, MANU-
FACTURES, DISEASES and METHOD of CURE, and other Particulars, fuffi-
cient to render it

A

COMPLETE INDIAN SYSTEM.

WITH

OBSERVATIONS on former HISTORIANS, the Conduct of our Colony
GOVERNORS, SUPERINTENDENTS, MISSIONARIES, &c.

ALSO

AN APPENDIX,

CONTAINING

A Defcription of the FLORIDAS, and the MISSISIPPI LANDS, with their PRODUC-
TIONS—The Benefits of colonifing GEORGIANA, and civilizing the INDIANS—
And the way to make all the Colonies more valuable to the Mother Country.

With a new MAP of the Country referred to in the Hiftory.

By J A M E S A D A I R, Efquire,
A TRADER with the INDIANS, and Refident in their Country for Forty Years.

L O N D O N:
Printed for EDWARD and CHARLES DILLY, in the Poultry,
MDCCLXXV.

Title page of the 1775 edition (courtesy of Tutwiler Collection of Southern History
and Literature, Birmingham Public Library, Birmingham, Alabama).

trade from the area of Mr. Bryan's proposed new settlement would have recognized James Adair.[251]

There were obvious benefits for a man in Adair's position to assist Bryan, including the fact that both were supporters of the American cause by this time.[252] Moreover, Bryan had important connections both in the colonies and in England. Bryan may have been among those who provided letters of introduction to Benjamin Franklin, for he had connections with Franklin in regard to botanical field experiments in Georgia.[253] Further, Bryan was involved with the religious community at Bethesda, Georgia, and had ties to churchmen in England—the very people from whom Adair sought support for missionaries to the Chickasaw and who would be interested in Adair's arguments concerning the origin of the American Indians.[254] Interestingly, one of Bryan's early supporters was East Florida Chief Justice William Drayton, who met Bryan in a Charleston bookshop.[255] There seems no doubt that Adair's involvement in Bryan's scheme speaks of an association designed to further the publication of the book. And for his part, Adair, in his *History*, promoted the colonization of the area sought by Bryan.[256]

Bryan was certainly not the only land speculator from whom Adair seems to have received assistance in the publication of his book. In his *History*, Adair called for the establishment of a new colony on the Mississippi River, which he referred to as Georgiana. He clearly echoed the sentiments of the times, and numerous colonization schemes for the Mississippi and Ohio country were afoot. It stands to reason that land speculators and those with colonization schemes would seek out Adair's advice, for he knew the lower Mississippi territory as did few others. And no doubt he counted such speculators among his unrecorded subscribers and supporters. The strong espousal for the establishment of "Georgiana" in his *History* seems to suggest his own involvement, but no concrete evidence has emerged to clarify his role in any colonization attempts. However, there is circumstantial evidence that links him to George Croghan's Illinois Company. Not only did Adair dedicate his volume to Croghan, whom he had known only briefly, but three prominent men from whom he would procure assistance in publishing his history were also members of the Illinois Company, including Sir William Johnson, Benjamin Franklin, and Joseph Galloway. Another individual closely associated with the effort was General Phineas Lyman, who worked tirelessly during the 1760s to secure a land grant in West Florida and establish a settlement on the Mississippi—Adair's Georgiana.[257] Without the discovery of additional evidence, Adair's participation in both schemes will remain unclear at best, but like his contemporary Bernard Romans, he would surely have counted supporters of colonization efforts among his readers.

When Adair's *History* reached American shores is unknown. At least some of those who subscribed to the book had to wait until after the Revolutionary War to obtain copies from London, and even in the South it was not generally known.[258] One person who evidently did receive a copy of the book before the war—most likely presented by Adair himself—was George Galphin. The book contains a number of handwritten corrections that appear to have been made by Adair himself. Galphin's copy was eventually donated to the Charleston Library Society in 1802. The book, still in Charleston, bears Galphin's name and the name of his property, "Silver Bluff." The inscription is dated 1775, suggesting an early presentation to the dedicatee by the author or his agent.[259] Galphin's book proved a rara avis indeed. In the 1850s, South Carolina historian John Logan searched the state for Adair's work and declared Galphin's book the "only remaining one that we know of in the state."[260]

Adair's last years, like so much of his life, remain a mystery. He apparently did not return to the Chickasaw country, and no credible reports of his activities after the appearance of his name on Jonathan Bryan's lease with the Creeks have surfaced to date.[261]

Adair's *History:* "A Complete Indian System"

Adair too had his kink. He believed all the Indians of America to be descended from the Jews. . . . His book contains a great deal of real instruction on it's subject, only requiring the reader to be constantly on his guard against the wonderful obliquities of his theory.
                    —Thomas Jefferson to John Adams, June 11, 1812

Since its publication in 1775, Adair's *History* has received considerable attention and acclaim. It remains one of the most frequently cited and best-known books on the late colonial South. L. H. Butterfield, who examined the eighteenth-century London publishing business, ranked the publishing house of Charles and Edward Dilly as "among the three or four leading publishers of American and American-related material in England" from 1750 to 1800. According to Butterfield, "in the field of general Americana the Dillys' outstanding publication was probably Adair's *History of the Indians.*"[262] Even so, it was rarely consulted by general readers or scholars until the early part of the twentieth century, when Samuel Cole Williams published in 1930 what quickly became the standard modernized version of the text: *Adair's History of the American Indians.* It has undergone numerous reprintings but is now out of print.[263]

Adair's *History,* as promised by early advertisements, is actually two volumes. The first, devoted to a disquisition on the origin of the American Indians, presents twenty-three arguments aimed at supporting the theory that the Indians are descended from the Lost Tribes of Israel. His purpose was not to provide a comprehensive discussion of native culture but to prove a thesis: thus his emphasis on such matters as ritual cleansing, the separation of the sick and wounded and women during their menses and at childbirth, and other parallels to Hebrew cultural traditions. Considerable facets of Indian social and political organization are simply not addressed since they do not elucidate the thesis presented. The second part of the work deals more particularly with each major southern Indian tribe and relates cultural information omitted from the first section. The sketches of tribal history are event-driven narratives encompassing not only famous events but also episodes from Adair's own life—presented from his point of view—as well as incidents that would have proved interesting to eighteenth-century readers. The majority of the text was written during the 1750s, although Adair continued to add information about events with which he was intimately connected after that date—notably, comments on the Cherokee war of 1759–60 and events in West Florida in 1765–67. In an appendix, Adair provided "Advice to Statesmen," concerning the proper management of the Indian trade and diplomacy, subjects upon which he considered himself an experienced hand, as well as a justification for establishing new colonies in the West. Throughout, the book also provides a platform for the opinionated author to air his views and complaints against various other aspects of his own society, from corpulence to Christianity.

Adair's seeming "obsession" with the Hebrew theory of Indian origin has resulted in harsh criticism and misunderstanding of the work, and some have even questioned the validity of his observations due to his supposedly fallacious beliefs.[264] Yet Adair's focus on the Hebraic origin of the American aborigines represents a continuing and intriguing line of inquiry begun centuries before his time: "a dispute agitated among the learned ever since the first discovery of America."[265] And the question continues to intrigue scholars into our own time. As Robert F. Berkhofer, Jr., noted, although Adair's theory is "unconvincing and even tedious to the modern reader, his position was an enlightened and not unusual one for the time."[266] In fact, Adair's well-organized and systematic approach to the question of Indian origins represented the most comprehensive and best-supported treatment of the problem by an American up to his time. The value in the theory is not the answer arrived at but the questioning itself, for, as John H. Powell observed, "How the Indians really did originate does not matter; what matters is how people think they originated."[267] And for Western thinkers, the question of origin had deeply profound significance.

For eighteenth-century North Americans, the inquiry into Indian origin concentrated not only on how they differed biologically and culturally from Europeans but also on how they resembled them. A people's origin seemingly predisposed them to certain physical and mental characteristics, and, by the same token, certain cultural traits provided evidence of distant origins. More important, a people's origins could provide clues to whether they were capable of "improving," i.e., of adapting to the "civilized" state reached by Europeans. The question of Indian suitability for attaining civilization was an important concern. What was civilization? While it certainly related to adoption of Christian beliefs, it really had more to do with general standards of living, concepts of property ownership and governance, family kinship structure, how household labor was divided between the sexes, manners, and standards of appearance and dress. For already by the middle of the eighteenth-century, Americans were seriously concerned as to how the Indian would fit into the rapidly changing world being wrested from the "wilderness" and civilized by intrepid Christians.

Adair's espousal of a Hebrew origin for American Indians supported larger aims, for it meant that as heirs of the Western Judaic tradition, their humanity was beyond doubt, and, therefore, they were suitable candidates for education and conversion to Christianity. He strongly rejected the theory espoused by Henry Home, Lord Kames, whose *Sketches of the History of Man* appeared in 1774. In his work, Kames wrote that the Indians were the products of a separate creation, clearly distinct from Europeans.[268] Adair was resolute in his view: Indians were the equals of Europeans physically, mentally, and spiritually: "Their notions of things are like ours, and their organical structure is the same. In them, the soul governs the body, according to the common laws of God in the creation of Adam."[269] Moreover, Adair believed that Indian culture had been "degenerating apace, on account of their great intercourse with foreigners."[270] Added to this belief was Adair's no-nonsense realization that Britain would—indeed, in Adair's view, should—expand and settle the backcountry. Adair accepted without comment that the dominant culture would be British. Thus, Adair's larger purpose was to save his Chickasaw countrymen from further decline and to integrate them fully into the emerging Anglocentric culture. His determined portrayal of the Chickasaw Indians as brave and true allies who would welcome both Christian missionaries and white settlers into their lands speaks to a deeper longing shared by many of those whose lives straddled both worlds and who hoped to reconcile diverse peoples into a harmonious frontier society defined by Western ideals and cultural norms.[271]

Viewed in the light of eighteenth-century intellectual inquiry—and the question of Indian origins was at the forefront of scientific debate throughout the Western world—Adair's framework not only provides evidence of the intellectual currents in British America but also can be viewed as a strength. Anthropologist Charles Hudson has observed, "Adair's Hebrew theory helped him understand the culture and society of the Indians more than it hindered him."[272] His attempt to find cultural parallels between Hebrew and Indian culture and his critical analysis of language in regard to both sounds and manner of speaking, though patently incorrect, led him to record careful and detailed information about Indian societies.[273] And if Adair could aver that "truth hath been my grand standard" in the relation of history and details of culture, he left no doubt that his method in forming the broader interpretations as to Indian origin was based on "probable arguments" based on a comparative study of Hebrew and "American" culture.[274]

Adair was a man of wide reading, particularly of the classics and biblical scholarship. Moreover, he consulted and cited many recent works, including those by French and Spanish authors.[275] Although he stated in his preface that the majority of his work was written in the Indian country far removed from the "conversation of the learned and from any libraries," he clearly had access to both.[276] Although it is impossible to say with certainty which southern book collections he consulted, there were substantial private collections in both Charleston and Savannah, and he also visited libraries and consulted the "learned" during his trip to New York and London. While he drew upon acknowledged sources and biblical history in his analysis of American Indian culture, the real strength of his argument is in his own careful observations, which he presents clearly and in detail, albeit frequently disjointed and clouded by attempts to connect them to Hebrew tradition.

In addition to his observations, Adair discussed matters of interest with his fellow deerskin traders, drawing on their experiences to supplement his own. In one memorable passage, Adair informs his readers that he had "recited" incidents described by La Page du Pratz in his *History of Louisiana* "to a body of gentlemen, well skilled in the languages, rites and customs of our East and West-Florida Indians, and they agreed that the Koran did not differ more widely from the divine oracles, than the accounts of this writer from the genuine customs of the Indian Americans."[277] Adair also took pains to obtain information from others that he could not acquire firsthand. The best example is his commission of William Bolsover to record information about the now famous Tuckabatchee plates. In typical fashion, Adair had Bolsover attest to his account.[278]

Adair's *History*, no doubt owing to the diligence of the Dillys in getting the book into the proper hands, was widely reviewed in British periodical literature, beginning with a favorable notice of the publication in the *London Magazine* in May 1775. A less enthusiastic report followed in June in the *Scots Magazine*.[279] *The Edinburgh Magazine and Review for August 1775* also provided a critical analysis of the book. The reviewer found special interest in Adair's comments on missionaries and included substantial excerpts on the Indian government and other cultural material but pronounced the author "unpractised in the arts of thinking and of composition, his facts are loose and his information vague." The review concluded with a derisive comment noting the inadequacies of writers "who are impelled to visit and reside in distant countries from no motives that are better, than a mere passion for wealth, or the gratification of a restless disposition." If Adair ever read the review, his pique at the rebuff might have been assuaged by the fact the reviewer likewise declared the works of Joseph Banks and Daniel Solander to be similarly deficient due to "inaccuracy and indistinctness."[280] The lengthiest and most thorough review appeared in *The Monthly Review; or Literary Journal* in 1776. The anonymous reviewer was not convinced by Adair's Hebrew origin theory, observing "a strong predisposition of our Author's imagination has led him to fancy resemblances where they do not really exist; and, in some cases, it certainly has induced him to misrepresent and explain away facts militating against his favourite hypothesis." The review concluded with lengthy excerpts.[281]

Adair's appeal to biblical authority, his antiquarian approach, tortured comparisons with Hebrew examples, and lapses of common sense revealed to early critics that Adair was out of step with the new thrust in natural history and modern historiography. Unlike Lord Kames, whose sources included Buffoon and Linnaeus, Adair looked to the past, citing early historical accounts, the Bible, and theological writers, including Thomas Thorowgood, Humphrey Prideaux, and even the Venerable Bede. One of Adair's critics laid this weakness bare in regard to Adair's discussion of the skin color of Indians. Adair's evidence was contradictory, as the reviewer observed. Adair claimed that the Indians' color resulted from artificial or environmental effects, such as the use of bear oil or various root dyes and exposure to the sun. Since such artificial color would not pass to succeeding generations, the reviewer chided Adair for turning to "maternal imagination, as the cause of the propagation of the pretended artificial Indian colour . . . a cause which modern philosophers will hardly admit, though it may be satisfactory to nurses and others equally ignorant and credulous." Specifically, Adair had cited examples of maternal impression from a popular work originally published in 1698, *Aristotle's Masterpiece,* that included the biblical example of Jacob's contrivance with a striped rod to produce spotted cattle. The reviewer challenged Adair with the self-assurance of a late-eighteenth-century natural philosopher: "let him repeat Jacob's experiment, and, the better to discover whether the varieties of colour which may happen among his herds in the course of it, are really produced by the source of imagination, let him paint his rods scarlet or green, and see if he can ever obtain a calf spotted with those colours."[282]

The continuing appeal of Adair's *History* would surely surprise his eighteenth-century reviewers, but modern readers need to be aware of a number of important biases in Adair's writings, apart from his origin theory and framework. Most important, the unrelenting struggle between France and Britain for control of the southeastern backcountry colored Adair's perception of events. As an ardent enemy of France, his propensity to see the struggle as English good against French duplicity and Spanish evil frequently rendered him blind to the true views and motives of Indian peoples whose lives were enmeshed in the deadly struggle. Moreover, his hard-line approach to both foreign powers and uncooperative Indian tribes made him favor an aggressive nonreconciliatory policy, which made him quick to espouse war over diplomacy. His views, largely shared by his colleagues in the Indian trade, frequently put him at odds with those who favored more moderate policies, including John Stuart, superintendent of Indian affairs.

There are several factors relating to Indian culture that bias his work. While he recognized that the Indians were divided into tribes or nations, he believed, based on his observations of ritual and language, that "all the various nations of Indians, seem to be of one descent." And he noted "there is a strong similarity of religious rites, and of civil and martial customs, among all the various American nations of Indians we have any knowledge of, on the extensive continent."[283] His belief that all southeastern tribes shared essentially the same culture meant that he frequently supplied composite descriptions of essential rituals, even omitting parts that do not provide evidence for this Hebrew theory. At times, it is difficult to tell which tribe he is writing about. On the other hand, the reports of other eighteenth-century observers leave no doubt that certain cultural traits were widespread. Careful comparison with other sources makes it possible to discern much from the broad descriptions provided by Adair.

Modern readers will acknowledge Adair as a talented writer, particularly his descriptive passages of events and places in the southeastern backcountry. At the same time, his undisciplined chronology, obvious bias, and florid style will surely elicit groans from some. His work is littered with Latin, Hebrew, and Indian words and quotations (as well as French, Greek, and Gaelic). Quotations from classical writers are usually identified and translated in the text by Adair but sometimes are not. Moreover, there are frequent inclusions of biblical quotations, as on page 286 of the original work, where he notes, without attribution as to its source from Hebrews 12:16, that some British appointees "have sold their birth-rights for a mess of pottage." Assiduous readers will doubtless find many such phrases buried in Adair's prose from both the Bible and classical literature. While Adair's descriptors are eminently quotable, readers should avoid embracing some of Adair's terminology for Indian council houses and leaders that he borrowed from Jewish history. He repeatedly referred to the Indian "statehouse" as a synedrion and religious leaders or old beloved men as priests, magi, or archi-magi.[284]

While a thorough textual deconstruction is not possible in the current edition, careful readers can note changes in tense and tone. Adair occasion-ally identifies his sources but often does not. Even so, it is often possible to discern when Adair is liberally paraphrasing other sources—usually in the context of ancient Jewish history—by careful attention to style shift.[285] But Adair was no mere copyist. In no place is this more evident than in his use of Thomas Thorowgood's 1650 work, *Jewes in America, or Probabilities That the Americans are of that Race . . . ,* as a source of information about the customs of South American tribes and Spanish accounts. However, a close compari-son of the two works reveals that while Adair, according to accepted prac-tice of the time, liberally paraphrases Thorowgood without attribution, he is not merely repeating Thorowgood's narrative. Rather, Adair creatively gleaned sources and information from the work, which he then cited in support of his own arguments.

His extended comparative analysis of southeastern Indian languages—no matter how flawed or incomplete—is the only such document from the eighteenth-century South. Adair reported that Priber had compiled a dic-tionary of Cherokee, but it was lost in the aftermath of his premature death while incarcerated at Fort Frederica. William Gerard De Brahm collected an extensive Cherokee vocabulary, but his work remained unpublished un-til the late twentieth century.[286] And there were other scattered attempts to collect lists of Indian words by various travelers, government officials, and interested persons, but nothing to compare to the analysis offered in print by Adair. For all its flawed imprecision, his work was remarkable for its time in that Adair, as a "linguist" and interpreter, had not only a working knowl-edge of the languages in question but a healthy respect for their complexity. In his *History,* he wrote "their words and sentences are expressive, concise, emphatical, sonorous, and bold."[287] His contemporaries were not always so charitable. Writing from New England, William Douglass reported in his account of British America, published in 1747, that the Indian "Manner of Expression is vehement and emphatick; their Ideas being few, their Lan-guage is not copious, it consists only of a few words; and many of these ill-contrived, by a rumbling noise or Sound of Many Syllables, they express an Idea or thing, which in the European Languages is done by a syllable or two."[288] Adair was not hobbled by such prejudice.

There has been no attempt to analyze the linguistic data presented by Adair in this edition. Professor Leon J. Weinberger examined the text and reported that Adair's knowledge of Hebrew is based on what was known about the language in the period 1735–44. He noted that with the discovery and decipherment of Akkadian, Hebrew's parent language, and Ugaritic, a close cognate of Hebrew, much more about the language is now known and better understood.[289] Thus, Adair's Hebrew should be evaluated in light of the state of knowledge in the early decades of the eighteenth century. Adair's contacts with the Jewish communities in Charleston and Savannah are unknown.[290] His use of native languages is likewise somewhat mystifying. Thomas Jefferson was perhaps the first to note that Adair "generalises . . . [and] brings himself to believe that the hundred languages of America, differing fundamentally every one from every other, as much as Greek from Gothic, have yet all one common prototype."[291] Professor Pat B. Kwachka, a specialist in the Choctaw language, recognized in Adair's discussion of Indian languages "sweeping, inaccurate generalizations" and "very Latinate" grammatical notions, as well as what appears to be a significant comprehension of Chickasaw.[292] Closer scrutiny of Adair's musing on "Indian dialects" is certainly required and is beyond the scope of this work. But readers would do well to keep in mind that regardless of the ultimate pronouncements by scholars on Adair's mastery of the Indian languages, his work is still useful for what it reveals about the knowledge of their interpreter. In his own society, he was an acknowledged expert in the Chickasaw language as well as Cherokee and Choctaw and, to a lesser extent, Muskogee.[293] Moreover, the use of a trader language that transcended tribal boundaries may explain some of Adair's anomalies.

One of the greatest puzzles to scholars concerning his work is his relative silence on matrilineal kinship. Although he mentions clans in passing, it is clear that he did not recognize the full significance of the Indians' social system, and his own prejudice and preconceptions muddled his understanding. Adair was not alone in his mystification, for matrilineal kinship clearly confused most eighteenth-century European men. It is also likely that he understood more than he presented for his readers, for the way in which Indians reckoned kinship does not support his Hebrew theory. Moreover, Adair was excluded from participation in essential tribal rituals and the governing process. Therefore his work fails to provide insight on Indian political organization and town life in general, particularly in regard to matters relating to Indian women, a subject upon which he said very little. And though he mentions many ritual practices and beliefs, he provides only the faintest outline of the annual ceremonial cycle. Oblique points of interest and curiosities take precedence over comprehensive lists of Indian villages, character sketches of their leaders, and an analysis of Indian political structure. It is incorrect to suppose that his lack of attention means that he did not observe these things or that they were not recognized by him. Rather, their absence speaks to the larger issues of what really mattered to the Anglocentric Adair and his audience—issues of diplomacy, French treachery, the Indian manner of war, the lives of deerskin traders, how women prepared

food, and how captives were treated. Adair and his readers were less interested in understanding arcane social and political structures than influencing
and changing them or manipulating them to their own advantage.

Overall, readers have praised the work since its appearance. Thomas Jefferson, in a letter to John Adams, wrote that Adair's book "contains a great
deal of real instruction on it's subject, only requiring the reader to be constantly on his guard against the wonderful obliquities of his theory."[294]
Benjamin Hawkins, the federal agent to the southern Indians in the early
national period, ordered a copy of Adair's *History* to assist him in understanding the southeastern Indians. Elias Boudinot, who would later produce
his own exposition on Indian origin under the title *A Star in the West,* used
Adair's *History* extensively after having its main facts corroborated by a
knowledgeable southern friend who declared "all leading facts mentioned
herein, fully confirmed, by his own personal knowledge."[295] Adair's contemporary Jonathan Carver, who published an account of his own American travels in London in 1778, liberally borrowed from Adair and other
writers—without attribution—passing off their observations as his own.
Edward King, Viscount Kingsborough, who also espoused a Jewish origin
for American Indians, reprinted Adair's twenty-three "arguments" in his
Antiquities of Mexico and provided commentary on Adair's work. John R.
Swanton, dean of American Indian ethnology, made extensive use of Adair's
book in his numerous works on the southeastern tribes, as did Charles Hudson in a later study of southeastern Indian culture.[296]

Modern historians of the eighteenth-century South have closely examined Adair's adventuresome life and his complex historical account in order
to ascertain if the book can be regarded as trustworthy historical evidence.
Wilcomb E. Washburn, author of perhaps the most insightful essay on Adair's
veracity, concluded that while Adair was "buoyant, cocky, [and] openly contemptuous of the statesmen at Charleston," his history, though "related
with sarcasm and asperity," deserved acclaim as "a hard-nosed account of a
hard life spent among the Indians."[297] Others, including Charles Paape, have
noted that Adair's account is "amply colored and distorted by prejudice."[298]
Such views, shared and espoused by South Carolina historian Eugene Sirmans, tend to dismiss Adair's sharply worded and frequently self-promoting
prose as hyperbole.[299] Wilbur R. Jacobs, the historian of Adair's contemporary Edmund Atkin, pointed to the "glaring prejudices and personal hatreds" in Adair's history.[300] But as Wilcomb Washburn sagely wrote, "an historian should be judged not by his attitude, but by his factual accuracy and
his logical analysis. Adair clearly stated his prejudices and hatreds as the consequences of certain facts and events. For an historian to fault Adair for these
attitudes, he must first prove, not the existence of prejudices and hatreds, but
their false factual basis. This, Adair's critics have not done."[301]

Among those who praised the historical accuracy of Adair's work is Lawrence Henry Gipson, who sanguinely noted that while it was true that Adair offered himself in a favorable light on many occasions and was driven by resentment against those who failed to recognize his services, "it is surprising how fully many of his assertions are verified in the official records of South Carolina and Louisiana."[302] Indeed, Adair's claims and observations are amply corroborated by contemporary government documents, manuscript letters, and newspaper accounts. In the most controversial part of his history, in which he explains his role in the so-called Choctaw Revolt, he cites and discusses still-extant contemporary records and official documents that support his version of events.[303] And throughout his work, he recalled "well-known circumstances" that could be corroborated by knowledgeable and respectable South Carolinians and Georgians like George Galphin, Lachlan McGillivray, and Peter Timothy from his own day.[304] There is no doubt that Adair made occasional errors of fact, but overall, his testimony concerning contemporary events is valid, even when dealing with matters that most strongly colored his judgment. His book, frequently neglected or maligned by historians, stands as a unique and worthy addition to the extant historical literature, providing details unavailable elsewhere as well as insights into the views and attitudes of those involved in the deerskin trade.

Ethnohistorians, perhaps more than any other readers, have come to respect Adair as a valid and engaging source. Cherokee scholar Raymond Fogelson wrote that Adair's work is "without doubt the most valuable eighteenth-century treatise on the Southern Indians."[305] Theda Perdue agreed that he was "arguably the most astute observer of eighteenth-century native life in the Southeast."[306] Patricia Galloway has pronounced his work "a truly exceptional body of ethnohistoric data."[307] And Charles Hudson, the author of the most critical examination of Adair's *History* as an ethnohistorical source, while pointing out both the strengths and failings of the methodology, pronounced Adair as "most impressive in grasping social nuances" and "a gifted interviewer."[308]

Taken as a whole, Adair's *History* provides a cornucopia of vitally interesting tidbits for modern readers. Adair's description of the deerskin trader's life, from trading path to domestic establishment, is unsurpassed, as are his musings on Indian rhetoric and recreation, subsistence activities, and ceremonial life. His discussion of the southeastern Indian way of war is unparalleled. Charles Hudson considers one of Adair's most important contributions to be the many Indian proverbs and sayings he repeats, almost certainly in the idiom of the Indians, thereby allowing readers to gain a new understanding of the worldview of Adair's subjects.[309] Adair's vignettes of life among the Indians are not merely instructive but entertaining, allowing a rare glimpse at everyday life in the eighteenth-century backcountry.

And Adair's *History* continues to engender scholarly discussion and debate. To date, his linguistic evidence remains underutilized and virtually ignored but holds promise as an immensely important source for southeastern Indian ethnohistory. Literary scholars and historians of intellectual studies have yet to attempt an analysis of Adair's historical sources and the intellectual milieu in which he lived or to explore the business and intellectual connections that bound the southern colonies to those of the North and to England. On the other hand, anthropologists are becoming increasingly aware of how Adair's interpretive framework has heavily influenced modern analyses of southeastern Indian culture. This is most strikingly evident in his emphasis on Indian cultural traditions that seemingly were devoted to maintaining purity and avoiding pollution. Modern scholars have begun to reevaluate and debate conceptualizations of southeastern Indian ritual that have relied on Western notions of purity and pollution—conceptualizations based heavily on Adair's evidence.[310] But Adair's book is not simply an antiquarian source fit for scholarly dissection. Modern readers who approach his *History* carefully, well aware of its shortcomings and flawed conclusions, will be rewarded with a rousing portrait of the eighteenth-century southeastern Indians and their world that surpasses all others.

The History of the American Indians

by James Adair

"A Map of the American Indian Nations. . . ." which accompanied the original edition of Adair's *History* (courtesy of Tutwiler Collection of Southern History and Literature, Birmingham Public Library, Birmingham, Alabama).

THE

HISTORY

OF THE

AMERICAN INDIANS,

PARTICULARLY

Those NATIONS adjoining to the MISSISIPPI, EAST AND
WEST FLORIDA, GEORGIA, SOUTH AND
NORTH CAROLINA, AND VIRGINIA:

CONTAINING

AN ACCOUNT OF their ORIGIN, LANGUAGE, MANNERS, RELIGIOUS
AND CIVIL CUSTOMS, LAWS, FORM OF GOVERNMENT, PUNISH-
MENTS, CONDUCT IN WAR AND DOMESTIC LIFE, THEIR HABITS,
DIET, AGRICULTURE, MANUFACTURES, DISEASES AND METHOD
OF CURE, AND OTHER PARTICULARS, sufficient to render it

A

COMPLETE INDIAN SYSTEM.

WITH

OBSERVATIONS on former HISTORIANS, the Conduct of our Colony
GOVERNORS, SUPERINTENDENTS, MISSIONARIES, &C.

ALSO

AN APPENDIX,

CONTAINING

A Description of the FLORIDAS, and the MISSISSIPPI LANDS, with their PRODUC-
TIONS—The Benefits of colonising GEORGIANA, and civilizing the INDIANS—
And the way to make all the Colonies more valuable to the Mother Country.

With a new MAP of the Country referred to in the History.

By JAMES ADAIR, Esquire,

A TRADER with the INDIANS, and Resident in their country for Forty Years.

LONDON:
Printed for EWARD and CHARLES DILLY, in the Poultry.
MDCCLXXV.

TO

The Hon. Colonel George Craghan, George Galphin, *and* Lachlan McGilwray[1],

ESQUIRES.★

GENTLEMEN,

To you, with the greatest propriety the following sheets are addressed. Your distinguished abilities—your thorough acquaintance with the North American Indians language, rites, and customs—your long application and services in the dangerous sphere of an Indian life, and your successful management of the savage natives, are well known over all the continent of America.

You often complained how the public had been imposed upon, either by fictitious and fabulous, or very superficial and conjectural accounts of the Indian nations—and as often wished me to devote my leisure hours to drawing up an Indian system. You can witness, that what I now send into the world, was composed more from a regard to your request, than any forward desire of my own. The prospect of your patronage inspired me to write, and it is no small pleasure and honor to me, that such competent judges of the several particulars now presented to public view, expressed themselves with so much approbation of the contents.

You well know the uprightness of my intentions as to the information here given, and that truth hath been my grand standard. I may have erred in the application of the rites and customs of the Indians to their origin and descent—and may have drawn some conclusions, exceeding the given evidence—but candor will excuse the language of integrity: and when the genuine principles, customs, &c. of the Indians are known, it will be easier afterwards for persons of solid learning, and free from secular cares, to trace their origin, clear up the remaining difficulties, and produce a more perfect history.

Should my performance be in the least degree instrumental to produce an

★The late Sir Wm. Johnson, Baronet, was another of the Author's friends, and stood at the head of the MS. Dedication.

accurate investigation and knowledge of the American Indians—their civilization—and the happy settlement of the fertile lands around them, I shall rejoice;
and the public will be greatly obliged to you, as your request incited to it; and
to you I am also indebted for many interesting particulars, and valuable observations.

I embrace this opportunity, of paying a public testimony of my gratitude, for
your many favours, to me. Permit me also to celebrate your public spirit—your
zealous and faithful service of your country—your social and domestic virtues,
&c. which have endeared you to your acquaintance, and to all who have heard
your names, and make you more illustrious, than can any high sounding titles.
All who know you, will readily acquit me of servility and flattery, in this address. Dedications founded on these motives, are the disgrace of literature, and
an insult to common sense. There are too many instances of this prostitution in
Great Britain, for it to be suffered in America. Numbers of high seated patrons
are praised for their divine wisdom and godlike virtues, and yet the whole
empire is discontented, and America in strong convulsions.

May you long enjoy your usual calm and prosperity! that so the widow, the
fatherless, and the stranger may always joyfully return (as in past years) from
your hospitable houses—while this Dedication stands as a small proof of that
sincere attachment with which I am,

Gentlemen,

Your most obedient,

Humble Servant,

JAMES ADAIR.

PREFACE.

The following history, and observations, are the production of one who hath been chiefly engaged in an Indian life ever since the year 1735: and most of the pages were written among our old friendly Chikkasah, with whom I first traded in the year 1744. The subjects are interesting, as well as amusing; but never was a literary work begun and carried on with greater disadvantages. The author was separated by his situation, from the conversation of the learned, and from any libraries—Frequently interrupted also by business, and obliged to conceal his papers, through the natural jealousy of the natives; the traders letters of correspondence always excited their suspicions, and often gave offence.— Another difficulty I had to encounter, was the secrecy and closeness of the Indians as to their own affairs, and their prying disposition into those of others—so that there is no possibility of retirement among them.

A view of the disadvantages of my situation, made me reluctant to comply with the earnest and repeated solicitation of many worthy friends, to give the public an account of the Indian nations with whom I had long resided, was so intimately connected, and of whom scarcely any thing had yet been published but romance, and a mass of fiction. My friends at last prevailed, and on perusing the sheets, they were pleased to approve the contents, as conveying true information, and general entertainment. Having no ambition to appear in the world as an author, and knowing that my history differed essentially from all former publications of the kind, I first resolved to suppress my name; but my friends advised me to own the work, and thus it is tendered to the public in the present form.

The performance, hath doubtless imperfections, *humanum est errare.*[2] Some readers may think, there is too much of what relates to myself, and to the adventures of small parties among the Indians and traders. But minute circumstances are often of great consequence, especially in discovering the descent and genius of a people—describing their manners and customs—and giving proper information to rulers at a distance. I thought it better to be esteemed prolix, than to omit any thing that might be useful on these points. Some repetitions, which occur, were necessary—The history of the several Indian nations being so much intermixed with each other, and their customs so nearly alike.

One great advantage my readers will here have; I sat down to draw the Indians on the spot—had them many years standing before me,—and lived with them as a friend and brother. My intentions were pure when I wrote, truth hath been my standard, and I have no sinister or mercenary views in publishing. With inexpressible concern I read the several imperfect and fabulous accounts of the Indians, already given to the world—Fiction and conjecture have no place in the following pages. The public may depend on the fidelity of the author, and that his descriptions are genuine, though perhaps not so polished and romantic as other Indian histories and accounts, they may have seen.

My grand objects, were to give the Literati proper and good materials for tracing the origin of the American Indians—and to incite the higher powers zealously to promote the best interests of the British colonies, and the mother country. For whose greatness and happiness, I have the most ardent desires.

The whole of the work is respectfully submitted to the candor and judgment of the impartial Public.

CONTENTS.

★Page numbers refer to the current edition. Numbers in brackets show the original page
numbers.

APPENDIX.

A History of the North-American Indians, Their customs, &c.

Observations on the colour, shape, temper, and dress of the Indians of America.

The Indians are of a copper or red-clay colour—and they delight in every thing, which they imagine may promote and increase it: accordingly, they paint their faces with vermilion, as the best and most beautiful ingredient. If we consider the common laws of nature and providence, we shall not be surprized at this custom; for every thing loves best its own likeness and place in the creation, and is disposed to ridicule its opposite. If a deformed son of burning Africa, was to paint the devil, he would not do it in black colours, nor delineate him with a shagged coarse woolly head, nor with thick lips, a short flat nose, or clumsy feet, like those of a bear: his devil would represent one of a different nation or people. But was he to draw an agreeable picture,—according to the African taste, he would daub it all over with sooty black. All the Indians are so strongly attached to, and prejudiced in favour of, their own colour, that they think as meanly of the whites, as we possibly can do of them. The English traders among them, experience much of it, and are often very glad to be allowed to pass muster with the Indian chieftains, as fellow-brethren [2] of the human species. One instance will sufficiently shew in what flattering glasses they view themselves.[3]

Some time past, a large body of the English Indian traders, on their way to the *Choktah* country, were escorted by a body of Creek and Choktah warriors. The Creeks having a particular friendship for some of the traders, who had treated them pretty liberally, took this opportunity to chide the Choktahs, before the traders, in a smart though friendly way, for not allowing to the English the name of human creatures:—for the general name they give us in their most favourable *war-speeches,* resembles that of a contemptible, heterogeneous animal.

The hotter, or colder the climate is, where the Indians have long resided, the greater proportion have they either of the red, or white, colour. I took particular notice of the Shawano Indians,[4] as they were passing from the northward, within fifty miles of the Chikkasah country, to that of the Creeks; and, by comparing them with the Indians which I accompanied to their camp, I observed the Shawano to be much fairer than the Chikkasah★; though I am satisfied, their endeavours to cultivate the copper colour, were alike. Many incidents and observations lead me to believe, that the Indian colour is not natural; but that the external difference between them and the whites, proceeds entirely from their customs and method of living, and not from any inherent spring of nature; which will entirely overturn Lord Kames's whole system of colour, and separate races of men.[5]

That the Indian colour is merely accidental, or artificial, appears pretty evident. Their own traditions record them to have come to their present lands by the way of the west, from a far distant country, and where there was no variegation of colour in human beings; and they are entirely ignorant which was the first or primitive colour. Besides, their rites, customs, &c. as we shall presently see, prove them to be orientalists:[6] and, as the difference of colour among the human species, is one of the principal causes of separation, strife, and bloodshed, would it not greatly reflect on the goodness and justice of the Divine Being, ignominiously to brand numerous tribes and their posterity, with a colour odious and hateful in the sight and opinion of those of a different colour. Some writers have contended, from [3] the diversity of colour, that America was not peopled from any part of Asia, or of the old world, but that the natives were a separate creation. Of this opinion, is Lord Kames, and which he labours to establish in his late publication, entitled, *Sketches of the History of Man*. But his reasoning on this point, for a local creation, is contrary both to revelation, and facts. His chief argument, that "there is not a single hair on the body of any American, nor the least appearance of a beard," is utterly destitute of foundation, as can be attested by all who have had any communication with them—of this more presently.—Moreover, to form one creation of *whites,* a second creation for the *yellows,* and a third for the *blacks,* is a weakness, of which infinite wisdom is incapable. Its operations are plain, easy, constant, and perfect. The variegation therefore of colours among the human race, depends upon a second cause. Lord Kames himself acknowledges, that "the Spanish inhabitants of Carthagena in South-America lose their vigour and colour in a few months."

★S is not a note of plurality with the Indians; when I mention therefore either their national, or proper names, that common error is avoided, which writers ignorant of their language constantly commit.[7]

We are informed by the anatomical observations of our American physicians, concerning the Indians, that they have discerned a certain fine cowl, or web, of a red gluey substance, close under the outer skin, to which it reflects the colour; as the epidermis, or outer skin, is alike clear in every different creature. And experience, which is the best medium to discover truth, gives the true cause why this corpus mucosum, or gluish web, is red in the Indians, and white in us; the parching winds, and hot sun-beams, beating upon their naked bodies, in their various gradations of life, necessarily tarnish their skins with the tawny red colour. Add to this, their constant anointing themselves with bear's oil, or grease, mixt with a certain red root, which, by a peculiar property, is able alone, in a few years time, to produce the Indian colour in those who are white born, and who have even advanced to maturity. These metamorphoses I have often seen.[8]

At the Shawano main camp[9]*, I saw a Pensylvanian, a white man by birth, and in profession a christian, who, by the inclemency of the sun, [4] and his endeavours of improving the red colour, was tarnished with as deep an Indian hue, as any of the camp, through they had been in the woods only the space of four years.

We may easily conclude then, what a fixt change of colour, such a constant method of life would produce: for the colour being once thoroughly established, nature would, as it were, forget herself, not to beget her own likeness. Besides, may we not suppose, that the imagination can impress the animalculæ, in the time of copulation, by its strong subtile power, with at least such an external similitude, as we speak of ?—The sacred oracles, and christian registers, as well as Indian traditions, support the sentiment;—the colour of Jacob's cattle resembled that of the peeled rods he placed before them, in the time of conception. We have good authority of a Spanish lady, who conceived, and was delivered of a negro child, by means of a black picture that hung on the wall, opposite to the bed where she lay. There is a record among the Chikkasah Indians, that tells us of a white child with flaxen hair, born in their country, long before any white people appeared in that part of the world; which they ascribed to the immediate power of the Deity impressing her imagination in a dream. And the Philosophical Transactions assure us of two white children having been born of black parents.[10] But waving all other arguments, the different method of living, connected

*In the year 1747, I headed a company of the cheerful, brave Chikkasah, with the eagles tails, to the camp of the Shawano Indians, to apprehend one Peter Shartee,[11] (a Frenchman) who, by his artful paintings, and the supine conduct of the Pensylvanian government, had decoyed a large body of the Shawano from the English, to the French, interest. But fearing the consequences, he went around an hundred miles, toward the Cheerake nation, with his family, and the head warriors, and thereby evaded the danger.

with the difference of climates, and extraordinary anointings and paintings, will effect both outward and inward changes in the human race, all round the globe: or, a different colour may be conveyed to the fœtus by the parents, through the channel of the fluids, without the least variation of the original stamina. For, though the laws of nature cannot be traced far, where there are various circumstances, and combinations of things, yet her works are exquisitely constant and regular, being thereto impelled by unerring divine Wisdom.

As the American Indians are of a reddish or copper colour,—so in general they are strong, well proportioned in body and limbs, surprisingly active and nimble, and hardy in their own way of living.

They are ingenious, witty, cunning, and deceitful; very faithful indeed to their own tribes, but privately dishonest, and mischievous to the Europeans and christians. Their being honest and harmless to each other, may be through fear of resentment and reprisal—which is unavoidable in case of any injury. [5] They are very close, and retentive of their secrets; never forget injuries; revengeful of blood, to a degree of distraction. They are timorous, and, consequently, cautious; very jealous of encroachments from their christian neighours; and, likewise, content with freedom, in every turn of fortune. They are possessed of a strong comprehensive judgment,—can form surprisingly crafty schemes, and conduct them with equal caution, silence, and address; they admit none but distinguished warriors, and old beloved men, into their councils. They are slow, but very persevering in their undertakings—commonly temperate in eating, but excessively immoderate in drinking.—They often transform themselves by liquor into the likeness of mad foaming bears. The women, in general, are of a mild, amiable, soft disposition: exceedingly modest in their behaviour, and very seldom noisy, either in the single, or married state.

The men are expert in the use of fire-arms,—in shooting the bow,—and throwing the feathered dart, and tomohawk, into the flying enemy. They resemble the lynx, with their sharp penetrating black eyes, and are exceedingly swift of foot; especially in a long chase: they will stretch away, through the rough woods, by the bare track, for two or three hundred miles, in pursuit of a flying enemy, with the continued speed, and eagerness, of a stanch pack of blood hounds, till they shed blood. When they have allayed this their burning thirst, they return home, at their leisure, unless they chance to be pursued, as is sometimes the case; whence the traders say, "that an Indian is never in a hurry, but when the devil is at his heels."

It is remarkable, that there are no deformed Indians[12]—however, they are generally weaker, and smaller bodied, between the tropics, than in the higher latitudes; but not in an equal proportion: for, though the Chikkasah and Choktah countries have not been long divided from each other, as appears by the similarity of their language, as well as other things, yet the Chikkasah are exceedingly taller, and stronger bodied than the latter, though their country is only two degrees farther north. Such a small difference of latitude, in so healthy a region, could not make so wide a difference in the constitution of their bodies. The former are a comely, pleasant looking people; their faces are tolerably round, contrary to the visage of the others, which inclines much to flatness, as is the case of most of the other Indian Americans. The lips of the Indians, in general, are thin.

[6] Their eyes are small, sharp, and black; and their hair is lank, coarse, and darkish. I never saw any with curled hair, but one in the Choktah country, where was also another with red hair; probably, they were a mixture of the French and Indians. Romancing travellers, and their credulous copyists, report them to be *imbarbes,* and as persons *impuberes,* and they appear so to strangers. But both sexes pluck all the hair off their bodies, with a kind of tweezers, made formerly of clam-shells, now of middle-sized wire, in the shape of a gun-worm; which, being twisted round a small stick, and the ends fastened therein, after being properly tempered, keeps its form: holding this Indian razor between their fore-finger and thumb, they deplume themselves,[13] after the manner of the Jewish novitiate priests, and proselytes.—As the former could not otherwise be purified for the function of his sacerdotal office; or the latter, be admitted to the benefit of religious communion.

Their chief *dress* is very simple, like that of the patriarchal age; of choice, many of their old head-men wear a long wide frock, made of the skins of wild beasts, in honour of that antient custom: It must be necessity that forces them to the pinching sandals for their feet. They seem quite easy, and indifferent, in every various scene of life, as if they were utterly divested of passions, and the sense of feeling. Martial virtue, and not riches, is their invariable standard for preferment; for they neither esteem, nor despise any of their people one jot more or less, on account of riches or dress. They compare both these, to paint on a warrior's face; because it incites others to a spirit of martial benevolence for their country, and pleases his own fancy, and the eyes of spectators, for a little time, but is sweated off, while he is performing his war-dances; or is defaced, by the change of weather.

They formerly wore shirts, made of drest deer-skins, for their summer visiting dress: but their winter-hunting clothes were long and shaggy, made of the skins of panthers, bucks, bears, beavers, and otters; the fleshy sides outward, sometimes doubled, and always softened like velvet-cloth, though they retained their fur and hair. The needles and thread they used formerly, (and now at times) were fish-bones, or the horns and bones of deer, rubbed sharp, and deer's sinews, and a sort of hemp, that grows among them spontaneously, in rich open lands. The women's dress consists only in a [7] broad softened skin, or several small skins sewed together, which they wrap and tye round their waist, reaching a little below their knees: in cold weather, they wrap themselves in the softened skins of buffalo calves, with the wintery shagged wool inward, never forgetting to anoint, and tie up their hair, except in their time of mourning. The men wear, for ornament, and the conveniencies of hunting, thin deer-skin boots, well smoked, that reach so high up their thighs, as with their jackets to secure them from the brambles and braky thickets. They sew them about five inches from the edges, which are formed into tossels [tassels], to which they fasten fawns trotters, and small pieces of tinkling metal, or wild turkey cock-spurs. The beaus used to fasten the like to their war-pipes, with the addition of a piece of an enemy's scalp with a tuft of long hair hanging down from the middle of the stem, each of them painted red: and they still observe that old custom, only they choose bell-buttons, to give a greater sound.[14]

The young Indian men and women, through a fondness of their ancient dress, wrap a piece of cloth round them, that has a near resemblance to the old Roman toga, or prætexta. 'Tis about a fathom square, bordered seven or eight quarters deep, to make a shining cavalier of the *beau monde*,[15] and to keep out both the heat and cold. With this frantic apparel, the red heroes swaddle themselves, when they are waddling, whooping, and prancing it away, in their sweltery town-houses, or supposed synhedria,[16] around the reputed holy fire. In a sweating condition, they will thus incommode themselves, frequently, for a whole night, on the same principle of pride, that the grave Spaniard's winter cloak must sweat him in summer.

They have a great aversion to the wearing of breeches; for to that custom, they affix the idea of helplessness, and effeminacy. I know a German of thirty years standing, chiefly among the Chikkasah Indians, who because he kept up his breeches with a narrow piece of cloth that reached across his shoulders, is distinguished by them, as are all his countrymen, by the despicable appellative, Kish-Kish Tarākshe, or *Tied Arse.*—They esteem the English much more than the Germans, because our limbs, they say, are less restrained by our apparel from manly exercise, than theirs. The Indian women also discreetly observe, that, as all their men sit down to make [8] water, the ugly breeches would exceedingly incommode them; and that, if they were allowed to wear breeches, it would portend no good to their country: however, they add, should they ever be so unlucky, as to have that pinching custom introduced among them, the English breeches would best suit their own female posture on that occasion; but that it would be exceedingly troublesome either way. The men wear a slip of cloth, about a quarter of an ell wide, and an ell and an half long, in the lieu of breeches; which they put between their legs, and tye round their haunches, with a convenient broad bandage. The women, since the time we first traded with them, wrap a fathom of the half breadth of Stroud cloth round their waist, and tie it with a leathern belt, which is commonly covered with brass runners or buckles: but this sort of loose petticoat, reaches only to their hams, in order to shew their exquisitely fine proportioned limbs.[17]

They make their shoes for common use, out of the skins of the bear and elk, well dressed and smoked, to prevent hardening; and those for ornament, out of deer-skins, done in the like manner: but they chiefly go bare-footed, and always bare-headed. The men fasten several different sorts of beautiful feathers, frequently in tufts; or the wing of a red bird, or the skin of a small hawk, to a lock of hair on the crown of their heads. And every different Indian nation when at war, trim their hair, after a different manner, through contempt of each other; thus we can distinguish an enemy in the woods, so far off as we can see him.

The Indians flatten their heads, in divers forms: but it is chiefly the crown of the head they depress, in order to beautify themselves, as their wild fancy terms it; for they call us *long heads,* by way of contempt. The Choktah Indians flatten their fore-heads, from the top of the head to the eye-brows with a small bag of sand; which gives them a hideous appearance; as the forehead naturally shoots upward, according as it is flattened: thus, the rising of the nose, instead of being equidistant from the beginning of the chin, to that of the hair, is, by their wild mechanism, placed a great deal nearer to the one, and farther from the other.[18] The Indian nations, round South-Carolina, and all the way to New Mexico, (properly called Mechiko) to effect this, fix the tender infant on a kind of cradle, where his feet are tilted, above a foot higher than a horizontal position [9],— his head bends back into a hole, made on purpose to receive it, where he bears the chief part of his weight on the crown of the head, upon a small bag of sand, without being in the least able to move himself. The skull resembling a fine cartilaginous substance, in its infant state, is capable of taking any impression. By this pressure, and their thus flattening the crown of the head, they consequently make their heads thick, and their faces broad: for, when the smooth channel of nature is stopped in one place, if a destruction of the whole system doth not thereby ensue, it breaks out in a proportional redundancy, in another. May we not to this custom, and as a necessary effect of this cause, attribute their fickle, wild, and cruel tempers? especially, when we connect therewith, both a false education, and great exercise to agitate their animal spirits. When the brain, in cooler people, is disturbed, it neither reasons, nor determines, with proper judgment? The Indians thus look on every thing around them, through their own false medium; and vilify our heads, because they have given a wrong turn to their own.

[10] *Observations on the origin and descent of the Indians.*

The very remote history of all nations, is disfigured with fable, and gives but little encouragement to distant enquiry, and laborious researches. Much of the early history and antiquities of nations is lost, and some people have no records at all, and to this day are rude and uncivilized. Yet a knowledge

of them is highly interesting, and would afford amusement, and even instruction in the most polished times, to the most polite. Every science has
certain principles, as its basis, from which it reasons and concludes. Mathe-
matical theorems, and logical propositions, give clear demonstrations, and
necessary conclusions: and thus other sciences. But, *history,* and the *origin*
of tribes and nations, have hitherto been covered with a great deal of ob-
scurity. Some antient historians were ignorant; others prejudiced. Some
searchers into antiquities adopted the traditional tales of their predecessors:
and others looking with contempt on the origin of tribes and societies, al-
together exploded them, without investigation. My design is, to examine,
and if possible, ascertain the genealogy and descent of the Indians, and to
omit nothing that may in the least contribute to furnish the public with a
full INDIAN SYSTEM.

In tracing the origin of a people, where there are no records of any kind,
either written, or engraved, who rely solely on oral tradition for the support
of their antient usages, and have lost great part of them—though the undertaking be difficult, yet where several particulars, and circumstances, strong
and clear, correspond, they not only make room for conjecture, but cherish
probability, and till better can be offered, must be deemed conclusive.

All the various nations of Indians, seem to be of one descent; they call a
buffalo, in their various dialects, by one and the same name, "*Yanasa.*" And
there is a strong similarity of religious rites, and of civil and martial customs, among all the various American nations of Indians we [11] have any
knowledge of, on the extensive continent; as will soon be shewn.

Their language is copious, and very expressive, for their narrow orbit of
ideas, and full of rhetorical tropes and figures, like the orientalists. In early
times, when languages were not so copious, rhetoric was invented to supply
that defect: and, what barrenness then forced them to, custom now continues
as an ornament.

Formerly, at a public meeting of the head-men, and chief orators, of the
Choktah nation, I heard one of their eloquent speakers deliver a very pathetic, elaborate, allegorical, tragic oration, in the high praise, and for the
great loss, of their great, judicious war-chieftain, *Shu-las-hum-másh-tà-be,* our
daring, brave friend, *red shoes.*[19] The orator compared him to the sun, that
enlightens and enlivens the whole system of created beings: and having carried the metaphor to a considerable length, he expatiated on the variety of
evils, that necessarily result from the disappearance and absence of the sun;
and, with a great deal of judgment, and propriety of expression, he concluded his oration with the same trope, with which he began.

They often change the sense of words into a different signification from
the natural, exactly after the manner also of the orientalists. Even, their
common speech is full of it; like the prophetic writings, and the book of

Job, their orations are concise, strong, and full of fire; which sufficiently con-
futes the wild notion which some have espoused of the North American
Indians being Præ-Adamites, or a separate race of men, created for that
continent.[20] What stronger circumstantial proofs can be expected, than that
they, being disjoined from the rest of the world, time immemorial, and destitute also of the use of letters, should have, and still retain the ancient standard of speech, conveyed down by oral tradition from father to son, to the
present generation? Besides, their persons, customs, &c. are not singular from
the rest of the world; which, probably, they would, were they not descended
from one and the same common head. Their notions of things are like ours,
and their organical structure is the same. In them, the soul governs the body,
according to the common laws of God in the creation of Adam. God employed six days, in creating the heavens, this earth, and the innumerable species [12] of creatures, wherewith it is so amply furnished. The works of a
being, infinitely perfect, must entirely answer the design of them: hence
there could be no necessity for a second creation; or God's creating many
pairs of the human race differing from each other, and fitted for different
climates: because, that implies imperfection, in the grand scheme, or a want
of power, in the execution of it—Had there been a prior, or later formation
of any new class of creatures, they must materially differ from those of the
six days work; for it is inconsistent with divine wisdom to make a vain, or
unnecessary repetition of the same act. But the American Indians neither
vary from the rest of mankind, in their internal construction, nor external
appearance, except in colour; which, as hath been shewn, is either entirely
accidental, or artificial. As the Mosaic account declares a completion of the
manifestations of God's infinite wisdom and power in creation, within that
space of time; it follows, that the Indians have lineally descended from
Adam, the first, and the great parent of all the human species.

Both the Chikkasah and Choktah Indians, call a deceitful person, *Seente,*
a snake: and they frequently say, they have not *Seente Soolish,* the snake's
tongue; the meaning of which, is very analogous to רמי, a name the Hebrews gave to a deceitful person; which probably proceeded from a traditional knowledge of Eve's being beguiled by the tempter, in that shape; for
the Indians never affix any bad idea to the present reptile fraternity, except that of poisonous teeth: and they never use any such metaphor, as that
of a snake's teeth.

Some have supposed the Americans to be descended from the *Chinese:*
but neither their religion, laws, customs, &c., agree in the least with those of
the Chinese: which sufficiently proves, they are not of that line. Besides, as
our best ships now are almost half a year in sailing to China, or from thence
to Europe; it is very unlikely they should attempt such dangerous discoveries, in early time, with their (supposed) small vessels, against rapid currents,

and in dark and sickly monsoons, especially, as it is very probable they were unacquainted with the use of the load-stone to direct their course. China is above eight thousand miles distant from the American continent, which is twice as far as across the Atlantic ocean.—And, we are not informed by any antient writer, of their maritime skill, or so much as any inclination that way, besides [13] small coasting voyages.—The winds blow likewise, with little variation, from east to west, within the latitudes of thirty and odd, north and south, and therefore they could not drive them on the American coast, it lying directly contrary to such a course.

Neither could persons sail to America, from the north, by the way of Tartary or ancient Scythia; that, from its situation, never was, or can be, a maritime power, and it is utterly impracticable for any to come to America, by sea, from that quarter. Besides, the remaining traces of their religious ceremonies, and civil and martial customs, are quite opposite to the like vestiges of the old Scythians.

Nor, even in the moderate northern climates, is to be seen the least vestige of any ancient stately buildings, or of any thick settlements, as are said to remain in the less healthy regions of Peru and Mexico. Several of the Indian nations assure us they crossed the Missisippi, before they made their present northern settlements; which, connected with the former arguments, will sufficiently explode that weak opinion, of the American Aborigines being lineally descended from the Tartars, or ancient Scythians.

It is a very difficult thing to divest ourselves, not to say, other persons, of prejudices and favourite opinions; and I expect to be censured by some, for opposing commonly received sentiments, or for meddling with a dispute agitated among the learned ever since the first discovery of America. But, TRUTH is my object: and I hope to offer some things, which, if they do not fully solve the problem, may lead the way, and enable others, possessing stronger judgment, more learning, and more leisure, to accomplish it. As I before suggested, where we have not the light of history, or records, to guide us through the dark maze of antiquity, we must endeavour to find it out by probable arguments; and in such subjects of enquiry, where no material objections can be raised against probability, it is strongly conclusive of the truth, and nearly gives the thing sought for.

From the most exact observations I could make in the long time I traded among the Indian Americans, I was forced to believe them lineally descended from the Israelites, either while they were a maritime power, [14] or soon after the general captivity; the latter however is the most probable.[21] This descent, I shall endeavour to prove from their religious rites, civil and martial customs, their marriages, funeral ceremonies, manners, language, traditions, and a variety of particulars.—Which will at the same time make the reader thoroughly acquainted with nations, of which it may be said to this day, very little have been known.

[15] *Observations, and arguments, in proof of the American Indians being descended from the Jews.*[22]

A number of particulars present themselves in favour of a Jewish descent. But to form a true judgment, and draw a solid conclusion, the following arguments must not be partially separated. Let them be distinctly considered—then unite them together, and view their force collectively.

ARGUMENT I.

As the Israelites were divided into Tribes, and had chiefs over them, so the Indians divide themselves: each tribe forms a little community within the nation—And as the nation hath its particular symbol, so hath each tribe the badge from which it is denominated. The sachem of each tribe, is a necessary party in conveyances and treaties, to which he affixes the mark of his tribe, as a corporation with us doth their public seal*.—If we go from nation to nation among them, we shall not find one, who doth not lineally distinguish himself by his respective family. The genealogical names which they assume, are derived, either from the names of those animals, whereof the *cherubim* are said in revelation, to be compounded; or from such creatures as are most familiar to them. They have the families of the *eagle, panther, tyger,* and *buffalo;* the family of the *bear, deer, racoon, tortoise, snake, fish;* and, likewise, of the *wind*.[23] The last, if not derived from the appearance of the divine glory, as expressed by the prophet Ezekiel, may [16] be of Tyrian extraction. We are told in the fragment of Sanchoniathon,[24] that the Tyrians worshipped fire, and the ærial wind, as gods; and that Usous, the son of Hypsouranias, built a sacred pillar to each of them: so that, if it is not of Israelitish extraction, it may be derived from the Tyrians their neighbours—as may, likewise, the appellative name of *fish;* especially, as the Indians, sometimes, invoke the eagle, and the fish, when they are curing their sick. The

---

*Many of the ancient heathens followed the Jewish custom of dividing themselves into tribes, or families. The city of Athens was divided into ten parts, or tribes, and which the Greeks called *Phule,* a tribe. They named each of the heads that presided over them, Archegos, Archiphulogos, &c. And writers inform us, that the East-Indian pagans have to this day tribes, or casts; and that each cast chuses a head to maintain its privileges, to promote a strict observance of their laws, and to take care that every thing be managed with proper order. The ancient heathens mimicked a great deal of the Jewish ceremonial law.

Tyrians were the people, in early times, who, above all others, enriched themselves in the natural element of the fish.

The Indians, however, bear no religious respect to the animals from which they derive the names of their tribes, but will kill any of the species, when opportunity serves. The *wolf* indeed, several of them do not care to meddle with, believing it unlucky to kill them; which is the sole reason that few of the Indians shoot at that creature, through a notion of spoiling their guns. Considering the proximity of Tyre to Egypt, probably this might be a custom of Egyptian extraction; though, at the same time, they are so far from esteeming it a deity, they reckon it the most abominable quadruped of the whole creation.

There is no tribe, or individual, among them, however, called by the name *opossum*★, which is with the Cheerake stiled *seequa;* and with the Chikkasah and Choktah Indians, *shookka,* synonymous with that of a *hog.* This may be more material than at first appears, as our natural histories tell us, that the opossum is common in other parts of the world. Several of the old Indians assure us, they formerly reckoned it as filthy uneatable an animal, as a hog; although they confess, and we know by long observation, that, from the time our traders settled among them, they are every year more corrupt in their morals; not only in this instance of eating an impure animal, but in many other religious customs of their forefathers.

When we consider the various revolutions these unlettered savages are likely to have undergone, among themselves, through a long-forgotten measure of time; and that, probably, they have been above twenty centuries, without the use of letters to convey down their traditions, it cannot be reasonably expected they should still retain the identical names of [17] their primo-genial tribes. Their main customs corresponding with those of the Israelites, sufficiently clears the subject. Besides, as hath been hinted, they call some of their tribes by the names of the cherubimical figures, that were carried on the four principal standards of Israel.

I have observed with much inward satisfaction, the community of goods that prevailed among them, after the patriarchal manner, and that of the primitive christians; especially with those of their own tribe. Though they are become exceedingly corrupt, in most of their ancient commendable qualities, yet they are so hospitable, kind-hearted, and free, that they would share with those of their own tribe, the last part of their provisions even to a single ear of corn; and to others, if they called when they were eating; for they have no stated meal-time.[25] An open generous temper is a standing virtue among them; to be narrow-hearted, especially to those in want, or to

★A creature that hath a head like a hog, and a tail like a rat.

any of their own family, is accounted a great crime, and to reflect scandal on the rest of the tribe. Such wretched misers they brand with bad characters, and wish them the fate of Prometheus, to have an eagle or vulture fastened to their liver: or of Tantalus, starving in the midst of plenty, without being able to use it. The Cheerake Indians have a pointed proverbial expression, to the same effect—*Sinnawàh nà wóra;* "The great hawk is at home."[26] However, it is a very rare thing to find any of them of a narrow temper: and though they do not keep one promiscuous common stock, yet it is to the very same effect; for every one has his own family, or tribe: and, when one of them is speaking, either of the individuals, or habitations, of any of his tribe, he says, "He is of my house;" or, "It is my house." Thus, when King David prayed that the divine wrath might only fall on his house, he might mean the tribe of Judah, as well as his own particular family, exclusive of the aggregate body of Israel.

When the Indians are travelling in their own country, they enquire for a house of their own tribe; and if there be any, they go to it, and are kindly received, though they never saw the persons before—they eat, drink, and regale themselves, with as much freedom, as at their own tables; which is the solid ground covered with a bear-skin. It is their usual custom to carry nothing along with them in the journies but a looking-glass, and red paint, hung to their back—their gun and shot pouch—or bow and quiver [18] full of barbed arrows; and, frequently, both gun and bow: for as they are generally in a state of war against each other, they are obliged, as soon as able, to carry those arms of defence. Every town has a state-house, or synedrion, as the Jewish sanhedrim, where, almost every night, the head men convene about public business; or the town's-people to feast, sing, dance, and rejoice, in the divine presence, as will fully be described hereafter. And if a stranger calls there, he is treated with the greatest civility and hearty kindness—he is sure to find plenty of their simple home fare, and a large cane-bed covered with the softened skins of bears, or buffaloes, to sleep on.[27] But, when his lineage is known to the people, (by a stated custom, they are slow in greeting one another) his relation, if he has any there, addresses him in a familiar way, invites him home, and treats him as his kinsman.

When a warrior dies a natural death, (which seldom happens) the war-drums, musical instruments, and all other kinds of diversion, are laid aside for the space of three days and nights. In this time of mourning for the dead, I have known some of the frolicksome young sparks to ask the name of the deceased person's tribe; and once, being told it was a *racoon,* (the genealogical name of the family) one of them scoffingly replied, "then let us away to another town, and cheer ourselves with those who have no reason to weep; for why should we make our hearts weigh heavy for an ugly, dead racoon?"

But notwithstanding they are commonly negligent of any other tribe but their own, they regard their own particular lineal descent in as strict a manner as did the Hebrew nation.[28]

ARGUMENT II.

By a strict, permanent, divine precept, the Hebrew nation were ordered to worship at Jerusalem, *Jehovah* the true and living God, and who by the Indians is stiled *Yohewah;* which the seventy-two interpreters, either from ignorance or superstition, have translated *Adonai;* and is the very same as the Greek *Kurios,* signifying Sir, Lord, or Master; which is commonly applied to earthly potentates, without the least signification of, or relation to, that most great and awful name, which describes the divine essence, who naturally [19] and necessarily exists of himself, without beginning or end.[29] The ancient heathens, it is well known, worshipped a plurality of gods—Gods which they formed to themselves, according to their own liking, as various as the countries they inhabited, and as numerous, with some, as the days of the year. But these Indian Americans pay their religious devoir to *Loak-Ishtōhoollo-Aba,* "the great, beneficent, supreme, holy spirit of fire," who resides (as they think) above the clouds, and on earth also with unpolluted people. He is with them the sole author of warmth, light, and of all animal and vegetable life. They do not pay the least perceivable adoration to any images, or to dead persons; neither to the celestial luminaries, nor evil spirits, nor any created being whatsoever. They are utter strangers to all the gestures practised by the pagans in their religious rites. They kiss no idols; nor, if they were placed out of their reach, would they kiss their hands, in token of reverence and a willing obedience.[30]

The ceremonies of the Indians in their religious worship, are more after the Mosaic institution, than of pagan imitation: which could not be, if the majority of the old natives were of heathenish descent; for all bigots and enthusiasts will fight to death for the very shadow of their superstitious worship, when they have even lost all the substance. There yet remain so many marks, as to enable us to trace the Hebrew extraction and rites, through all the various nations of Indians; and we may with a great deal of probability conclude, that, if any heathens accompanied them to the American world, or were settled in it before them, they became proselytes of justice, and their pagan rites and customs were swallowed up in the Jewish.

To illustrate the general subject, I shall give the Indian opinion of some of the heathen gods, contrasted with that of the pagan.

The American Indians do not believe the SUN to be any bigger than it appears to the naked eye. Conversing with the Chikkàsah archi-magus,[31] or high-priest, about that luminary, he told me, "it might possibly be as broad and round as his winter-house; but he thought it could not well exceed it."

We cannot be surprised at the stupidity of the Americans in this respect, when we consider the gross ignorance which now prevails among the general part of the Jews, not only of the whole system of nature, but of the essential meaning of their own religious ceremonies, received from the Divine Majesty. [20] —And also when we reflect, that the very learned, and most polite of the ancient Romans, believed (not by any new-invented mythology of their own) that the sun was drawn round the earth in a chariot. Their philosophic system was not very dissimilar to that of the wild Americans; for Cicero tells us, Epicurus thought the sun to be less than it appeared to the eye. And Lucretius says, *Tantillus ille sol,* "a diminutive thing." And, if the Israelites had not at one time thought the sun a portable god, they would not have thought of a chariot for it. This they derived from the neighbouring heathen; for we are told, that they had an house of the sun, where they danced in honour of him, in circuits, and had consecrated spherical figures; and that they, likewise, built a temple to it; for "they purified and sanctified themselves in the gardens; behind the house, or temple of Achad." In *Isa.* xvii. 8, we find they had *sun-images,* which the Hebrews called *chummanim,* made to represent the sun, or for the honour and worship of it: and the Egyptians met yearly to worship in the temple of Beth-Shemesh, a house dedicated to the sun. Most part of the old heathens adored all the celestial orbs, especially the sun; probably they first imagined its enlivening rays immediately issued from the holy fire, light, and spirit, who either resided in, or was the identical sun. That idolatrous ceremony of the Jews, Josiah utterly abolished about 640 years before our christian æra. The sacred text says, "He took away the horses, which the kings of Judah had given to the sun, and he burned the chariots of the sun with fire." At Rhodes, a neighbouring island to Judæa, they consecrated chariots to the sun, on account of his glorious splendour and benign qualities. Macrobius tells us, that the Assyrians worshipped Adad, or Achad, an idol of the sun; and Strabo acquaints us, the Arabians paid divine homage to the sun, &c. But the Indian Americans pay only a civil regard to the sun: and the more intelligent sort of them believe, that all the luminaries of the heavens are moved by the strong fixt laws of the great Author of nature.[32]

In 2 *Kings* xvii. 30, we read that the men of Babylon built Succoth-Benoth, "tents for young women;" having consecrated a temple to Venus, they fixed tents round it, where young women prostituted themselves in honour of the goddess. Herodotus, and other authors, are also sufficient witnesses on this point. Now, were the Americans originally heathens, or not of Israel, when they wandered there from captivity, in quest of [21] liberty, or on any other accidental account, that vicious precedent was so well calculated for America, where every place was a thick arbour, it is very improbable they should have discontinued it: But they are the very reverse. To commit such acts of pollution, while they are performing any of their religious ceremonies, is deemed so provoking an impiety, as to occasion even the supposed sinner to be excluded from all religious communion with the rest of the people. Or even was a man known to have gone in to his own wife, during the time of their fastings, purifications, &c. he would also be separated from them. There is this wide difference between the impure and obscene religious ceremonies of the ancient heathens, and the yet penal, and strict purity of the natives of America.

The heathens chose such gods, as were most suitable to their inclinations, and the situation of their country. The warlike Greeks and Romans worshipped *Mars* the god of war; and the savage and more bloody Scythians deified the *Sword.* The neighbouring heathens round Judæa, each built a temple to the supposed god that presided over their land. *Rimmon,* was the Syrian god of pomegranates: and the Philistines, likewise, erected a temple to *Dagon,* who had first taught them the use of wheat; which the Greeks and Romans changed into *Ceres,* the goddess of corn, from the Hebrew, *Geres,* which signifies grain. But the red Americans firmly believe, that their war-captains, and their reputed prophets, gain success over their enemies, and bring on seasonable rains, by the immediate reflection of the divine fire, co-operating with them.

We are informed by Cicero, that the maritime Sidonians adored *fishes:* and by the fragment of Sanchoniathon, that the Tyrians worshipped the element of *fire,* and the *ærial wind,* as gods:—probably having forgotten that the first and last names of the three celestial cherubic emblems, only typified the deity. Ancient history informs us, that Zoroaster, who lived An. M. 3480, made *light* the emblem of good, and *darkness* the symbol of evil—he taught an abhorrence of images, and instructed his pupils to worship God, under the figurative likeness of *fire:* but he asserted two contrary original principles; the one of good, and the other of evil. He allowed no temples, but enjoined sacrificing in the open air, and on the top of an hill. The ancient Persians kept up their reputed holy fire, without suffering it to be extinguished; which their pretended successors observe with the [22] strictest devotion, and affirm it has been burning, without the least intermission, several thousand years. But the Indian Americans are so far from the idolatry of the Sidonians, that they esteem fish only as they are useful to the support of human life; though one of their tribes is called the *fish:*—they are so far from paying any religious worship to the aerial wind, like the Tyrians, that they often call the bleak north-wind, explicatively, very evil, and accursed; which they probably, would not say, if they derived the great esteem they now have for the divine fire, from the aforesaid idolatrous nations: neither would they wilfully extinguish their old fire, before the annual sacrifice is offered up, if, like the former heathens, they paid religious worship to the elementary fire; for no society of people would kill their own gods, unless the papists, who go farther, even to eat him. The Indians esteem the old year's fire, as a most dangerous pollution, regarding only the supposed holy fire, which the archi-magus annually renews for the people.

They pay no religious worship to stocks, or stones, after the manner of the old eastern pagans; neither do they worship any kind of images whatsoever. And it deserves our notice, in a very particular manner, to invalidate the idle dreams of the jesuitical fry of South-America, that none of all the various nations, from Hudson's Bay to the Missisippi, has ever been known, by our trading people, to attempt to make any image of the great Divine Being, whom they worship. This is consonant to the Jewish observance of the second commandment, and directly contrary to the usage of all the ancient heathen world, who made corporeal representations of their deities— and their conduct, is a reproach to many reputed christian temples, which are littered round with a crowd of ridiculous figures to represent God, spurious angels, pretended saints, and notable villains.

The sacred penmen, and prophane writers, assure us that the ancient heathens had lascivious gods, particularly מפלצת, 2 *Chron.* xv.16. which was the abominable Priapus. But I never heard that any of our North-American Indians had images of any kind. There is a carved human statue of wood, to which, however, they pay no religious homage: It belongs to the head war-town of the upper Muskohge country, and seems to have been originally designed to perpetuate the memory of some distinguished hero, who deserved well of his country; for, when their *cusseena,* or bitter, black drink is about to [23] be drank in the synedrion, they frequently, on common occasions, will bring it there, and honour it with the first conch-shell-full, by the hand of the chief religious attendant: and then they return it to its former place. It is observable, that the same beloved waiter, or holy attendant, and his co-adjutant, equally observe the same ceremony to every person of reputed merit, in that quadrangular place. When I past that way, circumstances did not allow me to view this singular figure; but I am assured by several of the traders, who have frequently seen it, that the carving is modest, and very neatly finished, not unworthy of a modern civilized artist.[33] As no body of people we are acquainted with, have, in general, so great a share of strong natural parts as those savages, we may with a great deal of probability suppose, that their tradition of the second commandment, prevented them from having one, not to say the same plentiful variety of images, or idols, as have the popish countries.

Notwithstanding they are all degenerating apace, on account of their great intercourse with foreigners, and other concurring causes; I well remember, that, in the year 1746, one of the upper towns of the aforesaid Muskohge, was so exceedingly exasperated against some of our Chikkasah traders, for having, when in their cups, forcibly viewed the nakedness of one of their women, (who was reputed to be an hermaphrodite)[34] that they were on the point of putting them to death, according to one of their old laws against crimes of that kind.—But several of us, assisted by some of the Koosah town, rescued them from their just demerit. Connecting together these particulars, we can scarcely desire a stronger proof, that they have not been idolaters, since they first came to America; much less, that they erected, and worshipped any such lascivious and obscene idols, as the heathens above recited.

The Sidonians and Philistines worshipped Ashtaroth, in the figure of the *celestial luminaries;* or, according to others, in the form of a *sheep:* but the Americans pay the former, only, a civil regard, because of the beneficial influence with which the deity hath impressed them. And they reckon *sheep* as despicable and helpless, and apply the name to persons in that predicament, although a ram was the animal emblem of power, with the ancient eastern heathens. The Indians sometimes call a nasty fellow, *Chookphe* [24] *kussooma,* "a stinking sheep," and "a goat." And yet a goat was one of the Egyptian deities; as likewise were all the creatures that bore wool; on which account, the sacred writers frequently term idols, "the hairy." The despicable idea which the Indians affix to the species, shews, they neither use it as a divine symbol, nor have a desire of being named Dorcas, which, with the Hebrews, is a proper name, expressive of a wild she goat. I shall subjoin here, with regard to Ashtaroth, or Astarte, that though the ancients believed their deities to be immortal, yet they made to themselves both male and female gods, and, by that means, Astarte, and others, are of the fæminine gender. Trismegistus too, and the Platonics, affirmed there was deus masculo-fæmineus; though different sexes were needful for the procreation of human beings.

Instead of consulting such as the heathen oracles—or the Teraphim—the Dii Penates—or Dii Lares, of the ancients, concerning future contingencies, the Indians only pretend to divine from their dreams;[35] which may proceed from the tradition they still retain of the knowledge their ancestors obtained from heaven, in visions of the night, *Job* xxxiii. "God speaketh once, yea twice, yet man perceiveth it not. In a dream, in a vision of the night, when deep sleep falleth upon men, in slumberings upon the bed, then he openeth the ears of men, and sealeth their instruction." When we consider how well stocked with gods, all the neighbouring nations of Judæa were; especially the maritime powers, such as Tyre and Sidon, Carthage and Egypt, which continually brought home foreign gods, and entered them into their own Palladia; and that these Americans are utterly ignorant both of the gods and their worship, it proves, with sufficient evidence, that the gentlemen, who trace them from either of those states, only perplex themselves in wild theory, without entering into the merits of the question.

As the *bull* was the first terrestrial *cherubic emblem,* denoting fire, the ancient Egyptians, in length of time, worshipped Apis, Serapis, or Osiris, under the form of an ox; but, when he grew old, they drowned him, and lamented his death in a mourning habit; which occasioned a philosopher thus to jest them, *Si Dii sunt, cur plangitis? Si mortui, cur adoratis?* "If they be gods, why do you weep for them? And, if they are dead, why do you worship them?"[36] A bull, ox, cow, or calf, was the favourite deity of [25] the ancient idolaters. Even when YOHEWAH was conducting Israel in the wilderness, Aaron was forced to allow them a golden calf, according to the usage of the Egyptians: and at the defection of the ten tribes, they worshipped before the emblematical images of two calves, through the policy of Jeroboam. The Troglodites used to strangle their aged, with a cow's tail: and some of the East-Indians are said to fancy they shall be happy, by holding a cow's tail in their hand when dying: others imagine the Ganges to wash away all their crimes and pollution. The Indian Americans, on the contrary, though they derive the name of cattle from part of the divine essential name, (as shall be elsewhere observed) and use the name of a buffalo as a war appellative, and the name of a tribe; yet their regard to them, centres only in their usefulness for the support of human life: and they believe they can perform their religious ablutions and purifications, in any deep clean water.

The superstitious heathens, whom the Hebrews called, *Yedonim,* pretended that the bones of those they worshipped as gods when alive, revealed both present and future things, that were otherwise concealed: and the hieroglyphics, the priestly legible images, which the Egyptians inscribed on the tombs of the deceased, to praise their living virtue, and incite youth to imitate them, proved a great means of inducing them in process of time to worship their dead. But the Americans praise only the virtues of their dead, as fit copies of imitation for the living. They firmly believe that the hand of God cuts off the days of their dead friend, by his pre-determined purpose. They are so far from deifying fellow-creatures, that they prefer none of their own people, only according to the general standard of reputed merit.

The Chinese, likewise, though they call God by the appellative, *Cham Ti,* and have their temples of a quadrangular form, yet they are gross idolaters; like the ancient Egyptians, instead of offering up religious oblations to the great Creator and Preserver of the universe, they pay them to the pictures of their deceased ancestors, and erect temples to them, in solitary places without their cities—likewise to the sun, moon, planets, spirits, and inventors of arts; especially to the great Confucius, notwithstanding he strictly prohibited the like idolatrous rites. And the religious modes of the ancient inhabitants [26] of Niphon, or the Japanese, are nearly the same; which are diametrically opposite to the religious tenets of the wild Americans.

The diviners among the Philistines pretended to foretel things, by the flying, chirping, and feeding of wild fowls. The Greeks and Romans called fowls, Nuncii Deorum.[37] And Calchas is said to have foretold to Agamemnon, by the number of sparrows which flew before him, how many years the Trojan war should last. The Assyrians worshipped pigeons, and bore the figure of them on their standards, as the sacred oracles shew us, where the anger of the pigeon, and the sword of the pigeon, points at the destroying sword of the Assyrians. But, though the American woods swarm with a surprizing variety of beautiful wild fowl, yet the natives do not make the least pretension to auguries. They know it is by a certain gift or instinct, inferior to human reason, that the birds have a sufficient knowledge of the seasons of the year. I once indeed observed them to be intimidated at the voice of a small uncommon bird, when it pitched, and chirped on a tree over their war camp.[38] But that is the only trace of such superstition, as I can recollect among them. Instead of calling birds the messengers of the gods, they call the great eagle, Ooōle; which seems to be an imitation of Eloha.—This may be accounted for, from the eagle being one of the cherubic emblems, denoting the air, or spirit. They esteem pigeons only as they are salutary food, and they kill the turtle-dove, though they apply it as a proper name to their female children.

The Babylonians were much addicted to auguries: and they believed them to be unerring oracles, and able to direct them in doubtful and arduous things, Ezek. xxi. 21. Those auguries always directed their conduct, in every material thing they undertook; such as the beginning and carrying on war, going a journey, marriage, and the like. But, as we shall soon see, the Americans, when they go to war, prepare and sanctify themselves, only by fasting and ablutions, that they may not defile their supposed holy ark, and thereby incur the resentment of the Deity. And many of them firmly believe, that marriages are made above. If the Indian Americans were descended from any of the states or people above mentioned, they could not well have forgotten, much less could they have so essentially departed from their idolatrous worship. It is hence probable, they came here, [27] soon after the captivity, when the religion of the Hebrew nation, respecting the worship of Deity, was in its purity. And if any of the ancient heathens came with them, they became proselytes of habitation, or justice—hereby, their heathenish rites and ceremonies were, in process of time, intirely absorbed in the religious ceremonies of the Jews.

Had the nine tribes and half of Israel which were carried off by Shalmaneser, King of Assyria, and settled in Media, continued there long,[39] it is very probable, that by intermarrying with the natives, and from their natural fickleness and proneness to idolatry, and the force of example, they would have adopted, and bowed before the gods of the Medes and the Assyrians, and carried them along with them. But there is not a trace of this idolatry among the Indians. The severe afflictions they underwent in captivity, doubtless humbled their hearts, and reclaimed them from the service of the calves, and of Baalam, to the true divine worship—a glimpse of which they still retain. And that the first settlers came to America before the destruction of the first temple, may be inferred, as it is certain both from Philo and Josephus, that the second temple had no cherubim. To reflect yet greater light on the subject, I shall here add a few observations on the Indians supposed religious cherubic emblems, the cherubimical names of their tribes, and from whence they, and the early heathens, may be supposed to have derived them.

When the goodness of Deity induced him to promise a saviour to fallen man, in paradise, he stationed flaming *cherubim* in the garden. The type I shall leave; but when mankind became intirely corrupt, God renewed his promise to the Israelites, and to convey to posterity the true divine worship, ordered them to fix in the tabernacle, and in Solomon's temple, *cherubim,* over the mercy-seat,—the very curtains which lined the walls, and the veil of the temple, likewise, were to have those figures. The cherubim are said to represent the names and offices of *Yohewah Elohim,*[40] in redeeming lost mankind. The word כרבים, is drawn from כ, a note of resemblance, and רב, a great or mighty one; *i.e.* the "similitude of the great and mighty One," whose emblems were the bull, the lion, the man, and the eagle. The prophet Ezekiel has given us two draughts of the cherubim (certainly not without an instructive design) in his two visions, described in the first [28] and tenth chapters. In chap. x. ver. 20, he assures us that "he knew they were the cherubim." They were uniform, and had those four compounded animal emblems; "Every one had four faces—פנים," appearances, habits, or forms; which passage is illustrated by the similar divine emblems on the four principal standards of Israel. The standard of Judah bore the image of a *lion;* Ephraim's had the likeness of a *bull;* Reuben's had the figure of a *man's* head; and Dan's carried the picture of an *eagle,* with a serpent in his talons★: Each of the cherubim, according to the prophet, had the head and face of a man—the likeness of an eagle, about the shoulders, with expanded wings; their necks, manes, and breasts, resembled those of a lion; and their feet those of a bull, or calf. "The sole of their feet was like the sole of a calf's foot." One would conclude, from Ezekiel's visions, and *Psal.* xviii. 10.— *Ps.* xcix. 1. "He rode upon a cherub, and did fly:"—"The Lord reigneth,

---

★The MAN, which the lion on the standard of Judah, and the head on Reuben's, typified, was, in the fulness of time, united to the divine essence.

let the people tremble: he sitteth between the cherubim, let the earth be moved,"—that Elohim chose the cherubic emblems, in condescension to man, to display his transcendent glorious title of King of kings. We view him seated in his triumphal chariot, and as in the midst of a formidable war camp, drawn by those four creatures, the bull, the lion, the man, and the eagle; strong and descriptive emblems of the divine essence. What animal is equal to the *bull,* or ox, for strength, indefatigable service, and also for food? In eastern countries, they were always used to plough, and beat out the grain, besides other services omitted in modern times; the *lion* excels every other animal in courage, force, and prowess: *man* far surpasses all other creatures, in understanding, judgment, and wisdom; and there is no bird so sagacious, or can fly so swift, or soar so high as the eagle, or that bears so intense a love to its young ones.

These are the emblems of the *terrestrial cherubim:* and the Psalmist calls them Merabha Hashekina, "The chariot of Divine Majesty:" "God sitteth between, and rideth upon, the cherubim," or divine chariot. The *celestial cherubim* were *fire, light,* and *air,* or spirit, which were typified by the *bull,* the *lion,* and the *eagle.* Those divine emblems, in a long revolution of time, [29] induced the ancients by degrees, to divide them, and make images of the divine persons, powers, and actions, which they typified, and to esteem them gods. They consecrated the bull's head to the fire, the lion's to light, and the eagle's to the air, which they worshipped as gods. And, in proportion as they lost the knowledge of the emblems, they multiplied and compounded their heads with those of different creatures. The Egyptians commonly put the head of a lion, hawk, or eagle, and sometimes that of a ram, or bull, to their images; some of which resembled the human body. Their Apis, or Osiris, gave rise to Aaron's, and apostate Israel's, golden calf: and their sphynx had three heads. Diana of Ephesus was triformis; Janus of Rome, biformis, and, sometimes, quadriformis; and Jupiter, Sol, Mercury, Proserpine, and Cerberus, were triple-headed.

Hesiod tells us, the ancient heathens had no less than thirty thousand *gods.* It is well known that the ancient heathens, especially the Greeks and Romans, abounded with male and female deities; and commonly in human effigy. As they imagined they could not safely trust themselves to the care of any one god, they therefore chose a multiplicity. They multiplied and changed them from childhood to old age. The Romans proceeded so far, as to make Cloacina the guardian goddess of each house-of-office. The heathens in general, appointed one god to preside over the land, and another over the water; one for the mountains, and another for the valleys. And they were so diffident of the power of their gods, that they chose a god, or goddess, for each part of the body; contrary to the religious system of their best poets and philosophers, and that of the present savage Americans: the former affirmed, *sapiens dominabitur astris,* &c.; "A wise, good man, will always be ruled by divine reason; and not pretend to be drawn to this or that, by an over-bearing power of the stars, or fortune:" and the latter assert, "that temporal good or evil is the necessary effect of their own conduct; and that the Deity presides over life and death."[41]

If this first institution of the cherubic emblems was not religious, nor derived from the compounded figures of the scripture cherubim, how is it that so many various nations of antiquity, and far remote from each other, should have chosen them as gods, and so exactly alike? Is it not most reasonable to suppose, that as they lost the meaning of those symbolical figures, and [30] their archetypes, fire, light, and air, or spirit, which represented the attributes, names, and offices of *Yohewah Elohim,* they divided them into so many various gods, and paid them divine worship. Yet, though the Indian Americans have the supposed cherubimical figures, in their synhedria, and, through a strong religious principle, dance there, perhaps every winter's night, always in a bowing posture, and frequently sing *Halelu-Yah Yo He Wah,* I could never perceive, nor be informed, that they substituted them, or the similitude of any thing whatsoever, as objects of divine adoration, in the room of the great invisible divine essence. They use the feathers of the eagle's tail, in certain friendly and religious dances, but the whole town will contribute, to the value of 200 deer-skins, for killing a large eagle; (the bald eagle they do not esteem);[42] and the man also gets an honourable title for the exploit, as if he had brought in the scalp of an enemy. Now, if they reckoned the eagle a god, they would not only refuse personal profits, and honours, to him who killed it, but assuredly inflict on him the severest punishment, for committing so atrocious and sacrilegious an act.

I have seen in several of the Indian synhedria, two white painted eagles carved out of poplar wood, with their wings stretched out, and raised five feet off the ground, standing at the corner, close to their red and white imperial seats:[43] and, on the inner side of each of the deep-notched pieces of wood, where the eagles stand, the Indians frequently paint, with a chalky clay, the figure of a man, with buffalo horns—and that of a panther, with the same colour; from which I conjecture, especially, connected with their other rites and customs soon to be mentioned, that the former emblem was designed to describe the divine attributes, as that bird excels the rest of the feathered kind, in various superior qualities; and that the latter symbol is a contraction of the cherubimical figures, the man, the bull, and the lion. And this opinion is corroborated by an established custom, both religious and martial, among them, which obliges them to paint those sacred emblems anew, at the first fruit-offering, or the annual expiation of sins. Every one of their war-leaders must also make three successful *wolfish campaigns,* with their reputed holy ark, before he is admitted to wear a pair of a young buffalo-bull's horns on his forehead,[44] or to sing the triumphal war song, and to dance with the same animal's tail sticking up behind him, while he sings *Yo Yo,* &c.

[31] Now we know it was an usual custom with the eastern nations, to affix horns to their gods. The Sidonian goddess Ashtaroth was horned; and Herodotus says, the Egyptians painted their Venus, or Isis, after the same manner: and the Greek Jo, (which probably was Yo) had horns, in allusion to the bull's head, the chief emblem of the celestial cherubic fire, representing Yo (He Wah) as its name plainly indicates. A horn was, likewise, a Persian emblem of power★.

That the Indians derived those symbolical representations from the compounded figures of the cherubim, seems yet more clear, from the present cherubic names of their tribes, and the pre-eminence they formerly bore over the rest. At present, indeed, the most numerous tribe commonly bears the highest command; yet their old warriors assure us, it was not so even within their own remembrance. The title of the *old beloved men,* or *archimagi,* is still hereditary in the *panther,* or *tyger family:*[45] As North-America breeds no lions, the panther, of any animal it contains, is the nearest emblem of it. The Indian name of each cherub, both terrestrial and celestial, reflects great light on the present subject; for they call the buffalo (bull) *Yanasa;* the panther, or supposed lion, *Koè-Ishto,* or *Koè-O,* "the cat of God;" the man, or human creature, *Ya-we;* and the eagle, *Ooóle;* fire is *Loak;* the solar light, *Ashtahále;* and air, *Màhàle,* in allusion to מי, water, and אל, the omnipotent; the note of aspiration is inserted, to give the word a fuller and more vehement sound. Their eagle and buffalo tribes resemble two other cherubic names or emblems. They have one they call *Spháne,* the meaning of which they have lost; perhaps it might have signified the *man.*

Near to the red and white imperial seats, they have the representation of a full moon, and either a half moon, or a breast-plate, raised five or six feet high at the front of the broad seats, and painted with chalky clay; sometimes black paintings are intermixed.[46] But, let it be noticed, that in the [32] time of their most religious exercises, or their other friendly rejoicings there, they do not pay the least adoration to any of those expressive emblems; nor seem to take any notice of them: which is the very reverse to the usage of all the ancient heathen world. Hence one would conclude, that they not only brought with them the letter, but the meaning of those reputed cherubimi-

---

★The metaphorical expressions, and emblematical representations, of the law and the prophets, are generally suited to the usages of the eastern countries. And this metaphor, of a horn, is commonly so used, through all the divine registers, multiplying the number of horns of the object they are describing, to denote its various, great, and perfect power; unless where seven is mentioned as a number of perfection, as in St. John's figurative, magnificent, and sublime description of Christ.

cal figures, which were designed to represent the inseparable attributes of *Yohewah*.

It is universally agreed, by the Christian world, that every religious observance of the ancient heathens, which the Mosaic law approved of, was at first derived from divine appointment; and as we are assured in the first pages of the sacred oracles, concerning Cain, *Gen.* iv. 16. "that he went out from the *presence of the Lord,*" we learn, that God, in that early state of the world, chose a place for his more immediate presence,— פנים, his faces, appearances, or forms residing in, or between, the cherubim. We may, therefore, reasonably conclude, from the various gods, and religious worship of the ancient heathens, and from the remaining divine emblems, and family names of the Indian Americans, that the former deduced those emblems they deifyed, from the compounded cherubim in paradise: and that the Indians derived their cherubic figures, and names of tribes, from the cherubim that covered the mercy-seat, in the tabernacle, and in Solomon's temple, alluded to and delineated in several parts of the sacred oracles.

ARGUMENT III.

Agreeable to the THEOCRACY, or divine government of Israel, the Indians think the Deity to be the immediate head of their state.

All the nations of Indians are exceedingly intoxicated with religious pride, and have an inexpressible contempt of the white people, unless we except those half-savage Europeans, who are become their proselytes. *Nothings* is the most favourable name they give us, in their set speeches: even the Indians who were formerly bred in amity with us, and in enmity to the French, used to call us, in their war orations, *hottŭk ookproose,* "The accursed people." But they flatter themselves with the name *hottuk oretoopah,* "The beloved people," because their supposed ancestors, as they affirm, were under the immediate government of the Deity, who was present with them, in a [33] very particular manner, and directed them by prophets; while the rest of the world were aliens and out-laws to the covenant.

When the *archi-magus,* or any one of their magi, is persuading the people, at their religious solemnities to a strict observance of the old beloved, or divine speech, he always calls them, "The beloved," or holy people, agreeable to the Hebrew epithet, *Ammi,* during the theocracy of Israel: he urges them, with the greatest energy of expression he is capable of, a strong voice, and very expressive gestures, to imitate the noble actions of their great and virtuous forefathers, which they performed, in a surprizing manner, by their holy things, and a strict observance of the old, beloved speech. Then, he flourishes on their beloved land that flowed with milk and honey, telling them they had good, and the best things in the greatest plenty: and speaks largely of their present martial customs, and religious rites, which they derived from their illustrious predecessors,—strictly charging them not to deviate, in the least, out of that old, beloved, beaten path, and they will surely meet with all the success that attended their beloved forefathers.

I have heard the speaker, on these occasions, after quoting the war actions of their distinguished chieftains, who fell in battle, urging them as a copy of imitation to the living—assure the audience, that such a death, in defence of their beloved land, and beloved things, was far preferable to some of their living pictures, that were only spending a dying life, to the shame and danger of the society, and of all their beloved things, while the others died by their virtue, and still continue a living copy. Then, to soften the thoughts of death, he tells them, they who died in battle are only gone to sleep with their beloved forefathers; (for they always collect the bones)—and mentions a common proverb they have, *Neetak Intàhāh*, "The days appointed, or allowed him, were finished." And this is their firm belief; for they affirm, that there is a certain fixt time, and place, when, and where, every one must die, without any possibility of averting it. They frequently say, "Such a one was weighed on the path, and made to be light;" ascribing life and death to God's unerring and particular providence; which may be derived from a religious opinion, and proverb of the Hebrews, that "the divine care extended itself, from the horns of the unicorn, to the very feet of the lice." And the more refined part of the old heathens believed the like. The ancient Greeks and Romans, who were great copiers [34] of the rites and customs of the Jews, believed there were three destinies who presided over human life, and had each of them their particular office; one held the distaff of life, while another spun the thread, and Atropos cut it off: a strong but wild picture of the divine fire, light, and spirit. When Virgil is praising the extraordinary virtue of Ripheus, who was killed in defence of his native city, Troy, he adds, *Diis aliter visumest,*—submitting to the good and wise providence of the gods, who thought fit to call him off the stage. However, he seems to be perplexed on the subject; as he makes fate sometimes conditional;

> —————*Similis si cura fuisset,*
> *Nec pater omnipotens Trojam nec fata vetabant*
> *Stare,*——— [47]

"If the usual proper care had been taken, neither Jupiter nor fate would have hindered Troy from standing at this time." But, if the time of dying was unalterably fixed, according to the Indian system, or that of our fatalists, how would its votaries reconcile the scheme of divine Providence? which must be in conformity to truth, reason, and goodness,—and how explain the nature of moral good and evil? On their principle, self-murder would be a necessary act of a passive being set on work by the first mover; and his obligations would be proportionable, only to his powers and faculties; which would excuse the supposed criminal from any just future punishment for suicide. But religion, and true reason, deny the premises, and they themselves will not own the consequence.

It is their opinion of the THEOCRACY, or, that God chose them out of all the rest of mankind, as his peculiar and beloved people,—which animates both the white Jew, and the red American, with that steady hatred against all the world, except themselves, and renders them hated or despised by all. The obstinacy of the former, in shutting their eyes against the sacred oracles, which are very explicit and clear in the original text, and of which they were the trustees, incites both our pity and reproof; whereas the others firm adherence to, and strong retention of, the rites and customs of their fore-fathers, only attract our admiration.

The American Indians are so far from being *Atheists*, as some godless Europeans have flattered themselves, to excuse their own infidelity, that they have the great sacred name of God, that describes his divine essence, and [35] by which he manifested himself to Moses—and are firmly persuaded they now live under the immediate government of the Deity. The ascension of the smoke of their victim, as a sweet favour to *Yohewah*, (of which here-after) is a full proof to the contrary, as also that they worship God, in a smoke and cloud, believing him to reside above the clouds, and in the ele-ment of the, supposed, holy annual fire. It is no way material to fix any certain place for the residence of Him, who is omnipresent, and who sus-tains every system of beings. It is not essential to future happiness, whether we believe his chief place of abode is in *cælo tertio, paradiso terrestri,* or *ele-mento igneo.*[48] God hath placed conscience in us for a monitor, witness, and judge.—It is the guilty or innocent mind, that accuses, or excuses us, to Him. If any farther knowledge was required, it would be revealed; but St. Paul studiously conceals the mysteries he saw in the empyreal heavens.

The place of the divine residence is commonly said to be above the clouds; but that is because of the distance of the place, as well as our utter ignorance of the nature of Elohim's existence, the omnipresent spirit of the universe. Our finite minds cannot comprehend a being who is infinite. This inscrutable labyrinth occasioned Simonides, a discreet heathen poet and philosopher, to request Hiero, King of Sicily, for several days successively, to grant him a longer time to describe the nature of the Deity; and, at the end, to confess ingenuously, that the farther he waded in that deep mystery, the more he sunk out of his depth, and was less able to define it.

If we trace Indian antiquities ever so far, we shall find that not one of them ever retained, or imbibed, atheistical principles, except such whose in-terest as to futurity it notoriously appeared to be—whose practices made them tremble whenever they thought of a just and avenging God: but these rare instances were so far from infecting the rest, that they were the more confirmed in the opinion, of not being able either to live or die well, without a God. And this all nature proclaims in every part of the universe.

ARGUMENT IV.

We have abundant evidence of the Jews believing in the *ministration of angels,* during the Old-Testament dispensation; their frequent appearances, and their services, on earth, are recorded in the oracles, which the Jews themselves receive as given by divine inspiration. And St. Paul in his [36] epistle addressed to the Hebrews, speaks of it as their general opinion, that "Angels are ministring spirits to the good and righteous on earth." And that it was the sentiment of those Jews who embraced christianity, is evident from *Acts* xii. where an angel is said to deliver Peter from his imprisonment, and when the maid reported that Peter stood at the gate knocking, his friends doubting, said, "It is his angel." Women also are ordered to have their heads covered in religious assemblies, because of the presence of the angels, and to observe silence, the modest custom of the eastern countries. The Indian sentiments and traditions are the same.—They believe the higher regions to be inhabited by good spirits, whom they call *Hottuk Ishtohoollo,* and *Nana Ishtohoollo,* "holy people," and "relations to the great, holy One." The *Hottuk ookproose,* or *Nana ookproose,* "accursed people," or "accursed beings," they say, possess the dark regions of the west; the former attend, and favour the virtuous; and the latter, in like manner, accompany and have power over the vicious: on which account, when any of their relations die, they immediately fire off several guns, by one, two, and three at a time, for fear of being plagued with the last troublesome neighbours: all the adjacent towns also on the occasion, whoop and halloo at night; for they reckon, this offensive noise sends off the ghosts to their proper fixed place, till they return at some certain time, to repossess their beloved tract of land, and enjoy their terrestrial paradise. As they believe in God, so they firmly believe that there is a class of higher beings than men, and a future state and existence.[49]

There are not greater bigots in Europe, nor persons more superstitious, than the Indians, (especially the women) concerning the power of witches, wizards, and evil spirits. It is the chief subject of their idle winter night's chat: and both they, and several of our traders, report very incredible and shocking stories. They will affirm that they have seen, and distinctly, most surprizing apparitions, and heard horrid shrieking noises. They pretend, it was impossible for all their senses to be deluded at the same time; especially at *Okmulge,*[50] the old waste town, belonging to the *Muskohge,* 150 miles S.W. of Augusta in Georgia, which the South-Carolinians destroyed about the year 1715. They strenuously aver, that when necessity forces them to encamp there, they always hear, at the dawn of the morning, the usual noise of Indians singing their joyful religious notes, and dancing, as if going down to the river to purify themselves, and then returning to the old town-house: with a great deal more to the same effect. Whenever I have been [37] there, however, all hath been silent. Our noisy bacchanalian company might indeed have drowned the noise with a greater of their own. But as I have gone the tedious Chikkasah war path, through one continued desart, day and night, much oftener than any of the rest of the traders, and alone, to the Chikkasah country, so none of those frightful spirits ever appeared to, nor any tremendous noise alarmed me. But they say this was "because I am an obdurate infidel that way."

The Hebrews seem to have entertained notions pretty much resembling the Indian opinions on this head, from some passages in their rabbins, and which they ground even on the scriptures★. We read *Isa.* xiii. 21. "But wild beasts of the desart shall lie there, and their houses shall be full of doleful creatures, and owls shall dwell there, and satyrs shall dance there†."

Several warriors have told me, that their *Nana Ishtohoollo,* "concomitant holy spirits," or angels, have forewarned them, as by intuition, of a dangerous ambuscade, which must have been attended with certain death, when they were alone, and seemingly out of danger; and by virtue of the impulse, they immediately darted off, and, with extreme difficulty, escaped the crafty, pursuing enemy. Similar to this, was the opinion of many of the Jews, and several of the ancient and refined heathens, and is the sentiment of moderns, that intimations of this kind, for man's preservation and felicity, proceed from God by the instrumentality of good angels, or superior invisible beings, which he employs for that purpose—who can so impress the imagination, and influence the mind, as to follow the suggestions, but not so as to destroy the liberty of the will.—Thus Homer introduces Minerva as suggesting what was proper for the persons she favoured—and other superior beings; but they deliberated on the counsel, and chose that which appeared to be right.

ARGUMENT V.

The *Indian language,* and *dialects,* appear to have the very idiom and genius of the *Hebrew.* Their words and sentences are expressive, concise, emphatical, [38] sonorous, and bold—and often, both in letters and signification, syn-

---

★Lev. xix. 31. 1 Sam. xxviii. 3, &c. Isa. viii. 19.
†Bochart[51] supposes that *tsiim* signify *wild cats;* and that אחים is not any particular creature, but the crying or howling of wild beasts. His opinion is confirmed by many judicious writers.

onymous with the Hebrew language. It is a common and old remark, that there is no language, in which some Hebrew words are not to be found. Probably *Hebrew* was the first, and only language, till distance of time and place introduced a change, and then soon followed a mixture of others. The accidental position of the characters, might also coincide with some Hebrew words, in various dialects, without the least intention. As the true pronunciation of the Hebrew characters, is lost in a considerable degree, it is too difficult a task, for a skilful Hebraist, to ascertain a satisfactory identity of language, between the Jews, and American Aborigines; much more so to an Indian trader, who professes but a small acquaintance with the Hebrew, and that acquired by his own application. However, I will endeavour to make up the deficiency of *Hebrew,* with plenty of good solid *Indian roots.*[52]

The Indian nouns have neither cases nor declensions. They are invariably the same, through both numbers, after the Hebrew manner. In their verbs, they likewise sometimes use the preterperfect, instead of the present tense of the indicative mood; as *Blahsas Aiahre, Apeesahre,* "Yesterday I went and saw;" and *Eemmako Aiahre, Apeesahre,* "Now I go and see." Like the Hebrews, they have no comparative, or superlative degree. They express a preference, by the opposite extremes; as *Chekusteene,* "You are virtuous;" *Sahakse,* "I am vicious." But it implies a comparative degree, and signifies, "You are more virtuous than I am." By prefixing the adverbs, which express *little,* and *much,* to the former words, it conveys the same meaning; the former of which is agreeable to the Hebrew idiom. And a double repetition of the same adjective, makes a superlative, according to the Hebrew manner; as *Lawwa, Lawwa,* "most, or very many." To add *hah* to the end of an adjective, unless it is a noun of multitude like the former, makes it also a superlative; as *Hakse to hah,* "They are most, or very wicked." *Hakse* signifies vicious, probably when the vicious part of the Israelites were under the hand of the corrector, the judge repeated that word: *ta,* is a note of plurality, and *hah* an Hebrew accent of admiration; which makes it a superlative. To join the name of God, or the leading vowel of the mysterious, great, divine name, to the end of a noun, likewise implies a superlative; as *Hakse-ishto,* or *Hakse-o,* "He, or she, is very wicked." The former method of speech exactly agrees with the Hebrew idiom; as the original text shews, in innumerable instances.

[39] When the Hebrews compare two things, and would signify a parity between them, they double the particle of resemblance; "I am as thou art; and my people as thy people:" And the Indians, on account of that original defective standard of speech, are forced to use the like circumlocution; as *Che Ahōba sia,* "I am like you;" and *Sahottuk Chehottuk tooah,* &c. for *Hottuk* signifies people, and the *S* expresses the pronoun my, or mine: and it likewise changes an active, into a passive verb. Although this Indian and Hebrew method of speech, is rather tedious and defective, yet, at the same time, they

who attain any tolerable skill in the dialects of the one, and language of the other, will discover the sense plain enough, when a comparison is implied.

There is not, perhaps, any one language or speech, except the Hebrew, and the Indian American, which has not a great many prepositions. The Indians, like the Hebrews, have none in separate and express words. They are forced to join certain characters to words, in order to supply that great defect. The Hebrew consonants, called *serviles,* were tools to supply the place of the prepositions. The Indians, for want of a sufficient number of radical words, are forced to apply the same noun and verb, to signify many things of a various nature. With the Cheerake, *Eeankke,* signifies a *prisoner, captive, slave, awl, pin, needle,* &c.; which occasions the Indian dialects to be very difficult to strangers. The Jewish Rabbins tell us, that the Hebrew language contains only a few more than a thousand primitive words, of which their whole language is formed. So that the same word very often denotes various, though not contrary things. But there is one radical meaning, which will agree to every sense that word is used in.

By custom, a Hebrew noun frequently supplied the place of a pronoun; by which means, it caused a tedious, and sometimes an ambiguous circumlocution. From this original defective standard of speech, the Indians have forgotten all their pronouns, except two primitives and two relatives; as, *Anòwah, Ego,* and *Ishna, Tu:* the latter bears a great many significations, both as singular and plural, viz. *Eeàpa* and *Eeàko;* which signify he, she, this, that, &c.: And they are likewise adverbs of place; as here, there, &c. הוא *Hewa,* signifies he or she; אני *Ani,* we; and אנו, *Anowa,* he, she, him, her, &c.

[40] The Hebrew language frequently uses hyperboles, or magnifying numbers, to denote a long space of time: the Indians, accordingly, apply the words, *Neetak akroohah,* "all days," or, in other words, "for ever," to a long series of years. With the Jews, sitting, signified dwelling; and, with the Indians, it is the very same; for, when they ask a person where he dwells, they say, *Katèmuk Ishbeneele (chuak?),* which is literally, "where do you sit?" And when they call us irreligious, they say *Nāna U-bat,* "No thing," or literally, "a relation to nothing;" for *Nāna* signifies a relation: and the other is always a negative adverbial period; which seems also to proceed from a religious custom of the Hebrews, in giving despicable borrowed names to idols; as to בעלים, Baalim, "Particles of air," meaning, *nothing.* To which the Psalmist alludes, saying, "I will not take up their names in my lips." And St. Paul says, "We know that an idol is *nothing.*" This expression the Indians apply, in a pointed metaphor, to the white people, but never to each other.

Like the Hebrews, they seldom, if ever, double the liquid consonant *R;* for they generally seem desirous of shuffling over it, at any rate: And they often give it the sound of *L;* but, if it precedes a word, where the other consonant soon follows, they always give it its proper sound, contrary to the usage of the Chinese: as the name of a stone, they often call, *Tahle,* instead of *Tahrè;* but the Indians say, "*Tahre lakkàna,* literally, "Yellow stone," *i.e.* gold.

The Hebrews subjoined one of their serviles, to words, to express the pronoun relative, *thy* or *thine:* And as that particle was also a note of resemblance, it shews the great sterility of that language. As a specimen—They said אביך, (Abiche) "your father," and אמך, (Ameche) "Your mother," &c. Only that the Hebrew period is initial, in such a case, to the Indian nouns, they always use the very same method of expression. This I shall illustrate with two words in the dialects of the Chikkasah and Cheerake—as *Chinge* and *Chatokta,* "your father;" *Angge* and *Aketohta* signifying "my father," in resemblance of אב, *Abba,* of the same import; likewise *Chishke* and *Chacheeah,* "your mother;" for *Saske* and *Akachee* signify "my mother," in imitation of אשה, *Ashe.* Also *Sas Kish* signifies podex meus, *Chish Kish,* podex tuus, and *Kish Kish,* podex illius;[53] which I guess to be an [41] opprobrious allusion to Kish the father of Saul, for the son's assuming the throne at the end of the Jewish theocracy. In their adjectives and verbs, they use the same method of speech; as *Nahoorèso Chin-Chookoma,* "Your book is good." The former word is compounded of נא (*Na*) now, or the present time, and *Hoorèso,* delineated, marked, or painted. *Aia* signifies *to go,* and *Maia-Cha,* "Go along," or *Maia,* the same; for, by prefixing מ to it, it implies a requisite obedience. In like manner, *Apeesah,* to see, and *Peesàcha,* look, or "see you." And, when that particle is prefixed to a verb, it always expresses the accusative case of the same pronoun; as *Chepeesahre,* "I saw you," and *Chepeesahras,* "I shall see you." Each of the Hebrew characters are radicals; although half of them are *serviles,* according to that proper term of the scholiasts; for, when they are prefixed, inserted, or subjoined, either at the beginning, middle, or end of a radical word, *they serve* to form its various augments, inflexions, and derivatives. According to this difficult standard of speech, the Indian nouns, moods, and tenses, are variously formed to express different things. As there is no other known language or dialect, which has the same tedious, narrow, and difficult principles; must we not consider them to be twin-born sisters? The want of proper skill to observe the original fixed idea of the Indian words, their radical letters, and the due sounds in each of them, seems to have been the only reason why the writers on the American Aborigines, have not exhibited the true and genuine properties of any one of their dialects; as they are all uniform in principle: so far at least, as an extensive acquaintance reaches.

The Hebrew nouns are either derived from verbs, or both of them are one and the same; as ברכה, (Beroche) "Blessing," from ברך, (Beroch) "to bless," and דבר דבר, (Dabar Daber) "he spoke the speech." This proper name signifies "loquacious," like the Indian *Sekàkee,* signifying the "grasshopper." The Indian method of expression, exactly agrees with that Hebrew mode of speech; for they say *Anumbōle Anumbole (kis)* "I spake the speaking;" and *Anumbole Enumbole (kis)*, "he spoke the speaking, or speech." And by inserting the name of God between these two words, their meaning is the very same with those two first Hebrew words. I shall subjoin another word of the same sort—*Hookseelèta* signifies "a shutting instrument;" and they say *Ishtookseelèta,* or *Hookseelèta,Ish-hookseetas,* or *Hookseetà Cha,* "You shall, or, shut you the door." Their period of the last word, always denotes the second person singular of the imperative mood; [42] and that of the other preceding it, either the first or second person singular of the indicative mood; which is formed so by a fixed rule, on account of the variegating power of the serviles, by affixing, inserting, or suffixing them, to any root. According to the usage of the Hebrews, they always place the accusative case also before the verb; as in the former Indian words.

With the Hebrews, תפלה signified "a prayer," or a religious invocation, derived from פלח, Phelac, "to pray to, or invoke the Deity." In a strong resemblance thereof, when the Indians are performing their sacred dance, with the eagles tails, and with great earnestness invoking *Yo He Wah* to bless them with success and prosperity, *Phale* signifies, "waving," or invoking by waving, *Ishphāle,* you wave, *Phalècha,* wave you, *Aphalàle,* I waved, *Aphalèlas,* I will wave, &c. Psalmodists seem to have borrowed the notes *fa, la,* from the aforesaid Hebrew words of praying, singing to, or invoking Elohim. פעל, (Phoole) "to work," is evidently drawn from the former Hebrew word, which signifies to invoke (and probably to wave the feathers of the cherubic eagle before) *Yo He Wah.* The greatest part of the Levitical method of worshipping, consisted in laborious mechanical exercises, much after the Indian manner; which the popish priests copy after, in a great many instances, as pulling off their clothes, and putting on others; imagining that the Deity is better pleased with persons who variegate their external appearances, like Proteus, than with those who worship with a steady, sincere disposition of mind; besides a prodigious group of other superstitious ceremonies, which are often shamefully blended with those of the old pagans.

As the Hebrew word נא, *Na,* signifies the present time—so when the Indians desire a person to receive something from them speedily, they say, *Nà* (short and gutturally) *eescha,* "take it, now." He replies *Unta,* or *Omeh,* which are good-natured affirmatives. The pronoun relative, "you," which they term *Ishna,* is a compounded Hebrew word, signifying (by application) the person present, or "you."

With the Hebrews, הר הר, *Hara Hara,* signifies, "most, or very, hot;" the repetition of the word makes it a superlative. In a strict resemblance of that word, and mode of speech, when an Indian is baffled by any of their [43] humorous wits, he says, in a loud jesting manner, *Hara Hara,* or *Hala Hala,* according to their capacity of pronouncing the liquid *R:* and it signifies, "you are very hot upon me:" their word, which expresses "sharp," conveys the idea of bitter-heartedness with them; and that of bitterness they apply only to the objects of taste.

With the Cheerake, Chikkasah, and Choktah Indians, *Nannè* signifies "a hill:" and *Nannéh,* with the two last-mentioned nations, "a fish;" and *Unchàba,* "a mountain." But they call an alligator, or crocodile, *Nannéh Chunchàba,* literally, "the fish like a mountain;" which the English language would abbreviate into the name of a mountain-fish; but, instead of a hyphen, they use the Hebrew כ, a note of resemblance, which seems to point at the language from which they derived it. In like manner, *Aà* signifies to walk, and *Eette,* wood; but *Eette Chanáa,* any kind of wheel; which is consonant to the aforesaid Hebrew idiom; with many others of the like nature: but a specimen of this sort must suffice.

The Hebrew and Indian words, which express delineating, writing, decyphering, marking, and painting, convey the same literal meaning in both languages; as *Exod.* xvii. 14. שפר כחב, (*Chethéba Sepháre*) "delineate this with delineations;" and, with the Indians, *Hoorèso* is, in like manner, the radical name of books, delineating, &c.; and *Ootehna* that for numbering, instead of reading. The nearest approach they can make to it, is, *Anumbōle hoorèso Ishanumbōlas,* "You shall speak the speech, which is delineated."

They call a razor, *Baspoo Shaphe,* "A shaving knife:" and *Shaphe* always signifies to shave; probably, because when they first began to shave themselves, they were ridiculed by the higher, or more religious part of the people, for imitating that heathenish custom. The Hebrew שפה, (*Shaphe*) signifying lip, confession, or worship; which divine writ assures us, the descendants of Noah changed, when they opposed the divine will of settling various parts of the earth, and built the great tower of Babel, as an emblem of greatness, to get them a name*.

[44] *Loak* signifies fire, and *Loak Ishtohoollo,* "the holy or divine fire," or the anger of Ishtohoollo, "the great, holy One;" which nearly agrees with the Hebrew להט, that which flames, or scorches with vehement heat. And it is the scripture method of conveying to us a sensible idea of the divine wrath, according to the cherubic name אש, which likewise signifies fire. But the Persians worshipped the burning fire, by the name of *Oromazes;* and darkness, or the spirit, by that of *Aramanius;* quite contrary to the religious system of the Indian Americans: and the aforesaid Indian method of expression, seems exactly to coincide with the Hebrew idiom.

Buk-she-ah-ma is the name of their Indian flap, or broad slip of cloth with which the men cover their nakedness; but the word they use to express our

---

Skin signifies an eye; and *Skeeshāpha,* one-eyed; as if proceeding from the divine anger. They often change *i* into *ee.*

sort of breeches, is a compound, *Balaphooka,* derived from the Hebrew באל, which signifies, behind; and the Indian *Naphooka,* a coat, any kind of clothes, or covering; *Baloka* signifies, behind; silently telling us, they formerly wore a different sort of breeches to what they use at present. They likewise say, *Neeppe-Phú-ka,* "A flesh-covering."

The father of King Saul was called Kish, "podex;" which signifies also the rear of an army, or the hindermost person, according to the Hebrew idiom. Thus the Indians, by *Kish,* express the podex of any animal—the hindermost person—the gavel-end of an house, and the like. *Kish Kish,* is with them a superlative, and, as before hinted, used to convey the contempt they have for that proper name. May not the contemptible idea the West-Florida-Missisippi Indians affix to the name of Kish, be on account of his son's succession to the throne, at the end of the theocracy of Israel, and beginning a despotic regal government?

The Indians, according to the usage of the Hebrews always prefix the substantive to the adjective; as *Netak Chookòma,* "A good day;" *Nakkàne* and *Eho Chookòma,* "A good, or goodly man and woman." The former of which is termed, in Hebrew, *Yoma Tòbe,* signifying, according to our method of salutation, a good-day, a merry season, a festival day, &c. And the Indian appellatives are similarly exprest in Hebrew, *Behtobe* and *Ashe-Tòbe,* "A good, goodly, discreet, or wise man and woman." *Choòkoma,* with the Indians, is the proper name of a comely woman, when *A* is prefixed to it; as *A-chookòma,* "My goodly, or beautiful:" they use it for a warrior, [45] when it is compounded without the *A;* as *Chookoma hummáshtàbe,* "One who killed a beautiful, great, red, or war-chieftain;" which is compounded of *Chookoma,* comely, *Humma,* red, שא, *Ash,* fire, and *Abe,* a contraction of לבא, *Abele,* signifying grief, or sorrow. Hence it appears, that because the Hebrews affixed a virtuous idea to *Tòbe,* goodly; the Indians call white by the same name, and make it the constant emblem of every thing that is good, according to a similar Hebrew custom. Of this the sacred oracles make frequent mention.

The Jews called that, which was the most excellent of every thing, the *fat;* and the Indians, in like manner, say, *Oosto Neehe,* "The fat of the pompion," *Tranche Neehe,* "The fat of the corn." *Neeha* is the adjective, signifying *fat,* from which the word *Neeta,* "a bear," is derived. They apply the word *heart,* only to animate beings.

As the Deity is the soul of every system—and as every nation, from the remotest ages of antiquity, believed that they could not live well, without some god or other; when, therefore, we clearly understand the name, or names, by which any society of people express their notions of a deity, we can with more precision form ideas of the nature of their religious worship, and of the object, or objects, of their adoration. I shall therefore here give a plain description of the names by which the Indian Americans speak of God.

Ishtohoollo is an appellative for God. Ishtohoollo points at the greatness, purity, and goodness, of the Creator in forming אֵישׁ and אֵישָׁא: it is derived from *Ishto,* GREAT, which was the usual name of God through all the prophetic writings; likewise, from the present tense of the infinitive mood of the active verb, *Ahoollo,* "I love," and from the preter tense of the passive verb, *Hoollo,* which signifies "sanctifying, sanctified, divine, or holy." Women set apart, they term, *Hoollo, i.e.* sanctifying themselves to Ishtohoollo: likewise, *Netakhoollo* signifies "a sanctified, divine, or holy day;" and, in like manner, *Ookka Hoollo,* "water sanctified," &c. So that, *Ishtohoollo,* when applied to God, in its true radical meaning, imports, "The great, beloved, holy Cause;" which is exceedingly comprehensive, and more expressive of the true nature of God, than the Hebrew name *Adonai,* which is applicable to a human being. Whenever the [46] Indians apply the epithet, compounded, to any of their own religious men, it signifies the great, holy, beloved, and sanctified men of the Holy One.

They make this divine name point yet more strongly to the supreme author of nature; for, as אָב, signifies father; and as the omnipresent Spirit of the universe, or the holy father of mankind, is said to dwell above, they therefore call the immense space of the heavens, *Aba, Abáse,* and *Abatèra:* and, to distinguish the King of kings, by his attributes, from their own *Minggo Ishto,* or great chieftains, they frequently name him *Minggo Ishto Aba,* &c.; *Ishto Aba,* &c.; *Minggo Aba,* &c.; and, when they are striving to move the passions of the audience, *Ishtohoollo Aba.* The Hebrew servants were not allowed to call their master or mistress אָב, *Abba,* till they were adopted; to which custom St. Paul alludes, *Rom.* viii. 15.

They have another appellative, which with them is the mysterious, essential name of God—the *tetragrammaton,* or great four-lettered name—which they never mention in common speech,—of the time and place, when, and where, they mention it, they are very particular, and always with a solemn air.[54]

There is a species of tea, that grows spontaneously, and in great plenty, along the sea-coast of the two Carolinas, Georgia, and East and West-Florida, which we call *Yopon,* or *Cusseena:*[55] The Indians transplant, and are extremely fond of it; they drink it on certain stated occasions, and in their most religious solemnities, with awful invocations: but the women, and children, and those who have not successfully accompanied their holy ark, *pro Aris et Focis,*[56] dare not even enter the sacred square, when they are on this religious duty; otherwise, they would be dry scratched with snakes teeth, fixed in the middle of a split reed, or piece of wood, without the privilege of warm water to supple the stiffened skin.[57]

When this beloved liquid, or supposed holy drink-offering, is fully pre-pared, and fit to be drank, one of their *Magi* brings two old consecrated, large conch-shells,[58] out of a place appropriated for containing the holy things, and delivers them into the hands of two religious attendants, who, after a wild ceremony, fill them with the supposed sanctifying, bitter liquid: then they approach near to the two central red and white seats, (which the [47] traders call the war, and beloved cabbins) stooping with their heads and bodies pretty low; advancing a few steps in this posture, they carry their shells with both hands, at an instant, to one of the most principal men on those red and white seats, saying, on a bass key, Y'AH, quite short: then, in like manner, they retreat backward, facing each other, with their heads bowing forward, their arms across, rather below their breast, and their eyes half shut; thus, in a very grave, solemn manner, they sing on a strong bass key, the awful monosyllable, O[59], for the space of a minute: then they strike up ma-jestic HE, on the treble, with a very intent voice, as long as their breath allows them; and on a bass key, with a bold voice, and short accent, they at last utter the strong mysterious sound, WAH, and thus finish the great song, or most solemn invocation of the divine essence, The notes together com-pose their sacred, mysterious name, Y-O-HE-WAH.

That this seems to be the true Hebrew pronunciation of the divine es-sential name, יהוה,[60] JEHOVAH, will appear more obvious from the sound they seem to have given their characters.[61] The Greeks, who chiefly copied their alphabet from the Hebrew, had not *jod,* but ιοτα, very nearly resembling the sound of our *Y.* The ancient Teutonic and Sclavonian dialects, have *Yah* as an affirmative, and use the consonant *W* instead of *V.* The high importance of the subject, necessarily would lead these supposed red Hebrews, when sepa-rated from other people in America, to continue to repeat the favourite name of God, YO HE WAH, according to the ancient pronunciation.

Contrary to the usage of all the ancient heathen world, the American Indians not only name God by several strong compounded appellatives, ex-pressive of many of his divine attributes, but likewise say YAH at the begin-ning of their religious dances, with a bowing posture of body; then they sing YO YO, HE HE,[62] and repeat those sacred notes, on every religious oc-casion: the religious attendants calling to YAH to enable them humbly to supplicate, seems to point to the Hebrew custom of pronouncing, יה, *Yah,* which likewise signifies the divine essence. It is well known what sacred regard the Jews had to the four-lettered divine name, so as scarcely ever to mention it, but once a year, when the high-priest went into the holy sanc-tuary, at the expiation of sins. Might not the Indians copy from them, this sacred invocation? Their method of invoking God, in a [48] solemn hymn, with that reverential deportment, and spending a full breath on each of the two first syllables of the awful divine name, hath a surprizing analogy to the Jewish custom, and such as no other nation or people, even with the advantage of written records, have retained.

It may be worthy of notice, that they never prostrate themselves, nor bow their bodies, to each other, by way of salute, or homage, though usual with the eastern nations, except when they are making or renewing peace with strangers, who come in the name of YAH; then they bow their bodies in that religious solemnity—but they always bow in their religious dances, because then they sing what they call divine hymns, chiefly composed of the great, beloved, divine name, and addressed to YO HE WAH. The favoured persons, whom the religious attendants are invoking the divine essence to bless, hold up the shells with both hands, to their mouths, during the awful sacred invocation, and retain a mouthful of the drink, to spirt out on the ground, as a supposed drink-offering to the great self-existent Giver; which they offer at the end of their draught. If any of the traders, who at those times are invited to drink with them, were to neglect this religious observance, they would reckon us as godless and wild as the wolves of the desart★.[63] After the same manner, the supposed holy waiters proceed, from the highest to the lowest, in their synedrion[64]: and, when they have ended that awful solemnity, they go round the whole square, or quadrangular place, and collect tobacco from the sanctified sinners, according to ancient custom; "For they who serve at the altar, must live by the altar."

The Cheerake method of adjuring a witness to declare the truth, strongly corroborates the former hints, and will serve as a key to open the vowels of the great, mysterious, four-lettered name of God. On small affairs, the judge, who is an elderly chieftain, asks the witness, *Cheeakōhgà (sko?)* "Do you lie?" To which he answers, *Ansa*[65] *Kai-e-koh-gà,* "I do not lie." But [49] when the judge will search into something of material consequence, and adjures the witness to speak the naked truth, concerning the point in question, he says "O E A *(sko?)*" "What you have now said, is it true, by this strong emblem of the beloved name of the great self-existent God?" To which the witness replies, O E A, "It is true, by this strong pointing symbol of YO HE WAH." When the true knowledge of the affair in dispute, seems to be of very great importance, the judge swears the witness thus: O E A—YAH *(sko?)* This most sacred adjuration imports, "Have you now told me the real truth by the lively type of the great awful name of God, which describes his necessary

---

★The Mosaic law injoined the offering of libations; as *Exod.* xxix. and *Numb.* xv. And the heathens, especially the ancient Greeks and Romans, mimicked a great deal of the Mosaic institution. They observed the like ceremonies in their idolatrous sacrifices. The priests only tasted, and then spilt some wine, milk, or other liquor, in honour of the Deity, to whom the sacrifice was offered. Alexander is said to have sacrificed a bull to Neptune, and to have thrown a golden vessel used for the libation, into the sea.

existence, without beginning or end; and by his self-existent literal name, in which I adjure you." The witness answers, O E A—Yᴀʜ, "I have told you the naked truth, which I most solemnly swear, by this strong religious picture of the adorable, great, divine, self-existent name, which we are not to prophane; and I likewise attest it, by his other beloved, unspeakable,[66] sacred, essential name."

When we consider that the period of the adjurations, according to their idiom, only asks a question; and that the religious waiters say Yᴀʜ, with a profound reverence, in a bowing posture of body, immediately before they invoke YO Hᴇ Wᴀʜ,—the one reflects so much light upon the other, as to convince me, that the Hebrews, both invoked and pronounced the divine tetragrammaton, YO Hᴇ Wᴀʜ, and adjured their witnesses to give true evidence, on certain occasions, according to the Indian usage; otherwise, how could they possibly, in a savage state, have a custom of so nice and strong-pointing a standard of religious caution? It seems exactly to coincide with the conduct of the Hebrew witnesses even now on the like religious occasions—who being sworn, by the name of the great living God, openly to declare the naked truth, hold up their right hand, and answer, אמן אמן, *Amen Amen,* or "very true;" "I am a most faithful witness." The Hebrew word signifies faithful, and by being repeated twice, becomes a superlative, and O E A—Yᴀʜ is one of the highest degree.

St. John, in his gospel, according to the Hebrew method of adjuration, often doubles the *Amen.* And the same divine writer, at the beginning of each of his seven epistles, in describing the glorious and transcendant qualities of Jesus Christ, and particularly in the epistle to the church of Laodicea, points at the same custom, "These things saith the *Amen,* the faithful and true witness, the beginning of the creation of God."

[50] The Cheerake use another expression, which bears a strong analogy to the former method of adjuration; though it is not so sacred in their opinion, because of one letter prefixed, and another subjoined. The judge, in small controversies, asks the witness, *To e u (sko?)* To which he answers, *To eu,* or *To e u hah,* "It is very true," or "a most certain truth." Such an addition of any letter, or letters, to the vowels of the supposed divine, four-lettered name, seems to proceed from a strict religious custom of proportioning them to the circumstances of persons and things, lest, otherwise, they should blaspheme, or prophane the emblems of the great divine name. And the vowel *U* seems to allude to אחד, *i.e.* Oɴᴇ—a name of God, figuratively—for, in their dialect, when it is a period, it makes a superlative, according to their usage in applying the rest of the divine appellatives, symbols, or names.

They esteem *To e u hah* so strong an assent to any thing spoken, that *Cheesto Kaiēhre,* "the old rabbet," (the name of the interpreter) who formerly accompanied seven of their head warriors to London,[67] assured me, they held there a very hot debate, in their subterranean lodgings, in the dead hours of the night of September the 7th, 1730, whether they should not kill him, and one of the war-chieftains, because, by his mouth, the other answered *To e u hah* to his Majesty's speech, wherein he claimed, not only their land, but all the other unconquered countries of the neighbouring nations, as his right and property. When they returned home, they were tried again, by the national sanhedrim, for having betrayed the public faith, and sold their country, for acknowledged value, by firm compact, as representatives of their country; they having received a certain quantity of goods, and a decoying belt of white wampum: but, upon serious deliberation, they were honourably acquitted, because it was judged, the interpreter was bound, by the like oath, to explain their speeches; and that surprise, inadvertence, self-love, and the unusual glittering show of the courtiers, extorted the sacred assent, *To e u hah,* out of the other's mouth, which spoiled the force of it; being much afraid, lest they should say something amiss, on account of the different idiom of the English, and Indian American dialects★. As there is no alternative between a falsehood, and a lie, they [51] usually tell any person, in plain language, "You lie," as a friendly negative to his reputed untruth. The cheerful, inoffensive *old rabbet* told me, he had urged to them, with a great deal of earnestness, that it was certain death by our laws, to give his Majesty the lie to his face; and cautioned them to guard their mouths very strongly from uttering such dangerous language: otherwise, their hearts would become very heavy, and even sorrowful to death; as he would be bound as firmly by our holy books, to relate the bare naked truth, as they were by repeating *To e u ah,*[68] or even O-E-A—Yah.

The Chikkasah and Choktah method of adjuring a witness to give true evidence, is something similar to the former attestation, by *To e u hah:* when they ask them, whether they do not lie, they adjure them thus, *Chiklooska ke-e-u Chua?* The termination implies a question of the second person, sin-

---

★The strong sentiments, natural wit, and intense love of liberty, which the Indians shew themselves possessed of, in a high degree, should direct our colonists to pursue a different method [51] of contracting Indian covenants than they have commonly used. First, let them consider the general good of the community, who chose them for that end; and then make a plain agreement with the Indians, adapted to their fixed notion of liberty, and the good of their country, without any deluding sophisms. If they do not keep these essential points of amity in view, we shall fare again, as hath Georgia; for, by a childish treaty with the Muskohge Indians, when defeated An. 1715, its most northern boundaries are confined to the head of the ebbing and flowing of Savànnah river.[69] We are said to have flourished off very commodious Indian treaties in the *council-books,* with the Muskohge, which the community know nothing of, except a few plain common particulars, as they some years since declared.

gular number, and the whole oath signifies literally, "Do not you lie? Do you not, of a certain truth?" To which he answers by two strong negative asseverations, *Aklooska Ke-e-u-que-Ho,* "I do not lie; I do not, of a certain truth." When the Choktah are averring any thing asked of them, they assert it, by saying YAH. This shews their ignorance of the vowels of the supposed divine four-lettered name, in comparison of the Cheerake; and that they are become less religious, by prophaning the divine name, YAH; which confirms me in the opinion, that the Cheerake Indians were a more civilized people than any of the other neighbouring Indians.

We are told that the northern Indians, in the time of their rejoicings, repeat YO HA HAN; which, if true, evinces that their corruption advances, in proportion as they are distant from South-America, and wanted a [52] friendly intercourse with those who had an open communication with those southern regions★. Living in moderate high latitudes, would naturally prevent them from sinking into effeminacy, and inspire them with martial tempers, (as we are told of the Chili Indians) without being originally a bloodier people than any of the southern nations. However, we should be sparing of credit to what unskilful writers have carefully copied from each other, and transmitted to the learned world.

I shall hereafter, under another argument, shew, that the Indians variously transpose, shorten, and lengthen, each syllable of the great divine name, YO HE WAH, in a very extraordinary manner, when they are singing and dancing to, and before, the divine essence: and that they commonly derive

---

★They who have a desire to see the genuine oratory of the Indians, may find it partly exhibited to the public, by the laborious Mr. Colden, mostly in the manner, as I am told, he found it in the *council-books.* As that gentleman is an utter stranger to the language and customs of the Indians, it was out of his power to do justice to the original. Their speech, in general, abounds with bolder tropes and figures than illiterate interpreters can well comprehend, or explain. In the most essential part of his copied work, he committed a very material blunder, by writing in the first edition, the Indian solemn invocation, YO HA HAN. I was well assured by the intelligent Sir William Johnson, and the skilful, benevolent, pious, and reverend Mr. John Ogilvie, that the northern Indians always pronounce it YO HE A 'AH; and so it is inserted in the second edition. In justice to this valuable luminary of the church, and the worthy laity of the city of New-York, I must observe, that, while the rest of his sacerdotal brethren were much blamed for neglecting their office of teaching, and instead thereof, were militating for an *episcopate,* that gentleman was universally beloved by all ranks of people. He spent his time, like a true servant of God, in performing the various duties of his sacred office; and had the utmost pleasure in healing breaches, both in public society, and in private families. Great numbers of the poor negroe slaves, were instructed by him in the principles of christianity, while the other clergymen were earnestly employed in disturbing the quiet of the public, for the sake of their favourite Peter's pence.[70] [52]

such words as convey a virtuous idea, from, or compound them with that divine, essential name.

I shall now shew a farther parity, between the Hebrew language, and the Aboriginal American dialects.

Pushkoosh signifies an infant, *Neetta* a bear, *Nassooba* a wolf, &c.—By joining the word *Ooshe,* to the end of the names of animals, it makes a [53] distinction; as *Nassoob-ooshe,* a wolf-cub, *Neett'-ooshe* a bear-cub: but though the word *Oophe* signifies a dog, as an exception to their general method of speech, they call a puppy *Ooph-ishik,* because he is so domestic, or sociable, as שיק, to kiss, or fondle. In like manner, *Pishi* signifies milk; and *Pishik* a woman's breast, or the udder of any animal; as the young ones, by kissing, or sucking, shade the breast, פי, with their mouth, and thereby receive their nourishment. With the Hebrews, אפך (*Oophecha*) signifies active, or restless: which, according to the Indian idiom, expresses the quality of a dog; *Oophe* is therefore the name of this animal, and their period denotes a similarity, according to the usage of the Hebrews.

Shale and *Shatèra,* signify to carry, *Shapore,* a load. The former word consists of *Sheth* and *Ale. Illeh* imports dead, and *Kaneha* lost. They say *Shat Kaneha,* to carry a thing quite away, or to Canaan.—Likewise, *Illeht Kaneha,* literally, dead, and lost, or probably, gone to Canaan. Several old Indian American towns are called *Kanāai;* and it hath been a prevailing notion with many Jews, that when any of their people died in a strange land, they passed through the caverns of the earth, till they arrived at Canaan, their attractive centre. And the word *Oobèa,* likewise imports dead, or cut off by O E A, or *Yohewah;* for they firmly believe, as before hinted, they cannot outlive the time the Deity has prescribed them. They likewise say, *Hasse Ookkīlle Cheele,* "the sun is, or has been, caused to die in the water," *i.e.* sun-set. When they would say, "Do not obscure, or darken me," they cry *Ish-ookkīlle Chīnna,* verbatim, "Do not occasion *Ish,* me, to become like the sun, dead in the water." They call the new moon, *Hasse Awáhta,* "the moon is called upon to appear by Yohewah:" which plainly shews, that they believe the periodical revolutions of the moon to be caused, and the sun every day to die, or be extinguished in the ocean, by the constant laws of God. When we ask them, if to-day's sun is drowned in the western ocean, how another can rise out of the eastern ocean to-morrow? they only reply, *Pilla Yammi,* or *Yammi mung;* or such is the way of God with his people. It seems to be a plain contraction of יה and אממי *Ammi;* which was the name of Israel during the theocracy. Besides, *Aeemmi* signifies, "I believe;" as the peculiar people believed in Yohewah. And it likewise imports, "I am the owner of, &c."—according to the Hebrew idiom, the words and meaning nearly agree.

[54] *Eette* signifies wood; and they term any kind of chest, box, or trunk,

Eette Oobe; and frequently, *Oobe;* which seems to point to the "ark of the purifier," that was so fatal to the laity even to touch; a strong emanation of the holy fire, light, and spirit, residing in it, as well as in that which the priests carried to war, against the devoted enemy.

The Chikkasah settled a town, in the upper, or most western part of the Muskohge country, about 300 miles eastward of their own nation, and called it *Ooe-ása;*[71] which is derived from O E A, and *Asa,* "there," or "here, is;" *i.e.* "YO He Wah presides in this place." And, when a person is removing from his former dwelling, they ask him, *Ish-ooè-à (tūm?)* "are you removing hence, in the name, or under the patronage, of YO He Wah?" And it both signifies to ascend, and remove to another place. As, O E A, Aba, the omnipresent father of mankind, is said to dwell above, so the Indian hopes to remove there from hence, by the bounty of Ishtohoollo, the great holy One: according to their fixed standard of speech, had they made any nearer approach to O E A, the strong religious emblem of the beloved four-lettered name, it would have been reckoned a prophanation.

Phutchik signifies a star, and *Oonna* "he is arrived:" but *Phutchik Oonnache,* "the morning-star;" because he is the forerunner of light, and resembles the sun that reflects it. And *Oonna-hah* signifies to-morrow, or it is day. The termination denotes their gladness, that the divine light had visited them again: and, when they are asking if it is day, they say *Onna Hē (tak?).* The last monosyllable only asks a question; and the fæminine gender treble note is the mid syllable of the great divine name—which may reflect some light upon the former observations.

Although the Hebrews had a proper name for the human soul, calling it נפש; yet in *Prov.* xx. 27, it is called נר יהוה, "The candle, or lamp of God;" and figuratively applied, it conveys a strong idea of the human soul: Thus the Indians term it, *Nāna Ishtohoollo,* "something of, or a relation to, the great holy One;" very analogous to the former method of expressing the rational principle, in allusion to the celestial cherubic name אש, *Ashe,* Fire, as they believe the Deity resides in the new year's, supposed holy fire. Because *Ish,* Man, received his breath from the divine inspiration of the beneficent creator Yah, they term the human [55] species, in their strong-pointing language, *Yāhwè;* which, though different from the divine, essential, four-lettered name, in sound has יה, Yah, for its radix. But, because the monkey mimics *Yahweh,* or the rational creation, more than any other brute, in features, shape, gesture, and actions; in proportion to the similitude, they give him a similar name, *Shaw-we.* This indeed makes a near approach to *Ish* and *Yah,* and to *Yahwe;* but it wants the radix of both, and consequently bears no signification of relation to either. While they urge, that the regularity of the actions of the brute creatures around them, expresses a nice understanding or instinct; they deny their being endued with any portion of the reasoning, and living principle, but bear only a faint allusion to *Nana Ishtohoollo,* the rational soul. The most intelligent among them, say the human soul was not made of clay, like the brute creation, whose soul is only a corporeal substance, attenuated by heat, and thus rendered invisible.

Through a seeming war-contempt of each other, they all use a favourite termination to their adjectives, (very rarely to their substantives) and sometimes to their verbs; especially when they are flourishing away, in their rapid war-speeches, which on such occasions they always repeat with great vehemence. I shall give a specimen of two words, in the dialects of our southern Indians. *R I* is the favourite period of the Katāhba Indians; as *Mare-ŕi,* or *Wahre-ŕi,* "Good," and *Maretawah-ŕi,* or *Wahrètawàh-ŕi,* "best," or very good; *Wah,* the last syllable of the great divine name, is evidently the radix, and magnifies the virtuous idea to a superlative. In like manner, *Shegàre-Wahŕi,* "not bad," but *Sheekàre-ŕi,* signifies "bad." With these Indians, *Sheeke* is the name of a buzzard, which they reckon to be a most impure fowl, as it lives on putrid carcasses; upon which account, they choose that word to convey a vicious idea.

Quo is the sounding termination of the Cheerake; as *Seohsta-quo,* "good," —and *O-se-u,* "best," or very good. Here they seem to have studiously chosen the vowels:—As the following words will illustrate, *Tònàte-ū,* "very honest," or virtuous, and *Y-O-U,* "Evil," or very bad. To corroborate the hints I gave, concerning the Indian names of monkey,[72] and the human species, let it be observed, that though their words convey a virtuous or vicious idea, in proportion as they are constituted out of [56] any of their three divine names, YOHEWAH, YAH, and ISHTOHOOLLO; or contain the vowels of the great sacred name, yet the aforesaid word Y-O-U, is so far from being a deviation from that general custom, it is an emphatical, and emblematical term to express evil, by the negative of good; for, as it is the only substantive or adjective of that word, it is a strong expressive symbol of the nature, and physical cause of moral evil, by separating *YO,* the first syllable of the divine four-lettered name into two syllables; and adding *U,* as a superlative period, to make it *malum malorum.*[73]

Shèh is the sounding criterion of the Muskohge, or Creek Indians,—a kind of cant jargon, for example; *Heettla-sheh,* signifies "good," and *Heettla-wah-E-sheh,* "very good;" according to their universal standard of speech, it becomes a superlative, by subjoining that part of the divine name to it. With the Chikkasah and Choktah, *Heettla* signifies dancing; probably because that religious exercise was good and highly pleasing to them, when, according to ancient custom, they danced in their symbolical circles, to, and before, YO HE WAH. With the former, *Apullowhage sheh,* expresses "bad," or evil, thereby inverting the divine letters.

Skeh is the favourite termination of the Chikkasah and Choktah—as

Chookòma-skeh, "good," *Chookòmasto-skeh* (alluding to *Ishto*) "very good;" and *Ookproo-skeh,* "bad." Likewise, *Ookproosto,* "worst," or very bad; for, by annexing the contracted initial part of the divine name, *Ishtohoollo,* to the end of it, it is a superlative. These remarks may be of service to the inhabitants of our valuable and extensive barriers, in order to discover the national name of those savages, who now and then cut them off.

Ookproo-se, with those Indians, signifies "accursed;" the two last letters make only a *samech,* which implies a neuter passive: and, as *Ookproo* is the only substantive or adjective they use to express "evil," by doubling the leading vowel of the four-lettered divine name, both at the beginning and end of the word; may we not conjecture at its origin, as glancing at the introduction of sin or evil by man's overacting, or innovating, through a too curious knowledge, or choice? "Ye shall be as gods," and, in order to gain the resemblance, they ate what was forbidden.

[57] The greater number of their compounded words, (and, I believe, every one of them) which convey a virtuous or pure idea, either have some syllables of the three divine names, or visibly glance at them; or have one or two vowels of the sacred name, Yo HE WAH, and generally begin with one of them; which I shall exemplify, with a few Chikkasah and Cheerake words. *Isse-Ahowwè,* "Deer;" *Yanàsa,* Buffalo, which as it begins with the divine name, YAH, contains no more of their beloved vowels: in like manner, *Wahka,* "cattle;" *Ishke-Oochēa,* "a mother." This last seems to be drawn from *Isha,* the mother of all mankind. *Ehó* and *Enekia* signify "a woman." The latter is derived from the active verb, *Akekiuhah,* signifying "to love ardently," or like a woman; *Nakkàne Askai,* "a man." From this word, the Chikkasah derive *Nakke,* the name of an arrow or bullet: and with the Cheerake *Askai* signifies "to fear;" as all the American brute animals were afraid of man, &c.

Words, which imply either a vicious or impure idea, generally begin with a consonant, and double those favourite vowels, either at the beginning and end, or in the middle, of such words; as *Nassooba Woheea,* "a wolf." With the Chikkasah, *Eassooba* signifies "bewildered;" *Patche,* "a pigeon," and *Patche Eassooba,* "a turtle-dove." *Soore* and *Sheeke* are the Chikkasah and Cheerake names of a "Turkey-buzzard;" *Choola* and *Choochòla,* "a fox;" *Shookqua* and *Seequa,* an "opossum," or hog; *Ookoonne,* "a polecat;" *Ookoonna,* "a badger;" *Chookphe* and *Cheesto,* "a rabbet." The last word is derived from the defective verb *Chesti,* "forbear," or do not meddle with; and rabbets were prohibited to the Israelites. In like manner, *Ooppa* and *Ookookoo,* "a night-owl;" *Oophe* and *Keera,* "a dog;" *Nahoolla* and *U-nēhka,* "white people," or "impure animals." The Chikkasah both corrupt and transpose the last part of the divine name, Ishtohoollo; and the Cheerake invert their magnifying termination *U,* to convey an impure idea. And through the like faint allusion to this divine name, *Hoollo* signifies "idols, pictures, or images;" a sharp-pointed sarcasm ! for the word, *Hoollo,* signifies also "menstruous women," who were for the time an equal abomination to the Israelites, and with whom they were to have no communion. These two words seem to bear the same analogy to each other, as אל, *Al,* a name of God, and אלה, *Aleh,* signifying the covenant of the holy One to redeem man, אלוה, *Aloah,* execrated, or accursed of God, as idols were.

[58] With the Cheerake, *Awwa,* or *Amma,* signifies "water," and *Ammoi,* "a river;" not much unlike the Hebrew. They likewise term salt, *Hawa;* and both the conjunction copulative, and "to marry," is *Tawa.* The name of a wife is *Awah;* which written in Hebrew, makes הוה, *Eve,* or *Eweh,* the name of our general mother. So that the Indian name of a wife, is literally and emphatically, HIS AND, "One absolutely needful for the well-being of *Ish,* or man;" *Ishtawa (tim?)* signifies "have you married?" We gain additional light from the strong significant appellative, *Ish-ke,* "a mother;" which is an evident contraction of *Isha,* the mother of *Yawe,* or mankind, with their favourite termination, *ske,* subjoined; the word becomes thus smoother than to pronounce it at its full length, *Isha-ske.* If we consider that the Hebrews pronounced ו, *Vau,* when a consonant, as *W,* here is a very strong, expressive gradation, through those various words, up to the divine, necessary, AND, who formed and connected every system of beings; or to the Hebrew divine original YO HE WAH: at the same time, we gain a probable reason why so many proper names of old Indian places, in South-Carolina, and elsewhere, along the great continent, begin with our Anglo-Saxon borrowed character, *W;* as *Wampee, Watboo, Wappoo, Wadmolā, Wassamèsāh,* &c. Chance is fluctuating, and can never act uniformly.

To elucidate the aforesaid remarks, it may not be amiss to observe, that, according to the Israelitish custom both of mourning, and employing mourners for their dead, and calling weeping, the lifting up of their voices to God, the Choktah literally observe the same custom; and both they and the Chikkasah term a person, who through a pretended religious principle bewails the dead, *Yah-ah,* "Ah God!" and one, who weeps on other occasions, *Yāhma,* "pouring out salt tears to, or before God;" which is similar to יהמי. When a person weeps very bitterly, they say, *Yahmishto,* which is a compounded word, derived from יה, and ומי, with the initial part of the divine name, *Ishtohoollo,* subjoined, to magnify the idea, according to the usage of the Hebrews. When the divine penman is describing the creation, and the strong purifying wind, which swept along the surface of the waters, he calls it, "the air, or spirit;" and, more significantly, "the wind of God," or a very great wind: and, in other parts of the divine oracles, great hail, a [59] great lion, and the like, are by the same figure, called the hail of God. They also apply the former words, *Yah-ah, Yah-ma,* and the like, to express the very same ideas through all the moods and tenses as *Cheyaàras,* "I shall weep for you;" *Sawa Cheyaàra Awa,* "Wife, I will not weep for you." And when the violence of their grief for the deceased, is much abated, the women frequently, in their plaintive notes, repeat *Yo Hé (tà) Wāh, Yo Hé (tà) Wēh, Yò Hé ta Há, Yo Hê tà Héh;*[74] with a reference probably to the Hebrew custom of immoderately weeping and wailing for their dead, and invoking the name of God on such doleful occasions; and which may have induced these supposed red Hebrews to believe the like conduct, a very essential part of religious duty. *Neetak Yah-ah* signifies "a fast day," because they were then humbly to say *Ah,* and afflict their souls before YAH. In like manner, *Yah-`Abe* signifies "one who weeps for having killed, or murdered another." Its roots are הי, *Yah,* their continual war-period, and, אבל, *Abele,* signifying "sorrow or mourning;" for, as killing, or murdering, is an hostile act, it cannot be drawn from אבה, which signifies brotherly love, or tender affection. *Nana-Yah-Abe* describes a person weeping, while another is killing him. Now, as *Nana* is "a relation," *Yah* "God," and *Abe* as above, the true meaning seems to be, "One, like bleeding Abele, weeping to God." Likewise their name for salt, *Hawa,* may inform us, that though at present they use no salt in their religious offerings, they forbore it, by reason of their distant situation from the sea-shore, as well as by the danger of blood attending the bringing it through an enemy's country; for, according to the idiom of their language, if they had not thought salt an essential part of the law of sacrificature, they most probably, would not have derived it from the two last syllables of the great divine name; whereas they double the consonant, when they express water, without drawing it from the clear fountain of living waters, YO HE WAH.

With the Hebrews, as before observed*, טפל, *Tephale,* signifies "shaking or pulling of the hand, cohesion, conjunction, or entering into society;" and "praying, or invoking." In conformity to that original standard, when the Indians would express a strong, lasting friendship, they have no [60] other way, than by saying, *Aharattlè-la pheena chemanumbóle,* "I shall firmly shake hands with your discourse, or speech."

When two nations of Indians are making, or renewing peace with each other, the ceremonies and solemnities they use, carry the face of great antiquity, and are very striking to a curious spectator, which I shall here relate, so far as it suits the present subject. When strangers of note arrive near the place, where they design to contract new friendship, or confirm their old amity, they send a messenger a-head, to inform the people of their amicable intention. He carries a swan's wing in his hand, painted all over with streaks of white clay, as an expressive emblem of their embassy.[75] The next day,

*Page 42.

when they have made their friendly parade, with firing off their guns and whooping, and have entered the beloved square, their chieftain, who is a-head of the rest, is met by one of the old beloved men, or magi, of the place. He and the visitant approach one another, in a bowing posture. The former says, *Yô, Ish la chu Anggòna?* "Are you come a friend in the name of God?" Or, "Is God with you, friend?" for, *Yo* is a religious contraction of *Yohewah,*—*Ish* "the man," *La* a note of joy, *Chu* a query, and *Anggona* "a friend." The other replies, *Yah—Arahre-O, Anggona,* "God is with me, I am come, a friend, in God's name." The reply confirms the meaning of the questionary salute, in the manner before explained. The magus then grasps the stranger with both his hands, around the wrist of his right hand, which holds some green branches—again, about the elbow—then around the arm, close to his shoulder, as a near approach to the heart. Then his immediately waving the eagles tails over the head of the stranger, is the strongest pledge of good faith. Similar to the Hebrew word, *Phále* with the Indians, signifies "to wave," and likewise to shake; for they say, *Skooba—Phále,* "shaking one's head." How far the Indian oath, or manner of covenanting agrees with that of the Hebrews, on the like solemn occasion, I refer to the intelligent reader. Their method of embracing each other, seems to resemble also that custom of the Hebrews when a stranger became surety for another, by giving him his wrist; to which Solomon alludes, "If thou hast stricken hand with the stranger, &c."—Their common method of greeting each other, is analogous with the above; the host only says, *Ish-la Chu?* and the guest replies, *Arahre-O,* "I am come in the name of O E A," or Yo He Wah.

[61] When *O* is joined to the end of words, it always denotes a superlative, according to their universal figurative abbreviations of the great beloved name; thus with the Chikkasah, *Isse,* "deer," and *Isse-O,* "very great deer;" *Yanása,* "a buffalo," *Yanas-O,* "a very extraordinary great buffalo;" which is, at least, as strong a superlative, as אל ביח אל, signifying "the house of the Omnipotent," or "the temple."

With the Cheerake Indians, *A (wàh tà) howwe* signifies "a great deer-killer;" it is compounded of *Ahowwe,* "a deer," *Wah* —the period of the divine name, and *Ta,* a note of plurality. The title, "the deer-killer of God for the people," was, since my time, very honourable among them, as its radical meaning likewise imports. Every town had one solemnly appointed; him, whom they saw the Deity had at sundry times blessed with better success than the rest of his brethren, in supplying them with an holy banquet, that they might eat, and rejoice, before the divine essence. But now it seems, by reason of their great intercourse with foreigners, they have left off that old social, religious custom; and even their former noted hospitality. I will also observe, that though necessity obliged them to apply the bear's-grease, or oil, to religious uses, they have no such phrase as (*Wah ta) eeōna;*

not accounting the bear so clean an animal as the deer, to be offered, and eaten in their religious friendly feasts; where they solemnly invoked, ate, drank, sung, and danced in a circular form, to, and before, YO He Wah.

The Indian dialects, like the Hebrew language, have a nervous and emphatical manner of expression.—The Indians do not personify inanimate objects, as did the oriental heathens, but their style is adorned with images, comparisons, and strong metaphors like the Hebrews; and equal in allegories to any of the eastern nations. According to the ages of antiquity, their war-speeches, and public orations, always assume a poetical turn, not unlike the sound of the measures of the celebrated Anacreon and Pindar. Their poetry is seldom exact in numbers, rhymes, or measure: it may be compared to prose in music, or a tunable way of speaking. The period is always accompanied with a sounding vehemence, to inforce their musical speech: and the music is apparently designed to please the ear, and affect the passions.

[62] After what hath been said of their language, it may be proper here to shew how they accent the consonants: I shall range them in the order of our alphabet, except those they pronounce after our manner. When *CH* begins a word, or is prefixed to a vowel, it conveys a soft sound, as *Cháa*, "high;" but otherwise it is guttural: as is *D*, which is expressed by fixing the tip of the tongue between the teeth, as *Dawi*, for David. *G* is always guttural, as we accent *Go*. They cannot pronounce *Gn*; and they have not the *Hh*, neither can it be expressed in their dialects, as their leading vowels bear the force of guttural consonants. They have not the Jod, as I can any way recollect, or get information of; nor can they repeat it, any nearer than *Chot*. They pronounce *K*, as in *Ko*; *L* and *N*, as *D—S*, by fixing the tongue to the lower teeth; *T* like *D*, as in the old Hibernian, or Celtic affirmative, *Ta*. They cannot pronounce *V*, or *X*; they call the governor of Moveel, (Mobille) *Goweno-Moweeleh*: and they have not a word which begins or ends with *X*. *KS* are always divided into two syllables; as *Hak-se*, "mad," &c. They have not the letter *Z*; much less any such harsh sound as *Tz* although they have *Tl*. As they use the Hebrew consonants *Y* and *W*, in their most solemn invocation YO He Wah, instead of the present Hebrew *Jod* and *Vau*; so they seem to exclude them intirely out of their various dialects: the pronunciation therefore of the Hebrew characters, which are supposed to convey the other sounds, they are unacquainted with; and those which seem to be transposed, may be clearly ascertained by persons of proper capacity and leisure, by comparing a sufficient number of Hebrew and Indian words together. The Indian accents, *Oo*, and *O*, *Qu*, and *Tl*, may, prove a pretty good key to speculative enquirers.

Tl often occur in their words; as *Tlumba*, "to bleed with a lancet, to bore, scoop, or make any thing hollow;" and *Heettla*, "to dance." And the South-Americans, we are told, had likewise the same sound, as in that national name, *Tlaskala:* it seems to have been universal over the extensive continent. And, from a similarity of the Hebrew manners, religious rites, civil and martial customs, we have a strong presumptive proof, that they used the aforesaid double vowels, and likewise a single vowel, as a termination, to give their words a soft accent: and it is plain to me, that the Hebrew language did not sound so harsh, as it is now commonly expressed, but like the American dialects it was interspersed with vowels, [63] and a vowel was commonly subjoined to each word, for the sake of a soft cadence; as *Abele,* and *Ale,* instead of אבל, *Abel,* and אל, *Al,* &c.

The English characters cannot be brought any nearer to the true pronunciation of the Indian words, than as above set down: so that former writers have notoriously strayed, by writing conjecturally, or taking things on the wing of fame. What Indian words we had, being exceedingly mangled, either by the fault of the press, or of torturing pens, heretofore induced skilful persons to conjecture them to be hieroglyphical characters, in imitation of the ancient Egyptian manner of writing their chronicles.

The Indians express themselves with a great deal of vehemence, and with short pauses, in all their set speeches; but, in common discourse, they express themselves according to our usual method of speech, only when they scold each other: which I never observed, unless they were intoxicated with spiritous liquors, or casually overheard a husband when sober in his own family. They always act the part of a stoic philosopher in outward appearance, and never speak above their natural key. And in their philosophic way of reasoning, their language is the more sharp and biting, like keen irony and satyr, that kills whom it praises. They know, that thus they correct and subdue the first boilings of anger; which, if unchecked, proves one of the most dangerous passions to which human nature is subject. So that remote savages, who have heard only the jarring screeches of night-owls, and the roaring voices of ravenous beasts of prey, in this respect give lessons, and set a worthy example to our most civilized nations.

I have heard several eloquent Indian leaders, just as they were ready to set off for war, to use as bold metaphors and allegories in their speeches—and images almost as full and animating, as the eloquent penman of the old divine book of Job, even where he is painting, with his strong colours, the gladness and contempt of the beautiful war-horse, at the near approach of the enemy. I heard one of their captains, at the end of his oration for war, tell the warriors that stood outermost, he feelingly knew their guns were burning in their hands; their tomohawks thirsty to drink the blood of their enemy; and their trusty [64] arrows impatient to be on the wing; and, lest delay should burn their hearts any longer, he gave them the cool refreshing word, "Join the holy ark, and away to cut off the devoted enemy." They immediately sounded the shrill whoó-whoòp, and struck up the solemn, awful song, *Yŏ,* &c.

In Virginia, resides the remnant of an Indian tribe, who call themselves *Sepóne;*[76] which word, with the Egyptians, signifies the time of putting their wine into vessels; derived, according to mythologists, from *Saphan,* "to inclose or conceal." From thence they formed the fictitious *Tisiphone,* the punisher of sins, animated with hatred; and also the rest of their pretended furies, from the like circumstances of the year. Our early American writers have bestowed on these Indians an emperor, according to the Spanish copy, calling him *Pawhatan*—contrary to the Indian method of ending their proper names with a vowel; and have pictured them as a separate body of fierce idolatrous canibals. We however find them in the present day, of the same temper and religious tenets, as the rest of the Indian Americans, in proportion to their situation in life. Considering the nearness of Egypt to Judea, they might have derived that appellative from the Egyptians,— especially, as here, and in several of our American colonies, (particularly on the north side of Susquehāna river, in Pensylvania) are old towns, called *Kanāa.* There was about thirty years ago, a remnant of a nation, or sub-divided tribe of Indians, called *Kanāai;* which resembles the Hebrew proper name, כנען, (*Canaan,* or *Chanoona*). Their proper names always end with a vowel: and they seldom use a consonant at the end of any word★. I can-not recollect [65] any exceptions but the following, which are sonorous, and seem to be of an ancient date; *Ookkàh,* "a swan;" *Ilpàtak,* "a wing;" *Kooshàk,* "reeds;" *Sheenuk,* "sand;" *Shūtik,* "the skies;" *Phutchik,* "a star;" *Soonak,* "a kettle;" *Skin,* "the eye;" *Ai-eep,* "a pond;" and from which they

★If we consider the proximity of those Indians to a thick-settled colony, in which there are many gentlemen of eminent learning, it will appear not a little surprizing that the name *Canaanites,* in the original language, according to the Indian method of expressing it, as above, did not excite the attention of the curious, and prompt them to some enquiry into the language, rites, and customs, of those Aborigines: which had they effected, would have justly procured them those eulogia from the learned world, which their society profusely bestowed on the artful, improved strokes of a former prime magistrate of South-Carolina, whose conduct in Indian affairs, was so exceed-ingly singular, if not sordid and faulty,[77] (as I publicly proved when he presided there) that another year's such management would have caused the Cheerake to remove to the French barrier, or to have invited the French to settle a garrison, where the late unfortunate Fort-Loudon stood. But a true British administration succeeding, in the very critical time, it destroyed their immature, but most dangerous threatening scheme. This note I insert here, though rather out of place, to shew, that the northern gentlemen have not made all those observations and enquiries, with regard to the Indians, which might have been reasonably expected, from so numerous and learned a body.

derive the word *Ai-ee-pe,* "to bathe," which alludes to the eastern method of purifying themselves. *Ilbàk* signifies "a hand:" and there are a few words that end with *sh;* as *Soolish,* "a tongue," &c.

The Indians call the lightning and thunder, *Eloha,* and its rumbling noise, *Rowah,* which may not improperly be deduced from the Hebrew. To enlighten the Hebrew nation, and impress them with a reverential awe of divine majesty, God spoke to them at Sinai, and other times during the theocracy, with an awful or thundering voice. The greater part of the Hebrews seem to have been formerly as ignorant of philosophy, as are the savage Americans now. They did not know that thunder proceeded from any natural cause, but from the immediate voice of Elohim, above the clouds: and the Indians believe, according to this Hebrew system of philosophy, that *Minggo Ishto Eloha Alkaiasto,* "the great chieftain of the thunder, is very cross, or angry when it thunders:" and I have heard them say, when it rained, thundered, and blew sharp, for a considerable time, that the beloved, or holy people, were at war above the clouds. And they believe that the war at such times, is moderate, or hot, in proportion to the noise and violence of the storm.

I have seen them in these storms, fire off their guns, pointed toward the sky; some in contempt of heaven, and others through religion—the former, to shew that they were warriors, and not afraid to die in any shape; much less afraid of that threatening troublesome noise: and the latter, because their hearts directed them to assist *Ishtohoollo Eloha*★. May not this [66] proceed from an oral tradition of the war which the rebellious angels waged against the great Creator; and which the ancient heathens called the war of the giants? Nothing sounds bolder, or is more expressive, than the Cheerake name of thunder, *Eentaquàróske.* It points at the effects and report of the battles, which they imagine the holy people are fighting above. The smallpox, a foreign disease, no way connatural to their healthy climate, they call *Oonatàquára,* imagining it to proceed from the invisible darts of angry fate, pointed against them, for their young people's vicious conduct. When they say, "I shall shoot," their term is, *Ake-rooka.* The radix of this word is in the

★The first lunar eclipse I saw, after I lived with the Indians, was among the Cheerake, An. 1736: and during the continuance of it, their conduct appeared very surprizing to one who had not seen the like before; they all ran wild, this way and that way, like lunatics, firing their guns, whooping and hallooing, beating of kettles, ringing horse-bells, and making the most horrid noises that human beings possibly could. This was the effect of their natural philosophy, and done to assist the suffering moon. And it is an opinion of some of the East-Indians, that eclipses are occasioned by a great monster resembling a bull-frog, which now and then gnaws one edge of the sun and moon, and would totally destroy them, only that they frighten it away, and by that means preserve them and their light.[78]

two last syllables; the two first are expressive only of the first person singular; as *Akeeohoosa,* "I am dead, or lost;" and *Akeeohooséra,* "I have lost." *Rooka* seems to have a reference to the Hebrew name for the holy Spirit.

The most southern old town, which the Chikkasah first settled, after the Chokchoomah,[79] Choktah, and they, separated on our side of the Missisippi, into three different tribes, they called *Yanèka,*[80] thereby inverting *Yahkàne,* the name of the earth; as their former brotherhood was then turned into enmity★. The bold Creeks on the opposite, or north side of them, they named *Yahnàbe,* "killing to God," or devoting to death; for the mid consonant expresses the present time. And their proper names of persons, and places, are always expressive of certain circumstances, or things, drawn from roots, that convey a fixed determinate meaning.

With the Muskóhge, *Algeh* signifies "a language," or speech: and, because several of the Germans among them, frequently say *Yah-yah,* as an affirmative, they call them *Yah-yah Algeh,* "Those of the blasphemous speech;" which strongly hints to us, that they still retain a glimpse of the third moral command delivered at Sinai, "Thou shalt not take the name of the Lord thy God in vain," or apply the name of YOHEWAH, thy ELOHIM, to vain, or created things.

[67] These Indians, to inculcate on their young people, that YO HE WAH is the Author of vegetation, call the growth of vegetables, *Wahráah,* "moved by Yohewah;" for *Aàh* signifies to walk, or move; and the consonant is an expletive of distinction. In like manner, *Wah-àh* signifies, that "the fruits are ripe," or moved to their joy, by Yohewah. They likewise call the flying of birds, Wahkáàh; as Yohewah gave them that swift motion. And, when young pigeons are well feathered, they say, *Patche hishshè oolphotàháh—Patchè* signifies "a pidgeon," *Hishshè,* "leaves, hair, or feathers," *oolpha,* or *oolpho,* "a bud," *ta,* a note of plurality, and *háh* of admiration, to make it a plural superlative. But, when the pigeons, in winter, fly to a moderate climate in great clouds, they use the word, *Wah-àh,* which in every other application describes vegetation, and say, *Patche Wah-àh,* "the pigeons are moved to them by Yohewah;" which seems to allude to the quails in the wilderness, that were miraculously sent to feed the Israelites.

Clay basons they call *Ai-am-bo;* and their old round earthen forts, *Aiambo Cháah,* this last word signifying "high," or tall: but a stockade, or wooden fort, they term, *Hoorèta;* and to inswamp, *Book-Hoore,* from *Bookse,* "a swamp," and *Hoorèta,* "a fort, or place of difficult access." High waters, con-

---

★They call the earth Yahkàne, because Yah formed it, as his footstool, by the power of his word. In allusion also hereto, Nakkàne signifies a man, because of the mother-earth; and Nakke a bullet, or arrow. When the Cheerake ask a person, Is it not so? they say, Wahkane? The divine essential name, and Kane, are evidently the roots of these words.

veys to them, an idea only of deepness; as *Ookka phobe,* "deep waters." And they say, *Ookka chookòma intáa,* "The water glides, or moves along pleasantly, or goodly." That the word *Intâa,* has *Ya-ah* for its radix, is apparent from their name for a rapid current, *Yahnāle,* "it runs with a very extraordinary force;" the mid consonant is placed there, to give the word a suitable vehemence of expression—and the word is compounded of יה, *Yah,* and אל, *Ale,* two names of God. In like maner, *Yahnhà* signifies "a pleurisy," fever, and the like; because they reckon, when YAH says *ha* in anger, to any of their vicious people, he immediately fires the blood, and makes it run violently through all the veins of the body. *Ashtahále* signifies the reflection of the celestial luminaries, which is composed of two of the divine names; as אש, *Ash,* the celestial, cherubimical name of God, signifying fire, *ta,* a contraction of the conjunction copulative, and אל, *Ale,* the strong, or omnipotent. They say a river, or warm victuals, is *A-shù-pa;* that is, the former is become fordable, and the latter eatable. They here divide *Ash* into two syllables; and the termination alludes to the word, *Apà,* which signifies eating.

[68] *Páàh* signifies to raise the voice, *Vocifero*—for פי, *Phi,* signifies "the mouth," and *Aàh,* "to move." *Opáe* is the name of a war-leader, because he is to move his mouth to O E A, or invoke YO HE WAH, while he carries the beloved ark to war, and is sanctifying himself and his party, that they may obtain success against the enemy. But *Pae-Minggo* signifies a far-off, or distant chieftain. *Pa yak Matàháh,* is the high name of a war-leader, derived from *Páah,* to raise the voice to YAH, and *Tàhàh,* "finished," meaning his war-gradation: the *M* prefixed to it, makes it a substantive, according to the usage of the Hebrews. Any thing liquid they term *Ookche,* from *Ookka* and *che:* and *Ookchaah* signifies "alive." It is drawn from *Ookka,* "water," *Ch,* a note of resemblance, and *Aàh,* "moving;" *i.e.* a living creature resembles moving water. In like manner, *Ookchà* signifies to awake out of sleep; and also to plant any vegetable substance, alluding to their three different states—they first were enabled to move about—then rest, or sleep is necessary, and also being planted in the earth—but they hope that in due time, they shall be moved upward, after they have slept a while in the earth, by the omnipotent power of *Yah.* They have an idea of a resurrection of the dead body, according to the general belief of the Jews, and in conformity to St. Paul's philosophical axiom, that corruption precedes generation, and a resurrection.

Keenta signifies "a beaver," *Ookka* "water," and *Heenna* "a path;" but, for a smooth cadence, they contract them into one word, *Keentook-heenna;* which very expressively signifies "a beaver-dam."

The Indian compounded words, are generally pretty long; but those that are radical, or simple, are mostly short: very few, if any of them, exceed three or four syllables. And, as their dialects are guttural, every word contains some consonants; and these are the essential characteristics of language. Where they deviate from this rule, it is by religious emblems; which obviously proceeds from the great regard they paid to the names of the Deity; especially, to the four-lettered, divine, essential name, by using the letters it contains, and the vowels it was originally pronounced with, to convey a virtuous idea; or, by doubling, or transposing them, to signify the contrary. In this they all agree. And, as this general custom must proceed from one primary cause, it seems to assure us, they were not in a [69] savage state, when they first separated, and variegated their dialects, with so much religious care, and exact art. Blind chance could not direct so great a number of remote and warring savage nations to fix on, and unite in so nice a religious standard of speech. Vowels are inexpressive of things, they only typify them; as *Oo-E-A,* "to ascend, or remove:"—*O E A,* a most sacred affirmation of the truth. Similar to these are many words, containing only one consonant: as *To-e-u,* "it is very true;" *O-se-u,* "very good;" *Y-O-U,* "evil, or very bad;" *Y-â-a,* "he moves by the divine bounty;" *Nan-ne Y-a,* "the divine hill, or the mount of God," &c. If language was not originally a divine gift, which some of our very curious modern philosophers deny, and have taken great pains to set aside; yet human beings are possessed of the faculties of thinking and speaking, and, in proportion to their ideas, they easily invented, and learned words mixed with consonants and vowels, to express them. Natural laws are common and general. The situation of the Indian Americans, has probably been the means of sinking them into that state of barbarism we now behold—Yet, though in great measure they may have lost their primitive language, not one of them expresses himself by the natural cries of brute-animals, any farther than to describe some of the animals by the cries they make; which we ourselves sometimes imitate, as *Choo-qua-lê-qua-lôô,* the name they give that merry night-singing bird, which we call "Whip her will my poor wife," (much like our cuckoo) so termed from its musical monotony. No language is exempt from the like simple copyings. The nervous, polite, and copious Greek tongue had the loud-sounding *Bôô Böao,* which the Romans imitated, by their bellowing *Boves Böum;* and the Indians say *Pa-a,* signifying the loud noise of every kind of animals, and their own loud-sounding war *Whoô Whoóp.* Where they do not use divine emblems, their words have much articulation of consonants. Their radicals have not the inseparable property of three consonants, though frequently they have; and their words are not so long, as strangers conjecturally draw them out. Instead of a simple word, we too often insert the wild picture of a double, or triple-compounded one; and the conjugation of their verbs, utterly deceives us. A specimen of this, will shew it with sufficient clearness, and may exhibit some useful hints to the curious searchers of antiquity.

A-nô-wa signifies "a rambler, renegadoe, or a person of no settled place of abode." *A-nó-wah*, the first person, and *Ish-na*, the second person [70] singular, but they have not a particular pronoun for the third; they distinguish it by custom. *Si-a*, or *Sy-ah*, is "I am;" *Chee-a*, or *Chy-ak*, "you are;" and *Too-wah*, "he is." *Ay-ah* signifies "to go;" *Ay-a-sa*, "I remain;" *Ish-i-a-sa*, "you remain;" *A-sa*, "he remains." *A-OO-E-A* is a strong religious emblem, signifying "I climb, ascend, or remove to another place of residence." It points to *A-nò-wah*, the first person singular, and O-E-A, or YO HE WAH; and implies, putting themselves under his divine patronage. The beginning of that most sacred symbol, is, by studious skill, and a thorough knowledge of the power of letters, placed twice, to prevent them from applying the sacred name to vain purposes, or created things. In like manner they say, *Nas-sap-pe-O Ish-OO-E-A*, "You are climbing a very great acorn-tree," meaning an oak; for *Nas-se* is the name of an acorn; and the mid part of that triple compounded word, is derived from *Ap-pê-la*, "to help;" *Che-ap-pê-la A-wa*, "I do not help you." The termination, according to their fixed idiom, magnifies it to a superlative. *Quoo-ran-hê-qua*, a noted old camping place, fourteen miles above the settlement of *Ninety-six*, and eighty-two below the Cheerake, signifies, in their dialect, "the large white oaks." *Oos-sak* is the name of a "hickory-nut," and *Oos-sak Ap-pe-O*, as above. *Oot-te* signifies "a chestnut;" *Noot-te*, "a tooth;" *Soot-te*, "a pot;" and *Oo-te*, "to make a fire," which may be called an Indian type for eating boiled chestnuts.

When they say, "He is removing his camp," they express it in a most religious manner, *Al-bé-na-OO-E-A*. *Al-be-nâs-le* signifies "I camped;" *Al-be-nâs-le-chû*, "I shall, or will, camp:" but, according to their religious mode of speaking, *Al-bé-na A-OO-E-A-re*, expresses the former, and *Al-bé-na A-OO-E-A-rá-chû*, the latter phrase; likewise, *Al-bé-na OO-E-As* signifies *Castra Moveto*,[81] imperatively. It is worthy of notice, that as they have no pronoun relative to express the third person singular, they have recourse to the first syllable of the essential word, *Toowah*, "He is." In allusion to that word, they term the conjunction copulative, *Ta-wah*, and *Tee-U-Wah*, "resting." So mixed a train of nice and exact religious terms, could not be invented by people, as illiterate and savage as the Indians now are, any more than happen by accident.

Though they have lost the true meaning of their religious emblems, except what a very few of us occasionally revive in the retentive memories of their old inquisitive magi; yet tradition directs them to apply them properly. [71] They use many plain religious emblems of the divine names, YOHEWAH, YAH, and ALE,—and these are the roots of a prodigious number of words, through their various dialects. It is surprising they were unnoticed, and that no use was made of them, by the early voluminous Spanish writers, or by our own, for the information of the learned world, notwithstanding the bright lights they had to direct them in that æra, when the decorations of their holy temples and priests, their religious ceremonies, and sacred hymns of praise to the Deity, of which hereafter, so nearly corresponded with the Israelitish, and might have been readily discovered by any who eyed them with attention. In our time, by reason of their long intercourse with foreigners, we have necessarily but a few dark traces to guide our inquiries, in the investigation of what must have been formerly, shining truths.

I must beg to be indulged with a few more remarks on their verbs.—If we prefix *As* to *A-a*, "to move," it becomes *A-sâ-a*, "to offend." The monosyllables *Ish* and *Che*, variously denote the second person singular; but when the former is by custom prefixed to a verb, the latter then expresses either the accusative or ablative case singular of the pronoun relative; as *Ish-a-sâ-ah*, "you are offended, or moved to say Ah;" *Ish-a-sâ-a-re*, "you were displeased;" but *Che-a-sâ-ah* signifies "I am displeased with you;" and *Che-a-sâ-a-re* "I was offended by you;" *Che-a-sâ-a-chee-le* is "I occasion, or have occasioned you to be displeased," literally, "I produce, or have produced offence to you;" and *Che-a-sâ-a-cheê-la Awa*, "I shall not cause you to be displeased." In like manner, they say *A-ân-ha*, which signifies "I despise," or literally, "I move *ha*;" for the mid letter is inserted for distinction-sake, according to their idiom. So *A-chîn-ha-chu*, "I shall contemn you;" *A-chîn-ha-cheé-la A-wa*, "I shall not cause you to become despicable." *Chee-le* signifies literally, "to bring forth young." So that the former method of expression is very significant, and yet it shews a sterility of language, as that single word is applicable to every species of female animals, fowls not excepted: Thus, *Phoo-she Chee-le*, "the birds lay." *Oe-she* signifies "a young animal," of any kind—and likewise an egg. When mentioned alone, by way of excellence, it is the common name of an infant; but when the name of the species of animals is prefixed to it, it describes the young creature. *An-push-koosh oo-she*, is what the tender mother says to her well-pleased infant. The two words import the same thing. The former resembles the Hebrew, and the latter is likewise a substantive; they [72] say *Chool-loo-she Teeth-lâ-a-ta-hâh*, "the fox-cubs are run off;"—*Choo-la* being the name of a fox. *Phut-choos-oo-she Wah kâ-as*, "let the young duck fly away;" and *Phoo-soo-she Hish-she Ool-pha-quî-sa*, "the young wild bird's hairs, or feathers, are not sprung, or budded." *Pa-se* signifies the hair of a man's head, or the mane of animals. *Sha-le* signifies pregnant, literally, "to carry a burthen;" as *Oo-she Shâ-le*, "she bears, or carries, an infant;" but, when it is born, *Shoo-le* is the name for carrying it in their arms. This bears off from the divine radix, with great propriety of language. *Im* prefixed to a verb, denotes the masculine and feminine pronouns, *illum* and *illam*. As this is their fixed method of speech, the reader will easily understand the true idiom of their language. *Sal-le* signifies "I am dead," *Chil-le*, you, &c. *Il-leh*, he, &c. And this is likewise a substantive, as *Il-let Min-te*, "death is approaching," or coming: *Min-té-cha* signifies "come you;" and *A-min-té-la A-wa,* or *Ac-min-tá-qua-chù,* "I will not come."

The former word, *Shâ-le,* "to carry a burthen," or, she is pregnant, seems to be derived from ש and אל: and, as *A-shâ-le, Ish-shâ-le,* and *E-shâ-le,* are the first, second, and third persons singular of the present tense, the latter may allude to her conception by the power of the Deity: and it also points to שול, *Sha-wô-le,* or Saul, "the grave, or sepulchre," out of which the dead shall come forth to a new world of light. In like manner *Chee-le* "to bring forth," or *A-chee-lá-le,* "I brought forth," appears to be derived from כ, a note of resemblance, and אל, *A-le,* the fruitful Omnipotent. All the American nations, like the Jews, entertain a contemptible opinion of their females that are barren—sterility they consider as proceeding from the divine anger, on account of their conjugal infidelity.

To enable grammarians to form a clear idea of the Indian method of variegating their verbs, and of the true meaning they convey, we must again recur to the former essential word, or rather divine emblem, *A-ah,* "he moves." They say *A-as,* "let him move," and *Ee-má-ko,* or *Blâ-sas A-â-á-re,* "I now move," or "yesterday I moved;" for, like the Hebrews, they sometimes use the preterperfect, instead of the present tense. *A-â-a-ra-chû* is the first person singular of the future tense, in the indicative mood. *A-â-ta-hah* expresses the third person plural of the present tense, and same mood. *A-â-ta-hâh-ta-kô-a* signifies, by query, "have ye, or will ye move?" It is their method of conjugating their verbs, that occasions any of their [73] radical or derivative verbs to exceed three or four syllables; as we see by this, which, though composed only of two vowels, or short syllables, is yet so greatly deflected. With them two negatives make an affirmative, as *Ak-hish-ko-quá,* "I shall not drink;" add the strong negative termination *A-wa,* it is, "I will certainly drink." An affirmative question frequently implies a strong negative; as *Ai-a-râ-ta-kô-a,* literally, "will, or should, I go?" that is, "I really will not, or should not go:" and on the contrary, a negative query imports an affirmative assertion; as *A-kai-u-quâ-ta-kô-a,* "should not I go?" or, "I surely should go." *Ee-á ko A-pâ-ret Sa-kâi-a-qua-ta-kô-a,* is literally, "if I ate, should not I be satisfied?" which implies, "If I ate, I should be fully satisfied." To drinking, they apply a word that signifies content; and indeed, they are most eager to drink any sort of spiritous liquors, when their bellies are quite full. When they are tired with drinking, if we say to any of them, *Un-ta Ang-gó-na Che-ma-hîsh-kó-la Chû,* "Well, my friend, I will drink with you;" *Che-a-yôok-pa-chée-re Too-gat,* "for, indeed, I rejoice in your company;" he replies, *Hai-a, Ook-ka Hoo-me Hish-ko Sa-nook-tá-ra;* which is, "No; for I am content with drinking bitter waters." They constantly prefix the substantive before the adjective, and place the accusative case before the verb.

If we translate the following words, *Ook-ka Pangge Hum-ma Law-wa A-hish-kó-le Bla sas,* they literally signify, "yesterday I drank a great deal of red-grape water," meaning claret. Thus they say, *Tik-ké-ba, Ing-glee-she Fren-she Ee-lap A-bing-ga E-tee-be,* "formerly, when the English and French fought against each other;" *Fren-she Ing-glee-she A-be-tâ-le,* "the French were killed by the English."

The verbs are seldom defective, or imperfect: though they may seem to be so to persons who do not understand the idiom of their language, they are not; they only appear as such by the near resemblance of words, which convey a different meaning—as *A-kai-a,* "I go," *Sa-kai-a,* "I am satisfied with eating," and *Sal-kai-a,* "I am angry, cross, vexed, or disturbed in mind;" *Shee-a, Che-kai-a,* and *Chil-kai-a,* in the second person; *Ai-a, E-kai-a,* and *Al-kai-a,* in the third person singular. *A-pee-sa* signifies "to see," and *Al-pêê-sa,* "strait, even, or right;" *Al-poo-ê-ak,* the general name of mercantile goods, I subjoin, as such a word is uncommon with them; they seldom use so harsh a termination. I shall here close this argument, and hope [74] enough hath been said to give a clear idea of the principles of the Indian language and dialects, its genius and idiom, and strong similarity to, and near coincidence with the Hebrew—which will be not easily accounted for, but by considering the American Indians as descended from the Jews.

ARGUMENT VI.

They count TIME after the manner of the Hebrews.

They divide the year into spring—summer—autumn, or the fall of the leaf—and winter: which the Cheerake Indians call *Kogeh, Akooèa, Oolekóhste, Kóra;* and the Chikkasah and Choktah nation, *Otoolpha, Tŏme palle, Ashtòra-móona, Ashtòra. Kógeh* is drawn from *Anantóge,* the general appellation for the sun and moon; because, when the sun returns from the southern hemisphere, he covers the vegetable world with a green livery. *Akooèa* alludes strongly to the essential divine name, as we have seen in the former argument. With regard to *Oolekohste,* "the fall of the leaf," as they call a buzzard, *Soore,* or *Soole;* and as *Soolekohste* signifies troublesome, offensive, disagreeable, the word signifies, that "the fall of the year is as disagreeable a sight, as that of a buzzard." *Kora,* as with the Hebrews, signifies the winter; and is likewise the name of a bone: and by joining *Hah,* an Hebrew note of admiration, to the end of it, as *Kora-Hah,* it becomes the proper name of a man, signifying, "all bones," or very bony. *Otóol-phà,* "the spring season," is derived from *Oolpha,* the name of a bud, or to shoot out; because then the solar heat causes vegetables to bud and spring. *Tŏmeh* signifies "the solar light," and *Palle,* "warm or hot;" *Ashtora,* "winter," and *Moona,* "presently," &c.[82]

They number their years by any of those four periods, for they have no name for a year; and they subdivide these, and count the year by lunar months, like the Israelites, who counted by moons, as their name sufficiently testifies; for they called them ירחים, the plural of ירח, the moon.

The Indians have no distinct proper name for the sun and moon; one word, with a note of distinction, expresses both—for example; the Cheerake [75] call the sun *Eus-se A-nan-tó-ge,* "the day-moon, or sun;" and the latter, *Neus-se A-nan-tó-ge,* or "the night-sun, or moon." In like manner, the Chikkasah and Choktah term the one, *Neetak-Hasséh,* and the other, *Neennak-Hasséh;* for *Neetak* signifies "a day," and *Neennak,* "a night."

Here I canot forbear remarking, that the Indians call the penis of any animal, by the very same name, *Hasse;* with this difference only, that the termination is in this instance pronounced short, whereas the other is long, on purpose to distinguish the words. This bears a strong analogy to what the rabbins tell us of the purity of the Hebrew language, that "it is so chaste a tongue, as to have no proper names for the parts of generation." The Cheerake can boast of the same decency of style, for they call a corn-house, *Watóhre* and the penis of any creature, by the very same name; intimating, that as the sun and moon influence and ripen the fruits that are stored in it, so by the help of Ceres and Bacchus, Venus lies warm, whereas on the contrary, *sine Cerere & Bacchus, friget Venus.*[83]

They count certain very remarkable things, by knots of various colours and make, after the manner of the South-American Aborigines; or by notched square sticks, which are likewise distributed among the head warriors, and other chieftains of different towns, in order to number the winters, &c.—the moons also—their sleeps—and the days when they travel; and especially certain secret intended acts of hostility. Under such a circumstance, if one day elapses, each of them loosens a knot, or cuts off a notch, or else makes one, according to previous agreement; which those who are in the trading way among them, call broken days. Thus they proceed day by day, till the whole time is expired, which was marked out, or agreed upon; and they know with certainty, the exact time of any of the aforesaid periods, when they are to execute their secret purposes, be they ever so various. The authors of the romantic Spanish histories of Peru and Mexico, have wonderfully stretched on these knotted, or marked strings, and notched square sticks, to shew their own fruitful inventions, and draw the attention and surprise of the learned world to their magnified bundle of trifles.[84]

The method of counting time by weeks, or sevenths, was a very ancient custom, practised by the Syrians, Egyptians, and most of the oriental nations; [76] and it evidently is a remain of the tradition of the creation. The Creator, indeed, renewed to the Hebrews the old precept of sanctifying the seventh day, on a particular occasion. And christianity promoted that religious observance in the western world, in remembrance of the work of redemption. The Greeks counted time by decads, or tens; and the Romans by nones, or ninths. The number, and regular periods of the Indians public religious feasts, of which presently, is a good historical proof, that they counted time by, and observed a weekly sabbath, long after their arrival on the American continent.

They count the day also by the three sensible differences of the sun, like the Hebrews—sun-rise, they term, *Hassé kootcha meente,* "the sun's coming out;"—noon, or mid-day, *Tabookòre;*—and sun-set, *Hassé Oobèa,* literally, "the sun is dead;" likewise, *Hasse Ookka'tòra,* that is, "the sun is fallen into the water;" the last word is compounded of *Ookka,* water, and *Etòra,* to fall: it signifies also "to swim," as instinct would direct those to do, who fell into the water. And they call dark, *Ookklille*—derived from *Ookka,* water, and *Illeh,* dead; which shews their opinion of the sun's disappearance, according to the ancients, who said the sun slept every night in the western ocean. They subdivide the day, by any of the aforesaid three standards—as half way between the sun's coming out of the water; and in like manner, by midnight, or cock-crowing, &c.

They begin the year, at the first appearance of the first new moon of the vernal æquinox, according to the ecclesiastical year of Moses: and those synodical months, each consist of twenty-nine days, twelve hours, and forty odd minutes; which make the moons, alternately, to consist of twenty-nine and of thirty days. They pay a great regard to the first appearance of every new moon, and, on the occasion, always repeat some joyful sounds, and stretch out their hands towards her—but at such times they offer no public sacrifice.

Till the 70 years captivity commenced, (according to Dr. Prideaux,[85] 606 years before the Christian æra) the Israelites had only numeral names for the solar and lunar months, except אביב and האתנים; the former signifies a green ear of corn; and the latter, robust, or valiant. And by the first [77] name, the Indians, as an explicative, term their *passover,* which the trading people call the green-corn dance.[86] As the Israelites were a sensual people, and generally understood nothing but the shadow, or literal part of the law; so the Indians closely imitate them, minding only that traditional part, which promised them a delicious land, flowing with milk and honey. The two Jewish months just mentioned, were æquinoctial. Abib, or their present Nisan, was the seventh of the civil, and the first of the ecclesiastical year, answering to our March and April: and Ethanim, which began the civil year, was the seventh of that of the ecclesiastical, the same as our September and October. And the Indians name the various seasons of the year, from the planting, or ripening of the fruits. The green-eared moon is the most beloved, or sacred,—when the first fruits become sanctified, by being annually offered up. And from this period they count their beloved, or holy things.

When they lack a full moon, or when they travel, they count by sleeps; which is a very ancient custom—probably, from the Mosaic method of counting time, "that the evening and the morning were the first day." Quantity they count by tens, the number of their fingers; which is a natural method to all people. In the mercantile way, they mark on the ground their numbers, by units; or by X for ten; which, I presume they learned from the white people, who traded with them. They readily add together their tens, and find out the number sought. They call it *Yakâ-ne Tlápha,* or "scoring on the ground." But *old time* they can no way trace, only by remarkable circumstances, and æras. As they trade with each other, only by the hand, they have no proper name for a pound weight.

The Cheerake count as high as an hundred, by various numeral names; whereas the other nations of East and West-Florida, rise no higher than the decimal number, adding units after it, by a conjunction copulative; which intimates, that nation was either more mixed, or more skilful, than the rest: the latter seems most probable. They call a thousand, *Skoeh Chooke Kaiére,* "the old," or "the old one's hundred:" and so do the rest, in their various dialects, by interpretation; which argues their former skill in numbers.

[78] I shall here give a specimen of the Hebrew method of counting, and that of the Cheerake, Chikkasah, and Muskohge or Creeks, by which some farther analogy will appear between the savage Indians, and their supposed Israelitish brethren. The Hebrew characters were numeral figures: they counted by them alphabetically, א (1), ב (2), and so on to the letter י, the tenth letter of the alphabet, and which stands for ten; then, by prefixing י to those letters, they proceeded with their rising numbers, as יא (11), יב (12), יג (13), יד (14), &c. They had words also of a numeral power, as אחד (1), שני (2), שלשי (3), ארבע (4), &c. We shall now see how the Indian method of numbering agrees with this old standard, as well as with the idiom of the Hebrew language in similar cases.

The Cheerake number thus: *Soquo* 1, *Tahre* 2, *Choeh* 3, *Nankke* 4, *Ishke* 5, *Sootàre* 6, *Karekóge* 7, *Suhnâyra* 8, *Sohnáyra* 9, *Skoeh* 10, *Soàtoo* 11, *Taràtoo* 12, &c. And here we may see a parity of words between two of the Indian nations; for the Muskohge term a stone, *Tahre;* which glances at the Hebrew, as they not only built with such material, but used it as a word of number, expressive of two. In like manner, *Ishke* "five," signifies a mother, which seems to shew that their numeral words were formerly significant; and that they are one stock of people.

The Chikkasah and Choktah count in this manner—*Chephpha* 1, *Toogàlo* 2, *Tootchēna* 3, *Oosta* 4, *Tàthlàbe* 5, *Hannàhle* 6, *Untoogàlo* 7, *Untootchēna* 8, *Chakkále* 9, *Pokoole* 10, *Pokoole Aawa Chephpha,* "ten and one," and so on. The Cheerake have an old waste town, on the Georgia south-west branch of Savannah river, called *Toogàlo;*[87] which word may come under the former observation, upon the numerical word two: and they call a pompion, *Oosto,* which resembles *Oosta,* four.

The Cheerake call twenty, *Tahre Skoeh,* "two tens;" and the Chikkasah term it, *Pokoole Toogalo,* "ten twos:" as if the former had learned to number from the left hand to the right, according to the Syriac custom; and the latter, from the right to the left hand, after the Hebrew manner. The former call an hundred, *Skoeh Chooke;* and, as before observed, a thousand, *Skoeh Chooke Kaiére,* or "the old one's hundred;" for with them, *Kaiére* signifies "ancient," or aged; whereas *Eti,* or *Eti-u,* expresses former old time. [79] May not this have some explanation, by the "Ancient of days," as expressed by the prophet Daniel—magnifying the number, by joining one of the names of God to it—according to a frequent custom of the Hebrews? This seems to be illustrated with sufficient clearness, by the numerical method of the Chikkasah—for they call an hundred, *Pokoole Tathleepa;* and a thousand, *Pokoole Tathleepa Tathleepa Ishto;* the last of which is a strong double superlative, according to the usage of the Hebrews, by a repetition of the principal word; or by affixing the name of God to the end of it, to heighten the number. Ishto is one of their names of God, expressive of majesty, or greatness; and *Soottathleepa*★, the name of a drum, derived from *Sootte,* an earthen pot, and *Tathleepa,* perhaps the name or number of some of their ancient legions.

The Muskohge method of counting is, *Hommai* 1, *Hokkóle* 2, *Tootchēna* 3, *Ohsta* 4, *Chakàpe* 5, *Eepáhge* 6, *Hoolopháge* 7, *Cheenèpa* 8, *Ohstàpe* 9, *Pokóle* 10, &c. I am sorry that I have not sufficient skill in the Muskohge dialect, to make any useful observations on this head; however, the reader can easily discern the parity of language, between their numerical words, and those of the Chikkasah and Choktah nations; and may from thence conclude, that they were formerly one nation and people.

I have seen their symbols, or signatures, in a heraldry way, to count or distinguish their tribes, done with what may be called wild exactness. The Choktah use the like in the dormitories of their dead; which seems to argue, that the ancienter and thicker-settled countries of Peru and Mexico had formerly, at least, the use of hieroglyphic characters; and that they painted the real, or figurative images of things, to convey their ideas. The present American Aborigines seem to be as skilful Pantomimi, as ever were those of ancient Greece or Rome, or the modern Turkish mutes, who describe the meanest things spoken, by gesture, action, and the passions of the face. Two far-distant Indian nations, who understand not a word of each other's language, will intelligibly converse together, and contract engagements, with-

★The double vowels, *oo* and *ee,* are always to be joined in one syllable, and pronounced long.

out any interpreter, in such a surprizing manner, as is scarcely credible. As their dialects are guttural, the indications they use, with the hand or [80] fingers, in common discourse, to accompany their speech, is the reason that strangers imagine they make only a gaggling noise, like what we are told of the Hottentots, without any articulate sound; whereas it is an ancient custom of the eastern countries, which probably the first emigrants brought with them to America, and still retain over the far-extended continent★.

ARGUMENT VII.

In conformity to, or after the manner of the Jews, the Indian Americans have their PROPHETS, HIGH-PRIESTS, and others of a religious order. As the Jews had a *sanctum sanctorum,* or most holy place, so have all the Indian nations; particularly, the Muskohge. It is partitioned off by a mud-wall about breast-high, behind the white seat, which always stands to the left hand of the red-painted war-seat; there they deposit their consecrated vessels, and supposed holy utensils, none of the laity daring to approach that sacred place, for fear of particular damage to themselves, and general hurt to the people, from the supposed divinity of the place.[88]

With the Muskohge, *Hitch Lalàge* signifies "cunning men," or persons prescient of futurity, much the same as the Hebrew seers. *Ckeeràtahége* is the name of the pretended prophets, with the Cheerake, and nearly approaches to the meaning of נביא, *Nebia,* the Hebrew name of a prophet. *Cheera* is their word for "fire," and the termination points out men possest of, or endued with it. The word seems to allude to the celestial cherubim, fire, light, and spirit, which centered in O E A, or YOHEWAH. These Indians call their pretended prophets also *Loá-che,* "Men resembling the holy fire," or as Elohim; for the termination expresses a comparison, and *Loa,* is a contraction of *Loak,* drawn from אלה, *Elóah,* the singular number of אלהים, *Elohim,* the name of the holy ones. And, as the Muskohge[89] [81] call the noise of thunder, *Erowah,* so the Cheerake by inverting it, *Worah,* "He is;" thereby alluding to the divine essence: and, as those term the lightning *Elóa,* and believe it immediately to proceed from the voice of *Ishtohollo Elóa Aba,* it shews the analogy to the Hebrews, and their sentiments to be different from all the early heathen world.

The Indian tradition says, that their forefathers were possessed of an ex-

---

★The first numbering was by their fingers; to which custom Solomon alludes, *Prov.* iii. 16. "length of days is in her right hand." The Greeks called this, [Αποπεμπομαζειν], because they numbered on their five fingers: and Ovid says, *Seu, quia tot digitis, per quos numeráre solemus;* likewise Juvenal, *Sua dextrâ computat annos.* Others numbered on their ten fingers, as we may see in Bede de ratione temporum. And the ancients not only counted, but are said to speak with their fingers, *Prov.* vi. 13, "The wicked man he teacheth with his fingers." And Nævius, in Tarentilla, says, *dat digito literas.*[90]

traordinary divine spirit, by which they foretold things future, and con-
trouled the common course of nature: and this they transmitted to their
offspring, provided they obeyed the sacred laws annexed to it. They believe,
that by the communication of the same divine fire working on their *Loáche,*
they can now effect the like.[91] They say it is out of the reach of *Nana
Ookproo,* either to comprehend, or perform such things, because the beloved
fire, or the holy spirit of fire, will not co-operate with, or actuate *Hottuk
Ookproose,* "the accursed people." *Ishtohoollo* is the name of all their priestly
order, and their pontifical office descends by inheritance to the eldest: those
friend-towns, which are firmly confederated in their exercises and plays,
never have more than one *Archi-magus* at a time. But lameness, contrary to
the Mosaic law, it must be confessed, does not now exclude him from offi-
ciating in his religious function; though it is not to be doubted, as they are
naturally a modest people, and highly ridicule those who are incapable of
procreating their species, that formerly they excluded the lame and impo-
tent. They, who have the least knowledge in Indian affairs, know, that the
martial virtue of the savages, obtains them titles of distinction; but yet their
old men, who could scarcely correct their transgressing wives, much less go
to war, and perform those difficult exercises, that are essentially needful in
an active warrior, are often promoted to the pontifical dignity, and have
great power over the people, by the pretended sanctity of the office. Notwithstanding the Cheerake are now a nest of apostate hornets, pay little
respect to grey hairs, and have been degenerating fast from their primitive
religious principles, for above thirty years past—yet, before the last war, *Old
Hop,*[92] who was helpless and lame, presided over the whole nation, as *Archi-
magus,* and lived in Choàte,[93] their only town of refuge. It was entirely
owing to the wisdom of those who then presided in South-Carolina, that
his dangerous pontifical, and regal-like power, was impaired, by their setting
up *Atta Kulla Kulla,*[94] and supporting him so well, as to prevent the then
easy transition of an Indian [82] high-priesthood into a French American
bloody chair, with a bunch of red and black beads; where the devil and they
could as easily have instructed them in the infernal French catechism, as
they did the Canada Indians: as—Who killed Christ? *Answer,* The bloody
English; &c.★

   To discover clearly the origin of the Indian religious system, I must occasionally quote as much from the Mosaic institution, as the savages seem
to copy after, or imitate, in their ceremonies; and only the faint image of

---

★A wrong belief has a most powerful efficacy in depraving men's morals, and a right
one has a great power to reform them. The bloody Romish bulls, that France sent
over to their Indian converts, clearly prove the former; and our peaceable conduct, as
plainly shewed the latter, till Britannia sent out her lions to retaliate.

the Hebrew can now be expected to be discerned, as in an old, imperfect glass. The priesthood originally centered with the first male born of every family: with the ancient heathens, the royalty was annexed to it, in a direct line; and it descended in that manner, as low as the Spartans and Romans. But, to secure Israel from falling into heathenish customs and worship; God in the time of Moses, set apart the Levites for religious services in the room of the first-born; and one high-priest, was elected from the family of Aaron, and anointed with oil, who presided over the rest. This holy office descended by right of inheritance. However, they were to be free of bodily defects, and were by degrees initiated to their holy office, before they were allowed to serve in it. They were consecrated, by having the water of purifying sprinkled upon them, washing all their body, and their clothes clean, anointing them with oil, and offering a sacrifice.

It is not surprizing that the dress of the old savage *Archi-magus,* and that of the Levitical high-priest, is somewhat different. It may well be supposed, they wandered from captivity to this far-distant wilderness, in a distrest condition, where they could scarcely cover themselves from the inclemency of heat and cold. Besides, if they had always been possessed of the greatest affluence, the long want of written records would sufficiently excuse the difference; because oral traditions are liable to variation. However, there are some traces of agreement in their pontifical dress. Before the Indian *Archi-magus* officiates in making the supposed holy fire, for the yearly atonement [83] of sin, the Sagan clothes him with a white ephod, which is a waistcoat without sleeves. When he enters on that solemn duty, a beloved attendant spreads a white-drest buck-skin on the white seat, which stands close to the supposed holiest, and then puts some white beads on it, that are given him by the people. Then the *Archi-magus* wraps around his shoulders a consecrated skin of the same sort, which reaching across under his arms, he ties behind his back, with two knots on the legs, in the form of a figure of eight. Another custom he observes on this solemn occasion, is, instead of going barefoot, he wears a new pair of buck-skin white maccasenes made by himself, and stitched with the sinews of the same animal★. The upper leather across the toes, he paints, for the space of three inches, with a few streaks of red—not with vermilion, for that is their continual war-emblem, but with

★Observant ubi festa mero pede sabbata reges,
Et vetus indulget senibus clementa porcis.
JUVENAL, Sat. vi. [95]

When the high-priest entered into the holiest, on the day of expiation, he clothed himself in white; and, when he finished that day's service, he laid aside those clothes and left them in the tabernacle. *Lev.* xvi. 23.

When the Egyptian priests went to worship in their temples, they wore shoes of white parchment. HERODOTUS, Lib. ii. Cap. v.

a certain red root, its leaves and stalk resembling the ipecacuanha, which is their fixed red symbol of holy things.[96] These shoes he never wears, but in the time of the supposed passover; for at the end of it, they are laid up in the beloved place, or holiest, where much of the like sort, quietly accompanies an heap of old, broken earthen ware, conch-shells, and other consecrated things.

The Mosaic ceremonial institutions, are acknowledged by our best writers, to represent the Messiah, under various types and shadows; in like manner, the religious customs of the American Indians, seem to typify the same; according to the early divine promise, that the seed of the woman should bruise the head of the serpent; and that it should bruise his heel.— The Levitical high-priest wore a *breast-plate,* which they called *Hosechim,* and on it the *Urim* and *Thummim,* signifying lights and perfections; for they are the plurals of אור, *Awóra,* (which inverted makes *Erowa*) and חורה, *Thòràh,* [84] the law, as it directed them under dark shadows, to Messiah, the lamp of light and perfections. In resemblance of this sacred pectoral, or breast-plate, the American *Archi-magus* wears a breast-plate, made of a white conch-shell with two holes bored in the middle of it, through which he puts the ends of an otter-skin strap, and fastens a buck-horn white button to the outside of each,[97] as if in imitation of the precious stones of Urim, which miraculously blazoned from the high-priest's breast, the unerring words of the divine oracle. Instead of the plate of gold, which the Levite wore on his forehead, bearing these words קדש לי יהוה *Kadesh li Yohewah,* "holy, or separate to God," the Indian wears around his temples, either a wreath of swan-feathers, or a long piece of swan-skin doubled, so as only the fine snowy feathers appear on each side. And, in likeness to the *Tiara* of the former, the latter wears on the crown of his head, a tuft of white feathers, which they call *Yatèra.* He likewise fastens a tuft of blunted wild Turkey cock-spurs, toward the toes of the upper part of his maccasenes, as if in resemblance to the seventy-two bells, which the Levitical high-priest wore on his coat of blue. Those are as strong religious pontifical emblems, as any old Hebrews could have well chosen, or retained under the like circumstances of time and place. Thus appears the Indian Archimagus—not as *Merubha Begadim,* "the man with many clothes," as they called the high-priest of the second temple, but with clothes proper to himself, when he is to officiate in his pontifical function, at the annual expiation of sins★. As religion is the touchstone of every nation of people, and as these Indians cannot be supposed to have been deluded out of theirs, separated from the

★The only ornaments that distinguished the high-priest from the rest, were a coat with seventy-two bells, an ephod, or jacket without sleeves, a breast-plate set with twelve stones, a linen mitre, and a plate of gold upon his forehead.

rest of the world, for many long-forgotten ages—the traces which may be discerned among them, will help to corroborate the other arguments concerning their origin.

These religious, beloved men are also supposed to be in great favour with the Deity, and able to procure rain when they please. In this respect also, we shall observe a great conformity to the practice of the Jews. The Hebrew records inform us, that in the moon *Abib*, or Nisan, they prayed for [85] the spring, or latter rain, to be so seasonable and sufficient as to give them a good harvest. And the Indian Americans have a tradition, that their forefathers sought for and obtained such seasonable rains, as gave them plentiful crops; and they now seek them in a manner agreeable to the shadow of this tradition.

When the ground is parched, their *rain-makers*,[98] (as they are commonly termed) are to mediate for the beloved red people, with the bountiful holy Spirit of fire. But their old cunning prophets are not fond of entering on this religious duty, and avoid it as long as they possibly can, till the murmurs of the people force them to the sacred attempt, for the security of their own lives. If he fails, the prophet is shot dead, because they are so credulous of his divine power conveyed by the holy Spirit of fire, that they reckon him an enemy to the state, by averting the general good, and bringing desolating famine upon the beloved people. But in general, he is so discerning in the stated laws of nature, and skilful in priestcraft, that he always seeks for rain, either at the full, or change of the moon; unless the birds, either by instinct, or the temperature of their bodies, should direct him otherwise. However, if in a dry season, the clouds, by the veering of the winds, pass wide of their fields—while they are inveighing bitterly against him, some in speech, and others in their hearts, he soon changes their well-known notes—he assumes a displeased countenance and carriage, and attacks them with bitter reproaches, for their vicious conduct in the marriage-state, and for their notorious pollutions, by going to the women in their religious retirements, and for multifarious crimes that never could enter into his head to suspect them of perpetrating, but that the divinity his holy things were endued with, had now suffered a great decay, although he had fasted, purified himself, and on every other account, had lived an innocent life, according to the old beloved speech: adding, "*Loak Ishtohoollo* will never be kind to bad people." He concludes with a religious caution to the penitent, advising them to mend their manners, and the times will mend with them: Then they depart with sorrow and shame. The old women, as they go along, will exclaim loudly against the young people, and protest they will watch their manners very narrowly for the time to come, as they are sure of their own steady virtue.

[86] If a two-years drought happens, the synhedrim, at the earnest solicitation of the mortified sinners, convene in a body, and make proper en-

quiry into the true cause of their calamities; because (say they) it is better to spoil a few roguish people, than a few roguish people should spoil *Hottuk Oretoopah:* The lot soon falls upon Jonas, and he is immediately swallowed up. Too much rain is equally dangerous to those red prophets.—I was lately told by a gentleman of distinguished character, that a famous rain-maker of the Muskohge was shot dead, because the river over-flowed their fields to a great height, in the middle of August, and destroyed their weighty harvest. They ascribed the mischief to his ill-will; as the Deity, they say, doth not injure the virtuous, and designed him only to do good to the beloved people.

In the year 1747, a Nàchee warrior told me, that while one of their prophets was using his divine invocations for rain, according to the faint image of their ancient tradition, he was killed with thunder on the spot; upon which account, the spirit of prophecy ever after subsided among them, and he became the last of their reputed prophets. They believed the holy Spirit of fire had killed him with some of his angry darting fire, for wilful impurity; and by his threatening voice, forbad them to renew the like attempt—and justly concluded, that if they all lived well, they should fare well, and have proper seasons. This opinion coincides with that of the Israelites, in taking fire for the material emblem of Yohewah; by reckoning thunder the voice of the Almighty above, according to the scriptural language; by esteeming thunder-struck individuals under the displeasure of heaven—and by observing and enforcing such rules of purity, as none of the old pagan nations observed, nor any, except the Hebrews.

As the prophets of the Hebrews had oracular answers, so the Indian magi, who are to invoke YO He Wah, and mediate with the supreme holy fire, that he may give seasonable rains, have a transparent stone, of supposed great power in assisting to bring down the rain, when it is put in a bason of water; by a reputed divine virtue, impressed on one of the like sort, in time of old, which communicates it circularly. This stone would suffer a great decay, they assert, were it even seen by their own laity; but if by foreigners, it would be utterly despoiled of its divine [87] communicative power. Doth not this allude to the precious blazoning stones of Urim and Thummim?

In Tymáhse,[99] a lower Cheerake town, lived one of their reputed great divine men, who never informed the people of his seeking for rain, but at the change, or full of the moon, unless there was some promising sign of the change of the weather, either in the upper regions, or from the feathered kalender; such as the quacking of ducks, the croaking of ravens, and from the moistness of the air felt in their quills; consequently, he seldom failed of success, which highly increased his name, and profits; for even when it rained at other times, they ascribed it to the intercession of their great beloved man. Rain-making, in the Cheerake mountains, is not so dangerous an office, as in the rich level lands of the Chikkasah country, near the Mississippi. The above Cheerake prophet had a carbuncle, near as big as an egg, which they said he found where a great rattlesnake lay dead, and that it sparkled with such surprizing lustre, as to illuminate his dark winter-house, like strong flashes of continued lightning, to the great terror of the weak, who durst not upon any account, approach the dreadful fire-darting place, for fear of sudden death.[100] When he died, it was buried along with him according to custom, in the town-house of Tymáhse, under the great beloved cabbin, which stood in the westernmost part of that old fabric, where they who will run the risk of searching, may luckily find it; but, if any of that family detected them in disturbing the bones of their deceased relation, they would resent it as the basest act of hostility. The inhuman conduct of the avaricious Spaniards toward the dead Peruvians and Mexicans, irritated the natives, to the highest pitch of distraction, against those ravaging enemies of humanity. The intense love the Indians bear to their dead, is the reason that so few have fallen into the hands of our physicians to dissect, or anatomise. We will hope also, that from a principle of humanity, our ague-charmers, and water-casters, who like birds of night keep where the Indians frequently haunt, would not cut up their fellow-creatures, as was done by the Spanish butchers in Peru and Mexico.

Not long ago, at a friendly feast, or feast of love, in West-Florida, during the time of a long-continued drought, I earnestly importuned the old rain-maker, for a sight of the pretended divine stone, which he had assured me he was possessed of; but he would by no means gratify my request. He [88] told me, as I was an infidel, literally, "one who shakes hands with the accursed speech," and did not believe its being endued with a divine power, the sight of it could no ways benefit me; and that, as their old unerring tradition assured them, it would suffer very great damage in case of compliance, he hoped I would kindly acquiesce; especially, as he imagined, I believed every nation of people had certain beloved things, that might be easily spoiled by being polluted. I told him I was fully satisfied with the friendly excuse he made to my inconsiderate request; but that I could scarcely imagine there were any such beloved men, and beloved things, in so extremely fertile, but now sun-burnt soil. Their crops had failed the year before, by reason of several concurring causes: and, for the most part of the summer season, he had kept his bed through fear of incurring the punishment of a false prophet; which, joined with the religious regimen, and abstemious way of living he was obliged strictly to pursue, it sweated him so severely, as to reduce him to a skeleton. I jested him in a friendly way, saying, I imagined, the supreme holy fire would have proved more kind to his honest devotees, than to sicken him so severely, especially at that critical season, when the people's food, and his own, entirely depended on his health; that, though our beloved men never undertook to bring down sea-sonable rains, yet we very seldom failed of good crops, and always paid them the tenth basket-full of our yearly produce; because, they persuaded our young people, by the force of their honest example, and kind-hearted en-chanting language, to shun the crooked ways of *Hottuk Kallákse,* "the mad light people," and honestly to shake hands with the old beloved speech—that the great, supreme, fatherly Chieftain, had told his *Loáche* to teach us how to obtain peace and plenty, and every other good thing while we live here, and when we die, not only to shun the accursed dark place, where the sun is every day drowned, but likewise to live again for ever, very happily in the favourite country.

He replied, that my speech consisted of a mixture of good and ill; the beginning of it was crooked, and the conclusion straight. He said, I had wrongfully blamed him, for the effect of the disorderly conduct of the red people and himself, as it was well known he fasted at different times for several days together; at other times ate green tobacco-leaves; and some days drank only a warm decoction of the button snake-root,[101] without allowing [89] any one, except his religious attendant, to come near him; and, in every other respect, had honestly observed the austere rules of his religious place, according to the beloved speech that *Ishtohoollo Elóa Aba* gave to the *Loáche* of their forefathers: but *Loak Ishtohoollo* was sorely vexed with most of their young people for violating the chastity of their neighbours wives, and even among the thriving green corn and pease, as their beds here and there clearly proved; thus, they spoiled the power of his holy things, and tempted *Minggo Ishto Elóa,* "the great chieftain of the thunder," to bind up the clouds, and withold the rain. Besides, that the old women were less honest in paying their rain-makers, than the English women behaved to their beloved men, unless I had spoken too well of them. The wives of this and the other person, he said, had cheated him, in not paying him any portion of the last year's bad crop, which their own bad lives greatly contributed to, as that penurious crime of cheating him of his dues, sufficiently testified; not to mention a late custom, they had contracted since the general peace, of planting a great many fields of beans and pease, in distant places, after the summer-crops were over, on the like dishonest principle; likewise in affirm-ing, that when the first harvest was over, it rained for nothing; by that means they had blackened the old beloved speech, that *Ishtohoollo Eloa* of old spoke to his *Loáche,* and conveyed down to him, only that they might paint their own bad actions white. He concluded, by saying, that all the chieftains, and others present, as well as myself, knew now very well, from his honest speech, the true cause of the earth's having been so strangely burnt till lately; and that he was afraid, if the hearts of those light and mad people he complained of, did not speedily grow honest, the dreadful day would soon come, in which *Lóak Ishtohoollo* would send *Phutchik Keeraah Ishtò,* "the great blazing star," *Yahkàne eeklénna, Loak loáchàché,* "to burn up half of the earth with fire," *Pherimmi Aiùbe,* "from the north to the south," *Hassé oobèa perà,* "toward the setting of the sun," where they should in time arrive at the dreadful place of darkness, be confined there hungry, and otherwise sorely distrest among hissing snakes and many other frightful creatures, according to the ancient true speech that *Ishtohoollo Aba* spoke to his beloved *Loáche.*

Under this argument, I will also mention another striking resemblance to the Jews, as to their TITHES.—As the sacerdotal office was fixed in the tribe [90] of Levi, they had forty-eight cities allotted them from the other tribes. And Moses assures us, in *Deut.* xiv. 28, 29, that those tribes paid them also once in three years, the tithe, or tenth of all they possessed, which is supposed to be about the thirtieth part of their annual possessions; by which means they were reasonably maintained, as spiritual pastors, and enabled to fulfil the extensive and charitable application of their dues, as enjoined.

It hath been already hinted, that the Indian prophets undertake by the emanation of the divine spirit of fire, co-operating with them, to bring down proper rains for crops, on the penalty of loosing their own lives; as the Indians reckon that a regular virtuous life will sufficiently enable their great beloved men to bring blessings of plenty to the beloved people; and if they neglect it, they are dangerous enemies, and a great curse to the community. They imagine his prophetic power is also restrictive as to winter-rains, they doing more hurt than good; for they justly observe, that their ground seldom suffers by the want of winter-rains. Their sentiments on this head, are very strong; they say, *Ishtohoollo Aba* allows the winter-rain to fall unsought, but that he commanded their forefathers to seek for summer-rain, according to the old law, otherwise he would not give it to them. If the seasons have been answerable, when the ripened harvest is gathered in, the old women pay their reputed prophet with religious good-will, a certain proportional quantity of each kind of the new fruits, measured in the same large portable back-baskets, wherein they carried home the ripened fruits.[102] This stated method they yearly observe; which is as consonant to the Levitical institution, as can be reasonably expected, especially, as their traditions have been time out of mind preserved only by oral echo.

Modern writers inform us, that the Persees pay a tithe of their revenues to the chief Destour, or Archimagus of a city or province, who decides cases of conscience, and points of law, according to the institution of Zoroaster— a mixture of Judaism and paganism. Their annual religious offering to the Archimagi, is a misapplication of the Levitical law concerning tithes, contrary to the usage of the American Aborigines, which it may be supposed they immediately derived from the Hebrews; for, as the twelfth tribe was devoted to the divine service, they were by divine appointment, maintained at the public expense. However, when we consider that their government was [91] of mixed kind—first a theocracy—then by nobles, and by kings— and at other times by their high-priest, it seems to appear pretty plain, that the Deity raised, preserved, and governed those people to oppose idolatry, and continue, till the fulness of time came, the true divine worship on earth, under ceremonial dark shadows, without exhibiting their government in the least, as a plan of future imitation. Besides, as Messiah is come, according to the predictions of the divine oracles, which represented him under various strong types and shadows, surely christians ought to follow the copy of their humble Master and his holy disciples, and leave the fleecing of the flock to the avaricious Jews, whose religious tenets, and rapacious principles, support them in taking annual tithes from each other; who affect to believe that all the Mosaic law is perpetually binding, and that the predicted Shilo, who is to be their purifier, king, prophet, and high-priest, is not yet come. The *law of tithing,* was calculated only for the religious œconomy of the Hebrew nation; for as the merciful Deity, who was the immediate head of that state, had appropriated the Levites to his service, and prohibited them purchasing land, lest they should be seduced from their religious duties, by worldly cares, He, by a most bountiful law, ordered the state to give them the tithe, and other offerings, for the support of themselves and their numerous families, and also of the widow, the fatherless, and the stranger.

I shall insert a dialogue, that formerly passed between the Chikkasah Loáche and me, which will illustrate both this, and other particulars of the general subject; and also shew the religious advantages and arguments, by which the French used to undermine us with the Indians.[103]

We had been speaking of trade, which is the usual topic of discourse with those craftsmen. I asked him how he could reasonably blame the English traders for cheating *Tekapê húmmah,* "the red folks,"[104] even allowing his accusations to be just; as he, their divine man, had cheated them out of a great part of their crops, and had the assurance to claim it as his religious due, when at the same time, if he had shaked hands with the straight old beloved speech, or strictly observed the ancient divine law, his feeling heart would not have allowed him to have done such black and crooked things, especially to the helpless, the poor, and the aged; [92] it rather would have strongly moved him to stretch out to them a kind and helping hand, according to the old beloved speech of *Ishtohoollo Aba* to his *Hottuk Ishtohoollo,* who were sufficiently supported at the public expence, and strictly ordered to supply with the greatest tenderness, the wants of others.

He smartly retorted my objections, telling me, that the white people's excuses for their own wrong conduct, were as false and weak as my complaints were against him. The red people, he said, saw very clearly through such thin black paint; though, his sacred employment was equally hid from them and me; by which means, neither of us could reasonably pretend to be proper judges of his virtuous conduct, nor blame him for the necessary effect of our own crimes; or urge it as a plea for cheating him out of his yearly dues, contrary to the old divine speech, for the crops became light by their own vicious conduct, which spoiled the power of his holy things. So that it was visible, both the red and white people were commonly too partial to themselves; and that by the bounty of the supreme fatherly Chieftain, it was as much out of his power, as distant from his kindly heart, either to wrong the beloved red people, or the white nothings; and that it became none, except mad light people, to follow the crooked steps of *Hottuk Ookproose,* the accursed people.

As there was no interruption to our winter-night's chat, I asked him in a friendly manner, whether he was not afraid, thus boldly to snatch at the divine power of distributing rain at his pleasure, as it belonged only to the great beloved thundering Chieftain, who dwells far above the clouds, in the new year's unpolluted holy fire, and who gives it in common to all nations of people alike, and even to every living creature over the face of the whole earth, because he made them—and his merciful goodness always prompts him to supply the wants of all his creatures. He told me, that by an ancient tradition, their *Loáche* were possessed of an extraordinary divine power, by which they foretold hidden things, and by the beloved speech brought down showers of plenty to the beloved people; that he very well knew, the giver of virtue to nature resided on earth in the unpolluted holy fire, and likewise above the clouds and the sun, in the shape of a fine fiery substance, attended by a great many beloved people; and that he continually weighs us, and measures out good or bad [93] things to us, according to our actions. He added, that though the former beloved speech had a long time subsided, it was very reasonable they should still continue this their old beloved custom; especially as it was both profitable in supporting many of their helpless old beloved men, and very productive of virtue, by awing their young people from violating the ancient laws. This shewed him to be cunning in priestcraft, if not possessed of a tradition from the Hebrew records, that their prophets by the divine power, had, on material occasions, acted beyond the stated laws of nature, and wrought miracles.

My old prophetic friend told me, with a good deal of surprize, that though the beloved red people had by some means or other, lost the old beloved speech; yet *Frenshe Lakkàne ookproo,* "the ugly yellow French," (as they term the Missisippians) had by some wonderful method obtained it; for his own people, he assured me, had seen them at New Orleans to bring down rain in a very dry season, when they were giving out several bloody speeches to their head warriors against the English Chikkasah traders. On a mischievous politic invitation of the French, several of the Chikkasah had then paid them a visit, in the time of an alarming drought and a general fast, when they were praying for seasonable rains at mass. When they came, the interpreter was ordered to tell them, that the French had holy places and holy things, after the manner of the red people—that if their young people proved honest, they could bring down rain whenever they stood in need of it—and that this was one of the chief reasons which induced all the various nations of the beloved red people to bear them so intense a love; and, on the contrary, so violent and inexpressible an hatred even to the very name of the English, because every one of them was marked with *Anumbole Ookkproo,* "the curse of God."

The method the Chikkasah prophet used in relating the affair, has some humour in it—for their ignorance of the christian religion, and institutions, perplexes them when they are on the subject; on which account I shall literally transcribe it.

He told me, that the Chikkasah warriors during three successive days, accompanied the French *Loáche* and *Ishtohoollo* to the great beloved house, where a large bell hung a-top, which strange sight exceedingly surprized [94] them; for, instead of being fit for a horse, it would require a great many ten horses to carry it. Around the inside of the beloved house, there was a multitude of he and she beloved people, or male and female saints or angels, whose living originals, they affirmed, dwelt above the clouds, and helped them to get every good thing from *Ishtohoollo Aba,* when they earnestly crave their help. The French beloved men spoke a great deal with much warmth; the rest were likewise busily employed in imitation of their *Ishtohoollo* and *Loáche.* At one time they spoke high, at another low. One chose this, and another chose that song. Here the men kneeled before the images of their she-beloved people; there the women did the like before their favourite and beloved he-pictures, entreating them for some particular favour which they stood in need of. Some of them, he said, made very wild motions over their heads and breasts; and others struck their stomachs with a vehemence like their warriors, when they drink much *Ookka Homma,* "bitter waters," or spirituous liquor; while every one of them had a bunch of mixed beads, to which they frequently spoke, as well as counted over; that they loved these beads, for our people strictly observed, they did not give them to their *Loáche* and *Ishtohoollo,* as the red people would have done to those of their own country, though it was very plain they deserved them, for beating themselves so much for the young people's roguish actions; and likewise for labouring so strongly in pulling off their clothes, and putting them on again, to make the beloved physic work, which they took in small pieces, to help to bring on the rain. On the third day (added he) they brought it down in great plenty, which was certainly a very difficult performance; and as surprizing too, that they who are always, when opportunity answers, persuading the red people to take up the bloody hatchet against their old steady friends, should still have the beloved speech, which *Ishtoohoollo Aba Eloa* formerly spoke to his beloved *Loáche*. ——Thus ended our friendly discourse.

ARGUMENT VIII.

Their Festivals, Fasts, and Religious Rites, have also a great resemblance to those of the Hebrews. It will be necessary here to take a short view of the principal Jewish feasts, &c. They kept every year, a sacred feast called the Passover, in memory of their deliverance from Egyptian [95] bondage. Seven days were appointed, *Lev.* xxiii.—To these they added an eighth, through a religious principle, as preparatory, to clear their houses of all leaven, and to fix their minds before they entered on that religious duty. The name of this festival is derived from a word which signifies to "pass over;" because, when the destroying angel flew through the Egyptian houses, and killed their first-born, he passed over those of the Israelites, the tops of whose doors were stained with the blood of the lamb, which they were ordered to kill. This solemnity was instituted with the strongest injunctions, to let their children know the cause of that observance, and to mark that night through all their generations.

Three days before this sacred festival, they chose a lamb, without spot or blemish, and killed it on the evening of the fourteenth day of Abib, which was the first moon of the ecclesiastical, and the seventh of the civil year; and they ate it with bitter herbs, without breaking any of the bones of it, thus prefiguring the death of Messiah. This was the reason that this was the chief of the days of unleavened bread, and they were strictly forbidden all manner of work on that day; besides, no uncircumcised, or unclean persons ate of the paschal lamb. Those of the people, whom diseases or long journies prevented from observing the passover on that day, were obliged to keep it in the next moon.

On the sixteenth day, which was the second of the passover, they offered up to God a sheaf of the new barley-harvest, because it was the earliest grain. The priest carried it into the temple, and having cleaned and parched it, he grinded or pounded it into flower, dipt it in oil, and then waved it before the Lord, throwing some into the fire. The Jews were forbidden to eat any of their new harvest, till they had offered up a sheaf, the grain of which filled an omer, a small measure of about five pints. All was impure and unholy till this oblation was made, but afterwards it became hallowed, and every one was at liberty to reap and get in his harvest.

On the tenth day of the moon Ethanim, the first day of the civil year, they celebrated the great fast, or feast of expiation, afflicted their souls, and ate nothing the whole day. The high-priest offered several sacrifices, and having carried the blood of the victims into the temple, he sprinkled it upon the altar of incense, and the veil that was before the holiest; and went [96] into that most sacred place, where the divine Shekinah resided, carrying a censer smoking in his hand with incense, which hindered him from having a clear sight of the ark. But he was not allowed to enter that holy place, only once a year, on this great day of expiation, to offer the general sacrifice both for the sins of the people and of himself. Nor did he ever mention the divine four-lettered name, YO HE WAH, except on this great day, when he blessed the people.

Because the Israelites lived in tabernacles, or booths, while they were in the wilderness; as a memorial therefore of the divine bounty to them, they were commanded to keep the feast of tabernacles, on the fifteenth day of the month Tisri, which they called *Rosh Hosanah,* or *Hoshianah,* it lasted eight days; during which time, they lived in arbours, (covered with green boughs of trees) unless when they went to worship at the temple, or sung *Hoshaniyo* around the altar. When they were on this religious duty, they were obliged each to carry in their hands a bundle of the branches of willows, palm-trees, myrtles, and others of different sorts, laden with fruit, and tied together with ribbons; and thus rejoice together with the appointed singers, and vocal and instrumental music, in the divine presence before the altar. On the eighth day of the feast, one of the priests brought some water in a golden vessel, from the pool of Siloam, mixed it with wine, and poured it on the morning-sacrifice, and the first fruits of their latter crops which were then presented, as an emblem of the divine graces that should flow to them, when Shilo came, who was to be their anointed king, prophet, and bigh-priest—The people in the mean time singing out of Isaiah "with joy shall ye draw water out of the wells of salvation."

Let us now turn to the copper colour American Hebrews.—While their sanctified new fruits are dressing,[105] a religious attendant is ordered to call six of their old beloved women to come to the temple, and dance the beloved dance with joyful hearts, according to the old beloved speech. They cheerfully obey, and enter the supposed holy ground in solemn procession, each carrying in her hand a bundle of small branches of various green trees; and they join the same number of old magi, or priests, who carry a cane in one hand adorned with white feathers, having likewise green boughs in their other hand, which they pulled from their holy arbour, and carefully place there, encircling it with several rounds. Those beloved men have their heads [97] dressed with white plumes; but the women are decked in their finest, and anointed with bear's-grease, having small tortoise-shells, and white pebbles, fastened to a piece of white-drest deer-skin, which is tied to each of their legs.

The eldest of the priests leads the sacred dance, a-head of the innermost row, which of course is next to the holy fire. He begins the dance round the supposed holy fire, by invoking YAH, after their usual manner, on a bass key, and with a short accent; then he sings YO YO, which is repeated by the rest of the religious procession; and he continues his sacred invocations and praises, repeating the divine word, or notes, till they return to the same point of the circular course, where they began: then HE HE in like manner, and WAH WAH. While dancing they never fail to repeat those notes; and frequently the holy train strike up *Halelu, Halelu;* then *Haleluiah, Halelu-Yah,* and ALELUIAH and ALELU-YAH, "Irradiation to the divine essence," with great earnestness and fervor, till they encircle the altar, while each strikes the ground with right and left feet alternately, very quick, but well-timed. Then the awful drums join the sacred choir, which incite the old female singers to chant forth their pious notes, and grateful praises before the divine essence, and to redouble their former quick joyful steps, in imitation of the leader of the sacred dance, and the religious men a-head of them. What with the manly strong notes of the one, and the shrill voices of the other, in concert with the bead-shells, and the two sounding, drum-like earthen vessels, with the voices of the musicians who beat them, the reputed holy ground echoes with the praises of YO HE WAH. Their singing and dancing in three circles around their sacred fire, appears to have a reference to a like religious custom of the Hebrews. And may we not reasonably suppose, that they formerly understood the psalms, or divine hymns? at least those that begin with *Halelu-Yah;* otherwise, how came all the inhabitants of the extensive regions of North and South-America, to have, and retain those very expressive Hebrew words? or how repeat them so distinctly, and apply them after the manner of the Hebrews, in their religious acclamations? The like cannot be found in any other countries.

In like manner, they sing on other religious occasions, and at their feasts of love, *Ale-Yo Ale-Yo;* which is אל, the divine name, by his attribute of omnipotence; and י, alluding יהוה. They sing likewise *Hewah Hewah,* which is הוה "the immortal soul;" drawn from the divine essential name, [98] as deriving its rational faculties from YOHEWAH. Those words that they sing in their religious dances, they never repeat at any other time; which seems to have greatly occasioned the loss of the meaning of their divine hymns; for I believe they are now so corrupt, as not to understand either the spiritual or literal meaning of what they sing, any further than by allusion.

In their circuiting dances, they frequently sing on a bass key, *Alué Alué, Aluhé, Aluhé,* and *Aluwàh Aluwàh,* which is the Hebrew אלוה. They likewise sing *Shilù-Yŏ, Shilù-Yŏ, Shilù-Hé Shilù-Hé, Shilù-Wâh, Shilù-Wâh,* and *Shilù-Hàh Shilù-Hàh.* They transpose them also several ways, but with the very same notes. The three terminations make up in their order the four-lettered divine name. *Hah* is a note of gladness—the word preceding it, *Shilù*, seems to express the predicted human and divine שילוה, Shiloh, who was to be the purifier, and peace-maker.

They continue their grateful divine hymns for the space of fifteen minutes, when the dance breaks up. As they degenerate, they lengthen their dances, and shorten the time of their fasts and purifications; insomuch, that they have so exceedingly corrupted their primitive rites and customs, within the space of the last thirty years, that, at the same rate of declension, there will not be long a possibility of tracing their origin, but by their dialects, and war-customs.

At the end of this notable religious dance, the old beloved, or holy women return home to hasten the feast of the new-sanctified fruits. In the mean while, every one at the temple drinks very plentifully of the Cusseena and other bitter liquids, to cleanse their sinful bodies; after which, they go to some convenient deep water, and there, according to the ceremonial law of the Hebrews, they wash away their sins with water. Thus sanctified, they return with joyful hearts in solemn procession, singing their notes of praise, till they enter into the holy ground to eat of the new delicious fruits of wild Canaan★. The women now with the utmost cheerfulness, bring to [99] the outside of the sacred square, a plentiful variety of all those good things, with which the divine fire has blessed them in the new year; and the religious attendants lay it before them, according to their stated order and reputed merit. Every seat is served in a gradual succession, from the white and red imperial long broad seats, and the whole square is soon covered: frequently they have a change of courses of fifty or sixty different sorts, and thus they continue to regale themselves, till the end of the festival; for they reckon they are now to feast themselves with joy and gladness, as the divine fire is appeased for past crimes, and has propitiously sanctified their weighty harvest. They all behave so modestly, and are possessed of such an extraordinary constancy and equanimity, in the pursuit of their religious mysteries, that they do not shew the least outward emotion of pleasure, at the first sight of the sanctified new fruits; nor the least uneasiness to be tasting those tempting delicious fat things of Canaan. If one of them acted in a contrary manner, they would say to him, *Che-Hakset Kaneha*, "You resemble such as were beat in Canaan." This unconcern, doubtless proceeded originally from a virtuous principle; but now, it may be the mere

---

★They are so strictly prohibited from eating salt, or flesh-meat, till the fourth day, that during the interval, the very touch of either is accounted a great pollution: after that period, they are deemed lawful to be eaten. All the hunters, and able-bodied men, kill and barbecue wild game in the woods, at least ten days before this great festival, and religiously keep it for that sacred use.

effect of habit: for, jealousy and revenge excepted, they seem to be divested of every mental passion, and entirely incapable of any lasting affection.

I shall give an instance of this.—If the husband has been a year absent on a visit to another nation, and should by chance overtake his wife near home, with one of his children skipping along side of her; instead of those sudden and strong emotions of joy that naturally arise in two generous breasts at such an unexpected meeting, the self-interested pair go along as utter strangers, without seeming to take the least notice of one another, till a considerable time after they get home.

The Indians formerly observed the grand festival of the annual expiation of sin, at the beginning of the first new moon, in which their corn became full-eared;[106] but for many years past they are regulated by the season of their harvest. And on that head, they shew more religious patience than the Hebrews formerly did; who, instead of waiting till their grain was ripe, forced their barley, which ripened before any other sort they planted. And they are perhaps as skilful in observing the revolutions of the moon, as ever the Israelites were, at least till the end of the first temple; for during that period, instead of measuring time by astronomical calculations, they [100] knew it only by the phases of the moon. In like manner, the supposed red Hebrews of the American desarts, annually observed their festivals, and *Neetak Yáh-àh,* "days of afflicting themselves before the Deity," at a prefixed time of a certain moon. To this day, a war-leader, who, by the number of his martial exploits is entitled to a drum, always sanctifies himself, and his outstanding company, at the end of the old moon, so as to go off at the appearance of the new one by day-light; whereas, he who has not sufficiently distinguished himself, must set out in the night.

As the first of the *Neetak Hoollo,* precedes a long strict fast of two nights and a day, they gormandize such a prodigious quantity of strong food, as to enable them to keep inviolate the succeeding fast, the sabbath of sabbaths, the *Neetak Yah-ah:* the feast lasts only from morning till sun-set. Being great lovers of the ripened fruits, and only tantalized as yet, with a near view of them; and having lived at this season, but meanly on the wild products of nature—such a fast as this may be truly said to afflict their souls, and to prove a sufficient trial of their religious principles. During the festival, some of their people are closely employed in putting their temple in proper order for the annual expiation; and others are painting the white cabbin, and the supposed holiest, with white clay; for it is a sacred, peaceable place, and white is its emblem. Some, at the same time are likewise painting the war-cabbin with red clay, or their emblematical red root,[107] as occasion requires; while others of an inferior order, are covering all the seats of the beloved square with new mattresses, made out of the fine splinters of long canes, tied together with flags. In the mean time, several of them are busy in sweeping the temple, clearing it of every supposed polluting thing, and carrying out the ashes from the hearth which perhaps had not been cleaned six times since the last year's general offering. Several towns join together to make the annual sacrifice; and, if the whole nation lies in a narrow compass, they make but one annual offering: by which means, either through a sensual or religious principle, they strike off the work with joyful hearts. Every thing being thus prepared, the *Archi-magus* orders some of his religious attendants to dig up the old hearth, or altar, and to sweep out the remains that by chance might either be left, or drop down. Then he puts a few roots of the button-snake-root, with some green leaves of an uncommon small sort of tobacco, and a little of the new fruits, at the bottom of the fire-place, which he [102 (*sic*)] orders to be covered up with white marley clay, and wetted over with clean water★.

Immediately, the *magi* order them to make a thick arbour over the altar, with green branches of the various young trees, which the warriors had designedly chosen, and laid down on the outside of the supposed holy ground: the women, in the interim are busy at home in cleaning out their houses, renewing the old hearths, and cleansing all their culinary vessels, that they may be fit to receive the pretended holy fire, and the sanctified new fruits, according to the purity of the law; lest by a contrary conduct, they should incur damage in life, health, future crops, &c. It is fresh in the memory of the old traders, that formerly none of these numerous nations of Indians would eat, or even handle any part of the new harvest, till some of it had been offered up at the yearly festival by the *Archi-magus,* or those of his appointment, at their plantations, though the light harvest of the past year had forced them to give their women and children of the ripening fruits, to sustain life. Notwithstanding they are visibly degenerating, both in this, and every other religious observance, except what concerns war; yet their magi and old warriors live contentedly on such harsh food as nature affords them in the woods, rather than transgress that divine precept given to their fore-fathers.

Having every thing in order for the sacred solemnity, the religious wait-ers carry off the remains of the feast, and lay them on the outside of the square; others of an inferior order carefully sweep out the smallest crumbs, for fear of polluting the first-fruit offering; and before sun-set, the temple must be cleared, even of every kind of vessel or utensil, that had contained, or been used about any food in that expiring year. The women carry all off,

---

★Under the palladium of Troy, were placed things of the like nature, as a preservative from evil; but the above practice seems to be pretty much tempered with the Mosaic institution; for God commanded them to make an altar of earth, to sacrifice thereon. *Exod.* xx. 24.

but none of that sex, except half a dozen of old beloved women, are allowed in that interval to tread on the holy ground, till the fourth day. Now, one of the waiters proclaims with a loud voice, for all the warriors and beloved men, whom the purity of the law admits, to come and enter the beloved square, and observe the fast; he likewise exhorts all [102] the women and children, and those who have not initiated themselves in war, to keep apart from them, according to law. Should any of them prove disobedient, the young ones would be dry-scratched, and the others stript of every thing they had on them. They observe the same strict law of purity, in their method of sanctifying themselves for war, in order to obtain the divine protection, assistance, and success. But a few weeks since, when a large company of these warlike savages were on the point of setting off to commence war against the Muskohge, some of the wags decoyed a heedless trader into their holy ground, and they stript him, so as to oblige him to redeem his clothes with vermilion. And, on account of the like trespass, they detained two Indian children two nights and a day, till their obstinate parents paid the like ransom.[108]

Their great beloved man, or *Archi-magus,* now places four centinels, one at each corner of the holy square, to keep out every living creature as impure, except the religious order, and the warriors who are not known to have violated the law of the first-fruit-offering, and that of marriage, since the last year's expiation. Those centinels are regularly relieved, and firm to their sacred trust; if they discerned a dog or cat on the outlimits of the holy square, before the first-fruit-offering was made, they would kill it with their arrows on the spot.[109]

They observe the fast till the rising of the second sun; and be they ever so hungry in that sacred interval, the healthy warriors deem the duty so awful, and the violation so inexpressibly vicious, that no temptation would induce them to violate it; for, like the Hebrews, they fancy temporal evils are the necessary effect of their immoral conduct, and they would for ever ridicule and reproach the criminal for every bad occurrence that befel him in the new year, as the sinful author of his evils; and would sooner shoot themselves, than suffer such long-continued sharp disgrace. The religious attendants boil a sufficient quantity of button-snake-root, highly imbittered, and give it round pretty warm, in order to vomit and purge their sinful bodies.[110] Thus they continue to mortify and purify themselves, till the end of the fast. When we consider their earnest invocations of the divine essence, in this solemnity—their great knowledge of specific virtues in simples— that they never apply the aforesaid root, only on religious occasions—that they frequently drink it to such excess as to impair their health, [103] and sometimes so as to poison themselves by its acrid quality—and take into the account, its well-known medicinal property of curing the bite of the most dangerous sort of the serpentine generation; must not one think, that the Aboriginal Americans chose it, as a strong emblem of the certain cure of the bite of the old serpent in Eden.

That the women and children, and those worthless fellows who have not hazarded their lives in defence of their holy places and holy things, and for the beloved people, may not be entirely godless, one of the old beloved men lays down a large quantity of the small-leafed green tobacco, on the outside of a corner of the sacred square; and an old beloved woman, carries it off, and distributes it to the sinners without, in large pieces, which they chew heartily, and swallow, in order to afflict their souls. She commends those who perform the duty with cheerfulness, and chides those who seem to do it unwillingly, by their wry faces on account of the bitterness of the supposed sanctifying herb. She distributes it in such quantities, as she thinks are equal to their capacity of sinning, giving to the reputed, worthless old He-hen-pickers, the proportion only of a child, because she thinks such spiritless pictures of men cannot sin with married women; as all the females love only the virtuous manly warrior, who has often successfully accompanied the beloved ark.

In the time of this general fast, the women, children, and men of weak constitutions, are allowed to eat, as soon as they are certain the sun has begun to decline from his meridian altitude; but not before that period. Their indulgence to the sick and weak, seems to be derived from divine precept, which forbad the offering of sacrifice at the cost of mercy; and the snake-root joined with their sanctifying bitter green tobacco, seem to be as strong expressive emblems as they could have possibly chosen, according to their situation in life, to represent the sacred institution of eating the paschal lamb, with bitter herbs; and to shew, that though the old serpent bit us in Eden, yet there is a branch from the root of Jesse, to be hoped for by those who deny themselves their present sweet taste, which will be a sufficient purifier, and effect the cure.

The whole time of this fast may with truth be called a fast, and to the *Archi-magus,* to all the *magi,* and pretended prophets, in particular; for, by [104] ancient custom, the former is obliged to eat of the sanctifying small-leafed tobacco, and drink the snake-root, in a separate hut for the space of three days and nights without any other subsistence, before the solemnity begins; besides his full portion along with the rest of the religious order, and the old war-chieftains, till the end of the general fast, which he pretends to observe with the strictest religion. After the first-fruits are sanctified, he lives most abstemiously till the end of the annual expiation, only sucking water-melons now and then to quench thirst, and support life, spitting out the more substantial part.[111]

By the Levitical law, the priests were obliged to observe a stricter sanctity of life than the laity; all the time they were performing the sacerdotal offices, both women and wine were strictly forbidden to them. Thus the Indian religious are retentive of their sacred mysteries to death, and the *Archimagus* is visibly thin and meagre at the end of the solemnity. That rigid self-denial, seems to have been designed to initiate the Levite, and give the rest an example of leading an innocent simple life, that thereby they might be able to subdue their unruly passions; and that by mortifying and purifying himself so excessively, the sacrifice by passing through his pure hands, may be accepted, and the holy Spirit of fire atoned, according to the divine law. The superannuated religious are also emulous in the highest degree, of excelling one another in their long fasting; for they firmly believe, that such an annual self-denying method is so highly virtuous, when joined to an obedience of the rest of their laws, as to be the infallible means of averting evil, and producing good things, through the new year. They declare that a steady virtue, through the divine co-operating favour, will infallibly insure them a lasting round of happiness.

At the end of this solemn fast, the women by the voice of a crier, bring to the outside of the holy square, a plentiful variety of the old year's food newly drest, which they lay down, and immediately return home; for every one of them know their several duties, with regard both to time and place. The centinels report the affair, and soon afterward the waiters by order go, and reaching their hands over the holy ground, they bring in the provisions, and set them down before the famished multitude. Though most of the people may have seen them, they reckon it vicious and mean to shew a gladness for the end of their religious duties; and shameful [105] to hasten the holy attendants, as they are all capable of their sacred offices. They are as strict observers of all their set forms, as the Israelites were of those they had from divine appointment.

Before noon, the temple is so cleared of every thing the women brought to the square, that the festival after that period, resembles a magical entertainment that had no reality in it, consisting only in a delusion of the senses. The women then carry the vessels from the temple to the water, and wash them clean for fear of pollution. As soon as the sun is visibly declining from his meridian, this third day of the fast, the *Archi-magus* orders a religious attendant to cry aloud to the crowded town, that the holy fire is to be brought out for the sacred altar—commanding every one of them to stay within their own houses, as becomes the beloved people, without doing the least bad thing—and to be sure to extinguish, and throw away every spark of the old fire; otherwise, the divine fire will bite them severely with bad diseases, sickness, and a great many other evils, which he sententiously enumerates, and finishes his monitory caution, by laying life and death before them.

Now every thing is hushed.—Nothing but silence all around: the *Archi-magus,* and his beloved waiter, rising up with a reverend carriage, steady countenance, and composed behaviour, go into the beloved place, or holiest, to bring them out the beloved fire. The former takes a piece of dry poplar, willow, or white oak, and having cut a hole, so as not to reach through it, he then sharpens another piece, and placing that with the hole between his knees, he drills it briskly for several minutes, till it begins to smoke—or, by rubbing two pieces together, for about a quarter of an hour, by friction he collects the hidden fire; which all of them reckon to immediately issue from the holy Spirit of fire. The Muskohge call the fire their grandfather—and the supreme Father of mankind, *Esakàta-Emishe,* "the breath master," as it is commonly explained.[112] When the fire appears, the beloved waiter cherishes it with fine chips, or shaved splinters of pitch-pine, which had been deposited in the holiest: then he takes the unsullied wing of a swan, fans it gently, and cherishes it to a flame. On this, the *Archi-magus* brings it out in an old earthen vessel, whereon he had placed it, and lays it on the sacred altar, which is under an arbour, thick-weaved a-top with green boughs.[113] It is observable, that when the Levites laid wood on the sacred fire, it was unlawful [106] for them either to blow it with bellows, or their breath. The Magians, or followers of Zoroaster, poured oil on their supposed holy fire, and left it to the open air to kindle it into flame. Is not this religious ceremony of these desolate Indians a strong imitation, or near resemblance of the Jewish customs?

Their hearts are enlivened with joy at the appearance of the reputed holy fire, as the divine fire is supposed to atone for all their past crimes, except murder: and the beloved waiter shews his pleasure, by his cheerful industry in feeding it with dry fresh wood; for they put no rotten wood on it, any more than the Levites would on their sacred altars. Although the people without, may well know what is transacting within, yet, by order, a crier informs them of the good tidings, and orders an old beloved woman to pull a basket-full of the new-ripened fruits, and bring them to the beloved square. As she before had been appointed, and religiously prepared for that solemn occasion, she readily obeys, and soon lays it down with a cheerful heart, at the out-corner of the beloved square. By ancient custom, she may either return home, or stand there, till the expiation of sin hath been made, which is thus performed—The *Archi-magus,* or fire-maker, rises from his white seat and walks northward three times round the holy fire, with a slow pace, and in a very sedate and grave manner, stopping now and then, and speaking certain old ceremonial words with a low voice and a rapidity of expression, which none understand but a few of the old beloved men, who equally secrete their religious mysteries, that they may not be prophaned. He then takes a little of each sort of the new harvest, which the old woman had brought to the extremity of the supposed holy ground, rubs some bear's oil over it, and offers it up together with some flesh, to the bountiful holy Spirit of fire, as a first-fruit offering, and an annual oblation for sin. He likewise consecrates the button-snake-root, and the cusseena, by pouring a little of those two strong decoctions into the pretended holy fire. He then purifies the red and white seats with those bitter liquids, and sits down. Now, every one of the outlaws who had been catched a tripping, may safely creep out of their lurking holes, anoint themselves, and dress in their finest, to pay their grateful thanks at an awful distance, to the forgiving divine fire. A religious waiter is soon ordered to call to the women around, to come for the sacred fire: they gladly obey.—When they come to the outside of the quadrangular holy ground, the *Archi-magus* addresses the warriors, and gives [107] them all the particular positive injunctions, and negative precepts they yet retain of the ancient law, relating to their own manly station. Then he changes his note, and uses a much sharper language to the women, as suspecting their former virtue. He first tells them very earnestly, that if there are any of them who have not extinguished the old evil fire, or have contracted any impurity, they must forthwith depart, lest the divine fire should spoil both them and the people; he charges them to be sure not to give the children a bad example of eating any unsanctified, or impure food, otherwise they will get full of worms, and be devoured by famine and diseases, and bring many other dangerous evils both upon themselves, and all the beloved, or holy people. This seems to allude to the theocratic government of the Jews, when such daring criminals were afflicted with immediate and visible divine punishment.

In his female lecture, he is sharp and prolix: he urges them with much earnestness to an honest observance of the marriage-law, which may be readily excused, on account of the prevalent passion of self-interest. Our own christian orators do not exert themselves with half the eloquence or eagerness, as when that is at stake which they most value. And the old wary savage has sense enough to know, that the Indian female virtue is very brittle, not being guarded so much by inward principle, as the fear of shame, and of incurring severe punishment; but if every bush of every thicket was an hundred-eyed Argos, it would not be a sufficient guard over a wanton heart. So that it is natural they should speak much on this part of the subject, as they think they have much at stake. After that, he addresses himself to the whole body of the people, and tells them, in rapid bold language, with great energy, and expressive gestures of body, to look at the holy fire, which again has introduced all those shameful adulterous criminals into social privileges; he bids them not to be guilty of the like for time to come, but be sure to remember well, and strongly shake hands with the old beloved straight speech, otherwise the divine fire, which sees, hears, and knows them, will spoil them exceedingly, if at any time they relapse, and commit that detestable crime. Then he numerates all the supposed lesser crimes, and moves the audience by the great motives of the hope of temporal good, and the fear of temporal evil, assuring them, that upon their careful observance of the ancient law, the holy fire will enable their prophets, the rain-makers, to procure them plentiful harvests, and give their war-leaders victory over their enemies—and by the [108] communicative power of their holy things, health and prosperity are certain: but on failure, they are to expect a great many extraordinary calamities, such as hunger, uncommon diseases, a subjection to witchcraft, and captivity and death by the hands of the hateful enemy in the woods, where the wild fowls will eat their flesh, and beasts of prey destroy the remaining bones, so as they will not be gathered to their forefathers—because their ark abroad, and beloved things at home, would lose their virtual power of averting evil. He concludes, by advising them to a strict observance of their old rites and customs, and then every thing shall go well with them. He soon orders some of the religious attendants to take a sufficient quantity of the supposed holy fire, and lay it down on the outside of the holy ground, for all the houses of the various associated towns, which sometimes lie several miles apart. The women, hating sharp and grave lessons, speedily take it up, gladly carry it home, and lay it down on their unpolluted hearths, with the prospect of future joy and peace.

While the women are running about, and getting ready to dress the sanctified new-fruits on the sacred fire, the *Archi-magus* sends a religious attendant to pull some cusseena, or *yopon,* belonging to the temple; and having parched it brown on the altar, he boils it with clear running water in a large earthen pot, about half full; it has such a strong body, as to froth above the top by pouring it up and down with their consecrated vessels, which are kept only for that use: of this they drink now and then, till the end of the festival, and on every other religious occasion from year to year. Some of the old beloved men, through a religious emulation in sanctifying themselves, often drink this, and other bitter decotions, to such excess, as to purge themselves very severely—when they drink it, they always invoke YO He Wah.

If any of the warriors are confined at home by sickness, or wounds, and are either deemed incapable or unfit to come to the annual expiation, they are allowed one of the old consecrated conch-shells-full of their sanctifying bitter cusseena, by their magi. The traders hear them often dispute for it, as their proper due, by ancient custom: and they often repeat their old religious ceremonies to one another, especially that part which they imagine most affects their present welfare; the aged are sent to instruct the young ones in these particulars. The above allowance, seems to be derived from the divine precept of mercy, in allowing a second passover [109] in favour of those who could not go, or were not admitted to the first; and the latter custom, to be in obedience to the divine law, which their supposed progenitors were to write on the posts of the doors, to wear as frontlets before their eyes, and teach to their children.

Though the Indians do not use salt in their first-fruit-oblation till the fourth day; it is not to be doubted but they formerly did. They reckon they cannot observe the annual expiation of sins, without bear's oil, both to mix with that yearly offering, and to eat with the new sanctified fruits; and some years they have a great deal of trouble in killing a sufficient quantity of bears for the use of this religious solemnity, and their other sacred rites for the approaching year; for at such seasons they are hard to be found, and quite lean. The traders commonly supply themselves with plenty of this oil from winter to winter; but the Indians are so prepossessed with a notion of the white people being all impure and accursed, that they deem their oil as polluting on those sacred occasions, as Josephus tells us the Jews reckoned that of the Greeks. An Indian warrior will not light his pipe at a white man's fire if he suspects any unsanctified food has been dressed at it in the new year. And in the time of the new-ripened fruits, their religious men carry a flint, punk, and steel, when they visit us, for fear of polluting themselves by lighting their pipes at our supposed *Loak ookproose,* "accursed fire," and spoiling the power of their holy things. The polluted would, if known, be infallibly anathamatized, and expelled from the temple, with the women, who are suspected of gratifying their vicious taste. During the eight days festival, they are forbidden even to touch the skin of a female child: if they are detected, either in cohabiting with, or laying their hand on any of their own wives, in that sacred interval, they are stripped naked, and the offender is universally deemed so atrocious a criminal, that he lives afterwards a miserable life. Some have shot themselves dead, rather than stand the shame, and the long year's continual reproaches cast upon them, for every mischance that befalls any of their people, or the ensuing harvest,—a necessary effect of the divine anger, they say, for such a crying sin of pollution. An instance of this kind I heard happened some years ago in Talàse, a town of the Muskohge, seven miles above the Alebáma garrison.

When we consider how sparingly they eat in their usual way of living, it is surprising to see what a vast quantity of food they consume [110] on their festival days. It would equally surprize a stranger to see how exceedingly they vary their dishes, their dainties consisting only of dried flesh, fish, oil, corn, beans, pease, pompions, and wild fruit. During this rejoicing time, the warriors are drest in their wild martial array, with their heads covered with white down: they carry feathers of the same colour, either in their hands, or fastened to white scraped canes, as emblems of purity, and scepters of power, while they are dancing in three circles, and singing their religious praises around the sacred arbour, in which stands the holy fire. Their music consists of two clay-pot drums, covered on the top with thin wet deer-skins, drawn very tight, on which each of the noisy musicians beats with a stick, accompanying the noise with their voices; at the same time, the danc-ers prance it away, with wild and quick sliding steps, and variegated postures of body, to keep time with the drums, and the rattling calabashes shaked by some of their religious heroes, each of them singing their old religious songs, and striking notes *in tympano et choro.*[114] Such is the graceful dancing, as well as the vocal and instrumental music of the red Hebrews on religious and martial occasions, which they must have derived from early antiquity. Toward the conclusion of the great festival, they paint and dress themselves anew, and give themselves the most terrible appearance they possibly can. They take up their war-instruments, and fight a mock-battle in a very exact manner: after which, the women are called to join in a grand dance, and if they disobey the invitation they are fined. But as they are extremely fond of such religious exercise, and deem it productive of temporal good, all soon appear in their finest apparel, as before suggested, decorated with silver ear-bobs, or pendants to their ears, several rounds of white beads about their necks, rings upon their fingers, large wire or broad plates of silver on their wrists, their heads shining with oil, and torrepine-shells containing pebbles, fastened to deer-skins, tied to the outside of their legs. Thus adorned, they join the men in three circles, and dance a considerable while around the sacred fire, and then they separate.

At the conclusion of this long and solemn festival, the *Archi-magus* orders one of the religious men to proclaim to all the people, that their sacred annual solemnity is now ended, and every kind of evil averted from the beloved people, according to the old straight beloved speech; they must therefore paint themselves, and come along with him according to ancient [111] custom. As they know the stated time, the joyful sound presently reaches their longing ears: immediately they fly about to grapple up a kind of chalky clay, to paint themselves white. By their religious emulation, they soon appear covered with that emblem of purity, and join at the outside of the holy ground, with all who had sanctified themselves within it, who are likewise painted, some with streaks, and others all over, as white as the clay can make them: recusants would undergo a heavy penalty. They go along in a very orderly solemn procession, to purify themselves in running water. The *Archi-magus* heads the holy train—his waiter next—the beloved men according to their seniority—and the warriors by their reputed merit. The women follow them in the same orderly manner, with all the children that can walk, behind them, ranged commonly according to their height; the very little ones they carry in their arms. Those, who are known to have eaten of the unsanctified fruits, bring up the rear. In this manner the procession moves along, singing ALELUIAH to YO HE WAH, &c. till they get to the water, which is generally contiguous, when the *Archi-magus* jumps into it, and all the holy train follow him, in the same order they observed from the temple. Having purified themselves, or washed away their sins, they come out with joyful hearts, believing themselves out of the reach of temporal evil, for their past vicious conduct: and they return in the same religious cheerful manner, into the middle of the holy ground, where having made a few circles, singing and dancing around the altar, they thus finish their annual great festival, and depart in joy and peace.

Ancient writers inform us, that while the Scythians or Tartars were heathens, their priests in the time of their sacrifices, took some blood, and mixing it with milk, horse-dung, and earth, got on a tree, and having exhorted the people, they sprinkled them with it, in order to purify them, and defend them from every kind of evil: the heathens also excluded some from religious communion. The Egyptians excommunicated those who ate of animals that bore wool, or cut the throat of a goat*. And in ancient times, they, and the Phœnicians, Greeks, &c. adored the serpent, and expelled those who killed it. The East-Indians likewise, drive those from the [112] supposed benefit of their altars, who eat of a cow, and drink wine, or that eat with foreigners, or an inferior cast. Though the heathen world offered sacrifice, had ablutions, and several other sorts of purifications, and frequently by fire; yet at the best, their religious observances differed widely from the divine institutions; whereas the American Aborigines observe strict purity, in the most essential parts of the divine law. The former concealed their various worship from the light of the sun; some seeking thick groves, others descending into the deep valleys, others crawling to get into caverns, and under their favourite rocks. But we find the latter, in their state-houses and temples, following the Jerusalem copy in a surprizing manner. Those of them who yet retain a supposed most holy place, contrary to the usage of the old heathen world, have it standing at the west end of the holy quadrangular ground: and they always appoint those of the meanest rank, to sit on the seats of the eastern square, so that their backs are to the east, and faces to the west†. The red square looks north; and the second men's cabbin, as

*Lanatis animalibus abstinet omnis
Mensa; nefas illic fœtum jugulare capellæ.
JUVENAL, Sat. xv.[115]

†The Hebrews had two presidents in the great synhedrion. The first was called *Nashe Yo,* "a prince of God." They elected him on account of his wisdom: The second was called *Rosh Ha-Yoshibbah,* "the father of the assembly:" he was chief in the great council. And *Ab beth din,* or "the father of the consistory," sat at his right hand, as the chief of the seventy-two, of which the great synhedrion consisted, the rest sitting according to their merit, in a gradual declension from the prince, to the end of the

the traders term the other square, of course looks south,[116] which is a strong imitation of Solomon's temple, that was modelled according to the divine plan of the Israelitish camp in the wilderness. We find them also sanctifying themselves, according to the emblematical laws of purity, offering their annual sacrifice in the centre of their quadrangular temples, under the meridian light of the sun. Their magi are devoted to, and bear the name of the great holy One; their supposed prophets likewise that of the divine fire; and each of them bear the emblems of purity and holiness—while in their religious duties, they sing ALELUIAH, YO HE WAH, &c. both day and night. Thus different are the various gods, [113] temples, prophets, and priests of all the idolatrous nations of antiquity, from the savage Americans; which shews with convincing clearness, especially by recollecting the former arguments, that the American Aborigines were never idolaters, nor violated the second commandment in worshipping the incomprehensible, omnipresent, divine essence, after the manner described by the popish historians of Peru and Mexico; but that the greatest part of their civil and religious system, is a strong old picture of the Israelitish, much less defaced than might be reasonably expected from the circumstances of time and place.

Every spring season, one town or more of the Missisippi Floridians,[117] keep a great solemn feast of love, to renew their old friendship. They call this annual feast, *Hottuk Aimpa, Heettla, Tanáa,* "the people eat, dance, and walk as twined together"[118]—The short name of their yearly feast of love, is *Hottuk Impanáa,* "eating by a strong religious, or social principle;" *Impanáa* signifies several threads or strands twisted or warped together. *Hissoobistarákshe,* and *Yelphòba Panáa,* is "a twisted horse-rope," and "warped garter★." This is also contrary to the usage of the old heathen world, whose festivals were in honour to their chief idols, and very often accompanied with detestable lewdness and debauchery.

They assemble three nights previous to their annual feast of love; on the fourth night they eat together. During the intermediate space, the young men and women dance in circles from the evening till morning. The men masque their faces with large pieces of gourds of different shapes and

---

semicircle. The like order is observed by the Indians,—and *Jer.* ii. 27, God commanded the Israelites, that they should not turn their backs to him, but their faces toward the propitiatory, when they worshipped him. I remember, in Koosah,[119] the uppermost western town of the Muskohge, which was a place of refuge, their supposed holiest consisted of a neat house, in the centre of the western square, and the door of it was in the south gable-end close to the white cabbin, each on a direct line, north and south.

★The name of a horse-rope is derived from *Tarákshe* "to tie," and *Hìssooba* "an elk, or horse that carries a burthen;" which suggests that they formerly saw elks carry burthens, though perhaps not in the northern provinces.

hieroglyphic paintings.[120] Some of them fix a pair of young buffalo horns to their head; others the tail, behind. When the dance and their time is expired, the men turn out a hunting, and bring in a sufficient quantity of venison, for the feast of renewing their love, and confirming their friendship with each other. The women dress it, and bring the best they have along with it; which a few springs past, was only a variety of Esau's small red acorn pottage, as their crops had failed. When they have eaten together, they fix in the ground a large pole with a bush tied at the top, over which [114] they throw a ball. Till the corn is in, they meet there almost every day, and play for venison and cakes, the men against the women; which the old people say they have observed for time out of mind.

Before I conclude this argument, I must here observe, that when the Indians meet at night to gladden and unite their hearts before YOHEWAH, they sing *Yohèwà-shoo Yohèwà-shoo, Yohewàhshee Yohewàshee,* and *Yohewàhshai Yohewàhshai,* with much energy. The first word is nearly in Hebrew characters, יהושע, the name of Joshua, or saviour, *Numb.* xiii. 8. That ע is properly expressed by our double vowel *oo,* let it be observed, that as בעל is "a ruler," or "commanding"—so the Indians say *Boole Hakse* "strike a person, that is criminal." In like manner they sing *Meshi Yo, Meshi Yo, Meshi He, Meshi He, Meshi Wah Meshi Wah;* likewise, *Meshi Hah Yo,* &c.; and *Meshi Wàh Hàh Meshi Wàh Hè,* transposing and accenting each syllable differently, so as to make them appear different words. But they commonly make those words end with one syllable of the divine name, *Yo He Wah.* If we connect this with the former part of the subject, and consider they are commonly anointed all over, in the time of their religious songs and circuiting dances, the words seem to glance at the Hebrew original, and perhaps they are sometimes synonymous; for שמן signifies oil; the person anointed משח, *Messiah,* and he who anointed משיחו, which with the Indians is *Meshiháh Yo.*

That these red savages formerly understood the radical meaning, and emblematical design, of the important words they use in their religious dances and sacred hymns, is pretty obvious, if we consider the reverence they pay to the mysterious divine name YO HE WAH, in pausing during a long breath on each of the two first syllables; their defining good by joining *Wah* to the end of a word, which otherwise expresses moral evil, as before noticed; and again by making the same word a negative of good, by separating the first syllable of that divine name into two syllables, and adding *U* as a superlative termination, *Y-O-U:* all their sacred songs seem likewise to illustrate it very clearly; *Halelu-Yah, Shilu Wah, Meshi Wah, Meshiha Yo,* &c. The words which they repeat in their divine hymns, while dancing in three circles around their supposed holy fire, are deemed so sacred, that they have not been known ever to mention them at any other time: and as they are a most erect

[115] people, their bowing posture during the time of those religious acclamations and invocations, helps to confirm their Hebrew origin.

ARGUMENT IX.

The Hebrews offered DAILY SACRIFICE, which the prophet Daniel calls *Tamid,* "the daily." It was an offering of a lamb every morning and evening, at the charges of the common treasury of the temple, and except the skin and intrails, it was burnt to ashes—upon which account they called it, *Oolah Kalile,* to ascend and consume. The Indians have a similar religious service. The Indian women always throw a small piece of the fattest of the meat into the fire when they are eating, and frequently before they begin to eat. Sometimes they view it with a pleasing attention, and pretend to draw omens from it. They firmly believe such a method to be a great means of producing temporal good things, and of averting those that are evil: and they are so far from making this fat-offering through pride or hypocrisy, that they perform it when they think they are not seen by those of contrary principles, who might ridicule them without teaching them better.

Instead of blaming their religious conduct, as some have done, I advised them to persist in their religious duty to *Ishtohoollo Aba,* because he never failed to be kind to those who firmly shaked hands with the old beloved speech, particularly the moral precepts, and after they died, he would bring them to their beloved land; and took occasion to shew them the innumerable advantages their reputed forefathers were blest with, while they obeyed the divine law.

The white people, (I had almost said christians) who have become Indian proselytes of justice, by living according to the Indian religious system, assure us, that the Indian men observe the daily sacrifice both at home, and in the woods, with new-killed venison; but that otherwise they decline it.[121] The difficulty of getting salt for religious uses from the sea-shore, and likewise its irritating quality when eaten by those who have green wounds, might in time occasion them to discontinue that part of the sacrifice. [116] They make salt for domestic use, out of a saltish kind of grass, which grows on rocks, by burning it to ashes, making strong lye of it, and boiling it in earthen pots to a proper consistence.[122] They do not offer any fruits of the field, except at the first-fruit-offering: so that their neglect of sacrifice, at certain times, seems not to be the effect of an ignorant or vicious, but of their intelligent and virtuous disposition, and to be a strong circumstantial evidence of their Israelitish extraction.

Though they believe the upper heavens to be inhabited by *Ishtohoollo Aba,* and a great multitude of inferior good spirits; yet they are firmly persuaded that the divine omnipresent Spirit of fire and light resides on earth, in their annual sacred fire while it is unpolluted; and that he kindly accepts their lawful offerings, if their own conduct is agreeable to the old divine law, which was delivered to their forefathers. The former notion of the Deity, is agreeable to those natural images, with which the divine penmen, through all the prophetic writings, have drawn YOHEWAH ELOHIM. When God was pleased with Aaron's priesthood and offerings, the holy fire descended and consumed the burnt-offering on the altar, &c.

By the divine records of the Hebrews, this was the emblematical token of the divine presence; and the smoke of the victim ascending toward heaven, is represented as a sweet favour to God. The people who have lived so long apart from the rest of mankind, are not to be wondered at, if they have forgotten the end and meaning of the sacrifice; and are rather to be pitied for seeming to believe, like the ignorant part of the Israelites, that the virtue is either in the form of offering the sacrifice, or in the divinity they imagine to reside on earth in the sacred annual fire; likewise, for seeming to have forgotten that the virtue was in the thing typified.

In the year 1748, when I was at the Koosàh on my way to the Chikkasah country, I had a conversation on this subject, with several of the more intelligent of the Muskohge traders. One of them told me, that just before, while he and several others were drinking spirituous liquors with the Indians, one of the warriors having drank to excess, reeled into the fire, and burned himself very much. He roared, foamed, and spoke the worst things against God, that their language could express. He upbraided him with [117] ingratitude, for having treated him so barbarously in return for his religious offerings, affirming he had always sacrificed to him the first young buck he killed in the new year; as in a constant manner he offered him when at home, some of the fattest of the meat, even when he was at short allowance, on purpose that he might shine upon him as a kind God.—And he added, "now you have proved as an evil spirit, by biting me so severely who was your constant devotee, and are a kind God to those accursed nothings, who are laughing at you as a rogue, and at me as a fool, I assure you, I shall renounce you from this time forward, and instead of making you look merry with fat meat, you shall appear sad with water, for spoiling the old beloved speech. I am a beloved warrior, and consequently I scorn to lie; you shall therefore immediately fly up above the clouds, for I shall piss upon you." From that time, his brethen said, God forsook that terrestrial residence, and the warrior became godless. This information exactly agrees with many such instances of Indian impiety, that happened within my own observation—and shews the bad consequences of that evil habit of using spirituous liquors intemperately, which they have been taught by the Europeans.

The Indians have among them the resemblance of the Jewish SIN-

OFFERING, and TRESPASS-OFFERING, for they commonly pull their new-killed venison (before they dress it) several times through the smoke and flame of the fire, both by the way of a sacrifice, and to consume the blood, life, or animal spirits of the beast, which with them would be a most horrid abomination to eat. And they sacrifice in the woods, the milt, or a large fat piece of the first buck they kill, both in their summer and winter hunt; and frequently the whole carcass. This they offer up, either as a thanksgiving for the recovery of health, and for their former success in hunting; or that the divine care and goodness may be still continued to them.[123]

When the Hebrews doubted whether they had sinned against any of the divine precepts, they were obliged by the law to bring to the priest a ram of their flock, to be sacrificed, which they called *Ascham*. When the priest offered this, the person was forgiven. Their sacrifices and offerings were called *Shilomim,* as they typified *Shilo-Berith,* "the purifying root," who was to procure them peace, rest, and plenty. The Indian imitates the Israelite [118] in his religious offerings, according to the circumstances of things; the Hebrew laid his hands on the head of the clean and tame victim, to load it with his sins, when it was to be killed. The Indian religiously chuses that animal which in America comes nearest to the divine law of sacrifice, according to what God has enabled him; he shoots down a buck, and sacrifices either the whole carcass, or some choice part of it, upon a fire of green wood to burn away, and ascend to *Yohewah.* Then he purifies himself in water, and believes himself secure from temporal evils. Formerly, every hunter observed the very same religious œconomy; but now it is practiced only by those who are the most retentive of their old religious mysteries.

The Muskohge Indians sacrifice a piece of every deer they kill at their hunting camps, or near home; if the latter, they dip their middle finger in the broth, and sprinkle it over the domestic tombs of their dead, to keep them out of the power of evil spirits, according to their mythology; which seems to proceed from a traditional knowledge, though corruption of the Hebrew law of sprinkling and of blood.

The Indians observe another religious custom of the Hebrews, in making a PEACE-OFFERING, or sacrifice of gratitude, if the Deity in the supposed holy ark is propitious to their campaign against the enemy, and brings them all safe home. If they have lost any in war, they always decline it, because they imagine by some neglect of duty, they are impure: then they only mourn their vicious conduct which defiled the ark, and thereby occasioned the loss. Like the Israelites, they believe their sins are the true cause of all their evils, and that the divinity in their ark, will always bless the more religious party with the best success. This is their invariable sentiment, and is the sole reason of their mortifying themselves in so severe a manner while they are out at war, living very scantily, even in a buffalo-range, under a strict rule, lest by luxury their hearts should grow evil, and give them occasion to mourn.

The common sort of Indians, in these corrupt times, only sacrifice a small piece of unsalted fat meat, when they are rejoicing in the divine presence, singing *Yo Yo*, &c. for their success and safety: but, according to the religious custom of the Hebrews, who offered sacrifices of thanksgiving [119] for every notable favour that Elohim had conferred either on individuals, or the body,—both the war-leader and his religious assistant go into the woods as soon as they are purified, and there sacrifice the first deer they kill; yet, as hath been observed, they always celebrate the annual expiation of sins in their religious temples.

The red Hebrews imagine their temples to have such a typical holiness, more than any other place, that if they offered up the annual sacrifice elsewhere, it would not atone for the people, but rather bring down the anger of *Ishtohoollo Aba*, and utterly spoil the power of their holy places and holy things. They who sacrifice in the woods, do it only on the particular occasions now mentioned; unless incited by a dream, which they esteem a monitory lesson of the Deity, according to a similar opinion of the Hebrews. To conclude this argument, it is well known, that the heathens offered the most abominable and impure sacrifices to a multiplicity of idol gods; some on favourite high places, others in thick groves, yea, offerings of their own children were made! and they likewise prostituted their young women in honour of their deities. The former is so atrocious in the eyes of the American Hebrews, that they reckon there needs no human law to prevent so unnatural a crime; the vilest reptiles being endued with an intense love to their young ones: and as to the latter, if even a great war-leader is known to cohabit with his own wife, while sanctifying himself according to their mode on any religious occasion, he is deemed unclean for the space of three days and nights; or should he during the annual atonement of sins, it is deemed so dangerous a pollution, as to demand a strict exclusion from the rest of the sanctified head-men and warriors, till the general atonement has been made at the temple, to appease the offended Deity: besides, as a shameful badge of his impiety, his clothes are stripped off. Thus different are the various modes and subjects of the heathenish worship and offerings, from those of the savage Americans. The surprizing purity the latter still observe in their religious ceremonies, under the circumstances of time and place, points strongly at their origin. [120]

ARGUMENT X.

The Hebrews had various ABLUTIONS and ANOINTINGS, according to the Mosaic ritual—and all the Indian nations constantly observe similar customs from religious motives.[124] Their frequent bathing, or dipping themselves and their children in rivers, even in the severest weather, seems to be as truly Jewish, as the other rites and ceremonies which have been mentioned. Frequent washing of the body was highly necessary to the health of the Hebrews in their warm climate, and populous state—but it is useless in this point of view to the red Americans, as their towns are widely distant from each other, thin peopled, and situated in cold regions. However, they practise it as a religious duty, unless in very hot weather, which they find by experience to be prejudicial to their health, when they observe the law of mercy, rather than that of sacrifice. In the coldest weather, and when the ground is covered with snow, against their bodily ease and pleasure, men and children turn out of their warm houses or stoves, reeking with sweat, singing their usual sacred notes, *Yo Yo,* &c. at the dawn of day, adoring YO HE WAH, at the gladsome sight of the morn; and thus they skip along, echoing praises, till they get to the river, when they instantaneously plunge into it. If the water is frozen, they break the ice with a religious impatience: After bathing, they return home, rejoicing as they run for having so well performed their religious duty, and thus purged away the impurities of the preceding day by ablution. The neglect of this hath been deemed so heinous a crime, that they have raked the legs and arms of the delinquent with snake's teeth, not allowing warm water to relax the stiffened skin. This is called dry-scratching;[125] for their method of bleeding consists in scratching the legs and arms with goir-fish teeth, when the skin has been first well loosened by warm water. The criminals, through a false imitation of true martial virtue, scorn to move themselves in the least out of their erect posture, be the pain ever so intolerable; if they did, they would be laughed at, even by their own relations—first, for being vicious; and next, for being timorous. This will help to lessen our surprize at the uncommon patience and constancy with which they are endued, beyond the rest of mankind, in suffering long-continued torture; especially as it is one [121] of the first, and strongest impressions they take; and they have constant lessons and examples of fortitude, exhibited before their eyes.

The Hebrews had convenient separate places for their women to bathe in, and purify themselves as occasion required: and at the temple (and the synagogues, after the captivity) they worshipped apart from the men, lest they should attract one another's attention from the divine worship: and it was customary for the women to go veiled, for fear of being seen, when they walked the streets. No doubt but jealousy had as great a share in introducing this custom as modesty, especially while poligamy was suffered in the rich. But the scantiness of the Jewish American's circumstances, has obliged them to purify themselves in the open rivers, where modesty forbad them to expose their women; who by this means, are now less religious than the men in that duty, for they only purify themselves as their discretion directs them. In imitation of the Hebrew women being kept apart from the men at their worship, the Indians intirely exclude their females from their temples by ancient custom, except six old beloved women, who are admitted to sing, dance, and rejoice, in the time of their annual expiation of sins, and then retire. In their town-houses also they separate them from the warriors, placing them on the ground at each side of the entrance of the door within, as if they were only casual spectators.

It may be objected, that the ancient Egyptians, Greeks, and Romans worshipped their Gods, at the dawn of day: and the Persian Magi, with all the other worshippers of fire, paid their religious devoirs to the rising sun, but, as the Indians are plainly not idolaters, or poly-theists; as they sing to, and invoke YAH, and YO HE WAH, the divine essence, as they run along at the dawn of day to purify themselves by ablution; it seems sufficiently clear, they are not descended from either of the last mentioned states, but that their origin is from the Israelites. This law of purity, bathing in water, was essential to the Jews—and the Indians to this day would exclude the men from religious communion who neglected to observe it.

It was customary with the Jews also after bathing to anoint themselves with oil. All the orientalists had a kind of sacred respect to OIL; particularly the Jews. With them, the same word which signified "noon-day" or splendor, צהר, denoted also "lucid oil."—And the olive-tree is derived [122] from the verb, to shine—Because, the fruit thereof tended to give their faces a favourite glistering colour. 'Tis well known that oil was applied by the Jews to the most sacred, as well as common uses. Their kings, prophets and priests, at their inauguration and consecration were anointed with oil—and the promised Saviour was himself described, by the epithet "anointed," and is said Psal. xlv. 7. to be "anointed with the oil of gladness above his fellows." We shall on this point, discover no small resemblance and conformity in the American Indians.

The Indian priests and prophets are initiated by unction. The Chikkasah some time ago set apart some of their old men of the religious order. They first obliged them to sweat themselves for the space of three days and nights, in a small green hut, made on purpose, at a considerable distance from any dwelling; through a scrupulous fear of contracting pollution by contact, or from the effluvia of polluted people—and a strong desire of secreting their religious mysteries. During that interval, they were allowed to eat nothing but green tobacco, nor to drink any thing except warm water, highly imbittered with the button-snake-root, to cleanse their bodies, and prepare them to serve in their holy, or beloved office, before the divine essence, whom during this preparation they constantly invoke by his essential name, as before described. After which, their priestly garments and ornaments, mentioned under a former argument, page 84, are put on, and then bear's oil is poured upon their head.—If they could procure olive, or palm oil, instead of bear's oil, doubtless they would prefer and use it in their sacred ceremonies; especially, as they are often destitute of their favourite bear's oil for domestic uses.

The Jewish women were so exceedingly addicted to anoint their faces and bodies, that they often preferred oil to the necessaries of life; the widow who addressed herself to Elisha, though she was in the most pinching straits, and wanted every thing else, yet had a pot of oil to anoint herself. This custom of anointing became universal, among the eastern nations. They were not satisfied with perfuming themselves with sweet oils and fine essences; but anointed birds—as in the ninth ode of Anacreon;

Tot unde nunc odores?
Huc advolans per auras,
Spirasque, depluisque;[126]

[123] The poet introduces two doves conversing together; one of which carried a letter to Bathyllus, the anointed beau; and the other wishes her much joy, for her perfumed wings that diffused such an agreeable smell around. And the same poet orders the painter to draw this Samian beau, with his hair wet with essence, to give him a fine appearance. Nitidas comas ejus facilto. Ode 29. Virgil describes Turnus, just after the same manner,

Vibratos calido ferro, myrrhaque madentes.
ÆNEID, l. 12.[127]

Homer tells us, that Telemachus and Philistratus anointed their whole bodies with essences, after they had visited the palace of Menelaus, and before they sat down at table. Odyss. l. 4.

The Jews reckoned it a singular piece of disrespect to their guest, if they offered him no oil. When any of them paid a friendly visit, they had essences presented to anoint their heads; to which custom of civility the Saviour alludes in his reproof of the parsimonious Pharisee, at whose house he dined. Luke vii. 46.

All the Indian Americans, especially the female sex, reckon their bear's oil or grease, very valuable, and use it after the same manner as the Asiatics did their fine essences and sweet perfumes; the young warriors and women are uneasy, unless their hair is always shining with it; which is probably the reason that none of their heads are bald. But enough is said on this head, to shew that they seem to have derived this custom from the east.[128]

ARGUMENT XI.

The Indians have customs consonant to the Mosaic LAWS OF UNCLEAN-NESS.[129] They oblige their women in their *lunar retreats,* to build small huts, at as considerable a distance from their dwelling-houses, as they imagine may be out of the enemies reach; where, during the space of that period, they are obliged to stay at the risque of their lives.[130] Should they be known to violate that ancient law, they must answer for every misfortune that befalls [124] any of the people, as a certain effect of the divine fire; though the lurking enemy sometimes kills them in their religious retirement. Notwithstanding they reckon it conveys a most horrid and dangerous pollution to those who touch, or go near them, or walk any where within the circle of their retreats; and are in fear of thereby spoiling the supposed purity and power of their holy ark, which they always carry to war; yet the enemy believe they can so cleanse themselves with the consecrated herbs, roots, &c. which the chieftain carries in the beloved war-ark, as to secure them in this point from bodily danger, because it was done against their enemies.

The non-observance of this separation, a breach of the marriage-law, and murder, they esteem the most capital crimes. When the time of the women's separation is ended, they always purify themselves in deep running water, return home, dress, and anoint themselves. They ascribe these monthly periods, to the female structure, not to the anger of *Ishtohoollo Aba.*

Correspondent to the Mosaic law of women's purification after *travel* [travail], the Indian women absent themselves from their husbands and all public company, for a considerable time.—The *Muskōhge* women are separate for three moons, exclusive of that moon in which they are delivered. By the Jewish law, women after a male-birth were forbidden to enter the temple; and even, the very touch of sacred things, forty days.—And after a female, the time of separation was doubled.

Should any of the Indian women violate this law of purity, they would be censured, and suffer for any sudden sickness, or death that might happen among the people, as the necessary effect of the divine anger for their polluting sin, contrary to their old traditional law of female purity. Like the greater part of the Israelites, it is the fear of temporal evils, and the prospect of temporal good, that makes them so tenacious and observant of their laws. At the stated period, the Indian womens impurity is finished by ablution, and they are again admitted to social and holy privileges.

By the Levitical law, the people who had *running issues,* or *sores,* were deemed unclean, and strictly ordered apart from the rest, for fear of polluting them; for every thing they touched became unclean. The Indians, in as strict a manner, observe the very same law; they follow the ancient [125] Israelitish copy so close, as to build a small hut at a considerable distance from the houses of the village, for every one of their warriors wounded in war, and confine them there, (as the Jewish lepers formerly were, without the walls of the city) for the space of four moons, including that moon in which they were wounded, as in the case of their women after travel [travail]: and they keep them strictly separate, lest the impurity of the one should prevent the cure of the other. The reputed prophet, or divine physician, daily pays them a due attendance, always invoking YO HE WAH to bless the means they apply on the sad occasion; which is chiefly mountain allum, and medicinal herbs, always injoyning a very abstemious life, prohibiting them women and salt in particular, during the time of the cure, or sanctifying the reputed sinners. Like the Israelites, they firmly believe that safety, or wounds, &c. immediately proceed from the pleased, or angry deity, for their virtuous, or vicious conduct, in observing, or violating the divine law.

In this long space of purification, each patient is allowed only a superannuated woman to attend him, who is past the temptations of sinning with men, lest the introduction of a young one should either seduce him to folly; or she having committed it with others—or by not observing her appointed time of living apart from the rest, might thereby defile the place, and totally prevent the cure. But what is yet more surprising in their physical, or rather theological regimen, is, that the physician is so religiously cautious of not admitting polluted persons to visit any of his patients, lest the defilement should retard the cure, or spoil the warriors, that before he introduces any man, even any of their priests, who are married according to the law, he obliges him to assert either by a double affirmative, or by two negatives, that he has not known even his own wife, in the space of the last natural day. This law of purity was peculiar to the Hebrews, to deem those unclean who cohabited with their wives, till they purified themselves in clean water. Now as the heathen world observed no such law, it seems that the primitive Americans derived this religious custom also from divine precept; and that these ceremonial rites were originally copied from the Mosaic institution.

The Israelites became unclean only by *touching their dead,* for the space of seven days; and the high-priest was prohibited to come near the dead. 'Tis much the same with the Indians to this day. To prevent pollution, when the sick person is past hope of recovery, they [126] dig a grave, prepare the tomb, anoint his hair, and paint his face; and when his breath ceases, they hasten the remaining funeral preparations, and soon bury the corpse. One of a different family will never, or very rarely pollute himself for a stranger; though when living, he would cheerfully hazard his life for his safety: the relations, who become unclean by performing the funeral duties, must live apart from the clean for several days, and be cleansed by some of their religious order, who chiefly apply the button-snake-root for their purification, as formerly described: then they purify themselves by ablution. After three days, the funeral assistants may convene at the town-house, and follow their usual diversions. But the relations live recluse a long time, mourning the dead.★

The Cheerake, notwithstanding they have corrupted most of their primitive customs, observe this law of purity in so strict a manner, as not to touch the corpse of their nearest relation though in the woods. The fear of pollution (not the want of natural affection, as the unskilful observe) keeps them also from burying their dead, in our reputed unsanctified ground, if any die as they are going to Charles-town, and returning home; because they are distant from their own holy places and holy things, where only they could perform the religious obsequies of their dead, and purify themselves according to law. An incident of this kind happened several years since, a little below *Ninety-six,* as well as at the Conggarees, in South-Carolina:—at the former place, the corpse by our humanity was interred; but at the latter, even the twin-born brother of an Indian christian lady well known by the name of the *Dark-lanthorn,*[131] left her dead and unburied.

The conversion of this *rara avis*[132] was in the following extraordinary manner.—There was a gentleman who married her according to the manner of the Cheeràke; but observing that marriages were commonly of a short [127] duration in that wanton female government, he flattered himself of ingrossing her affections, could he be so happy as to get her sanctified by one of our own beloved men with a large quantity of holy water in baptism—and be taught the conjugal duty, by virtue of her new christian name, when they were married a-new. As she was no stranger in the English settlements, he soon persuaded her to go down to the Conggarees, to get the beloved speech, and many fine things beside. As the priest was one of those sons of wisdom, the church sent us in her maternal benevolence, both to keep and draw us from essential errors, he readily knew the value of a convert, and grasping at the opportunity, he changed her from a wild savage to a believing christian in a trice.

He asked her a few articles of her creed, which were soon answered by

---

★One of the Cheeràke traders, who now resides in the Choktah country, assures me, that a little before the commencement of the late war with the Cheerake, when the *Buck,* a native of Nuquòse-town, died, none of the warriors would help to bury him, because of the dangerous pollution, they imagined they should necessarily contract from such a white corpse; as he was begotten by a white man and a half-breed Cheerake woman—and as the women are only allowed to mourn for the death of a warrior, they could not assist in this friendly duty. By much solicitation, the gentleman (my author) obtained the help of an old friendly half-bred-warrior. They interred the corpse; but the savage became unclean, and was separate from every kind of communion with the rest, for the space of three days.

the bridegroom, as interpreter, from some words she spoke on a trifling question he asked her. When the priest proposed to her a religious question, the bridegroom, by reason of their low ideas, and the idiom of their dialects, was obliged to mention some of the virtues, and say he recommended to her a very strict chastity in the married state. "Very well, said she, that's a good speech, and fit for every woman alike, unless she is very old—But what says he now?" The interpreter, after a short pause, replied, that he was urging her to use a proper care in domestic life. "You evil spirit, said she, when was I wasteful, or careless at home?" He replied, "never": "Well then, said she, tell him his speech is troublesome and light.—But, first, where are those fine things you promised me?" He bid her be patient a little, and she should have plenty of every thing she liked best; at this she smiled. Now the religious man was fully confirmed in the hope of her conversion; however, he asked if she understood, and believed that needful article, the doctrine of the trinity. The bridegroom swore heartily, that if he brought out all the other articles of his old book, she both knew and believed them, for she was a sensible young woman.

The bridegroom had a very difficult part to act, both to please the humour of his Venus, and to satisfy the inquisitive temper of our religious son of Apollo; he behaved pretty well however, till he was desired to ask her belief of the uni-trinity, and tri-unity of the deity; which the beloved man endeavoured to explain. On this, she smartly asked him the subject of their long and crooked-like discourse. But, as his patience was now exhausted [128], instead of answering her question, he said with a loud voice, that he believed the religious man had picked out all the crabbed parts of his old book, only to puzzle and stagger her young christian faith; otherwise how could he desire him to persuade such a sharp-discerning young woman, that one was three, and three, one? Besides, that if his book had any such question, it belonged only to the deep parts of arithmetic, in which the very Indian beloved men were untaught. He assured the priest, that the Indians did not mind what religion the women were of, or whether they had any; and that the bride would take it very kindly, if he shortened his discourse, as nothing can disturb the Indian women so much as long lectures.

The *Dark-lanthorn,* (which was the name of the bride) became very uneasy, both by the delay of time, and the various passions she attentively read in the bridegroom's face and speech, and she asked him sharply the meaning of such a long discourse. He instantly cried out, that the whole affair was spoiled, unless it was brought to a speedy conclusion: but the religious man insisted upon her belief of that article, before he could proceed any farther. But by way of comfort, he assured him it should be the very last question he would propose, till he put the holy water on her face, and read over the marriage ceremony. The bridegroom revived at this good news, immediately sent the bowl around, with a cheerful countenance; which the bride observing, she asked him the reason of his sudden joyful looks.—But, what with the length of the lecture, the close application of the bowl, and an over-joy of soon obtaining his wishes, he proposed the wrong question; for instead of asking her belief of the mysterious union of the tri-une deity, he only mentioned the manly faculties of nature. The bride smiled, and asked if the beloved man borrowed that speech from his beloved marriage-book? Or whether he was married, as he was so waggish, and knowing in those affairs.—The priest imagining her cheerful looks proceeded from her swallowing his doctrine, immediately called for a bowl of water to initiate his new convert. As the bridegroom could not mediate with his usual friendly offices in this affair, he persuaded her to let the beloved man put some beloved water on her face, and it would be a sure pledge of a lasting friendship between her and the English, and intitle her to every thing she liked best. By the persuasive force of his promises, she consented: and had the constancy, though so ignorant a [129] novitiate in our sacred mysteries, to go through her catechism, and the long marriage ceremony,—although it was often interrupted by the bowl. This being over, she proceeded to go to bed with her partner, while the beloved man sung a psalm at the door, concerning the fruitful vine. Her name he soon entered in capital letters, to grace the first title-page of his church book of converts; which he often shewed to his English sheep, and with much satisfaction would inform them how, by the co-operation of the Deity, his earnest endeavours changed an Indian *Dark-lanthorn* into a lamp of christian light. However, afterward to his great grief, he was obliged on account of her adulteries, to erase her name from thence, and enter it anew in some of the crowded pages of female delinquents.

When an Israelite died in any house or tent, all who were in it, and the furniture belonging to it contracted a pollution, which continued for seven days. All likewise who touched the body of a dead person, or his grave, were impure for seven days. Similar notions prevail among the Indians. The Choktah are so exceedingly infatuated in favour of the infallible judgment of their pretended prophets, as to allow them without the least regret, to dislocate the necks of any of their sick who are in a weak state of body, to put them out of their pain, when they presume to reveal the determined will of the Deity to shorten his days, which is asserted to be communicated in a dream;[133] by the time that this theo-physical operation is performed on a patient, they have a scaffold prepared opposite to the door, whereon he is to lie till they remove the bones in the fourth moon after, to the remote bone-house of that family: they immediately carry out the corpse, mourn over it, and place it in that dormitory, which is strongly pallisadoed around, lest the children should become polluted even by passing under the dead.

Formerly when the owner of a house died, they set fire to it, and to all the provisions of every kind; or sold the whole at a cheap rate to the trading people, without paying the least regard to the scarcity of the times. Many of them still observe the same rule, through a wild imitation of a ceremonial observance of the Israelites, in burning the bed whereon a dead person lay, because of its impurity. This is no copy from the ancient heathens, but from the Hebrews. [130]

ARGUMENT XII.

Like the Jews, the greatest part of the southern Indians *abstain* from most things that are either in themselves, or in the general apprehension of mankind, loathsome, or *unclean:* where we find a deviation from that general rule among any of them, it is a corruption—either owing to their intercourse with Europeans, or having contracted an ill habit from necessity. They generally affix very vicious ideas to the eating of impure things; and all their prophets, priests, old warriors and war-chieftains, before they enter on their religious duties, and while they are engaged in them, observe the strictest abstinence in this point. Formerly, if any of them did eat in white people's houses, or even of what had been dressed there, while they were sanctifying themselves, it was deemed a dangerous sin of pollution. When some of them first corrupted their primitive virtue, by drinking of our spirituous liquors, the religious spectators called it *ooka hoome,* "bitter waters;" alluding, I conjecture, to the bitter waters of jealousy, that produced swelling and death to those who committed adultery, but had no power over the innocent. That this name is not accidental, but designedly pointed, and expressive of the bitter waters of God, seems obvious, not only from the image they still retain of them, but likewise when any of them refuse our invitation of drinking spirituous liquors in company with us, they say *Ahiskòla Awa, Ooka Hoomeh Iishto,* "I will not drink, they are the bitter waters of the great One." Though *Ishto,* one of the names of God, subjoined to nouns, denotes a superlative degree, in this case they deviate from that general rule—and for this reason they never affix the idea of bitter to the spirituous liquors we drink among them. *Hoomeh* is the only word they have to convey the meaning of bitter; as *Aneh Hoomeh,* "bitter ears," or pepper.

They reckon all birds of prey, and birds of night, to be unclean, and unlawful to be eaten. Not long ago, when the Indians were making their winter's hunt, and the old women were without flesh-meat at home, I shot a small fat hawk, and desired one of them to take and dress it; but though I strongly importuned her by way of trial, she, as earnestly refused it for [131] fear of contracting pollution, which she called the "accursed sickness," supposing disease would be the necessary effect of such an impurity. Eagles of every kind they esteem unclean food; likewise ravens (though the name of a tribe with them) crows, buzzards, swallows, bats, and every species of owls: and they believe that swallowing flies, musketoes, or gnats, always breeds sickness, or worms, according to the quantity that goes into them; which though it may not imply extraordinary skill in physic, shews their retention of the ancient law, which prohibited the swallowing of flies: for to this that divine sarcasm alludes, "swallowing a camel, and straining at a gnat." Such insects were deemed unclean, as well as vexatious and hurtful. The God of Ekron was *Beelzebub,* or the God and ruler of flies.

None of them will eat of any animal whatsoever, if they either know, or suspect that it died of itself. I lately asked one of the women the reason of throwing a dung-hill-fowl[134] out of doors, on the corn-house; she said, that she was afraid, *Oophe Abeeka Hakset Illeh,* "it died with the distemper of the mad dogs," and that if she had eaten it, it would have affected her in the very same manner. I said, if so, she did well to save herself from danger, but at the same time, it seemed she had forgotten the cats. She replied, "that such impure animals would not contract the accursed sickness, on account of any evil thing they eat; but that the people who ate of the flesh of the swine that fed on such polluting food, would certainly become mad."

In the year 1766, a madness seized the wild beasts in the remote woods of West-Florida, and about the same time the domestic dogs were attacked with the like distemper; the deer were equally infected.[135] The Indians in their winter's hunt, found several lying dead, some in a helpless condition, and others fierce and mad. But though they are all fond of increasing their number of deer-skins, both from emulation and for profit, yet none of them durst venture to slay them, lest they should pollute themselves, and thereby incur bodily evils. The head-man of the camp told me, he cautioned one of the *Hottuk Hakse,* who had resided a long time at Savannah, from touching such deer, saying to him *Chehaksinna,* "Do not become vicious and mad," for *Isse Hakset Illehtàhah,* "the deer were mad, and are dead;" adding, that if he acted the part of *Hakse,* he would cause both himself, [132] and the rest of the hunting camp to be spoiled; nevertheless he shut his ears against his honest speech, and brought those dangerous deer-skins to camp. But the people would not afterward associate with him; and he soon paid dear for being *Hakse,* by a sharp splintered root of a cane running almost through his foot, near the very place where he first polluted himself; and he was afraid some worse ill was still in wait for him.

In 1767, the Indians were struck with a disease, which they were unacquainted with before. It began with sharp pains in the head, at the lower part of each of the ears, and swelled the face and throat in a very extraordinary manner, and also the testicles. It continued about a fortnight, and in the like space of time went off gradually, without any dangerous consequence, or use of outward or inward remedies: they called it *Wahka Abeeka,* "the cattle's distemper," or sickness.[136] Some of their young men had by stealth killed and eaten a few of the cattle which the traders had brought up, and they imagined they had thus polluted themselves, and were smitten in that strange manner, by having their heads, necks, &c. magnified like the same parts of a sick bull. They first concluded, either to kill all the cattle, or send them immediately off their land, to prevent the like mischief, or greater ills from befalling the beloved people—for their cunning old physicians or prophets would not undertake to cure them, in order to inflame the people to execute the former resolution; being jealous of encroachments, and afraid the cattle would spoil their open corn-fields; upon which account, the traders arguments had no weight with these red Hebrew philosophers. But fortunately, one of their head warriors had a few cattle soon presented to him, to keep off the wolf; and his reasoning proved so weighty, as to alter their resolution, and produce in them a contrary belief.

They reckon all those animals to be unclean, that are either carnivorous, or live on nasty food; as hogs, wolves, panthers, foxes, cats, mice, rats. And if we except the bear, they deem all beasts of prey unhallowed, and polluted food; all amphibious quadrupeds they rank in the same class. Our old traders remember when they first began the custom of eating beavers: and to this day none eat of them, except those who kill [133] them; though the flesh is very wholesome, on account of the bark of trees they live upon. It must be acknowledged, they are all degenerating apace, insomuch, that the Choktah Indians, on account of their scantiness of ammunition while they traded with the French, took to eat horse-flesh, and even snakes of every kind; though each of these species, and every sort of reptiles, are accounted by the other neighbouring nations, impure food in the highest degree. And they ridicule the Choktah for their cannibal apostacy, and term them in common speech, "the evil, ugly, Choktah."

They abhor moles so exceedingly, that they will not allow their children even to touch them, for fear of hurting their eye-sight; reckoning it contagious. They believe that nature is possest of such a property, as to transfuse into men and animals the qualities, either of the food they use, or of those objects that are presented to their senses; he who feeds on venison, is according to their physical system, swifter and more sagacious than the man who lives on the flesh of the clumsy bear, or helpless dunghill fowls, the slow-footed tame cattle, or the heavy wallowing swine. This is the reason that several of their old men recommend, and say, that formerly their greatest chieftains observed a constant rule in their diet, and seldom ate of any animal of a gross quality, or heavy motion of body, fancying it conveyed a dullness through the whole system, and disabled them from exerting themselves with proper vigour in their martial, civil, and religious duties.

I have already shewn their aversion to eating of unsanctified fruits; and in this argument, that they abstain from several other things, contrary to the usage of all the old heathen world. It may be objected, that now they seldom refuse to eat hogs flesh, when the traders invite them to it; but this proceeds entirely from vicious imitation, and which is common with the most civilized nations. When swine were first brought among them, they deemed it such a horrid abomination in any of their people to eat that filthy and impure food, that they excluded the criminal from all religious communion in their circular town-house, or in their quadrangular holy ground at the annual expiation of sins, equally as if he had eaten unsanctified fruits. After the yearly atonement was made at the temple, he was indeed re-admitted to his usual privileges. Formerly, none of their beloved [134] men, or warriors, would eat or drink with us on the most pressing invitation, through fear of polluting themselves, they deemed us such impure animals. Our eating the flesh of swine, and venison, with the gravy in it, helped to rivet their dislike, for this they reckon as blood.

I once asked the *Archimagus,* to sit down and partake of my dinner; but he excused himself, saying, he had in a few days some holy duty to perform, and that if he eat evil or accursed food, it would spoil him,—alluding to swine's flesh. Though most of their virtue hath lately been corrupted, in this particular they still affix vicious and contemptible ideas to the eating of swine's flesh; insomuch, that *Shúkàpa,* "swine eater," is the most opprobious epithet they can use to brand us with: they commonly subjoin *Akanggàpa,* "eater of dunghill fowls." Both together, signify "filthy, helpless animals." By our surprising mismanagement in allowing them a long time to insult, abuse, rob, and murder the innocent British subjects at pleasure, without the least satisfaction, all the Indian nations formerly despised the English, as a swarm of tame fowls, and termed them so, in their set speeches.

The Indians through a strong principle of religion, abstain in the strictest manner, from eating the BLOOD of any animal; as it contains the life, and spirit of the beast, and was the very essence of the sacrifices that were to be offered up for sinners. And this was the Jewish opinion and law of sacrifice, Lev. xvii. 11. "for the life of the flesh is in the blood, and I have given it to you upon the altar, to make an atonement for your souls; for it is the blood, which maketh an atonement for the soul." When the English traders have been making sausages mixt with hog's blood, I have observed the Indians to cast their eyes upon them, with the horror of their reputed fore-fathers, when they viewed the predicted abomination of desolation, fulfilled by Antiochus, in defiling the temple.

An instance lately happened, which sufficiently shews their utter aversion to blood. A Chikkesah woman, a domestic of one of the traders, being very ill with a complication of disorders, the Indian physician seemed to use his best endeavours to cure her, but without the least visible effect. [135] To preserve his medical credit with the people, he at last ascribed her ailment to the eating of swine's flesh, blood, and other polluting food: and said, that such an ugly, or accursed sickness, overcame the power of all his beloved songs, and physic; and in anger, he left his supposed criminal patient to be punished by Loak Ishtohoollo. I asked her some time afterwards, what her ailments were, and what she imagined might have occasioned them? She said, she was full of pain, that she had *Abeeka Ookproo,* "the accursed sickness," because she had eaten a great many fowls after the manner of the white people, with the *Issish Ookproo,* "accursed blood," in them. In time she recovered, and now strictly abstains from tame fowls, unless they are bled to death, for fear of incurring future evil, by the like pollution.

There is not the least trace among their ancient traditions, of their deserving the hateful name of cannibals, as our credulous writers have carefully copied from each other. Their taste is so opposite to that of the Anthrophagi, that they always over-dress their meat whether roasted or boiled.

The Muskoghe who have been at war, time out of mind, against the Indians of Cape-Florida, and at length reduced them to thirty men, who removed to the Havannah along with the Spaniards;[137] affirm, they could never be informed by their captives, of the least inclination they ever had of eating human flesh, only the heart of the enemy—which they all do, sympathetically (blood for blood) in order to inspire them with courage; and yet the constant losses they suffered, might have highly provoked them to exceed their natural barbarity. To eat the heart of an enemy will in their opinion, like eating other things, before mentioned, communicate and give greater heart against the enemy. They also think that the vigorous faculties of the mind are derived from the brain, on which account, I have seen some of their heroes drink out of a human skull; they imagine, they only imbibe the good qualities it formerly contained.

When speaking to the *Archimagus* concerning the Hottentots, those heterogeneous animals according to the Portuguese and Dutch accounts, he asked me, whether they builded and planted—and what sort of food they [136] chiefly lived upon. I told him, I was informed that they dwelt in small nasty huts, and lived chiefly on sheep's guts and crickets. He laughed, and said there was no credit to be given to the far-distant writers of those old books, because they might not have understood the language and customs of the people; but that those, whom our books reported to live on such nasty food, (if they did not deceive us) might have been forced to it for the want of better, to keep them from dying; or by the like occasion, they might have learned that ugly custom, and could not quit it when they were free from want, as the Choktah eat horse-flesh, though they have plenty of venison: however, it was very easy, he said, to know whether they were possessed of human reason, for if they were endued with shame to have a desire of covering their nakedness, he concluded them to be human. He then asked me, whether I had been informed of their having any sort of language, or method of counting as high as the number of their fingers, either by words or expressive motion; or of bearing a nearer resemblance to *Yáwe,* the human creature, in laughter, than *Shawe* the ape bore; or of being more social and gregarious than those animals of the country where they lived. If they were endued with those properties, he affirmed them to be human creatures; and that such old lying books should not be credited.

The more religious, or the least corrupted, of the various remote Indian nations, will not eat of any young beast when it is newly yeaned; and their old men think they would suffer damage, even by the bare contact: which seems to be derived from the Mosaic law, that prohibited such animals to be offered up, or eaten, till they were eight days old; because, till then, they were in an imperfect and polluted state! They appear, however, to be utterly ignorant of the design and meaning of this appointment and practice, as well as of some other customs and institutions. But as the time of circumcising the Israelitish children was founded on this law of purity, it seems probable, that the American Aborigines observed the law of circumcision, for some time after they arrived here, and desisted from it, when it became incompatible with the hard daily toils and sharp exercises, which necessity must have forced them to pursue, to support life: especially when we consider, that the sharpest and most lasting affront, the most opprobious, indelible epithet, with which one Indian can possibly brand another, is to call him in public company, *Hoobuk Waske,* Eunuchus, præputio detecto.[138] They resent it so highly, that in the year [137] 1750, when the Cheerakee were on the point of commencing a war against us, several companies of the northern Indians, in concert with them, compelled me in the lower Cheerakee town to write to the government of South-Carolina, that they made it their earnest request to the English not to mediate in their war with the Katáhba Indians, as they were fully resolved to prosecute it, with the greatest eagerness, while there was one of that hateful name alive;[139] because in the time of battle, they had given them the ugly name of short-tailed eunuchs. Now as an eunuch was a contemptible name with the Israelites, and none of them could serve in any religious office; it should seem that the Indians derived this opprobious and singular epithet from Jewish tradition, as castration was never in use among the ancient or present Americans.

The Israelites were but forty years in the wilderness, and would not have renewed the painful act of circumcision, only that Joshua inforced it: and by the necessary fatigues and difficulties, to which as already hinted, the primitive Americans must be exposed at their first arrival in this waste and extensive wilderness, it is likely they forbore circumcision, upon the divine principle extended to their supposed predecessors in the wilderness, of not accepting sacrifice at the expence of mercy. This might soothe them after-wards wholly to reject it as a needless duty, especially if any of the eastern heathens accompanied them in their travels in quest of freedom. And as it is probable, that by the time they reached America, they had worn out their knives and every other sharp instrument fit for the occasion; so had they performed the operation with flint-stones, or sharp splinters, there is no doubt that each of the mothers would have likewise said, "This day, thou art to me a bloody husband★." However, from the contemptible idea the Americans fix to castration, &c. it seems very probable the more religious among them used circumcision in former ages.[140]

Under this argument, I must observe that *Ai-ú-be* signifies "the thigh" of any animal; and *E-ee-pattáh Tekále,* "the lower part of the thigh," or literally, "the hanging of the foot." And when in the woods, the Indians cut a small piece out of the lower part of the thighs of the deer they kill, length-ways and pretty deep. Among the great number of venison-hams they bring to our trading houses, I do not remember to [138] have observed one without it; from which I conjecture, that as every ancient custom was designed to convey, either a typical, or literal instructive lesson of some useful thing; and as no usage of the old heathen world resembled this custom; it seems strongly to point at Jacob's wrestling with an angel, and obtaining for him-self and his posterity, the name, ישר-אל, (perhaps, *Yosher-ale*) "divine guide," or "one who prevails with the omnipotent," and to the children of Israel not eating the sinew of the thigh of any animal, to perpetuate the memory of their ancestor's sinew being shrunk, which was to obtain the blessing.

The Indians always sew their maccasenes with deer's sinews, though of a sharp cutting quality, for they reckon them more fortunate than the wild hemp: but to eat such, they imagine would breed worms, and other ail-ments, in proportion to the number they eat. And I have been assured by a gentleman of character, who is now an inhabitant of South-Carolina, and well acquainted with the customs of the northern Indians, that they also cut a piece out of the thigh of every deer they kill, and throw it away; and reckon it such a dangerous pollution to eat it, as to occasion sickness and other misfortunes of sundry kinds, especially by spoiling their guns from shooting with proper force and direction. Now as none of the old heathens had such a custom, must it not be considered as of Israelitish extraction?

ARGUMENT XIII.

The Indian MARRIAGES, DIVORCES, and PUNISHMENTS of adultery, still re-tain a strong likeness to the Jewish laws and customs in these points.

The Hebrews had sponsalia de presenti, and sponsalia de futuro:[141] a con-

★Exod. iv. 25, 26.

siderable time generally intervened between their contract and marriage: and their nuptial ceremonies were celebrated in the night. The Indians observe the same customs to this day; insomuch, that it is usual for an elderly man to take a girl, or sometimes a child to be his wife, because she is capable of receiving good impressions in that tender state: frequently, a moon elapses after the contract is made, and the value received, before [139] the bridegroom sleeps with the bride, and on the marriage day, he does not appear before her till night introduces him, and then without tapers.

The grandeur of the Hebrews consisted pretty much in the multiplicity of their wives to attend them, as a showy retinue: as the meaner sort could not well purchase one, they had a light sort of marriage suitable to their circumstances, called by the scholiasts, *usu capio;*[142] "taking the woman for present use." When they had lived together about a year, if agreeable, they parted good friends by mutual consent. The Indians also are so fond of variety, that they ridicule the white people, as a tribe of narrow-hearted, and dull constitutioned animals, for having only one wife at a time; and being bound to live with and support her, though numberless circumstances might require a contrary conduct. When a young warrior cannot dress *alamode America,* he strikes up one of those matches for a few moons, which they term *Toopsa Tǎwah,* "a make haste marriage," because it wants the usual ceremonies, and duration of their other kind of marriages.

The friendliest kind of marriage among the Hebrews, was eating bread together. The bridegroom put a ring on the fourth finger of the bride's left hand before two witnesses, and said, "Be thou my wife, according to the law of Moses." Her acceptance and silence implying consent, confirmed her part of the marriage contract, because of the rigid modesty of the eastern women. When the short marriage contract was read over, he took a cake of bread and broke it in two, for himself and her; or otherwise, he put some corn between their hands: which customs were used as strong emblems of the necessity of mutual industry and concord, to obtain present and future happiness. When an Indian makes his first address to the young woman he intends to marry, she is obliged by ancient custom to sit by him till he hath done eating and drinking, whether she likes or dislikes him; but afterward, she is at her own choice whether to stay or retire★.

When the bridegroom marries the bride, after the usual prelude, he takes a choice ear of corn, and divides it in two before witnesses, gives her one half in her hand, and keeps the other half to himself; or otherwise, [140] he

★Cant. iii. 4. I held him and would not let him go, until I had brought him to my father's house, and into the chambers of her that conceived me: See Gen. xxiv. 67. Such was the custom of the Hebrews.

gives her a deer's foot, as an emblem of the readiness with which she ought to serve him: in return, she presents him with some cakes of bread, thereby declaring her domestic care and gratitude in return for the offals; for the men feast by themselves, and the women eat the remains. When this short ceremony is ended, they may go to bed like an honest couple.

Formerly, this was an universal custom among the native Americans; but this, like every other usage of theirs, is wearing out apace. The West-Floridans, in order to keep their women subject to the law of adultery, bring some venison or buffalo's flesh to the house of their nominal wives, at the end of every winter's hunt: that is reckoned a sufficient annual tye of their former marriages, although the husbands do not cohabit with them. The Muskóhge men, if newly married, are obliged by ancient custom, to get their own relations to hoe out the corn-fields of each of their wives, that their marriages may be confirmed: and the more jealous, repeat the custom every year, to make their wives subject to the laws against adultery. But the Indians in general, reckon that before the bridegroom can presume to any legal power over the bride, he is after the former ceremonies, or others something similar, obliged to go into the woods to kill a deer, bring home the carcass of venison, and lay it down at her house wrapt up in its skin; and if she opens the pack, carries it into the house, and then dresses and gives him some of it to eat with cakes before witnesses, she becomes his lawful wife, and obnoxious to all the penalties of an adultress.

The Hebrews had another sort of marriage—by purchase: the bride-groom gave the father of the bride as much as he thought she was worth: and according to the different valuation, so sooner or later she went off at market. The only way to know the merit of a Hebrew lady, was to enquire the value for which her father would sell her, and the less rapacious he was, the sooner she might get an husband. Divine writ abounds with instances of the like kind; as Gen. xxxiv. 12. "Ask me never so much dowry and I will give it." David bought Michal, and Jacob dearly purchased Rachel, &c. The women brought nothing with them, except their clothes, rings and bracelets, and a few trinkets. When the Indians would express a proper mar-riage, they have a word adapted according to their various dialects, to give them a suitable idea of it; but when they are [141] speaking of their sensual marriage bargains, they always term it, "buying a woman;" for example— they say with regard to the former, *Che-Awalas,* "I shall marry you," the last syllable denotes the first person of the future tense, the former, "I shall make you, as *Awa,* or *Hewa* was to *Ish,*" which is confirmed by a strong nega-tive similar expression, *Che-Awala Awa,* "I shall not marry you." But the name of their market marriages, is *Otoolpha, Eho Achumbàras, Saookchàa,* "In the spring, I shall buy a woman, if I am alive." Or *Eho Achumbàra Awa,* "I shall not buy a woman," *Sàlbasa toogat,* "for indeed I am poor:" the former usage, and method of language is exactly calculated to express that singular custom of the Hebrews, per coemptionem.[143]

They sometimes marry by deputation or proxy. The intended bride-groom sends so much in value to the nearest relations of the intended bride, as he thinks she is worth: if they are accepted, it is a good sign that her relations approve of the match, but she is not bound by their contract alone; her consent must likewise be obtained, but persuasions most commonly prevail with them. However, if the price is reckoned too small, or the goods too few, the law obliges them to return the whole, either to himself, or some of his nearest kindred. If they love the goods, as they term it, according to the like method of expression with the Hebrews, the loving couple may in a short time bed together upon trial, and continue or discontinue their love according as their fancy directs them. If they like each other, they become an honest married couple when the nuptial ceremony is performed, as already described. When one of their chieftains is married, several of his kinsmen help to kill deer and buffalos, to make a rejoicing marriage feast, to which their relations and neighbours are invited: there the young warriors sing with their two chief musicians, who beat on their wet deer skin tied over the mouth of a large clay-pot, and raise their voices, singing *Yo Yo,* &c. When they are tired with feasting, dancing, and singing the Epithalamium, they depart with friendly glad hearts, from the house of praise.

If an Israelite lay with a bond woman betrothed, and not redeemed, she was to be beaten, but not her fellow criminal; for in the original text, Lev. xix. 20. the word is in the fœminine gender. When offenders were beaten, they were bowed down, as Deut. xxv. 2.—so that they [142] neither sat nor stood, and their whip had a large knot to it, which commanded the thongs, so as to expand, or contract them; the punishment was always to be suited to the nature of the crime, and the constitution of the criminal. While the offenders were under the lash, three judges stood by to see that they received their full and just due. The first repeated the words of Deut. xxviii. 58. the second counted the stripes, and the third said, "Hack, or lay on." The offender received three lashes on the breast, three on the belly, three on each shoulder, &c. But adultery was attended with capital punishment, as Deut. xxii. 22. The parties when legally detected, were tried by the lesser judicatory, which was to consist, at least of twenty-three: the Sanhedrim gave the bitter waters to those women who were suspected of adultery. The former were stoned to death; and the latter burst open, according to their imprecation, if they were guilty: the omnipotent divine wisdom impressed those waters with that wonderful quality, contrary to the common course of nature. The men married, and were divorced as often as their caprice directed them; for if they imagined their wives did not value them, according to their own partial opinion of themselves, they notified the occasion of the dislike, in a small billet, that her virtue might not be suspected: and when they gave any of them the ticket, they ate together in a very civil manner, and thus dissolved the contract.

I have premised this, to trace the resemblance to the marriage divorces and punishments of the savage Americans.[144] The middle aged people of a place, which lies about half-way to Mobille, and the Illinois, assure us, that they remember when adultery was punished among them with death, by shooting the offender with barbed arrows, as there are no stones there. But what with the losses of their people at war with the French and their savage confederates, and the constitutional wantonness of their young men and women, they have through a political desire of continuing, or increasing their numbers, moderated the severity of that law, and reduced it to the present standard of punishment; which is in the following manner. If a married woman is detected in adultery by one person, the evidence is deemed good in judgment against her; the evidence of a well grown boy or girl, they even reckon sufficient, because of the heinousness of the crime, and the difficulty of discovering it in their thick forests. This is a corruption of the Mosaic law, which required two evidences, and exempted both women [143] and slaves from public faith; because of the reputed fickleness of the one, and the base, groveling temper of the other. When the crime is proved against the woman, the enraged husband accompanied by some of his relations, surprises and beats her most barbarously, and then cuts off her hair and nose, or one of her lips. There are many of that sort of disfigured females among the Chikkasah, and they are commonly the best featured, and the most tempting of any of their country-women, which exposed them to the snares of young men. But their fellow-criminals, who probably first tempted them, are partially exempted from any kind of corporal punishment.

With the Muskohge Indians, it was formerly reckoned adultery, if a man took a pitcher of water off a married woman's head, and drank of it. But their law said, if he was a few steps apart, and she at his request set it down, and retired a little way off, be might then drink without exposing her to any danger. If we seriously reflect on the rest of their native customs, this old law, so singular to themselves from the rest of the world, gives us room to think they drew it from the Jewish bitter waters that were given to real, or suspected adulteresses, either to prove their guilt, or attest their innocence.

Among those Indians, when adultery is discovered, the offending parties commonly set off speedily for the distant woods, to secure themselves from the shameful badge of the sharp penal law, which they inevitably get, if they can be taken before the yearly offering for the atonement of sin; afterward, every crime except murder is forgiven. But they are always pursued, and frequently overtaken; though perhaps, three or four moons absent, and two hundred miles off, over hills and mountains, up and down many creeks and rivers, on contrary courses, and by various intricate windings—the pursuers are eager, and their hearts burn within them for revenge. When the husband has the chilling news first whispered in his ear, he steals off with his witness to some of his kinsmen, to get them to assist him in revenging his injury: they are soon joined by a sufficient number of the same family, if the criminal was not of the same tribe; otherwise, he chuses to confide in his nearest relations. When the witness has asserted to them the truth of his evidence by a strong asseveration, they separate to avoid suspicion, and meet commonly in the dusk of the evening, near the town of the adulterer, [144] where each of them provides a small hoop-pole, tapering to the point, with knobs half an inch long, (allowed by ancient custom) with which they correct the sinners; for as their law in this case doth not allow partiality, if they punished one of them, and either excused or let the other escape from justice, like the Illinois, they would become liable to such punishment as they had inflicted upon either of the parties.

They commonly begin with the adulterer, because of the two, he is the more capable of making his escape: they generally attack him at night, by surprise, lest he should make a desperate resistance, and blood be shed to cry for blood. They fall on eager and merciless, whooping their revengeful noise, and thrashing their captive, with their long-knobbed hoop-flails; some over his head and face; others on his shoulders and back. His belly, sides, legs, and arms, are gashed all over, and at last, he happily seems to be insensible of pain: then they cut off his ears★.

★Among these Indians, the trading people's ears are often in danger, by the sharpness of this law, and their suborning false witnesses, or admitting foolish children as legal evidence; but generally either the tender-hearted females or friends, give them timely notice of their danger. Then they fall to the rum-keg,—and as soon as they find the pursuers approaching, they stand to arms in a threatning parade. Formerly, the traders like so many British tars, kept them in proper awe, and consequently prevented them from attempting any mischief. But since the patenteed race of Daublers set foot in their land, they have gradually become worse every year, murdering valuable innocent British subjects at pleasure: and when they go down, they receive presents as a tribute of fear, for which these Indians upbraid, and threaten us. The Muskohge lately clipt off the ears of two white men for supposed adultery.[145] One had been a disciple of *Black Beard,* the pirate; and the other, at the time of going under the hands of those Jewish clippers, was deputed by the whimsical war-governor of Georgia, to awe the traders into an obedience of his despotic power. His successor lost his life on the Chikkasah war-path, twenty miles above the Koosah, or uppermost western town of the Muskohge, in an attempt to arrest the traders; which should not by any means be undertaken in the Indian country.

They observe, however, a gradation of punishment, according to the criminality of the adulteress. For the first breach of the marriage faith, they crop her ears and hair, if the husband is spiteful: either of those badges proclaim her to be a whore, or *Hakse Kaneha,* "such as were evil in Canaan," for the hair of their head is their ornament: when loose it commonly reaches below their back; and when tied, it stands below the crown of the head, about four inches long, and two broad. As the [145] offender cuts a comical figure among the rest of the women, by being trimmed so sharp, she always keeps her dark winter hot house, till by keeping the hair moistened with grease, it grows so long as to bear tying. Then she accustoms herself to the light by degrees; and soon some worthless fellow, according to their standard, buys her for his *And;* which term hath been already explained.

The adulterer's ears are slashed off close to his head, for the first act of adultery, because he is the chief in fault. If the criminals repeat the crime with any other married persons, their noses and upper lips are cut off. But the third crime of the like nature, is attended with more danger; for their law says, that for public heinous crimes, satisfaction should be made visible to the people, and adequate to the injuries of the virtuous,—to set their aggrieved hearts at ease, and prevent others from following such a dangerous crooked copy. As they will not comply with their mitigated law of adultery, nor be terrified, nor shamed from their ill course of life; that the one may not frighten and abuse their wives, nor the other seduce their husbands and be a lasting plague and shame to the whole society, they are ordered by their ruling magi and war-chieftains, to be shot to death, which is accordingly executed: but this seldom happens.

When I asked the Chikkasah the reason of the inequality of their marriage-law, in punishing the weaker passive party, and exempting the stronger, contrary to reason and justice; they told me, it had been so a considerable time—because their land being a continual seat of war, and the lurking enemy for ever pelting them without, and the women decoying them within, if they put such old cross laws of marriage in force, all their beloved brisk warriors would soon be spoiled, and their habitations turned to a wild waste. It is remarkable, that the ancient Egyptians cut off the ears and nose of the adulteress; and the prophet alludes to this sort of punishment, Ezek. xxiii. 25. "They shall deal furiously with thee: they shall take away thy nose and thine ears." And they gave them also a thousand stripes, with canes on the buttocks★. The Cheerake are an exception to all civilized or savage nations, in having no laws against adultery; they [146] have been

★When human laws were first made, they commanded that if the husband found the adulterer in the fact, he should kill them both. Thus the laws of Solon and Draco ordained: but the law of the twelve tables softened it.

a considerable while under petticoat-government, and allow their women full liberty to plant their brows with horns as oft as they please, without fear of punishment. On this account their marriages are ill observed, and of a short continuance; like the Amazons, they divorce their fighting bed-fellows at their pleasure, and fail not to execute their authority, when their fancy directs them to a more agreeable choice. However, once in my time a number of warriors, belonging to the family of the husband of the adulteress, revenged the injury committed by her, in her own way; for they said, as she loved a great many men, instead of a husband, justice told them to gratify her longing desire—wherefore, by the information of their spies, they followed her into the woods a little way from the town, (as decency required) and then stretched her on the ground, with her hands tied to a stake, and her feet also extended, where upwards of fifty of them lay with her, having a blanket for a covering. The Choktah observe the same savage custom with adulteresses. They term their female delinquents, *Ahowwe Ishto;* the first is a Cheerake word, signifying, "a deer."—And through contempt of the Chikkasah, they altered their penal law of adultery.

The Muskohge Indians, either through the view of mitigating their law against adultery, that it might be adapted to their patriarchal-like government; or by misunderstanding the Mosaic precept, from length of time, and uncertainty of oral tradition, oblige the adulteress under the penalty of the severest law not to be free with any man, (unless she is inclined to favour her fellow sufferer) during the space of four moons, after the broken moon in which they suffered for each other, according to the custom of the Maldivians. But her husband exposes himself to the utmost severity of the marriage law, if he is known to hold a familiar intercourse with her after the time of her punishment.

ARGUMENT XIV.

Many other of the INDIAN PUNISHMENTS, resemble those of the Jews. Whosoever attentively views the features of the Indian, and his eye, and [147] reflects on his fickle, obstinate, and cruel disposition, will naturally think on the Jews. English America, feelingly knows the parity of the temper of their neighbouring Indians, with that of the Hebrew nation.

The Israelites cut off the hands and feet of murderers, 2 Sam. iv. 12.— strangled false prophets—and sometimes burned, stoned, or beheaded those malefactors who were condemned by the two courts of judgment. The Indians either by the defect of tradition, or through a greedy desire of revenge, torture their prisoners and devoted captives, with a mixture of all those Jewish capital punishments. They keep the original so close in their eye, as to pour cold water on the sufferers when they are fainting, or overcome by the fiery torture—to refresh, and enable them to undergo longer tortures.

The Hebrews gave wine mixt with the juice of myrrh, to their tortured criminals, to revive their spirits; and sometimes vinegar to prevent too great an effusion of blood, lest they should be disappointed in glutting their greedy eyes, with their favourite tragedy of blood: which was eminently exemplified in their insulting treatment of Christ on the cross.

The Indians, beyond all the rest of mankind, seem in this respect to be actuated with the Jewish spirit. They jeer, taunt, laugh, whoop, and rejoice at the inexpressible agonies of those unfortunate persons, who are under their butchering hands; which would excite pity and horror in any heart, but that of a Jew. When they are far from home, they keep as near to their distinguishing customs, as circumstances allow them: not being able formerly to cut off the heads of those they killed in war, for want of proper weapons; nor able to carry them three or four hundred miles without putrefaction, they cut off the skin of their heads with their flint-stone knives, as speaking trophies of honour, and which register them among the brave by procuring them war titles. Though now they have plenty of proper weapons, they vary not from this ancient barbarous custom of the American aborigines: which has been too well known by many of our northern colonists, and is yet shamefully so to South-Carolina and Georgia barriers, by the hateful name of scalping.[146]

The Indians strictly adhere more than the rest of mankind to that positive, unrepealed law of Moses, "He who sheddeth man's blood, by [148] man shall his blood be shed:" like the Israelites, their hearts burn violently day and night without intermission, till they shed blood for blood.[147] They transmit from father to son, the memory of the loss of their relation, or one of their own tribe or family, though it were an old woman—if she was either killed by the enemy, or by any of their own people. If indeed the murder be committed by a kinsman, the eldest can redeem: however, if the circumstances attending the fact be peculiar and shocking to nature, the murderer is condemned to die the death of a sinner, "without any one to mourn for him," as in the case of suicide; contrary to their usage toward the rest of their dead, and which may properly be called the death or burial of a Jewish ass.

When they have had success in killing the enemy, they tie fire-brands in the most frequented places, with grape vines which hang pretty low, in order that they may be readily seen by the enemy. As they reckon the aggressors have loudly declared war, it would be madness or treachery in their opinion to use such public formalities before they have revenged crying blood; it would inform the enemy of their design of retaliating, and destroy the honest intention of war. They likewise strip the bark off several large trees in conspicuous places, and paint them with red and black hieroglyphics, thereby threatening the enemy with more blood and death. The last were strong and similar emblems with the Hebrews, and the first is analogous to one of their martial customs; for when they arrived at the enemies territories, they threw a fire-brand within their land, as an emblem of the anger of *Ash,* "the holy fire" for their ill deeds to his peculiarly beloved people. To which custom Obadiah alludes, when he says (ver. 18.) "they shall kindle in them and devour them, there shall not be any remaining of the house of Esau, &c." which the Septuagint translates, "one who carries a fire-brand." The conduct of the Israelitish champion, Sampson, against the Philistines, proceeded from the same war custom, when he took three-hundred *Shugnalim,* (which is a bold strong metaphor) signifying *Vulpes,* foxes or sheaves of corn; and tying them tail to tail, or one end to the other in a continued train, he set fire to them, and by that means, burned down their standing corn.

In the late Cheerake war, at the earnest persuasions of the trading people, several of the Muskohge warriors came down to the barrier-settlements of Georgia, [149] to go against the Cheerake, and revenge English crying blood: but the main body of the nation sent a running embassy to the merchants there, requesting them immediately to forbear their unfriendly proceedings, otherwise, they should be forced by disagreeable necessity to revenge their relations blood if it should chance to be spilt contrary to their ancient laws: this alludes to the levitical law, by which he who decoyed another to his end, was deemed the occasion of his death, and consequently answerable for it. If an unruly horse belonging to a white man, should chance to be tied at a trading house and kill one of the Indians, either the owner of the house, or the person who tied the beast there, is responsible for it, by their lex talionis;[148] which seems to be derived also from the Mosaic precept,—if an ox known by its owner to push with its horn, should kill a person, they were both to die the death. If the Indians have a dislike to a person, who by any casualty was the death of one of their people, he stands accountable, and will certainly suffer for it, unless he takes sanctuary.

I knew an under trader, who being intrusted by his employer with a cargo of goods for the country of the Muskohge, was forced by the common law of good faith, to oppose some of those savages in the remote woods, to prevent their robbing the camp: the chieftain being much intoxicated with spirituous liquors, and becoming outrageous in proportion to the resistance he met with, the trader like a brave man, opposed lawless force by force: some time after, the lawless bacchanal was attacked with a pleurisy, of which he died. Then the heads of the family of the deceased convened the lesser judicatory, and condemned the trader to be shot to death for the supposed murder of their kinsman; which they easily effected, as he was off his guard, and knew nothing of their murdering design. His employer however had such a friendly intercourse with them, as to gain timely notice of any thing that might affect his person or interest; but he was so far from assisting the unfortunate brave man as the laws of humanity and common honour obliged him, that as a confederate, he not only concealed their bloody intentions, but went basely to the next town, while the savages painted themselves red and black, and give them an opportunity of perpetrating the horrid murder. The poor victim could have easily escaped to the English settlements if forewarned, and got the affair accommodated by the mediation of the government. In acts of blood, if the supposed murderer [150] escapes, his nearest kinsman either real or adopted, or if he has none there, his friend stands according to their rigorous law, answerable for the fact. But though the then governor of South Carolina was sufficiently informed of this tragedy, and that it was done contrary to the treaty of amity, and that there is no possibility of managing them, but by their own notions of virtue, he was passive, and allowed them with impunity to shed this innocent blood; which they ever since have improved to our shame and sorrow. They have gradually become worse every year; and corrupted other nations by their contagious copy, so as to draw them into the like bloody scenes, with the same contempt, as if they had killed so many helpless timorous dunghill fowls, as they despitefully term us.

There never was any set of people, who pursued the Mosaic law of *retaliation* with such a fixt eagerness as these Americans. They are so determined in this point, that formerly a little boy shooting birds in the high and thick corn-fields, unfortunately chanced slightly to wound another with his childish arrow; the young vindictive fox, was excited by custom to watch his ways with the utmost earnestness, till the wound was returned in as equal manner as could be expected. Then, "all was straight," according to their phrase. Their hearts were at rest, by having executed that strong law of nature, and they sported together as before. This observation though small in itself, is great in its combined circumstances, as it is contrary to the usage of the old heathen world. They forgive all crimes at the annual atonement of sins, except murder, which is always punished with death. The Indians constantly upbraid us in their bacchanals, for inattention to this maxim of theirs; they say, that all nations of people who are not utterly sunk in cowardice, take revenge of blood before they can have rest, cost what it will. The Indian Americans are more eager to revenge blood, than any other people on the whole face of the earth. And when the heart of the revenger of blood in Israel was hot within him, it was a terrible thing for the casual *manslayer* to meet him, Deut. xix. 6. "Lest the avenger of blood pursue the slayer while his heart is hot, and overtake him, because the way is long, and slay him; whereas he was not worthy of death, inasmuch as he hated him not in time past."

I have known the Indians to go a thousand miles, for the purpose of revenge, in pathless woods; over hills and mountains; through large cane [151] swamps, full of grape-vines and briars; over broad lakes, rapid rivers, and deep creeks; and all the way endangered by poisonous snakes, if not with the rambling and lurking enemy, while at the same time they were exposed to the extremities of heat and cold, the vicissitude of the seasons; to hunger and thirst, both by chance, and their religious scanty method of living when at war, to fatigues, and other difficulties. Such is their over-boiling revengeful temper, that they utterly contemn all those things as imaginary trifles, if they are so happy as to get the scalp of the murderer, or enemy, to satisfy the supposed craving ghosts of their deceased relations. Though they imagine the report of guns will send off the ghosts of their kindred that died at home, to their quiet place, yet they firmly believe, that the spirits of those who are killed by the enemy, without equal revenge of blood, find no rest, and at night haunt the houses of the tribe to which they belonged*: but, when that kindred duty of retaliation is justly executed, they immediately get ease and power to fly away: This opinion, and their method of burying and mourning for the dead, of which we shall speak presently, occasion them to retaliate in so earnest and fierce a manner. It is natural for friends to study each others mutual happiness, and we should pity the weakness of those who are destitute of our advantages; whose intellectual powers are unimproved, and who are utterly unacquainted with the sciences, as well as every kind of mechanical business, to engage their attention at home. Such persons cannot well live without war; and being destitute of public faith to secure the lives of embassadors in time of war, they have no sure method to reconcile their differences: consequently, when any casual thing draws them into a war, it grows every year more spiteful till it advances to a bitter enmity, so as to excite them to an implacable hatred to one another's very national names. Then they must go abroad to spill the enemy's blood, and to revenge crying blood. We must also consider, it is by scalps they get all their war-titles, which distinguish them among the brave: and these they hold in as high esteem, as the most ambitious Roman general ever did a great triumph. By how much the deeper any society of people are sunk in ignorance, so much the more they value themselves on their bloody merit. This was [152] long the characteristic of the Hebrew nation, and has been conveyed down to these their supposed red descendants.

However, notwithstanding their bloody temper and conduct towards

---

*As the Hebrews supposed there was a holiness in Canaan, more than in any other land, so they believed that their bodies buried out of it, would be carried through caverns, or subterraneous passages of the earth to the holy land, where they shall rise again and dart up to their holy attracting centre.

enemies, when their law of blood does not interfere, they observe that Mosiac precept, "He shall be dealt with according as he intended to do to his neighbour, but the innocent and righteous man thou shalt not slay." I must observe also that as the Jewish prists were by no means to shed human blood, and as king David was forbidden by the prophet to build a temple because he was a man of war and had shed blood—so, the Indian *Ishtohoollo* "holy men" are by their function absolutely forbidden to slay; notwithstanding their propensity thereto, even for small injuries. They will not allow the greatest warrior to officiate, when the yearly grand sacrifice of expiation is offered up, or on any other religious occasion, except the leader. All must be performed by their beloved men, who are clean of every stain of blood, and have their foreheads circled with streaks of white clay.

As this branch of the general subject cannot be illustrated, but by well-known facts, I shall exemplify it with the late and long-continued conduct of the northern Indians, and those of Cape Florida, whom our navigators have reported to be cannibals. The Muskohoge, who have been bitter enemies to the Cape Florida Indians, time immemorial, affirm their manners, tempers and appetites, to be the very same as those of the neighboring Indian nations. And the Florida captives who were sold in Carolina,[149] have told me, that the Spaniards of St. Augustine and St. Mark's garrisons, not only hired and paid them for murdering our seamen, who were so unfortunate as to be shipwrecked on their dangerous coast, but that they delivered up to the savages those of our people they did not like, to be put to the fiery torture. From their bigotted persecuting spirit, we may conclude the victims to have been those who would not worship their images and crucifixes. The Spaniards no doubt could easily influence this decayed small tribe to such a practice, as they depended upon them for the necessaries of life: and though they could never settle out of their garrisons in West-Florida, on account of the jealous temper of the neighboring unconquered Indians, yet the Cape-Floridans were only Spanish mercenaries, shedding blood for their maintenance. A seduced Indian [153] is certainly less faulty than the apostate Christian who instigated him; when an Indian sheds human blood, it does not proceed from wantonness, or the view of doing evil, but solely to put the law of retaliation in force, to return one injury for another; but, if he has received no ill, and has no suspicion of the kind, he usually offers no damage to those who fall in his power, but is moved with compassion, in proportion to what they seem to have undergone. Such as they devote to the fire, they flatter with the hope of being redeemed, as long as they can, to prevent the giving them any previous anxiety or grief, which their law of blood does not require.

The French Canadians are highly censurable, and their bloody popish clergy, for debauching our peaceable northern Indians, with their *infernal catechism,*—the first introduction into their religious mysteries. Formerly, when they initiated the Indian sucklings into their mixt idolatrous worship, they fastened round their necks, a bunch of their favourite red and black beads, with a silver cross hanging down on their breasts, thus engaging them, as they taught, to fight the battles of God. Then they infected the credulous Indians with a firm belief, that God once sent his own beloved son to fix the red people in high places of power, over the rest of mankind; that he passed through various countries, to the universal joy of the inhabitants, in order to come to the beloved red people, and place them in a superior station of life to the rest of the American world; but when he was on the point of sailing to America, to execute his divine embassy, he was murdered by the bloody monopolizing English, at the city of London, only to make the red people weigh light. Having thus instructed, and given them the catechism by way of question and answer, and furnished them with 2000 gross of scalping knives and other murdering articles, the catechumens soon sallied forth, and painted themselves all over with the innocent blood of our fellow-subjects, of different stations, and ages, and without any distinction of sex,—contrary to the standing Indian laws of blood.

The British lion at last however triumphed, and forced the French themselves to sue for that friendly intercourse and protection, which their former catechism taught the Indians to hate, and fly from, as dangerous to their universal happiness.

[154] When I have reasoned with some of the old headmen, against their barbarous custom of killing defenceless innocent persons, who neither could nor would oppose them in battle, but begged that they might only live to be their slaves, they told me that formerly they never waged war, but in revenge of blood; and that in such cases, they always devoted the guilty to be burnt alive when they were purifying themselves at home, to obtain victory over their enemies. But otherwise they treated the vanquished with the greatest clemency, and adopted them in the room of their relations, who had either died a natural death, or had before been sufficiently revenged, though killed by the enemy.

The Israelites thus often devoted their captives to death, without any distinction of age or sex,—as when they took Jericho, they saved only merciful Rahab and her family;—after they had plundered the Midianites of their riches, they put men women and children to death, dividing among themselves a few virgins and the plunder;—with other instances that might be quoted. The Indian Americans, beyond all the present race of Adam, are actuated by this bloody war-custom of the Israelites; they put their captives to various lingering torments, with the same unconcern as the Levite, when he cut up his beloved concubine into eleven portions, and sent them to the eleven tribes, to excite them to revenge the affront, the Benjamites had given him. When equal blood has not been shed to quench the crying blood of their relations, and give rest to their ghosts, according to their credenda, while they are sanctifying themselves for war, they always allot their captives either to be killed or put to the fiery torture: and they who are thus devoted, cannot by any means be saved, though they resembled an angel in beauty and virtue.

Formerly, the Indians defeated a great body of the French, who at two different times came to invade their country.[150] They put to the fiery torture a considerable number of them; and two in particular, whom they imagined to have carried the French ark against them. The English traders solicited with the most earnest entreaties, in favour of the unfortunate captives; but they averred, that as it was not our business to intercede in behalf of a deceitful enemy who came to shed blood, unless we were resolved to share their deserved fate, so was it entirely out of the reach of goods, though piled as high as the skies, to redeem them, [155] because they were not only the chief support of the French army, in spoiling so many of their warriors by the power of their ugly ark, before they conquered them; but were delivered over to the fire, before they entered into battle.

When I was on my way to the Chikkasah, at the Okchai,[151] in the year 1745, the conduct of the Muskohge Indians was exactly the same with regard to a Cheerake stripling, whose father was a white man, and mother an half-breed—regardless of the pressing entreaties and very high offers of the English traders, they burned him in their usual manner. This seems to be copied from that law which expressly forbad the redeeming any devoted persons, and ordered that they should be surely put to death, Lev. xxvii. 29. This precept had evidently a reference to the law of retaliation.—Saul in a superstitious and angry mood, wanted to have murdered or sacrificed to God his favourite son Jonathan, because when he was fainting he tasted some honey which casually fell in his way, just after he had performed a prodigy of martial feats in behalf of Israel: but the gratitude, and reason of the people, prevented him from perpetrating that horrid murder. If devoting to death was a divine extraction, or if God delighted in human sacrifices, the people would have been criminal for daring to oppose the divine law,—which was not the case. Such a law if taken in an extensive and literal sense, is contrary to all natural reason and religion, and consequently in a strict sense, could not be enjoined by a benevolent and merciful God; who commands us to do justice and shew mercy to the very beasts; not to muzzle the ox while he is treading out the grain; nor to insnare the bird when performing her parental offices. "Are ye not of more value than many sparrows?"

The Indians use no stated ceremony in immolating their devoted captives, although it is the same thing to the unfortunate victims, what form their butcherers use. They are generally sacrificed before their conquerors set off for war with their ark and supposed holy things. And sometimes the Indians devote every one they meet in certain woods or paths, to be killed there, except their own people; this occasioned the cowardly Cheerake in the year 1753, to kill two white men on the Chikkasah war-path, which leads from the country of the Muskohge.[152] And the Shawànoh Indians who [156] settled between the *Ooe-Asa* and *Koosah-towns,*[153] told us that their people to the northward had devoted the English to death for the space of six years; but when that time was expired and not before, they would live in friendship as formerly. If the English had at that time executed their own law against them, and demanded equal blood from the Cheeràke, and stopt all trade with them before they dipt themselves too deep in blood, they would soon have had a firm peace with all the Indian nations. This is the only way of treating them now, for when they have not the fear of offending, they will shed innocent blood, and proceed in the end to lay all restraint aside.

The late conduct of the Chikkasah war-council, in condemning two pretended friends to death, who came with a view of shedding blood; shews their knowledge of that equal law of divine appointment to the Jews, "he shall be dealt with exactly as he intended to do to his neighbour."

It ought to be remarked, that they are careful of their youth, and fail not to punish them when they transgress. Anno 1766, I saw an old head man, called the *Dog-King* (from the nature of his office)[154] correct several young persons—some for supposed faults, and others by way of prevention. He began with a lusty young fellow, who was charged with being more effeminate than became a warrior; and with acting contrary to their old religious rites and customs, particularly, because he lived nearer than any of the rest to an opulent and helpless German, by whom they supposed he might have been corrupted. He bastinadoed the young sinner severely, with a thick whip, about a foot and a half long, composed of plaited silk grass, and the fibres of the button snake-root stalks, tapering to the point, which was secured with a knot. He reasoned with him, as he corrected him: he told him that he was *Chehakse Kanèha-He,* literally, "you are as one who is wicked, and almost lost★." The grey-hair'd corrector said, he treated him in that manner according to ancient custom, through an effect of love, to induce him to shun vice, and to imitate the virtues of [157] his illustrious forefathers, which he endeavoured to enumerate largely: when the young sinner had received his supposed due, he went off seemingly well pleased.

This Indian correction lessens gradually in its severity, according to the

★As *Chin-Kanehah* signifies, "you have lost," and *Che-Kanehah,* "you are lost," it seems to point at the method the Hebrews used in correcting their criminals in Canaan, and to imply a similarity of manners. The word they use to express "forgetfulness," looks the very same way, *Ish Al Kanehah,* "you forget," meaning that *Ish* and *Canaan* are forgotten by *Ale.*

age of the pupils. While the *Dog-King* was catechising the little ones, he said *Che Haksinna,* "do not become vicious." And when they wept, he said *Che-Abela Awa,* "I shall not kill you," or "I shall not put you into the state of bleeding *Abéle*★."

Like the present Jews, their old men are tenacious of their ancient rites and customs; imagining them to be the sure channel through which all temporal good things flow to them, and by which the opposite evils are averted. No wonder therefore, that they still retain a multiplicity of Hebrew words, which were repeated often with great reverence in the temple; and adhere to many of their ancient rules and methods of punishment.

[158] ARGUMENT XV.

The Israelites had CITIES OF REFUGE, or places of safety, for those who killed a person unawares, and without design; to shelter them from the blood-thirsty relations of the deceased, or the revenger of blood, who always pursued or watched the unfortunate person, like a ravenous wolf: but after the death of the high-priest the man-slayer could safely return home, and nobody durst molest him.

According to the same particular divine law of mercy, each of these In-

---

★The Indians use the word *Hakse,* to convey the idea of a person's being criminal in any thing whatsoever. If they mention not the particular crime, they add, *Hakset Kanehah,* pointing as it were to those who were punished in Canaan. Such unfortunate persons as are mad, deaf, dumb or blind, are called by no other name than *Hakse.* In like manner *Kallakse* signifies "contemptible, unsteady, light, or easily thrown aside,"—it is a diminutive of קלל, of the same meaning. And they say such an one is *Kallaks'-Ishto,* "execrated, or accursed to God," because found light in the divine balance. As the American Aborigines used no weights, the parity of language here with the Hebrew, seems to assure us, they originally derived this method of expression from the Israelites, who took the same idea from the poise of a balance, which divine writ frequently mentions. Job, chap. xxxi, describes justice with a pair of scales, "Let me be weighed in an even balance, that I may know my perfection." And they call weighing, or giving a preference, *Tekále,* according to the same figure of speech: and it agrees both in expression and meaning, with the Chaldean *Tekel,* if written with Hebrew characters, as in that extraordinary appearance on the wall of the Babylonish monarch, interpreted by the prophet Daniel. When they prefer one person and would lessen another, they say *Eeàpa Wĕhke Tekále,* "this one weighs heavy," and *Eeàko Kallakse,* or *Kall'aks'ooshe Tekále,* "that one weighs light, very light." When any of their people are killed on any of the hunting paths, they frequently say, *Heenna tungga Tannip Tekále,* "right on the path, he was weighed for the enemy, or the opposite party," for *Tannip* is the only word they have to express the words *enemy* and the *opposite;* as *Ook'heenna Tannip,* "the opposite side of the water path:" hence it is probable, they borrowed that notable Assyrian expression while in their supposed captivity, brought it with them to America, and introduced it into their language, to commemorate so surprising an event.

dian nations have either a house or town of refuge, which is a sure asylum to protect a man-slayer, or the unfortunate captive, if they can once enter into it. The Cheerake, though now exceedingly corrupt, still observe that law so inviolably, as to allow their beloved town the privilege of protecting a wilful murtherer: but they seldom allow him to return home afterwards in safety—they will revenge blood for blood, unless in some very particular case when the eldest can redeem. However, if he should accept of the price of blood to wipe away its stains, and dry up the tears of the rest of the nearest kindred of the deceased, it is generally productive of future ills; either when they are drinking spirituous liquors, or dancing their enthusiastic war dances, a tomohawk is likely to be sunk into the head of some of his relations.

Formerly, when one of the Cheerake murdered an English trader he immediately ran off for the town of refuge; but as soon as he got in view of it, the inhabitants discovered him by the close pursuit of the shrill war-whoo-whoop; and for fear of irritating the English, they instantly answered the war cry, ran to arms, intercepted, and drove him off into Tennàse river (where he escaped, though mortally wounded) lest he should have entered the reputed holy ground, and thus it had been stained with the blood of their friend; or he had obtained sanctuary to the danger of the community, and the foreign contempt of their sacred altars.

[159] This town of refuge called *Choate,* is situated on a large stream of the Missisippi, five miles above the late unfortunate *Fort-Loudon,*—where some years ago, a brave Englishman was protected after killing an Indian warrior in defense of his property. The gentleman told me, that as his trading house was near to that town of refuge, he had resolved with himself, after some months stay in it, to return home; but the head-man assured him, that though he was then safe, it would prove fatal if he removed thence; so he continued in his asylum still longer, till the affair was by time more obliterated, and he had wiped off all their tears with various presents. In the upper or most western part of the country of the Muskóhge, there was an old beloved town, now reduced to a small ruinous village, called *Koosah,* which is still a place of safety for those who kill undesignedly. It stands on commanding ground, over-looking a bold river, which after running about forty leagues, sweeps close by the late mischievous French garrison *Alebámah,* and down to *Mobille-Sound,* 200 leagues distance, and so into the gulph of Florida.

In almost every Indian nation, there are several *peaceable towns,* which are called "old-beloved," "ancient, holy, or white towns★;" they seem to have been formerly "towns of refuge," for it is not in the memory of their oldest

---

★White is their fixt emblem of peace, friendship, happiness, prosperity, purity, holiness, &c. as with the Israelites.

people, that ever human blood was shed in them; although they often force persons from thence, and put them to death elsewhere.[155]

ARGUMENT XVI.

Before the Indians go to WAR, they have many preparatory ceremonies of *purification* and *fasting*,[156] like what is recorded of the Israelites.

In the first commencement of a war, a party of the injured tribe turns out first, to revenge the innocent crying blood of their own bone and flesh, as they term it. When the leader begins to beat up for volunteers, he goes three times round his dark winter-house, contrary to the course of the sun, sounding the war-whoop, singing the war-song, and beating the drum. [160] Then he speaks to the listening crowd with very rapid language, short pauses, and an awful commanding voice, tells them of the continued friendly offices they have done the enemy, but which have been ungratefully returned with the blood of his kinsmen; therefore as the white paths have changed their beloved colour, his heart burns within him with eagerness to tincture them all along, and even to make them flow over with the hateful blood of the base contemptible enemy. Then he strongly persuades his kindred warriors and others, who are not afraid of the enemies bullets and arrows, to come and join him with manly cheerful hearts: he assures them, he is fully convinced, as they are all bound by the love-knot, so they are ready to hazard their lives to revenge the blood of their kindred and country-men; that the love of order, and the necessity of complying with the old religious customs of their country, had hitherto checked their daring generous hearts, but now, those hindrances are removed: he proceeds to whoop again for the warriors to come and join him, and sanctify themselves for success against the common enemy, according to their ancient religious law.

By his eloquence, but chiefly by their own greedy thirst of revenge, and intense love of martial glory, on which they conceive their liberty and happiness depend, and which they constantly instil into the minds of their youth—a number soon join him in his winter-house, where they live separate from all others, and purify themselves for the space of three days and nights, exclusive of the first broken day. In each of those days they observe a strict fast till sun-set, watching the young men very narrowly who have not been initiated in war-titles, lest unusual hunger should tempt them to violate it, to the supposed danger of all their lives in war, by destroying the power of their purifying beloved physic, which they drink plentifully during that time. This purifying physic, is warm water highly imbittered with button-rattle-snake-root, which as hath been before observed, they apply only to religious purposes.[157] Sometimes after bathing they drink a decoction made of the said root—and in like manner the leader applies aspersions, or sprinklings, both at home and when out at war. They are such strict observers of the law of purification, and think it so essential in obtaining health and success in war, as not to allow the best beloved trader that ever lived among them, even to enter the beloved ground, appropriated to the religious duty of being sanctified [161] for war; much less to associate with the camp in the woods, though he went (as I have known it to happen) on the same war design; —they oblige him to walk and encamp separate by himself, as an impure dangerous animal, till the leader hath purified him, according to their usual time and method, with the consecrated things of the ark. With the Hebrews, the ark of *Berith,* "the purifier," was a small wooden chest, of three feet nine inches in length, two feet three inches broad, and two feet three inches in height. It contained the golden pot that had manna in it, Aaron's rod, and the tables of the law. The INDIAN ARK is of a very simple construction, and it is only the intention and application of it, that makes it worthy of notice; for it is made with pieces of wood securely fastened together in the form of a square. The middle of three of the sides extend a little out, but one side is flat, for the conveniency of the person's back who carries it. Their ark has a cover, and the whole is made impenetrably close with hiccory-splinters;[158] it is about half the dimensions of the divine Jewish ark, and may very properly be called the red Hebrew ark of the purifier, imitated. The leader, and a beloved waiter, carry it by turns. It contains several consecrated vessels, made by beloved superannuated women, and of such various antiquated forms, as would have puzzled Adam to have given significant names to each. The leader and his attendant, are purified longer than the rest of the company, that the first may be fit to act in the religious office of a priest of war, and the other to carry the awful sacred ark. All the while they are at war, the *Hetissu,* or "beloved waiter," feeds each of the warriors by an exact stated rule, giving them even the water they drink, out of his own hands, lest by intemperance they should spoil the supposed communicative power of their holy things, and occasion fatal disasters to the war camp.

The ark, mercy-seat, and cherubim, were the very essence of the levitical law, and often called "the testimonies of *Yohewah.*" The ark of the temple was termed his throne, and David calls it his foot-stool. In speaking of the Indian places of refuge for the unfortunate, I observed, that if a captive taken by the reputed power of the beloved things of the ark, should be able to make his escape into one of these towns,—or even into the winter-house of the Archi-magus, he is delivered from the fiery torture, otherwise inevitable. This when joined to the rest of the faint images of the Mosaic customs they still retain, seems to point at the mercy-seat in the sanctuary. It is also highly worthy of notice, that they [162] never place the ark on the ground, nor sit on the bare earth while they are carrying it against the enemy. On hilly ground where stones are plenty, they place it on them: but in level land upon short logs, always resting themselves on the like materials.

Formerly, when this tract was the Indian Flanders of America, as the French and all their red Canadian confederates were bitter enemies to the inhabitants, we often saw the woods full of such religious war-reliques. The former is a strong imitation of the pedestal, on which the Jewish ark was placed, a stone rising three fingers breadth above the floor. And when we consider—in what a surprising manner the Indians copy after the ceremonial law of the Hebrews, and their strict purity in their war camps; that *Opae,* "the leader," obliges all during the first campaign they make with the beloved ark, to stand, every day they lie by, from sun-rise to sun-set—and after a fatiguing day's march, and scanty allowance, to drink warm water imbittered with rattle-snake-root very plentifully, in order to be purified— that they have also as strong a faith of the power and holiness of their ark, as ever the Israelites retained of their's, ascribing the superior success of the party, to their stricter adherence to the law than the other; and after they return home, hang it on the leader's red-painted war pole—we have strong reason to conclude their origin is Hebrew. From the Jewish ark of the tabernacle and the temple, the ancient heathens derived their arks, their *cistiæ* or religious chests, their Teraphim or Dii Lares, and their tabernacles and temples. But their modes and objects of worship, differed very widely from those of the Americans.

The Indian ark is deemed so sacred and dangerous to be touched, either by their own sanctified warriors, or the spoiling enemy, that they durst not touch it upon any account★. It is not to be meddled with by any, except the war chieftain and his waiter, under the penalty of incurring great evil. [163]

★A gentleman who was at the Ohio, in the year 1756, assured me he saw a stranger there very importunate to view the inside of the Cheerake ark, which was covered with a drest deer-skin, and placed on a couple of short blocks.[159] An Indian centinel watched it, armed with a hiccory bow, and brass-pointed barbed arrows, and he was faithful to his trust; for finding the stranger obtruding to pollute the supposed sacred vehicle, he drew an arrow to the head, and would have shot him through the body, had he not suddenly withdrawn; the interpreter, when asked by the gentleman what it contained, told him there was nothing in it but a bundle of conjuring traps. This shews what conjurers our common interpreters are, and how much the learned world have really profited by their informations. The Indians have an old [163] tradition, that when they left their own native land, they brought with them a *sanctified rod* by order of an oracle, which they fixed every night in the ground; and were to remove from place to place on the continent towards the sun-rising, till it budded in one night's time; that they obeyed the sacred mandate, and the miracle took place after they arrived to this side of the Missisippi, on the present land they possess. This, they say, was the sole cause of their settling here—of fighting so firmly for their reputed holy land and holy things—and that they may be buried with their beloved fore-fathers.[160] I have seen other Indians who pretend to the like miraculous direction, and I think it plainly to refer to Aaron's rod, which was a branch of an almond-tree, and that budded and blossomed in one night.

Nor would the most inveterate enemy touch it in the woods for the very same reason; which is agreeable to the religious opinion and customs of the Hebrews, respecting the sacredness of their ark, witness what befel Uzzah, for touching it, though with a religious view, and the Philistines for carrying it away, so that they soon thought proper to return it, with presents.

The leader virtually acts the part of a priest of war, *pro tempore,*[161] in imitation of the Israelites fighting under the divine military banner. If they obtain the victory, and get some of the enemies scalps, they sanctify themselves when they make their triumphal entrance, in the manner they observed before they set off to war; but, if their expedition proves unfortunate, they only mourn over their loss, ascribing it to the vicious conduct of some of the followers of the beloved ark. What blushes should this savage virtue raise in the faces of nominal christians, who ridicule the unerring divine wisdom, for the effects of their own imprudent or vicious conduct. May they learn from the rude uncivilized Americans, that vice necessarily brings evil—and virtue, happiness.

The Indians will not cohabit with women while they are out at war; they religiously abstain from every kind of intercourse even with their own wives, for the space of three days and nights before they go to war, and so after they return home, because they are to sanctify themselves. This religious war custom, especially in so savage a generation, seems to be derived from the Hebrews, who thus sanctified themselves, to gain the divine protection, and victory over their common enemies: as in the precept of Moses to the war camp when he ascended Mount Sinai; and in Joshua's prohibition to the Israelites★; and in the case of Uriah. The warriors consider themselves as devoted to God apart from the rest of the [164] people, while they are at war accompanying the sacred ark with the supposed holy things it contains.

The French Indians are said not to have deflowered any of our young women they captivated, while at war with us; and unless the black tribe, the French Canadian priests, corrupted their traditions, they would think such actions defiling, and what must bring fatal consequences on their own heads. We have an attested narrative of an English prisoner, who made his escape from the Shawanoh Indians, which was printed at Philadelphia, anno 1757, by which we were assured, that even that blood-thirsty villain, Capt. Jacob,[162] did not attempt the virtue of his female captives, lest (as he told one of them) it should offend the Indian's God; though at the same time his pleasures heightened in proportion to the shrieks and groans of our people of different ages and both sexes, while they were under his tortures.

★Joshua commanded the Israelites the night before they marched, to sanctify themselves by washing their clothes, avoiding all impurities, and abstaining from matrimonial intercourse.

Although the Choktah are libidinous, and lose their customs apace, yet I have known them to take several female prisoners without offering the least violence to their virtue, till the time of purgation was expired;—then some of them forced their captives, notwithstanding their pressing entreaties and tears.[163] As the aforesaid Shawanoh renegado professed himself so observant of this law of purity, so the other northern nations of Indians, who are free from adulteration by their far-distance from foreigners, do not neglect so great a duty: and it is highly probable, notwithstanding the silence of our writers, that as purity was strictly observed by the Hebrews in the temple, field and wilderness, the religious rites and customs of the northern Indians, differ no farther from those of the nations near our southern settlements than reason will admit, allowing for their distant situation from Peru and Mexico, whence they seem to have travelled.

When they return home victorious over the enemy, they sing the triumphal song to Yo-He-Wah, ascribing the victory to him, according to a religious custom of the Israelites, who were commanded always to attribute their success in war to Jehovah, and not to their swords and arrows.

In the year 1765, when the Chikkasah returned with two French scalps, from the Illinois, (while the British troops were on the Missisippi, about 170 leagues below the Illinois)[164] as my trading house was near the Chikkasah [165] leader, I had a good opportunity of observing his conduct, as far as it was exposed to public view.

Within a day's march of home, he sent a runner a-head with the glad tidings—and to order his dark winter house to be swept out very clean, for fear of pollution. By ancient custom, when the out-standing party set off for war, the women are so afraid of the power of their holy things, and of prophaning them, that they sweep the house and earth quite clean, place the sweepings in a heap behind the door, leaving it there undisturbed, till *Opáe*, who carries the ark, orders them by a faithful messenger to remove it. He likewise orders them to carry out every utensil which the women had used during his absence, for fear of incurring evil by pollution. The party appeared next day painted red and black, their heads covered all over with swan-down, and a tuft of long white feathers fixt to the crown their heads. Thus they approached, carrying each of the scalps on a branch of the evergreen pine*, singing the awful death song, with a solemn striking air, and sometimes Yo He Wah; now and then sounding the shrill death *Whóo*

---

*As the Indians carry their enemies scalps on small branches of ever-green pine, and wave the martial trophies on a pine-branch before YO He Wah; I cannot help thinking that the pine was the emblematical tree so often mentioned in divine writ, by the plural name, *Shittim;* especially as the mountain Cedar, comparatively speaking, is low and does not seem to answer the description of the inspired writers; besides that כפר *Chepher* is figuratively applied to the mercy-seat, signifying, literally, a screen, or cover against storms; which was pitched over with the gum of the pine-tree.

Whoop Whoop. When they arrived, the leader went a-head of his company, round his winter hot house, contrary to the course of the sun, singing the monosyllable YO, for about the space of five seconds on a tenor key; again, HE HE: short, on a bass key; then WAH WAH, gutturally on the treble, very shrill, but not so short as the bass note. In this manner they repeated those sacred notes, YO, HE HE, WAH WAH, three times, while they were finishing the circle, a strong emblem of the eternity of Him, "who is, was, and is to come," to whom they sung their triumphal song, ascribing the victory over their enemies to his strong arm, instead of their own, according to the usage of the Israelites by divine appointment. The duplication of the middle and last syllables of the four-lettered essential name of the deity, and the change of the key from their established method of invoking YO HE WAH, when they are drinking their bitter drink, (the *Cusseena*) in their temples, where they always spend a long breath on each of the two first [166] syllables of that awful divine song, seems designed to prevent a prophanation.

The leader's *Hetissu,* "or waiter," placed a couple of new blocks of wood near the war pole, opposite to the door of the circular hot-house, in the middle of which the fire-place stood; and on these blocks he rested the supposed sacred ark, so that it and the holy fire faced each other. The party were silent a considerable time. At length, the chieftain bade them sit down, and then enquired whether his house was prepared for the solemn occasion, according to his order the day before: being answered in the affirmative, they soon rose up, sounded the death whoop, and walked round the war pole; during which they invoked and sung three times, YO, HE HE, WAH WAH, in the manner already described. Then they went with their holy things in regular order into the hot-house, where they continued, exclusive of the first broken day, three days and nights apart from the rest of the people, purifying themselves with warm lotions, and aspersions of the emblematical button-snake-root, without any other subsistence between the rising and the setting of the sun.

During the other part of the time, the female relations of each of the company, after having bathed, anointed, and drest themselves in their finest, stood in two rows, one on each side of the door, facing each other, from the evening till the morning, singing HA HA, HA HE, with a soft shrill voice and a solemn moving air for more than a minute, and then paused about ten minutes, before, they renewed their triumphal song. While they sung, they gave their legs a small motion, by the strong working of their muscles, without seeming to bend their joints. When they had no occasion to retire, they have stood erect in the same place, a long frosty night; and except when singing, observed a most profound silence the whole time. During that period, they have no intercourse with their husbands; and they avoided several other supposed pollutions, as not to eat or touch salt, and the like.

The leader, once in two or three hours came out at the head of his company, and raising the death whoop, made one circle round the red painted war pole, holding up in their right hands the small boughs of pine with the scalps fixt to them, singing as above, waving them to and fro, and then returned again. This religious order they strictly observed the whole time [167] they were purifying themselves, and singing the song of safety, and victory, to the goodness and power of the divine essence. When the time of their purification and thanksgiving expired, the men and women went and bathed themselves separately, returned in the same manner, and anointed again, according to their usual custom.

They joined soon after in a solemn procession, to fix the scalps on the tops of the houses of their relations who had been killed without revenge of blood. The war chieftain went first—his religious attendant followed him; the warriors next, according to their rising merit; and the songstresses brought up the rear. In this order they went round the leader's winter-house from the east to the north, the men striking up the death whoop, and singing the death song; and then YO, HE HE, WAH WAH, as described; the women also warbling HA HA, HA HE, so that one might have said according to the sacred text, "great was the company of the women who sung the song of triumph."* Then they fixed on the top of the house, a twig of the pine they had brought with them, with a small piece of one of the scalps fastened to it: and this order they observed from house to house till in their opinion they had appeased the ghosts of their dead. They went and bathed again; and thus ended their purification, and triumphal solemnity—only the leader and his religious waiter kept apart three days longer, purifying themselves. I afterward asked the reason of this—they replied they were *Ishtohoolo*. This seems to be so plain a copy of the old Jewish customs, I am satisfied the reader will easily discern the analogy, without any farther observations.

I cannot however conclude this argument, without a few remarks concerning the Indian methods of *making peace,* and of renewing their old friendship.[165] They first smoke out of the friend-pipe, and eat together; then they drink of the *Cusseena,* using such invocations as have been mentioned, and proceed to wave their large fans of eagles-tails,—concluding with a dance. The persons visited, appoint half a dozen of their most active and expert young warriors to perform this religious duty, who have had their own temples adorned with the swan-feather-cap. They paint their bodies with white clay, and cover their heads with swan-down; then approaching the chief [168] representative of the strangers, who by way of honour, and

---

*Last year I heard the Choktah women, in those towns which lie next to New Orleans, sing a regular anthem and dirge, in the dusk of the evening, while their kinsmen were gone to war against the Muskohge.

strong assurance of friendship, is seated on the central white or holy seat, "the beloved cabbin" (which is about nine feet long and seven feet broad), they wave the eagles tails backward and forward over his head★. Immediately they begin the solemn song with an awful air; and presently they dance in a bowing posture; then they raise themselves so erect, that their faces look partly upwards, waving the eagles tails with their right hand toward heaven, sometimes with a slow, at others with a quick motion; at the same time they touch their breast with their small callabash and pebbles fastened to a stick of about a foot long, which they hold in their left hand, keeping time with the motion of the eagles tails: during the dance, they repeat the usual divine notes, YO, &c. and wave the eagles tails now and then over the stranger's head, not moving above two yards backward or forward before him. They are so surprisingly expert in their supposed religious office, and observe time so exactly, with their particular gestures and notes, that there is not the least discernible discord. If the Hebrews danced this way, (as there is strong presumptive proof) they had very sweating work, for every joint, artery, and nerve, is stretched to the highest pitch of exertion; and this may account for Saul's daughter Michal, chiding David for falling in with the common dancers.

The Indians cannot shew greater honour to the greatest potentate on earth, than to place him in the white seat—invoke YO He Wah, while [169] he is drinking the Cusseena, and dance before him with the eagles tails. When two chieftains are renewing, or perpetuating friendship with each

---

★When they are disaffected, or intend to declare war, they will not allow any of the party against whom they have hostile views, to approach the white seat; as their holy men, and holy places, are considered firmly bound to keep good faith, and give sure refuge. Indeed in the year 1750, after having narrowly escaped with my life from the Cheerake lower towns, I met two worthy gentlemen at the settlement of Ninety-six, who were going to them.[166] I earnestly dissuaded them against pursuing their journey, but without effect: when they arrived at the middle Cheerake towns, the old beloved men and war chieftains invited them and twenty of the traders to go in the evening to their town-house, to sit on their white beloved seat, partake of their feast, and smoke together with kindly hearts, according to their old friendly custom. The gentlemen happily rejected the invitation, and boldly told them they were apprised of their treacherous intentions: they braved a little, to surprise and intimidate the Indians, and then mounted, directed their course toward the place where a treacherous ambuscade had been laid for them—but they soon silently took another course, and passing through an unsuspected difficult marsh, and almost pathless woods, by the dawn of the morning they reached the Georgia side of Savannah river, which was about 80 miles, where a body of the Muskohge chanced to be preparing for war against the treacherous Cheerake. These protected them from their pursuers, and the gentlemen arrived safe at Augusta, the upper barrier and Indian mart of Georgia.[167]

other, they are treated with the same ceremonies. And in their circular friendly dances, when they honour their guests, and pledge themselves to keep good faith with them, they sometimes sing their divine notes with a very awful air, pointing their right hand towards the sky. Some years ago, I saw the Kooasahte Indians (two hundred miles up Mobille river)[168] perform this rite with much solemnity; as if invoking the deity by their notes and gestures, to enable them to shew good-will to their fellow-creatures, and to bear witness of their faithful vows and conduct. This custom is plainly not derived from the old Scythians, or any other part of the heathen world. Their forms and usages when they make peace, or pledged faith, and contracted friendship with each other, were widely different: but to those of the Jews it hath the nearest resemblance.

ARGUMENT XVII.

The Indian origin and descent may also be in some measure discerned by their taste for, and kind of ORNAMENTS.

The Israelites were fond of wearing beads and other ornaments, even as early as the patriarchal age, and the taste increased to such a degree that it became criminal, and was sharply reprehended by the prophets, particularly Isaiah. The Israelitish women wore rich garters about their legs, and against the rules of modesty, they shortened their under garments, in order to shew how their legs and feet were decorated; Isaiah, chap. iii. 18. "The Lord will take away the bravery of their tinkling ornaments about their feet," which loaded them so heavy that they could scarcely walk; and ver. 19, 20, 21. "The chains and the bracelets—The ornaments of the legs—and the ear-rings—The rings and nose jewels." In resemblance to these customs, the Indian females continually wear a beaded string round their legs, made of buffalo-hair, which is a species of coarse wool; and they reckon it a great ornament, as well as a preservative against miscarriages, hard labour, and other evils. They wear also a heap of land [170] tortoise-shells with pebbles or beads in them, fastened to pieces of deer-skins, which they tie to the outside of their legs, when they mix with the men in their religious dances.

The Indian nations are agreed in the custom of thus adorning themselves with beads of various sizes and colours; sometimes wrought in garters, sashes, necklaces, and in strings round their wrists; and so from the crown of their heads sometimes to the cartilage of the nose. And they doat on them so much as to make them their current money in all payments to this day.

Before we supplied them with our European beads, they had great quantities of wampum; (the Buccinum of the ancients) made out of conch-shell, by rubbing them on hard stones, and so they form them according to their liking.[169] With these they bought and sold at a stated current rate, without the least variation for circumstances either of time or place; and now they will hear nothing patiently of loss or gain, or allow us to heighten the price of our goods, be our reasons ever so strong, or though the exigencies and changes of time may require it. Formerly, four deer-skins was the price of a large conch-shell bead, about the length and thickness of a man's forefinger; which they fixed to the crown of their head, as an high ornament—so greatly they valued them. Their beads bear a very near resemblance to ivory, which was highly esteemed by the Hebrews.

The New-England writers assure us, that the Naragansat Indians paid to the colony of Massachusetts, two hundred fathoms of wampum, only in part of a debt; and at another payment one-hundred fathoms: which shews the Indian custom of wearing beads has prevailed far north on this continent, and before the first settling of our colonies.

According to the oriental custom, they wear ear-rings and finger-rings in abundance. Tradition says, they followed the like custom before they became acquainted with the English.

The men and women in old times used such coarse diamonds, as their own hilly country produced, when each had a bit of stone fastened with a [171] deer's sinew to the tying of their hair, their nose, ears, and maccaseenes: but from the time we supplied them with our European ornaments, they have used brass and silver ear-rings, and finger-rings; the young warriors now frequently fasten bell-buttons, or pieces of tinkling brass to their maccaseenes, and to the outside of their boots, instead of the old turky-cock-spurs which they formerly used. Both sexes esteem the above things, as very great ornaments of dress, and commonly load the parts with each sort, in proportion to their ability of purchasing them: it is a common trading rule with us, to judge of the value of an Indian's effects, by the weight of his fingers, wrists, ears, crown of his head, boots, and maccaseenes—by the quantity of red paint daubed on his face, and by the shirt about the collar, shoulders, and back, should he have one.

Although the same things are commonly alike used or disused, by males and females; yet they distinguish their sexes in as exact a manner as any civilized nation. The women bore small holes in the lobe of their ears for their rings, but the young heroes cut a hole round almost the extremity of both their ears, which till healed, they stretch out with a large tuft of buffalo's wool mixt with bear's oil: then they twist as much small wire round as will keep them extended in that hideous form. This custom however is wearing off apace.[170] They formerly wore *nose-rings,* or jewels, both in the northern and southern regions of America, according to a similar custom of the Jews and easterns; and in some places they still observe it. At present, they hang a piece of battered silver or pewter, or a large bead to the nostril, like the European method of treating swine, to prevent them from rooting the earth; this, as well as the rest of their customs, is a true picture and good copy of their supposed early progenitors.

I have been among the Indians at a drinking match, when several of their beaus have been humbled as low as death, for the great loss of their big ears. Being so widely extended, it is as easy for a person to take hold of, and pull them off, as to remove a couple of small hoops were they hung within reach; but if the ear after the pull, stick to their head by one end, when they get sober, they pare and sew it together with a needle and deer's sinews, after sweating him in a stove. Thus the disconsolate warrior recovers his former cheerfulness, and hath a lasting caution of not putting his ears a second time in danger with bad company: [172] however, it is not deemed a scandal to lose their ears by any accident, because they became slender and brittle, by their virtuous compliance with that favourite custom of their ancestors.

ARGUMENT XVIII.

The Indian manner of CURING THEIR SICK, is very similar that of the Jews. They always invoke YO HE WAH, a considerable space of time before they apply any medicines, let the case require ever so speedy an application. The more desperately ill their patients are, the more earnestly they invoke the deity on the sad occasion. Like the Hebrews, they firmly believe that diseases and wounds are occasioned by the holy fire, or divine anger, in proportion to some violation of the old beloved speech. The Jews had but small skill in physic.—They called a physician "a binder of wounds," for he chiefly poured oil into the wounds and bound them up. They were no great friends to this kind of learning and science; and their Talmud has this proverb, "the best physicians go to hell." King Asa was reproved for having applied to physicians, for his disease in his feet. The little use they made of the art of medicine, especially for internal maladies; and their persuasion that distempers were either the immediate effects of God's anger, or caused by evil spirits, led them to apply themselves to the prophets, or to diviners, magicians and enchanters. Hezekiah's boil was cured by Isaiah—Benhadad king of Syria, and Naaman the Syrian applied to the prophet Elisha, and Ahaziah king of Israel sent to consult Baal-zebub. The Indians deem the curing their sick or wounded a very religious duty; and it is chiefly performed by their supposed prophets, and magi, because they believe they are inspired with a great portion of the divine fire. On these occasion they sing YO YO, on a low bass key for two or three minutes very rapidly; in like manner, HE HE, and WA WA. Then they transpose and accent those sacred notes with great vehemence, and supplicating fervor, rattling all the while a calabash with small pebble-stones, in imitation of the old Jewish rattles, to make a greater sound, and [173] as it were move the deity to co-operate with their simple means and finish the cure★.

When the Indian physicians visit their supposed irreligious patients, they approach them in a bending posture, with their rattling calabash, preferring that sort to the North-American gourds:[171] and in that bent posture of body, they run two or three times round the sick person, contrary to the course of the sun, invoking God as already exprest. Then they invoke the raven, and mimic his croaking voice: Now this bird was an ill omen to the ancient heathens, as we may see by the prophet Isaiah; so that common wisdom, or self-love, would not have directed them to such a choice, if their traditions had represented it as a bad symbol. But they chose it as an emblem of recovery, probably from its indefatigableness in flying to and fro when sent out of the ark, till he [174] found dry ground to rest on†. They also place a

---

★Formerly, an old Nachee warrior who was blind of one eye, and very dim-sighted in the other, having heard of the surprising skill of the European oculists, fancied I could cure him. He frequently importuned me to perform that friendly office, which I as often declined. But he imagining all my excuses were the effect of modesty and caution, was the more importunate, and would take no denial. I was at last obliged to commence Indian oculist. I had just drank a glass of rum when he came to undergo the operation at the time appointed; he observing my glass, said, it was best to defer it till the next day.—I told him, I drank so on purpose, for as the white people's physic and beloved songs were quite different from what the red people applied and sung, it was usual with our best physicians to drink a little, to heighten their spirits, and enable them to sing with a strong voice, and likewise to give their patients a little, to make their hearts weigh even within them; he consented, and lay down as if he was dead, according to their usual custom. After a good many wild ceremonies, I sung up *Sheela na Guira,* "will you drink wine?" Then I drank to my patient, which on my raising him up, he accepted: I gave him several drinks of grogg, both to divert myself, and purify the obtruding supposed sinner. At last, I applied my materia medica, blowing a quill full of fine burnt allum and roman vitriol into his eye. Just as I was ready to repeat it, he bounded up out of his seemingly dead state, jumped about, and said, my songs and physic were not good. When I could be heard, I told him the English beloved songs and physic were much stronger than those of the red people, and that when they did not immediately produce such an effect as he found, it was a sure sign they were good for nothing, but as they were taking place, he would soon be well. He acquiesced because of the soporific dose I gave him. But ever after, he reckoned he had a very narrow chance of having his eye burnt out by *Loak Ishtohoollo,* for drinking *Ooka Hoome,* "the bitter waters," and presuming to get cured by an impure accursed nothing, who lied, drank, ate hog's flesh, and sung *Tarooa Ookproo'sto,* "the devil's tune," or the song of the evil ones.[172]

†The ancients drew bad presages from the situation, and croaking of ravens and crows. They looked on that place as unhappy, where either of them had croaked in the morning. Hesiod forbids to leave a house unfinished, lest a crow should chance to come and croak when sitting on it. And most of the illiterate peasants in Europe are tinctured with the like superstition, pretending to draw ill omens from its voice.

bason of cold water with some pebbles in it on the ground, near the patient, then they invoke the fish, because of its cold element, to cool the heat of the fever. Again, they invoke the eagle, (*Oóóle*) they solicit him as he soars in the heavens, to bring down refreshing things for their sick, and not to delay them, as he can dart down upon the wing, quick as a flash of lightning. They are so tedious on this subject, that it would be a task to repeat it: however, it may be needful to observe, that they chuse the eagle because of its supposed communicative virtues; and that it is according to its Indian name, a cherubimical emblem, and the king of birds, of prodigious strength, swiftness of wing, majestic stature, and loving its young ones so tenderly, as to carry them on its back, and teach them to fly.

Josephus tells us, that Solomon had a divine power conferred upon him, of driving evil spirits out of possessed persons—that he invented several incantations by which diseases were cured—and left behind him such a sure method of exorcising, as the dæmons never returned again: and he assures us, the Jews followed the like custom as late as his own time; and that he saw such a cure performed by one Eleazar. They likewise imagined, that the liver of a fish would keep away evil spirits, as one of the apocryphal writers acquaints us⋆.

[175] In the Summer-season of the year 1746, I chanced to see the Indians playing at a house of the former Missisippi-Nachee, on one of their old sacred musical instruments. It pretty much resembled the Negroe-Banger in shape,[173] but far exceeded it in dimensions; for it was about five feet long, and a foot wide on the head-part of the board, with eight strings made out of the sinews of a large buffalo. But they were so unskilful in acting the part of the Lyrick, that the *Loache,* or prophet who held the instrument between

⋆They imagined incense also to be a sure means to banish the devil; though asafœtida, or the devil's dung, might have been much better. On Cant. iv. 6. "1 will get me to the hill of incense," the Chaldee paraphrast says, that, while the house of Israel kept the art of their holy fore-fathers, both the morning and mid-day evil spirits fled away, because the divine glory dwelt in the sanctuary, which was built on Mount Moriah; and that all the devils fled when they smelled the effluvia of the fine incense that was there. They likewise believed that herbs and roots had a power to expel dæmons. And Josephus tells us, that the root *Bara,* immediately drives out the devil. I suppose it had such a physical power against fevers and agues, as the jesuit's bark.[174]

The church of Rome, in order to have powerful holy things, as well as the Jews, applies salt, spittle, holy-water, and consecrated oil, to expel the devils from the credulous of their [175] own persuasion; and the oil alone is used as a viaticum, on account of its lubricous quality, to make them slippery, and thereby prevent the devil from laying hold, and pulling them down when they ascend upward. They reckon that observance a most religious duty, and an infallible preservative against the legions of evil spirits who watch in the ærial regions; and also necessary to gain celestial admission for believers.

his feet, and along side of his chin, took one end of the bow, whilst a lusty fellow held the other; by sweating labour they scraped out such harsh jarring sounds, as might have been reasonably expected by a soft ear, to have been sufficient to drive out the devil if he lay any where hid in the house. When I afterward asked him the name, and the reason of such a strange method of diversion, he told me the dance was called *Keetla Ishto Hoollo,* "a dance to, or before, the great holy one;" that it kept off evil spirits, witches, and wizards, from the red people; and enabled them to ordain elderly men to officiate in holy things, as the exigency of the times required.

He who danced to it, kept his place and posture, in a very exact manner, without the least perceivable variation: yet by the prodigious working of his muscles and nerves, he in about half an hour, foamed in a very extraordinary manner, and discontinued it proportionally, till he recovered himself. This surprising custom I have mentioned here, because it was usual among the Hebrews, for their prophets to become furious, and as it were beside themselves, when they were about to prophesy. Thus with regard to Saul, it seems that he became furious, and tortured his body by violent gestures: and when Elisha sent one of the children of the prophets to anoint Jehu, one said to him, wherefore cometh this mad fellow? The Chaldee paraphrast, on I Sam. xviii. 10. concerning Saul's prophesying, paraphrases it, cæpit furire, "he began to grow mad, &c."[175]

When the East-Indian Fakirs are giving out their pretended prophecies, they chuse drums and trumpets, that by such confused striking sounds, [176] their senses may be lulled asleep or unsettled, which might otherwise render them uncapable of receiving the supposed divine inspiration. And they endeavour to become thus possest before crowds of people with a furious rage, by many frantic and violent motions of body, and changes of posture, till they have raised it to the highest pitch they are capable of, and then fall on the ground almost breathless; when they recover themselves a little, they give out their prophecies, which are deemed oracular.

Lactantius[176] and others tell us, that the Sibyls were possest of the like fury; and most part of the ancients believed they ought to become furious, the members of the body to shake, and the hairs of their head to stand an end before they could be divinely inspired: which seems plainly to shew, that though the ancient heathens mimicked a great deal of the Mosaic law, yet theirs had but a faint glance on the Hebrew manner of consulting Yohewah; whereas the Indian Americans invoke the true God, by his favourite essential name, in a bowing posture, on every material occasion, whether civil, martial, or religious, contrary to the usage of all the old heathen world.

In the year 1765, an old physician, or prophet, almost drunk with spirituous liquors, came to pay me a friendly visit: his situation made him more communicative than he would have been if quite sober. When he came to the door, he bowed himself half bent, with his arms extended north and south, continuing so perhaps for the space of a minute. Then raising himself erect, with his arms in the same position, he looked in a wild frightful manner, from the south-west toward the north, and sung on a low bass key *Yo Yo Yo Yo,* almost a minute, then *He He He He,* for perhaps the same space of time, and *Wa Wa Wa Wa,* in like manner; and then transposed, and accented those sacred notes several different ways, in a most rapid guttural manner. Now and then he looked upwards, with his head considerably bent backward;—his song continued about a quarter of an hour. As my door which was then open stood east, his face of course looked toward the west; but whether the natives thus usually invoke the deity, I cannot determine; yet as all their winter houses have their doors toward the east, had he used the like solemn invocations there, his face would have consequently looked the same way, contrary to the usage of [177] the heathens. After his song, he stepped in: I saluted him, saying, "Are you come my beloved old friend?" he replied, *Arahre-O.* "I am come in the name of O E A." I told him, I was glad to see, that in this mad age, he still retained the old Chikkasah virtues. He said, that as he came with a glad heart to see me his old friend, he imagined he could not do me a more kind service, than to secure my house from the power of the evil spirits of the north, south, and west,—and, from witches, and wizards, who go about in dark nights, in the shape of bears, hogs, and wolves, to spoil people: "the very month before, added he, we killed an old witch, for having used destructive charms." Because a child was suddenly taken ill, and died, on the physician's false evidence, the father went to the poor helpless old woman who was sitting innocent, and unsuspecting, and sunk his tomohawk into her head, without the least fear of being called to an account. They call witches and wizards, *Ishtabe,* and *Hoollabe,* "man-killers," and "spoilers of things sacred." My prophetic friend desired me to think myself secure from those dangerous enemies of darkness, for (said he) *Tarooa Ishtohoollo-Antarooare,* "I have sung the song of the great holy one." The Indians are so tenacious of concealing their religious mysteries, that I never before observed such an invocation on the like occasion—adjuring evil spirits, witches, &c. by the awful name of deity.[177]

ARGUMENT XIX.

The Hebrews have at all times been very careful in the BURIAL of their dead—to be deprived of it was considered as one of the greatest of evils. They made it a point of duty to perform the funeral obsequies of their friends—often embalmed the dead bodies of those who were rich, and even buried treasure in the tombs with their dead. Josephus tells us, that in king David's sepulchre, was buried such a prodigious quantity of treasures, that

Hyrcanus the Maccabean, took three thousand talents out of it, about thirteen hundred years after, to get rid of Antiochius then besieging Jerusalem. And their people of distinction, we are told, followed the like custom of burying gold and silver with the dead. Thus it was an universal custom with the ancient Peruvians, when the owner died to bury his [178] effects with him, which the avaricious Spaniards perceiving, they robbed these storehouses of the dead of immense quantity of treasures. The modern Indians bury all their moveable riches, according to the custom of the ancient Peruvians and Mexicans, insomuch, that the grave is heir of all.[178]

Except the Cheerake, only one instance of deviation, from this ancient and general Indian custom occurs to me: which was that of *Malahche,* the late famous chieftain of the *Kowwetah* head war-town of the lower part of the Muskohge country,[179] who bequeathed all he possessed to his real, and adopted relations,—being sensible they would be much more useful to his living friends, than to himself during his long sleep: he displayed a genius far superior to the crowd.

The Cheerake of late years, by the reiterated persuasion of the traders, have entirely left off the custom of burying effects with the dead body; the nearest of blood inherits them. They, and several other of our Indian nations, used formerly to shoot all the live stock that belonged to the deceased, soon after the interment of the corpse; not according to the Pagan custom of the funeral piles, on which they burned several of the living, that they might accompany and wait on the dead, but from a narrow-hearted avaricious principle, derived from their Hebrew progenitors.

Notwithstanding the North-American Indians, like the South-Americans, inter the whole riches of the deceased with him, and so make his corpse and the grave heirs of all, they never give them the least disturbance; even a blood-thirsty enemy will not despoil nor disturb the dead. The grave proves an asylum, and a sure place of rest to the sleeping person, till at some certain time, according to their opinion, he rises again to inherit his favourite place,—unless the covetous, or curious hand of some foreigner, should break through his sacred bounds. This custom of burying the dead person's treasures with him, has entirely swallowed up their medals, and other monuments of antiquity, without any probability of recovering them*.

---

*In the Tuccabatches on the Tallapoose river, thirty miles above the Allabahamah garrison, are two brazen tables, and five of copper. They esteem them so sacred as to keep [179] them constantly in their holy of holies, without touching them in the least, only in the time of their compounded first-fruit-offering, and annual expiation of sins; at which season, their magus carries one under his arm, a-head of the people, dancing round the sacred arbour; next to him their head-warrior carries another; and those warriors who chuse it, carry the rest after the manner of the high-priest; all the others carry white canes with swan-feathers at the top. Hearing accidentally of these

[179] As the Hebrews carefully buried their dead, so on any accident, they gathered their bones and laid them in the tombs of their fore-fathers: Thus, all the numerous nations of Indians perform the like friendly office to every deceased person of their respective tribe; insomuch, that those who [180] lose their people at war, if they have not corrupted their primitive customs, are so observant of this kindred duty, as to appropriate some time to collect the bones of their relations; which they call *bone gathering,* or "gathering the bones to their kindred," according to the Hebrew idiom★.[180] The Cheerake, by reason of their great intercourse with foreigners, have dropped that

important monuments of antiquity, and enquiring pretty much about them, I was certified of the truth of the report by four of the southern traders, at the most eminent Indian-trading house of all English America. One of the gentlemen informed me, that at my request he endeavoured to get a liberty of viewing the aforesaid tables, but it could not possibly be obtained, only in the time of the yearly grand sacrifice, for fear of polluting their holy things, at which time gentlemen of curiosity may see them. *Old Bracket,*[181] an Indian of perhaps 100 years old, lives in that old beloved town, who gave the following description of them:

Old Bracket's account of the *five copper* and *two brass plates* under the beloved cabbin in Tuccabatchey-square.

The shape of the five copper plates; one is a foot and half long and seven inches wide, the other four are shorter and narrower.

The largest stamped thus

The shape of the two brass plates,—about a foot and a half in diameter.

He said—he was told by his forefathers that those plates were given to them by the man we call God; that there had been many more of other shapes, some as long as he could stretch with both his arms, and some had writing upon them which were buried with particular men; and that they had instructions given with them, viz. they must only be handled by particular people, and those fasting; and no unclean woman must be suffered to come near them or the place where they are deposited. He said, none but this town's people had any such plates given them, and that they were a different people from the Creeks. He only remembered three more, which were buried with three of his family, and he was the only man of the family now left. He said, there were two copper plates under the king's cabbin, which had lain there from the first settling of the town.

This account was taken in the Tuccabatchey-square, 27th July, 1759, per *Will. Bolsover.*[182]

★With the Hebrews, "to gather," usually signified to die. Gen. xlix. 33. Jacob is said to be gathered to his people. Psal. xxvi. 9. Gather not my soul with sinners. And Numb. xx. 24. Aaron shall be gathered to his people.

friendly office: and as they seem to be more intelligent than the rest of our English-American Indians in their religious rites, and ceremonial observances, so I believe, the fear of pollution has likewise contributed to obliterate that ancient kindred duty. However, they separate those of their people who die at home, from others of a different nation; and every particular tribe indeed of each nation bears an intense love to itself, and divides every one of its people from the rest, both while living, and after they are dead.

When any of them die at a distance, if the company be not driven and pursued by the enemy, they place the corpse on a scaffold, covered with notched logs to secure it from being torn by wild beasts, or fowls of prey: when they imagine the flesh is consumed, and the bones are thoroughly dried, they return to the place, bring them home, and inter them in a very solemn manner. They will not associate with us, when we are burying any of our people, who die in their land: and they are unwilling we should join with them while they are performing this kindred duty to theirs. Upon which account, though I have lived among them in the raging time of the small pox, even of the confluent sort, I never saw but one buried, who was a great favourite of the English, and chieftain of *Ooeasa,* as formerly described.[183]

The Indians use the same ceremonies to the bones of their dead, as if they were covered with their former skin, flesh, and ligaments. It is but a few days since I saw some return with the bones of nine of their people, who had been two months before killed by the enemy. They were tied in white deerskins, separately; and when carried by the door of one of the houses of their family, they were laid down opposite to it, till the female [181] relations convened, with flowing hair, and wept over them about half an hour. Then they carried them home to their friendly magazines of mortality, wept over them again, and then buried them with the usual solemnities; putting their valuable effects, and as I am informed, other convenient things in along with them, to be of service to them in the next state. The chieftain carried twelve short sticks tied together, in the form of a quadrangle; so that each square consisted of three. The sticks were only peeled, without any paintings; but there were swans feathers tied to each corner, and as they called that frame, *Tereekpe tobeh,* "a white circle," and placed it over the door, while the women were weeping over the bones, perhaps it was originally designed to represent the holy fire, light, and spirit, who formerly presided over the four principal standards of the twelve tribes of Israel.

When any of their people die at home, they wash and anoint the corpse, and soon bring it out of doors for fear of pollution; then they place it opposite to the door, on the skins of wild beasts, in a sitting posture, as looking into the door of the winter house, westward, sufficiently supported with all his moveable goods; after a short elogium, and space of mourning, they carry him three times around the house in which he is to be interred, stopping half a minute each time, at the place where they began the circle, while the religious man of the deceased person's family, who goes before the hearse, says each time, *Yâh,* short with a bass voice, and then invokes on a tenor key, *Yo,* which at the same time is likewise sung by all the procession, as long as one breath allows. Again, he strikes up, on a sharp treble key, the fœminine note, *He,* which in like manner, is taken up and continued by the rest: then all of them suddenly strike off the solemn chorus, and sacred invocation, by saying, on a low key, *Wâh;* which constitute the divine essential name, *Yohewah.* This is the method in which they performed the funeral rites of the chieftain before referred to; during which time, a great many of the traders were present, as our company was agreeable at the interment of our declared patron and friend.[184] It seems as if they buried him in the name of the divine essence, and directed their plaintive religious notes to the author of life and death, in hopes of a resurrection of the body; which hope engaged the Hebrews to stile their burying places, "the house of the living."

[182] When they celebrated these funeral rites of the above chieftain, they laid the corpse in his tomb, in a sitting posture, with his face towards the east, his head anointed with bear's oil, and his face painted red, but not streaked with black, because that is a constant emblem of war and death; he was drest in his finest apparel, having his gun and pouch, and trusty hiccory bow, with a young panther's skin, full of arrows, along side of him, and every other useful thing he had been possessed of,—that when he rises again, they may serve him in that tract of land which pleased him best before he went to take his long sleep. His tomb was firm and clean in-side. They covered it with thick logs, so as to bear several tiers of cypress-bark, and such a quantity of clay as would confine the putrid smell, and be on a level with the rest of the floor. They often sleep over those tombs; which, with the loud wailing of the women at the dusk of the evening, and dawn of the day, on benches close by the tombs, must awake the memory of their relations very often: and if they were killed by an enemy, it helps to irritate and set on such revengeful tempers to retaliate blood for blood.

The Egyptians either embalmed, or buried, their dead: other heathen nations imagined that fire purified the body; they burned therefore the bodies of their dead, and put their ashes into small urns, which they religiously kept by them, as sacred relicks. The Tartars called *Kyrgessi,* near the frozen sea, formerly used to hang their dead relations and friends upon trees, to be eaten by ravenous birds to purify them. But the Americans seem evidently to have derived their copy from the Israelites, as to the place where they bury their dead, and the method of their funeral ceremonies, as well as the persons with whom they are buried, and the great expences they are at in their burials. The Hebrews buried near the city of Jerusalem, by the brook Kedron; and they frequently hewed their tombs out of rocks, or buried their dead opposite to their doors, implying a silent lesson of friendship, and a pointing caution to live well. They buried all of one family together; to which custom David alludes, when he says, "gather me not with the wicked:" and Sophronius said with regard to the like form, "noli me tangere, hæretice, neque vivum nec mortuum."[185] But they buried strangers apart by themselves, and named the place, *Kebhare Galeya,* "the burying place of strangers." And these rude Americans are so strongly partial to the same custom, that they imagine if any of us [183] were buried in the domestic tombs of their kindred, without being adopted, it would be very criminal in them to allow it; and that our spirits would haunt the eaves of their houses at night, and cause several misfortunes to their family.

In resemblance to the Hebrew custom of embalming their dead, the Choktah treat the corpse just as the religious Levite did his beloved concubine, who was abused by the Benjamites; for having placed the dead on a high scaffold stockaded round, at the distance of twelve yards from his house opposite to the door, the whole family convene there at the beginning of the fourth moon after the interment, to lament and feast together: after wailing a while on the mourning benches, which stand on the east side of the quadrangular tomb, they raise and bring out the corpse, and while the feast is getting ready, a person whose office it is, and properly called the *bone-picker,* dissects it, as if it was intended for the shambles in the time of a great famine, with his sharp-pointed, bloody knife. He continues busily employed in his reputed sacred office, till he has finished the task, and scraped all the flesh off the bones; which may justly be called the Choktah method of enbalming their dead. Then, they carefully place the bones in a kind of small chest, in their natural order, that they may with ease and certainty be some time afterward reunited, and proceed to strike up a song of lamentation, with various wailing tunes and notes: afterwards, they join as cheerfully in the funeral feast, as if their kinsman was only taking his usual sleep. Having regaled themselves with a plentiful variety, they go along with those beloved relicks of their dead, in solemn procession, lamenting with doleful notes, till they arrive at the bone-house, which stands in a solitary place, apart from the town: then they proceed around it, much after the manner of those who performed the obsequies of the Chikkasah chieftain, already described, and there deposit their kinsman's bones to lie along side of his kindred-bones, till in due time they are revived by *Ishtohoollo Aba,* that he may repossess his favourite place.

Those bone-houses are scaffolds raised on durable pitch-pine forked posts, in the form of a house covered a-top, but open at both ends. I saw three of them in one of their towns, pretty near each other—the place seemed to be unfrequented; each house contained the bones of one tribe, [184] separately, with the hieoglyphical figures of the family on each of the old-shaped arks: they reckon it irreligious to mix the bones of a relation with those of a stranger, as bone of bone, and flesh of the same flesh, should be always joined together; and much less will they thrust the body of their beloved kinsman into the abominable tomb of a hateful enemy. I observed a ladder fixed in the ground, opposite to the middle of the broad side of each of those dormitories of the dead, which was made out of a broad board, and stood considerably bent over the sacred repository, with the steps on the inside. On the top was the carved image of a dove, with its wings stretched out, and its head inclining down, as if earnestly viewing or watching over the bones of the dead: and from the top of the ladder to almost the surface of the earth, there hung a chain of grape-vines twisted together, in circular links, and the same likewise at their domestic tombs.[186] Now the dove after the deluge, became the emblem of *Rowah,* the holy spirit, and in process of time was deified by the heathen world, instead of the divine person it typified: the vine was likewise a symbol of fruitfulness, both in the animal and vegetable world.

To perpetuate the memory of any remarkable warriors killed in the woods, I must here observe, that every Indian traveller as he passes that way throws a stone on the place, according as he likes or dislikes the occasion, or manner of the death of the deceased.

In the woods we often see innumerable heaps of small stones in those places, where according to tradition some of their distinguished people were either killed, or buried, till the bones could be gathered: there they add *Pelion* to *Ossa,* still increasing each heap, as a lasting monument, and honour to them, and an incentive to great actions.[187]

Mercury was a favourite god with the heathens, and had various employments; one of which was to be god of the roads, to direct travellers aright—from which the ancient Romans derived their *Dii Compitales,* or *Dei Viales,*[188] which they likewise placed at the meeting of roads, and in the high ways, and esteemed them the patrons and protectors of travellers. The early heathens placed great heaps of stones at the dividing of [185] the roads, and consecrated those heaps to him by unction★, and other religious ceremonies. And in honour to him, travellers threw a stone to them, and thus exceedingly increased their bulk: this might occasion Solomon to compare the giving honour to a fool, to throwing a stone into a heap, as each were

★They rubbed the principal stone of each of those heaps all over with oil, as a sacrifice of libation; by which means they often became black, and slippery; as Arnobius relates of the idols of his time; Lubricatum lapidem, et ex olivi unguine sordidatum, tanquam inesset vis presens, adulabar. *Arnob. Advers. Gent.*[189]

alike insensible of the obligation; and to cause the Jewish writers to call this custom a piece of idolatrous worship. But the Indians place those heaps of stones where there are no dividings of the roads, nor the least trace of any road★. And they then observe no kind of religious ceremony, but raise those heaps merely to do honour to their dead, and incite the living to the pursuit of virtue. Upon which account, it seems to be derived from the ancient Jewish custom of increasing Absalom's tomb; for the last things are easiest retained, because people repeat them oftenest, and imitate them most.

[186] ARGUMENT XX.

The Jewish records tell us, that their women MOURNED for the loss of their deceased husbands, and were reckoned vile, by the civil law, if they married in the space, at least, of ten months after their death. In resemblance to that custom, all the Indian widows, by an established strict penal law, mourn for the loss of their deceased husbands; and among some tribes for the space of three or four years. But the East-India Pagans forced the widow, to sit on a pile of wood, and hold the body of her husband on her knees, to be consumed together in the flames.

The Muskohge widows are obliged to live a chaste single life, for the tedious space of four years; and the Chikkasah women, for the term of three, at the risque of the law of adultery being executed against the recusants.[190] Every evening, and at the very dawn of day, for the first year of her widowhood, she is obliged through the fear of shame to lament her loss, in very intense audible strains. As *Yah ah* signifies weeping, lamenting, mourning, or Ah God; and as the widows, and others, in their grief bewail and cry *Yo He (ta) Wah, Yohetaweh; Yohetaha Yohetahe,* the origin is sufficiently clear. For the

---

★Laban and Jacob raised a heap of stones, as a lasting monument of their friendly covenant. And Jacob called the heap *Galeed,* "the heap of witness." Gen. xxxi. 47.

Though the Cheerake do not now collect the bones of their dead, yet they continue to raise and multiply heaps of stones, as monuments for their dead; this the English army remembers well, for in the year 1760, having marched about two miles along a wood-land path, beyond a hill where they had seen a couple of these reputed tombs, at the war-woman's creek, they received so sharp a defeat by the Cheerake, that another such must have inevitably ruined the whole army.[191]

Many of those heaps are to be seen, in all parts of the continent of North-America: where stones could not be had, they raised large hillocks or mounds of earth, wherein they carefully deposited the bones of their dead, which were placed either in earthen vessels, or in a simple kind of arks, or chests. Although the Mohawk Indians may be reasonably expected to have lost their primitive customs, by reason of their great intercourse with foreigners, yet I was told by a gentleman of distinguished character, that they observe the aforesaid sepulchral custom to this day, insomuch, that when they are performing that kindred-duty, they cry out, *Mahoom Taguyn Kameneh,* "Grandfather, I cover you."

Hebrews reckoned it so great an evil to die unlamented, like Jehoiakim, Jer. xxii. 18. "who had none to say, Ah, my brother! Ah, my sister! Ah, my Lord! Ah, his glory!" that it is one of the four judgments they pray against, and it is called the burial of an ass. With them, burying signified lamenting, and so the Indian widows direct their mournful cries to the author of life and death, insert a plural note in the sacred name, and again transpose the latter, through an invariable religious principle, to prevent a prophanation.

Their law compels the widow, through the long term of her weeds, to refrain all public company and diversions, at the penalty of an adulteress; [187] and likewise to go with flowing hair, without the privilege of oil to anoint it. The nearest kinsmen of the deceased husband, keep a very watchful eye over her conduct, in this respect. The place of interment is also calculated to wake the widow's grief, for he is intombed in the house under her bed. And if he was a war-leader, she is obliged for the first moon, to sit in the day-time under his mourning war-pole★, which is decked with all his martial trophies, and must be heard to cry with bewailing notes. But none of them are fond of that month's supposed religious duty, it chills, or sweats, and wastes them so exceedingly; for they are allowed no shade, or shelter. This sharp rigid custom excites the women to honour the marriage-state, and keeps them obliging to their husbands, by anticipating the visible sharp difficulties which they must undergo for so great a loss. The three or four years monastic life, which she lives after his death, makes it her interest to strive by every means, to keep in his lamp of life, be it ever so dull and worthless; if she is able to shed tears on such an occasion, they often proceed from self-love. We can generally distinguish between the widow's natural mourning voice, and her tuneful laboured strain. She doth not so much bewail his death, as her own recluse life, and hateful state of celibacy; which to many of them, is as uneligible, as it was to the Hebrew ladies, who preferred death before the unmarried state, and reckoned their virginity a bewailable condition, like the state of the dead.

The Choktah Indians hire mourners to magnify the merit and loss of their dead, and if their tears cannot be seen to flow, their shrill voices will be heard to cry, which answers the solemn chorus a great deal better†.

★The war-pole is a small peeled tree painted red, the top and boughs cut off short: it is fixt in the ground opposite to his door, and all his implements of war, are hung on the short boughs of it, till they rot.
†Jer. ix. 17. 19. Thus saith the Lord of hosts: consider ye, and call for the mourning-women, that they may come; and send for cunning women, that they may come. For a voice of wailing is heard out of Zion, how are we spoiled? we are greatly confounded, because we have forsaken the land, because our dwellings have cast us out.

However, they are no way churlish of their tears, for I have seen them, on the occasion, pour them out, like fountains of water: but after having [188] thus tired themselves, they might with equal propriety have asked by-standers in the manner of the native Irish, Ara ci fuar bass—"And who is dead?"

They formerly dressed their heads with black moss on those solemn oc-casions; and the ground adjacent to the place of interment, they now beat with laurel-brushes, the women having their hair disheveled: the first of which customs seems to be derived from the Hebrew custom of wearing sack-cloth at their funeral solemnities, and on other occasions, when they afflicted their souls before God—to which divine writ often alludes, in de-scribing the blackness of the skies: and the laurel being an ever-green, is a lively emblem of the eternity of the human soul, and the pleasant state it enters into after death, according to antiquity. They beat it on the ground, to express their sharp pungent grief; and, perhaps, to imitate the Hebrew trumpeters for the dead, in order to make as striking a sound as they possibly can on so doleful an occasion.

Though the Hebrews had no positive precept that obliged the widow to mourn the death of her husband, or to continue her widowhood, for any time; yet the gravity of their tempers, and their scrupulous nicety of the law of purity, introduced the observance of those modest and religious customs, as firmly under the penalty of shame, as if they bore the sanction of law★. In imitation of them, the Indians have copied so exactly, as to compel the widow to act the part of the disconsolate dove, for the irreparable loss of her mate. Very different is the custom of other nations:—the Africans, when any of their head-men die, kill all their slaves, their friends that were dearest to them, and all their wives whom they loved best, that they may accompany and serve them, in the other world, which is a most diabolical Ammonitish sacrifice of human blood. The East-India widows may refuse to be burned on their husbands funeral piles, with impunity, if they become prostitutes, or public women to sing and dance at marriages, or on other occasions of rejoicing. How superior [189] is the virtuous custom of the savage Ameri-cans, concerning female chastity during the time of their widowhood?

The Indian women mourn three moons, for the death of any female of their own family or tribe. During that time, they are not to anoint, or tie up their hair; neither is the husband of the deceased allowed, when the offices of nature do not call him, to go out of the house, much less to join any company: and in that time of mourning he often lies among the ashes.

★Theodosius tells us, Lib. 1. Legum de fecundis nuptiis, that women were infamous by the civil law, who married a second time before a year, or at least ten months were expired.

The time being expired, the female mourners meet in the evening of the beginning of the fourth moon, at the house where their female relation is intombed, and stay there till morning, when the nearest surviving old kinswoman crops their fore-locks pretty short. This they call *Ehó Intànáah,* "the women have mourned the appointed time." *Eho* signifies "a woman," *Inta* "finished by divine appointment," *Aà* "moving" or walking, and *Ah,* "their note of grief, sorrow, or mourning:" the name expresses, and the custom is a visible certificate of, their having mourned the appointed time for their dead. When they have eaten and drank together, they return home by sunrise, and thus finish their solemn *Yah-ah.*

ARGUMENT XXI.

The surviving brother, by the Mosaic law, was to RAISE SEED to a deceased brother who left a widow childless, to perpetuate his name and family, and inherit his goods and estate, or be degraded: and, if the issue he begat was a male child, it assumed the name of the deceased. The Indian custom looks the very same way; yet it is in this as in their law of blood—the eldest brother can redeem.

Although a widow is bound, by a strict penal law, to mourn the death of her husband for the space of three or four years; yet, if she be known to lament her loss with a sincere heart, for the space of a year, and her circumstances of living are so strait as to need a change of her station—and the elder brother of her deceased husband lies with her, she is thereby exempted [190] from the law of mourning, has a liberty to tie up her hair, anoint and paint herself in the same manner as the Hebrew widow, who was refused by the surviving brother of her deceased husband, became free to marry whom she pleased.

The warm-constitutioned young widows keep their eye so intent on this mild beneficent law, that they frequently treat their elder brothers-in-law with spirituous liquors till they intoxicate them, and thereby decoy them to make free, and so put themselves out of the reach of that mortifying law. If they are disappointed, as it sometimes happens, they fall on the men, calling them *Hoobuk Wakse,* or *Skoobále, Hassé kroopha,* "Eunuchus præputio detecto, et pene brevi;"[192] the most degrading of epithets. Similar to the Hebrew ladies, who on the brother's refusal loosed his shoe from his foot, and spit in his face, (Deut. xxv. 9.); and as some of the Rabbies tell us they made water in the shoe, and threw it with despite in his face, and then readily went to bed to any of his kinsmen, or most distant relations of the same line that she liked best; as Ruth married Boaz. Josephus, to palliate the fact, says she only beat him with the shoe over his face. David probably alludes to this custom, Psal. lx. 8. "Over Edom I will cast out my shoe," or detraction.

Either by corruption, or misunderstanding that family-kissing custom of the Hebrews, the corrupt Cheerake marry both mother and daughter at once; though, unless in this instance, they and all the other savage nations observe the degrees of consanguinity in a stricter manner than the Hebrews, or even the christian world. The Cheerake do not marry their first or second cousins; and it is very observable, that the whole tribe reckon a friend in the same rank with a brother, both with regard to marriage, and any other affair in social life. This seems to evince that they copied from the stable and tender friendship between Jonathan and David; especially as the Hebrews had legal, or adopted, as well as natural brothers.

[191] ARGUMENT XXII.

When the Israelites gave names to their children or others, they chose such appellatives as suited best with their circumstances, and the times. This custom was as early as the Patriarchal age; for we find Abram was changed into Abraham; Sarai into Sarah, Jacob into Israel;—and afterwards Oshea, Joshua, Solomon, Jedidiah, &c. &c. This custom is a standing rule with the Indians, and I never observed the least deviation from it. They give their children names, expressive of their tempers, outward appearances, and other various circumstances; a male child, they will call *Choola,* "the fox;" and a female, *Pakahle,* "the blossom, or flower." The father and mother of the former are called *Choollingge,* and *Choollishke,* "the father and mother of the fox;" in like manner, those of the latter, *Pakahlingge,* and *Pakahlishke;* for *Ingge* signifies the father, and *Ishke* the mother. In private life they are so termed till that child dies; but after that period they are called by the name of their next surviving child, or if they have none, by their own name: and it is not known they ever mention the name of the child that is extinct. They only faintly allude to it, saying, "the one that is dead," to prevent new grief, as they had before mourned the appointed time. They who have no children of their own, adopt others, and assume their names, in the manner already mentioned. This was of divine appointment, to comfort the barren, and was analogous to the kindred method of counting with the Hebrews: instead of surnames, they used in their genealogies the name of the father, and prefixed *Ben,* "a son," to the person's name. And thus the Greeks, in early times. No nation used surnames, except the Romans after their league and union with the Sabines. And they did not introduce that custom, with the least view of distinguishing their families, but as a politic seal to their strong compact of friendship; for as the Romans prefixed Sabine names to their own, the Sabines took Roman names in like manner. A specimen of the Indian war-names, will illustrate this argument with more clearness.

[192] They crown a warrior, who has killed a distinguished enemy, with the name, *Yanasabe,* "the buffalo-killer;" *Yanasa* is a buffalo, compounded of *Yah,* the divine essence, and *Asa,* "there, or here is," as formerly mentioned:

and *Abe* is their constant war-period, signifying, by their rhetorical figure "one who kills another." It signifies also to murder a person, or beat him severely. This proper name signifies, the prosperous killer, or destroyer of the buffalo, or strong man—it cannot possibly be derived from אבה, *Abeh,* which signifies good-will, brotherly love, or tender affection; but from אבל, *Abele,* grief, sorrow, or mourning, as an effect of that hostile act.

Anoah, with the Indians, is the name of a rambling person, or one of unsettled residence, and *Anoah ookproo,* is literally a bad rambling person, "a renagadoe:" likewise *Anoah ookproo'shto* makes it a superlative, on account of the abbreviation of *Ishto,* one of the divine names which they subjoin. In like manner, *Noabe* is the war-name of a person who kills a rambling enemy, or one detached as a scout, spy, or the like. It consists of the patriarchal name, *Noah,* and *Abe,* "to kill," according to the Hebrew original, of which it is a contraction, to make it smoother, and to indulge a rapidity of expression. There is so strong an agreement between this compounded proper name, and two ancient Hebrew proper names, that it displays the greatest affinity between the warfaring red and white Hebrews; especially as it so clearly alludes to the divine history of the first homicide, and the words are adapted to their proper significations.

Because the Choktah did not till lately trim their hair, the other tribes through contempt of their custom, called them *Pas' Pharáàh,* "long hair," and they in return, gave them the contemptuous name, *Skoobálè'shtó,* "very naked, or bare heads," compounded of *Skooba, Ale,* and *Ishto:* the same word, or *Waksishto,* with *Hasseh* prefixed, expresses the *penem præputio detecto;*[193] which shews they lately retained a glimmering, though confused notion of the law of circumcision, and the prohibition of not polling their hair. They call a crow, *Pharah;* and *Pas'pharáàbe* is the proper name of a warrior, who killed an enemy wearing long hair. It is a triple compound from *Pásèh,* "the hair of one's head," *Pharaah* "long," and *Abe,* "killing," which they croud together. They likewise say, their tongue is not [193] *Pharakto,* "forked," thereby alluding probably to the formerly-hateful name of the Egyptian kings, Pharaoh.

When the Indians distinguish themselves in war, their names are always compounded,—drawn from certain roots suitable to their intention, and expressive of the characters of the persons, so that their names joined together, often convey a clear and distinct idea of several circumstances—as of the time and place, where the battle was fought, of the number and rank of their captives, and the slain. The following is a specimen: one initiating in war-titles, is called *Tannip-Abe,* "a killer of the enemy;"—he who kills a person carrying a kettle, is crowned *Soonak-Abe-Tuska;* the first word signifies a kettle, and the last a warrior. *Minggáshtàbe* signifies "one who killed a very great chieftain," compounded of *Mingo, Ash,* and *Abe. Pae-Máshtàbe,* is, one in the way of war-gradation, or below the highest in rank, *Pae* signifying "far off." *Tisshu Mashtabe* is the name of a warrior who kills the war-chieftain's waiter carrying the beloved ark. *Shulashum-mashtabe,* the name of the late Choktah great war-leader, our firm friend Red-shoes, is compounded of *Shulass',* "Maccaseenes," or deer skin-shoes, *Humma,* "red," *Ash,* "the divine fire;" *T* is inserted for the sake of a bold sound, or to express the multiplicity of the exploits he performed, in killing the enemy.[194] In treating of their language, I observed, they end their proper names with a vowel, and contract their war-titles, to give more smoothness, and a rapidity of expression. *Etehk* is the general name they give to any female creature, but by adding their constant war-period to it, it signifies "weary;" as *Chetehkabe,* "you are weary:" to make it a superlative, they say *Chetehkabe-O:* or *Chetehkabeshto.*

The Cheerake call a dull stalking fellow, *Sooreh,* "the turkey-buzzard," and one of an ill temper, *Kana Cheesteche,* "the wasp," or a person resembling the dangerous Canaan rabbit, being compounded of the abbreviated name of Canaan, and *Cheesto* "a rabbit," which the Israelites were not to meddle with. One of our chief traders, who was very loquacious, they called *Sekakee,* "the grass-hopper," derived from *Sekako,* "to make haste." To one of a hoarse voice, they gave the name, *Kanoona,* "the bull-frog."

[194] The Katahba Indians call their chief old interpreter, on account of his obscene language, *Emate-Atikke,* "the smock-interpreter." The *"raven,"* is one of the Cheerake favourite war-names. Carolina and Georgia remember *Quorinnah,* "the raven," of *Huwhase-town;*[195] he was one of the most daring warriors of the whole nation, and by far the most intelligent, and this name, or war-appellative, admirably suited his well-known character. Though with all the Indian nations, the raven is deemed an impure bird, yet they have a kind of sacred regard to it, whether from the traditional knowledge of Noah's employing it while he was in the ark, or from that bird having fed Elijah in the wilderness (as some suppose) cannot be determined; however with our supposed red Hebrews the name points out an indefatigable, keen, successful warrior.

ARGUMENT XXIII.

Although other resemblances of the Indian rites and customs to those of the Hebrews, might be pointed out; not to seem tedious, I proceed to the last argument of the origin of the Indian Americans, which shall be from their own traditions,—from the accounts of our English writers—and from the testimonies which the Spanish writers have given, concerning the primitive inhabitants of Peru and Mexico.[196]

The Indian tradition says, that their forefathers in very remote ages came from a far distant country, where all the people were of one colour; and that in process of time they moved eastward, to their present settlements. So that, what some of our writers have asserted is not just, who say the Indians affirm, that there were originally three different tribes in those countries, when the supreme chieftain to encourage swift running, proposed a proportionable reward of distinction to each, as they excelled in speed in passing a certain distant river; as, that the first should be polished white—the second red—and the third black; which took place accordingly after the race was over.[197] This story sprung from the innovating superstitious [195] ignorance of the popish priests, to the south-west of us. Our own Indian tradition is literal, and not allegorical, and ought to be received; because people who have been long separated from the rest of mankind, must know their own traditions the best, and could not be deceived in so material, and frequently repeated an event. Though they have been disjoined through different interests, time immemorial; yet, (the rambling tribes of northern Indians excepted) they aver that they came over the Missisippi from the westward, before they arrived at their present settlements. This we see verified by the western old towns they have left behind them; and by the situation of their old beloved towns, or places of refuge, lying about a west course from each different nation. Such places in Judea were chiefly built in the most remote parts of the country; and the Indians deem those only as beloved towns, where they first settled.

This tradition is corroborated by a current report of the old Chikkasah Indians to our traders, "that about forty years since, there came from Mexico some of the old Chikkasah nation, (the Chichemicas, according to the Spanish accounts) in quest of their brethren, as far north as the Aquahpah nation,[198] about 130 miles above the Nachee old towns, on the south side of the Missisippi; but through French policy, they were either killed, or sent back, so as to prevent their opening a brotherly intercourse, as they had proposed." And it is worthy of notice, that the Muskohgeh cave, out of which one of their politicians persuaded them their ancestors formerly ascended to their present terrestrial abode, lies in the Nanne Hamgeh old town, inhabited by the Missisippi-Nachee Indians, which is one of the most western parts of their old-inhabited country.[199]

I hope I shall be excused in reciting their ancient oral tradition, from father to son to the present time. They say, that one of their cunning old religious men finding that religion did not always thrive best, resolved with himself to impose on his friends credulity, and alter in some respects their old tradition; he accordingly pretended to have held for a long time a continual intercourse with their subterranean progenitors in a cave, above 600 miles to the westward of Charles-town in South-Carolina, adjoining to the old Chikkasah trading path; this people were then possest of every thing convenient for human life, and he promised them fully to supply their wants, [196] in a constant manner, without sweating in the field; the most troublesome of all things to manly brisk warriors. He insisted, that all who were desirous of so natural and beneficial a correspondence, should contribute large presents, to be delivered on the embassy, to their brethren—terræ filii,[200]—to clear the old chain of friendship from the rust it had contracted, through the fault of cankering time. He accordingly received presents from most of the people, to deliver them to their beloved subterranean kindred: but it seems, they shut up the mouth of the cave, and detained him there in order to be purified.

The old waste towns of the Chikkasah lie to the west and south-west, from where they have lived since the time we first opened a trade with them; on which course they formerly went to war over the Missisippi, because they knew it best, and had disputes with the natives of those parts, when they first came from thence. Wisdom directed them then to connive at some injuries on account of their itinerant camp of women and children; for their tradition says, it consisted of ten thousand men, besides women and children, when they came from the west, and passed over the Missisippi. The fine breed of running wood horses they brought with them, were the present Mexican or Spanish barbs.[201] They also aver, that their ancestors cut off, and despoiled the greatest part of a caravan, loaded with gold and silver; but the carriage of it proved so troublesome to them, that they threw it into a river where it could not benefit the enemy.

If we join together these circumstances, it utterly destroys the fine Peruvian and Mexican temples of the sun, &c.—which the Spaniards have lavishly painted from their own fruitful imaginations, to shew their own capacity of writing, though at the expence of truth; and to amuse the gazing distant world, and lessen our surprise at the sea of reputed heathenish blood, which their avaricious tempers, and flaming superstitious zeal, prompted them to spill.

If any English reader have patience to search the extraordinary volumes of the Spanish writers, or even those of his catholic majesty's chief historiographer,[202] he will not only find a wild portrait, but a striking resemblance and unity of the civil and martial customs, the religious rites, and traditions, of the [197] ancient Peruvians and Mexicans, and the North-Americans, according to the manner of their moresque paintings: likewise, the very national name of the primitive Chikkasah, which they stile Chichemicas, and whom they repute to have been the first inhabitants of Mexico. However, I lay little stress upon Spanish testimonies, for time and ocular proof have convinced us of the laboured falshood of almost all their historical narrations concerning every curious thing relative to South America. They were so divested of those principles inherent to honest enquirers after truth, that they have recorded themselves to be a tribe of prejudiced bigots, striving to aggrandise the Mahometan valour of about nine hundred spurious catholic christians, under the patronage of their favourite saint, as persons by whom heaven designed to extirpate those two great nominal empires of pretended cannibals. They found it convenient to blacken the natives with ill names, and report them to their demi-god the mufti of Rome, as sacrificing every day, a prodigious multitude of human victims to numerous idol-gods.

The learned world is already fully acquainted with the falsehood of their histories; reason and later discoveries condemn them. Many years have elapsed, since I first entered into Indian life, besides a good acquaintance with several southern Indians, who were conversant with the Mexican Indian rites and customs; and it is incontrovertible, that the Spanish monks and jesuits in describing the language, religion, and customs, of the ancient Peruvians and Mexicans, were both unwilling, and incapable to perform so arduous an undertaking, with justice and truth. They did not converse with the natives as friends, but despised, hated, and murdered them, for the sake of their gold and silver: and to excuse their own ignorance, and most shocking, cool, premeditated murders, they artfully described them as an abominable swarm of idolatrous cannibals offering human sacrifices to their various false deities, and eating of the unnatural victims. Nevertheless, from their own partial accounts, we can trace a near agreement between the civil and martial customs, the religious worship, traditions, dress, ornaments, and other particulars of the ancient Peruvians and Mexicans, and those of the present North American Indians.

[198] Acosta[203] tells us, that though the Mexicans have no proper name for God, yet they allow a supreme omnipotence and providence: his capacity was not sufficient to discover the former; however, the latter agrees with the present religious opinion of the English-American Indians, of an universal divine wisdom and government. The want of a friendly intercourse between our northern and southern Indians, has in length of time occasioned some of the former a little to corrupt, or alter the name of the self-existent creator and preserver of the universe, as they repeat it in their religious invocations, YO HE A AH. But with what show of truth, consistent with the above concession, can Acosta describe the Mexicans as offering human sacrifices also to devils, and greedily feasting on the victims!

We are told also that the Nauatalcas believe, they dwelt in another region before they settled in Mexico; that they wandered eighty years in search of it, through a strict obedience to their gods, who ordered them to go in quest of new lands, that had such particular signs;—that they punctually obeyed the divine mandate, and by that means found out, and settled the fertile country of Mexico. This account corresponds with the Chikkasah tradition of settling in their present supposed holy land, and seems to have been derived from a compound tradition of Aaron's rod, and the light or divine presence with the Israelites in the wilderness, when they marched. And probably the Mexican number of years, was originally *forty,* instead of *eighty.*

Lopez de Gomara tells us,[204] that the Mexicans were so devout, as to offer to the sun and earth, a small quantity of every kind of meat and drink, before any of themselves tasted it; and that they sacrificed part of their corn, fruits, &c. in like manner; otherwise, they were deemed haters of, and contemned by their gods. Is not this a confused Spanish picture of the Jewish daily sacrifice, and first-fruit-offering, as formerly observed? and which, as we have seen, are now offered up by the northern Indians, to the bountiful giver, the supreme holy spirit of fire, whom they invoke in that most sacred and awful song, YO He Wah, and loudly ascribe to him *Hallelu-Yah,* for his continued goodness to them.

The Spanish writers say, that when Cortes approached Mexico, Montezuma shut himself up, and continued for the space of eight days in [199] prayers and fasting: but to blacken him, and excuse their own diabolical butcheries, they assert he offered human sacrifices at the same time to abominable and frightful idols. But the sacrifices with more justice may be attributed to the Spaniards than to the Mexicans—as their narratives also are a sacrifice of truth itself. Montezuma and his people's fastings, prayers, &c. were doubtless the same with those of the northern Indians, who on particular occasions, by separate fastings, ablutions, purgations, &c. seek to sanctify themselves, and so avert the ill effects of the divine anger, and regain the favour of the deity.

They write, that the Mexicans offered to one of their gods, a sacrifice compounded of some of all the seeds of their country, grinded fine, and mixed with the blood of children, and of sacrificed virgins; that they plucked out the hearts of those victims, and offered them as first-fruits to the idol; and that the warriors imagined, the least relic of the sacrifice would preserve them from danger. They soon afterwards tell us of a temple of a quadrangular form, called *Teucalli,* "God's house," and *Chacalmua,* "a minister of holy things," who belonged to it. They likewise speak of "the hearth of God,—the continual fire of God,—the holy ark," &c. If we cut off the jesuitical paintings of the unnatural sacrifice, the rest is consonant to what hath been observed, concerning the North American Indians. And it is very obvious, the North and South American Indians are alike of vindictive tempers, putting most of their invading enemies that fall into their power to the fiery torture. The Spaniards looking upon themselves as divine embassadors, under the imperial signature of the Holy Lord of Rome, were excessively enraged against the simple native South-Americans, because they tortured forty of their captivated people by reprisal, devoting them to the fire, and ate their hearts, according to the universal war-custom of our northern Indians, on the like occasion. The Spanish terror and hatred on this account, their pride, religious bigotry, and an utter ignorance of the Indian dialects, rites, and customs, excited them thus to delineate the Mexicans;—and equally hard names, and unjust charges, the bloody members of their diabolical inquisition used to bestow on those pretended heretics, whom they gave over to be tortured and burnt by the secular power. But it is worthy of notice, the Spanish writers acknowledge that the Mexicans brought their human sacrifices from the opposite sea; and did not offer up any of their own people: so that this was but the same [200] as our North American Indians still practice, when they devote their captives to death; which is ushered in with ablutions, and other method of sanctifying themselves, as have been particularly described and they perform the solemnity with singing the sacred triumphal song, with beating of the drum, dances, and various sort of rejoicings, through gratitude to the beneficent and divine author of success against their common enemy. By the description of the Portuguese writers, the Indian-Brasilian method of war, and of torturing their devoted captives, very nearly resembles the customs of our Indians.

Acosta, according to his usual ignorance of the Indian customs, says, that some in Mexico understood one another by whistling, on which he attempts to be witty—but notwithstanding the great contempt and surprise of the Spaniards at those Indians who whistled as they went; this whistle was no other than the war-whoop, or a very loud and shrill shout, denoting death, or good or bad news, or bringing in captives from war. The same writer says they had three kinds of knighthood, with which they honoured the best soldiers; the chief of which was the red ribbon; the next the lion, or tyger-knight; and the meanest was the grey knight. He might with as much truth, have added the turky-buzzard knight, the sun-blind bat knight, and the night-owl knight. His account of the various gradations of the Indian war-titles, shews the unskilfulness of that voluminous writer, even in the first principles of his Indian subject, and how far we ought to rely on his marvellous works.

The accounts the Spaniards formerly gave us of Florida and its inhabitants, are written in the same romantic strain with those of Mexico. Ramusius[205] tells us, that Alvaro Nunes and his company reported the Apalahchee Indians to be such a gigantic people, as to carry bows, thick as a man's arm, and of eleven or twelve spans long, shooting with proportional force and direction. It seems they lived then a sober and temperate life, for Morgues says, one of their kings was three hundred years old; though Laudon reckons him only two hundred and fifty and Morgues assures us, he saw this young Indian Methusalah's father, who was fifty years older than his son, and that each them was likely by the common course of nature to live thirty or forty years longer, although they had seen their fifth generation.[206] Since that time they have so exceedingly degenerated, in height of body, largeness of [201] defensive arms, and ante-deluvian longevity, that I am afraid, these early and extraordinary writers would scarcely know the descendants of those Apalahche Anakim, if they now saw them. They are at present the same as their dwarfish red neighbours; sic transit gloria mundi.[207]

Nicholaus Challusius[208] paints Florida full of winged serpents; he affirms he saw one there, and that the old natives were very careful to get its head, on account of some supposed superstition. Ferdinando Soto tells us, that when he entered Florida, he found a Spaniard, (J. Ortez)[209] whom the natives had captivated during the space of twelve years, consequently he must have gained in that time, sufficient skill in their dialect to give a true interpretation and account—and he assures us, that Ucita, the Lord of the place, made that fellow, "Temple-keeper," to prevent the night-wolves from carrying away the dead corpse; that the natives worshipped the devil, and sacrificed to him the life and blood of most of their captives;—who spoke with them face to face, and ordered them to bring those offerings to quench his burning thirst. And we are told by Benzo,[210] that when Soto died, the good-natured Cacique ordered two likely young Indians to be killed according to custom, to wait on him where he was gone.—But the Christian Spaniards denied his death, and assured them he was the son of God, and therefore could not die. If we except the last sentence, which bears a just analogy to the presumption and arrogance of the popish priests and historians, time and opportunity have fully convinced us, that all the rest is calumny and falshood. It must be confessed however, that none, even of the Spanish monks and friars, have gone so deep in the marvellous, as our own sagacious David Ingram[211]—he assures us, "that he not only heard of very surprising animals in these parts of the world, but saw elephants, horses, and strange wild animals twice as big as our species of horses, formed like a grey-hound in their hinder parts; he saw likewise bulls with ears like hounds; and another surprising species of quadrupeds bigger than bears, without head or neck, but nature had fixed their eyes and mouths more securely in their breasts." At the end of his monstrous ideal productions, he justly introduces the devil in the rear, sometimes assuming the likeness of a dog; at other times the shape of a calf, &c. Although this legendary writer has transcended the bounds of truth, yet where he is not emulous of outdoing the jesuitical romances, it would require a good knowledge of America to confute him in many particulars: [202] this shews how little the learned world can rely on American narrators; and that the origin of the Indian Americans, is yet to be traced in a quite different path to what any of those hyperbolical, or wild conjectural writers have prescribed.

The Spaniards have given us many fine polished Indian orations, but they were certainly fabricated at Madrid; the Indians have no such ideas, or methods of speech, as they pretend to have copied from a faithful interpretation on the spot: however, they have religiously supported those monkish dreams, and which are the chief basis of their Mexican and Peruvian treaties.

According to them, the Mexican arms was an eagle on a tunal or stone, with a bird in his talons,—which may look at the armorial ensign of Dan. And they say, the Mexicans worshipped *Vitzliputzli,* who promised them a land exceedingly plenty in riches, and all other good things; on which account they set off in quest of the divine promise, four of their priests carrying their idol in a coffer of reeds, to whom he communicated his oracles, giving them laws at the same time—teaching them ceremonies and sacrifices they should observe; and directed them when to march, and when to stay in camp, &c. So much, might have been collected from them by signs, and other expressive indications; for we are well assured, that the remote uncorrupted part of the Mexicans still retain the same notions as our northern Indians, with regard to their arriving at, and settling in their respective countries, living under a theocratic government, and having the divine war-ark, as a most sacred seal of success to the beloved people, against their treacherous enemies, if they strictly observe the law of purity, while they accompany it. This alone, without any reflection on the rest, is a good glass to shew us, that the South and North American Indians are twin-born brothers; though the Spanish clergy, by their dark but fruitful inventions, have set them at a prodigious variance.

Acosta tells us, that the Peruvians held a very extraordinary feast called *Ytu,*—which they prepared themselves for, by fasting two days, not accompanying with their wives, nor eating salt-meat or garlic, nor drinking Chica during that period—that they assembled all together in one place, and did not allow any stranger or beast to approach them; that they had clothes and [203] ornaments which they wore, only at that great festival; that they went silently and sedately in procession, with their heads veil'd, and drums beating—and thus continued one day and night; but the next day they danced and feasted; and for two days successively, their prayers and praises were heard. This is another strong picture of the rites of the Indian North-Americans, during the time of their great festival, to atone for sin; and with a little amendment, would exhibit a surprising analogy of sundry essential rites and customs of the Northern and South American Indians, which equally glance at the Mosaic system.

Lerius[212] tells us, that he was present at the triennial feast of the Caribbians, where a multitude of men, women, and children, were assembled; that they soon divided themselves into three orders, apart from each other, the women and children being strictly ordered to stay within, and to attend diligently to the singing: that the men sung in one house, *He, He, He,* while the others in their separate houses, answered by a repetition of the same notes: that having thus continued a quarter of an hour, they all danced in three different rings, each with rattles, &c. And the natives of Sir Francis Drake's New Albion,[213] were desirous of crowning him *Hio,* or *Ohio,* a name well known in North America, and hath an evident relation to the great beloved name. Had the former been endued with a proper capacity, and given a suitable attention to the Indian general law of purity, he would probably have described them singing *Yo-He Wah, Hallelu-Yah,* &c. after the present manner of our North American red natives; and as giving proper names to persons and things from a religious principle, to express the relation they bore to the sacred four-lettered name.

These writers report also, that the Mexicans sacrificed to the idol *Haloc,* "their God of water," to give them seasonable rains for their crops: and they tell us, that the high-priest was anointed with holy oil, and dressed with pontifical ornaments, peculiar to himself, when he officiated in his sacred function; that he was sworn to maintain their religion, rights, and liberties, according to their ancient law; and to cause the sun to shine, and all their vegetables to be properly refreshed with gentle showers. If we throw down the "monkish idol god of water," we here find a strong parity of religious customs and ceremonies, between the pretended prophets, and high-priests of the present northern Indians, and the ancient Mexicans.

[204] Acosta tells us, that the Peruvians acknowledged a supreme God, and author of all things, whom they called *Viracocha,* and worshipped as the chief of all the gods, and honoured when they looked at the heavens or any of the celestial orbs; that for want of a proper name for that divine spirit of the universe, they, after the Mexican manner, described him by his attributes,—as *Pachacamac,* "the Creator of heaven and earth." But, though he hath described them possessed of these strong ideas of God, and to have dedicated a sacred house to the great first cause, bearing his divine prolific name; yet the Spanish priesthood have at the same time, painted them as worshipping the devil in the very same temple. Here and there a truth may be found in their writings, but if we except the well-designed performance of Don Antonio de Ulloa, one duodecimo volume would have contained all the accounts of any curious importance, which the Spaniards have exhibited to the learned world, concerning the genuine rites and customs, of the ancient Peruvians and Mexicans, ever since the seisure of those countries, and the horrid murders committed on the inhabitants.[214]

But among all the Spanish friars, *Hieronimo Roman* was the greatest champion in hyperbolical writing.[215] He has produced three volumes concerning the Indian American rites and ceremonies;—he stretches very far in his second part of the commonwealths of the world; but when he gets to

Peru and Mexico, the distance of those remote regions enables him to exceed himself: beyond all dispute, the other writers of his black fraternity, are only younger brethren, when compared to him in the marvellous. His, is the chief of all the Spanish romances of Peru and Mexico.

He says, the Indian natives, from Florida to Panama, had little religion or policy; and yet he affirms a few pages after, that they believed in one true, immortal and invisible God, reigning in heaven, called *Yocahuuagnamaorocoti;* and is so kind as to allow them images, priests, and popes, their high-priest being called *papa* in that language. The origin of images among them, is accounted for in a dialogue he gives us, between a shaking tree and one of the Indian priests: after a great deal of discourse, the tree ordered the priest to cut it down, and taught him how to make images thereof, and erect a temple. The tree was obeyed, and every year their votaries solemnized the dedication. The good man has [205] laboured very hard for the images, and ought to have suitable applause for so useful an invention; as it shews the universal opinion of mankind, concerning idols and images. With regard to that long conjectural divine name, by which they expressed the one true God, there is not the least room to doubt, that the South-Americans had the divine name, *Yohewah,* in as great purity as those of the north, especially, as they were at the fountain head; adding to it occasionally some other strong compound words.

He says also, that the metropolis of *Cholola* had as many temples as there were days in the year; and that one of them was the most famous in the world, the basis of the spire being as broad as a man could shoot with a cross bow, and the spire itself three miles high. The temples which the holy man speaks of, seem to have been only the dwelling-houses of strangers, who incorporated with the natives, differing a little in their form of structure, according to the usual custom of our northern Indians: and his religious principles not allowing him to go near the reputed shambles of the devil, much less to enter the supposed territories of hell, he has done pretty well by them, in allowing them golden suns and moons—vestry keepers, &c. The badness of his optic instruments, if joined with the supposed dimness of his sight, may plead in excuse for the spiral altitude, which he fixes at 15,480 feet; for from what we know of the northern Indians, we ought to strike off the three first figures of its height, and the remaining 40 is very likely to have been the just height of the spire, alias the red-painted, great, *war-pole.*

The same writer tells us, that the Peruvian pontifical office belonged to the eldest son of the king, or some chief lord of the country: and that it devolved by succession. But he anoints him after a very solemn manner, with an ointment which he carefully mixes with the blood of circumcised infants. This priest of war dealing so much in blood himself, without doubt, suspected them of the like; though at the same time no Indian priest will either shed, or touch human blood: but that they formerly circumcised, may with great probability be allowed to the holy man.

The temples of Peru were built on high grounds, or tops of hills, he says, and were surrounded with four circular mounds of earth, the one rising [206] gradually above the other, from the outermost circle; and that the temple stood in the center of the inclosed ground, built in a quadrangular form, having altars, &c. He has officiously obtruded the sun into it; perhaps, because he thought it dark within. He describes another religious house, on the eastern part of that great inclosure, facing the rising sun, to which they ascended by six steps, where, in the hollow of a thick wall, lay the image of the sun, &c. This thick wall having an hollow part within it, was no other than their sanctum sanctorum, conformably to what I observed, concerning the pretended holiest place of the Muskohge Indians. Any one who is well acquainted with the language, rites, and customs of the North-American Indians, can see with a glance when these monkish writers stumble on a truth, or ramble at large.

Acosta says, that the Mexicans observed their chief feast in the month of May, and that the nuns two days before mixed a sufficient quantity of beets with honey, and made an image of it. He trims up the idol very genteelly, and places it on an azure-coloured chair, every way becoming the scarlet-coloured pope. He soon after introduces flutes, drums, cornets, and trumpets, to celebrate the feast of *Eupania Vitzliputzli,* as he thinks proper to term it: on account of the nuns, he gives them *Pania,* "feminine bread," instead of the masculine *Panis;* which he makes his nuns to distribute at this love-feast, to the young men, in large resembling great bones. When they receive them, they religiously lay them down at the feast of the idol, and call them the flesh and bones of the God *Vitzliputzli.*

Then he brings in the priests vailed, with garlands on their heads and chains of flowers about their necks, each of them strictly observing their place: if the inquisitive reader should desire to know how he discovered those garlands and flowery chains; (especially as their heads were covered, and they are secret in their religious ceremonies) I must inform him, that Acosta wrought a kind of cotton, or woollen cloth for them, much finer than silk, through which he might have easily seen them—besides, such a religious dress gave him a better opportunity of hanging a cross, and a string of beads afterwards round their necks.

[207] Next to those religious men, he ushers in a fine company of gods and goddesses, in imagery, dressed like the others, the people paying them divine worship; this without doubt, is intended to support the popish saint-worship. Then he makes them sing, and dance round the paste, and use several other ceremonies. And when the eyes are tired with viewing those wild

circlings, he solemnly blesses, and consecrates those morsels of paste, and thus makes them the real flesh and bones of the idol, which the people honour as gods. When he has ended his feast of transubstantiation, he sets his sacrificers to work, and orders them to kill and sacrifice more men than at any other festival;—as he thinks proper to make this a greater carnival than any of the rest.

When he comes to finish his bloody sacrifices, he orders the young men and women into two rows, directly facing each other, to dance and sing by the drums, in praise of the feast and the god; and he sets the oldest and the greatest men to answer the song, and dance around them, in a great circle. This with a little alteration, resembles the custom of the northern Indians. He says, that all the inhabitants of the city and country came to this great feast,—that it was deemed sacrilegious in any person to eat of the honeyed paste, on this great festival-day, or to drink water, till the afternoon; and that they earnestly advised those, who had the use of reason, to abstain from water till the afternoon, and carefully concealed it from the children during the time of this ceremony. But, at the end of the feast, he makes the priests and ancients of the temple to break the image of paste and consecrated rolls, into many pieces, and give them to the people by the way of sacrament, according to the strictest rules of order, from the greatest and eldest, to the youngest and least, men, women and children: and he says, they received it with bitter tears, great reverence, and a very awful fear, with other strong signs of devotion, saying at the same time,—"they did not eat the flesh and bones of their God." He adds, that they who had sick people at home, demanded a piece of the said paste, and carried and gave it to them, with the most profound reverence and awful adoration; that all who partook of this propitiating sacrifice, were obliged to give a part of the seed of Maiz, of which the idol was made; and then at the end of the solemnity, a priest of high authority preached to [208] the people on their laws and ceremonies, with a commanding voice, and expressive gestures; and thus dismissed the assembly.

Well may Acosta blame the devil in the manner he does, for introducing among the Mexicans, so near a resemblance of the popish superstitions and idolatry. But whether shall we blame or pity this writer, for obscuring the truth with a confused heap of falshoods? The above is however a curious Spanish picture of the Mexican passover, or annual expiation of sins, and of their second passover in favour of their sick people,—and paying their tythes,—according to similar customs of our North-American Indians. We are now sufficiently informed of the rites and customs of the remote, and uncorrupt South-Americans, by the Missisippi Indians, who have a communication with them, both in peace and war.

Ribault Laudon[216] describing the yearly festival of the Floridans, says that the day before it began, the women swept out a great circuit of ground, where it was observed with solemnity;—that when the main body of the people entered the holy ground, they all placed themselves in good order, stood up painted, and decked in their best apparel, when three *Iawas,* or priests, with different paintings and gestures followed them, playing on musical instruments, and singing with a solemn voice—the others answering them: that when they made three circles in this manner, the men ran off to the woods, and the women staid weeping behind, cutting their arms with muscle-shells, and throwing the blood towards the sun; and that when the men returned, the three days feast was finished. This is another confused Spanish draught of the Floridan passover, or feast of love; and of their universal method of bleeding themselves after much exercise, which according to the Spanish plan, they offered up to the sun. From these different writers, it is plain that where the Indians have not been corrupted by foreigners, their customs and religious worship are nearly alike; and also that every different tribe, or nation of Indians, uses such-like divine proper name, and awful sounds, as *Yah-Wah, Hetovah,* &c. being transpositions of the divine essential name, as our northern Indians often repeat in their religious dances. As the sound of *Yah-wah* jarred in Laudon's ear, he called it *Java,* in resemblance to the Syriac and Greek method of expressing the tetra-grammaton, from which Galatinus imposed it upon us, calling it *Jehowah,* instead of *Yohewah.*[217]

[209] The Spanish writers tell us, that the Mexicans had a feast, and month, which they called *Hueitozolti,* when the maiz was ripe; every man at that time bringing an handful to be offered at the temple, with a kind of drink, called *Utuli,* made out of the same grain.—But they soon deck up an idol with roses, garlands, and flowers, and describe them as offering to it sweet gums, &c. Then they speedily dress a woman with the apparel of either the god, or goddess, of salt, which must be to season the human sacrifices, as they depicture them according to their own dispositions. But they soon change the scene, and bring in the god of gain, in a rich temple dedicated to him, where the merchants apart sacrifice vast numbers of purchased captives. It often chagrines an inquisitive and impartial reader to trace the contradictions, and chimerical inventions, of those aspiring bigoted writers; who speak of what they did not understand, only by signs, and a few chance words. The discerning reader can easily perceive them from what hath been already said, and must know that this Spanish mountain in labour, is only the Indian first fruit-offering, according to the usage of our North-American Indians.

It is to be lamented that writers will not keep to matters of fact: Some of our own historians have described the Mohawks as cannibals, and continually hunting after man's flesh; with equal truth Diodorus Siculus, Strabo, and others report, that in Britain there were formerly Anthropophagi, "man-eaters."[218]

Garcillasso de La Vega, another Spanish romancer, says, that the Peruvian shepherds worshipped the star called Lyra, as they imagined it preserved their flocks: but he ought first to have supplied them with flocks, for they had none except a kind of wild sheep, that kept in the mountains, and which are of so fætid a smell, that no creature is fond to approach them.[219]

The same aspiring fictitious writer tells us, the Peruvians worshipped the Creator of the world, whom he is pleased to call *Viracocha Pachuyacha ha hic:* any person who is in the least acquainted with the rapid flowing manner of the Indian American dialects, will conclude from the wild termination that the former is not the Peruvian divine name. Next to this great Creator of the universe, he affirms, they worshipped the sun; and [210] next to the solar orb, they deified and worshipped thunder, believing it proceeded from a man in heaven, who had power over the rain, hail, and thunder, and every thing in the ærial regions; and that they offered up sacrifices to it, but none to the universal Creator. To prefer the effect to the acknowledged prime cause, is contrary to the common reason of mankind, who adore that object which they esteem either the most beneficent, or the most powerful.

Monsieur Le Page Du Pratz[220] tells us, he lived seven years among the Nachee Indians, about one hundred leagues up the Missisippi from New-Orleans; and in order to emulate the Spanish romances of the Indians, in his performance, he affirms their women are double-breasted, which he particularly describes: and then following the Spanish copy, he assures us, the highest rank of their nobles is called suns, and that they only attend the sacred and eternal fire; which he doubtless mentioned, merely to introduce his convex lens, by which he tells us with a great air of confidence, he gained much esteem among them, as by the gift of it, he enabled them to continue their holy fire, if it should casually be near extinguished. According to him, the Chikkasah tongue was the court language of the Missisippi Indians, and it had not the letter *R.*—The very reverse of which is the truth;[221] for the French and all their red savages were at constant war with them, because of their firm connection with the English and hated their national name; and as to the language, they could not converse with them, as their dialects are so different from each other. I recited a long string of his well-known stories to a body of gentlemen, well skilled in the languages, rites and customs of our East and West-Florida Indians, and they agreed that the Koran did not differ more widely from the divine oracles, than the accounts of this writer from the genuine customs of the Indian Americans.

The Spanish artists have furnished the savage war-chieftain, or their Emperor Montezuma, with very spacious and beautiful palaces, one of which they raised on pillars of fine jasper; and another wrought with exquisite skill out of marble, jasper, and other valuable stones, with veins glistering like rubies,—they have finished the roof with equal skill, composed of carved and painted cypress, cedar, and pine-trees, without any kind of nails. They should have furnished some of the chambers with suitable pavilions [211] and beds of state; but the bedding and furniture in our northern Indian huts, is the same with what they were pleased to describe, in the wonderful Mexican palaces. In this they have not done justice to the grand red monarch, whom they raised up, (with his 1000 women, or 3000 according to some,) only to magnify the Spanish power by overthrowing him.

Montezuma in an oration to his people, at the arrival of the Spaniards, is said by Malvendar,[222] to have persuaded his people to yield to the power of his Catholic Majesty's arms, for their own fore-fathers were strangers in that land, and brought there long before that period in a fleet. The emperor, who they pretend bore such universal arbitrary sway, is raised by their pens, from the usual rank of a war chieftain, to his imperial greatness: But despotic power is death to their ears, as it is destructive of their darling liberty, and reputed theocratic government; they have no name for a subject, but say, "the people." In order to carry on the self-flattering war-romance, they began the epocha of that great fictitious empire, in the time of the ambitious and formidable Montezuma, that their handful of heaven-favoured popish saints might have the more honour in destroying it: had they described it of a long continuance, they foresaw that the world would detect the fallacy, as soon as they learned the language of the pretended empire; correspondent to which, our own great Emperor Powhatan of Virginia, was soon dethroned. We are sufficiently informed by the rambling Missisippi Indians, that *Motehshuma* is a common high war-name of the South-American leaders; and which the fate he is said to receive, strongly corroborates. Our Indians urge with a great deal of vehemence, that as every one is promoted only by public virtue, and has his equals in civil and martial affairs, those Spanish books that have mentioned red emperors, and great empires in America, ought to be burnt in some of the remaining old years accursed fire. And this Indian fixed opinion seems to be sufficiently confirmed by the situation of Mexico, as it is only about 315 miles from south to north; and narrower than 200 miles along the northern coast—and lies between Tlascala and Mechoacan, to the west of the former, and east of the latter, whence the Mexicans were continually harassed by those lurking swift-footed savages, who could secure their retreat home, in the space of two or three days. When we consider the vicinity of those two inimical states to the pretended puissant empire of Mexico, which might have easily crushed them to pieces, with her formidable [212] armies, in order to secure the lives of the subjects, and credit of the state, we may safely venture to affirm, from the long train of circumstances already exhibited, that the Spanish Peruvian and Mexican empires are without the least foundation in nature; and that the Spaniards defeated the tribe of Mexico (properly called *Mechiko*) &c. chiefly, by the help of their red allies.

In their descriptions of South-America and its native inhabitants, they treat largely of heaven, hell, and purgatory; lions, salamanders, maids of honour, maids of penance, and their abbesses; men whipping themselves with cords; idols, mattins, monastic vows, cloisters of young men, with a prodigious group of other popish inventions: and we must not forget to do justice to those industrious and sagacious observers, who discovered two golgothas, or towers made of human skulls, plaistered with lime. Acosta tells us, that Andrew de Topia assured him, he and Gonsola de Vimbria reckoned one hundred and thirty-six thousand human skulls in them. The temple dedicated to the air, is likewise worthy of being mentioned, as they assert in the strongest manner, that five thousand priests served constantly in it, and obliged every one who entered, to bring some human sacrifice; that the walls of it were an inch thick, and the floor a foot deep, with black, dry, clotted blood. If connected herewith, we reflect, that beside this blood-thirsty god of the air, the Spaniards have represented them as worshipping a multitude of idol gods and goddesses, (no less than two thousand according to Lopez de Gomara) and sacrificing to them chiefly human victims; and that the friars are reported by a Spanish bishop of Mexico, in his letters of the year 1532, to have broken down twenty thousand idols, and desolated five hundred idol temples, where the natives sacrificed every year more than twenty thousand hearts of boys and girls; and that if the noblemen were burnt to ashes, they killed their cooks, butlers, chaplains, and dwarfs★—and had a plenty of targets, maces, and ensigns hurled into their funeral piles: this terrible slaughter, points out to us clearly from their own accounts, that these authors either gave the world a continued chain of falsehoods, or those sacrifices, and human massacres [213] they boastingly tell us of, would have, long before they came, utterly depopulated Peru and Mexico.

I shall now quote a little of their less romantic description, to confirm the account I have given concerning the genuine rites, and customs, of our North-American Indians.

The ornaments of the Indians of South and North America, were formerly, and still are alike, without the least difference, except in value. Those superficial writers agree, that the men and women of Peru and Mexico wore golden ear-rings, and bracelets around their necks and wrists; that the

★With regard to Indian dwarfs, I never heard of, or saw any in the northern nations, but one in Ishtatoe, a northern town of the middle part of the Cheerake country,— and he was a great beloved man.

men wore rings of the same metal in their nose, marked their bodies with various figures, painted their faces red, and the women their cheeks, which seems to have been a very early and general custom. They tell us, that the coronation of the Indian kings, and installment of their nobles, was solemnized with comedies, banquets, lights, &c. and that no plebeians were allowed to serve before their kings; they must be knights, or noblemen. All those sounding high titles are only a confused picture of the general method of the Indians in crowning their warriors, performing their war-dances, and esteeming those fellows as old women, who never attended the reputed holy ark with success for the beloved brethren.

Don Antonio de Ulloa informs us, that some of the South-American natives cut the lobes of their ears, and for a considerable time, fastened small weights to them, in order to lengthen them; that others cut holes in their upper and under lips; through the cartilege of the nose, their chins, and jaws, and either hung or thrust through them, such things as they most fancied, which also agrees with the ancient customs of our Northern Indians.[223]

Emanuel de Moraes and Acosta affirm, that the Brasilians marry in their own family, or tribe. And Jo. de Laet.[224] says, they call their uncles and aunts, "fathers and mothers," which is a custom of the Hebrews, and of all our North-American Indians: and he assures us they mourn very much for their dead; and that their clothes are like those of the early Jews.

[214] Ulloa assures us, that the South American Indians have no other method of weaving carpets, quilts, and other stuffs, but to count the threads one by one, when they are passing the woof;—that they spin cotton and linnen, as their chief manufacture, and paint their cloth with the images of men, beasts, birds, fishes, trees, flowers, &c. and that each of those webs was adapted to one certain use, without being cut, and that their patience was equal to so arduous a task. According to this description, there is not the least disparity between the ancient North-American method of manufacturing, and that of the South Americans.

Acosta writes, that the clothes of the South-American Indians are shaped like those of the ancient Jews, being a square little cloak, and a little coat: and the Rev. Mr. Thorowgood,[225] anno 1650, observes, that this is a proof of some weight in shewing their original descent; especially to such who pay a deference to Seneca's parallel arguments of the Spaniards having settled Italy; for the old mode of dress is universally alike, among the Indian Americans.

Laet. in his description of America, and Escarbotus, assure us, they often heard the South American Indians to repeat the sacred word *Halleluiah*, which made them admire how they first attained it. And Malvenda says, that the natives of St. Michael had tomb-stones, which the Spaniards digged up, with several ancient Hebrew characters upon them, as, "Why is God gone away?" And, "He is dead, God knows." Had his curiosity induced him to transcribe the epitaph, it would have given more satisfaction; for, as they yet repeat the divine essential name, *Yo He (ta) Wah,* so as not to prophane it, when they mourn for their dead, it is probable, they could write or engrave it, after the like manner, when they first arrived on this main continent.

We are told, that the South American Indians have a firm hope of the resurrection of their bodies, at a certain period of time; and that on this account they bury their most valuable treasures with their dead, as well as the most useful conveniences for future domestic life, such as their bows and arrows: And when they saw the Spaniards digging up their graves for gold and silver, they requested them to forbear scattering the bones of their [215] dead in that manner, lest it should prevent their being raised and united again★.[226]

Monsieur de Poutrincourt[227] says, that, when the Canada Indians saluted him, they said *Ho Ho Ho;* but as we are well assured, they express *Yo He a Ah,* in the time of their festivals and other rejoicings, we have reason to conclude he made a very material mistake in setting down the Indian solemn blessing, or invocation. He likewise tells us, that the Indian women will not marry on the graves of their husbands, i.e. "soon after their decease,"— but wait a long time before they even think of a second husband. That, if the husband was killed, they would neither enter into a second marriage, nor eat flesh, till his blood had been revenged: and that after child-bearing, they observe the Mosaic law of purification, shutting up themselves from their husbands, for the space of forty days.

Peter Martyr[228] writes, that that Indian widow married the brother of her deceased husband, according to the Mosaic law: and he says, the Indians worship that God who created the sun, moon, and all invisible things, and who gives them every thing that is good. He affirms the Indian priests had chambers in the temple, according to the custom of the Israelites, by divine appointment, as I Chron. ix. 26, 27. And that there were certain places in it, which none but their priests could enter, i.e. "the holiest." And Key[229] says also, they have in some parts of America, an exact form of king, priest, and prophet, as was formerly in Canaan.

Robert Williams, the first Englishman in New-England, who is said to have learned the Indian language, in order to convert the natives, believed them to be Jews: and he assures us, that their tradition records that their ancestors came from the south-west, and that they return there at death; that their women separate themselves from the rest of the people at certain periods; and that their language bore some affinity to the Hebrew.

Baron Lahontan[230] writes, that the Indian women of Canada purify them-

★Vid. Ceuto ad Solin. Benz. & Hist. Peruv.

selves after travail; thirty days for a male child—and forty for a female: that during the said time, they live apart from their husband—that the unmarried brother of the deceased husband marries the widow, six months [216] after his decease; and that the outstanding parties for war, address the great spirit every day till they set off, with sacrifices, songs, and feasting.

We are also told, that the men in Mexico sat down, and the women stood, when they made water, which is an universal custom among our North-American Indians. Their primitive modesty, and indulgence to their women, seem to have introduced this singular custom, after the manner of the ancient Mauritanians, on account of their scantiness of clothing, as I formerly observed.

Lerius tells us, that the Indians of Brasil wash themselves ten times a day; and that the husbands have no matrimonial intercourse with their wives, till their children are either weaned, or grown pretty hardy; which is similar to the custom of these northern Indians, and that of the Israelites, as Hos. i. 8. He says, if a Peruvian child was weaned before its time, it was called *Ainsco,* "a bastard." And that if a Brasilian wounds another, he is wounded in the same part of the body, with equal punishment; limb for limb, or life for life, according to the Mosaic law;—which, within our own memory, these Indian nations observed so eagerly, that if a boy shooting at birds, accidentally wounded another, though out of sight, with his arrow ever so slightly, he, or any of his family, wounded him after the very same manner; which is a very striking analogy with the Jewish retaliation. He likewise tells us, that their Sachems, or Emperors, were the heads of their church: and according to Laet. Descrip. America, the Peruvians had one temple consecrated to the creator of the world; besides four other religious places, in resemblance of the Jewish synagogues. And Malvenda says, the American idols were mitred, as Aaron was. He likewise affirms, as doth Acosta, that the natives observed a year of jubilee, according to the usage of the Israelites.

Benzo says, that the men and women incline very much to dancing; and the women often by themselves, according to the manner of the Hebrew nation; as in I Sam. xxi. 11. especially after gaining a victory over the enemy, as in Judg. xi. 34.–xxi. 21, 23, and I Sam. xviii. 6, 7. Acosta tells us, that though adultery is deemed by them a capital crime, yet they at the same time set little value by virginity, and it seems to have been a bewailable condition, in Judea. He likewise says, they wash their [217] new born infants, in resemblance of the Mosaic law; as Ezek. xvi. 9. And the Spaniards say, that the priests of Mexico, were anointed from head to foot; that they constantly wore their hair, till they were superannuated; and that the husband did not lie with his wife, for two years after she was delivered. Our northern Indians imitate the first custom; though in the second, they resemble that of the heathen by polling or trimming their hair; and with regard to the third, they always sleep apart from their wives, for the greater part of a year, after delivery.

By the Spanish authorities, the Peruvians and Mexicans were Polygamists, but they had one principal wife, to whom they were married with certain solemnities; and murder, adultery, theft, and incest, were punished with death.—But there was an exception in some places, with regard to incestuous intercourses: which is entirely consonant to the usage of the northern Indians. For as to incest, the Cheerake marry both mother and daughter, or two sisters; but they all observe the prohibited laws of consanguinity, in the strictest manner. They tell us, that when the priests offered sacrifice, they abstained from women and strong drink, and fasted several days, before any great festival; that all of them buried their dead in their houses, or in high places; that when they were forced to bury in any of the Spanish church-yards, they frequently stole the corpse, and interred it either in one of their own houses, or in the mountains; and that Juan de la Torre took five hundred thousand Pezoes out of one tomb. Here is a long train of Israelitish customs: and, if we include the whole, they exhibit a very strong analogy between all the essential traditions, rites, customs, &c. of the South and North American Indians; though the Spaniards mix an innumerable heap of absurd chimeras, and romantic dreams, with the plain material truths I have extracted.

I lately perused the first volume of the History of North-America, from the discovery thereof by Sylvanus Americanus, printed in New Jersey, Anno 1761, from, I believe, the Philadelphia monthly paper[231]—and was not a little surprised to find in such a useful collection, the conjectural, though perhaps well-intended accounts of the first adventurers, and settlers, in North-America, concerning the natives: and which are laid as the only basis for inquisitive writers to trace their origin, instead of later and more substantial observations. Though several of those early writers were undoubtedly [218] sagacious, learned, and candid; yet under the circumstances in which they wrote, it was impossible for them to convey to us any true knowledge of the Indians, more than what they gained by their senses, which must be superficial, and liable to many errors. Their conjectural accounts ought to have been long since examined, by some of that learned body, or they should not have given a sanction to them. However, they are less faulty than the Spanish accounts.

I presume, enough hath been said to point out the similarity between the rites and customs of the native American Indians, and those of the Israelites.—And that the Indian system is derived from the moral, ceremonial, and judicial laws of the Hebrews, though now but a faint copy of the divine original.—Their religious rites, martial customs, dress, music, dances, and domestic forms of life, seem clearly to evince also, that they came to

America in early times, before sects had sprung up among the Jews, which was soon after their prophets ceased, and before arts and sciences had arrived to any perfection; otherwise, it is likely they would have retained some knowledge of them, at least where they first settled, it being in a favourable climate, and consequently, they were in a more compact body, than on this northern part of the American continent.

The South-American natives wanted nothing that could render life easy and agreeable: and they had nothing superfluous, except gold and silver. When we consider the simplicity of the people, and the skill they had in collecting a prodigious quantity of treasures, it seems as if they gained that skill from their countrymen, and the Tyrians; who in the reign of Solomon exceedingly enriched themselves, in a few voyages. The conjecture that the aborigines wandered here from captivity, by the north east parts of Asia, over Kamschatska, to have their liberty and religion; is not so improbable, as that of their being driven by stress of weather into the bay of Mexico, from the east.

Though a single argument of the general subject, may prove but little, disjoined from the rest; yet, according to the true laws of history, and the best rules for tracing antiquities, the conclusion is to be drawn from clear corresponding circumstances united: the force of one branch of the subject ought to be connected with the others, and then judge by the whole. Such [219] readers as may dissent from my opinion of the Indian American origin and descent, ought to inform us how the natives came here, and by what means they formed the long chain of rites, customs, &c. so similar to the usage of the Hebrew nation, and in general dissimilar to the modes, &c. of the Pagan world.

Ancient writers do not agree upon any certain place, where the Ophir[232] of Solomon lay; it must certainly be a great distance from Joppa, for it was a three years voyage. After the death of Solomon, both the Israelites and Tyrians seem to have utterly discontinued their trading voyages to that part of the world. Eusebius and Eupolemus say, that David sent to Urphe, an island in the red sea, and brought much gold into Judea; and Ortelius reckons this to have been Ophir: though, agreeably to the opinion of the greater part of the modern literati, he also conjectures Cephala, or Sophala, to have been the Ophir of Solomon. Junius imagines it was in Aurea Chersonesus; Tremellius and Niger are of the same opinion. But Vatablus reckons it was Hispaniola, discovered, and named so by Columbus: yet Postellus, Phil. Mornay, Arias Montanus, and Goropius, are of opinion that Peru is the ancient Ophir; so widely different are their conjectures. Ancient history is quite silent, concerning America; which indicates that it has been time immemorial rent asunder from the African continent, according to Plato's Timeus. The north-east parts of Asia also were undiscovered, till of late.

Many geographers have stretched Asia and America so far, as to join them together: and others have divided those two quarters of the globe, at a great distance from each other. But the Russians, after several dangerous attempts, have clearly convinced the world, that they are now divided, and yet have a near communication together, by a narrow strait, in which several islands are situated; through which there is an easy passage from the north-east of Asia to the north-west of America by the way of Kamschatska; which probably joined to the north-west point of America. By this passage, supposing the main continents were separated, it was very practicable for the inhabitants to go to this extensive new world; and afterwards, to have proceeded in quest of suitable climates,—according to the law of nature, that directs every creature to such climes as are most convenient and agreeable.

[220] Having endeavoured to ascertain the origin and descent of the North-American Indians—and produced a variety of arguments that incline my own opinion in favour of their being of Jewish extraction—which at the same time furnish the public with a more complete INDIAN SYSTEM of religious rites, civil and martial customs, language, &c. &c. than hath ever been exhibited, neither disfigured by fable, nor prejudice—I shall proceed to give a general historical description of those Indian nations among whom I have chiefly resided.

AN
ACCOUNT
OF THE
KATAHBA, CHEERAKE, MUSKOHGE, CHOKTAH, AND CHIKKASAH NATIONS:

WITH
OCCASIONAL OBSERVATIONS
ON
Their LAWS, and the Conduct of our GOVERNORS, SUPERINTENDANTS, MISSIONARIES, &c. towards them.

[223]An Account of the Katahba Nation, &c.

I begin with the KATAHBA, because their country is the most contiguous to Charles-Town in South-Carolina.[233] It is placed in our modern maps, in 34 degrees north latitude, but proper care hath not yet been taken to ascertain the limits and site of any of the Indian nations. It is bounded on the north and north-east, by North-Carolina—on the east and south, by South-Carolina—and about west-south-west by the Cheerake nation. Their chief settlement is at the distance of one hundred and forty-five miles from the Cheerake, as near as I can compute it by frequent journies, and about 200 miles distant from Charles-Town.

Their soil is extremely good; the climate open and healthy; the water very clear, and well-tasted. The chief part of the Katahba country, I observed during my residence with them, was settled close on the east side of a broad purling river, that heads in the great blue ridge of mountains, and empties itself into Santee-river, at Amelia township; then running eastward of Charles-town, disgorges itself into the Atlantic. The land would produce any sort of Indian provisions, but, by the continual passing and repassing of the English, between the northern and southern colonies, the Katahba live perhaps the meanest of any Indians belonging to the British American empire. They are also so corrupted by an immoderate use of our spirituous liquors, and of course, indolent, that they scarcely plant any thing fit for the support of human life. South-Carolina has supplied their wants, either [224] through a political, or charitable view; which kindness, several respectable inhabitants in their neighbourhood say, they abuse in a very high degree; for they often destroy the white people's live stock, and even kill their horses for mischief sake.

It was bad policy of a prime magistrate of South-Carolina, who a little more than twenty years ago, desired me to endeavour to decoy the Chikkasah nation to settle near New-Windsor, or Savanna town.[234] For the Indians will not live peaceable with a mixed society of people. It is too recent to need enlarging on, that the English inhabitants were at sundry times forced by necessity, to take shelter in New-Windsor and Augusta garrisons, at the alarm of the cannon, to save themselves from about an hundred of the Chikkasah, who formerly settled there, by the inticement of our traders: the two colonies of South-Carolina and Georgia were obliged on this occasion to send up a number of troops, either to drive them off, or check their insolence. By some fatality, they are much addicted to excessive drinking, and spirituous liquors distract them so exceedingly, that they will even eat live coals of fire. Harsh usage alone, will never subdue an Indian: and too much indulgence is as bad; for then they would think, what was an effect of politic friendship, proceeded from a tribute of fear. We may observe of them as of the fire, "it is safe and useful, cherished at proper distance; but if too near us, it becomes dangerous, and will scorch if not consume us."

We are not acquainted with any savages of so warlike a disposition, as the Katahba and the Chikkasah. The six united northern nations have been time immemorial engaged in a bitter war with the former, and the Katahba are now reduced to a very few above one hundred fighting men—the small pox, and intemperate drinking, have contributed however more than their wars to their great decay. When South-Carolina was in its infant state, they mustered fifteen hundred fighting men: and they always behaved as faithful and friendly to the English as could be reasonably expected, from cunning, suspicious, and free savages. About the year 1743, their nation consisted of almost 400 warriors, of above twenty different dialects. I shall mention a few of the national names of those, who make up this mixed language;— the *Kátahba,* is the standard, or court-dialect—the *Wataree,* who make up a large town; *Eenó,* [225] *Charàh,wah* now *Chowan, Canggaree, Nachee, Yamasee, Coosah,* &c.[235] Their country had an old waste field of seven miles extent, and several others of smaller dimensions; which shews that they were formerly a numerous people, to cultivate so much land with their dull stone-axes, before they had an opportunity of trading with the English, or allowed others to incorporate with them.

[226]Account of the Cheerake Nation, &c.

We shall now treat of the Cheerake nation, as the next neighbour to South-Carolina.

Their national name is derived from *Chee-ra,* "fire," which is their reputed lower heaven, and hence they call their magi, *Cheerà-tahge,* "men possessed of the divine fire."[236] The country lies in about 34 degrees north latitude, at the distance of 340 computed miles to the north-west of Charles-town,—140 west-south-west from the Katahba nation,—and almost 200 miles to the north of the Muskohge or Creek country.

They are settled, nearly in an east and west course, about 140 miles in length from the lower towns where Fort-Prince-George stands, to the late unfortunate Fort-Loudon. The natives make two divisions of their country, which they term *Ayrate,* and *Ottare,* signifying "low," and "mountainous."[237] The former division is on the head branches of the beautiful Savanah river, and the latter on those of the easternmost river of the great Missisippi. Their towns are always close to some river, or creek; as there the land is commonly very level and fertile, on account of the frequent washings off the mountains, and the moisture it receives from the waters, that run through their fields. And such a situation enables them to perform the ablutions, connected with their religious worship.

The eastern, or lower parts of this country, are sharp and cold to a Carolinian in winter, and yet agreeable: but those towns that lie among the [227] Apalahche mountains, are very pinching to such who are unaccustomed to a savage life. The ice and snow continue on the north-side, till late in the spring of the year: however, the natives are well provided for it, by their bathing and anointing themselves. This regimen shuts up the pores of the body, and by that means prevents too great a perspiration; and an accustomed exercise of hunting, joined with the former, puts them far above their climate: they are almost as impenetrable to cold, as a bar of steel, and the severest cold is no detriment to their hunting.

Formerly, the Cheerake were a very numerous and potent nation. Not above forty years ago, they had 64 towns and villages, populous, and full of women and children. According to the computations of the most intelligent old traders of that time, they amounted to upwards of six-thousand fighting men; a prodigious number to have so close on our settlements, defended by blue-topped ledges of inaccessible mountains: where, but three of them can make a successful campaign, even against their own watchful red-colour enemies. But they were then simple, and peaceable, to what they are now.

As their western, or upper towns, which are situated among the Apalahche-mountains, on the eastern branches of the Misisisippi, were always engaged in hot war with the more northern Indians; and the middle and lower towns in constant hostility with the Muskohge, till reconciled by a governor of South-Carolina for the sake of trade,—several of their best towns, on the southern branch of Savanah-river, are now forsaken and destroyed: as *Ishtatohe, Echia, Toogalo,* &c.,[238] and they are brought into a narrower compass. At the conclusion of our last war with them, the traders calculated the number of their warriors to consist of about two thousand three-hundred,[239] which is a great diminution for so short a space of time: and if we may conjecture for futurity, from the circumstances already past, there will be few of them alive, after the like revolution of time. Their towns are still scattered wide of each other, because the land will not admit any other settlement: it is a rare thing to see a level tract of four hundred acres. They are also strongly attached to rivers,—all retaining the opinion of the ancients, that rivers are necessary to constitute a paradise. Nor is it only ornamental, but likewise beneficial to them, on account of purifying themselves, and also for the services of common life,—such as fishing, [228] fowling, and killing of deer, which come in the warm season, to eat the saltish moss and grass, which grow on the rocks, and under the surface of the waters. Their rivers are generally very shallow, and pleasant to the eye; for the land being high, the waters have a quick descent; they seldom overflow their banks, unless when a heavy rain falls on a deep snow.—Then, it is frightful to see the huge pieces of ice, mixed with a prodigious torrent of water, rolling down the high mountains, and over the steep craggy rocks, so impetuous, that nothing can resist their force. Two old traders saw an instance of this kind, which swept away great plantations of oaks and pines, that had their foundation as in the center of the earth.—It overset several of the higher rocks, where the huge rafts of trees and ice had stopped up the main channel, and forced itself across through the smaller hills.

From the historical descriptions of the Alps, and a personal view of the Cheerake mountains—I conclude the Alps of Italy are much inferior to several of the Cheerake mountains, both in height and rockiness: the last are also of a prodigious extent, and frequently impassable by an enemy. The *Allegeny,* or "great blue ridge," commonly called the *Apalahche*-mountains, are here above a hundred miles broad; and by the best accounts we can get from the Missisippi Indians, run along between Peru and Mexico, unless where the large rivers occasion a break. They stretch also all the way from the west of the northern great lakes, near Hudson's Bay, and across the Missisippi, about 250 leagues above New-Orleans. In the lower and middle parts of this mountainous ragged country, the Indians have a convenient passable path, by the foot of the mountains: but farther in, they are of such a prodigious height, that they are forced to wind from north to south, along the rivers and large creeks, to get a safe passage: and the paths are so steep in many places, that the horses often pitch, and rear an end, to scramble up. Several of the mountains are some miles from bottom to top, according to the ascent of the paths: and there are other mountains I have seen from these, when out with the Indians in clear weather, that the eye can but faintly discern, which therefore must be at a surprising distance.

Where the land is capable of cultivation, it would produce any thing suitable to the climate. Hemp, and wine-grapes grow there to admiration: [229] they have plenty of the former, and a variety of the latter that grow spontaneously. If these were properly cultivated, there must be a good return. I have gathered good hops in the woods opposite to Nuquose, where our troops were repelled by the Cheerake, in the year 1760.[240] There is not a more healthful region under the sun, than this country; for the air is commonly open and clear, and plenty of wholesome and pleasant water. I know several bold rivers, that fill themselves in running about thirty miles, counting by a direct course from their several different fountains, and which are almost as transparent as glass. The natives live commonly to a great age; which is not to be wondered at, when we consider the high situation of their country,—the exercise they pursue,—the richness of the soil that produces plenty for a needful support of life, without fatiguing, or overheating the planters,—the advantages they receive from such excellent good water, as gushes out of every hill; and the great additional help by a plain abstemious life, commonly eating and drinking, only according to the solicitations of nature. I have seen strangers however, full of admiration at beholding so few old people in that country; and they have concluded from thence, and reported in the English settlements, that it was a sickly short-lived region: but we should consider, they are always involved in treacherous wars, and exposed to perpetual dangers, by which, infirm and declining people generally fall, and the manly old warrior will not shrink. And yet many of the peaceable fellows, and women, especially in the central towns, see the grey hairs of their children, long before they die; and in every Indian country, there are a great many old women on the frontiers, perhaps ten times the number of the men of the same age and place—which plainly shews the country to be healthy. Those reach to a great age, who live secure by the fire-side, but no climates or constitutions can harden the human body, and make it bullet-proof.

The Cheerake country abounds with the best herbage, on the richer parts of the hills and mountains; and a great variety of valuable herbs is promiscuously scattered on the lower lands. It is remarkable, that none of our botanists should attempt making any experiments there, notwithstanding the place invited their attention, and the public had a right to expect so generous an undertaking from several of them; while at the same time, they would be recovering, or renewing their health, at a far easier, cheaper, and safer rate, than coasting it to our northern colonies.

[230] On the level parts of the water-side, between the hills, there are plenty of reeds: and, formerly, such places abounded with great brakes of winter-canes.—The foilage of which is always green, and hearty food for horses and cattle.[241] The traders used to raise there flocks of an hundred, and a hundred and fifty excellent horses; which are commonly of a good size, well-made, hard-hoofed, handsome, strong and fit for the saddle or draught: but a person runs too great a risk to buy any to take them out of the country, because, every spring-season most of them make for their native range. Before the Indian trade was ruined by our left-handed policy, and the natives were corrupted by the liberality of our dim-sighted politicians, the Cheerake were frank, sincere, and industrious. Their towns then, abounded with hogs, poultry, and every thing sufficient for the support of a reasonable life, which the traders purchased at an easy rate, to their mutual satisfaction: and as they kept them busily employed, and did not make themselves too cheap, the Indians bore them good-will and respect—and such is the temper of all the red natives.

I will not take upon me to ascertain the real difference between the value of the goods they annually purchased of us, in former and later times; but, allowing the consumption to be in favour of the last, what is the gain of such an uncertain trifle, in comparison of our charges and losses by a merciless savage war? The orderly and honest system, if resumed, and wisely pursued, would reform the Indians, and regain their lost affections; but that of general licences to mean reprobate pedlars, by which they are inebriated, and cheated, is pregnant with complicated evils to the peace and welfare of our valuable southern colonies.[242]

As the Cheerake began to have goods at an under price, it tempted them to be both proud, and lazy. Their women and children are now far above taking the trouble to raise hogs for the ugly white people, as the beautiful red heroes proudly term them. If any do—they are forced to feed them in small penns, or inclosures, through all the crop-season, and chiefly on long pursly, and other wholsome weeds, that their rich fields abound with. But at the fall of the leaf, the woods are full of hiccory-nuts, acorns, chesnuts, and the like; which occasions the Indian bacon to be more streaked, firm, and better tasted, than any we meet with in [231] the English settlements. Some of the natives are grown fond of horned cattle, both in the Cheerake and Muskohge countries, but most decline them, because the fields are not regularly fenced. But almost every one hath horses, from two to a dozen; which makes a considerable number, through their various nations. The Cheerake had a prodigious number of excellent horses, at the beginning of their late war with us; but pinching hunger forced them to eat the greatest part of them, in the time of that unfortunate event. But as all are now become very active and sociable, they will soon supply themselves with plenty of the best sort, from our settlements—they are skilful jockies, and nice in their choice.

From the head of the southern branch of Savanah-river, it does not exceed half a mile to a head spring of the Missisippi-water, that runs through the middle and upper parts of the Cheerake nation, about a north-west course,—and joining other rivers, they empty themselves into the great Missisippi. The above fountain, is called "Herbert's spring ★:"[243] and it was natural for strangers to drink thereof, to quench thirst, gratify their curiosity, and have it to say they had drank of the French waters. Some of our people, who went only with the view of staying a short time, but by some allurement or other, exceeded the time appointed, at their return, reported either through merriment or superstition, that the spring had such a natural bewitching quality, that whosoever drank of it, could not possibly quit the nation, during the tedious space of seven years. All the debauchees readily fell in with this superstitious notion, as an excuse for their bad method of living, when they had no proper call to stay in that country; and in process of time, it became as received a truth, as any ever believed to have been spoken by the delphic oracle. One cursed, because its enchantment had marred his good fortune; another condemned his weakness for drinking down witchcraft, against his own secret suspicions; one swore he would never taste again such known dangerous poison, even though he should be forced to go down to the Missisippi for water; and another comforted himself, that so many years out of the seven, were already passed, and wished that if ever he tasted it again, though under the greatest necessity, he might be confined to the stygian waters. Those who had their minds more inlarged, diverted themselves much at their cost, [232] for it was a noted favourite place, on account of the name it went by; and being a well-situated and good spring, there all travellers commonly drank a bottle of choice: But

★So named from an early commissioner of Indian affairs.

now, most of the packhorse-men, though they be dry, and also matchless sons of Bacchus, on the most pressing invitations to drink there, would swear to forfeit sacred liquor the better part of their lives, rather than basely renew, or confirm the loss of their liberty, which that execrable fountain occasions.

About the year 1738, the Cheerake received a most depopulating shock, by the small pox, which reduced them almost one half, in about a year's time: it was conveyed into Charles-town by the Guinea-men, and soon after among them, by the infected goods.[244] At first it made slow advances, and as it was a foreign, and to them a strange disease, they were so deficient in proper skill, that they alternately applied a regimen of hot and cold things, to those who were infected. The old magi and religious physicians who were consulted on so alarming a crisis, reported the sickness had been sent among them, on account of the adulterous intercourses of their young married people, who the past year, had in a most notorious manner, violated their ancient laws of marriage in every thicket, and broke down and polluted many of the honest neighbours bean-plots, by their heinous crimes, which would cost a great deal of trouble to purify again. To those flagitious crimes they ascribed the present disease, as a necessary effect of the divine anger; and indeed the religious men chanced to suffer the most in their small fields, as being contiguous to the town-house, where they usually met at night to dance, when their corn was out of the stalks; upon this pique, they shewed their priest-craft. However, it was thought needful on this occasion, to endeavour to put a stop to the progress of such a dangerous disease: and as it was believed to be brought on them by their unlawful copulation in the night dews, it was thought most practicable to try to effect the cure, under the same cool element. Immediately, they ordered the reputed sinners to lie out of doors, day and night, with their breast frequently open to the night dews, to cool the fever: they were likewise afraid, that the diseased would otherwise pollute the house, and by that means, procure all their deaths. Instead of applying warm remedies, they at last in every visit poured cold water on their naked breasts, sung their religious mystical song, *Yo Yo,* &c. with a doleful tune, [233] and shaked a callabash with the pebble-stones, over the sick, using a great many frantic gestures, by way of incantantion. From the reputed cause of the disease, we may rationally conclude their physical treatment of it, to be of a true old Jewish descent; for as the Israelites invoked the deity, or asked a blessing on every thing they undertook, so all the Indian Americans seek for it, according on the remaining faint glimpse of their tradition.

When they found their theological regimen had not the desired effect, but that the infection gained upon them, they held a second consultation, and deemed it the best method to sweat their patients, and plunge them into the river,—which was accordingly done.[245] Their rivers being very cold in summer, by reason of the numberless springs, which pour from the hills and mountains—and the pores of their bodies being open to receive the cold, it rushing in through the whole frame, they immediately expired: upon which, all the magi and prophetic tribe broke their old consecrated physic-pots, and threw away all the other pretended holy things they had for physical use, imagining they had lost their divine power by being polluted; and shared the common fate of their country. A great many killed themselves; for being naturally proud, they are always peeping into their looking glasses, and are never genteelly drest, according to their mode, without carrying one hung over their shoulders: by which means, seeing themselves disfigured, without hope of regaining their former beauty, some shot themselves, others cut their throats, some stabbed themselves with knives, and others with sharp-pointed canes; many threw themselves with sullen madness into the fire, and there slowly expired, as if they had been utterly divested of the native power of feeling pain.

I remember, in *Tymáse,*[246] one of their towns, about ten miles above the present Fort Prince-George, a great head-warrior, who murdered a white man thirty miles below *Cheeòwhee,*[247] as was proved by the branded deerskins he produced afterward—when he saw himself disfigured by the small pox, he chose to die, that he might end as he imagined his shame. When his relations knew his desperate design, they narrowly watched him, and took away every sharp instrument from him. When he found he was balked of his intention, he fretted and said the worst things their language [234] could express, and shewed all the symptoms of a desperate person enraged at his disappointment, and forced to live and see his ignominy; he then darted himself against the wall, with all his remaining vigour,—his strength being expended by the force of his friends opposition, he fell sullenly on the bed, as if by those violent struggles he was overcome, and wanted to repose himself. His relations through tenderness, left him to his rest—but as soon as they went away, he raised himself, and after a tedious search, finding nothing but a thick and round hoe-helve, he took the fatal instrument, and having fixed one end of it in the ground, he repeatedly threw himself on it, till he forced it down his throat, when he immediately expired.—He was buried in silence, without the least mourning.

Although the Cheerake shewed such little skill in curing the small pox, yet they, as well as all other Indian nations, have a great knowledge of specific virtues in simples; applying herbs and plants, on the most dangerous occasions, and seldom if ever, fail to effect a thorough cure, from the natural bush. In the order of nature, every country and climate is blest with specific remedies for the maladies that are connatural to it—Naturalists tell us they have observed, that when the wild goat's sight begins to decay, he rubs his head against a thorn, and by some effluvia, or virtue in the vegetable, the sight is renewed. Thus the snake recovers after biting any creature, by his knowledge of the proper antidote; and many of our arts and forms of living, are imitated by lower ranks of the animal creation: the Indians, instigated by nature, and quickened by experience, have discovered the peculiar properties of vegetables, as far as needful in their situation of life. For my own part, I would prefer an old Indian before any chirurgeon [surgeon] whatsoever, in curing green wounds by bullets, arrows, &c. both for the certainty, ease, and speediness of cure; for if those parts of the body are not hurt, which are essential to the preservation of life, they cure the wounded in a trice. They bring the patient into a good temperament of body, by a decoction of proper herbs and roots, and always enjoin a most abstemious life: they forbid them women, salt, and every kind of flesh-meat, applying mountain allum, as the chief ingredient.[248]

[235] In the year 1749, I came down, by the invitation of the governor of South-Carolina, to Charles-Town, with a body of our friendly Chikkasah Indians: one of his majesty's surgeons, that very day we arrived, cut off the wounded arm of a poor man. On my relating it to the Indians, they were shocked at the information, and said, "The man's poverty should have induced him to exert the common skill of mankind, in so trifling an hurt; especially, as such a butchery would not only disfigure, but disable the poor man the rest of his life; that there would have been more humanity in cutting off the head, than in such a barbarous amputation, because it is much better for men to die once, than to be always dying, for when the hand is lost, how can the poor man feed himself by his daily labour—By the same rule of physic, had he been wounded in his head, our surgeons should have cut that off, for being unfortunate." I told the benevolent old warriors, that the wisdom of our laws had exempted the head from such severe treatment, by not settling a reward for the severing it, but only so much for every joint of the branches of the body, which might be well enough spared, without the life; and that this medical treatment was a strong certificate to recommend the poor man to genteel lodgings, where numbers belonging to our great canoes, were provided for during life. They were of opinion however, that such brave hardy fellows would rather be deemed men, and work for their bread, than be laid aside, not only as useless animals, but as burdens to the rest of society.

I do not remember to have seen or heard of an Indian dying by the bite of a snake, when out at war, or a hunting; although they are then often bitten by the most dangerous snakes—every one carries in his shot-pouch, a piece of the best snake-root, such as the *Seneeka,* or fern-snake-root,—or the wild hore-hound, wild plantain, St. Andrew's cross, and a variety of other herbs and roots, which are plenty, and well known to those who range the American woods, and are exposed to such dangers, and will effect a thorough and speedy cure if timely applied.[249] When an Indian perceives he is struck by a snake, he immediately chews some of the root, and having swallowed a sufficient quantity of it, he applies some to the wound; which he repeats as occasion requires, and in proportion to the poison the snake has infused into the wound. For a short space of time, there is a terrible conflict through all the body, by the jarring qualities of [236] the burning poison, and the strong antidote; but the poison is soon repelled through the same channels it entered, and the patient is cured.

The Cheerake mountains look very formidable to a stranger, when he is among their valleys, incircled with their prodigious, proud, contending tops; they appear as a great mass of black and blue clouds, interspersed with some rays of light. But they produce, or contain every thing for health, and wealth, and if cultivated by the rules of art, would furnish perhaps, as valuable medicines as the eastern countries; and as great quantities of gold and silver, as Peru and Mexico, in proportion to their situation with the æquator. On the tops of several of those mountains, I have observed tufts of grass deeply tinctured by the mineral exhalations from the earth; and on the sides, they glistered from the same cause. If skilful alchymists made experiments on these mountains, they could soon satisfy themselves, as to the value of their contents, and probably would find their account in it.

Within twenty miles of the late Fort-Loudon, there is great plenty of whet-stones for razors, of red, white, and black colours. The silver mines are so rich, that by digging about ten yards deep, some desperate vagrants found at sundry times, so much rich ore, as to enable them to counterfeit dollars, to a great amount;[250] a horse load of which was detected in passing for the purchase of negroes, at Augusta, which stands on the south-side of the meandering beautiful Savanah river, half way from the Cheerake country, to Savanah, the capital of Georgia. The load-stone is likewise found there, but they have no skill in searching for it, only on the surface; a great deal of the magnetic power is lost, as being exposed to the various changes of the weather, and frequent firing of the woods. I was told by a trader, who lives in the upper parts of the Cheerake country, which is surrounded on every side, by prodigious piles of mountains called Cheèowhée, that within about a mile of the town of that name, there is a hill with a great plenty of load-stones—the truth of this any gentleman of curiosity may soon ascertain, as it lies on the northern path that leads from South-Carolina, to the remains of Fort-Loudon: and while he is in search of this, he may at the same time make a great acquest of riches, for the load-stone is known to accompany rich metals. I was once near that load-stone [237] hill, but the heavy rains which at that time fell on the deep snow, prevented the gratifying my curiosity, as the boggy deep creek was thereby rendered impassable.

In this rocky country, are found a great many beautiful, clear, chrystaline stones, formed by nature into several angles, which commonly meet in one point: several of them are transparent, like a coarse diamond—others resemble the onyx, being engendered of black and thick humours, as we see water that is tinctured with ink, still keeping its surface clear. I found one stone like a ruby, as big as the top of a man's thumb, with a beautiful dark shade in the middle of it. Many stones of various colours, and beautiful lustre, may be collected on the tops of those hills and mountains, which if skilfully managed, would be very valuable, for some of them are clear, and very hard. From which, we may rationally conjecture that a quantity of subterranean treasures is contained there; the Spaniards generally found out their southern mines, by such superficial indications. And it would be an useful, and profitable service for skilful artists to engage in, as the present trading white savages are utterly ignorant of it. Manifold curious works of the wise author of nature, are bountifully dispersed through the whole of the country, obvious to every curious eye.

Among the mountains, are many labyrinths, and some of a great length, with many branches, and various windings; likewise different sorts of mineral waters, the qualities of which are unknown to the natives, as by their temperate way of living, and the healthiness of their country, they have no occasion to make experiments in them. Between the heads of the northern branch of the lower Cheerake river, and the heads of that of Tuckasehchee, winding round in a long course by the late Fort-Loudon, and afterwards into the Missisippi, there is, both in the nature and circumstances, a great phænomenon—Between two high mountains, nearly covered with old mossy rocks, lofty cedars, and pines, in the valleys of which the beams of the sun reflect a powerful heat, there are, as the natives affirm, some bright old inhabitants, or rattle snakes, of a more enormous size than is mentioned in history. They are so large and unwieldy, that they take a circle, almost as wide as their length, to crawl round in their shortest orbit: but bountiful nature compensates the heavy motion of their bodies, for [238] as they say, no living creature moves within the reach of their sight, but they can draw it to them;[251] which is agreeable to what we observe, through the whole system of animated beings. Nature, endues them with proper capacities to sustain life;—as they cannot support themselves, by their speed, or cunning to spring from an ambuscade, it is needful they should have the bewitching craft of their eyes and forked tongues.

The description the Indians give us of their colour, is as various as what we are told of the camelion, that seems to the spectator to change its colour, by every different position he may view it in; which proceeds from the piercing rays of light that blaze from their foreheads, so as to dazzle the eyes, from whatever quarter they post themselves—for in each of their heads, there is a large carbuncle, which not only repels, but they affirm, sullies the meridian beams of the sun. They reckon it so dangerous to disturb those creatures, that no temptation can induce them to betray their secret recess to the prophane. They call them and all of the rattle-snake kind, kings, or chieftains of the snakes; and they allow one such to every different species of the brute creation. An old trader of Cheeowhee told me, that for the reward of two pieces of stroud-cloth, he engaged a couple of young warriors to shew him the place of their resort; but the head-men would not by any means allow it, on account of a superstitious tradition—for they fancy the killing of them would expose them to the danger of being bit by the other inferior species of that serpentine tribe, who love their chieftains, and know by instinct those who maliciously killed them, as they fight only in their own defence, and that of their young ones, never biting those who do not disturb them. Although they esteem those rattle snakes as chieftains of that species, yet they do not deify them, as the Egyptions did all the serpentine kind, and likewise Ibis, that preyed upon them; however, it seems to have sprung from the same origin, for I once saw the Chikkasah Archimagus to chew some snake-root, blow it on his hands, and then take up a rattle snake without damage—soon afterwards he laid it down carefully, in a hollow tree, lest I should have killed it. Once on the Chikkasah trading war-path, a little above the country of the Muskohge, as I was returning to camp from hunting, I found in a large cane swamp, a fellow-traveller, an old Indian trader, inebriated and naked, except his Indian breeches and maccaseenes; in that habit he sat, [239] holding a great rattle-snake round the neck, with his left hand besmeared with proper roots, and with the other, applying the roots to the teeth, in order to repel the poison, before he drew them out; which having effected, he laid it down tenderly at a distance. I then killed it, to his great dislike, as he was afraid it would occasion misfortunes to himself and me. I told him, as he had taken away its teeth, common pity should induce one to put it out of misery, and that a charitable action could never bring ill on any one; but his education prevented his fears from subsiding. On a Christmas-day, at the trading house of that harmless, brave, but unfortunate man, I took the foot of a guinea-deer out of his shot-pouch—and another from my own partner, which they had very safely sewed in the corner of each of their otter-skin-pouches, to enable them, according to the Indian creed, to kill deer, bear, buffaloe, beaver, and other wild beasts, in plenty: but they were so infatuated with the Indian superstitious belief of the power of that charm, that all endeavours of reconciling them to reason were ineffectual: I therefore returned them, for as they were Nimrods, or hunters of men, as well as of wild beasts, I imagined, I should be answerable to myself for every accident that might befal them, by depriving them of what they depended upon as their chief good, in that wild sphere of life. No wonder that the long-desolate savages of the far extending desarts of America, should entertain the former superstitious notions of ill luck by that, and good fortune by this; as those of an early christian education, are so soon imprest with the like opinions. The latter was killed on the old Chikkasah, or American-Flanders path, in company with another expert brave man, in the year 1745, by twenty Choktah savages, set on by the christian French of Tumbikpe garrison;[252] in consequence of which, I staid by myself the following summer-season, in the Chikkasah country, and when the rest of the trading people and all our horses were gone down to the English settlements, I persuaded the Choktah to take up the bloody tomohawk against those perfidious French, in revenge of a long train of crying blood: and had it not been for the self-interested policy of a certain governor, those numerous savages, with the war-like Chikkasah, would have destroyed the Missisippi settlements, root and branch, except those who kept themselves closely confined in garrison. When I treat of the Choktah country, I shall more particularly relate that very material affair.

[240] The superior policy of the French so highly intoxicated the light heads of the Cheerake, that they were plodding mischief for twenty years before we forced them to commit hostilities. The illustration of this may divert the reader, and shew our southern colonies what they may still expect from the masterly abilities of the French Louisianians, whenever they can make it suit their interest to exert their talents among the Indian nations, while our watch-men are only employed in treating on paper, in our far-distant capital seats of government.

In the year 1736, the French sent into South-Carolina, one Priber,[253] a gentleman of a curious and speculative temper. He was to transmit them a full account of that country, and proceed to the Cheerake nation, in order to seduce them from the British to the French interest. He went, and though he was adorned with every qualification that constitutes the gentleman, soon after he arrived at the upper towns of this mountainous country, he exchanged his clothes and every thing he brought with him, and by that means, made friends with the head warriors of great Telliko, which stood on a branch of the Missisippi. More effectually to answer the design of his commission, he ate, drank, slept, danced, dressed, and painted himself, with the Indians, so that it was not easy to distinguish him from the natives,—he married also with them, and being endued with a strong understanding and retentive memory, he soon learned their dialect, and by gradual advances, impressed them with a very ill opinion of the English, representing them as a fraudulent, avaritious, and encroaching people: he at the same time, inflated the artless savages, with a prodigious high opinion of their own importance in the American scale of power, on account of the situation of their country, their martial disposition, and the great number of their warriors, which would baffle all the efforts of the ambitious, and ill-designing British colonists. Having thus infected them by his smooth deluding art, he easily formed them into a nominal republican government—crowned their old Archi-magus, emperor, after a pleasing new savage form, and invented a variety of high-sounding titles for all the members of his imperial majesty's red court, and the great officers of state; which the emperor conferred upon them, in a manner according to their merit. He himself received the honourable title of his imperial majesty's principal secretary of state, and as such he subscribed himself, in all the letters he wrote to our government, and lived in open defiance [241] of them. This seemed to be of so dangerous a tendency, as to induce South-Carolina to send up a commissioner, Col. F—x,[254] to demand him as an enemy to the public repose—who took him into custody, in the great square of their state-house: when he had almost concluded his oration on the occasion, one of the head warriors rose up, and bade him forbear, as the man he entended to enslave, was made a great beloved man, and become one of their own people. Though it was reckoned, our agent's strength was far greater in his arms than his head, he readily desisted—for as it is too hard to struggle with the pope in Rome, a stranger could not miss to find it equally difficult to enter abruptly into a new emperor's court, and there seize his prime minister, by a foreign authority; especially when he could not support any charge of guilt against him. The warrior told him, that the red people well knew the honesty of the secretary's heart would never allow him to tell a lie; and the secretary urged that he was a foreigner, without owing any allegiance to Great Britain,—that he only travelled through some places of their country, in a peaceable manner, paying for every thing he had of them; that in compliance with the request of the kindly French, as well as from his own tender feelings for the poverty and insecure state of the Cheerake, he came a great way, and lived among them as a brother, only to preserve their liberties, by opening a water communication between them and New Orleans; that the distance of the two places from each other, proved his motive to be the love of doing good, especially as he was to go there, and bring up a sufficient number of Frenchmen of proper skill to instruct them in the art of making gunpowder, the materials of which, he affirmed their lands abounded with.— He concluded his artful speech, by urging that the tyrannical design of the English commissioner toward him, appeared plainly to be levelled against them, because, as he was not accused of having done any ill to the English, before he came to the Cheerake, his crime must consist in loving the Cheerake.—And as that was reckoned so heinous a transgression in the eye of the English, as to send one of their angry beloved men to enslave him, it confirmed all those honest speeches he had often spoken to the present great war-chieftains, old beloved men, and warriors of each class.

An old war-leader repeated to the commissioner, the essential part of the speech, and added more of his own similar thereto. He bade him to inform [242] his superiors, that the Cheerake were as desirous as the English to continue a friendly union with each other, as "freemen and equals." That they hoped to receive no farther uneasiness from them, for consulting their own interests, as their reason dictated.—And they earnestly requested them to send no more of those bad papers to their country, on any account; nor to reckon them so base, as to allow any of their honest friends to be taken out of their arms, and carried into slavery. The English beloved man had the honour of receiving his leave of absence, and a sufficient passport of safe conduct, from the imperial red court, by a verbal order of the secretary of state,—who was so polite as to wish him well home, and ordered a convoy of his own life-guards, who conducted him a considerable way, and he got home in safety.

From the above, it is evident, that the monopolizing spirit of the French had planned their dangerous lines of circumvallation, respecting our envied colonies, as early as the before-mentioned period. Their choice of the man, bespeaks also their judgment.—Though the philosophic secretary was an utter stranger to the wild and mountainous Cheerake country, as well as to their language, yet his sagacity readily directed him to chuse a proper place, and an old favourite religious man, for the new red empire; which he formed by slow, but sure degrees, to the great danger of our southern colonies. But the empire received a very great shock, in an accident that befel the secretary, when it was on the point of rising into a far greater state of puissance, by the acquisition of the Muskohge, Choktah, and the western Missisippi Indians. In the fifth year of that red imperial æra, he set off for Mobille, accompanied by a few Cheerake. He proceeded by land, as far as a navigable part of the western great river of the Muskohge; there he went into a canoe prepared for the joyful occasion, and proceeded within a day's journey of Alebahma garrison—conjecturing the adjacent towns were under the influence of the French, he landed at Tallapoose town, and lodged there all night. The traders of the neighbouring towns soon went there, convinced the inhabitants of the dangerous tendency of his unwearied labours among the Cheerake, and of his present journey, and then took him into custody, with a large bundle of manuscripts, and sent him down to Frederica in Georgia; the governor committed him to a place of confinement, though not with common felons, as he was a foreigner, and was said to have held a place of considerable rank in [243] the army with great honour. Soon after, the magazine took fire, which was not far from where he was confined, and though the centinels bade him make off to a place of safety, as all the people were running to avoid danger from the explosion of the powder and shells, yet he squatted on his belly upon the floor, and continued in that position, without the least hurt: several blamed his rashness, but he told them, that experience had convinced him, it was the most probable means to avoid imminent danger. This incident displayed the philosopher and soldier, and after bearing his misfortunes a considerable time with great constancy, happily for us, he died in confinement,—though he deserved a much better fate. In the first year of his secretaryship I maintained a correspondence with him; but the Indians becoming very inquisitive to know the contents of our marked large papers, and he suspecting his memory might fail him in telling those cunning sifters of truth, a plausible story, and of being able to repeat it often to them, without any variation,— he took the shortest and safest method, by telling them that, in the very same manner as he was their great secretary, I was the devil's clerk, or an accursed one who marked on paper the bad speech of the evil ones of darkness. Accordingly, they forbad him writing any more to such an accursed one, or receiving any of his evil-marked papers, and our correspondence ceased. As he was learned, and possessed of a very sagacious penetrating judgment, and had every qualification that was requisite for his bold and difficult enterprize, it is not to be doubted, that as he wrote a Cheerake dictionary, designed to be published at Paris, he likewise set down a great deal that would have been very acceptable to the curious, and serviceable to the representatives of South-Carolina and Georgia; which may be readily found in Frederica, if the manuscripts have had the good fortune to escape the despoiling hands of military power.[255]

When the western Cheerake towns lost the chief support of their imperial court, they artfully agreed to inform the English traders, that each of them had opened their eyes, and rejected the French plan as a wild scheme, inconsistent with their interests; except great Telliko, the metropolis of their late empire,[256] which they said was firmly resolved to adhere to the French proposals, as the surest means of promoting their welfare and happiness. Though the inhabitants of this town were only dupes to the rest, yet for [244] the sake of the imagined general good of the country, their constancy enabled them to use that disguise a long time, in contempt of the English, till habit changed into a real hatred of the object, what before was only fictitious. They corresponded with the French in the name of those seven towns, which are the most warlike part of the nation: and they were so strongly prepossessed with the notions their beloved secretary had infused into their heads, in that early weak state of Louisiana, that they had resolved to remove, and settle so low down their river, as the French boats could readily bring them a supply. But the hot war they fell into with the northern Indians, made them postpone the execution of that favourite design; and the settling of Fort Loudon, quieted them a little, as they expected to get presents, and spirituous liquors there, according to the manner of the French promises, of which they had great plenty.

The French, to draw off the western towns, had given them repeated assurances of settling a strong garrison on the north side of their river, as high up as their large pettiaugres could be brought with safety, where there was a large tract of rich lands abounding with game and fowl, and the river with fish.—They at the same time promised to procure a firm peace between the Cheerake and all the Indian nations depending on the French; and to bestow on them powder, bullets, flints, knives, scissars, combs, shirts, looking glasses, and red paint,—beside favourite trifles to the fair sex: in the same brotherly manner the Alebahma French extended their kindly hands to their Muskohge brethren. By their assiduous endeavours, that artful plan was well supported, and though the situation of our affairs, in the remote, and leading Cheerake towns, had been in a ticklish situation, from the time their project of an empire was formed; and though several other towns became uneasy and discontented on sundry pretexts, for the space of two years before the unlucky occasion of the succeeding war happened—yet his excellency our governor neglected the proper measures to reconcile the wavering savages, till the gentleman who was appointed to succeed him, had just reached the American coast:[257] then, indeed, he set off, with a considerable number of gentlemen, in flourishing parade, and went as far as Ninety-six★ settlement;[258] from whence, as most probably he expected, he was fortunately recalled, and joyfully superseded. I saw him on his way up, and plainly observed he was unprovided for the journey; it must unavoidably have proved abortive [245] before he could have proceeded through the Cheerake country,—gratifying the inquisitive disposition of the people, as he went, and quieting the jealous minds of the inhabitants of those towns, who are settled among the Apalahche mountains, and those seven towns, in particular, that lie beyond them. He neither sent before, nor carried with him, any presents wherewith to soothe the natives; and his kind promises, and smooth speeches, would have weighed exceedingly light in the Indian scale.

Having shewn the bad state of our affairs among the remotest parts of the Cheerake country, and the causes.—I shall now relate their plea, for commencing war against the British colonies;[259] and the great danger we were exposed to by the incessant intrigues of the half-savage French garrisons, in those hot times, when all our northern barriers were so prodigiously harrassed. Several companies of the Cheerake, who joined our forces under General Stanwix at the unfortunate Ohio,[260] affirmed that their alienation

---

★So called from its distance of miles from the Cheerake.

from us, was—because they were confined to our martial arrangement, by unjust suspicion of them—were very much contemned,—and half-starved at the main camp: their hearts told them therefore to return home, as free-men and injured allies, though without a supply of provisions. This they did, and pinching hunger forced them to take as much as barely supported na-ture, when returning to their own country. In their journey, the German inhabitants, without any provocation, killed in cool blood about forty of their warriors, in different places—though each party was under the com-mand of a British subject. They scalped all, and butchered several, after a most shocking manner, in imitation of the barbarous war-custom of the savages; some who escaped the carnage, returned at night, to see their kin-dred and war-companions, and reported their fate.[261] Among those who were thus treated, some were leading men, which had a dangerous tendency to disturb the public quiet. We were repeatedly informed, by public account, that those murderers were so audacious as to impose the scalps on the gov-ernment for those of French Indians; and that they actually obtained the premium allowed at that time by law in such a case. Although the vindictive disposition of Indians in general, impetuously forces them on in quest of equal revenge for blood, without the least thought of consequences; yet as a misunderstanding had subsisted some time, between several distant towns, and those who chanced to lose their people in Virginia, the chiefs of those families being afraid of a civil war, [246] in case of a rupture with us, dis-suaded the furious young warriors from commencing hostilities against us, till they had demanded satisfaction, agreeable to the treaty of friendship between them and our colonies; which if denied, they would fully take of their own accord, as became a free, warlike, and injured people. In this state, the affair lay, for the best part of a year, without our using any proper con-ciliating measures, to prevent the threatening impending storm from de-stroying us: during that interval, they earnestly applied to Virginia for satis-faction, without receiving any; in like manner to North-Carolina; and afterwards to South-Carolina, with the same bad success. And there was an-other incident at Fort Prince-George, which set fire to the fuel, and kindled it into a raging flame: three light-headed, disorderly young officers of that garrison, forcibly violated some of their wives, and in the most shameless manner, at their own houses, while the husbands were making their winter hunt in the woods—and which infamous conduct they madly repeated, but a few months before the commencement of the war: in other respects, through a haughty over-bearing spirit, they took pleasure in insulting and abusing the natives, when they paid a friendly visit to the garrison.[262] No wonder that such a behaviour, caused their revengeful tempers to burst forth into action. When the Indians find no redress of grievances, they never fail to redress themselves, either sooner or later. But when they begin, they do not know where to end. Their thirst for the blood of their reputed enemies, is not to be quenched with a few drops.—The more they drink, the more it inflames their thirst. When they dip their finger in human blood, they are restless till they plunge themselves in it.

Contrary to the wise conduct of the French garrisons in securing the affection of the natives where they are settled—our sons of Mars imbittered the hearts of those Cheerake, that lie next to South-Carolina and Georgia colonies, against us, with the mid settlements and the western towns on the streams of the Missisippi: who were so incensed as continually to upbraid the traders with our unkind treatment of their people in the camp at Monongahela,—and for our having committed such hostilities against our good friends, who were peaceably returning home through our settlements, and often under pinching wants. The lying over their dead, and the wailing of the women in their various towns, and tribes, for their deceased relations, at the dawn of day, and in the dusk of the evening, proved another strong provocative to them to retaliate blood for blood. The Muskohge [247] also at that time having a friendly intercourse with the Cheerake, through the channel of the governor of South-Carolina, were, at the instance of the watchful French, often ridiculing them for their cowardice in not revenging the crying blood of their beloved kinsmen and warriors. At the same time, they promised to assist them against us, and in the name of the Alebahma French, assured them of a supply of ammunition, to enable them to avenge their injuries, and maintain their lives and liberties against the mischievous and bloody English colonists; who, they said, were naturally in a bitter state of war against all the red people, and studied only how to steal their lands, on a quite opposite principle to the open steady conduct of the generous French, who assist their poor red brothers, a great way from their own settlements, where they can have no view, but that of doing good. Notwithstanding the repeated provocations we had given to the Cheerake,—and the artful insinuations of the French, inculcated with proper address; yet their old chiefs not wholly depending on the sincerity of their smooth tongues and painted faces, nor on the assistance, or even neutrality of the remote northern towns of their own country, on mature deliberation, concluded that, as all hopes of a friendly redress for the blood of their relations now depended on their own hands, they ought to take revenge in that equal and just manner, which became good warriors. They accordingly sent out a large company of warriors, against those Germans, (or Tied-arse people, as they term them) to bring in an equal number of their scalps, to those of their own murdered relations.—Or if they found their safety did not permit, they were to proceed as near to that settlement, as they conveniently could, where having taken sufficient satisfaction, they were to bury the bloody tomohawk they took with them. They set off, but advancing pretty far into the high settlements of North-Carolina, the ambitious young leaders separated into small companies, and killed as many of our people, as unfortunately fell into their power, contrary to the wise orders of their seniors, and the number far exceeded that of their own slain. Soon after they returned home, they killed a reprobate old trader; and two soldiers also were cut off near Fort Loudon. For these acts of hostility, the government of South-Carolina demanded satisfaction, without receiving any; the hearts of their young warriors were so exceedingly enraged, as to render their ears quite deaf to any remonstrance of their seniors, respecting an amicable accommodation; for as they expected to be exposed to very little danger, on our remote, dispersed, and [248] very extensive barrier settlements, nothing but war-songs and war-dances could please them, during this flattering period of becoming great warriors, "by killing swarms of white dung-hill fowls, in the corn-fields, and asleep," according to their war-phrase.

Previous to this alarming crisis, while the Indians were applying to our colonies for that satisfaction, which our laws could not allow them, without a large contribution of white scalps, from Tyburn, with one living criminal to suffer death before their eyes,—his excellency William Henry Lyttleton, governor of South-Carolina,[263] strenuously exerted himself in providing for the safety of the colony; regardless of fatigue, he visited its extensive barriers, by land and water, to have them put in as respectable a condition, as circumstances could admit, before the threatening storm broke out: and he ordered the militia of the colony, under a large penalty, to be trained to arms, by an adjutant general, (the very worthy Col. G. P.)[264] who saw those manly laws of defence duly executed. We had great pleasure to see his excellency on his summer's journey, enter the old famous New-Windsor garrison, like a private gentleman, without the least parade; and he proceeded in his circular course, in the same retired easy manner, without incommoding any of the inhabitants. He fully testified, his sole aim was the security and welfare of the valuable country over which he presided, without imitating the mean self-interested artifice of any predecessor. At the capital seat of government, he busily employed himself in extending, and protecting trade, the vital part of a maritime colony; in redressing old neglected grievances, of various kinds; in punishing corruption wheresoever it was found, beginning at the head, and proceeding equally to the feet; and in protecting virtue, not by the former cobweb-laws, but those of old British extraction. In so laudable a manner, did that public-spirited governor exert his powers, in his own proper sphere of action: but on an object much below it, he failed, by not knowing aright the temper and customs of the savages.

The war being commenced on both sides, by the aforesaid complicated causes, it continued for some time a partial one: and according to the well-known temper of the Cheerake in similar cases, it might either have remained so, or soon have been changed into a very hot civil war, had we [249] been so wise as to have improved the favourable opportunity. There were seven northern towns, opposite to the middle parts of the Cheerake country, who from the beginning of the unhappy grievances, firmly dissented from the hostile intentions of their suffering and enraged countrymen, and for a considerable time before, bore them little good-will, on account of some family disputes, which occasioned each party to be more favourable to itself than to the other: These, would readily have gratified their vindictive disposition, either by a neutrality, or an offensive alliance with our colonists against them. Our rivals the French, never neglected so favourable an opportunity of securing, and promoting their interests.— We have known more than one instance, wherein their wisdom has not only found out proper means to disconcert the most dangerous plans of disaffected savages, but likewise to foment, and artfully encourage great animosities between the heads of ambitious rival families, till they fixed them in an implacable hatred against each other, and all of their respective tribes. Had the French been under such circumstances, as we then were, they would instantly have sent them an embassy by a proper person, to enforce it by the persuasive argument of interest, well supported with presents to all the leading men, in order to make it weigh heavy in the Indian scale; and would have invited a number of those towns to pay them a brotherly visit, whenever it suited them, that they might shake hands, smoke out of the white, or beloved pipe, and drink physic together, as became old friends of honest hearts, &c.

Had we thus done, many valuable and innocent persons might have been saved from the torturing hands of the enraged Indians! The favourite leading warrior of those friendly towns, was well known to South-Carolina and Georgia, by the trading name—"*Round O.*"[265] on account of a blue impression he bore in that form. The same old, brave, and friendly warrior, depending firmly on our friendship and usual good faith, came down within an hundred miles of Charles-town, along with the head-men, and many others of those towns, to declare to the government, an inviolable attachment to all our British colonies, under every various circumstance of life whatsoever; and at the same time, earnestly to request them to supply their present want of ammunition, and order the commanding officer of Fort-Prince-George to continue to do them the like service, when necessity should force them to apply for it; as they were fully determined to war [250] to the very last, against all the enemies of Carolina, without regarding who they were, or the number they consisted of. This they told me on the spot; for having been in a singular manner recommended to his excellency the general, I was pre-engaged for that campaign—but as I could not obtain orders to go a-head of the army, through the woods, with a body of the Chikkasah, and commence hostilities, I declined the affair. Had our valuable, and well-meaning Cheerake friends just mentioned, acted their usual part of evading captivity, it would have been much better for them, and many hundreds of our unfortunate out-settlers; but they depending on our usual good faith, by their honest credulity were ruined. It was well-known, that the Indians are unacquainted with the custom and meaning of hostages; to them, it conveyed the idea of slaves, as they have no public faith to secure the lives of such—yet they were taken into custody, kept in close confinement, and afterwards shot dead: their mortal crime consisted in sounding the war-whoop, and hollowing to their countrymen, when attacking the fort in which they were imprisoned, to fight like strong-hearted warriors, and they would soon carry it, against the cowardly traitors, who deceived and inslaved their friends in their own beloved country.[266] A white savage on this cut through a plank, over their heads, and perpetrated that horrid action, while the soldiery were employed like warriors, against the enemy: to excuse his baseness, and save himself from the reproaches of the people, he, like the wolf in the fable, falsely accused them of intending to poison the wells of the garrison.

By our uniform misconduct, we gave too plausible a plea to the disaffected part of the Muskohge to join the Cheerake, and at the same time, fixed the whole nation in a state of war against us—all the families of those leading men that were so shamefully murdered, were inexpressibly imbittered against our very national name, judging that we first deceived, then inslaved, and afterwards killed our best, and most faithful friends, who were firmly resolved to die in our defence. The means of our general safety, thus were turned to our general ruin. The mixed body of people that were first sent against them, were too weak to do them any ill; and they soon returned home with a wild, ridiculous parade. There were frequent desertions among them—some were afraid of the small-pox, which then raged in the country—others abhorred an inactive life; this fine silken body chiefly consisted of citizens and planters from the low settlements, unacquainted with the hardships of a wood-land, savage [251] war, and in case of an ambuscade attack, were utterly incapable of standing the shock. In Georgiana, we were assured by a gentleman of character, a principal merchant of Mobille, who went a voluntier on that expedition,[267] that toward the conclusion of it, when he went round the delicate camp, in wet weather, and late at night, he saw in different places from fifteen to twenty of their guns in a cluster, at the distance of an equal number of paces from their tents, seemingly so rusty and peaceable, as the loss of them by the usual sudden attack of Indian savages, could not in the least affect their lives. And the Cheerake nation were sensible of their innocent intentions, from the disposition of the expedition in so late a season of the year: but their own bad situation by the ravaging small-pox, and the danger of a civil war, induced the lower towns to lie dormant. However, soon after our people returned home, they firmly united in the generous cause of liberty, and they acted their part so well, that our traders suspected not the impending blow, till the moment they fatally felt it: some indeed escaped by the assistance of the Indians. In brief, we forced the Cheerake to become our bitter enemies, by a long train of wrong measures, the consequences of which were severely felt by a number of high assessed, ruined, and bleeding innocents—May this relation, be a lasting caution to our colonies against the like fatal errors! and induce them, whenever necessity compels, to go well prepared, with plenty of fit stores, and men, against any Indian nation, and first defeat, and then treat with them. It concerns us to remember, that they neither shew mercy to those who fall in their power, by the chance of war; nor keep good faith with their enemies, unless they are feelingly convinced of its reasonableness, and civilly treated afterward.

Had South-Carolina exerted herself in due time against them, as her situation required, it would have saved a great deal of innocent blood, and public treasure: common sense directed them to make immediate preparations for carrying the war into their country, as the only way to conquer them; but they strangely neglected sending war-like stores to Ninety-six, our only barrier-fort, and even providing horses and carriages for that needful occasion, till the troops they requested arrived from New-York: and then they sent only a trifling number of those, and our provincials, under the gallant Col. Montgomery, (now Lord Eglington).[268] His twelve hundred brave, hardy highlanders, though but a handful, were much abler, however, to [252] fight the Indians in their country than six thousand heavy-accoutered and slow moving regulars: for these, with our provincials, could both fight and pursue, while the regulars would always be surrounded, and stand a sure and shining mark. Except a certain provincial captain who escorted the cattle, every officer and private man in this expedition, imitated the intrepid copy of their martial leader; but being too few in number, and withal, scanty of provisions, and having lost many men at a narrow pass, called Crow's Creek, where the path leads by the side of a river, below a dangerous steep mountain,—they proceeded only a few miles, to a fine situated town called Nuquose; and then wisely retreated under cover of the night, toward Fort-Prince-George, and returned to Charles-town, in August 1760. Seven months after the Cheerake commenced hostilities, South-Carolina by her ill-timed parsimony again exposed her barriers to the merciless ravages of the enraged Indians—who reckoning themselves also superior to any resistance we could make, swept along the valuable out-settlements of North-Carolina and Virginia, and like evil ones licensed to destroy, ruined every thing near them. The year following, Major Grant, the present governor of East-Florida,[269] was sent against them with an army of regulars and provincials, and happily for him, the Indians were then in great want of ammunition: they therefore only appeared, and suddenly disappeared. From all probable circumstances, had the Cheerake been sufficiently supplied with ammunition, twice the number of troops could not have defeated them, on account of the declivity of their stupendous mountains, under which their paths frequently run; the Virginia troops likewise kept far off in flourishing parade, without coming to our assistance, or making a diversion against those warlike towns which lie beyond the Apalahche mountains,—the chief of which are, *Tennàse, Choàte, Great-Telliko,* and *Huwhàse.*

At the beginning of the late Cheerake war, I had the pleasure to see, at *Augusta* in *Georgia,* the honourable gentleman who was our first Indian super-intendant;[270] he was on his way to the Muskohge country, to pacify their ill disposition toward us, which had irritated the Cheerake, and engaged them in a firm confederacy against us. They had exchanged their bloody tomohawks, and red and black painted swans wings, a strong emblem of blood and death, in confirmation of their offensive and defensive treaty. But, notwithstanding our dangerous situation ought to have directed any gentleman worthy of public trust, to [253] have immediately proceeded to their country, to regain the hearts of those fickle and daring savages, and thereby elude the deep-laid plan of the French; and though Indian runners were frequently sent down by our old friendly head-men, urging the absolute necessity of his coming up soon, otherwise it would be too late—he trifled away near half a year there, and in places adjoining, in raising a body of men with a proud uniform dress, for the sake of parade, and to escort him from danger, with swivels, blunderbusses, and many other such sorts of blundering stuff, before he proceeded on his journey. This was the only way to expose the gentleman to real danger, by shewing at such a time, a diffidence of the natives—which he accordingly effected, merely by his pride, obstinacy, and unskilfulness. It is well known, the whole might have been prevented, if he had listened to the entreaties of the Indian traders of that place, to request one (who would neither refuse, nor delay to serve his country on any important occasion) to go in his stead, as the dangerous situation of our affairs demanded quick dispatch. But pride prevented, and he slowly reached there, after much time was lost.

The artful French commander,[271] had in the mean while a very good opportunity to distract the giddy savages, and he wisely took advantage of the delay, and persuaded a considerable body of the Shawano Indians to fly to the northward,—as our chief was affirmed to be coming with an army and train of artillery to cut them off, in revenge of the blood they had formerly spilled. We soon heard, that in their way, they murdered a great many of the British subjects, and with the most despiteful eagerness committed their bloody ravages during the whole war.

After the head-men of that far-extending country, were convened to know the import of our intendants long-expected embassy, he detained them from day to day with his parading grandeur; not using the Indian friendly freedom, either to the red, or white people, till provisions grew scanty. Then their hearts were imbittered against him, while the French Alebahma commander was busy, in taking time by the forelock. But the former, to be uniform in his stiff, haughty conduct, crowned the whole, in a longer delay, and almost gained a supposed crown of martydom,—by prohibiting, in an obstinate manner, all the war-chieftains and beloved men then assembled together in the great beloved square, from handing the friendly white pipe to a certain great [254] war-leader, well-known by the names of *Yah-Yah-Tustanage,* or "the Great Mortar,"[272] because he had been in the French interest. Our great man, ought to have reclaimed him by strong reasoning and good treatment: but by his misconduct, he inflamed the hearts of him and his relations with the bitterest enmity against the English name, so that when the gentleman was proceeding in his laconic stile,—a warrior who had always before been very kind to the British traders, (called "the *Tobacco-eater,*" on account of his chewing tobacco) jumped up in a rage, and darted his tomohawk at his head,—happily for all the traders present, and our frontier colonies, it sunk in a plank directly over the superintendant; and while the tobacco-eater was eagerly pulling it out, to give the mortal blow, a warrior, friendly to the English, immediately leaped up, saved the gentleman, and prevented those dangerous consequences which must otherwise have immediately followed.[273] Had the aimed blow succeeded, the savages would have immediately put up the war and death whoop, destroyed most of the white people there on the spot, and set off in great bodies, both to the Cheerake country, and against our valuable settlements. Soon after that gentleman returned to Carolina, the Great Mortar persuaded a party of his relations to kill our traders, and they murdered ten;—very fortunately, it stopped there for that time.[274] But at the close of the great congress at Augusta,[275] where four governors of our colonies, and his majesty's superintendant, convened the savages and renewed and confirmed the treaty of peace, the same disaffected warrior returning home, sent off a party, who murdered fourteen of the inhabitants of Long-Cane settlement, above Ninety-Six.[276] The result of that dangerous congress, tempted the proud savages to act such a part, as they were tamely forgiven, and unasked, all their former scenes of blood.

During this distracted period, the French used their utmost endeavours to involve us in a general Indian war, which to have saved South-Carolina and Georgia, would probably have required the assistance of a considerable number of our troops from Canada. They strove to supply the Cheerake, by way of the Missisippi, with warlike stores; and also sent them powder, bullets, flints, knives, and red paint, by their staunch friend, the disaffected Great Mortar, and his adherents. And though they failed in executing their mischievous plan, both on account of the manly escape of our traders, and the wise conduct of those below, they did not despair. Upon studious deliberation, they concluded, that, if the aforesaid chieftain [255] *Yah Yah Tustanàge,* his family, and warriors, settled high up one of their leading rivers, about half way toward the Cheerake, it would prove the only means then left, of promoting their general cause against the British colonists: And, as the lands were good for hunting,—the river shallow, and abounding with saltish grass, for the deer to feed on in the heat of the day, free of troublesome insects,— and as the stream glided by the Alebahma garrison to Mobille, at that time in the French hands, it could not well fail to decoy a great many of the ambitious young warriors, and others, to go there and join our enemies, on any occasion which appeared most conducive to their design of shedding blood, and getting a higher name among their wolfish heroes. He and his numerous pack, confident of success, and of receiving the French supplies by water, set off for their new seat, well loaded, both for their Cheerake friends and themselves. He had a French commission, with plenty of beeswax, and decoying pictures; and a flourishing flag, which in dry weather, was displayed day and night, in the middle of their anti-anglican theatre. It in a great measure answered the serpentine design of the French, for it became the general rendezvous of the Missisippi Indians, the Cheerake, and the more mischievous part of the Muskohge. The latter became the French carriers to those high-land savages: and had they received the ammunition sent them by water, and that nest been allowed to continue, we should have had the French on our southern colonies at the head of a dreadful confederated army of savages, carrying desolation where-ever they went. But, the plan miscarried, our friendly gallant Chikkasah, being well informed of the ill design of this nest of hornets, broke it up. A considerable company of their resolute warriors marched against it; and, as they readily knew the place of the Great Mortar's residence, they attacked it, and though they missed him, they killed his brother. This, so greatly intimidated him, and his clan, that they suddenly removed from thence; and their favourite plan was abortive. When he got near to a place of safety, he shewed how highly irritated he was against us, and our allies. His disappointment, and disgrace, prevented him from returning to his own native town, and excited him to settle in the remotest, and most northern one of the whole nation, toward the Cheerake, in order to assist them, (as far as the French, and his own corroding temper might enable him) against the innocent objects of his enmity: and during the continuance of the war we held with those savages, he and a [256] numerous party of his adherents kept passing, and repassing, from thence to the bloody theatre. They were there, as their loud insulting bravadoes testified, during our two before-mentioned campaigns, under Hon. Col. Montgomery, and Major Grant. The wise endeavours of Governor Bull, of South-Carolina, and the unwearied application of Governor Ellis, of Georgia, in concert with the gentlemen of two great trading houses, the one at Augusta, and the other on the Carolina side of the river, not far below, where the Indians crowded day and night, greatly contributed to demolish the plan of the French and their ally, the Great Mortar.[277]

When public spirit, that divine spark, glows in the breast of any of the American leaders, it never fails to communicate its influence, all around, even to the savages in the remotest wilderness; of which Governor Ellis is an illustrious instance. He speedily reconciled a jarring colony—calmed the raging Muskohge, though set on by the mischievous Alebahma French,—pacified the Cheerake, and the rest of their confederates—sent them off well pleased, without executing their base design, and engaged them into a neutrality. The following, is one instance—As soon as the Indians killed our traders, they sent runners to call home their people, from our settlements: a friendly head warrior, who had notice of it at night, near Augusta, came there next day with a few more, expressed his sorrow for the mischief his countrymen had done us, protested he never had any ill intentions against us, and said that, though by the law of blood, he ought to die, yet, if we allowed him to live as a friend, he should live and die one. Though thousands of regular troops would most probably have been totally cut off, had they been where the intended general massacre began, without an escortment of our provincials; yet an unskilful, haughty officer of Fort-Augusta laboured hard for killing this warrior, and his companion, which of course, would have brought on what the enemy sought, a complicated, universal war. But his excellency's humane temper, and wise conduct, actuating the Indian trading gentlemen of Augusta, they suffered him to set off to strive to prevent the further effusion of innocent blood, and thus procured the happy fruits of peace, to the infant colonies of Georgia and South-Carolina.

ACCOUNT
OF THE
MUSKOHGE NATION, &C.

Their country is situated, nearly in the centre, between the Cheerake, Georgia, East and West-Florida, and the Choktah and Chikkasah nations, the one 200, and the other 300 miles up the Missisippi. It extends 180 computed miles, from north to south. It is called the Creek country, on account of the great number of Creeks, or small bays, rivulets and swamps, it abounds with. This nation is generally computed to consist of about 3500 men fit to bear arms; and has fifty towns, or villages. The principal are *Ok-whûs-ke, Ok-chai, Tuk-ke-bat-che, Tal-lâ-se, Kow-hé-tah,* and *Cha-hâh.*[278] The nation consists of a mixture of several broken tribes, whom the Muskohge artfully decoyed to incorporate with them, in order to strengthen themselves against hostile attempts. Their former national names were *Ta-mé-tah, Tae-keo-ge, Ok-chai, Pak-ká-na, Wee-tam-ka;* with them is also one town of the *Sha-wa-no,* and one of the *Nah-chee* Indians; likewise two great towns of the *Koo-a-sâh-te.*[279] The upper part of the Muskohge country is very hilly—the middle less so—the lower towns, level: These are settled by the remains of the *Oosécha, Okone,* and *Sawakola* nations.[280] Most of their towns are very commodiously and pleasantly situated, on large, beautiful creeks, or rivers, where the lands are fertile, the water clear and well tasted, and the air extremely pure. As the streams have a quick descent, the climate is of a most happy temperature, free from disagreeable heat or cold, unless for the space of a few days, in summer and winter, according to all our American climes. In their country are four bold rivers, which spring from the Apalahche mountains, and interlock with the eastern branches of the Missisippi. The Koosah river is the western boundary of their towns: It is 200 yards broad, and runs by the late Alebahma, to [258] Mobille, eastward. Okwhuske lies 70 miles from the former, which taking a considerable southern sweep, runs a western course, and joins the aforesaid great stream, a little below that deserted garrison; since the year 1764, the Muskohge have settled several towns, seventy miles eastward from Okwhuske, on the Chatahooche river, near to the old trading path. This great lympid stream is 200 yards broad, and lower down, it passes by the Apalahche, into Florida; so that this nation extends 140 miles in breadth from east to west, according to the course of the trading path.

Their land is generally hilly, but not mountainous; which allows an army an easy passage into their country, to retaliate their insults and cruelties—that period seems to advance apace; for the fine flourishing accounts of those who gain by the art, will not always quiet a suffering people. As the Muskohge judge only from what they see around them, they firmly believe they are now more powerful than any nation that might be tempted to invade them. Our passive conduct toward them, causes them to entertain a very mean opinion of our martial abilities: but, before we tamely allowed them to commit acts of hostility, at pleasure, (which will soon be mentioned) the traders taught them sometimes by strong felt lessons, to conclude the English to be men and warriors. They are certainly the most powerful Indian nation we are acquainted with on this continent, and within thirty years past, they are grown very warlike. Toward the conclusion of their last war with the Cheerake,[281] they defeated them so easily, that in contempt, they sent several of their women and small boys against them, though, at that time, the Cheerake were the most numerous. The Choktah were also much inferior to them, in several engagements they had with them; though, perhaps, they are the most artful ambuscaders, and wolfish savages, in America.—But, having no rivers in their own country, very few of them can swim, which often proves inconvenient and dangerous, when they are in pursuit of the enemy, or pursued by them. We should be politically sorry for their differences with each other to be reconciled, as long experience convinces us they cannot live without shedding human blood somewhere or other, on account of their jealous and fierce tempers, in resentment of any kind of injury, and the martial preferment each obtains for every scalp of an enemy. They are so extremely anxious to be distinguished by high war-titles, that sometimes a small party of warriors, on failing of success in their campaign, have been detected in murdering [259] some of their own people, for the sake of their scalps. We cannot expect that they will observe better faith towards us—therefore common sense and self-love ought to direct us to chuse the least of two unavoidable evils; ever to keep the wolf from our own doors, by engaging him with his wolfish neighbours: at least, the officious hand of folly should not part them, when they are earnestly engaged in their favourite element against each other.

All the other Indian nations we have any acquaintance with, are visibly and fast declining, on account of their continual merciless wars, the immoderate use of spirituous liquors, and the infectious ravaging nature of the small pox: but the Muskohge have few enemies, and the traders with them have taught them to prevent the last contagion from spreading among their towns, by cutting off all communication with those who are infected, till the danger is over. Besides, as the men rarely go to war till they have helped the women to plant a sufficient plenty of provisions, contrary to the usual method of warring savages, it is so great a help to propagation, that by this means also, and their artful policy of inviting decayed tribes to incorporate with them, I am assured by a gentleman of distinguished character, who speaks their language as well as their best orators, they have increased double in number within the space of thirty years past, notwithstanding their widows are confined to a strict state of celibacy, for the full space of four years after the death of their husbands. When we consider that two or three will go several hundred miles, to way-lay an enemy—the contiguous situation of such a prodigious number of corrupt, haughty, and mischievous savages to our valuable colonies, ought to draw our attention upon them. Those of us who have gained a sufficient knowledge of Indian affairs, by long experience and observation, are firmly persuaded that the seeds of war are deeply implanted in their hearts against us; and that the allowing them, in our usual tame manner, to insult, plunder, and murder peaceable British subjects, only tempts them to engage deeper in their diabolical scenes of blood, till they commence a dangerous open war against us: the only probable means to preserve peace, is either to set them and their rivals on one another, or by prudent management, influence them to employ themselves in raising silk, or any other staple commodity that would best suit their own temper and climate. Prudence points out this, but the task is too arduous for strangers ever to be able to effect, or they care not about it.

[260] Before the late cession of East and West Florida to Great Britain, the country of the Muskohge lay between the territories of the English, Spaniards, French, Choktah, Chikkasah, and Cheerake.—And as they had a water carriage, from the two Floridas; to secure their liberties, and a great trade by land from Georgia and South-Carolina, this nation regulated the Indian balance of power in our southern parts of North-America; for the French could have thrown the mercenary Choktah, and the Missisippi savages, into the scale, whenever their interest seemed to require it. The Muskohge having three rival christian powers their near neighbours, and a French garrison on the southern extremity of the central part of their country ever since the war of the year 1715;[282] the old men, being long informed by the opposite parties, of the different views, and intrigues of those European powers, who paid them annual tribute under the vague appellation of presents, were become surprisingly crafty in every turn of low politics. They held it as an invariable maxim, that their security and welfare required a perpetual friendly intercourse with us and the French; as our

political state of war with each other, would always secure their liberties: whereas, if they joined either party, and enabled it to prevail over the other, their state, they said, would then become as unhappy as that of a poor fellow, who had only one perverse wife, and yet must bear with her froward temper; but a variety of choice would have kept off such an afflicting evil, either by his giving her a silent caution against behaving ill, or by enabling him to go to another, who was in a better temper. But as the French Alebahma Garrison had been long directed by skilful officers, and supplied pretty well with corrupting brandy, taffy,[283] and decoying trifles at the expence of government, they industriously applied their mischievous talents in impressing many of the former simple and peaceable natives with false notions of the ill intentions of our colonies. In each of their towns, the French gave a considerable pension to an eloquent head-man, to corrupt the Indians by plausible pretexts, and inflame them against us; who informed them also of every material occurrence, in each of their respective circles. The force of liquors made them so faithful to their trust, that they poisoned the innocence of their own growing families, by tempting them, from their infancy, to receive the worst impressions of the British colonists: and as they very seldom got the better of those prejudices, they alienated the affections of their offspring, and riveted their bitter enmity against us. That conduct of the Christian French has fixed many of the Muskohge [261] in a strong native hatred to the British Americans, which being hereditary, must of course increase, as fast as they increase in numbers; unless we give them such a severe lesson, as their annual hostile conduct to us, has highly deserved since the year 1760. I shall now speak more explicitly on this very material point.

By our superintendant's strange pursuit of improper measures to appease the Muskohge, as before noticed, the watchful French engaged the irritated Great Mortar to inspire his relations to cut off some of our traders by surprise, and follow the blow at the time the people were usually employed in the corn-fields, lest our party should stop them, in their intended bloody career. They accordingly began their hostile attack in the upper town of the nation, except one, where their mischievous red abettor lived: two white people and a negroe were killed, while they were in the horse-pen, preparing that day to have set off with their returns to the English settlements. The trader, who was surly and ill-natured, they chopped to pieces, in a most horrid manner, but the other two they did not treat with any kind of barbarity; which shews that the worst people, in their worst actions, make a distinction between the morally virtuous, and vicious.[284] The other white people of that trading house, happily were at that time in the woods;—they heard the savage platoon, and the death, and war-whoop, which sufficiently warned them of their imminent danger, and to seek their safety by the best means they could. Some of them went through the woods after night, to our friend towns; and one who happened to be near the town when the alarm was given, going to bring in a horse, was obliged to hide himself under a large fallen tree, till night came on. The eager savages came twice, pretty near him, imagining he would chuse rather to depend on the horse's speed, than his own: when the town was engaged in dividing the spoils, his wife fearing she might be watched, took a considerable sweep round, through the thickets, and by searching the place, and making signals, where she expected he lay concealed, fortunately found him, and gave him provisions to enable him to get to our settlements, and then returned home in tears: he arrived safe at Augusta, though exceedingly torn with the brambles, as his safety required him to travel through unfrequented tracts. In the mean while, the savages having by this inflamed their greedy thirst for blood, set off swiftly, and as they darted [262] along sounding the news of war, they from a few, increased so fast, that their voices conveyed such thrilling shocks to those they were in quest of, as if the infernal legions had broken loose through their favourite Alebahma, and were invested with power to destroy the innocent. The great Okwhuske-town, where they reached, lay on the western side of the large easternmost branch of Mobille river, which joins a far greater western river, almost two miles below the late Alebahma; and the English traders store-houses lay opposite to the town. Those red ambassadors of the French, artfully passed the river above the town, and ran along silently to a gentleman's dwelling house, where they first shot down one of his servants, and in a minute or two after, himself: probably, he might have been saved, if he had not been too desperate; for a strong-bodied leading warrior of the town was at his house when they came to it, who grasped him behind, with his face toward the wall, on purpose to save him from being shot; as they durst not kill himself, under the certain pain of death. But very unluckily, the gentleman struggled, got hold of him, threw him to the ground, and so became too fair a mark.—Thus the Frenchified savages cut off, in the bloom of his youth, the son of J. R. Esq;[285] Indian trading merchant of Augusta, who was the most stately, comely, and gallant youth, that ever traded in the Muskohge country, and equally blest with every social virtue, that attracts esteem. The very savages lament his death to this day, though it was usual with him to correct as many of the swaggering heroes, as could stand round him in his house, when they became impudent and mischievous, through the plea of drinking spirituous liquors: when they recover from their bacchanal phrenzy, they regard a man of a martial spirit, and contemn the pusillanimous.

While the town was in the utmost surprise, the ambitious warriors were joyfully echoing—"all is spoiled;" and sounding the death-whoop, they, like so many infernal furies commissioned to destroy, set off at full speed, dispersing their bloody legions to various towns, to carry general destruction along with them. But before any of their companies reached to the Okchai war-town, (the native place of the Great Mortar) the inhabitants had heard the massacre was begun, and according to their rule, killed two of our traders in their house, when quite off their guard: as these traders were brave, and regardless of danger by their habit of living, the savages were afraid to bring their arms with them, it being unusual, [263] by reason of the secure situation of the town. A few therefore entered the house, with a specious pretence, and intercepted them from the fire-arms, which lay on a rack, on the front of the chimney; they instantly seized them, and as they were loaded with large shot, they killed those two valuable and intrepid men, and left them on the fire—but if they had been a few minutes fore-warned of the danger, their lives would have cost the whole town very dear, unless they had kindled the house with fire-arrows.

Like pestilential vapours driven by whirlwinds, the mischievous savages endeavoured to bring desolation on the innocent objects of their fury, wherever they came: but the different flights of the trading people, as well as their own expertness in the woods, and their connections with the Indians, both by marriage and other ties of friendship, disappointed the accomplishment of the main point of the French diabolical scheme of dipping them all over in blood. By sundry means, a considerable number of our people met at the friendly house of the old Wolf-King,[286] two miles from the Alebahma Fort, where that faithful stern chieftain treated them with the greatest kindness. But, as the whole nation was distracted, and the neighbouring towns were devoted to the French interest, he found that by having no fortress, and only forty warriors in his town, he was unable to protect the refugees. In order therefore to keep good faith with his friends, who put themselves under his protection, he told them their situation, supplied those of them with arms and ammunition who chanced to have none, and conveyed them into a contiguous thick swamp, as their only place of security for that time; "which their own valour, he said, he was sure would maintain, both against the French, and their mad friends." He was not mistaken in his favourable opinion of their war abilities, for they ranged themselves so well, that the enemy found it impracticable to attack them, without sustaining far greater loss than they are known to hazard.—He supplied them with necessaries, and sent them safe at length to a friendly town, at a considerable distance, where they joined several other traders, from different places, and were soon after safely escorted to Savanah.

It is surprising how those hardy men evaded the dangers they were surrounded with, especially at the beginning, and with so little loss. One of [264] them told me, that while a party of the savages were on a corn-house scaffold, painting themselves red and black, to give the cowardly blow to him and his companion, an old woman overheard them concerting their bloody design, and speedily informed him of the threatening danger: he mentioned the intended place of meeting to his friends, and they immediately set off, one this way, and another that, to prevent a pursuit, and all met safe, to the great regret of the Christian French and their red hirelings. I was informed that another considerable trader, who lived near a river, on the outside of a town, where he stood secure in the affection of his savage brethren, received a visit from two lusty ill-looking strangers, without being discovered by any of the inhabitants. They were anointed with bear's oil, and quite naked, except a narrow slip of cloth for breeches, and a light blanket. When they came in, they looked around, wild and confused, not knowing how to execute the French commission, consistently with their own safety, as they brought no arms, lest it should have discovered their intentions, and by that means exposed them to danger. But they seated themselves near the door, both to prevent his escape, and watch a favourable opportunity to perpetrate their murdering scheme. His white domestics were a little before gone into the woods; and he and his Indian wife were in the storehouse, where there chanced to be no arms of defence, which made his escape the more hazardous. He was nearly in the same light dress, as that of his visitants, according to the mode of their domestic living: he was about to give them some tobacco, when their countenances growing more gloomy and fierce, were observed by his wife, as well as the mischievous direction of their eyes; presently therefore as they bounded up, the one to lay hold of the white man, and the other of an ax that lay on the floor, she seized it at the same instant, and cried, "husband fight strong, and run off, as becomes a good warrior." The savage strove to lay hold of him, till the other could disengage himself from the sharp struggle the woman held with him; but by a quick presence of mind, the husband decoyed his pursuer round a large ladder that joined the loft, and being strong and swift-footed, he there took the advantage of his too eager adversary, dashed him to the ground, and ran out of the house, full speed to the river, bounded into it, soon made the opposite shore, and left them at the store-house, from whence the woman, as a trusty friend, drove them off, with the utmost despight,—her family was her [265] protection. The remaining part of that day, he ran a great distance through the woods, called at night on such white people, as he imagined his safety allowed him, was joined by four of them, and went together to Pensacola. Within three or four days march of that place, the lands, they told me, were in general, either boggy and low, or consisting of sandy pine-barrens. Although they were almost naked, and had lived for many days on the produce of the woods, yet the dastardly Spaniards were so hardened against the tender feelings of nature in favour of the distressed, who now took sanctuary under the Spanish flag, as to refuse them every kind of assistance; contrary to the hospitable custom of the red savages, even towards those they devote to the fire. A north-country skipper, who rode in the harbour, was equally divested of the bowels of compassion toward them, notwithstanding their pressing entreaties, and offers of bills on very respectable persons in Charles-Town. But the commandant of the place soon instructed him very feelingly in the common laws of humanity; for on some pretext, he seized the vessel and cargo, and left the narrow-hearted miser to shift for himself, and return home as he could: those unfortunate traders were kindly treated however by the head-man of an adjacent town of the Apalahche Indians, who being a considerable dealer, supplied them with every thing they stood in need of, till, in time, they were recalled; for which they soon very thankfully paid him and the rest of his kind family, with handsome presents, as a token of their friendship and gratitude.[287]

In the mean while, some of the eloquent old traders continued in their towns, where the red flag of defiance was hung up day and night, as the French had no interest there: and, in a few other towns, some of our thoughtless young men, who were too much attached to the Indian life, from an early pursuit in that wild and unlimited country, chose to run any risk, rather than leave their favourite scenes of pleasure. In the day-time, they kept in the most unfrequented places, and usually returned at night to their friend's house: and they followed that dangerous method of living a considerable time, in different places, without any mischance. One of them told me, that one evening, when he was returning to his wife's house on horseback, before the usual time, he was overtaken by a couple of young warriors, who pranced up along aside of him. They spoke very kindly according to their custom, that they might shed blood, like wolves, without hazarding their own carcases. As neither of them had any weapons, except a long knife hanging round their neck in a sheath, they were afraid to attack him, on [266] so hazardous a lay. Their questions, cant language, and discomposed countenances, informed him of their bloody intentions, and cautioned him from falling into any of their wily stratagems, which all cowards are dextrous in forming. When they came to a boggy cane-branch, they strove to persuade him to alight, and rest a little, but finding their labour in vain, they got down: one prepared a club to kill him, and the other a small frame of split canes tied together with bark, to bear his scalp—seeing this, he set off with the bravado whoop, through the high lands, and as he rode a swift horse, he left them out of sight in an instant. He took a great sweep round, to avoid an after-chase. At night, he went to the town, got fire-arms, and provisions, and soon arrived safe in Georgia.

Other instances may be related, but these will suffice to shew how serviceable such hardy and expert men would be to their country, as heretofore, if our Indian trade was properly regulated; and how exceedingly preferable the tenth part of their number would prove against boasted regular troops, in the woods. Though the british legions are as warlike and formidable in the field of battle, as any troops whatever, as their martial bravery has often testified; yet in some situations they would be insignificant and helpless. Regular bred soldiers, in the American woods, would be of little service. The natives and old inhabitants, by being trained to arms from their infancy, in their wood-land sphere of life, could always surround them, and sweep them off entirely, with little damage to themselves. In such a case, field-pieces are a mere farce. The abettors of arbitrary power, who are making great advances through the whole British empire, to force the people to decide this point, and retrieve their constitutional rights and liberties, would do well to consider this.[288] Is it possible for tyranny to be so weak and blind, as to flatter its corrupt greatness with the wild notion of placing a despotic military power of a few thousand regular troops, over millions of the Americans, who are trained to arms of defence, from the time they are able to carry them—generally inured to dangers, and all of them possessing, in a high degree, the social virtues of their manly free-minded fore-fathers, who often bled in the noble cause of liberty, when hateful tyranny persisted in stretching her rod of oppression over their repining country? Tyrants are obstinately deaf, and blind; they will see and hear only through the false medium of self-interested court-flatterers, and, instead of redressing the grievances of the people, have sometimes openly [267] despised and insulted them, for even exhibiting their modest prayers at the foot of the throne, for a restoration of their rights and privileges. Some however have been convinced in the end they were wrong, and have justly suffered by the anathematizing voice of God and a foederal union. That "a prince can do no ill" is a flat contradiction of reason and experience, and of the English Magna Charta.

Soon after West-Florida was ceded to Great-Britain, two warlike towns of the *Koo-a-sah te* Indians[289] removed from near the late dangerous Alabahma French garrison, to the Choktah country about twenty-five miles below Tumbikbe—a strong wooden fortress, situated on the western side of a high and firm bank, overlooking a narrow deep point of the river of Mobile, and distant from that capital, one hundred leagues.[290] The discerning old war-chieftain of this remnant, perceived that the proud Muskohge, instead of reforming their conduct towards us, by our mild remonstrances, grew only more impudent by our lenity; therefore being afraid of sharing the justly deserved fate of the others, he wisely withdrew to this situation; as the French could not possibly supply them, in case we had exerted ourselves, either in defence of our properties, or in revenge of the blood they had shed. But they were soon forced to return to their former place of abode, on account of the partiality of some of them to their former confederates;

which proved lucky in its consequences, to the traders, and our southern colonies: for, when three hundred warriors of the Muskohge were on their way to the Choktah to join them in a war against us, two Kooasahte horsemen, as allies, were allowed to pass through their ambuscade in the evening, and they gave notice of the impending danger. These Kooasahte Indians, annually sanctify the mulberries by a public oblation, before which, they are not to be eaten; which they say, is according to their ancient law.[291]

I am assured by a gentleman of character, who traded a long time near the late Alebahma garrison, that within six miles of it, live the remains of seven Indian nations, who usually conversed with each other in their own different dialects, though they understood the Muskohge language; but being naturalized, they were bound to observe the laws and customs of the main original body.[292] These reduced, broken tribes, who have helped to multiply the Muskohge to a dangerous degree, have also a fixed oral tradition, that they formerly came from South-America, and, after sundry struggles [268] in defence of liberty, settled their present abode: but the Muskohge record themselves to be terræ filii, and believe their original predecessors came from the west, and resided under ground, which seems to be a faint image of the original formation of mankind out of the earth, perverted by time, and the usual arts of priest-craft.

It will be fortunate, if the late peace between the Muskohge and Choktah, through the mediation of a superintendant,[293] doth not soon affect the security of Georgia, and East and West-Florida, especially should it continue long, and Britain and Spain engage in a war against each other: for Spain will supply them with warlike stores, and in concert, may without much opposition, retake the Floridas; which they seem to have much at heart. A Cuba vessel, in the year 1767,[294] which seemed to be coasting on purpose to meet some of the Muskohge, found a camp of them almost opposite to the Apalache old fields, and proposed purchasing those lands from them; in order to secure their liberties, and, the same time, gratify the inherent, ardent desire they always had to oppose the English nation. After many artful flourishes, well adapted to soothe the natives into a compliance on account of the reciprocal advantages they proposed, some of the Muskohge consented to go in the vessel to the Havannah, and there finish the friendly bargain. They went, and at the time proposed, were sent back to the same place, but, as they are very close in their secrets, the traders know not the result of that affair; but when things in Europe require, time will disclose it.

As the Muskohge were well known to be very mischievous to our barrier-inhabitants, and to be an over-match for the numerous and fickle Choktah, the few warlike Chikkasah, by being put in the scale with these, would in a few years, have made the Muskohge kick the beam. Thus our southern colonists might have sat in pleasure, and security, under their fig-trees, and in their charming arbours of fruitful grape-vines. But now, they are uncertain whether they plant for themselves, or for the red savages, who frequently take away by force or stealth, their horses and other effects. The Muskohge chieftain, called the "Great Mortar," abetted the Cheerake against us, as hath been already noticed, and frequently, with his warriors and relations, carried them as good a supply of ammunition, as the French of the Alebahmah-garrison could well spare: for by order of their govern-ment, they were bound to reserve a certain quantity, for any unforeseen occasion [269] that might happen. If they had been possest of more, they would have given with a liberal hand, to enable them to carry on a war against us, and they almost effected their earnest wishes, when the English little expected it; for as soon as the watchful officer of the garrison, was informed by his trusty and well instructed red disciple, the Great Mortar, that the Cheerake were on the point of declaring against the English, he saw the consequence, and sent a pacquet by a Muskohge runner, to Tumbikbe-fort in the Choktah country, which was forwarded by another, and soon delivered to the governor of New-Orleans: the contents informed him of the favourable opportunity that offered for the French to settle themselves in the Cheerake country, where the late Fort-Loudon stood, near the con-flux of Great Telliko and Tennase-rivers, and so distress our southern colo-nies, as the body of the Cheerake, Muskohge, Choktah, Aquahpa, and the upper Missisippi-Indians headed by the French, would be able to maintain a certain successful war against us, if well supplied with ammunition. Their deliberations were short—they soon sent off a large pettiaugre, sufficiently laden with warlike stores, and decoying presents; and in obedience to the orders the crew had received of making all the dispatch they possibly could, in the third moon of their departure from New Orleans, they arrived within a hundred and twenty computed miles of those towns that are a little above the unhappy Fort-Loudon: there they were luckily stopped in their mischievous career, by a deep and dangerous cataract; the waters of which rolled down with a prodigious rapidity, dashed against the opposite rocks, and from thence rushed off with impetuous violence, on a quarter-angled course. It appeared so shocking and unsurmountable to the mon-sieurs, that after staying there a considerable time, in the vain expectation of seeing some of their friends, necessity forced them to return back to New Orleans, about 2600 computed miles, to their inconsolable disappoint-ment.[295]

These circumstances are now well known to our colonies: and, if our state policy had not sufficiently discovered itself of late, it would appear not a little surprising that the Great Mortar, should have such influence on the great beloved man, (so the Indians term the superintendant) as to move him, at a congress in Augusta, to write by that bitter enemy of the English name,

a conciliating letter to the almost-vanquished and desponding Choktah—
for where the conquerors have not an oblique point in [270] view, the conquered are always the first who humbly sue for peace. This beloved epistle,
that accompanied the eagles-tails, swans-wings, white beads, white pipes,
and tobacco, was sent by a white interpreter, and *Meshesheke,* a Muskohge
war-chieftain,[296] to the perfidious Choktah, as a strong confirmation of
peace. Without doubt it was a master stroke of court-policy, to strive to gain
so many expert red auxiliaries; and plainly shews how extremely well he
deserves his profitable place of public trust. I am assured by two respectable,
intelligent, old Indian traders, G. G. and L. M. G. Esq;[297] that they frequently
dissuaded him from ever dabling in such muddy waters; for the consequence would unavoidably prove fatal to our contiguous colonies. This was
confirmed by a recent instance—the late Cheerake war, which could not
have commenced, if the Muskohge and Cheerake had not been reconciled,
by the assiduous endeavours of an avaricious, and self-interested governor. If
any reader reckons this too bold, or personal, I request him to peruse a performance, entitled, "A modest reply to his Excellency J. G. Esq;" printed in
Charles-town, in the year 1750, in which every material circumstance is
sufficiently authenticated.[298]

When we consider the defenceless state, and near situation of our three
southern barrier colonies to the numerous Muskohge and Choktah—what
favourable opinion can charity reasonably induce us to form of the continued train of wrong measures the managers of our Indian affairs have
studiously pursued, by officiously mediating, and reconciling the deep-
rooted enmity which subsisted between those two mischievous nations? If
they could not, consistent with the tenour of their political office, encourage
a continuance of the war, they might have given private instructions to
some discreet trader to strive to influence them, so as to continue it.

It is excusable in clergymen that live in England to persuade us to inculcate, an endeavour to promote peace and good will, between the savages of
the remote desarts of America; especially if they employ their time in spiritual affairs, to which they ought to be entirely devoted, and not as courtiers,
in the perplexing labyrinths of state affairs: but what can be said of those
states-men, who instead of faithfully guarding the lives and privileges of
valuable subjects, extend mercy to their murderers, who have [271] a long
time wantonly shed innocent blood, and sometimes with dreadful tortures?
The blood cries aloud to the avenging God, to cause justice to be executed
on their execrable heads: for a while they may escape due punishment, but
at last it will fall heavy upon them.

When the superintendant's deputy convened most of the Muskohge
head-men, in order to write a friendly mediating letter to the Chikkasah,[299]
in behalf of the Muskohge, the Great Mortar, animated with a bitter resent-

ment against any thing transacted by any of the British nation, introduced a considerable number of his relations, merely to disconcert this plan. The letter, and usual Indian tokens of peace and friendship, were however carried up by a Chikkasah trader: but the Great Mortar timed it so well, that he soon set off after the other with ninety warriors, till he arrived within 150 miles of the Chikkasah country, which was half way from the western barriers of his own; there he encamped with 83, and sent off seven of the staunchest to surprize and kill whomsoever they could. Two days after the express was delivered, they treacherously killed two young women, as they were hoeing in the field; all the people being off their guard, on account of the late friendly tokens they received, and the assurance of the white man that there were no visible tracks of any person on the long trading path he had come. This was the beginning of May, in the year 1768, a few hours after I had set off for South-Carolina. As soon as the sculking barbarians had discharged the contents of their guns into their innocent victims, they tomohawked them, and with their long sharp knives, took off the scalps, put up the death *whoo-whoop-whoop,* and bounded away in an oblique course, to shun the dreaded pursuit. The Chikkasah soon put up their shrill war-whoop, to arm and pursue, and sixty set off on horse-back, full speed. They over-shot that part of the woods the enemy were most likely to have fled through; and four young sprightly Chikkasah warriors who outran the rest, at last discovered, and intercepted them;—they shot dead the Great Mortar's brother, who was the leader, scalped him, and retook one of the young women's scalps that was fastened to his girdle. Three continued the chase, and the fourth in a short time overtook them: soon afterward, they came up again with the enemy, at the edge of a large cane-swamp, thick-warped with vines, and china briers; there they stopped, and were at first in doubt of their being some of [272] their own company: the pursued soon discovered them, and immediately inswamped, whereupon the four were forced to decline the attack, the disadvantage being as four to eight in an open engagement. In a few days after, I fell in with them; their gloomy and fierce countenances cannot be expressed; and I had the uncourted honour of their company, three different times before I could reach my destined place, on account of a very uncommon and sudden flow of the rivers, without any rain. Between sunset and eleven o'clock the next day, the river, that was but barely our height in the evening, was swelled to the prodigious height of twenty-five feet perpendicular, and swept along with an impetuous force.

It may not be improper here to mention the method we commonly use in crossing deep rivers.—When we expect high rivers, each company of traders carry a canoe, made of tanned leather, the sides over-lapped about three fingers breadth, and well sewed with three seams. Around the gunnels, which are made of sapplings, are strong loop-holes, for large deer-skin strings to hang down both the sides: with two of these, is securely tied to the stem and stern, a well-shaped sappling, for a keel, and in like manner the ribs. Thus, they usually rig out a canoe, fit to carry over ten horse loads at once, in the space of half an hour; the apparatus is afterwards commonly hidden with great care, on the opposite shore. Few take the trouble to paddle the canoe; for, as they are commonly hardy, and also of an amphibious nature, they usually jump into the river, with their leathern barge a-head of them, and thrust it through the deep part of the water, to the opposite shore. When we ride only with a few luggage horses, as was our case at *Sip-se,* or "Poplar," the above-mentioned high-swelled river, we make a frame of dry pines, which we tie together with strong vines, well twisted; when we have raised it to be sufficiently buoyant, we load and paddle it across the stillest part of the water we can conveniently find, and afterward swim our horses together, we keeping at a little distance below them.[300]

At the time we first began to search for convenient floating timber, I chanced to stand at the end of a dry tree, overset by a hurricane, within three feet of a great rattle snake, that was coiled, and on his watch of self-defence, under thick herbage. I soon espied, and killed [273] him. But an astrologer, of twenty years standing among the Indians, immediately declared with strong asseverations, we should soon be exposed to imminent danger; which he expatiated upon largely, from his imagined knowledge of a combination of second causes in the celestial regions, actuating every kind of animals, vegetables, &c. by their subtil and delegated power. I argued in vain to hush his groundless fears: however, while the raft was getting ready, another gentleman, to quiet his timorous apprehensions, accompanied me with fire-arms, pretty near the path in the beforementioned cane-swamp, and we staid there a considerable while, at a proper distance apart—at last we heard the well-mimicked voice of partridges, farther off than our sight could discover, on which one of us struck up the whoop of friendship and indifference; for I knew that the best way of arguing on such occasions, was by a firmness of countenance and behaviour. I then went near to my companion, and said, our cunning man was an Aberdeen wizard, as he had so exactly foretold the event. The savages had both discovered our tracks, and heard the sound of the ax. We soon met them; they were nine of the mischievous *Ohchai* town, who had separated from the rest of their company. We conversed a little while together upon our arms, and in this manner exchanged provisions with each other—then we went down to the bank of the river, where they opened their packs, spread out some hairy deer and bear skins with the fleshy side undermost, and having first placed on them their heavy things, and then the lighter, with the guns which lay uppermost, each made two knots with the shanks of a skin, and in the space of a few minutes, they had their leathern barge afloat, which they soon thrust before them to the other shore, with a surprisingly small deviation from a direct course, considering the strong current of the water. When our astrologer saw them safe off, he wished them a speedy journey home, without being exposed to the necessity of any delay. He was soon after carried safe over on our raft, though once he almost over-set it, either by reason of the absence, or disturbance, of his mind. Had he contracted a fever, from the impending dangers his knowledge assured him were not yet past, the cold sweat he got when left by himself, while we were returning with the raft, and afterward swimming with the horses, must have contributed a good deal to the cure. Soon afterwards, we came in sight of their camp in a little spot of clear land, surrounded by a thick cane-swamp, where some traders formerly had been killed by the Choktah. Our astrologer [274] urged the necessity of proceeding a good way farther, to avoid the danger. I endeavored to convince him by several recent instances, that a timorous conduct was a great incentive to the base-minded savages, to do an injury, not expecting any defence; while an open, free, and resolute behaviour, a show of taking pleasure in their company, and a discreet care of our fire-arms, seldom failed to gain the good will of such as are not engaged in actual war against our country: he acquiesced, as I engaged to sit next to the Indian camp, which was about a dozen yards apart from our's. He chose his place pretty near to mine, but in the evening, I told him, that as I did not understand the Muskohge dialect, nor they much of the Chikkasah language, I would give him the opportunity of diverting himself at leisure with them, whilst on account of the fatigues of the day, I would repose myself close at the root of a neighbouring tree. This method of encamping in different places, on hazardous occasions, is by far the safest way. I told them, before my removal to my night quarters, that he was almost their countryman, by a residence of above twenty years among them,—their chieftain therefore readily addressed him, and according to what I expected, gave me an opportunity of decently retiring. But when he expected a formal reply, according to their usual custom, our astrological interpreter spoke only a few words, but kept pointing to the river, and his wet clothes, and to his head, shaking it two or three times; thereby informing them of the great danger he underwent in crossing the water, which gave him so violent a head-ach, as to prevent his speaking with any pleasure. I laughed, and soon after endeavoured to persuade him to go over a little while to their camp, as I had done, and by that means, he might know better their present disposition; he replied with a doleful accent, that he was already too near them, to the great danger of his life, which he now too late saw exposed, by believing my doctrine of bringing them to observe friendly measures, instead of pushing beyond them as he had earnestly proposed. I asked him how he could reasonably fear, or expect to shun a sudden death, on account of his knowledge of the starry influences, and skill in expounding dreams, and especially as he seemed firmly to believe the deity had pre-determined the exact time of every living creature's continuance here: upon this he prevaricated, and told me, that as I knew nothing of astrology, nor of the useful and skilful exposition of important dreams, neither believed any thing of witches and wizards being troublesome and hurtful to others, he could not imagine I believed any thing of a divine providence or a resurrection of the dead; which were evidently, [275] alike true, as appeared both by divine writ, and the united consent of every ancient nation. He said, people were ordered to watch and pray; I therefore could not be ruled by the scripture, for why did I go to bed so soon, and leave all that trouble to him. I told him, I wished he might by prayer, obtain a calm composure of mind. He said, I was the cause of all his uneasiness, by inducing him, contrary to his over night's bloody dream, to lie so near those wolfish savages. Then, in an angry panic, he cursed me, and said, he should not that night have prayed there, only that the devil tempted him to believe my damned lies, and sin against the divine intimations he had received just before.

Within half a day's ride of Augusta, I met the gentlemen who were appointed to meet certain head-men of the Muskohge, to run a line, between Georgia and the Muskohge country. The superintendant's deputy before-mentioned,[301] accompanying them; I then informed him of the bad situation of the Indian trade, both in the Chikkasah, and Muskohge nations —The cause thereof—The dangerous policy of having reconciled those jarring warlike savages—the ill disposition of the latter toward us,—and it was the opinion of all the traders (one excepted) that nothing, but their hot war with the Choktah, prevented them from executing their mischievous intentions against us. I said this to the commissary before the several gentlemen; but his conduct, and that of his brother officer in the Chikkasah country, were no way correspondent to the advice. While he benefited the ungrateful Muskohge, and gave them a plea to injure the traders, he was free from personal danger, from the red quarter; but one night at camp, after the line had been, at the friendly and artful persuasions of G. G. Esq;[302] run above twenty miles beyond the southern limits agreed upon, he almost fatally experienced the effects of their revengeful temper; which cannot be restrained when they imagine themselves really injured, and afterwards insulted: for as he was chiding a noted warrior with sharp language, the savage leaped up, seized the other's gun, cocked, and presented it against his breast; but luckily he could not discharge it, as it was double-tricker'd, contrary to the model of their smooth-bored guns. The public prints, however, echoed the success of our directors of Indian affairs, on this important occasion; though it was entirely owing to the abilities and [276] faithful application, first, of Mr. G. G. and afterwards of Mr. L. M. G.[303] which the deputy almost prevented by his imprudent conduct, that had nearly cost him also his life, and endangered the public tranquility.

In the year 1749, when I was going to Charles-town, under the provincial seal of South-Carolina, with a party of the Chikkasah Indians, the small-pox attacked them, not far from the Muskohge country; which becoming general through the camp, I was under the necessity of setting off by myself, between Flint river, and that of the Okmulgeh. I came up with a large camp of Muskohge traders, returning from the English settlements: the gentlemen told me, they had been lately assured at Augusta by the Cheerake traders, that above a hundred and twenty of the French Shawano might be daily expected near that place, to cut off the English traders, and plunder their camps, and cautioned me, with much earnestness at parting, to keep a watchful eye during that day's march. After having rode fifteen miles, about ten o'clock, I discovered ahead through the trees, an Indian ascending a steep hill: he perceived me at the same instant, for they are extremely watchful on such dangerous attempts—Ambuscade is their favourite method of attack. As the company followed their leader in a line, each at the distance of a few yards from the other, all soon appeared in view. As soon as I discovered the foremost, I put up the shrill whoop of friendship, and continually seemed to look earnestly behind me, till we approached near to each other, in order to draw their attention from me, and fix it that way, as supposing me to be the foremost of a company still behind. Five or six soon ran at full speed on each side of the path, and blocked up two vallies, which happened to be at the place of our meeting, to prevent my escape. They seemed as if their design was to attack me with their barbed arrows, lest they should alarm my supposed companions by the report of their guns. I observed that instead of carrying their bow and quiver over their shoulder, as is the travelling custom, they held the former in their left hand, bent, and some arrows. I approached and addressed them, and endeavoured to appear quite indifferent at their hostile arrangement. While I held my gun ready in my right hand about five yards distant from them, their leader who stood foremost came and struck my breast with the but-end of one of my pistols, which I had in my left hand:[304] I told him with that vehemence of speech, which is always requisite on such an occasion, that I was an English Chikkasah; and informed him by expressive gestures that there were two tens of Chikkasah [277] warriors, and more than half that number of women, besides children, a little behind, just beyond the first hill. At this news, they appeared to be much confused, as it was unexpected for such a number of warlike enemies to be so near at hand. This Shawano party consisted only of twenty-three middle sized, but strong bodied men, with large heads and broad flat crowns, and four tall young persons, whom I conjectured to be of the Cheerake nation. I spoke a little to a hair-lipped warrior among them, who told me he lived in *Tukkasêhche*,[305] a northern town of that country. The leader whispered something to his waiter, which, in like manner, was communicated to the rest, and then they all passed by me, with sullen looks and glancing eyes. I kept my guard till they were out of arrow-shot, when I went on at a seemingly indifferent pace. But, as soon out of their view,[306] I rode about seventy miles with great speed, to avoid the danger of a pursuit, as I imagined they would be highly enraged against me for their double disappointment. About sun-set of the same day, I discovered more Indians a-head; but, instead of sounding the usual whoop of defiance, I went on slowly, and silently, a little way, reasoning with myself about the safest method in so dangerous a situation: I had apprehensions of their being another party of the Shawano company, separated in that manner to avoid a pursuit; which otherwise might be very easy, by the plainness of their tracks, through the long grass and herbage. But, at the critical time, when I had concluded to use no chivalry, but give them leg-bail instead of it, by leaving my baggage-horses, and making, for a deep swamp, I discovered them to be a considerable body of the Muskohge head-men, returning home with presents from Charles Town, which they carried chiefly on their backs. The wolf-king (as the traders termed him)[307] our old steady friend of the Amooklasah Town, near the late Alebahma, came foremost, harnessed like a jack-ass, with a saddle on his back, well girt over one shoulder, and across under the other. We seemed equally glad to meet each other; they, to hear how affairs stood in their country, as well as on the trading path; and I to find, that instead of bitter-hearted foes, they were friends, and would secure my retreat from any pursuit that might happen. I told them the whole circumstances attending my meeting the Shawano, with their being conducted by our deceitful Cheerake friends, who were desirous of spoiling the old beloved white path, by making it red; and earnestly persuaded them to be on their guard that night, as I imagined the enemy had pursued me when they [278] found I had eluded their bloody intention. After a long conversation together, I advised them to go home through the woods, to prevent a larger body of the lurking enemy from spoiling them, and their beloved country, by the loss of so many old beloved men, and noted warriors. I said this, to rouse them against the Cheerake; well knowing that one pack of wolves, was the best watch against another of the same kind. They thanked me for the friendly notice I gave them, and the care I shewed for their safety, and engaged me to call the next day at a hunting camp, where was a war-leader, the son of the dog-king of the Huphale-Town, with a considerable number of their people, and desire them to remove with all speed to their camp, at the place they then fixed on. We smoked tobacco, and parted well pleased. According to promise, I went the next day to the camp, and delivered their message, which was readily complied with. The Shawano whom

I had eluded, after rambling about, and by viewing the smoke of fires from the tops of high hills and trees, and carefully listening to the report of guns, fell in with two Chikkasah hunters, who were adopted relations of the Muskohge, and killed, and scalped them, and then ran off to the northern towns of the Cheerake. This was the true and sole cause of the last war between the Muskohge and Cheerake: and the following account of the cause of those nations entering into amity with each other, will, on the strictest enquiry, be found as true.[308] The cause and direful effects are still feelingly known to great numbers of the suffering inhabitants, which I insert by way of caution to states-men hereafter.

As the Indians have no public faith to secure the lives of friendly messengers in war-time, their wars are perpetuated from one generation to another, unless they are ended by the mediation of some neutral party. A very polished courtier presided in South Carolina, who was said to have cast a very earnest eye on the supposed profits of the Cheerake trade, which were much lessened by the Muskohge war; and, in order to establish it at its former value, so as to be worth some hazard, he exerted himself to reconcile the Muskohge and Cheerake.[309] If he succeeded, he was sure to be something in pocket, and could report at home, the profound peace he had effected between those nations by his unwearied endeavours. He accordingly applied to some of the most intelligent and leading traders among those warring savages,[310] and attempted to persuade them [279] by the ruling motive of mutual interest, to be reconciled through his brotherly mediation. Though the Cheerake were great losers in the war, yet the surviving relations of those who had been killed without equal revenge of blood, were at first inflexible, and deaf to the mediation: but, by the oratory of some of their own speakers who had not suffered, connected with our traders persuasions, each separate family at last consented to meet their enemies, at the time and place appointed by brotherly request, and there bury the bloody tomohawk under ground, and smoke together, out of the friendly white pipe. But, as the Muskohge were conquerors, and frequently returned home in their favourite and public triumphant manner, and had then no mischievous views against the English, as at present, it was a very difficult task to reconcile them to our beloved man's pacific measures: their head-men had great sway over the ambitious, and young rising warriors, and by the former manly conduct of South-Carolina, in obtaining speedy redress for every material injury, the more sensible and honest part of the old leading men were as much averse to peace, as the light-headed warriors. They well knew the fickle and ungovernable temper of their young men and ambitious leaders, when they had no red enemies to war with, to obtain higher war-titles by scalps—and their wisdom saw at a distance, the dangerous consequences that must attend a general peace: for a considerable time, therefore, they highly inveighed, and firmly guarded against it. But when a man's private interest coincides with what he intends to accomplish, he is assiduous and more intent to effect it. This was verified by the unwearied diligence of the prime magistrate alluded to; he knew the Indians could not kill so many deer and beaver in the time of war as of peace, and by his address, he persuaded several of the leading traders, even contrary to their own outward security and inward choice, to exert their strongest endeavours with the Muskohge for a reconciliation with the Cheerake. The chief of those trading gentlemen, who unwillingly involved himself in this pernicious affair, was the humane and intelligent L. M'G—l—wr—, Esq.[311] Each had their lessons, to set forth the reciprocal advantages of the contending parties, by such a coalition; but it was finished by that gentleman's earnest and well-timed application, connected with his great natural sense, and easy flow of their own bold figurative way of expression—and their favourable opinion of his steady, honest principles. Since that unlucky period, he has as often lamented his success in that affair, as the discerning honest rulers of the Muskohge opposed it. He told me, that [280] when he was soliciting some of the head-men to comply with the fraternal proposals of our kindly ruler, he unexpectedly met with a very sharp repulse;—for, when he had finished his oration, on the disadvantages of frowning war, and the advantages of smiling peace, an old war-leader retorted every paragraph he had spoken, and told him, that till then he always had reckoned the English a very wise people, but now he was sorry to find them unwise, in the most material point: adding, "You have made yourself very poor, by sweating, far and near, in our smoky town-houses and hot-houses, only to make a peace between us and the Cheerake, and thereby enable our young mad people to give you, in a short time, a far worse sweat than you have yet had, or may now expect. But, forasmuch as the great English chieftain in Charles Town, is striving hard to have it so, by ordering you to shut your eyes, and stop your ears, lest the power of conviction should reach your heart, we will not any more oppose you in this mad scheme. We shall be silent concerning it; otherwise, I should be as mad as you, if I reasoned any more with one who is wilfully blind and deaf."

A number of their warriors met at Charles Town, at the time appointed:[312] their high-stationed English friend then took a great deal of pains to inform them of the mutual advantages, that would accrue to them, by a firm peace, and he convinced their senses of it, by a visible proof; for he borrowed from one of them an arrow, and holding each end of it in his hands, he readily broke it, which surprized none of the red spectators, except the owner,—they did not then regard it as a symbolical performance, but a boyish action. He again requested from the same young warrior, the loan of his remaining sheaf of arrows, who reluctantly gave them, as he feared they would all singly fare the fate of the former. But, when he held the bundle by each end in his hands, and could only bend it a little, he revived the watchful owner, and pleasingly surprized the attentive savages, as he thereby had strongly demonstrated to them, that *vis unita fortior,*[313] upon which he expatiated, in easy fine language, to the great joy of his red audience. By such evidence, they were induced to shake hands firmly together; and likewise to endeavour to preserve a perpetual union with all their neighbouring nations, lest the wolf should attack them separately. And ever since that impolitic mediation, they have been so strongly convinced of their great advantage and security, [281] by a close friendly union with each other, that all the efforts of the wise and honest Georgia patriot, Governor Ellis, in concert with the Indian trading merchants, to dissolve it in the year 1760,[314] proved abortive with the wary and jealous Muskohge, while we were at war with the Cheerake—and many of the out-settlers of Georgia and South Carolina were plundered and murdered by them, without sparing women or children; many instances of which we were too often well acquainted with on the spot. The Cheerake, however, stood in such great awe of about sixty Chikkasah warriors, that except once when they were repulsed by a treble inferior number, they durst not attempt any sort of attack on Georgia barriers, during the whole continuance of the war. The wisdom of the ruling members of that weak colony directed them, in their dangerous circumstances, to chuse the least of two evils,—to humour, and bear with those mischievous Muskohge, rather than involve themselves in a complicated war with those two confederated nations; which must have ruined Georgia, in the weak condition it then was. And, notwithstanding they have considerably increased since, both in wealth and number of inhabitants, it is probable, the colony is now less capable of bearing with any sort of firmness, a sudden shock from these savages, than they were at that time. For, though the people were then fewer in numbers; yet their settlements were more compact. By this means, they could easily join in social defense, on any alarm: and, as the circumstances of most of them did not tempt them to enervating luxury, so the needful exercises they daily pursued, enabled them to make a diversion of ranging the woods, when occasion required. Plantations are now settled, often at a great distance from each other, even to the outmost boundaries of the colony, where commonly the best gunsmen reside, but who probably would be cut off by surprize, at the first onset: and, lower down, their dispersed settlements are often separated, either by difficult or unpassable morasses,—slow running black waters,—or broken salt-water sounds; which of course would be a great impediment to the people supporting each other: so that each plantation is exposed to a separate assault, by a superior body of those cunning savages, who attack, and fly away like a sudden thunder gust. We have no sure way to fight them, but in carrying the war into the bowels of their own country, by a superior body of the provincial troops, mixed with regulars; and as we can expect no mercy in case of a defeat, we should not despise their power, but prepare ourselves for a sure conquest.

[282]Account of the Choktah Nation, &c.

The Choktah country lies in about 33 and 34 Deg. N. L. According to the course of the Indian path, their western lower towns are situated two hundred computed miles to the northward of New Orleans; the upper ones an hundred and sixty miles to the southward of the Chikkasah nation; 150 computed miles to the west of the late dangerous French Alebahma garrison, in the Muskohge country; and 150 to the north of Mobille, which is the first settlement, and only town, except New Orleans, that the French had in West-Florida.[315]

Their country is pretty much in the form of an oblong square. The barrier towns, which are next to the Muskohge and Chikkasah countries, are compactly settled for social defense, according to the general method of other savage nations; but the rest, both in the center, and toward the Missisippi, are only scattered plantations, as best suits a separate easy way of living. A stranger might be in the middle of one of their populous extensive towns, without seeing half a dozen of their houses, in the direct course of his path.[316] The French, to intimidate the English traders by the prodigious number of their red legions in West-Florida, boasted that the Choktah consisted of nine thousand men fit to bear arms: but we find the true amount of their numbers, since West-Florida was ceded to us, to be not above half as many as the French report ascertained. And, indeed, if the French and Spanish writers of the American Aborigines, had kept so near the truth, as to mix one half of realities, with their flourishing [283] wild hyperboles, the literati would have owed them more thanks than is now their due.

Those who know the Choktah, will firmly agree in opinion with the French, concerning them, that they are in the highest degree, of a base, ungrateful, and thievish disposition—fickle, and treacherous—ready-witted, and endued with a surprizing flow of smooth artful language on every subject, within the reach of their ideas; in each of these qualities, they far exceed any society of people I ever saw. They are such great proficients in the art of stealing, that in our store-houses, they often thieve while they are speaking to, and looking the owner in the face.[317] It is reckoned a shame to be detected in the act of theft; but, it is the reward they receive, which makes it shameful: for, in such a case, the trader bastinadoes the covetous sinner, almost as long as he seems sensible of pain. A few years ago, one of the Chikkasah warriors told me, he heard a middle-aged Choktah warrior, boast in his own country, at a public ball-play, of having artfully stolen several things from one and another trader, to a considerable amount, while he was cheapening goods of us, and we were blind in our own houses.

As their country is pleasantly interspersed with hills, and generally abounds with springs and creeks, or small brooks; and is in a happy climate, it is extremely healthful. Having no rivers in their country, few of them can swim, like other Indians; which often proves hurtful to them, when high freshes come on while they are out at war.[318] Their towns are settled on small streams that purl into Mobille river, and another a little to the southward of it. Koosah, the largest town in their nation, lies within 180 miles of Mobille, at a small distance from the river which glides by that low, and unhealthy old capital.[319] The summer-breezes pass by Mobille, in two opposite directions, along the channel of the river; and very unhealthy vapors keep floating over the small semicircular opening of the town, which is on the south-side of the river, opposite to a very low marsh, that was formed by great torrents of water, sweeping down rafts of fallen trees, till they settled there, and were mixt with the black soil of the low lands, carried, and subsiding there in the like manner. From thence, to the opposite shore, the river hath a sandy bottom, and at low water is so very shallow, that a person could almost walk across, though [284] it is two leagues broad. The southern side of the river is so full of great trees, that sloops and schooners have considerable difficulty in getting up abreast: and for a considerable distance from the sea-coast, the land is low, and generally unfit for planting, even on the banks of the river. About forty miles up, the French had a small settlement of one plantation deep, from the bank of Mobille river. The rest of the land is sandy pine barrens, till within forty miles of the Choktah country, where the oak and the hiccory-trees first appear; from whence, it is generally very fertile, for the extensive space of about six hundred miles toward the north, and in some places, two hundred and fifty, in others, two hundred and sixty in breadth, from the Missisippi: This tract far exceeds the best land I ever saw besides in the extensive American world. It is not only capable of yielding the various produce of all our North-American colonies on the main continent, as it runs from the south, towards the north; but, likewise, many other valuable commodities, which their situation will never allow them to raise. From the small rivers, which run through this valuable large tract, the far-extending ramifications are innumerable; each abounding with evergreen canes and reeds, which are as good to raise cattle in winter, as the best hay in the northern colonies. I need not mention the goodness of the summer-ranges; for, where the land is good, it always produces various sorts of good timber, such as oak of different kinds; hiccory, wall-nut, and poplar-trees. The grass is commonly as long and tender, as what the best English meadows yield; and, if those vacant fertile lands of the Missisippi were settled by the remote inhabitants of Virginia, the Ohio, and North-Carolina, they, from a small stock, could in a few years raise a prodigious number of horses, horned cattle, sheep, and swine, without any more trouble than branding, marking, and keeping them tame, and destroying the beasts of prey, by hunting them with dogs, and shooting them from the trees. Soon they might raise abundance of valuable productions, as would both enrich themselves and their off-spring, and, at the same time, add in a very high degree to the naval trade and manufactures of Great-Britain.

The Choktah flatten their foreheads with a bag of sand, which with great care they keep fastened on the scull of the infant, while it is in its tender and imperfect state. Thus they quite deform their face, and give themselves an appearance, which is disagreeable to any but those of their own [285] likeness. Their features and mind, indeed, exactly correspond together; for, except the intense love they bear to their native country, and their utter contempt of any kind of danger, in defence of it, I know no other virtue they are possessed of: the general observation of the traders among them is just, who affirm them to be divested of every property of a human being, except shape and language. Though the French at Mobille, and some at New Orleans, could speak the Choktah language extremely well, and consequently guide them much better than the English (notwithstanding we gave them a far greater supply of every kind of goods than they could purchase) yet, the French allowed none of them arms and ammunition, except such who went to war against our Chikkasah friends. One of those outstanding companies was composed also of several towns; for, usually one town had not more than from five, to seven guns. When the owners therefore had hunted one moon, they lent them for hire to others, for the like space of time; which was the reason, that their deer-skins, by being chiefly killed out of season, were then much lighter than now. The French commandant of Tumbikpe garrison[320] supervised the trade, as none was ever chosen to preside in so critical a place, unless well and early acquainted in the dialect, manners, and customs of the savages. The French Indian garrisons consisted of chosen provincial families, who had not the least spark of that haughty pride and contempt, which is too often predominant, at least among the ignorant part of the soldiery, against all, except their own fraternity. The Choktah were known to be of so fickle, treacherous, and bloody a disposition, that only three or four pedlars were allowed to go among them at a time: when they returned to the fort, the same number went out again, with as many trifles as a small barrel would conveniently contain. Thus they continued to amuse the savages of low rank, but they always kept the head-men in pay. These, at every public meeting, and convenient occasion, gave stated energetic orations in praise of the French; and, by this means, the rest were influenced. The pedlars thus got almost what they were pleased to ask, in return for their worthless trifles. All the way up the numerous streams of the Missisippi, and down those of Canada river, their wisdom directed them to keep up the price of their goods, and, by that means, they retained the savages in the firmest amity with them; no trader was allowed among them, except those of sufficient skill, in that dangerous sphere of life, and of faithful principles to government. The French very justly say, the English spoil the savages, wherever their trade extends among [286] them. They were too wise ever to corrupt them, according to our modern mad schemes. They had two great annual marts, where the Indians came to traffic for their deer-skins, beaver, and peltry; the one, at Montreal; and the other, at the Illinois, under the cannon of those garrisons. But the Philadelphians, in order to ingross the trade of the latter place, by a foolish notion of under-selling the old French traders, have ruined, and, as I am lately informed, entirely discontinued it. They who speak so much in favour of lowering the Indian trade, ought first to civilize the savages, and convince them of the absolute necessity there is of selling the same sort of goods, at various prices, according to different circumstances, either of time or place. While the present ill adapted measures are continued, nothing less than the miraculous power of deity can possibly effect the Indians reformation; many of the present traders are abandoned, reprobate, white savages. Instead of shewing good examples of moral conduct, besides their other part of life, they instruct the unknowing and imitating savages, in many diabolical lessons of obscenity and blasphemy.

When the English were taking possession of Mobille, the French commander had given previous orders to a skilful interpreter, to inform the Choktah, that his Christian Majesty, for peace-sake, had given up Mobille garrison to the avaricious English nation; but at the end of three years, the French would return and see to what purpose they had applied it.[321] The Choktah believed the declaration to be as true, as if several of their old head-men had dreamed it. The fore-sighted French knew their fickle and treacherous disposition, and that by this story, well supported with presents, they would be able, when occasion required, to excite them to commence a new war against us. The masterly skill of the French enabled them to do more with those savages, with trifles, than all our experienced managers of Indian affairs have been able to effect, by the great quantities of valuable goods, they gave them, with a very profuse hand. The former bestowed their small favours with exquisite wisdom; and their value was exceedingly inhanced, by the external kindly behaviour, and well adapted smooth address of the giver. But our wise men in this department, bestow the presents of the government, too often, in such a manner as to rivet the contempt they have imbibed against us; for I have been frequently upbraided, even by the old friendly Chikkasah, when inebriated, that the English in general despised their friends, and [287] were kindest to those who most insulted and injured them; and, that the surest way for the red people to get plenty of presents, was not to deserve them, but to act the murdering part of the ill-hearted Muskohge. In confirmation of their strong invectives, they recited above seventy instances of the Muskohge having murdered the English, not only with impunity, but with silent approbation; as they soon afterward received large presents, which must be either as a due for the bloodshed, or tribute given through fear. They enumerated some facts, which were attended with shocking circumstances: as, an innocent mother of good report, and two of her little children, put to slow torture in boiling water; and several of the like nature, which the Muskohge themselves had informed them of in a way of boasting, and to induce them to imitate their mischievous, but profitable example. While we bear any cool premeditated acts of Indian hostility with that crouching base behaviour, such passive conduct will serve only to tempt the Indians to advance in their favourite science of blood, and commence a general war. For cowards they always insult and despise, and will go any distance to revenge the blood of one of their tribe, even that of an old woman.

As it was confidently reported, that a military government would be continued by us in West Florida, till it was thick settled, the French inhabitants imagining that event could not happen till doom's-day, mostly retired to New Orleans, in order to shun such a tyrannic police. They were afraid of being imprisoned, and whipped, at the Governor's caprice, and even for things unnoticeable in the eye of the law; for as he ruled imperial over the soldiery, he would expect all his orders to be readily obeyed by every other person, without any hesitation. Such things are too common in a military government, and it was fatally experienced in this. In order to establish his absolute power, as the merchants, and other gentlemen at Mobille, of generous principles despised it, he found a plea to contend with one of them, though it was both illegal, and entirely out of his element. A Choktah having bought a small brass-kettle of one of the principal merchants of that place, was persuaded by a Frenchman, to return it, bring the value to him, and he would give him a better one in its stead; for there happened to be a very small crack of no consequence, and scarcely discernible, just above the rim. The Indian accordingly went to return it; but the gentleman would not receive it, as it was good, and fairly sold at [288] the usual price. The Chok-tah went back to the Frenchman to excuse himself in not being able to deal with him, as proposed; who persuaded him to complain to the Governor of the pretended injustice he had received from the merchant—he did, and the ruler gladly embraced the opportunity to gratify his pride, and aggrandize his power. He immediately sent some of his underlings, with a positive ver-bal command to the gentleman, to cancel the bargain with the Choktah, and deliver to him what he claimed, on receiving his own: the free-born Briton excused his non-compliance, in a rational and polite manner, according to his constant easy behaviour. Upon this, like a petty tyrant, the chief sent a file of musqueteers for him. When he appeared before his greatness, he as-serted the common privileges of a trading free subject of Great Britain, with decent firmness; and set forth the ill consequences of giving the troublesome savages an example so hurtful to trade, with other arguments well adapted to the occasion. The return was, an order to thrust the gentle-man into the black-hole of the garrison, where he was detained and treated as a capital criminal, till, by the loss of health through the dampness of that horrid place, the love of life prompted him to comply with every de-mand.[322] Had he waited the award of a court-martial, probably he would have had justice done him; for, except a couple of the officers of the com-mander's own principles, all the rest blamed, if not despised him for his haughtiness and ungenerous principles. This is a genuine sample of military governments—the Canadians may expect many such instances of justice and humanity in consequence of the late Quebec act, if it be not repealed.[323] While this military man acted in the magisterial office, though in pain when not triumphing over those peaceable subjects who would not stoop before him below the character of freemen, to flatter his lordly ambition; yet it was affirmed, he could not stand the sight of the inebriated Choktah. One instance of his passive conduct toward them, deserves to be recorded— As the centinels at the gates of his house, were strictly ordered not to resist the savages, these soon became so impudent as to insult them at pleasure; and one of them, without the least provocation, struck a soldier (while on his duty standing centry) with a full bottle on his head, with that violence, as to break his scull, the unfortunate soldier languished, and died, by the blow, without the least retaliation; though so absolutely needful in our early state of settling that part of the continent.

[289] We well know the fate of the British Americans in general, as to property, liberty, and life, if their court-enemies could but metamorphose them into asses, and quietly impose upon them military men as governors, and magistrates, to inforce a strict obedience to their grasping hand, and boundless will. But, may our wise statesmen henceforth rather keep them at home, and place them over such mean spirits as have sold their birth-rights

for a mess of pottage, and are degenerated from every virtue of the true and brave Englishman!

Though the French Americans were as desirous of purchasing Indian deer-skins and beaver as the English could well be; yet they wisely declined, where the public peace and security required it. By their wisdom, they employed the savages, as occasion offered, and kept them entirely dependant. They distributed through each nation, a considerable number of medals and flourishing commissions, in a very artful gradation, so as to gratify their proud tempers, and obtain an universal sway over them. They also sent a gun-smith to each of their countries, to mend the locks of their guns, at the expence of government: and any warrior who brought his chieftain's medal as a certificate, was waited on, and sent off with honour, and a very *bon grace,* to his entire satisfaction: with this, and other instances of good conduct, they led the savages at pleasure. When the French evacuated the Alebahma garrison, the Muskohge despitefully objected against receiving any such favours from us.[324] Even our old friendly Chikkasah were only tantalized with our friendship on that occasion, for the gun-smith was recalled— which, joined with the rest of the bad conduct of our managers of Indian affairs, vexed them so exceedingly, that they were on the point of committing hostilities against us, in the year 1769: so widely different is our Indian-trading conduct from that of the French.[325]

They wisely preferred the security of their valuable, but weak country to the dangerous profits of trade; they kept the best orators and the headmen as pensioners, on their side, and employed the rest of the warriors in their favourite science against the Chikkasah. As with the high placed mercenaries in Great Britain, so it will be a very difficult task (for some time) to manage any of the Indians well, particularly the Choktah, unless they in [290] some manner receive a favourite bribe, under the name of presents, as they usually had from the French. By reason of our misconduct, and the foolish distribution of presents, since Florida was ceded to us, they have been twice on the point of breaking with us, though the managers of our Indian affairs were at the same time echoing in the public papers of Georgia and South-Carolina, the peaceable and friendly disposition of all the savage nations around the colonies. The Choktah were designed to strike the first blow on their traders, and immediately to follow it on the inhabitants of Mobille; which, they imagined, they could easily effect by surprise in the night, and so enrich themselves with an immense booty. The first of those bloody plans was concerted against us, October the 18th 1765. The cause of which I shall relate.

In the eastern part of the Chikkasah nation, there is a young, and very enterprising war-leader, called "the Torrepine Chieftain," or "The leader of the land-tortoise family:"[326] his ambitious temper, which one of the traders at first imprudently supported against our old friendly war chieftain, *Pa-Yah-Matahah,* has unhappily divided the nation into two parties, which frequently act in opposition to any salutary measure, which is either proposed, or pursued by the other. The Torrepine chief received an embassy from the Muskohge Great Mortar to engage him against us, through a false pretence that we intended to take their lands, and captivate their women and children; as the vast strides we lately made through that extensive tract, from Georgia to New Orleans, and up the Missisippi, all the way to the Illinois, he said, would clearly convince so wise a people. He exhorted the Choktah war-leaders and old beloved men to rouse their martial tempers to defend their liberty and property, and preserve their holy places, and holy things, from the ambitious views of the impure and covetous English people, to listen to the loud call of liberty, and join heart and hand in its generous defence, which they now could easily effect, by crushing the snake in its infant state; whereas delay would allow it time to collect strength, to the utter danger of every thing they held as valuable—that now was the time to avert those dangerous evils, and that their mutual safety was at stake. He assured them from repeated experience, that the very worst that could befall them would be only a trifling scolding in their ears, and presents in their hands to make up the breach. The aspiring Chikkasah leader was, in a great measure, induced to fall [291] in with that cunning deceiver's measures by having seen above sixty of the Muskohge head-men and warriors, who received considerable presents from Geo. Johnstone, Esq; Governor of West-Florida, at Pensacola.[327] They told him our liberality proceeded intirely from fear; that when they killed any of our despicable and helpless swarms, they always received the like quantity, to quiet the martial hearts of their gallant young warriors; and that the sole reason we were so frugal to the Chikkasah, was owing to their unwise attachments to us; but if they followed their copy, they would soon become as rich as themselves.

If the sagacious, and gallant governor could have executed his will, they would not have thus boasted—he warmly debated in council to order each of them to be secured, as hostages, and kept aboard a man of war in the harbour, till satisfaction was remitted for the unprovoked, and wilful murders that nation had committed on several of his majesty's peaceable subjects: but his spirited resolution was overborne by a considerable majority of votes.[328] However, when they got home, they told our traders that his excellency's speech was quite different to that of the beloved white man, meaning the super-intendant, for it was very sharp and wounding; and that his eyes spoke, and glanced the fire also which was burning in his heart. No people are more observant of the passions in the honest face than they. Their eyes and judgment are surprisingly piercing; and in consequence of this

Governor's open, steady, virtuous conduct, all our neighbouring nations honour and love him, to this very day.

The Chikkasah chief sent his bloody embassy to the Choktah by a cunning and trusty uncle, who accompanied me to the late Tumbikpe-fort. I was ignorant of the mischievous plan, till we arrived at camp, near the Great Red Captain's: there, in bed at night, I plainly overheard the whole, and saw the white swan's wings, and others painted red and black,—persuasive and speaking emblems of friendship to the one party, and war, blood, and death to the other. They received those base tokens, according to the mischievous intention of those who sent them. As they are fond of novelty, the news was conveyed through the nation, with profound secresy: besides, they were very much rejoiced at so favourable an opportunity of making peace with the Muskohge, who awed them exceedingly, on account of their repeated losses, which were chiefly occasioned by their want [292] of skill in swimming. Tumbikpe garrison, a little before this time, was very unwisely removed; but, to supply that wrong measure, our super-intendant of Indian affairs, stationed here one of his representatives.[329] He was as much unacquainted with the language, manners, and customs of the Indians, as his employer: and yet wrote a considerable volume how to regulate Indian affairs in general, and particularly in the Choktah country. Besides his want of proper qualifications in so nice and difficult an office, he was in his temper so turbulent, proud, and querulous, that his presence instead of quieting the savages, was more than sufficient to disoblige, and distract them, in the most friendly times. He lived in the deserted garrison, as a place of security, kept weighty pullies to the gates, and his own door shut, as if the place had been a monastery; which was the worst measure he could possibly have pursued, considering the proud and familiar temper of those he had to deal with, and the late soothing treatment of the French to them. *Kapteny Humma Echeto* "the Great Red Captain,"[330] sent word to him he would call there, on a certain day, to confer with him on some material business. On account of their fluctuating councils in so weighty an affair as the intended war, he prolonged the time of going there, for the space of eight days; the gentleman engaged me to stay till the affair was decided. I continued without the least reluctance, as I saw the black storm gathering, and hoped I might be able in some measure to dispel it. When the Red Captain came, his chief business was to demand presents, in the same manner they received them from the French, as the war-chiefs and beloved men were grown very poor; and to know whether our government would enable them to revenge their dead, by bestowing on them ammunition to continue the war against the Muskohge, who highly despised us, and frequently committed acts of hostility against our people. Contrary to my advice, he gave a plain negative to each of his queries, without considering contingencies—Because the neighbouring town was silent, and very few of them came near the fort, he flattered himself that those dangerous tokens proceeded intirely from the cold reception, and frequent denials he had given them; and that for the future, he could live there in a retired and easy manner. But had he taken the trouble to go among them, as I did, he might have seen by their gloomy faces what bitter rancour was in their hearts. Next day, I discovered at the most unfrequented part of the fort, which was near the south east corner, on the river-side,[331] that the wary savages had in the night time [293] forced two of the great posts so far apart, as one person could easily pass through at a time; as such ocular proof might have made my host uneasy, I thought it wrong to molest his tranquillity by the discovery. The Red Chief would now drink no spirituous liquors, though I pressed him to it. They know their weakness then, which might lead them to divulge their country's secrets,—a great disgrace to a warrior. He went home with his heart greatly inebriated however, on account of the flat denials he had received; especially, as the warriors would depreciate him for his ill success.

In a few days after, I set off with my red companion, and lay all night at the Red Captain's house, which stands in one of their northern barrier towns. He walked out with me in the evening, but in his discourse, he used as much evasion and craft, as an old fox in his intricate windings to beguile the earnest pursuers. At night his house was very quiet, as if their long heads and treacherous hearts were equally at rest;—but I plainly saw into their favourite and laboured plan, and one of their females told me there was at that time, a great many head-men of different towns, at a neighbouring house, conferring together concerning the white people; and that she believed their speech was not good, as they did not allow any women or boys to hear it. The Red Chief and I parted like courtiers; it soon began to rain, so as to swell the waters to such a considerable height, as rendered them unpassable to horsemen, whose circumstances were not quite desperate. The Choktah leader sent a sprightly young man, his nephew, with me, under pretence of accompanying me and the above-mentioned Chikkasah warrior; but I was not without strong suspicion, that he was sent to shoot me by surprise, as soon as he heard the whooping death-signal in pursuit of me. For they had sent runners to call home those who were hunting in the woods, and the last company of them we met, reaching our camp in the night, staid there till the morning. We conversed together without the least disguise; they were confident the traders were killed, and their favourite war and death-cry would soon reach their listening ears. I thought it improper to make a jest of so serious an affair, and determined to set off, though my red companions endeavored to delay me as much as they could. Early in the morning I took out my saddle, which the Choktah mentioned to the others through a suspicion I intended to make my escape: but they quieted his jealousy, by telling him I did so, only because I was lazy to walk. About half a mile from camp, I soon catched and mounted one of [294] my horses, and set off, keeping clear of the trading path for about four miles, in order to perplex any pursuers that might be sent after me. When my horse tired, I led it on foot through the pathless woods about fifty miles, and heard no more of them. Had the Choktah known how to obtain a sufficient supply of ammunition, they would at this very time, have commenced war against us. That only checked their bloody aim, to their unspeakable grief, and prevented our being engaged in a dangerous war.

All our Indian-traders well know, that the misconduct and obstinacy of the first super-intendant of Indian affairs,[332] was the sole occasion of irritating the Great Mortar to become bitter-hearted against us, and devoting himself with a blood-thirsty desire to injure us, wherever his black policy could reach. And as the first, by his stiff behaviour set on the Mortar,—his successor, by ill-timed presents instead of demanding satisfaction, gave him as good an opportunity as he could have desired, to impress the warriors of his own and other nations, with a strong opinion of our timid disposition, and incapacity of opposing them. The impression of Governor Johnstone's speech, plainly declares they would not have been so weak as to utter their base threats against us, to the Chikkasah leader at Pensacola, only that they were previously corrupted by the mismanagement of Indian affairs. I am well assured, they frequently applauded his martial conduct when they returned home, and said he was a man and a warrior, which is as great an encomium, as they can bestow on any mortal. May West-Florida, and New Georgiana on the extensive and fertile lands of the meandring Missisippi,[333] have a continual succession of such chief magistrates as Mr. Johnstone, and his worthy successor Montfort Browne, Esq;[334] to study and promote the public good, and cause the balance of justice to be held with an even hand!

The following relation will serve to display what should be our manner of treating the Indians—A white man, on Mobille river, sold spirituous liquors to a couple of the Choktah, till they were much intoxicated, and unable to purchase any more; he then strenuously denied to credit them: their usual burning thirst exciting them to drink more, they became too troublesome for any spirited person to bear with. He took up an ax, at first in his own defence, but when they endeavoured to run off, he, in the heat of passion pursued, and unhappily killed one of them. The other ran, and told his [295] relations the sad disaster. Presently, nothing could be heard through the nation, but heavy murmurs and sharp threats. Governor Johnstone had the murderer soon apprehended, and confined him to be tried in due course of law. This delay of executing justice on one, and whom we only secured from their resentment as they imagined, tempted them to think on a general massacre. Soon after the sitting of the general court, their revengeful hearts became easy: for the man was fairly tried, and condemned, because he did not kill the savage in his own defence, but while he was retreating from him.[335] I have reason to believe the Indians would not have allowed the French, when in garrison among them, to delay shooting any of their people, whom they but even suspected of having killed the meanest of their kindred: for, in the year 1740, the Muskohge, on a false suspicion, forced the commanding officer of the Alebahma garrison, by their loud threats, to kill one of the militia soldiers. When they were leading him to the place of execution, he requested the favour of a bottle of wine, to enable him to die with the firm constancy of an honest French warrior: he received, and drank it off, and declared his innocence of the imputed crime, with his last words. The signal was given, and the soldiers, by order, quickly shot the unfortunate man. But the Englishman, who had been likewise a soldier, would not have been condemned by the mere assertion of the Choktah savage, cost what it would; as it was both repugnant to our law, and too dangerous a precedent to give to so treacherous a people. He was justly condemned on his companion's oath. His excellency Governor Johnstone acted so fairly and tenderly in this affair, that, by his request, one of the Chikkasah traders was summoned to sit on the trial, as he of a long time knew the base disposition of the Choktah; but no favourable circumstances appearing on his side, he was condemned.[336]

Although the Choktah had their desired revenge, yet, when their leader came parading into Tumbikpe garrison, with a gun he had taken from a white man, whom he murdered on the Chikkasah trading path; our superintendant's representative shamefully refused to act the part of the magistrate, or to impower the commanding officer of the Fort to secure the murderer, though he pressed him with manly earnestness, and protested that he would gladly confine him, were it not contrary to the tenour of his commission. The savage having boasted a while after his triumphal entrance, [296] returned exultingly to his country-men, to the shame and regret of the traders. Our white beloved man thought himself best employed in other affairs than these, and doubtless, profitable family jobbs ought to be well minded.[337]

His successor was equally skilful in managing the Indians as himself, though much his inferior.[338] His only merit was, the having been a clerk to the Chikkasah white beloved man, who resigned his place, on account of the discontinuance of his British pay. He corrupted and practised with the Indians, according to the system his teacher pursued. One instance, among many, will shew this: a gentleman came to view the Missisippi lands, from the settlements which are on the Yadkin, a large and beautiful river, that, after gliding down 300 miles to the Sand-hill, Wilmington, and the waste

Brunswick, is stiled Cape-Fear-River. He was highly pleased with the soil, climate, and situation of the lands he came in quest of: but told me, in a humorous manner, that, when he was at a French man's house, on the Spanish side of the river, a very lusty Choktah called there, in company with others upon a hunt. As the French Choktah was desirous of ingratiating himself into the favour of the host, he began to ridicule my friend with gestures, and mocking language: the more civilly the Englishman behaved, so much the more impudently the savage treated him. At length, his passions were inflamed, and he suddenly seized him in his arms, carried him a few steps off, and threw him down the bank into the Missisippi. The laugh now turned against him loud; for, if the Indians saw their grandmother break her neck by a fall from a horse, or any other accident, they would whoop and halloo. The Baptist, or dipped person, came out ashamed, but appeared to be very good-humoured after his purification, as he found he had not one of the French wood-peckers to deal with. However, one night, when the gentleman was on his return, the savages pursued, and endeavoured to kill him, and did seize his horses and baggage. He had a narrow escape for his life before he came to Quansheto, where the towns-people of the late Great Red Shoes had settled, and our white beloved man resided.[339] He made his complaint to him, which might have been expected to produce both pity and justice in any heart that was not callous. But, instead of endeavouring to redress his grievance, which he could have easily effected, he aggravated his sufferings [297] by abuse. As the savage had been brought up with the English traders, so as to be called the boy of one of them, and lived in *Yashoo,* the town of the present Red Shoes,[340] our chief could easily have had every thing returned, had he only demanded it in form. But, like his predecessor, he endeavoured to keep in with the Indians—he deemed their favourable report of his friendly conduct toward them, to be the main point he ought to observe, in order to secure the embassy from suffering damage, whatever became of truth, or justice.

The Choktah have a remote, but considerable town, called *Yowanne,* which is the name of a worm that is very destructive to corn in a wet season.[341] It lies forty miles below the seven southernmost towns of the nation, toward Mobille, and 120 computed miles from thence, on a pleasant small river, that runs south of the town. As it is a remote barrier, it is greatly harrassed by the Muskohge, when at war with them. Here, a company of them came lately looking for prey; but missing it, as the Choktah were apprized, and staid at home, their pride and disappointment excited them to injure those strangers who chanced to fall in their way. About six miles below the town, they came to the camp of two white men, who were just ready to set off to Mobille, with loaded horses; being resolved not entirely to miss their errand of blood and plunder, they attacked them with their tomohawks, cautious of not alarming the neighbouring enemy by the report of their guns. They speedily dispatched one of them; but the other being strong bodied, very fiery, and desperate, held them a sharp struggle, as it appeared afterward: his gun was found much battered, and the long grass quite beat down for a considerable way round the place where the Yowanne Indians found him suspended in the air. For as soon as those savages perpetrated that diabolical act, they hanged each of them on trees, with the horses halters, and carried away six of the horses loaded with drest deer-skins, as far as Mobille-river. *Minggo Humma Echeto,* the Great Red Chieftain, of the aforesaid town, on his return from war with the Muskohge, fortunately intercepted them, killed and scalped two, and retook the horses and leather.[342] These, he sent home, as he imagined the owner then resided in the nation, and would gladly redeem them with reasonable presents: while he went down to Mobille to shew his trophies of war, in full hopes of getting a new supply of ammunition from the deputy super-intendant,[343] to be used against the common enemy. He flattered himself that the scalps brought into our maritime town, in solemn [298] triumph, would prove a gladsome sight to our people, and enlarge their hearts towards him and his fatigued poor warriors. But he perceived nothing of this kind, of which he complained to me with very sharp language, and returned home, highly incensed against his new English friends.

I have reason to remember this too well; for, a little after those white men were murdered, business calling me to Mobille by myself, I chose to decline the eastern path, and the middle one that leads by the *Chakchooma* old fields, as they were much exposed to the incursions of the Muskohge; and rode through the chief towns of the nation, along the horse-path that runs from the Chikkasah, nearest the Missisippi, to Mobille.[344] About six miles below the seven-towns that lie close together, and next to New Orleans, I met a considerable party of the leaders and head-warriors returning home from war. We shook hands together, and they seemed very glad to see me. They earnestly dissuaded me from proceeding any farther, advised me to return to their friendly town, and rest awhile among them, declaring, that if my ears were mad, and would not hear their friendly speech, I should surely be killed, the enemy were ranging the woods so very thick. They were good judges of the danger, as they knew the treacherous plan they had concerted together at *Yowanne.* But the memory of past times, moved them to give me that kindly caution. I thanked them, and said, I wished business allowed me to act according to their advice, and accept of their generous invitation; but it did not: however, if my limited days were not finished before, I would shortly have the pleasure to see them again. I proceeded, and met several parties of the same main company, several miles distant from each other, carrying small pieces of a scalp, singing the triumphal song, and sounding the shrill death-whoop, as if they had killed hundreds. On my resting and smoking with the last party, they informed me, that their camp consisted of two hundred and fifty warriors, under great leaders, who were then return-ing from war against a town of the Koosaahte Indians, who had settled twenty-five miles above Mobille, on the eastern side of the river; that they had killed and wounded several of them, suspecting them of abetting the Muskohge, and fortunately got one of their scalps, which the warriors of separate towns divided, and were carrying home, with joyful hearts.[345]

A stranger would be much surprised to see the boasting parade these savages made with one scalp of a reputed enemy. To appearance, more [299] than a thousand men, women, lusty boys, and girls, went loaded with provi-sions to meet them; and to dance, sing, and rejoice at this camp, for their success in war, and safe return. Their camps were made with the green bark and boughs of trees, and gave a striking picture of the easy and simple modes of early ages. Their chieftains and great warriors sat in state, with the assuming greatness of the ancient senators of imperial Rome. I had the hon-our to sit awhile with them, and was diverted with the old circling and wheeling dances of the young men and women. I smoked with them, and then took my leave of this last camp of rejoicing heroes. The Choktah are the most formal in their addresses, of all the Indian nations I am acquainted with: and they reckon the neglect of observing their usual ceremonies, pro-ceeds from contempt in the traders, and from ignorance in strangers.

I encamped early, and within two leagues of *Yowanne,* as it seemed to be a good place for killing wild game. I imagined also, that here the people were awed by the Muskohge from ranging the woods, but, it happened otherwise: for, soon after the horse-bells began to ring, two sprightly young fellows came through the cane-swamp, and as enemies, they crawled up the steep bank of the creek, near to me, before I discovered them. My fire-arms were close at hand, and I instantly stood on my guard. They looked earnestly around, to see for the rest of my company, as it is very unusual for any of the traders, to take that journey alone. I asked them who they were, from whence they came, and what they were so earnestly searching for. They evaded answering my queries, and asked me if I did not come by myself. I told them, without hesitation, that some way behind, my companion rode out of the path to kill deer, as his gun was good, and he could use it ex-tremely well. On this, they spoke a little together, with a low voice; and then told me, that they belonged to *Yowanne,* and were part of a hunting camp, which was near at hand, and in view of the path. I asked them to sit down, which they did, but their discourse was disagreeable, as my supposed fellow-traveller was the chief subject of it. They said they would go back to their camp, and return to mine soon, to see whether the white man was come from hunting. They went, and were as good as their word; for, they did me the honour to pay me a second visit. As they were so very earnest in that which did not concern them, unless they had ill intentions, the sight of them would have instantly inflamed the heart of one not infected with stoicism, to wish for a proper [300] place to make a due retribution. At this time, the sun was near three hours from setting. The white hunter's absence was the first and chief subject of their discourse, till evening. As on a level place, all the savages sit cross-legged, so my visitors did, and held their guns on their knee, or kept them very near, with their otter-skin shot pouch over one of their shoulders, as is usual in time of danger. I observed their mischievous eyes, instead of looking out eastwardly toward the Muskohge country, were generally pointed toward the N. W. the way I had come. As by chance, I walked near to one of them, he suddenly snatched up his gun. No friendly Indians were ever known to do the like, especially so near home, and a considerable camp of his own people: innocence is not suspicious, but guilt. He knew his own demerit, and, perhaps imagined I knew it, from concurring circumstances. To see whether his conduct proceeded from a fear of danger, or from accident, I repeated the trial, and he did the same; which confirmed me in my opinion of their base intentions.

In this uneasy and restless manner we continued till sun-set, when one of them artfully got between me and my arms. Then they ordered me to stop the bells of my horses, which were grazing near the camp, (used partly on account of the number of big flies that infest the country.) I asked them the reason—they told me, because the noise frightened away the deer. I took no notice at first of their haughty command, but they repeated it with spiteful vehemence, and I was forced to obey their mandate. They looked, and listened earnestly along the edge of the swamp, but being disappointed of their expected additional prey, in about the space of ten minutes they ordered me to open the bells again. Of the manifold dangers I ever was in, I deemed this by far the greatest, for I stood quite defenceless. Their language and behaviour plainly declared their mischievous designs. I expected every minute to have been shot down: and though I endeavoured to shew a manly aspect, the cold sweat trickled down my face through uneasiness, and a crowd of contrary passions. After some time, in this alarming situation, they told me the ugly white man staid long, and that they would go to their camp a little while, and return again,—they did as they said. To deceive them, I had made my bed as for two people, of softened bear and buffalo skins, with the long hair and wool on, and blankets. My two watchmen came the third time, accompanied with one older than themselves: he spoke little, was artful, [301] and very designing. They seemed much concerned at the absence of my supposed companion, lest he should by unlucky mischance be bewildered, or killed by the Muskohge. I gave them several reasons to shew the futility of their kindly fears, and assured them he usually staid late to barbicue the meat, when he killed much, as he could not otherwise bring it to camp; but that he never failed, on such an occasion, to come some time in the night. The cunning fox now and then asked me a studied short question, in the way of cross examination, concerning the main point they had in view, and my answers were so cool and uniform, that I almost persuaded them firmly to credit all I said. When he could no way trepan me, and there was silence for several minutes, he asked me, if I was not afraid to be at camp alone. I told him I was an English warrior,—my heart was honest— and as I spoiled nobody, why should I be afraid? Their longing eyes by this time were quite tired. The oldest of them very politely took his leave of me in French; and the others, through an earnest friendly desire of smoking, and chatting a little with my absent companion, told me at parting to be sure to call them, by sounding the news-whoop, as soon as he arrived at camp. I readily promised to comply, for the sake of the favour of their good company: and to prevent any suspicion of the truth of my tale, I added, that if he failed in his usual good luck, they ought to supply us with a leg of venison, or we would give them as much, if he succeeded.

And now all was well, at least, with me; for I took time by the fore-lock, and left them to echoe the news-whoop. *Yowanne* lay nearly south-east from me; but to avoid my being either intercepted on the path, or heard by the quick-ear'd savages, I went a quarter of a mile up the large cane swamp, and passed through it on a south west course, but very slow, as it was a dark thicket of great canes and vines, over-topped with large spreading trees. I seldom had a glimpse of any star to direct my course, the moon being then far spent. About an hour before day-light, I heard them from the top of an high hill, fire off a gun at camp; which I supposed was when they found me gone, and in order to decoy my supposed companion to answer them with the like report; conjecturing he would imagine it was I who fired for him, according to custom in similar cases. I kept nearly at the distance of three miles from the path, till I arrived at the out-houses of Yowanne. As I had never before seen that town, nor gone to Mobille that way, one of the warriors at my request [302] conducted me to the river, which we waded breast-high, and went to the palisadoed fort of *Minggo Humma Echeto,* which stood commodiously on the bank of the river. He received and treated me very kindly; I concealed what befel me at camp, though I had reason to believe, he was informed of my escape by a runner, as I saw fresh tracks when I returned. I pretended to have come from camp, only to confer with him, concerning the situation of Mobille path, and follow his advice, either to proceed on, or return home, being convinced so great a chieftain as he, who lived in defiance of the Muskohge on that remote barrier, must be a better judge, than any of those I had met. He commended me for my caution, and assured me there were several companies of the Muskohge, then out at war on the path; and that as they hated and despised the English, they would surely kill me, if I continued my journey. I thanked him for his friendly caution, and told him it should not fall to the ground. I soon discovered his great resentment against the English, on account of the impolitic and unkind treatment he had received at Mobille. He reasoned upon it with strong natural good sense, and shewed me in his museum, the two red-painted scalps of the Muskohge who had murdered our people, and left them in contempt hanging like mangy dogs, with a horse's rope round each of their necks. He then shewed me the flourishing commissions he had received from both French and English. He descanted minutely on the wise and generous liberality of the former, on every material occasion; and on the niggardly disposition and discouraging conduct of the latter, when they ought to stretch out both their hands to those red people who avenged their wrongs, and brought them the scalps of the very enemy who had lately shed their blood. The French never so starved the public cause; and though they frequently gave sparingly, they bestowed their favours with a winning grace, and consummate wisdom.

This conduct of ours excited the crafty *Minggo Humma Echeto,* to give loose to his vindictive temper; and at the same time, to make it coincide with the general welfare of his country. For as the Muskohge had proved an over-match for them in almost every engagement, and had lately committed hostilities against us in their neighbourhood, he persuaded those head-men I had met, when convened in a council of war, that if they with proper secresy repeated the like hostile act on any of our people who first came that way, and reported it to have been done by the Muskohge, it would [303] certainly obtain that favourite point they had long wished for, of drawing us into an alliance with them against the common enemy, as we must have some of the inward feelings of men for our lost people. Probably, the decree of that red council would have been soon put in execution had it not been for me. When I took my leave of the red chief to return, the drum was beat to convene the people to tell them the cause of my coming to him, and returning home; and that as the women and children had seen me in the town, their late plan of execution must be entirely laid aside. One of the warriors was sent to accompany me, though rather by way of escortment. In my return I called at the before mentioned camp, and put up the whoop; my two former watchmen, on seeing me, resembled wolves catched in a pit, they hung down their heads, and looked gloomy, and wrathful. I asked them why they were ashamed, and why their hearts weighed so heavy; they said they were ashamed for me, I was so great a liar, and had earnestly told them so many ugly falshoods. I said, my speech to them could hurt no honest persons.—My head, my eyes, my heart, assured me their hearts were then like the snakes; and my tongue only spoke the speech of honest wisdom, so as to save myself from being bitten—That it was the property of poisonous snakes, when they miss their aim, to be enraged, and hide their heads in their hateful coil; and concluded, by telling them I went through the woods to Yowanne, to shew them publicly I was not hurt by lurking snakes—and that I would now return to the harmless Chikkasah, and tell them so—on this we parted.

A timely application of proper measures with the savages, is our only method to secure their feeble affections. If those, who are employed for that salutary purpose, justly pursued that point, its effect would soon be openly declared, by the friendly behaviour and honest conduct of the various western nations. But where interest governs, iniquitous measures are pursued, and painters can be got who will flatter the original, be it ever so black. Some of our chiefs, with a certain military officer in West-Florida, like trembling mice, humbly voted not to demand any satisfaction from the savages, for that most shocking act of cool murder I have just mentioned, lest it should provoke them to do us more mischief. But to the honour of George Johnstone, Esq; then Governor of West-Florida, as a representative of the suffering people, he despised such obsequious and pusillanimous councils, and insisted, in his usual manly manner, on an equal [304] revenge of blood, and had it speedily granted, as far as the situation of affairs could possible allow: for by a council of the red Sanhedrim, they condemned three of the chief murderers to be killed, and formally sent down to him two of their scalps to stop the loud voice of blood: but the third made off to the Cheerake, by which means he evaded his justly deserved fate—and too nice a scrutiny at such a time would not have been convenient.[346] All the western Indian nations, bear the highest regard to that paternal governor, and plain friend of all the people: and I record his conduct to do justice to so uncommon a character in America, as well as to engage his successors to pursue the same measures, and copy after him.

The Choktah, by not having deep rivers or creeks to purify themselves by daily ablutions, are become very irreligious in other respects, for of late years, they make no annual atonement for sin. As very few of them can swim, this is a full proof that the general opinion of the young brood of savages being able to swim like fish, as soon as they come into the world, ought to be intirely exploded. The Indian matrons have sense enough to know, that the swimming of human creatures is an art to keep the head above water, which is gained by experience; and that their helpless infants are incapable of it. Probably, the report sprung from their immersing the new-born infants in deep running water by the way of purification.

The Choktah are the craftiest, and most ready-witted, of any of the red nations I am acquainted with. It is surprising to hear the wily turns they use, in persuading a person to grant them the favour they have in view. Other nations generally behave with modesty and civility, without ever lessening themselves by asking any mean favours. But the Choktah, at every season, are on the begging lay. I several times told their leading men, they were greater beggars, and of a much meaner spirit, than the white-haired Chik-kasah women, who often were real objects of pity. I was once fully con-vinced that none was so fit to baffle them in those low attempts without giving offence, as their own country-men. One, in my presence, expatiated on his late disappointment and losses, with the several unexpected causes, and pressingly sollicited his auditor as a benevolent kinsman, to assist him in his distress: but the other [305] kept his ear deaf to his importunity, and entirely evaded the artful aim of the petitioner, by carrying on a discourse he had begun, before his relation accosted him as a suppliant. Each alter-nately began where they had left off, the one to inforce the compliance of his prayer, and the other, like the deaf adder, to elude the power of its charming him. Nature has in a very surprising manner, endued the Indian Americans, with a strong comprehensive memory, and great flow of lan-guage. I listened with close attention to their speeches, for a considerable time; at last the petitioner despairing of impressing the other with senti-ments in his favour, was forced to drop his false and tragical tale, and become seemingly, a patient hearer of the conclusion of the other's long narrative, which was given him with a great deal of outward composure, and cool good-nature.

In the years 1746 and 1747, I was frequently perplexed by the Choktah mendicants; which policy directed me to bear, and conceal as well as I could, because I was then transacting public business with them.[347] In 1747, one of their warriors and a Chokchooma came to me for presents; which according to my usual custom in those times, I gave, though much less than they pre-sumed to expect. The former, strongly declaimed against the penurious spirit of the French, and then highly applauded the open generous tempers of the English traders: for a considerable time, he contrasted them with each other, not forgetting, in every point of comparison, to give us the preference in a high degree. He was endued with so much eloquence and skill as to move the passions, and obtain his point. A considerable number of Chikkasah warriors who were present, told me soon after, that his skilful method of addressing me for a bottle of spirituous liquors, seemed to them astonishing: an old beloved man replied, that the worst sort of snakes were endued with the greatest skill to insnare and suck their prey, whereas, the harmless have no such power.

The Indians in general do not chuse to drink any spirits, unless they can quite intoxicate themselves.[348] When in that helpless and sordid condition, weeping and asking for more *ookka hoome,* "bitter waters," I saw one of the drunkard's relations, who some time before had taken a like dose, hold the rum-bottle to the other's head, saying, when he had drank deep, "Hah, you were very poor for drinking." Though I appealed to all the Chikkasah warriors present, that rum never stood on hand with me, when the [306] people were at home, and several times affirmed to the importunate Choktah, that it was entirely expended; yet my denial served only to make him more earnest: upon this, I told him, that though I had no *ookka hoome,* I had a full bottle of the water of *ane hoome,* "bitter ears," meaning long pepper, of which he was ignorant, as he had seen none of that kind. We were of opinion that his eager thirst for liquor, as well as his ignorance of the burning quality of the pepper, and the resemblance of the words, which signify things of a hot, though different nature, would induce the bacchanal to try it. He accordingly applauded my generous disposition, and said, "his heart had all the while told him I would not act beneath the character I bore among his country-people." The bottle was brought: I laid it on the table, and told him, as he was then spitting very much, (a general custom with the Indians, when they are eager for any thing) "if I drank it all at one sitting, it would cause me to spit in earnest, as I used it, only when I ate, and then very moderately; but though I loved it, if his heart was very poor for it, I should be silent, and not in the least grudge him for pleasing his mouth." He said, "your heart is honest indeed; I thank you, for it is good to my heart, and makes it greatly to rejoice." Without any farther ceremony, he seized the bottle, uncorked it, and swallowed a large quantity of the burning liquid, till he was near strangled. He gasped for a considerable time, and as soon as he recovered his breath, he said *Hah,* and soon after kept stroaking his throat with his right hand. When the violence of this burning draught was pretty well over, he began to flourish away, in praise of the strength of the liquor, and bounty of the giver. He then went to his companion, and held the bottle to his mouth, according to custom, till he took several hearty swallows. This Indian seemed rather more sensible of its fiery quality, than the other, for it suffocated him for a considerable time; but as soon as he recovered his breath, he tumbled about on the floor in various postures like a drunken person, overcome by the force of liquor. In this manner, each of them renewed their draught, till they had finished the whole bottle, into which two others had been decanted. The Chikkasah spectators were surprised at their tasteless and voracious appetite, and laughed heartily at them, mimicking the actions, language, and gesture of drunken savages. The burning liquor so highly inflamed their bodies that one of the Choktah to cool his inward parts, drank water till he almost burst: the other rather than bear the ridicule of the people, and the inward fire that [307] distracted him, drowned himself the second night after in a broad and shallow clay hole,[349] contiguous to the dwelling house of his uncle, who was the Chikkasah Archimagus.

There was an incident, something similar, which happened in the year 1736, in *Kanootare,* the most northern town of the Cheerake.[350] When all the liquor was expended, the Indians went home, leading with them at my request, those who were drunk. One, however, soon came back, and earnestly importuned me for more *Nawohti,* which signifies both physic and spirituous liquors. They, as they are now become great liars, suspect all others of being infected with their own disposition and principles. The more I excused myself, the more anxious he grew, so as to become offensive. I then told him, I had only one quarter of a bottle of strong physic, which sick people might drink in small quantities, for the cure of inward pains: and laying it down before him, I declared I did not on any account choose to part with it, but as his speech of few words, had become very long and troublesome, he might do just as his heart directed him concerning it. He took it up, saying his heart was very poor for physic, but that would cure it, and make it quite streight. The bottle contained almost three gills of strong spirits of turpentine, which in a short time, he drank off. Such a quantity of the like physic would have demolished me, or any white person. The Indians in general, are either capable of suffering exquisite pain longer than we are, or of shewing more constancy and composure in their torments. The troublesome visitor soon tumbled down and foamed prodigiously.—I then sent for some of his relations to carry him home. They came—I told them he drank greedily, and too much of the physic. They said, it was his usual custom, when the red people bought the English physic. They gave him a decoction of proper herbs and roots, the next day sweated him, repeated the former draught, and he soon got well. As those turpentine spirits did not inebriate him, but only inflamed his intestines, he well remembered the burning quality of my favourite physic, which he had so indiscreetly drank up, and cautioned the rest from ever teizing me for any physic I had concealed, in any sort of bottles, for my own use; otherwise they might be sure it would spoil them, like the eating of fire.

The Choktah are in general more slender than any other nation of savages I have seen. They are raw-boned, and surprisingly active in ball-playing [308]; which is a very sharp exercise, and requires great strength and exertion. In this manly exercise, no persons are known to be equal to them, or in running on level ground, to which they are chiefly used from their infancy, on account of the situation of their country, which hath plenty of hills, but no mountains; these lie at a considerable distance between them and the Muskohge. On the survey of a prodigious space of fertile land up the Missisippi, and its numberless fine branches, we found the mountains full three hundred miles from that great winding mass of waters.

Though the lands of West-Florida, for a considerable distance from the sea-shore, are very low, sour, wet, and unhealthy, yet it abounds with valuable timber for ship-building, which could not well be expended in the long space of many centuries. This is a very material article to so great a maritime power, as Great Britain, especially as it can be got with little expence and trouble. The French were said to deal pretty much that way; and the Spaniards, it is likely, will now resume it, as the bounty of our late ministry has allowed the French to transfer New-Orleans to them, and by that means they are able to disturb the British colonies at pleasure. It cannot fail of proving a constant bone of contention: a few troops could soon have taken it during the late war, for it was incapable of making any considerable resistance; and even French effrontery could not have presumed to withhold the giving it up, if the makers of our last memorable peace had not been so extremely modest, or liberal to them. If it be allowed that the first discoverers and possessors of a foreign waste country, have a just title to it, the French by giving up New Orleans to Great Britain, would have only ceded to her, possessions, which they had no right to keep; for Col. Wood was the first discoverer of the Missisippi, who stands on public record, and the chief part of ten years he employed in searching its course. This spirited attempt he began in the year 1654, and ended 1664. Capt. Bolton made the like attempt, in the year 1670. Doctor Cox of New Jersey sent two ships Anno 1698, which discovered the mouth of it; and having sailed a hundred miles up, he took possession of the whole country, and called it Carolana: whereas the French did not discover it till the year 1699, when they gave it the name of Colbert's-river, in honour of their favourite minister, and the whole country they called Loisinana,[351] which may soon be exchanged for Philippiana—till the Americans give it another and more desirable name.

[309] The Choktah being employed by the French, together with their other red confederates, against the English Chikkasah, they had no opportunity of inuring themselves to the long-winded chace, among a great chain of steep craggy mountains. They are amazingly artful however in deceiving an enemy; they will fasten the paws and trotters of panthers, bears, and buffalos, to their feet and hands, and wind about like the circlings of such animals, in the lands they usually frequent. They also will mimick the different notes of wild fowl, and thus often outwit the savages they have disputes with. Their enemies say, that when at war, it is impossible to discover their track, unless they should be so lucky as to see their persons. They act very timorously against the enemy abroad, but behave as desperate veterans when attacked in their own country. 'Till they were supplied by the English traders with arms and ammunition, they had very little skill in killing deer; but they improve very fast in that favourite art: no savages are equal to them in killing bears, panthers, wild cats, &c. that resort in thick cane-swamps; which swamps are sometimes two or three miles over, and an hundred in length, without any break either side of the stream.

About Christmas, the he and she bears always separate. The former usually snaps off a great many branches of trees, with which he makes the bottom of his winter's bed, and carefully raises it to a proper height, with the green tops of large canes; he chooses such solitary thickets as are impenetrable by the sun-beams. The she bear takes an old large hollow tree for her yeaning winter-house, and chuses to have the door above, to enable her to secure her young ones from danger. When any thing disturbs them, they gallop up a tree, champing their teeth, and bristling their hair, in a frightful manner: and when they are wounded, it is surprising from what a height they will pitch on the ground, with their weighty bodies, and how soon they get up, and run off. When they take up their winter-quarters, they continue the greater part of two months, in almost an entire state of inactivity: during that time, their tracks reach no farther than to the next water, of which they seldom drink, as they frequently suck their paws in their lonely recess, and impoverish their bodies, to nourish them. While they are employed in that surprising task of nature, they cannot contain themselves in silence, but are so well pleased with their repast, that they continue singing *hum um um:* as their pipes are none of the weakest, the Indians by this [310] means often are led to them from a considerable distance, and then shoot them down. But they are forced to cut a hole near the root of the tree, wherein the she bear and her cubs are lodged, and drive them out by the force of fire and suffocating smoke; and as the tree is partly rotten, and the inside dry, it soon takes fire. In this case, they become very fierce, and would fight any kind of enemy; but, commonly, at the first shot, they are either killed or mortally wounded. However, if the hunter chance to miss his aim, he speedily makes off to a sappling, which the bear by over-clasping cannot climb: the crafty hunting dogs then act their part, by biting behind, and gnawing its hams, till it takes up a tree. I have been often assured both by Indians and others, who get their bread by hunting in the woods, that the she-bear always endeavours to keep apart from the male during the helpless state of her young ones; otherwise he would endeavour to kill them; and that they had frequently seen the she bear kill the male on the spot, after a desperate engagement for the defence of her young ones. Of the great numbers I have seen with their young cubs, I never saw a he bear at such times, to associate with them: so that it seems one part of the Roman Satyrist's fine moral lesson, inculcating peace and friendship, is not just, *Sævis inter se convenit Ursis.*[352]

At the time Mobille (that grave-yard for Britons) was ceded to Great-Britain, the lower towns of the Choktah brought down all the Chikkasah scalps they had taken, in their thievish way of warring, and had them new painted, and carried them in procession on green boughs of pine, by way of bravado, to shew their contempt of the English. They would not speak a

word to the Chikkasah traders, and they sollicited the French for their consent to re-commence war against us, and establish them again by force of
arms, in their western possessions; but they told them, their king had firmly
concluded upon the cession, through his own benevolence of heart, to prevent the further effusion of innocent blood.—By this artful address, they
supported their credit with the savages, in the very point which ought to
have ruined it.

When the Choktah found themselves dipped in war with the Muskohge;
they sollicited the English for a supply of ammunition, urging with much
truth, that common sense ought to direct us to assist them, and deem the
others our enemies as much as theirs. But Tumbikpe-garrison was evacuated
through the unmanly fear of giving umbrage to the Muskohge [311], at the
very time it would have been of the utmost service to the general interest
of our colonies to have continued it.[353]

The commander concealed his timorous and precipitate retreat, even
from me and another old trader, till the very night he confusedly set off for
Mobille by water, and left to us the trouble of apologizing to the savages for
his misconduct. But after he got to a place of safety, he flourished away of
his wisdom and prowess. As a just stigma on those who abuse their public
trust, I cannot help observing, that in imitation of some other rulers, he
persuaded the Indians not to pay us any of our numerous out-standing debts,
though contrary to what was specified in our trading licences. They have
not courage enough to venture their own valuable lives to those red marts
of trade; if they had, they would persuade the Indians rather to pay their
debts honestly, year by year, as we trust them in their want, and depend on
their promise and fidelity. The gentlemen, who formerly traded with the
Muskohge, told me that the Georgia-governor, through a like generous
principle, forgave that nation once all the numerous debts they owed the
traders. But as soon as the Indians understood they would not be credited
again, under any circumstances whatsoever, they consented to pay their
debts, and declared the Governor to be a great mad-man, by pretending to
forgive debts contracted for valuable goods, which he never purchased, nor
intended to pay for.

Though the French Louisianians were few, and far dispersed, as well as
surrounded by the savages, yet close application and abilities in their various appointments, sufficiently made up their lack of numbers. When, and
where, their security seemed to require it, they with a great deal of art
fomented divisions among their turbulent red neighbours, and endeavoured
to keep the balance of power pretty even between them. Though they had
only one garrison in the country of the Muskohge, and another in that of
the Choktah, yet the commanders of those two posts, managed so well, that
they intimidated those two potent nations, by raising misunderstandings

between them, and threatening (when occasion required) to set the one against the other, with their red legions of the north, unless ample satisfaction was speedily given by the offending party, and solemn promises of a strict observance of true friendship for the time to come. How far our super-intendants, and commissioners of Indian affairs, have imitated that wise [312] copy, our traders can feelingly describe: and it will be a happiness, if our three western colonies have not the like experience, in the space of a few years. We assure them, that either the plan, or the means, for producing such an effect, has been pretty well concerted by the authors of that dangerous and fatal peace between the Muskohge and Choktah. Their own party indeed will greatly applaud it, and so will the much obliged Spaniards, especially if they soon enter into a war with Great Britain. It is to be wished, that those who preach peace and good-will to all the savage murderers of the British Americans, would do the same as to their American fellow-subjects,—and not, as some have lately done, cry peace to the Indians, and seek to plunge the mercenary swords of soldiers into the breasts of those of our loyal colonists, who are the most powerful of us, because they oppose the measures of an arbitrary ministry, and will not be enslaved.

In the year 1766, the Choktah received a considerable blow from the Muskohge.[354] Their old distinguished war-leader, before spoken of, *Minggo Humma Echéto,* set off against the Muskohge, with an hundred and sixty warriors, to cut off by surprise one of their barrier towns: as the waters were low, a couple of runners brought him a message from the nation, acquainting him there were two white men on their way to the Muskohge, and therefore desired him to send them back, lest they should inform them of the expedition, and by that means, endanger the lives of the whole. But though he treated these traders kindly at his war-camp, and did not shew the least diffidence of them respecting their secrecy; and sent this account back by the running messengers to his advisers, that the English were his friends, and could not be reasonably suspected of betraying them, if it were only on the situation of their own trading business, which frequently called them to various places,—yet those base-minded and perfidious men violated the generous faith reposed in them, and betrayed the lives of their credulous friends. They set off with long marches, and as soon as they arrived in the country of the Muskohge, minutely informed them of the Choktah's hostile intentions, and number, and the probable place of attacking the aforesaid camp, to the best advantage. The news was joyfully received, and, as they had reason to believe they could surprise the enemy, or take them at a disadvantage, in some convenient [313] place near their own barriers, a number of chosen warriors well prepared, set off in order to save their former credit, by revenging the repeated affronts the Choktah leader had given them in every engagement. He, in the most insulting manner, had often challenged their whole nation to meet him and his at any fixt time of a moon, and place, and fight it out, when the conquerors should be masters of the conquered—for the Muskohge used to ridicule the Choktah, by saying, they were like wolf-cubs, who would not take the water, but the thick swamp, as their only place of security against the enemy. It must here be remembered, that the Indians in general, are guided by their dreams when they attend their holy ark to war, reckoning them so many oracles, or divine intimations, designed for their good: by virtue of those supposed, sacred dictates, they will sometimes return home, by one, two, or three at a time, without the least censure, and even with applause, for this their religious conduct. Thus, one hundred and twenty of these Choktah, after having intimidated themselves apart from the rest, with visionary notions, left the war-camp and returned home. Our gallant friend, *Minggo Humma Echeto,* addressed his townsmen on this, and persuaded them to follow him against the enemy, saying, it was the part of brave warriors to keep awake, and not dream like old women. He told them their national credit was at stake for their warlike conduct under him; and that honour prompted him to proceed against the hateful enemy, even by himself, though he was certain his townsmen and warlike relations would not forsake him. Forty of them proceeded, and next day they were surrounded by an hundred and sixty of the Muskohge, several of whom were on horseback to prevent their escape. When the Choktah saw their dangerous situation, and that they had no alternative but a sudden, or lingering death, they fought as became desperate men, deprived of hope. While their arrows and ammunition lasted, they killed and wounded a considerable number of the opposite party: but the enemy observing their distressed situation, drew up into a narrow circle, and rushed upon the remaining and helpless few, with their guns, darts, clubs, and tomohawks, and killed thirty-eight. They were not able to captivate but two, whom they destined for the fiery torture: but at night, when the camp was asleep in too great security, one of them fortunately made his escape out of a pair of wooden stocks. They had flattered him with the hopes of being redeemed; but he told them he was [314] too much of a warrior to confide in their false promises. He got safe home, and related the whole affair.

Formerly, by virtue of the pressing engagement of a prime magistrate of South-Carolina, I undertook to open a trade with the Choktah, and reconcile their old-standing enmity with the Chikkasah.[355] I was promised to be indemnified in all necessary charges attending that attempt. As the Choktah, by the persuasions of the French, had killed my partner in the trade, I was desirous of any favourable opportunity of retaliating: especially, as we were exposed to perpetual dangers and losses, by the French rewards offered either for our scalps or horses-tails; and as the French were usually short of goods, while Great Britain was at war with them, we were liable to most damages from them in time of peace. They used to keep an alphabetical list of all the names of leading savages, in the various nations where they ingarrisoned themselves; and they duly paid them, every year, a certain quantity of goods besides, for all the damages they did to the Chikkasah, and our traders; which tempted them constantly to exert their abilities, to the good liking of their political employers. It happened, however, that one of the French of Tumbikpe-fort, being guided by Venus instead of Apollo, was detected in violating the law of marriage with the favourite wife of the warlike chieftain of Quansheto, *Shulashummashtabe,* who by his several transcendant qualities, had arrived to the highest pitch of the red glory. He was well known in Georgia and South-Carolina, by the name of Red Shoes; as formerly noticed.[356] As there lived in his town, a number of the Chok-choomah,[357] the senior tribe of the Chikkasah and Choktah, and who had a free intercourse with each of their countries, we soon had an account of every material thing that passed there. I therefore resolved to improve so favourable an opportunity as seemed to present itself, and accordingly soon privately convened two of the leading men of the Chikkasah nation, to assist me to execute the plan I had in view. One was the Archimagus, *Pastabe,* known in our colonies, by the name of "the Jockey,"—and the other, by that of *Pahemingo-Amalahta,*[358] who was the only Indian I ever knew to die of a consumption; which he contracted by various engagements with the enemy when far off at war, contrary to their general rule of martial purification. The violent exercise of running a great distance under the violent rays of the sun, and over sandy, or hilly grounds, would not allow him to [315] inswamp, and he fired his blood to such a degree, that a few years after this, when on a visit to our English settlement, he died at Augusta with this ailment. It is needful to mention those well-known circumstances, as the following relation of facts, depends in a considerable measure on them.

We three agreed to send some presents to *Red Shoes,* with a formal speech, desiring him to accept them with a kind heart, and shake hands with us as became brothers, according to the old beloved speech. Their own friendly messages, and treaties of peace, are always accompanied with so many sorts of presents, as their chiefs number. We in a few days packed up a sufficient quantity, to bury the tomohawk which the French had thrust into their unwilling hands, and to dry up the tears of the injured, and set their hearts at ease, for the time to come, by joining with the English and their old friendly Chikkasah, *Inggona Sekanoopa toochenase,* "in the triple knot of friendship," in order to cut off the dangerous snake's head, and utterly destroy the power of its forked tongue. As our real grievances were mutually the same, and numerous, we gave liberally. Having every thing as well concerted for the embassy, as such occasions require, my two red friends sent a trusty messenger for a couple of the foresaid neutral Indians, who had been a few days in the Chikkasah country, to accompany him late at night to my trading house. They readily obeyed; and, as the good-natured men and their families, through friendship to us, must infallibly have been sacrificed to French policy, if we failed of success, or they were discovered by captives, or any other means, we used the greatest secrecy, and placed a centinel to keep off all other persons during our private congress. After we had conversed with them a considerable time, on the necessity of the proposed attempt, and the certainty of succeeding in it, we opened our two large budgets, and read over the strong emblematical contents, according to their idiom, till we gave them a true impression of the whole. The next day we took care to send them off well pleased: and as several material circumstances conspired to assure us they would faithfully discharge the office of trust, which we reposed in them, we in a short time had the satisfaction to hear by other private runners of their countrymen, from our brave and generous patron, Red Shoes, that they were so far from breaking the public faith, that they read to him every material head of our embassy, and urged it with all their powers.

[316] That red chieftain introduced our friendly embassy, with such secresy and address to all the head-men he could confide in, that he soon persuaded most of them in all the neighbouring towns, to join heartily with him in his laudable plan. The sharpness of his own feelings for the base injury he had received from the French, and the well-adapted presents we sent him and his wife and gallant associates, contributed greatly to give a proper weight to our embassy. Such motives as these are too often the mainsprings that move the various wheels of government, even in the christian world. In about a month from the time we began to treat with Red-Shoes, he sent a considerable body of his warriors, with presents to me, as the representative of the English traders, and to my Chikkasah friends, consisting of swans-wings, white beads, pipes and tobacco; which was a strong confirmation of our treaty of peace,—and he earnestly requested of me to inform them with that candour, which should always be observed by honest friends, whether I could firmly engage that our traders would live, and deal among them, as we did with the Chikkasah; for a disappointment that way, he said, would prove fatal, should we entangle them with the French, in resentment of the many injuries they had long unprovokedly done us. I quieted their apprehensions on that material point of jealousy, to their entire satisfaction, and my two Chikkasah friends soon expatiated upon the subject to him, with a great deal of that life, wit and humour, so peculiar to the red Americans. We explained and confirmed anew, the whole contents of our former talk concerning the dangerous French snake; assuring them, that if they did

not soon exert themselves against it, as became brave free-men, they would still continue not only poor, and shamefully naked, below the state of other human beings, but be despised, and abused, in proportion to their mean passive conduct,—their greatest and most favourite war-chieftains not excepted, as they saw verified in their chief leader, *Shoolashummashtabe.* But if they exerted themselves, they would be as happy as our friendly, brave, and free Chikkasah, whom the French armies, and all their red confederates, could no way damage but as hidden snakes, on account of their own valour, and the steady friendship of the English,—who were always faithful to their friends even to death, as every river and creek sufficiently testified, all the way from the English settlements to the Chikkasah country. We mentioned how many were killed at several places, as they were going in a warlike manner to supply their beloved friends, without any being ever captivated by the numerous enemy, [317] though often attacked at a disadvantage— which ought to assure them, that whenever the English shaked hands with people, their hearts were always honest. We requested them therefore to think, and act, as our brotherly Chikkasah, who by strongly holding the chain of friendship between them and the English, were able in their open fields, to destroy the French armies, and in the woods bravely to fight, and baffle all the efforts of their despicable mercenary enemies, though their numbers of fighting men consisted of few more than one hundred to what the Choktah contained in old hundreds, or thousands. The French, we added, were liberal indeed; but to whom, or for what? They gave presents to the head-men, and the most eloquent speakers of their country, to inslave the rest, but would not supply them with arms and ammunition, without the price of blood against our traders and the friendly Chikkasah; that they themselves were witnesses, a whole town of sprightly promising young men had not now more than five or six guns; but they would learn to kill as many deer as the distinguished Chikkasah hunters, if they firmly shook hands with the English. We convinced them, that the true emblem of the English was a drest white deer-skin, but that the French dealt with them only in long scalping knives; that we had a tender feeling, when we heard the mourning voice of the tender-hearted widow, and only supplied our friends in their own defence, or in revenge of crying blood; but that the French delighted in blood, and were always plotting how to destroy them, and take away their lands, by setting them at war against those who loved them, and would secure their liberties, without any other view than as became brothers, who fairly exchanged their goods. We desired them to view the Chikkasah striplings, how readily their kindly hearts led them to listen to the friendly speech of their English trading speaker, because they knew we loved them, and enabled them to appear in the genteel dress of red people.

At the whoop, they soon appeared, and cheerfully complied with our various requests, to the great satisfaction of our new Choktah friends. The Chikkasah head-men told them with pleasure, that they were glad their own honest eyes had seen the pure effects of love to their English trader; and that their old people, time out of mind, had taught them so. Then they humourously enlarged on the unfriendly conduct of the French in a comparative manner, and persuaded them to keep their eyes open, and remember [318] well what they had seen and heard, and to tell it to all their head-men.

We adjusted every thing in the most friendly manner, to the intire satisfaction of the Choktah. I supplied each of them with arms, ammunition, and presents in plenty—gave them a French scalping knife which had been used against us, and even vermilion, to be used in the flourishing way, with the dangerous French snakes, when they killed and scalped them. They returned home extremely well pleased, echoed every thing they had seen and heard; and declared that the Chikkasah, in their daily dress, far exceeded the best appearance their country-men could make in the most showy manner, except those whom the French paid to make their lying mouths strong. They soon went to work—they killed the strolling French pedlars,—turned out against the Missisippi Indians and Mobillians, and the flame speedily raged very high. One of the Choktah women, ran privately to inform a French pedlar of the great danger he was in, and urged him immediately to make his escape. He soon saddled a fine strong sprightly horse he chanced to have at hand: just as he mounted, the dreadful death whoo whoop was sounded in pursuit of him, with the swift-footed red Asahel, *Shoolashum-mashtabe,* leading the chace. Though, from that place, the land-path was mostly level to Tumpikbe-garrison (about half a day's march) and though the Chikkasah and Choktah horses are Spanish barbs, and long winded, like wolves; yet Red-Shoes, far ahead of the rest, ran him down in about the space of fifteen miles, and had scalped the unfortunate rider some time before the rest appeared.[359]

It is surprising to see the long continued speed of the Indians in general—though some of us have often ran the swiftest of them out of sight, when on the chase in a collective body, for about the distance of twelve miles; yet, afterward, without any seeming toil, they would stretch on, leave us out of sight, and out-wind any horse. When this retaliating scheme was planned and executing, I was the only British subject in the Chikkasah country; and as I had many goods on hand, I staid in the nation, while we sent down our horses to the first English settlements,—which was full eight hundred miles distant, before the two Floridas were ceded to us. Seventeen were the broken days, according to the Indian phrase, when the Choktah engaged to return with the French scalps, as a full confirmation of their having [319] declared war against them, and of their ardent desire of always shaking hands with the English. The power of the French red mercenaries was however so very great, that Red Shoes could not with safety comply with his deputy's promise to me, to send the French snake's head, in the time appointed by our sticks hieroglyphically painted, and notched in due form.[360] The fall time drawing on, obliged me to set off for the Koosah-town, which is the most western of the Muskohge nation, about three hundred miles distant. I was accompanied by my two cheerful and gallant Chikkasah friends, already mentioned, with forty of their chosen warriors, brave as ever trod the ground, and faithful under the greatest dangers even to the death. On our way down, escorting the returning cargo, four Chikkasah, who were passing home through the woods, having discovered us, and observing in the evening a large camp of 80 French Choktah in pursuit of us; they returned on our tracks at full speed, to put us on our guard; but though we were so few, and had many women and children to protect, besides other incumbrances, yet as the enemy knew by our method of camping, and marching, we had discovered them, they durst not attack us.

Another time there was a hunting camp of only seventeen Chikkasah, with their wives and children, who were attacked by above sixty Choktah; but they fought them a long time, and so desperately, that they killed and wounded several, and drove them shamefully off, without any loss. It is usual for the women to sing the enlivening war song in the time of an attack; and it inflames the men's spirits so highly, that they become as fierce as lions. I never knew an instance of the Indians running off, though from a numerous enemy, and leaving their women and children to their barbarous hands.

Soon after we arrived at the upper western town of the Muskohge, which was called *Ooe-Asah,*[361] and settled by the Chikkasah and Nahchee, a great company of Red Shoes warriors came up with me, with the French scalps, and other trophies of war: but because a body of our Muskohge mercenary traders found their account in dealing with the French at the Alebahma-fort, they to the great risk of their own country's welfare, lodged so many caveats in my way by the mediation [320] of the Muskohge, that I found it necessary to consent that the scalps should be sent with the other trophies, in a Muskohge white deer-skin, to the French fort at the distance of seventy miles, to be buried deep in the ground,[362] instead of sending them by the Choktah runners, to his excellency the governor of South-Carolina, who had engaged me to strive to open a trade with those Indians. These opulent and mercenary white savages being now dead, I shall not disgrace the page with their worthless names. Soon after we had reached the Chikkasah country, Red Shoes came to pay us a friendly visit, accompanied with a great many head-men and warriors, both to be relieved in their poverty, and to concert the best measures of still annoying the common enemy.

We behaved kindly and free to them, to their entire satisfaction, and sent considerable presents to many head-men who staid at home, in confirmation of our strong friendship; acquainting them of our various plans of opera-tion against the enemy, in defence of their lives, freedom, and liberty of trade, in which the English and Chikkasah would faithfully support them. Every thing was delivered to them according to our intention, and as kindly received. And as all the Indians are fond of well-timed novelty, especially when they expect to be gainers by it, the name of the friendly and generous English was now echoed, from town to town, except in those few which had large pensions from the French.

In the beginning of the following spring, which was 1747, above fifty warriors from several towns of the Muskohge, came to the Chikkasah country, on their way to war against the Aquahpah Indians, on the western side of the Missisippi, one hundred and fifty miles above the Nahchee old fields.[363] By our good treatment of them, and well-timed application, they joined a body of Chikkasah warriors under *Payah Matahah,* and made a fleet of large cypress-bark-canoes, in which they embarked under the direc-tion of three red admirals, in long pettiaugers that had been taken from the French, as they were passing from New Orleans up to the Illinois. They proceeded down the Missisippi to the French settlements, and at-tacked and burned a large village at break of day, though under the com-mand of a stockade-fort; from which the Chikkasah leader was wounded with a grape-shot in his side. On this, as they despaired of his life, according to their universal method in such a case, they killed most of their unfortu-nate captives on the western bank of the Missisippi; and enraged with [321] fury, they overspread the French settlements, to a great distance, like a dreadful whirlwind, destroying every thing before them, to the astonish-ment and terror even of those who were far remote from the skirts of the direful storm. The French Louisianians were now in a desponding state, as we had beaten them in their own favourite political element, in which they had too often been successful even at the British court, after our troops and navies had scoured them out of the field and the ocean. They had no reason here to expect any favour of us, as we were only retaliating the long train of innocent blood of our fellow-subjects they had wantonly caused to be shed by their red mercenaries, and their fears now became as great as their danger—but they were needless; for though the Alebahma French, and many towns of the Muskohge, were in a violent ferment, when the foresaid warriors returned home, yet by the treacherous mediation of the above-mentioned traders and their base associates, the breach was made up. Had they been blest with the least spark of that love for the good of their coun-try, which the savages and French are, they could have then persuaded the Indians, to have driven the French from the dangerous Alebahma; and an alliance with the Chikkasah and Choktah would have effectually destroyed the dangerous line of circumvallation they afterwards drew around our valuable colonies. And as the Cheerake, by their situation, might easily have been induced to join in the formidable treaty, they with encouragement, would have proved far superior to all the northern red legions the French were connected with.

At that time I sent to the Governor of South Carolina, a large packet, relating the true situation of our Indian affairs, directed on his majesty's service: but though it contained many things of importance, (which the French, under such circumstances, would have faithfully improved) and required immediate dispatch; our Muskohge traders, to whose care I had sent it by some Chikkasah runners, were so daringly base as to open it, and destroy what their self-interested views seemed to require, and delayed the conveyance of the rest a considerable time, to prevent others from reaping the benefit of the trade before them. When I went down, I complained of their misconduct, and the Governor having promised me a public seal, threatened them loudly; but some after circumstances in trade made him to think it not worth while to put his threats in execution. When the French were destitute of goods at Tumbikpe-garrison, while [322] they were at war with the English, their policy allowed them to suffer several of our traders to deal with the Choktah, without any interruption, in order to keep them quiet; but as soon as they had a proper supply, they excited their treacherous friends to plunder, and kill our people. They, who had the fortune to get safe away, made great returns; which induced some to entertain too high notions of their profits, and so strangers hazarded too much at once. While the French had possession of Tumbikpe, we, who knew them, used to send there only small cargoes from the Chikkasah country, to avoid tempting them too far: but one of our great men was reported to have persuaded a couple of gentlemen to join in company with his brother (well known by the name of the Sphynx company)[364] in the Choktah trade, and to have supplied them very largely. They loaded, and sent off 360 valuable horses, which with all other concomitant charges, in going to such a far-distant country, swelled it to a high amount.[365] The traders, who were employed to vend the valuable cargo, gave large presents to six of the Muskohge leaders, known to be most attached to the British interest, to escort them, with a body of the Choktah, into the country. They passed by Alebahma, in the usual parade of the Indian traders, to the terror of the people in the fort. They proceeded as far as a powerful body of our Choktah friends had appointed to meet them, but considerably overstaid the fixed time there, in want of provisions, as their common safety would not allow them to go a hunting: by the forcible persuasion of the Muskohge head-men, they unluckily returned about one hundred and forty miles back on a north-east-course. But a few days after, a party of Choktah friends came to their late camp, in order to encourage them to come on without the least dread, as a numerous party were watching an opportunity to attack the French, and their own slavish countrymen; and that they would surely engage them very successfully, while the traders were fording Mobille-river, eight miles above Tumbikpe-fort, under a powerful escortment of their faithful friends. So wisely had they laid their plan, though it was disconcerted by the cautious conduct of the Muskohge head-men: for they are all so wary and jealous, that when they send any of their people on a distant errand, they fix the exact time they are to return home; and if they exceed but one day, they on the second send out a party on discovery★.

★I shall here mention an instance of that kind: at this time, a hunting camp of the Chikkasah went out to the extent of their winter-limits between the Choktah and Muskohge [323] countries: but being desirous of enlarging their hunt, they sent off a sprightly young warrior to discover certain lands they were unacquainted with, which they pointed to by the course of the sun, lying at the distance of about thirty miles. Near that place, he came up with a camp of Choktah, who seemed to treat him kindly, giving him venison and parched corn to eat: but while he was eating what some of the women had laid before him, one of the Choktah creeped behind him, and sunk his tomohawk into his head. His associates helped him to carry away the victim, and they hid it in a hollow tree, at a considerable distance from their camp; after which they speedily removed. When the time for his return was elapsed, the Chikkasah, next day, made a place of security for their women and children, under the protection of a few warriors; and the morning following, painted themselves red and black, and went in quest of their kinsman. Though they were strangers to the place, any farther than by their indications to him before he set off, yet so swift and skilful woods-men were they, that at twelve o'clock that day, they came to the Chok-tah camping place, where, after a narrow search, they discovered the trace of blood on a fallen tree, and a few drops of fresh blood on the leaves of trees, in the course they had dragged the corpse; these directed them to the wooden urn, wherein the remains of their kinsman were inclosed. They said, as they were men and warriors, it belonged to the female relations to weep for the dead, and to them to revenge it. They soon concluded to carry off the corpse, to the opposite side of a neighboring swamp, and then to pursue. Having deposited the body out of the reach of beasts of prey, they set off in pursuit of the Choktah: they came up with them before day-light, surrounded their camp, attacked them, killed one, and wounded several, whooping aloud, "that they were Chikkasah, who never first loosed the friend-knot between them and oth-ers, nor failed in revenging blood; but ye are roguish Choktah; you know you are like-wise cowards; and that you are worse than wolves, for they kill, only that they may eat, but you give your friends something to eat, that you may kill them with safety." They told them, as they had left their gallant relation unscalped in a tree, they left their cowardly one in like manner, along-side of another tree. They put up the death whoo whoop, returned, scaffolded their dead kinsman, and joined their own camp without any interruption. The reader will be able to form a proper judgment of the temper and abilities of the Indian savages, from these facts.

[323] Our Choktah traders having been thus induced to return to the Muskohge country, proceeded soon afterwards seventy miles on almost a northern course, and from thence to the Chikkasah about west by north— 300 miles of very mountainous land, till within forty miles of that extensive and fertile country—afterward, on a southern direction to the Choktah, 160 miles. This was a very oblique course, somewhat resembling the letter G reverted, its tail from Charles-town, consisting of 720 miles, and the head of 530, in all 1250 miles—a great distance to travel through woods, with loaded horses, where they shifted as they could, when the day's march was over; and through the varying seasons of the year. These traders were charged with great neglect, in being so long [324] before they reached the Choktah country;[366] this was to invalidate the pretensions of two other gentlemen, towards obtaining bills of exchange on the government, according to the strong promises they had, for any losses they might sustain in their Choktah cargo of goods, &c. Notwithstanding the former were utter strangers to the Chikkasah and Choktah, and in justice could only expect the common privilege of British subjects, yet his Excellency bestowed on them a large piece of written sheep-skin, bearing the impression of the threatening lion and unicorn to frighten every other trader from dealing with the Choktah, at their peril. The Chikkasah traders were much terrified at the unusual sight of the enlivened pictures of such voracious animals.[367] My situation caused me then to be silent, on that strange point; but when the chief of them, who carried those bees-wax-pictures, came to my trading house, chiefly to inlarge on the dreadful power of those fierce creatures,—I told him, as they answered the design, in making so many trembling believers, among the Indians, I did not imagine him so weak as to attempt to impose his scare-crows upon me; but that, as his Excellency had dipped me too deep in a dangerous and very expensive affair, and had done me the honour to send for me to Charles-town on his majesty's service, at the very time I could have secured them in the esteem of the fickle Choktah, I should not by any means oppose their aim of grasping the whole Choktah trade, be their plan ever so unwise and unfair. The letter the gentleman delivered to me was dated April 22, Anno 1747, in which his excellency acknowledged, in very obliging terms, that I had been very serviceable to the government, by my management among the Choktah, and might be assured of his countenance and friendship. As the rest of it concerned myself in other matters, and contained some things of the measures of government relating to the point in view, it may be right not to publish it: but it is among the public records in Charles-town, and may be seen in the secretary's office.[368] The traders, after this interview, set off for the Choktah; and I in a few days to South Carolina.

Soon after I arrived at Charles-town, I could not but highly resent the governor's ungenerous treatment of, and injustice to me, in sending for me to the neglect of my trade, only to carry on his unparalleled favourite scheme,—and I soon set off for the Chikkasah, without taking the least formal leave of his Excellency. By some means, he soon knew of my departure, [325] and persuaded G. G——n, Esq; (one of the two friends in South-Carolina, who only could influence me against my own liking)[369] to follow till he overtook me, and urge me to return, and accompany me to his Excellency's house. At his earnest sollicitations, the gentleman complied, came up with me, and prevailed on me to go back according to request. I had plenty of courtly excuses for my complaints and grievances, and in the hearing of my friend was earnestly pressed to forget and forgive all that was past; with solemn promises of full redress, according to his former engagement of drawing bills of exchange in my favour, on the government, if South-Carolina had not honour enough to repay me what I had expended in opening a trade with the numerous Choktah—besides gratuities for hardships, hazards, &c.

I wish I could here also celebrate his sincerity and faithfulness on this occasion—As I could not well suspect a breach of public faith, after it had been pledged in so solemn a manner, he had not much difficulty in detaining me on sundry pretexts, till the expected great Choktah crop of deerskins and beaver must have been gathered, before I could possibly return to the Chikkasah country, and from thence proceed to rival the Sphynx-company. Under those circumstances, I was detained so late in November, that the snow fell upon me at Edisto, the first day, in company with Captain W——d, an old trader of the Okwhuske, who was going to Savanah.[370] In the severity of winter, frost, snow, hail, and heavy rains succeed each other, in these climes, so that I partly rode, and partly swam to the Chikkasah country; for not expecting to stay long below, I took no leathern canoe. Many of the broad deep creeks, that were almost dry when I went down, had now far overflowed their banks, ran at a rapid rate, and were unpassable to any but desperate people: when I got within forty miles of the Chikkasah, the rivers and swamps were dreadful, by rafts of timber driving down the former, and the great fallen trees floating in the latter, for near a mile in length. Being forced to wade deep through cane-swamps or woody thickets, it proved very troublesome to keep my fire-arms dry, on which, as a second means, my life depended; for, by the high rewards of the French, some enemies were always rambling about in search of us. On the eastern side of one of the rivers, in taking a sweep early in a wet morning, in quest of my horses, I discovered smoke on a small piece of rising ground in a swamp, pretty near the edge; I [326] moved nearer from tree to tree, till I discovered them to be Choktah creeping over the fire. I withdrew without being discovered, or the least apprehension of danger, as at the worst, I could have immediately inswamped, secured a retreat with my trusty fire-arms, and taken through the river and the broad swamp, which then resembled a mixt ocean of wood and water. I soon observed the tracks of my horses, found them, and set off. At the distance of an hundred yards from the river, there was a large and deep lagoon, in the form of a semi-circle. As soon as I swam this, and got on the bank, I drank a good draught of rum:—in the middle of the river, I was forced to throw away one of my belt-pistols, and a long French scalping knife I had found, where the Choktah killed two of our traders. When I got on the opposite shore, I renewed my draught, put my fire-arms in order, and set up the war-whoop. I had often the like scenes, till I got to the Chikkasah country, which was also all afloat. The people had been saying, a little before I got home, that should I chance to be on the path, it would be near fifty days before I could pass the neighbouring deep swamps; for, on account of the levelness of the land, the waters contiguous to the Chikkasah, are usually in winter so long in emptying, before the swamps become passable. As I had the misfortune to lose my tomohawk, and wet all the punk in my shot-pouch by swimming the waters, I could not strike fire for the space of three days, and it rained extremely hard, during that time. By being thoroughly wet so long, in the cold month of December, and nipped with the frost, seven months elapsed before I had the proper use of the fingers of my right-hand. On that long and dangerous war-path, I was exposed to many dangers, and yet so extricated myself, that it would appear like Quixotism to enumerate them.

I often repented of trusting to the governor's promises, and so have many others. The Cheerake, *Attah Kullah Kullah,* whose name is the superlative of a skilful cutter of wood, called by us, "The Little Carpenter," had equal honour with me of receiving from his Excellency a considerable number of letters, which he said were not agreeable to the old beloved speech. He kept them regularly piled in a bundle, according to the time he received them, and often shewed them to the traders, in order to expose their fine promising contents. The first, he used to say, contained a little [327] truth, and he excused the failure of the greater part of it, as he imagined much business might have perplexed him, so as to occasion him to forget complying with his strong promise. "But count, said he, the lying black marks of this one:" and he descanted minutely on every circumstance of it. His patience being exhausted, he added, "they were an heap of black broad papers, and ought to be burnt in the old years fire."

Near the Muskohge country, on my way to the Chikkasah, I met my old friends, *Pa Yah-Matahah,* the Chikkasah head war-chieftain, and *Minggo-Pushkoosh,* the great Red-Shoes' brother, journeying to Charles-town, with one of the beaus of the Sphynx-company,[371] to relate the loss of the most part of that great cargo they so unwisely carried at once, and to solicit for a further supply. Those traders, one excepted, were very indiscreet, proud and stubborn. They strove who could out-dress, or most vilify the other even before the Indians, who were surprised, as they never heard the French to degrade one another. The haughty plan they laid, against the repeated persuasions of the other, was the cause of all their losses—they first lost the affection of the free, and equally proud Choktah; for they fixed as an invariable rule, to keep them at a proper distance, as they termed it; whereas I, according to the frequent, sharp, upbraiding language of the familiar savages to them, sat and smoked with the head-men on bear-skins, set the young people to their various diversions, and then viewed them with pleasure.

Notwithstanding the bad treatment I had received; as I was apprehensive of the difficulties they would necessarily be exposed to, on account of their ignorance and haughtiness, I wrote to them, by a few Chikkasah warriors, truly informing them of the temper of the Indians, and the difficulties they would probably be exposed to, from the policy of the French at Tumbikpe; and that though I had purposed to set off for South-Carolina, I would postpone going so soon, if they were of my opinion, that Mr. J. C—l (who joined with me in the letter)[372] and I could be of any service to their mercantile affairs. They received our well-intended epistle, and were so polite as to order their black interpretress to bid our red couriers tell us, they thanked us for our friendly offer, but did not stand in need of our assistance. They walked according to the weak crooked rule they had received below, and fared accordingly: for the disobliged [328] savages took most part of the tempting cargo. At this time, the French had only two towns and a half in their interest, and they were so wavering, that they could not rely on their friendship, much less on their ability of resisting the combined power of the rest of the nation; and they were on the very point of removing that useful and commanding garrison Tumbikpe, and settling one on another eastern-branch of the river, called Potagahatche, in order to decoy many of the Choktah to settle there by degrees, and intercept the English traders, on their way up from our settlements. This was as wise a plan as could possibly have been concerted, under the difficult circumstances they laboured at that time. But the unjust and unwise measures of the governor of South-Carolina, in sending his favourite traders with a scare-crow of bees-wax, to keep off others who were more intelligent, gave the desponding French a favourable opportunity to exert their powers, and regain the lost affections of a considerable number of our red allies; for none of our traders had now any goods in the Choktah country, nor were likely soon to carry any there.

Mr. C—l, the trader I just mentioned, was of a long standing among the Chikkasah, and indefatigable in serving his country, without regarding those dangers that would chill the blood of a great many others; and he was perfect master of the Indian language. About a year after this period, he went to Red Shoes' town, and in a summer's night, when he was chatting with our great English friend along-side of his Chikkasah wife, a party of the corrupt savages, that had been sent by the French, shot him through the shoulder, and her dead on the spot.[373] Red Shoes afterwards fared the same fate, by one of his own country-men, for the sake of a French reward, while he was escorting the foresaid gallant trader, and others, from the Chikkasah to his own country.[374] He had the misfortune to be taken very sick on the path, and to lye apart from the camp, according to their usual custom: a Judas, tempted by the high reward of the French for killing him, officiously pretended to take great care of him. While Red Shoes kept his face toward him, the barbarian had such feelings of awe and pity, that he had not power to perpetrate his wicked design; but when he turned his back, then he gave the fatal shot. In a moment the wretch ran off, and though the whole camp were out in an instant, to a considerable breadth, he evaded their pursuit, by darting himself like a snake, into a deep crevice of the [329] earth. The old trader, who was shot through the shoulder, going two years after the death of this our brave red friend, unfortunately a quarter of a mile into the woods, from the spacious clearing of the Chikkasah country, while all the men were on their winter hunt, and having only a tomohawk in his hand, the cowardly French Indians attacked him by surprise, shot him dead, and carried his scalp to Tumbikpe-fort: another white man unarmed, but out of the circle they had suddenly formed, ran for his fire-arms; but he and the traders came too late to overtake the blood-hounds. In this manner, fell those two valuable brave men, by hands that would have trembled to attack them on an equality.

The French having drawn off some towns from the national confederacy, and corrupted them, they began to shew themselves in their proper colours, and publicly offered rewards for our scalps. Of this I was soon informed by two Choktah runners, and in a few days time, I sent them back well pleased. I desired them to inform their head-men, that about the time those days I had marked down to them, were elapsed, I would be in their towns with a cargo, and dispose of it in the way of the French, as they were so earnest in stealing the English people. I charged them with a long relation of every thing I thought might be conducive to the main point in view; which was, the continuance of a fair open trade with a free people, who by treaty were become *allies* of Great Britain; not *subjects,* as our public records often wrongly term them—but people of one fire. As only merit in war-exploits, and flowing language and oratory, gives any of them the least preference above the rest, they can form no other idea of kings and subjects than that of tyrants domineering over base slaves: of course, their various dialects have no names for such.

I left the Chikkasah, and arrived in the Choktah country before the expiration of the broken days, or time we had appointed, with a considerable cargo. By the intended monopoly of our great beloved man, in frightening the Chikkasah traders, there were no English goods in the nation, when I went: and the necessity of the times requiring a liberal distribution, according to my former message, that alone must have fallen heavy upon me under the public faith, without any additional expences. A day before I got there, *Minggo Pushkoosh,* the half-brother of Red Shoes, was returned home from Charles-town, and by him I had the honour of receiving [330] a friendly and polite letter from the governor.[375] His main aim, at this sickened time of Indian trade, was to recover the value of the goods that had been lost in the Choktah country. He recommended one of the traders of the Sphynx-company to my patronage, pressing me to assist him as far as I possibly could, and likewise to endeavour to storm Tumbikpe-fort, promising at the same time, to become answerable to me for all my reasonable charges in that affair. I complied with every tittle of the gentleman's request, as far as I could, without charging him for it in the least. As I had then, the greatest part of my cargo on hand, I lent the other what he stood in need of, that he might regain what his former pride and folly had occasioned to be lost. At that time, powder and ball were so very scarce, that I could have sold to the Choktah, as much as would have produced fifteen hundred buck-skins, yet the exigency was so pressing, I gave them the chief part of my ammunition, though as sparingly as I could—for the French by our pursuit of wrong measures, (already mentioned) and their own policy, had dipped them into a civil war. As I had then no call to sacrifice my private interest for the emolument of the public, without indemnity, so I was not willing to suspect another breach of public faith. Red Shoes' brother came up freighted with plenty of courtly promises, and for his own security he was not backward in relating them to his brethren; otherwise, they would have killed both him and me; which would have reconciled them to the French, who a few days before, had proposed our massacre by a long formal message to them, as they afterwards informed me. I plainly saw their minds were unfixed, for their civil war proved very sharp. *Minggo Pushkoosh* and several head-men conducted me from town to town, to the crowd of the seven lower towns, which lie next to New Orleans: but they took proper care to make our stages short enough, that I might have the honour to converse with all their beloved men and chief warriors, and have the favour to give them plenty of presents, in return for so great an obligation. The Indian headmen deem it a trifle to go hundreds of miles, on such a gladsome errand; and very few of them are slow in honouring the traders with a visit, and a long, rapid, poetic speech. They will come several miles to dispose of a deer-skin.

When I arrived at the thick settlement of these lower towns, I began to imagine they had opened a communication with their subterranean brethren of Nanne Yah;[376] I was honoured with the company of a greater number [331] of red chiefs of war, and old beloved men, than probably ever appeared in imperial Rome. They in a very friendly manner, tied plenty of bead-garters round my neck, arms, and legs, and decorated me, *a la mode America.* I did myself the honour to fit them out with silver arm-plates, gorgets, wrist-plates, ear-bobs, &c. &c. which they kindly received, and protested they would never part with them, for the sake of the giver. However, by all my persuasions, they would not undertake to storm Tumbikpe-fort, though I offered to accompany them, and put them in a sure way of carrying it. They told me I was mad, for the roaring of the cannon was as dreadful as the sharpest thunder, and that the French with one of their great balls would tear me in pieces, as soon as I appeared in view.

While they declined a French war, their own civil war became bitter beyond expression. They frequently engaged, one party against the other, in the open fields: when our friends had fired away all their ammunition, they took to their hiccory-bows and barbed arrows, and rushed on the opposite party, with their bare tomohawks, like the most desperate veterans, regardless of life. They did not seem to regard dying so much, as the genteel appearance they made when they took the open field, on purpose to kill or be killed. They used to tell the English traders they were going on such a day to fight, or die for them, and earnestly importuned them for a Stroud blanket, or white shirt a-piece, that they might make a genteel appearance in English cloth, when they died. It was not safe to refuse them, their minds were so distracted by the desperate situation of their affairs; for as they were very scarce of ammunition, the French wisely headed their friend-party, with small cannon, battered down the others stockaded-forts, and in the end reduced them to the necessity of a coalition. These evils were occasioned merely by the avarice and madness of those I have stiled the Sphynx-Company.

At this dangerous time, the small-pox also was by some unknown means conveyed into the Choktah country, from below: and it depopulated them as much as the civil war had done.[377] The Choktah who escorted me into the Chikkasah nation, were infected with that malady in the woods, and soon spread it among others; these, a little time after, among the Muskohge, who were in company with me, on our way to Charles-town. I unluckily had [332] the honour to receive from the Governor, another polite letter, dated September 17th, anno 1749, citing me, under the great seal of the province, to come down with a party of Indians, as I had given his excellency notice of their desire of paying a friendly visit to South Carolina. And having purchased and redeemed three French captives which the Chikkasah had taken in war, under their leader *Pa-Yah-Matahah,* I now bestowed them on him, to enable him to make a flourishing entrance into Charles-town, after the manner of their American triumphs. He was very kind to them, though their manners were as savage as his own: excepting a few beads they used to count, with a small silver cross fastened to the top of them, they had nothing to distinguish them, and were ignorant of every point of Christianity. I set off with above twenty warriors, and a few women, along with the aforesaid war-leader, for Charles-town. As the French kept a watchful eye on my conduct, and the commanding officers of Tumbikpe garrison in the Choktah, and the Alebahma in the Muskohge country kept a continual communication with each other, the former equipped a party of their Choktah to retake the French captives by force, if we did not previously deliver them to a French party of the Muskohge, who were sent by the latter as in the name of the whole nation, though falsely, to terrify us into a compliance. We had to pass through the Muskohge country in our way to the British settlements; and though the French were at a great distance, yet they planned their schemes with consummate wisdom: for the two companies met at the time appointed, from two opposite courses of about a hundred and fifty miles apart, on the most difficult pass from Charles-town to the Missisipi, where the path ran through a swamp of ten miles, between high mountains; which were impassable in any other place for a great distance, on either side.[378] Here, the Muskohge left the Choktah company, and met us within half-a-day's march of their advantageous camping place. The foremost of our party had almost fired on those Muskohge who were a-head of the rest; but, as soon as they saw their white emblems of peace, they forebore, and we joined company. As soon as I heard them tell their errand, I sent out three warriors to reconnoitre the place, lest we should unawares be surrounded by another party of them; but there was no ambuscade. The Muskohge leader was called by the traders, "the Lieutenant," and had been a steady friend to their interest, till by our usual mismanagement in Indian affairs, he became [333] entirely devoted to the French; his behaviour was confident, and his address artful.[379]

The red ambassador spoke much of the kindly disposition of the French to such of his countrymen as were poor, and of their generous protection to the whole; contrasted with the ambitious views of the English, who were not content with their deer-skins and beaver, but coveted their lands. He said, "the Muskohge were sorry and surprised that their old friends the Chikkasah, in concert with a mad Englishman, should seduce their warriors to join with them to spill the blood of their French beloved friends, when they were by national consent, only to revenge crying blood against the Aquahpah; and that the former would be ashamed to allow the latter to carry those captives, who were their friends, through their nation to Charles-town. But, said he, as the Muskohge are desirous always to shake hands with the Chikkasah, the head-men have sent me in their name, to request you *Pa-Yah-Matahah* and other beloved warriors, to deliver to me those unfortunate prisoners, as a full proof you are desirous of tying fast the old friend-knot, which you have loosed in some measure." In this manner, the red ambassador of the dangerous Alebahma French captain flourished away and waited for a favourable answer, according to the confident hopes his employer had taught him to entertain, by the strong motive of self-interest.

But though the daring Chikkasah leader, and each of us, according to custom were silent, during the recital of the disagreeable harangue, only by stern-speaking countenances, *Pa-Yah-Matahah* replied, "O you Muskohge corrupted chieftain, who are degenerated so low as to become a strong-mouthed friend of the French, whose tongues are known of a long time, to be forked like those of the dangerous snakes; your speech has run through my ears, like the noise of a threatening high wind, which attacks the traveller as soon as he climbs to the top of a rugged steep mountain: though as he came along, the air was scarcely favourable enough for him to breathe in. You speak highly in praise of the French; and so do the baser sort of the Choktah, because every year they receive presents to make their lying mouths strong. That empty sounding kettle, fastened at the top of your bundle along side of you, I know to be French, and a true picture both of their messages, and methods of sending them. The [334] other things it contains, I guess, are of the same forked-tongued family; for if your speech had come from your own heart, it must have been straighter. What can be more crooked than it now is? Though I have no occasion to make any reply to your unjust complaints against the English people, as their chieftain, my friend, has his ears open, and can easily confute all you said against his people and himself; yet to prevent any needless delay on our day's march, I shall give as full an answer to your speech, as the short time we can stay here will allow. Since the time the English first shaked hands with you, have not they always held you fast by the arm, close to their heart, contrary to the good liking of your favourite French? And had they not helped you with a constant supply of every thing you stood in need of, in what manner could you have lived at home? Besides, how could you have secured your land from being spoiled by the many friendly red people of the French, issuing from the cold north? Only for their brotherly help, the artful and covetous French, by the weight of presents and the skill of their forked tongues, would before now, have set you to war against each other, in the very same manner they have done by the Choktah; and when by long and sharp struggles, you had greatly weakened yourselves, they by the assistance of their northern red friends, would have served you in the very same manner, their lying mouths, from their own guilty hearts, have taught you so un-

justly and shamefully to repeat of the English. You have openly acknowledged your base ingratitude to your best and old steady friends, who, I
believe, could damage you as much as they have befriended you, if you provoke them to it. Allowing the speech you have uttered with your mouth to
be true, that you are sent by all the red chieftains of your Muskohge people,
were your hearts so weak as to imagine it could any way frighten the Chikkasah? Ye well know, the ugly yellow French have proved most bitter enemies to us, ever since we disappointed them in their spiteful design of inslaving and murdering our poor, defenceless, and inoffensive red brethren,
the Nahchee, on the banks of the Meshesheepe water-path.[380] Ye may love
them, if it seems good to your hearts; your example that way shall have no
weight with us. We are born and bred in a state of war with them: and
though we have lost the greater part of our people, chiefly through the
mean spirit of their red hirelings, who were continually stealing our people
for the sake of a reward; yet they feelingly know we beat them, and their
employers, in every public engagement. We are the same people, and we
shall certainly live and die, in [335] such a manner as not to sully the ancient character of our warlike fore-fathers. As the French constantly employed their red people in acts of enmity against our English traders, as well
as us,—my beloved friend, standing there before you, complained of it to
the *Goweno-Minggo* in Charles-town, (the Governor of South-Carolina) and
he gave him *Hoolbo Hooreso Paraska Orehtoopa,* (their method of expressing
our provincial seal, for *hoolbo* signifies a picture, *hooreso* marked, or painted,
paraska made bread of, and *oretoopa* beloved, or of high note or power,) I and
my warriors gladly shaked hands with his speech; and so did those of your
own country, who assured us, they always scorned to be servants to the
crafty lying French. At their own desire, our old beloved men crowned them
warriors, in the most public and solemn manner. They were free either to
shut or open their ears to the English beloved speech. And why should we
not be as free to go to war against our old enemies, as you are against yours?
We are your friends by treaty; but we scorn a mean compliance to any demand, that would cast a disgrace on our national character. You have no right
to demand of me those ugly French prisoners. We took them in war, at the
risque of blood: and at home in our national council, we firmly agreed not
to part with any of them, in a tame manner, till we got to Charles-town. If
the Muskohge are as desirous as we, to continue to hold each other firmly
by the hand, we shall never loose the friend-knot: we believe such a tie is
equally profitable to each of us, and hope to continue it, to the latest times."

When the French ambassador found he must fail in his chief aim, he
with a very submissive tone, requested the Chikkasah war-leader to give
him a token, whereby he might get the other captives who were left at
home: but as they usually deny with modesty, he told him, he could not

advise him to take the trouble to go there, as he believed the head-men had kept them behind on purpose that they should be burnt at the stake, if any mischance befell him and his warriors, before they returned home, on account of his French prisoners. Finding that his threats and entreaties both proved ineffectual, he was obliged to acquiesce. Soon after, we set off, and he and his chagrined mercenaries quietly took up their travelling bundles, and followed us.

On that day's march, a little before we entered the long swamp, all our Chikkasah friends staid behind, killing and cutting up buffalo:[381] [336] By this means, I was a considerable way before the pack-horses, when we entered into that winding and difficult pass, which was a continued thicket. After riding about a mile, I discovered the fresh tracks of three Indians. I went back, put the white people on their guard, gave my horse and sword to a corpulent member of the Sphynx-company, and set off a-head, shunning the path in such places where the savages were most likely to post themselves. Now and then I put up the whoop on different sides of the path, both to secure myself and intimidate the opposite scout-party; otherwise, I might have paid dear for it, as I saw from a rising point, the canes where they were passing, to shake. I became more cautious, and they more fearful of being inclosed by our party. They ran off to their camp, and speedily from thence up the craggy rocks, as their tracks testified. Their lurking place was as artfully chosen, as a wolf could have fixed on his den. When our friendly Indians came to our camp, it was too late to give chase: they only viewed their tracks. At night, the Chikkasah war-leader gave out a very enlivening war speech, well adapted to the circumstances of time and place, and each of us lay in the woodland-form of a war-camp. As we were on our guard, the enemy did not think it consistent with their safety to attack us— ambuscading is their favourite plan of operation. The next day by agreement, the Indians led the van, and I brought up the rear with the French prisoners. A short way from our camp, there were steep rocks, very difficult for loaded horses to rear and ascend. Most of them had the good fortune to get safe up, but some which I escorted, tumbled backwards; this detained us so long, that the van, gained near three miles upon us. I posted myself on the top of one of the rocks, as a centinel to prevent our being surprised by the Choktah, and discovered them crawling on the ground behind trees, a considerable way off, on the side of a steep mountain, opposite to us. I immediately put up the war whoop, and told a young man with me the occasion of it; but he being fatigued and vexed with his sharp exercise, on account of the horses, only cursed them, and said, we were warriors, and would fight them, if they durst come near enough. As I was cool, I helped and hastened him off: in the mean while, I cautioned the captives against attempting to fly to the enemy in case they attacked us, as their lives should certainly pay for it—and they promised they would not. We at last set off, and met with no interruption: the enemy having a sharp [337] dread of our party ahead, who would have soon ran back to our assistance, had they attacked us—About an hour after our company, we got to camp. The Choktah at night came down from the mountains, and creeped after us. Our camp was pitched on very convenient ground, and as they could not surprise us, they only viewed at a proper distance, and retired. But they used an artful stratagem, to draw some of us into their treacherous snares; for they stole one of the bell horses, and led it away to a place near their den, which was about a mile below us, in a thicket of reeds, where the creek formed a semi-circle. This horse was a favourite with the gallant and active young man I had escorted the day before to camp.

As he was of a chearful and happy temper, the people were much surprised to find him at night peevish and querulous, contrary to every part of his past conduct; and though he delighted in arms, and carried them constantly when he went from camp, yet he went out without any this night, though I pressed him to take them. In less than an hour, he returned safe, but confused and dejected. When he sat down, he drooped his head on his hands, which were placed on his knees, and said, the enemy were lurking, and that we should soon be attacked, and some of us killed. As I pitied the state of his mind, I only told him, that yesterday, he and I knew the French savages were watching to take an advantage of us; but for his satisfaction I would take a sweep, on foot, while the Chikkasah painted themselves, according to their war-custom when they expect to engage an enemy. I went out with my gun, pouch, and belt-pistols, and within two hundred yards of the camp, discovered the enemies tracks; they had passed over a boggy place of the creek, upon an old hurricane-tree. I proceeded with the utmost caution, posting myself now and then behind large trees, and looking out sharply lest I should fall into an ambuscade, which the Choktah are cunning artists in forming. In this manner I marched for three quarters of an hour, and then took to high ground, a little above the enemies camp, in order to return for help to attack them. But the aforesaid brave youth, led on by his ill genius, at this time mounted a fiery horse, which soon ran into the ambuscade, where they shot him with a bullet in his breast, and another entered a little below the heart. The horse wheeled round in an instant, and sprung off, but in pitching over a large fallen tree, the unfortunate rider, by reason of his mortal wounds, [338] fell off, a victim to the barbarians. One of them soon struck a tomohawk into his head, just between his eyes, and jerked off a piece of scalp about the bigness of a dollar—they took also his Indian breeches, and an handkerchief he had on his head, and immediately flew through a thicket of briars, to secure their retreat. When they fired their two guns, I immediately gave the shrill war-whoop, which was resounded by one of the Chikkasah that had been out a hunting from the camp. They instantly set off full speed, naked, except their Indian breeches and maccasenes. I put myself in the same flying trim, on the enemies firing; we soon came to the tragical spot, but without stopping, we took their tracks, gave chase, and continued it a great way: unluckily, as we were running down a steep hill, they discovered us from the top of another, and soon dispersed themselves; by which means, not being able to discover one track of those foxes on the hard hilly ground, we were obliged to give over the chace, and returned to camp. We buried our friend, by fixing in a regular manner a large pile of great logs for the corpse, with big tough sapplings bent over it, and on each side, thrust deep into the ground, to secure it from the wild beasts. Though the whole camp at first imagined the enemy had killed me and captivated the other, yet the warriors did not shew the least emotion of gladness, nor even my favourite friend, the war-leader, when they first saw me safe: but the women received me with tears of joy. I mention this to shew the force of education and habit—those who are used to scenes of war and blood, become obdurate and are lost to all the tender feelings of nature; while they, whose employment it is to mourn for their dead, are susceptible of the tender impressions they were orginally endued with by Deity.

As the French frequently had been great sufferers by the Chikkasah, ever since the year 1730, necessity obliged them to bear their losses with patience, till they could get them revenged by the friendly hands of their red mercenaries. As soon as they had ingratiated themselves into the affections of all those Indians who were incorporated among the Muskohge, and had settled them near the Alebahma-garrison; and other towns, besides headmen, in sundry parts of the nation, being devoted to their service, they imagined they had now interest enough to get several of those warriors killed, who had joined the Chikkasah against their people over the Missisippi. But the old head-men of the Muskohge convened together, [339] and agreed to send a peremptory message to the French, ordering them, forthwith, to desist from their bloody politics, otherwise the river should carry their blood down to Mobille, and tell that garrison, their own treachery was the sole occasion of it, by mischievously endeavouring to foment a civil war between them, as they boasted they had done among the foolish Choktah. With much regret they laid aside their scheme, and were forced openly to wipe away the memory of every thing which had before given them offence; and to include all indiscriminately in the treaty of friendship, as all had only one fire. This proved a mortifying stroke to the French on sundry accounts: and during the continuance of this distracted scene, if any British governor of capacity and public spirit, had properly exerted himself, they must have withdrawn to Mobille, without any possibility of ever returning. For the enmity would soon have advanced to a most implacable hatred, as in the case of the Chikkasah and French: but such a conduct was incompatible with the private views of some among us.

As the small-pox broke out in our camp, when we got nigh to the Muskohge country, and detained the Indians there till they recovered, I set off without them for Charles-town. By the benefit of the air, and their drinking a strong decoction of hot roots, they all recovered. A Choktah warrior of Yahshoo-town,[382] humorously told me afterwards, that *ookka hoomeh,* "the bitter waters," meaning spirituous liquors, cured some people, while it killed others. He, by the advice of one of the English traders, administered it in pretty good doses to seven of his children in the small-pox, which kept out the corrupt humour, and in a short time perfectly cured each of them, he said, without the least appearance of any dangerous symptoms; whereas the disorder proved very mortal to the young people in the neighbourhood, who pursued a different course of physic. As most of the Indian traders are devotees of Bacchus, their materia medica consists of spirituous liquors, compounded with strong herbs and roots, of which they commonly have a good knowledge: and I have observed those who have left off the trade, and reside in the British settlements, to give their negroes for an anti-venereal, a large dose of old Jamaica and qualified mercury mixt together,—which, they say, the blacks cheerfully drink, without making a wry face, contrary to their usage [340] with every other kind of physic; and it is affirmed, that by this prescription, they soon get well.

The small pox with which the upper towns of the Muskohge were infected, was of the confluent sort, and it would have greatly depopulated them, if the officious advice of some among us, for all the other towns to cut off every kind of communication with them, on the penalty of death to any delinquent, had not been given and pursued. They accordingly posted centinels at proper places, with strict orders to kill such, as the most dangerous of all enemies: and these cautious measures produced the desired effect. And by the mean mediation of several of our principal traders, joined with the interest of their red friends, the commandant of the Alebahma fort, prevailed at last on the Chikkasah chieftain to take the three French prisoners to him, as he would pay him to his own satisfaction, give him presents, and drink with him as a friend, who had buried the bloody tomohawk deep in the ground. They were delivered up; and by that means the French were enabled to discourage those Muskohge warriors, who had joined the Chikkasah in the aforesaid acts of hostility against the Missisippi inhabitants.[383] In about the space of three months from the time the Chikkasah left their own country with me, they arrived at the late New-Windsor garrison, the western barrier of South-Carolina, and beautifully situated on a high commanding bank of the pleasant meandering Savanah river; so termed on account of the Shawano Indians having formerly lived there, till by our foolish measures, they were forced to withdraw northward in defence of their freedom.

At the request of the governor and council I rode there, to accompany our Chikkasah friends to Charles-town, where, I believe, on my account, they met with a very cold reception: for as something I wrote to the two gentlemen who fitted out, and sustained the loss of the Sphynx-company, had been inserted in the "modest reply to his Excellency the Governor," formerly mentioned, in order to obtain bills of exchange on Great Britain, I was now become the great object of his displeasure, and of a certain sett, who are known to patronise any persons if they chance to be born in the same corner of the world with themselves.[384] The Chikkasah had a very ungracious audience: On account [341] of the excessive modesty of this warlike people, their chieftain gave out a short oration, without hinting in the most distant manner, at any difficulties they underwent, by reason of their strong attachment to the British Americans,—concluding, that as the English beloved men were endowed with a surprising gift of expressing a great deal in few words, long speeches would be troublesome to them. He intended to have spoken afterwards of the Choktah affairs, and that I was a great sufferer by them, without any just retribution, and accordingly was very desirous of a second public interview; but our cunning beloved man artfully declined it, though they staid as late as the middle of April. It was a custom with the colony of South-Carolina towards those Indians who came on a friendly visit, to allow them now and then a tolerable quantity of spirituous liquors, to cheer their hearts, after their long journey; but, if I am not mistaken, those I accompanied, had not a drop, except at my cost. And when the Governor gave them, at the entrance of the council-chamber, some trifling presents, he hurried them off with such an air as vexed them to the heart; which was aggravated by his earnestly pointing at a noted war-leader, and myself, with an angry countenance, swearing that Indian had been lately down from Savanah, and received presents. They had so much spirit that they would not on any account have accepted his presents, but for my persuasions. As for myself, I could not forbear saying, honour compelled me as solemnly to declare that his assertion was not true, and that I had often given more to the Choktah at one time, than he had ever given to the Chikkasah, in order to rivet their enmity against the French of Louisiana, and thereby open a lasting trade with them, from which I was unfairly excluded, on account of a friendly monopoly, granted by him for a certain end to mere strangers. My words seemed to lie pretty sharp upon him, and I suppose contributed not a little to the uncourtly leave he took of our gallant, and faithful old friends. Soon after, at the request of the Governor and council however, I accompanied them the first day's march, on their way

home from Charles-town: they had no public order of credit for their needful travelling charges, though I sollicited his Excellency and the council to
grant them one, according to the ancient, hospitable, and wise custom of
South-Carolina, to all Indians who paid them a friendly visit, whose journey
was far shorter, were often uninvited, and of much less service, than the
Chikkasah to the British interest. As their horses were [342] very poor, I
told the Governor they could travel only at a slow pace, and as the wild
game was scarce in our settlements, hunger, and resentment for their unkind
usage, would probably tempt them to kill the planters stock, which might
produce bad consequences, and ought to be cautiously guarded against; but
I was an unfortunate solicitor.

With a flow of contrary passions I took my leave of our gallant Chikkasah friends. I viewed them with a tender eye, and revolved in my mind
the fatigues, difficulties, and dangers, they had cheerfully undergone, to
testify the intense affection they bore to the British Americans,—with the
ill treatment they had received from our chief magistrate, on account of
his own disappointments, and sharp-felt censures, for some supposed mismanagement, or illicit measures in trade. He is reported to have been no
way churlish to several of the dastardly Choktah, notwithstanding his un-
precedented and unkind treatment of our warlike Chikkasah—two hundred of which would attack five hundred of the others, and defeat them
with little loss. Their martial bravery has often testified this against enemies
even of a greater spirit.

Not long after the Chikkasah returned homeward, I advertised in the
weekly paper, that as I intended to leave Charles-town in a short time, I was
ready and willing to answer any of the legislative body such questions as
they might be pleased to propose to me concerning our Indian affairs, before the expiration of such a time; and that if his Excellency desired my
attendance, and either notified it in writing, or by a proper officer, I might
be found at my old lodgings.[385] On the evening of the very last day I had
proposed to stay, he sent me a peremptory written order to attend that
night, on public business, concerning Indian affairs; I punctually obeyed,
with respect to both time and place. He was now in a dilemma, by reason
of his (supposed) self-interested conduct concerning the Choktah trade,
which occasioned the aforesaid *modest reply,* that arraigned his proceedings
with severity and plainness. As I came down with the Indians, and was detained by his Excellency, under the great seal of the province, till this period,
April 1750, I had just reason to expect that good faith would have been kept
with me—that I should have been paid according to promise, at least for all
the goods I gave the Indians, by virtue thereof; and have had a just compensation for the great expenses I [343] was at in serving the government;—but

except the trifling sum of four pounds sterling, when I was setting off for the Indian country, I never received one farthing of the public money, for my very expensive, faithful, and difficult services.

In most of our American colonies, there yet remain a few of the natives, who formerly inhabited those extensive countries: and as they were friendly to us, and serviceable to our interests, the wisdom and virtue of our legislature secured them from being injured by the neighbouring nations. The French strictly pursued the same method, deeming such to be more useful than any others on alarming occasions. We called them "Parched-corn-Indians," because they chiefly use it for bread, are civilized, and live mostly by planting.[386] As they had no connection with the Indian nations, and were desirous of living peaceable under the British protection, none could have any just plea to kill or inslave them. But the grasping plan of the French required those dangerous scout-parties, as they termed them, to be removed out of the way; and the dormant conduct of the South-Carolina chief, gave them an opportunity to effect that part of their design; though timely notice, even years before, had been given by the Cheerake traders, that the French priests were poisoning the minds of those Indians against us, who live among the Apalahche mountains, and were endeavouring to reconcile them to all the various nations of the Missisippi and Canada savages; and that there was the greatest probability they would accomplish their dangerous plan, unless we soon took proper measures to prevent it. The informers had ill names and resentment for their news, and the assembly was charged with mispending their time, in taking notice of the wild incoherent reports of illiterate obscure persons. But it afterwards appeared, that according to their testimony, the interest and security of South-Carolina were in great danger. By the diligence of the French, their Indians entered into a treaty of friendship with the Cheerake: and their country became the rendezvous of the red pupils of the black Jesuits. Hence they ravaged South-Carolina, beginning at the frontier weak settlements, and gradually advanced through the country, for the space of eight years, destroying the live stock, insulting, frightening, wounding, and sometimes killing the inhabitants, burning their houses, carrying away their slaves, and committing every kind of devastation, till they proceeded so low as within thirty miles of Charles-town. The sufferers often exhibited their complaints, in the most pathetic and public manner; and [344] the whole country felt the ill effects of the late overbearing and negligent conduct. False colouring could serve no longer, and a few inconsiderable parties were sent out—but not finding any enemy, they were in a few months disbanded, and peaceable accounts were again sent home.

Our Settlement-Indians were at this time closely hunted, many were killed, and others carried off. A worthy gentleman, G. H. Esq; who lived at the Conggarees, suffered much on the occasion—he was employed to go to the Cheerake country, in quest of valuable minerals, in company with an Indian commissioner:[387]—in one of their middle towns, he retook some of our Settlement-Indians from the Canada-savages, whom a little before they had captivated and carried off from South-Carolina in triumph. While they were beating the drum, singing, dancing, and pouring the utmost contempt on the English name, honour prompted him to prefer the public credit to his own safety. By the earnest mediation of one of the traders, the head-men of the town consented to be neutral in the affair, and act as impartial friends to both parties. He then, with Col. F—x,[388] and some of the traders, went in a warlike gallant manner, and regardless of the savages threats, took and brought to a trader's house, our captivated friends:—they stood all night on their arms, and at a convenient interval, supplied those whom they had liberated, with necessaries to carry them to our settlements, where their trusty heels soon carried them safe. The gallant behaviour of those gentlemen gained the applause of the Cheerake—and each soon returned in safety, without any interruption, to their respective homes, where I wish they had ever after continued. But Mr. G. H. having considerably engaged himself in trade with the Katahba Indians, set off afterwards in company with an half-bred Indian of that nation, the favourite son of Mr. T. B. a famous old trader: in their way to the Katahba,[389] they were intercepted, and taken by some of the very savages who had threatened him among the Cheerake, when he released our domestic Indians. The government of South-Carolina was soon informed of the unhappy affair: and they dispatched a friendly embassy to the lower towns of the Cheerake, requesting them to intercept and retake the prisoners, if they passed near their country, and offered a considerable reward. Our friends were carried a little to the northward of the Cheerake nation, where their captors camped several days, and the Cheerake held with them an open friendly intercourse, as in despite to the English. The head men of the lower towns, not only stopped the traders and their red friends from going to rescue them, [345] but likewise threatened them for their generous intention. The savages, instead of keeping a due northern course homeward, took a large compass north-west, by the side of the Cheerake mountains, being afraid of a pursuit from the Katahba Indians. They marched fast with their two captives, to secure their retreat till they got within the bounds of the French treaty of peace, and then steered a due northern course, continuing it till they got nigh to their respective countries, where they parted in two bodies, and each took one of the prisoners with them. But as travelling so great a way in the heat of summer, was what Mr. G. H. was unaccustomed to, he was so much overcome by fatigue and sickness, that for several days before, he could not possibly walk. He then requested them to put him out of his misery, but they would not; for they reckoned his civil language to them proceeded from bodily pains, and from a martial spirit, which they regard. They consented to carry him on a bier, which they did both with care and tenderness. But on parting with his companion, he refused absolutely to proceed any farther with them, when they tomohawked him, just as his parted friend was out of the hearing of it. The last afterwards got home, and told us this melancholy exit of our worthy and much-lamented friend—who died as he lived, always despising life, when it was to be preserved only in a state of slavery. Though he was thus lost to his family and the community, by a manly performance of the duties of his office, in which he engaged by the pressing entreaties of the Governor, yet his widow was treated ungenerously and basely, as was Capt. J. P. at the Conggarees.[390]—But there would be no end, if we were to enter into particulars of court policy, and government honor and gratitude.

If our watch-men had not been quite remiss, they would have at least opposed the French emissaries on their first approach to our colonies, and have protected our valuable civilized Indians; for our negroes were afraid to run away, lest they should fall into their hands. The scheming French knew of what importance they were to us, and therefore they employed their red friends to extirpate them. And while those remote savages of Missisippi and Canada were pretending to seek the revenge of some old grievance, they wounded us at the same time in two very material points,—in getting a thorough knowledge of the situation of our most valuable, but weak southern colonies, and thus could strike us the [346] deeper,—and in destroying such of our inhabitants, as were likely to prove the greatest check to their intended future depredations. By our own misconduct, we twice lost the Shawano Indians; who have since proved very hurtful to our colonies in general. When the French employed them to weaken South-Carolina, a small company of them were surrounded and taken in a remote house of the lower settlements: and though they ought to have been instantly put to death, in return for their frequent barbarities to our people, yet they were conveyed to prison, confined a considerable time, and then discharged, to the great loss of many innocent lives. For as the Indians reckon imprisonment to be inslaving them, they never forgive such treatment; and as soon as these got clear, they left bloody traces of their vindictive tempers, as they passed along. About this time, a large company of French savages came from the head-streams of Monongahela-river to the Cheerake, and from thence were guided by one of them to where our settlement-Indians resided. They went to a small town of the *Euhchee,* about twelve miles below Savanah-town, and two below Silver-bluff, where G. G. Esq; lives,[391] and there watched like wolves, till by the mens making a day's hunt, they found an opportunity to kill the women and children. Immediately after which, they scouted off different ways, some through Savanah-river, which is about

200 yards broad; and others to the hunting place, both for their own security, and to give the alarm: We had on this occasion, a striking instance of
the tender affection of the Indian women to their children, for all those who
escaped, carried off their little ones. The men, by the alarming signal of the
shrill-sounding war-cry, soon joined, ran home, and without staying to view
the bloody tragedy, instantly took the enemies tracks, and eagerly gave
chase. To avoid the dreaded pursuit, the Cheerake guide led the French mercenaries a northern course, as far as the thick woods extended, which was
about fifteen miles from the place of their murders. From thence they
shifted toward the north-west, and were stretching away about 10 miles to
the north of Augusta, for Ninety-Six, which lay in a direct line to the lower
towns of the Cheerake; when unluckily for them, just as they were entering
into the open, and long-continued pine-barren, they were discovered by one
of our hunting white men, who was mounted on an excellent white horse,
and therefore a fine mark to be shot, which they would have done for their
own security, only he outstripped them, and kept in their back-tracks,
to trace them to their theatre of blood—their posture and countenances
plainly told him what they had done, on [347] some of our barriers. He had
not proceeded far, when he met the enraged Euhchee, on the hot pursuit.
He told them their course, and that their number was twenty-six. In running about twelve miles farther, they came in sight of the objects of their
hatred and rage: presently, they ran on each side of them, engaged them
closely, and killed several. Those who escaped, were forced to throw away
nine guns, (they had taken from some of our people) and almost every
thing, even their light breeches, to save their lives. They were so exceedingly terrified, lest the enraged pursuers should continue the chase, that they
passed wide of our then weak settlement of Ninety-Six, and kept on day
and night, till they got near to their conductor's mountainous country. This
was in the beginning of May 1750: and in our Indian-trading way, we say
that, when the heat of the new year enables the snakes to crawl out of their
lurking holes, the savages are equally moved to turn out to do mischief.
Many have experimentally felt the truth of this remark.

I had at this time occasion to go to the Cheerake country; and happened to have a brave chearful companion, Mr. H. F. of Ninety-Six settlement. We had taken a hearty draught of punch, about ten miles from
Keeohwhee-town,[392] opposite to which the late Fort-Prince-George stood,
and were proceeding along, when we discovered the fresh tracks of Indians
in the path, who were gone a-head. As we could not reasonably have the
least suspicion of their being enemies, we rode quite carelessly: but they
proved to be the above-mentioned Monongahela-Indians. Their watchfulness, and our singing, with the noise of our horses feet, made them hear us
before they could possibly see us,—when they suddenly posted themselves

off the path, behind some trees, just in the valley of Six-mile-creek, in order to revenge their loss by the Euhchee, which they ascribed to the information of the white man. But their Cheerake guide prevented them from
attempting it, by telling them, that as his country was not at war with us,
his life must pay for it, if they chanced to kill either of us; and as we were
fresh and well-armed, they might be sure we would fight them so successfully, as at least one of us should escape and alarm the towns: with this caution they forbore the hazardous attempt. They squatted, and kept close therefore, so as we did not see one of them; and we suspected no danger. By the
discontinuance of their tracks, we soon knew we had passed them: but, just
when we had hidden two cags of [348] rum, about two miles from the
town, four of them appeared, unarmed, stark naked, and torn by the thickets.
When we discovered them, we concluded they had been below on mischief.
If we had not been so nigh the town, my companion would have fired at
them. We went into the town, and the traders there soon informed us of
their cowardly design.

We went as far as the mid-settlements, and found most of the towns
much disaffected to us, and in a fluctuating situation, through the artifice of
the French. In a few days we returned, but found they had blocked up all
the trading paths, to prevent our traders from making their escape. Just as
we descended a small mountain, and were about to ascend a very steep one,
a hundred yards before us, which was the first of the Apalahche, or blue
ridge of mountains, a large company of the lower town Indians started out
from the sloping rocks, on the north side of the path, a little behind us. As
they were naked except their breech-cloth, were painted red and black, and
accoutered every way like enemies, I bid my companion leave the luggage-
horses and follow me: but as he left his arms at the lower town, and was not
accustomed to such surprises, it shocked him, till they ran down upon him.
On this I turned back, and stood on my arms, expecting they would have
fired upon us. However, they proposed some questions, which I answered, as
to where we had been, and were going, and that we were not any of their
traders. Had it been otherwise, the dispute would have been dangerous. We
got over the mountain, and safe to Tymahse; here we rested two nights, and
found the people distracted for mischief, to which the many causes before
mentioned prompted them. The governor, in less than a month after this
period, had the strongest confirmation of the ill intention of these savages
and their allies. Many expresses[393] with intelligence I sent, but the news was
pocketed, and my services traduced—because I would not assist the prime
magistrate in a bad cause, he and his humble servants depreciated the long
series of public services I had faithfully performed, and called them mere
accidental trifles; contrary to his former acknowledgments, both verbal and
in writing.[394] The French, however, had a different opinion of my services;

they were so well acquainted with the great damages I had done to them, and feared others I might occasion, as to confine me a close prisoner for a fortnight when I went to the Alebahma-garrison, in [349] the Muskohge country. They were fully resolved to have sent me down to Mobille or New Orleans, as a capital criminal, to be hanged for having abetted the Muskohge, Chikkasah, and Choktah, to shed a torrent of their christian blood; though I had only retaliated upon them, the long train of blood they had years before wantonly spilled. They wanted to have confronted me with the French prisoners I formerly mentioned, and with the Long Lieutenant, whom we met two days before the Choktah killed one of our people below *Book'pharaah,* or the long swamp. I was well assured, he was to have gone down to be baptized, and so become a good West-Florida-French christian, in order to condemn me, the poor[395] bloody heretic. I saw him, and they had by this time taught him to count beads; but I doubted not of being able to extricate myself some way or other. They appointed double centries over me, for some days before I was to be sent down in the French king's large boat. They were strictly charged against laying down their weapons, or suffering any hostile thing to be in the place where I was kept, as they deemed me capable of any mischief. I was not indeed locked up, only at night, lest it should give umbrage to our friendly Indians, but I was to have been put in irons, as soon as the boat passed the Indian towns, that lay two miles below the fort, in the forks of the Koosah and Okwhuske rivers.[396] About an hour before we were to set off by water, I escaped from them by land: and though they had horses near at hand, and a corrupt town of savages settled within 150 yards of the garrison, yet under those disadvantages, besides heavy rains that loosened the ground the very night before, I took through the middle of the low land covered with briers, at full speed. I heard the French clattering on horse-back along the path, a great way to my left hand, and the howling savages pursuing my tracks with careful steps, but my usual good fortune enabled me to leave them far enough behind, on a needless pursuit. As they had made my arms prisoners, I allowed them without the least regret to carry down my horses, clothes, &c. and punish them by proxy, in the manner they intended to have served the owner, for his faithful services to his country.[397]

While Governor G— presided in South-Carolina, it was needless to apply for a payment of the large debt the government owed me: but on his being succeeded by his Excellency W. H. L. Esq;[398] I imagined this a [350] favourable time to make my address. This worthy patriot had been well informed, by several Indian trading merchants of eminent character, of the expensive, difficult, and faithful services I had cheerfully done my country, to the amount of above one thousand pounds sterling on the public faith, and of the ungenerous returns I had received: he according to his natural kindness and humanity, promised to assist me. I then laid my case, with the well-known and important facts, before the members of the house of assembly in Charles-town; and when they convened, presented a memorial to the legislative body.[399] But several of the country representatives happened to be absent; and as the governor could not be reasonably expected in a short time, to purify the infected air which had prevailed in that house for fourteen years, a majority of the members had evidently determined not to alleviate my long complaint of grievances. To invalidate its force, they objected, that my claim was old; but did not attempt to prove the least tittle of what I exhibited to them to be false; they knew they could not. After a long and warm debate, when my secret enemies observed the clerk of the house was drawing near to the conclusion of my memorial, they seized on a couple of unfortunate monosyllables. I had said, that "the Indian Choktah had a great many *fine* promises;" the word *fine* was put to the torture, as reflecting on the very fine-promising gentleman. And in another sentence, I mentioned the time his excellency the late Governor of South-Carolina did me the honour to write me a very *smooth* artful letter, by virtue of which I went all the way to Charles-town, &c. The word *smooth,* so highly ruffled the smooth tempers of those gentlemen, that they carried a vote by a majority, and had it registered, importing, that they objected against the indelicacy, or impropriety, of the language in my memorial, but not against the merit of its contents. The minute, I here in a more public manner record anew, to the lasting honour of the persons who promoted it. The voice of oppressed truth, and injured innocence, can never be wholly stifled. Lest my memorial should again appear at the public bar of justice, in a less infected time, it was not sent to the office; which indicates that the former art of pocketing was not yet entirely forgotten. Indeed every state suffers more or less, from some malign influence, one time or other; but I have the happiness to say that the infection was not universal. South-Carolina has always been blessed with steady patriots, even in the most corrupt times: and may she abound with firm pillars of the constitution, according to our Magna Charta Americana, as [351] in the present trying æra of blessed memory, so long as the heavenly rays shall beam upon us!

As the power and happiness of Great Britain greatly depends on the prosperity of her American colonies, and the heart-soundness of her civil and ecclesiastical rulers—and as the welfare of America hangs on the balance of a proper intercourse with their Indian neighbours, and can never be continued but by observing and inforcing on both sides, a strict adherence to treaties, supporting public faith, and allowing only a sufficient number of such faithful and capable subjects to deal with them, as may gain their affections, and prove faithful centinels for the public security—I presume that the above relations, and observations, instead of being thought to be foreign, will be deemed essential to an history of the Indians. The remarks may be conducive also to the public welfare. Ignorance, or self-interest, has hitherto wrongly informed the community of the true situation of our Indian affairs westward.

[352]Account of the Chikkasah Nation.

The Chikkasah country lies in about 35 Deg. N. L. at the distance of 160 miles from the eastern side of the Missisippi; 160 miles to the N. of the Choktah, according to the course of the trading path; about half way from Mobille, to the Illinois, from S. to N; to the W. N. W. of the Muskohge (Creeks) about 300 computed miles, and a very mountainous winding path; from the Cheerake nearly W. about 540 miles; the late Fort-Loudon is by water 500 miles to the Chikkasah landing place, but only 95 computed miles by land.[400]

The Chikkasah are now settled between the heads of two of the most western branches of Mobille-river; and within twelve miles of the eastern main source of *Tahre Hache*, which lower down is called *Chokchooma*-river, as that nation made their first settlements there, after they came on the other side of the Missisippi. Where it empties into this, they call it *Yahshoo*-river.[401] Their tradition says they had ten thousand men fit for war, when they first came from the west, and this account seems very probable; as they, and the Choktah, and also the Chokchooma, who in process of time were forced by war to settle between the two former nations, came together from the west as one family.[402] The Chikkasah in the year 1[7]20, had four large contiguous settlements, which lay nearly in the form of three parts of a square, only that the eastern side was five miles shorter than the western, with the open part toward the Choktah. One was called *Yaneka*, about a mile wide, and six miles long, at the distance of twelve [353] miles from their present towns. Another was ten computed miles long, at the like distance from their present settlements, and from one to two miles broad. The towns were called *Shatara, Chookheereso, Hykehah, Tuskawillao,* and *Phalacheho.* The other square was single, began three miles from their present place of residence, and ran four miles in length, and one mile in breadth. This was called *Chookka Pharáah,* or "the long house." It was more populous than their whole nation contains at present. The remains of this once formidable people make up the northern angle of that broken square. They now scarcely consist of four hundred and fifty warriors, and are settled three miles westward from the deep creek, in a clear tract of rich land, about three miles square, running afterward about five miles toward the N. W. where the old fields are usually a mile broad. The superior number of their enemies forced them to take into this narrow circle, for social defence; and to build their towns, on commanding ground, at such a convenient distance from one another, as to have their enemies, when attacked, between two fires.[403]

Some of the old Nahchee Indians who formerly lived on the Missisippi, two hundred miles west of the Choktah, told me the French demanded from every one of their warriors a drest buck-skin, without any value for it, i.e. they taxed them; but that the warriors hearts grew very cross, and loved the deer-skins. According to the French accounts of the Missisippi-Indians, this seems to have been in the year 1729. As those Indians were of a peaceable and kindly disposition, numerous and warlike, and always kept a friendly intercourse with the Chikkasah, who never had any good-will to the French; these soon understood their heart-burnings, and by the advice of the old English traders, carried them white pipes and tobacco in their own name and that of South-Carolina,—persuading them with earnestness and policy to cut off the French, as they were resolved to inslave them in their own beloved land. The Chikkasah succeeded in their embassy. But as the Indians are slow in their councils on things of great importance, though equally close and intent, it was the following year before they could put their grand scheme in execution. Some of their head-men indeed opposed the plan, yet they never discovered it. But when these went a hunting in the woods, the embers burst into a raging flame. They attacked the French, who were flourishing away in the greatest security; and, as was affirmed, they entirely cut off the garrison, and neighbouring settlements, [354] consisting of fifteen hundred men, women, and children—the misconduct of a few indiscreet persons, occasioned so great a number of innocent lives to be thus cut off.[404]

The Nahchee afterwards built and settled a strong stockade fort, westward of their old fields, near a lake that communicates with *Bayouk Dargent;* but the ensuing summer, near 2000 French regulars and provincials, besides a great body of the Choktah and other savages invested it. The besieged sallied on them, with the utmost fury, killed a considerable number, and in all probability, would have totally destroyed the white soldiery, but for the sharp opposition of the Choktah in their own method of fighting. The Nahchee were at length repulsed, and bombarded with three mortars, which forced them to fly off different ways. The soldiers were too slow footed to pursue; but the Choktah, and other red allies, captivated a great number of them, and carried them to New Orleans, where several were burned, and the rest sent as slaves to the West India Islands: the greater part however went to the Chikkasah, where they were secured from the power of their French enemies. The French demanded them, but being absolutely refused, unluckily for many thousands of them, they formally declared war against the Chikkasah. In the open fields the Chikkasah bravely withstood, and repelled the greatest combined armies they were able to bring against them, north and south, and gave them and their swarms of red allies several notable defeats.

A body of the lower French, and about fourteen hundred Choktah, attacked the Long House Town, when only sixty warriors were at home; yet they fought so desperately, as to secure themselves, their women and children, till some of the hunters, who had been immediately sent for, came home to their assistance; when, though exceedingly inferior in number, they drove them off with great loss. Another time, the lower and upper Louisiana-French, and a great body of red auxiliaries, surprised late at night all their present towns, except Amalahta, that had about forty warriors, and which stood at some distance from the others. A considerable number of the enemy were posted at every door, to prevent their escape; and what few ran out were killed on the spot. The French seemed quite sure of their prey, having so well inclosed it. But, at the dawn of day, when they were capering and using those flourishes, that are peculiar [355] to that volatile nation, the other town drew round them stark naked, and painted all over red and black; thus they attacked them, killed numbers on the spot, released their brethren, who joined them like enraged lions, increasing as they swept along, and in their turn incircled their enemies. Their release increased their joy and fury, and they rent the sky with their sounds. Their flashy enemies, now changed their boasting tune, into "Oh morblieu!" and gave up all for lost. Their red allies out-heel'd them, and left them to receive their just fate. They were all cut off but two, an officer, and a negroe who faithfully held his horse till he mounted, and then ran along side of him. A couple of swift runners were sent after them, who soon came up with them, and told them to live and go home and inform their people, that as the Chikkasah hogs had now a plenty of ugly French carcases to feed on till next year, they hoped then to have another visit from them and their red friends; and that, as messengers, they wished them safe home. They accordingly returned with heavy hearts to the Chikkasah landing place, N. W. on the Missisippi, at the distance of 170 miles, where they took boat, and delivered their unexpected message:—grief and trembling spread through the country,—and the inhabitants could not secure themselves from the fury of these war-like, and enraged Chikkasah. Every one of their prisoners was put to the fiery torture, without any possibility of redemption, their hearts were so exceedingly imbittered against them.[405]

Flushed with this success, many parties turned out against the French, and from time to time hunted them far and near:—some went to the Missisippi, made a fleet of cypress-bark canoes, watched their trading boats, and cut off many of them without saving any of the people. The French finding it impracticable for a few boats to pass those red men of war, were obliged to go in a fleet, carry swivel-guns in their long pettiaugres, with plenty of men; but always shunning the Chikkasah side of the river, and observing the strictest order in their movements by day, and in their stations at night. The walking of a wild beast, I have been assured, has frequently called them to their arms, and kept them awake for the whole night, they were in so great dread of this warlike nation. The name of a Chikkasah became as dreadful, as it was hateful to their ears. And had it not been more owing to French policy than bravery, in uniting all the Missisippi and Canada-Indians in a confederacy and enmity against them, Louisiana-settlements [356] would have been long since, either entirely destroyed, or confined to garrisons.

When any of the French armies made a tolerable retreat, they thought themselves very happy. Once, when the impression was pretty much worn out of their minds, and wine inspired them with new stratagems, and hopes of better success, a great body of them, mixed with a multitude of savages, came to renew their attack. But as their hostile intentions were early discovered, the Chikkasah had built a range of strong stockade forts on ground which could not safely be approached, as the contiguous land was low, and chanced then to be wet. A number of the French and their allies drew near the western fort, but in the manner of hornets, flying about to prevent their enemies from taking a true aim, while several ranks followed each other in a slow and solemn procession, like white-robed, tall, midnight-ghosts, and as if fearless, and impenetrable. The Indians did not at first know what sort of animals they were, for several shots had been fired among them, without incommoding them, or retarding their direct course to the fort:—as they advanced nearer, the Chikkasah kept a continual fire at them, with a sure aim, according to their custom; this was with as little success as before, contrary to every attempt they had ever made before against their enemies. The warriors concluded them to be wizards, or old French-men carrying the ark of war against them. In their council, they were exceedingly perplexed: but just as they had concluded to oppose some of their own reputed prophets to destroy the power of those cunning men, or powerful spirits of the French, lo! those uncommon appearances spread themselves in battle-array, along the south-side of the fort, and threw hand-granadoes into the fort. Hoop Hoop

Ha was now joyfully sounded every where by the Chikkasah, being convinced they had skin and bone to fight with, instead of spirits. The matches
of the few shells the French had time to throw, were too long; and as our
traders had joined their friends by this time, they pulled out some, and threw
out other shells, as near to the enemy as they possibly could. They soon
found those dreadful phantoms were only common French-men, covered
with wool-packs, which made their breasts invulnerable to all their well-
aimed bullets. They now turned out of the fort, fell on, fired at their legs,
brought down many of them and scalped them, and drove the others with
considerable loss quite away to the southern hills, where the [357] trembling army had posted themselves out of danger. In the midst of the night
they decamped, and saved themselves by a well-timed retreat, left the Chikkasah triumphant, and inspired them with the fierceness of so many tygers;
which the French often fatally experienced, far and near, till the late cession
of West-Florida to Great Britain. I have two of these shells, which I keep
with veneration, as speaking trophies over the boasting Monsieurs, and their
bloody schemes.[406]

In the year 1748, the French sent a party of their Indians to storm some
of the Chikkasah traders' houses. They accordingly came to my trading
house first, as I lived in the frontier: finding it too dangerous to attempt to
force it, they patted with their hands a considerable time on one of the
doors, as a decoy, imitating the earnest rap of the young women who go a
visiting that time of night. Finding their labour in vain, one of them lifted
a billet of wood, and struck the side of the house, where the women and
children lay; so as to frighten them and awake me—my mastiffs had been
silenced with their venison. At last, the leader went a-head with the beloved
ark, and pretending to be directed by the divine oracle, to watch another
principal trader's house, they accordingly made for it, when a young woman,
having occasion to go out of the house, was shot with a bullet that entered
behind one of her breasts and through the other, ranging the bone; she
suddenly wheeled round, and tumbled down within the threshold of the
house—the brave trader instantly bounded up, sounding the war-whoop,
and in a moment grasped his gun, (for the traders beds are always hung
round with various arms of defence) and rescued her—the Indian physician
also, by his skill in simples, soon cured her.

As so much hath been already said of the Chikkasah, in the accounts of
the Cheerake, Muskohge, and Choktah, with whose history, theirs was necessarily interwoven, my brevity here, I hope will be excused.—The Chikkasah live in as happy a region, as any under the sun. It is temperate; as cool
in summer, as can be wished, and but moderately cold in winter. There is
frost enough to purify the air, but not to chill the blood; and the snow does
not lie four-and-twenty hours together. This extraordinary benefit, is not

from its situation to the equator, for the Cheerake country, among the Apalahche mountains is colder, in a surprising degree; but from the nature and levelness of the extensive circumjacent lands, which in general are very fertile. They have no running stream in [358] their present settlement. In their old fields, they have banks of oyster-shells, at the distance of four hundred miles from the sea-shore; which is a visible token of a general deluge, when it swept away the loose earth from the mountains, by the force of a tempestuous north-east wind, and thus produced the fertile lands of the Missisippi, which probably was sea, before that dreadful event.

As the Chikkasah fought the French and their red allies, with the utmost firmness, in defense of their liberties and lands, to the very last, without regarding their decay, only as an incentive to revenge their losses; equity and gratitude ought to induce us to be kind to our steady old friends, and only purchase so much of their land, as they would dispose of, for value. With proper management, they would prove extremely serviceable to a British colony, on the Missisippi. I hope no future misconduct will alienate their affections, after the manner of the super-intendant's late deputy, which hath been already mentioned. The skilful French could never confide in the Choktah, and we may depend on being forced to hold hot disputes with them, in the infant state of the Missisippi settlements: it is wisdom to provide against the worst events that can be reasonably expected to happen. The remote inhabitants of our northern colonies are well acquainted with the great value of those lands, from their observations on the spot.[407] The soil and climate are fit for hemp, silk, indigo, wine, and many other valuable productions, which our merchants purchase from foreigners, sometimes at a considerable disadvantage—The range is so good for horses, cattle, and hogs, that they would grow large, and multiply fast, without the least occasion of feeding them in winter, or at least for a long space of time, by reason of the numberless branches of reeds and canes that are interspersed, with nuts of various kinds. Rice, wheat, oats, barley, Indian corn, fruit-trees, and kitchen plants, would grow to admiration. As the ancients tell us, "Bacchus amat montes,"[408] so grape-vines must thrive extremely well on the hills of the Missisippi, for they are so rich as to produce winter-canes, contrary to what is known at any distance to the northward. If British subjects could settle West-Florida in security, it would in a few years become very valuable to Great Britain: and they would soon have as much profit, as they could desire, to reward their labour. Here, five hundred families would in all probability, be more beneficial to our mother-country, than the whole colony of North Carolina: besides innumerable branches toward Ohio and Monongahela.

[359] Enemies to the public good, may enter caveats against our settling where the navigation is precarious; and the extraordinary kindness of the late ministry to the French and Spaniards prevented our having an exclu-

sive navigation on the Missisippi. Aberville might still become a valuable mart to us; and from New Orleans it is only three miles to Saint John's Creek, where people pass through the lake of Saint Louis, and embark for Mobille and Pensacola. The Spaniards have wisely taken the advantage of our misconduct, by fortifying Louisiana, and employing the French to conciliate the affections of the savages; while our legislators, fermented with the corrupt lees of false power, are striving to whip us with scorpions. As all the Florida Indians are grown jealous of us, since we settled E. and W. Florida, and are unacquainted with the great power of the Spaniards in South America, and have the French to polish their rough Indian politics, Louisiana is likely to prove more beneficial to them, than it did to the French. They are fortifying their Missisippi settlements like a New Flanders, and their French artists, on account of our ministerial lethargy, will have a good opportunity, if an European war should commence, to continue our valuable western barriers as wild and waste, as the French left them. The warlike Chikkasah proved so formidable to them, that, except a small settlement above New Orleans, which was covered by the Choktah bounds, they did not attempt to make any other on the eastern side of the Missisippi, below the Illinois; though it contains such a vast tract of fine land, as would be sufficient for four colonies of two hundred and fifty miles square. Had they been able by their united efforts, to have destroyed the Chikkasah, they would not have been idle; for, in that case, the Choktah would have been soon swallowed up, by the assistance of their other allies, as they never supplied them with arms and ammunition, except those who went to war against the Chikkasah.

From North-Carolina to the Missisippi, the land near the sea, is, in general, low and sandy; and it is very much so in the two colonies of Florida, to a considerable extent from the sea-shore, when the lands appear fertile, level, and diversified with hills. Trees indicate the goodness or badness of land. Pine-trees grow on sandy, barren ground, which produces long coarse grass; the adjacent low lands abound with canes, reeds, [360] or bay and laurel of various sorts, which are shaded with large expanding trees—they compose an evergreen thicket, mostly impenetrable to the beams of the sun, where the horses, deer, and cattle, chiefly feed during the winter: and the panthers, bears, wolves, wild cats, and foxes, resort there, both for the sake of prey, and a cover from the hunters. Lands of a loose black soil, such as those of the Missisippi, are covered with fine grass and herbage, and well shaded with large and high trees of hickory, ash, white, red, and black oaks, great towering poplars, black walnut-trees, sassafras, and vines. The low wet lands adjoining the rivers, chiefly yield cypress-trees, which are very large, and of a prodigious height. On the dry grounds is plenty of beach, maple, holly, the cotton-tree, with a prodigious variety of other sorts. But we must not omit the black mulberry-tree, which, likewise, is plenty. It is high, and, if it had proper air and sun-shine, the boughs would be very spreading. On the fruit, the bears and wild fowl feed during their season; and also swarms of paroquets, enough to deafen one with their chattering, in the time of those joyful repasts. I believe the white mulberry-tree does not grow spontaneously in North-America. On the hills, there is plenty of chesnut-trees, and chesnut-oaks. These yield the largest sort of acorns, but wet weather soon spoils them. In winter, the deer and bears fatten themselves on various kinds of nuts, which lie thick over the rich land, if the blossoms have not been blasted by the north-east winds. The wild turkeys live on the small red acorns, and grow so fat in March, that they cannot fly farther than three or four hundred yards; and not being able soon to take the wing again, we speedily run them down with our horses and hunting mastiffs. At many unfrequented places of the Missisippi, they are so tame as to be shot with a pistol, of which our troops profited, in their way to take possession of the Illinois-garrison. There is a plenty of wild parsley, on the banks of that river, the roots of which are as large as those of parsnips, and it is as good as the other sort. The Indians say, they have not seen it grow in any woods remote from their country. They have a large sort of plums, which their ancestors brought with them from South-America, and which are now become plenty among our colonies, called Chikkasah plums.[409]

To the North West, the Missisippi lands are covered with filberts, which are as sweet, and thin-shelled, as the scaly bark hiccory-nuts. [361] Hazelnuts are very plenty, but the Indians seldom eat them. Black haws grow here in clusters, free from prickles: and pissimmons, of which they make very pleasant bread, barbicuing it in the woods. There is a sort of fine plums in a few places, large, and well-tasted; and, if transplanted, they would become better. The honey-locusts are pods about a span-long, and almost two inches broad, containing a row of large seed on one side, and a tough sweet substance the other. The tree is large, and full of long thorns; which forces the wild beasts to wait till they fall off, before they can gather that part of their harvest.—The trees grow in wet sour land, and are plenty, and the timber is very durable.[410] Where there is no pitch-pine, the Indians use this, or the sassafras, for posts to their houses; as they last for generations, and the worms never take them. Chinquapins are very plenty, of the taste of chesnuts, but much less in size. There are several sorts of very wholesome and pleasant-tasted ground nuts, which few of our colonists know any thing of. In wet land, there is an aromatic red spice, and a sort of cinnamon, which the natives seldom use. The Yopon, or Cusseena, is very plenty, as far as the salt air reaches over the low lands. It is well tasted, and very agreeable to those who accustom themselves to use it: instead of having any noxious quality, according to what many have experienced of the East-India insipid and costly tea, it is friendly to the human system, enters into a contest with the peccant humours, and expels them through the various channels of nature: it perfectly cures a tremor in the nerves. The North-American tea has a pleasant aromatic taste, and the very same salubrious property, as the Cusseena. It is an evergreen, and grows on hills. The bushes are about a foot high, each of them containing in winter a small aromatic red berry, in the middle of the stalk: such I saw it about Christmas, when hunting among the mountains, opposite to the lower Mohawk Castle, in the time of a deep snow.[411] There is no visible decay of the leaf, and October seems to be the proper time to gather it. The early buds of sassafras, and the leaves of ginseng, make a most excellent tea, equally pleasant to the taste, and conducive to health. The Chinese have sense enough to sell their enervating and slow-poisoning teas, under various fine titles, while they themselves prefer Ginseng-leaves. Each of our colonies abounds with ginseng, among the hills that lie far from the sea. Ninety-six settlement, is the lowest place where I have seen it grow in South Carolina. It is very plenty on the fertile parts of the Cheerake [362] mountains; it resembles Angelica, which in most places is also plenty. Its leaves are of a darker green, and about a foot and half from the root; the stalk sends out three equal branches, in the center of which a small berry grows, of a red colour, in August.—The seeds are a very strong and agreeable aromatic: it is plenty in West-Florida. The Indians use it on religious occasions. It is a great loss to a valuable branch of trade, that our people neither gather it in a proper season, nor can cure it, so as to give it a clear shining colour, like the Chinese tea. I presume it does not turn out well to our American traders; for, up the Mohawk river, a gentleman who had purchased a large quantity of it, told me that a skippel, or three bushels, cost him only nine shillings of New York currency: and in Charles-Town, an inhabitant of the upper Yadkin settlements in North Carolina, who came down with me from viewing the Nahchee old fields on the Missisippi, assured me he could not get from any of the South Carolina merchants, one shilling sterling a pound for it, though his people brought it from the Alehgany, and Apalahche mountains, two hundred miles to Charles-Town.[412]

It would be a service, worthy of a public-spirited gentleman, to inform us how to preserve the Ginseng, so as to give it a proper colour; for could we once effect that, it must become a valuable branch of trade. It is an exceeding good stomachic, and greatly supports nature against hunger and thirst. It is likewise beneficial against asthmatic complaints, and it may be said to promote fertility in women, as much as the East-India tea causes sterility in proportion to the baneful use that is made of it. A learned physician and botanist assured me, that the eastern teas are slow, but sure poison, in our American climates; and that he generally used the Ginseng very successfully in clysters, to those who had destroyed their health, by that dangerous habit. I advised my friend to write a treatise on its medical virtues, in the posterior application, as it must redound much to the public good. He told me, it would be needless; for quacks could gain nothing from the best directions; and that already several of his acquaintance of the faculty mostly pursued his practice in curing their patients. The eastern tea is as much inferior to our American teas, in its nourishing quality, as their album græcum is to our pure venison, from which we here sometimes collect it; let us, therefore, like frugal and wise people, use our own valuable aromatic tea, and thus induce our British [363] brethren to imitate our pleasant and healthy regimen; shewing the utmost indifference to any duties the statesmen of Great-Britain, in their assumed prerogative, may think proper to lay on their East-India poisoning, and dear-bought teas.

The industry of the uncorrupt part of the Indians, in general, and of the Chikkasah, in particular, extends no farther than to support a plain simple life, and secure themselves from the power of the enemy, and from hunger and cold. Indeed most of them are of late grown fond of the ornaments of life, of raising live stock, and using a greater industry than formerly, to increase wealth. This is to be ascribed to their long intercourse with us, and the familiar easy way in which our traders live with them, begetting imperceptibly an emulous spirit of imitation, according to the usual progress of human life. Such a disposition, is a great advance towards their being civilized; which, certainly must be effected, before we can reasonably expect to be able to bring them to the true principles of christianity. Instead of reforming the Indians, the monks and friars corrupted their morals: for, in the place of inculcating love, peace, and good-will to their red pupils, as became messengers of the divine author of peace, they only impressed their flexible minds with an implacable hatred against every British subject, without any distinction. Our people will soon discover the bad policy of the late Quebec act, and it is to be hoped that Great-Britain will in due time, send those black croaking clerical frogs of Canada home to their infallible mufti of Rome.[413]

I must here beg leave to be indulged, in a few observations on our own American missionaries. Many evils are produced by sending out ignorant and wicked persons as clergymen. Of the few I know,—two among them dare not venture on repeating but a few collects in the common prayer. A heathen could say, "if thou wouldst have me weep, thou must first weep thyself:" and how is it possible we should be able to make good impressions on others, unless they are first visible on ourselves? The very rudiments of learning, not to say of religion, are wanting in several of our missionary Evangelists; the best apology I have heard in their behalf, is, "an English nobleman asked a certain bishop, why he conferred holy orders on such a parcel of arrant blockheads? He replied, because it was better to have the ground plowed by asses, than leave it a waste full of thistles."

[364] It seems very surprising, that those who are invested with a power of conferring ecclesiastical orders, should be so careless in propagating the holy gospel, and assiduous to prophane holy things, in appointing and ordaining illiterate and irreligious persons to the service. What is it? but saying, "go teach the American fools. My blessing is enough. Cherish confidence, and depend upon it, they will not have confidence to laugh at you: Leave the remote and poor settlements to the care of divine providence, which is diffusive of its rich gifts. The harvest is great elsewhere. Only endeavour to episcopize the northern colonies; it is enough: there they are numerous, and able to pay Peter's pence, as well as our old jewish, and new parliamentary tithes; and in time your labours will be crowned with success."

That court however, which sends abroad stupid embassadors to represent it, cannot be reasonably expected to have success, but rather shame and derision. What can we think at this distance, when we see the number of blind guides, our spiritual fathers at home have sent to us, to lead us clear of the mazes of error? but, that they think of us with indifference, and are studiously bent on their own temporal interest, instead of our spiritual welfare. There are thousands of the Americans, who I believe have not heard six sermons for the space of above thirty years—and in fact they have more knowledge than the teachers who are sent to them, and too much religion to communicate with them. And even the blinder sort of the laity not finding truth sufficiently supported by their purblind guides, grow proud of their own imaginary knowledge, and some thereby proudly commence teachers,—by which means they rend the church asunder; and, instead of peace and love, they plant envy, contempt, hatred, revilings, and produce the works of the flesh, instead of those of the spirit.

Not so act the uncivilized Indians. Their supposed holy orders are obtained from a close attention to, and approved knowledge of their sacred mysteries. No temptations can corrupt their virtue on that head: neither will they convey their divine secrets to the known impure. This conduct is worthy to be copied, by all who pretend to any religion at all, and especially by those who are honoured with the pontifical dignity, and assume the name of "Right reverend, and Most reverend Fathers in God." I have been importunately requested at different times, by several eminent gentlemen, [365] who wish well to both church and state, to represent the evils resulting from such missionaries, in hope of redress; and on this occasion, I thought it criminal to refuse their virtuous request. The representation is true, and the writer is persuaded he cannot give the least offence by it, to any but the guilty.

My situation does not allow me, to fix the bounds our legislators claim on the Missisippi: but I have good reason to believe that the fine court title which France, in her late dying will, has transferred to Great-Britain, mostly consists in ideal possessions she never enjoyed. The monopolies already made, are equally unjust and pernicious. They, who take up valuable lands, especially on such a barrier, ought to settle them in a reasonable time, or be prevented from keeping out industrious inhabitants, and causing the place to continue in a defenceless condition.[414] Before we can settle the Missisippi, with any reasonable view of success, the government must build sufficient places of strength, both to make the colony appear respectable in the eyes of the Indians, and guard it from the evil eye of the Spaniards, who are watching at New Orleans, and over the river, to impede our interests, in that valuable but dangerous quarter. It might become an impenetrable barrier, if proper encouragement was given to the laborious and hardy inhabitants of our northern settlements, on the various branches of the Ohio, and in the back settlements of North Carolina, who are now almost useless to the community. As Great-Britain would be the chief gainer by their removal, she ought to encourage them to remove. Great numbers of them were preparing to come down, even in the years 1768 and 1769; but finding too many inconveniences and hazards in their way, they declined the attempt. As it is natural for every colony to endeavour to increase its number of industrious inhabitants, it cannot be expected, even if the mother country behaved more prudently than of late, that any of them would exert themselves much on such an occasion, as to raise dangerous rivals in their own staple commodity—However rice, indigo, silk, hemp, wine, and many other valuable productions are suitable to so fine a soil and climate; besides great quantities of beef, pork, and every kind of useful timber for Jamaica, which is contiguous to the mouth of the Missisippi. So great an acquisition of raw materials would soon prove very beneficial to Great-Britain, as well as a great safe-guard to the best part of our other colonies, and a very needful check to Spanish insolence. [366] Such a material undertaking, as the colonizing of so important a barrier, deserves public encouragement to put it in a fair way of doing well; and the continuance of a supply, and protection through its infant state, to secure it from any artful attempts the Spaniards and their French subjects might plot to disturb its tranquility, and thereby check its growth.

There might be introduced even among the Indian nations I have described, a spirit of industry, in cultivating such productions as would agree with their land and climates; especially, if the super-intendency of our Indian affairs, westward, was conferred on the sensible, public-spirited, and judicious Mr. George Galphin, merchant, or Lachlan M'Gilwray, Esq; of equal merit. Every Indian trader knows from long experience, that both these gentlemen have a greater influence over the dangerous Muskohge, than any others besides. And the security of Georgia requires one or other of them speedily to superintend our Indian affairs. It was, chiefly, the skilful management of these worthy patriots, which prevented the Muskohge from joining the Cheerake, according to treaty, against us in the years 1760 and 1761,—to their great expence and hazard of life, as they allowed those savages to eat, drink, and sleep at Silver-Bluff, below New Windsor garrison, and at Augusta fifteen miles apart, and about 150 miles from Savanah. I write from my own knowledge, for I was then on the spot, with a captain's commission from South Carolina.[415] A Muskohge war against us, could easily be prevented by either of those gentlemen, if chosen, and the destructive plan of general licences was repealed. It is to be hoped, that they who are invested with the power, will retract their former error, and have the pleasure of knowing the good effect it would produce, by giving an opportunity of civilizing and reforming the savages; which can never be effected by the former usual means. Admit into Indian countries, a sufficient number of discreet orderly traders.—This needful regulation will likewise benefit trade, which is almost ruined; and our valuable weak frontier colonies would thereby increase in numbers, proportionable to their security.

Formerly, each trader had a licence for two towns, or villages; but according to the present unwise plan, two, and even three Arab-like pedlars sculk about in one of those villages. Several of them also frequently emigrate into the woods with spirituous liquors, and cheating trifles, [367] after the Indian hunting camps, in the winter season, to the great injury of a regular trader, who supplies them with all the conveniences of hunting: for, as they will sell even their wearing shirt for inebriating liquors, they must be supplied anew in the fall of the year, by the trader. At my first setting out among them, a number of traders who lived contiguous to each other, joined through our various nations in different companies, and were generally men of worth: of course, they would have a living price for their goods, which they carried on horseback to the remote Indian countries, at very great expences. These set an honest copy for the imitation of the natives, for as they had much at stake, their own interest and that of the government coincided. As the trade was in this wise manner kept up to its just standard, the savages were industrious and frugal. But, lowering it, through a mistaken notion of regaining their affections, we made ourselves too cheap to them, and they despised us for it.[416] The trade ought to be raised to a reasonable fixed price, the first convenient opportunity—thus we shall keep them employed, and ourselves secure. Should we lower the trade, even fifty per cent below the prime cost, they would become only the more discontented, by thinking we had cheated them all the years past. A mean submissive temper can never manage our Indian affairs. The qualities of a kind friend, sensible speaker, and active brisk warrior, must constitute the character of a super-intendant. Great care ought to be taken, not to give the Indians offence, or a mean opinion of the people or government our Indian superintendants represent.

At a general congress in Mobille, Anno 1765, where were present his Ex-cellency the learned, cheerful, patriotic Governor of West-Florida, George Johnstone Esquire, the present superintendant of Indian affairs, and the head-men and warriors of the Choktah, and warlike Chikkasah nations, a tariff of trade was settled on every material article, in the most public and solemn manner, mostly according to the Muskohge standard, and to the great satisfaction of the Indians.[417] The price for which the corrupt and shamefully-indulged vagrant pedlars forced the traders at the risque of their lives, to traffic with them, being then about 70 per cent. below the French tariff in Indian trade up the Missisippi. Each of these traders took out In-dian trading licences, to which the fixed prices of various goods were an-next, thereby impowering them to traffic during the space of a twelve-month; and they gave penal bonds of security to the [368] secretary, for the just observance of their instructions. This proved however, through a bare-faced partiality, only a shameful farce on œconomy and good order. His Excellency, and the honourable Col. W—n,[418] were so strongly convinced of my former integrity, that in order to testify publicly their approbation of my good conduct, they did me the honour to pass security in the secretary's office, for my dealing with the Indians in strict conformity to the laws of trade. As I lost in the space of a year, to the amount of two and twenty hundred dollars-worth of goods at prime cost, by the disorderly conduct of other licensed traders, and had just reason to hope for redress on exhibiting a well-supported complaint; I drew up on my own account, and at the im-portunate request of the Chikkasah head-men, a memorial, setting forth their having notoriously violated every essential part of their instructions, enticing the Indians also to get drunk, and then taught them to blaspheme their maker.[419] This I proved, and that some of the lawless traders had fur-nished the Indians, in the space of a few months, with so great a quantity of prohibited liquors, as either did, or might enable some of them to decoy the savages to squander away thousands of drest deer-skins,—but they es-caped with impunity.

A few months before this period, some family disputes rose very high between the Chikkasah, on the following account. The Indians being am-bitious, free, and jealous of their liberties as well as independent of each other, where mutual consent is not obtained; one half of the nation were exceedingly displeased with the other, because, by the reiterated persuasions of a certain deputy, the latter had disposed of a tract of land, twelve miles toward the south, on the upper trading Choktah, or Mobille path, to one of those disorderly traders. By the application of the deputy, the head-men of both parties met him according to appointment, and partook of a plentiful barbicued feast, with plenty of spirituous liquors. As such conduct was against his majesty's proclamation, and appeared to me to be calculated, either for a clandestine trade, or family-job, I rejected the invitation, lest otherwise I might be charged as a party.[420] When they became intoxicated with liquor, a war-leader of the dissenting party, struck his tomohawk at the head of a noted chieftain, upbraiding him for bringing a strange fire into their land; but happily the blow missed its aim. Their disputes consequently rose higher every day; and the [369] dissidents informed the Muskohge of their then situation, and future intentions. *Yah-Yah-Tustanage,* "the Great Mortar," a bitter enemy of the English, soon sent up a company of his war-relations, to persuade them to guard in time, against our dangerous encroachments, by killing all the English, that planted their lands without the general consent of the owners, and to take their black people as a good prize; because they were building and planting for the reception of an English garrison, which was to come from the Missisippi and be the first means of enslaving them. While their transport of madness lasted, it was fruitless to reason with them; but at every convenient opportunity, I used such plain, friendly, and persuasive arguments to sooth them, as I imagined might regain their lost affections, and procrastinate the dangerous impending blow. They consented at last to forbear every kind of resentment against our late suspicious conduct, on condition of my writing to those who could redress them, and our people speedily withdrawing from their land the intruding planters. This I did; and at Mobille I delivered my remonstrance to the superintendant. Upon my urging the absolute necessity of pacifying our old steady friends, by removing the ungenerous cause of their jealousy, he assured me, that he would gladly comply with so just a request, especially, as it exactly coincided with his majesty's proclamation, then fixed on the fort-gate.

In the space of about ten days after, by order of Governor Johnstone, all the Chikkasah and Choktah traders were cited to appear before him and the superintendant, in order to know the merit of, and answer to, my numerous complaints. When they appeared, and every thing was properly adjusted, his secretary read paragraph by paragraph, and his excellency, very minutely examined all the reputable traders, who confirmed to his full satisfaction, the truth of every thing in my complaint. But tho' the memorial set forth, among other instances, that "but a few minutes after I had once a troublesome dispute with the abovementioned Chikkasah leader, on account of the traders prohibited and poisoning liquors, he went home distracted, and finding none but his aged mother, he would have killed her with his tomohawk, only for her earnest entreaties, and then sudden escape,"[421]—-yet none of those disorderly people were either suspended from trading with the Indians, or forfeited the penalty of their bonds—neither was the Indians request complied with. Though, I believe, the termination was to the no small mortification of his excellency.

[370] Anno 1767, the super-intendant's deputy convened all the Chikkasah traders and head-men of the nation, declaring that he had received positive orders from the superior over Indian affairs, to bring the trade to the late standard of the Muskohge. The head-men replied, that if their traders, or the super-intendant acted unwisely, they were not bound to follow the copy. We urged, that he had already exceedingly lowered the Mississippi-Indian trade, and had, at the Mobille congress, fixed a Tariff, a copy of which every one of us had, as well as a regular licence, having given approved security for our peaceable conduct, and fair dealing with the Indians, for the space of a year: and that besides the wrong policy of such an edict, as he now proposed, if we proved rogues to our own interest with them, we ought to be arrested as fools below. We concluded, by observing the great disadvantage of navigation that Mobille lay under, to which Charles-town was no way exposed in imports and exports; and that if the aforesaid Indian trade should, by any act be reduced below its present standard, it must necessarily cease of itself, unless as free-men, we said No to the command. Which the traders did, and resolved to support it.

The deputies treatment of Capt. J. C—l—b—rt, who has lived among the Chikkasah from his childhood, and speaks their language even with more propriety than the English,[422] deserves to be recorded—but I hope the gentleman will soon do it himself, to shew the higher powers the consequences of appointing improper, mercenary, and haughty persons to such offices. Sir William Johnson acted very differently—he was kind, intelligent, intrepid—he knew when to frown and when to smile on the Indian nations he was connected with, and blended the serpent with the dove. He chose his deputies or representatives in the Indian countries, according to their qualifications in the Indian life; and not unskilful men, and mere strangers, like some who have been obtruded into our southern nations. His prudent and brave deputy Col. Craghan,[423] did our chain of colonies more real service in a few months, than all our late southern commissioners of Indian affairs could possibly have done in ages. In the dangerous time of our settling the Illinois-garrison, 500 leagues up the Missisippi, he went from Johnson's Hall, in the lower part of the Mohawk country, and from thence coursed through the various nations of Indians, to the head-branches of Canada; and in like manner, down those of the Missisippi, to the garrison, amidst the greatest dangers; pleasing and reconciling the savages as he proceeded. [371] The Chikkasah first informed me of his journey and success—and I had it some time after, circumstantially confirmed to me by

Sir W. Johnson. When I spoke to the Col. himself on his fatigues and perils, he modestly replied "that while he was performing the needful duties of his office, and acting the part of a beloved man with the swan's wing, white pipe, and white beads, for the general good of his country, and of its red neighbours, he had no leisure to think of any personal dangers that might befall a well-meaning peace-maker." Having reconciled the Kuskuske Indians,[424] whom the French garrison had decoyed by their false painting of us, to remove with them over the Missisippi,—he from thence proceeded down by water to New Orleans; afterwards, along the gulph-stream of Mexico, to the place from whence he set off, amounting nearly to 5000 miles, in the oblique course he was forced to take.

In brief, able superintendants of Indian affairs, and who will often visit the Indians, are the safest and strongest barrier garrisons of our colonies— and a proper number of prudent honest traders dispersed among the savages would be better than all the soldiers, which the colonies support for their defence against them. The Indians are to be persuaded by friendly language; but nothing will terrify them to submit to what opposes their general idea of liberty. In the disputes between governors, superintendants, their deputies, and the traders, care should be taken to keep them very secret from the Indians,—for they love such traders as are governed by principle, and are easily influenced by them. Several agents of governors and superintendants have experienced this, when dispatched into their countries to seize either the goods or persons of one and another trader, who was obnoxious by not putting the neck under their lordly feet. Some have hardly escaped from being tomohawked and cut to pieces on the spot by the enraged Indians, for the violence offered to their friendly traders.—When an Indian and trader contract friendship, they exchange the clothes then upon them, and afterwards they cherish it by mutual presents, and in general, will maintain it to the death. As early as 1736 the Georgia governor began to harrass the licensed traders, and sent a commissioner to seize the goods of several Carolinian traders: in executing his commission, he was soon encircled by twenty-three Indians, and would have been instantly dispatched, but for the intercession of one of the suffering traders, Mr. J. G—r of Tennase.[425] When a governor of any of our colonies, is either weak in his [372] intellects, or has self-interested pursuits in view, incompatible with the public good, he will first oppress the Indian traders, and misrepresent all under his government who oppose him; and then adopt and pursue the low and tyrannical court maxim "divide, and you will subdue and rule them." Whether the animosities that subsisted among the inhabitants of Georgia, when Mr. Ellis went to preside there, sprung from any such cause, I will not say, but I well know that by his wisdom, cheerful and even temper, and an easy winning behaviour, he soon reconciled the contending parties in his gay and friendly hall.

The grateful and polite in that colony, have taught their rising families to revere his name, on account of his generous and patriotic spirit. He instructed the inhabitants of that infant colony, by example, how to fortify themselves against hostile dangers. The people were few, weak, harrassed, and disheartened: but as soon as the father and general put to his helping hand, their drooping spirits recovered. Then, defensible garrisons sprung up, after the manner of ancient Thebes; but as he knew that peace with the numerous nations of neighbouring Indians was essential to the welfare of a trading colony, he acted the part of the Archimagus, or great beloved man, with the swan's wing, white pipes, and tobacco, between the mischievous Muskohge and our colonies, at Savanah, in concert with the two worthy gentlemen before-mentioned. At that time our Indian affairs in general wore a most dangerous aspect—and the public stock was expended:—when the governor saw that he could not shake hands with the Indians, empty handed, he cheerfully supplied their discontented head-men with his own effects, and even his domestic utensils. They set a high value on each gift, chiefly for the sake of the giver, whom they adopted as brother, friend, father. He gave the colony a strong example of public spirit, by sacrificing his ease, and private interest, to the welfare of the people; whom he faithfully patronized (during his too short stay) according to the paternal intentions of his late Majesty. He was never ordered by his Prince to inform the legislative body of the colony, that, if the electors petitioned his majesty for the liberty of chusing representatives, he, through his own grace and goodness, would order his governor to inform them he was pleased to indulge them in the object of their submissive prayer. But had it been otherwise, Mr. Ellis would have deemed such a ministerial order, a gross attack upon his honour, if not on the constitutional rights of British subjects, and [373] have rejected it with contempt. When a gentleman of abilities employs his talents, in his proper sphere, in promoting the general good of society (instead of forwarding only his own interest) he is both an honour and a blessing to the community: the grateful public always revere such a character, and fail not to hand it down to the latest posterity, to stimulate others to follow the example. Such was Mr. Ellis in Georgia; and such was the learned, wise, polite, affable, and now much lamented Sir Henry Moore Bart. the late governor of New-York colony. His virtues so strongly endeared him to those he governed, and to every one who had the pleasure of his acquaintance, that his memory will never be forgotten. He came to his government at the most confused time America ever knew. He found the senior member of the council strongly barricaded in the fort,—but presently he ordered away the cannon, and put a stop to other hostile preparations. He conversed with the people as a father. They were soon convinced of his upright intentions, and he lived triumphant in their hearts. If strict integrity, great abilities, and the most ardent desires and endeavours to promote the mutual interests of prince and people,—if the most impartial administration of justice to every denomination of faithful subjects—if indefatigable application to public business, and a cheerfulness to redress every grievance that had the least tendency to affect the lives or property even of the meanest person: if these be the characteristics of one of the best of governors, our hearts feelingly testify, and the tears of a grateful people plainly shewed, he enjoyed them in the most eminent degree. His stay, however, among them was but short, for having given a finished copy for others to pursue, heaven called him home to reward him for his shining virtues: and, though the other worthy patriot is in being, yet the honest sons of Georgia deeply lament his being lost to them.

GENERAL
OBSERVATIONS
ON THE
NORTH AMERICAN INDIANS;
DISPLAYING

Their love to their country—Their martial spirit—Their caution in war—
Method of fighting—Barbarity to their captives—Instances of their fortitude
and magnanimity in the view of death—Their rewards of public services—
The manner of crowning their warriors after victory—Their games—
Method of fishing, and of building—Their utensils and manufactures—
Conduct in domestic life—Their laws, form of government, &c. &c.

[377]General Observations on the North American Indians.

In the following pages, the reader will find as great a variety of entertainment, as can well be expected in describing a rude and uncivilized people. The Indians having for a long time no intercourse with the rest of the world, and seldom one nation of them with another, their rites and customs are in several respects different. But as they agree in essentials through the whole extent of the American world, such agreement is apparently owing to tradition, and the usage of their ancestors, before they were subdivided as at present. Uniformity cannot be attributed to chance.

Through the whole continent, and in the remotest woods, are traces of their ancient warlike disposition. We frequently met with great mounds of earth, either of a circular, or oblong form, having a strong breast-work at a distance around them, made of the clay which had been dug up in forming the ditch, on the inner side of the inclosed ground, and these were their forts of security against an enemy. Three or four of them, are in some places raised so near to each other, as evidently for the garrison to take any enemy that passed between them. They were mostly built in low lands; [378] and some are overspread with large trees, beyond the reach of Indian tradition. About 12 miles from the upper northern parts of the Choktah country, there stand on a level tract of land, the north-side of a creek, and within arrow-shot of it, two oblong mounds of earth, which were old garrisons, in an equal direction with each other, and about two arrow-shots apart. A broad deep ditch inclosed those two fortresses, and there they raised an high breast-work, to secure their houses from the invading enemy. This was a stupendous piece of work, for so small a number of savages, as could support themselves in it; their working instruments being only of stone and wood. They called those old fortresses *Nanne Yah,* "the hills, or mounts of God."[426]

Probably, different parties, and even nations, were formed at first, either by caprice, differences, or the fear of punishment for offences. The demon of persecution however was never among them—not an individual durst ever presume to infringe on another's liberties. They are all equal—the only precedence any gain is by superior virtue, oratory, or prowess; and they esteem themselves bound to live and die in defence of their country. A warrior will accept of no hire for performing virtuous and heroic actions; they have exquisite pleasure in pursuing their own natural dictates. The headmen reward the worthy with titles of honour, according to their merit in speaking, or the number of enemies scalps they bring home. Their hearts are fully satisfied, if they have revenged crying blood, enobled themselves by war actions, given cheerfulness to their mourning country, and fired the breasts of the youth with a spirit of emulation to guard the beloved people from danger, and revenge the wrongs of their country. Warriors are to protect all, but not to molest or injure the meanest. If they attempted it, they would pay dear for their folly. The reason they are more earnest than the rest of mankind, in maintaining that divine law of equal freedom and justice, I apprehend, is the notion imbibed from their (supposed) Hebrew ancestors of the divine theocracy, and that inexpressible abhorrence of slavery, which must have taken place after their captivity by the Assyrians, or the Babylonians.

Every warrior holds his honour, and the love of his country, in so high esteem, that he prefers it to life, and will suffer the most exquisite tortures [379] rather than renounce it: there is no such thing among the Indians as desertion in war, because they do not fight like the Swiss for hire, but for wreaths of swan-feathers. If the English acted on that noble principle, or were encouraged by an able, public-spirited ministry, to cherish it, Britannia need neither sue, nor pay any of the German princes for protection, or alliances.

The equality among the Indians, and the just rewards they always confer on merit, are the great and leading—the only motives that warm their hearts with a strong and permanent love to their country. Governed by the plain and honest law of nature, their whole constitution breathes nothing but liberty: and, when there is that equality of condition, manners, and privileges, and a constant familiarity in society, as prevails in every Indian nation, and through all our British colonies, there glows such a chearfulness and warmth of courage in each of their breasts, as cannot be described. It were to be wished, that our military and naval officers of all ranks, instead of their usual harsh and imperious behaviour, would act the part of mild and good-natured patrons to those under them: kind, persuasive language has an irresistible force, and never fails to overcome the manly and generous heart, and love is strong as death. If the governed are convinced that their superiors have a real affection for them, they will esteem it their duty and interest to serve them and take pleasure in it. The late gallant Lord Howe, General

Wolfe, and Admiral Warren, are still alive in the grateful hearts of the Americans, and also of the soldiers and seamen, who fought under them.[427] No service was too difficult to oblige them, and they were ashamed to do any thing amiss. If every British officer set the like example, there would be little occasion for new mutiny acts, and other such like penal regulations. We have frequent instances in America, that merely by the power of affability, and good-natured language, the savage Indian, drunk and foaming with rage and madness, can be overcome and brought to weep. Lately, some came among us, inflamed and distracted foes; we persuaded them of our constant kindly intentions, and they repented, made atonement in regard to themselves, and checked the mad conduct of others.

The Indians are not fond of waging war with each other, unless prompted by some of the traders: when left to themselves, they consider [380] with the greatest exactness and foresight, all the attending circumstances of war. Should any of the young warriors through forwardness, or passion, violate the treaty of peace, the aggressing party usually send by some neutral Indians, a friendly embassy to the other, praying them to accept of equal retribution, and to continue their friendship, assuring them that the rash unfriendly action did not meet with the approbation, but was highly condemned by the head-men of the whole nation. If the proposal be accepted, the damage is made up, either by sacrificing one of the aggressors, of a weak family, or by the death of some unfortunate captive, who had been ingrafted in a wasted tribe. If a person of note was killed, the offended party take immediate satisfaction of their own accord, and send back the like embassy, acquainting them, that as crying blood is quenched with equal blood, and their beloved relation's spirit is allowed to go to rest, they are fond of continuing the friend-knot, and keeping the chain of friendship clear of rust, according to the old beloved speech: but, if they are determined for war, they say *Mattle, Mattle,* "it is finished, they are weighed, and found light." In that case, they proceed in the following manner.

A war captain announces his intention of going to invade the common enemy, which he, by consent of the whole nation, declares to be such: he then beats a drum three times round his winter house, with the bloody colours flying, marked with large strokes of black,—the grand war signal of blood and death. On this, a sufficient number of warriors and others, commonly of the family of the murdered person, immediately arm themselves, and each gets a small bag of parched corn-flour, for his war-stores. They then go to the aforesaid winter house, and there drink a warm decoction of their supposed holy consecrated herbs and roots for three days and nights, sometimes without any other refreshment. This is to induce the deity to guard and prosper them, amidst their impending dangers. In the most promising appearance of things, they are not to take the least nourishment of

food, nor so much as to sit down, during that time of sanctifying themselves, till after sunset. While on their expedition, they are not allowed to
lean themselves against a tree, though they may be exceedingly fatigued,
after a sharp day's march; nor must they lie by, a whole day to refresh themselves, or kill and barbicue deer and bear for their war journey. The more
virtuous they are, they reckon the greater will be their success against
the enemy, by the bountiful smiles of the deity. To [381] gain that favourite
point, some of the aged warriors narrowly watch the young men who are
newly initiated, lest they should prove irreligious, and prophane the holy fast,
and bring misfortunes on the out-standing camp. A gentleman of my acquaintance, in his youthful days observed one of their religious fasts, but
under the greatest suspicion of his virtue in this respect, though he had
often headed them against the common enemy: during their three days
purification, he was not allowed to go out of the sanctified ground, without
a trusty guard, lest hunger should have tempted him to violate their old
martial law, and by that means have raised the burning wrath of the holy
fire against the whole camp. Other particulars of this sacred process for war,
have been related in their proper place.★

When they have finished their fast and purifications, they set off, at the
fixed time, be it fair or foul, firing their guns, whooping, and hallooing, as
they march. The war-leader goes first, carrying the supposed holy ark: he
soon strikes up the awful and solemn song before mentioned, which they
never sing except on that occasion. The rest follow, in one line, at the distance of three or four steps from each other, now and then sounding the war
whoo-whoop, to make the leader's song the more striking to the people.[428]
In this manner they proceed, till quite out of the sight, and hearing of their
friends. As soon as they enter the woods, all are silent; and, every day they
observe a profound silence in their march, that their ears may be quick to
inform them of danger: their small black eyes are almost as sharp also as
those of the eagle, or the lynx; and with their feet they resemble the wild
cat, or the cunning panther, crawling up to its prey. Thus they proceed,
while things promise them good success; but, if their dreams portend any
ill, they always obey the supposed divine intimation and return home, without incurring the least censure. They reckon that their readiness to serve
their country, should not be subservient to their own knowledge or wishes,
but always regulated by the divine impulse. I have known a whole company
who set out for war, to return in small parties, and sometimes by single
persons, and be applauded by the united voice of the people; because they
acted in obedience to their *Nana Ishtohoollo,* "or guardian angels," who impressed them in the visions of night, with the friendly caution. As their

★Vide p. 143 &c.

dreams are reckoned ominous, so there is a small uncommon bird, called the "kind ill messenger," which they [382] always deem to be a true oracle of bad news. If it sings near to them, they are much intimidated: but, if it perches, and sings over the war-camp, they speedily break up. This superstitious custom prevailed with the early heathens, who pretended to prophesy by the flight of birds, and it reached even down to the time of the Romans.[429]

Every war captain chuses a noted warrior, to attend on him and the company. He is called *Etissú,* or "the waiter." Every thing they eat or drink during their journey, he gives them out of his hand, by a rigid abstemious rule—though each carries on his back all his travelling conveniences, wrapt in a deer skin, yet they are so bigoted to their religious customs in war, that none, though prompted by sharp hunger or burning thirst, dares relieve himself. They are contented with such trifling allowance as the religious waiter distributes to them, even with a scanty hand. Such a regimen would be too mortifying to any of the white people, let their opinion of its violation be ever so dangerous.

When I roved the woods in a war party with the Indians, though I carried no scrip, nor bottle, nor staff, I kept a large hollow cane well corked at each end, and used to sheer off now and then to drink, while they suffered greatly by thirst. The constancy of the savages in mortifying their bodies, to gain the divine favour, is astonishing, from the very time they beat to arms, till they return from their campaign. All the while they are out, they are prohibited by ancient custom, the leaning against a tree, either sitting or standing: nor are they allowed to sit in the day-time, under the shade of trees, if it can be avoided; nor on the ground, during the whole journey, but on such rocks, stones, or fallen wood, as their ark of war rests upon. By the attention they invariably pay to those severe rules of living, they weaken themselves much more than by the unavoidable fatigues of war: but, it is fruitless to endeavour to dissuade them from those things which they have by tradition, as the appointed means to move the deity, to grant them success against the enemy, and a safe return home.

It may be expected I should describe the number of men their war companies consist of, but it is various, and uncertain: sometimes, two or three only will go to war, proceed as cautiously, and strike their prey as panthers. In [383] the year 1747, a couple of the Mohawk Indians came against the lower towns of the Cheerake, and so cunningly ambuscaded them through most part of the spring and summer, as to kill above twenty in different attacks, before they were discovered by any part of the enraged and dejected people. They had a thorough knowledge of the most convenient ground for their purpose, and were extremely swift and long winded—whenever they killed any, and got the scalp, they made off to the neighbouring mountains,

and ran over the broad ledges of rocks, in contrary courses, as occasion offered, so as the pursuers could by no means trace them. Once, when a large
company was in chace of them, they ran round a steep hill at the head of
the main eastern branch of Savana river, intercepted, killed, and scalped the
hindmost of the party, and then made off between them and Keeowhee: as
this was the town to which the company belonged, they hastened home in
a close body, as the proper place of security from such enemy wizards. In
this manner, did those two sprightly gallant savages perplex and intimidate
their foes for the space of four moons, in the greatest security; though they
often were forced to kill and barbicue what they chiefly lived upon, in the
midst of their watchful enemies. Having sufficiently revenged their relations' blood, and gratified their own ambition with an uncommon number of scalps, they resolved to captivate one, and run home with him, as a
proof of their having killed none but the enemies of their country. Accordingly, they approached very near to Keeowhee, about half-a-mile below
the late Fort Prince George, advancing with the usual caution on such an
occasion—one crawled along under the best cover of the place, about the
distance of an hundred yards a-head, while the other shifted from tree to
tree, looking sharply every way. In the evening, however, an old beloved
man discovered them from the top of an adjoining hill, and knew them to
be enemies, by the cut of their hair, light trim for running, and their postures; he returned to the town, and called first at the house of one of our
traders, and informed him of the affair, enjoining him not to mention it to
any, lest the people should set off against them without success, before their
tracks were to be discovered, and he be charged with having deceived them.
But, contrary to the true policy of traders among unforgiving savages, that
thoughtless member of the Choktah Sphynx-company busied himself as
usual out of his proper sphere, sent for the head-men, and told them the
story. As the Mohawks were our allies and not known to molest any of the
traders [384] in the paths and woods, he ought to have observed a strict
neutrality. The youth of the town, by order of their head-men, carried on
their noisy public diversions in their usual manner, to prevent their foes
from having any suspicion of their danger, while runners were sent from the
town to their neighbours, to come silently and assist them to secure the prey,
in its state of security. They came like silent ghosts, concerted their plan of
operation, passed over the river at the old trading ford, opposite to the late
Fort, which lay between two contiguous commanding hills, and proceeding downward over a broad creek, formed a large semi-circle from the river
bank, while the town seemed to be taking its usual rest. They then closed
into a narrower compass, and at last discovered the two brave unfortunate
men lying close under the tops of some fallen young pine-trees. The company gave the war signal, and the Mohawks bounding up, bravely repeated

it: but, by their sudden spring from under thick cover, their arms were useless; they made desperate efforts however to kill or be killed, as their situation required. One of the Cheerake, the noted half breed of Istanare town,[430] which lay two miles from thence, was at the first onset, knocked down and almost killed with his own cutlass, which was wrested from him, though he was the strongest of the whole nation. But they were over-powered by numbers, captivated, and put to the most exquisite tortures of fire, amidst a prodigious crowd of exulting foes.

One of the present Choktah traders who was on the spot, told me, that when they were tied to the stake, the younger of the two discovering our traders on a hill pretty near, addressed them in English, and entreated them to redeem their lives. The elder immediately spoke to him, in his own lan-guage, to desist—on this, he recollected himself, and became composed like a stoic, manifesting an indifference to life or death, pleasure or pain, accord-ing to their standard of martial virtue; and their dying behaviour did not reflect the least dishonour on their former gallant actions. All the pangs of fiery torture served only to refine their manly spirits: and as it was out of the power of the traders to redeem them, they according to our usual cus-tom retired, as soon as the Indians began the diabolical tragedy.

The common number of an Indian war company, is only from twenty to forty, lest their tracks should be discovered by being too numerous: [385] but if the warring nations are contiguous to each other, the invading party generally chuses to out-number a common company, that they may strike the blow with greater safety and success, as their art of war is chiefly killing by surprise; confident that in case of a disappointment, their light heels will ensure their return to their own country. When a small company go to war, they always chuse to have a swamp along side of them, with a thick covert for their shelter, because a superior number will scarcely pursue them where they might reasonably expect to lose any of their warriors. When they ar-rive at the enemies hunting ground, they act with the greatest caution and policy. They separate themselves, as far as each can hear the other's travelling signal, which is the mimicking such birds and beasts as frequent the spot. And they can exactly imitate the voice and sound of every quadruped and wild fowl through the American woods. In this way of travelling, they usu-ally keep an hundred yards apart on the course agreed upon at camp. When the leader thinks it the surest way of succeeding against the enemy, he sends a few of the best runners to form an ambuscade near their towns: there, they sometimes fix the broad hoofs of buffalos, and bear's paws upon their feet, to delude the enemy: and they will for miles together, make all the windings of these beasts with the greatest art. But, as both parties are extremely wary and sagacious, I have known such arts to prove fatal to the deluders. At other times, a numerous company will walk in three different rows, by way of a decoy, every one lifting his feet so high, as not to beat down the grass or herbage; and each row will make only one man's track, by taking the steps of him who went before, and a gigantic fellow takes the rear of each rank, and thereby smooths the tracks with his feet. When they are convinced the enemy is in pursuit of them, at so considerable a distance from the country, as for themselves not to be over-powered by numbers, they post themselves in the most convenient place, in the form of an half-moon, and patiently wait a whole day and night, till the enemy runs into it; and in such a case, the victory at one broad-side is usually gained.

When they discover the tracks of enemies in their hunting ground, or in the remote woods, it is surprising to see the caution and art they use, both to secure themselves, and take advantage of the enemy. If a small company be out at war, they in the day time crawl through [386] thickets and swamps in the manner of wolves—now and then they climb trees, and run to the top of hills, to discover the smoke of fire, or hear the report of guns: and when they cross through the open woods, one of them stands behind a tree, till the rest advance about a hundred yards, looking out sharply on all quarters. In this manner, they will proceed, and on tiptoe, peeping every where around; they love to walk on trees which have been blown down, and take an oblique course, till they inswamp themselves again, in order to conceal their tracks, and avoid a pursuit. As we can gain nothing by blows, with such warriors, it is certainly our interest, as a trading people, to use proper measures to conciliate their affections; for whether we are conquerors, or conquered, we are always great losers in an Indian war.

When the invaders extend themselves cross the woods, in quest of their prey, if they make a plain discovery, either of fresh tracks, or of the enemy, they immediately pass the war-signal to each other, and draw their wings toward the centre. If the former, they give chace, and commonly by their wild-cat-method of crawling, they surround, and surprise the pursued, if unguarded—however, I have known them to fail in such attempts; for the Indians generally are so extremely cautious, that if three of them are in the woods, their first object is a proper place for defence, and they always sit down in a triangle, to prevent a surprise. When enemies discover one another, and find they can take no advantage, they make themselves known to each other; and by way of insulting bravado, they speak aloud all the barbarities they ever committed against them;—that they are now, to vindicate those actions, and make the wound for ever incurable; that they are their most bitter enemies, and equally contemn their friendship and enmity. In the mean while, they throw down their packs, strip themselves naked, and paint their faces and breast red as blood, intermingled with black streaks. Every one at the signal of the shrill-sounding war-cry, instantly covers himself behind a tree, or in some cavity of the ground where it admits of the best safety. The leader, on each side, immediately blows the small whistle he carries for the occasion, in imitation of the ancient trumpet, as the last signal of engagement. Now hot work begins—The guns are firing; the chewed bullets flying; the strong hiccory bows a twanging; the dangerous barbed arrows whizzing as they fly; the sure-shafted javelin striking death wherever it reaches; and the well-aimed tomohawk killing, or disabling its enemy. Nothing scarcely can be heard [387] for the shrill echoing noise of the war and death-whoop, every one furiously pursues his adversary from tree to tree, striving to incircle him for his prey; and the greedy jaws of pale death are open on all sides, to swallow them up. One dying foe is intangled in the hateful and faltering arms of another: and each party desperately attempts both to save their dead and wounded from being scalped, and to gain the scalps of their opponents. On this the battle commences anew—But rash attempts fail, as their wary spirits always forbid them from entering into a general close engagement. Now they retreat: then they draw up into various figures, still having their dead and wounded under their eye. Now they are flat on the ground loading their pieces—then they are up firing behind trees, and immediately spring off in an oblique course to recruit—and thus they act till winged victory declares itself.

The vanquished party makes for a swampy thicket, as their only asylum: but should any of them be either unarmed, or slightly wounded, the speedy pursuers captivate them, and usually reserve them for a worse death than that of the bullet. On returning to the place of battle, the victors begin, with mad rapture, to cut and slash those unfortunate persons, who fell by their arms and power; and they dismember them, after a most inhuman manner. If the battle be gained near home, one hero cuts off and carries this member of the dead person, another that, as joyful trophies of a decisive victory. If a stranger saw them thus loaded with human flesh, without proper information, he might conclude them to be voracious canibals, according to the shameful accounts of our Spanish historians. Their first aim however is to take off the scalp, when they perceive the enemy hath a proper situation, and strength to make a dangerous resistance. Each of them is so emulous of exceeding another in this point of honour, that it frequently stops them in their pursuit.

This honourable service is thus performed—They seize the head of the disabled, or dead person, and placing one of their feet on the neck, they with one hand twisted in the hair, extend it as far as they can—with the other hand, the barbarous artists speedily draw their long sharp-pointed scalping knife out of a sheath from their breast, give a slash round the top of the skull, and with a few dexterous scoops, soon strip it off. [388] They are so expeditious as to take off a scalp in two minutes.[431] When they have performed this part of their martial virtue, as soon as time permits, they tie with bark or deer's sinews, their speaking trophies of blood in a small hoop, to preserve it from putrefaction, and paint the interior part of the scalp, and the hoop, all round with red, their flourishing emblematical colour of blood.[432]

They are now satiated for the present, and return home. Tradition, or the native divine impression on human nature, dictates to them that man was not born in a state of war; and as they reckon they are become impure by shedding human blood, they hasten to observe the fast of three days, as formerly mentioned, and be sanctified by the war-chieftain, as a priest of war, according to law. While they are thus impure, though they had a fair opportunity of annoying the common enemy again, yet on this account they commonly decline it, and are applauded for their religious conduct, by all their countrymen. Indeed, formerly, when the whole combined power of the French, and their Indians, was bent against the warlike Chikkasah, I have known the last sometimes to hazard their martial virtue and success, and to fight three or four companies of French Indians, before they returned home; but the leaders excused themselves, by the necessity of self-defence. They have no such phrase as the "fortune of war." They reckon the leader's impurity to be the chief occasion of bad success; and if he lose several of his warriors by the enemy, his life is either in danger for the supposed fault, or he is degraded, by taking from him his drum, war-whistle, and martial titles, and debasing him to his boy's name, from which he is to rise by a fresh gradation. This penal law contributes, in a good measure, to make them so exceedingly cautious and averse to bold attempts in war, and they are usually satisfied with two or three scalps and a prisoner.

It has been long too feelingly known, that instead of observing the generous and hospitable part of the laws of war, and saving the unfortunate who fall into their power, that they generally devote their captives to death, with the most agonizing tortures.[433] No representation can possibly be given, so shocking to humanity, as their unmerciful method of tormenting their devoted prisoner; and as it is so contrary to the standard of the rest of [389] the known world, I shall relate the circumstances, so far as to convey proper information thereof to the reader. When the company return from war, and come in view of their own town, they follow the leader one by one, in a direct line, each a few yards behind the other, to magnify their triumph. If they have not succeeded, or any of their warriors are lost, they return quite silent; but if they are all safe, and have succeeded, they fire off the Indian platoon, by one, two, and three at a time, whooping and insulting their prisoners. They camp near their town all night, in a large square plot of ground, marked for the purpose, with a high war-pole fixed in the middle of it, to which they secure their prisoners. Next day they go to the leader's house in a very solemn procession, but stay without, round his red-painted war-pole, till they have determined concerning the fate of their prisoners. If any one of the captives should be fortunate enough to get loose, and run into the house of the archi-magus, or to a town of refuge, he by ancient custom, is saved from the fiery torture—these places being a sure asylum to them if they were invaded, and taken, but not to invaders, because they came to shed blood.

Those captives who are pretty far advanced in life, as well as in war-gradations, always atone for the blood they spilt, by the tortures of fire.—They readily know the latter, by the blue marks over their breasts and arms; they being as legible as our alphabetical characters are to us. Their ink is made of the soot of pitch-pine, which sticks to the inside of a greased earth-ern pot; then delineating the parts, like the ancient Picts of Britain, with their wild hieroglyphics, they break through the skin with gair-fish-teeth, and rub over them that dark composition, to register them among the brave; and the impression is lasting. I have been told by the Chikkasah, that they formerly erazed any false marks their warriors proudly and privately gave themselves—in order to engage them to give real proofs of their martial virtue, being surrounded by the French and their red allies; and that they degraded them in a public manner, by stretching the marked parts, and rub-bing them with the juice of green corn, which in a great degree took out the impression.[434]

The young prisoners are saved, if not devoted while the company were sanctifying themselves for their expedition; but if the latter be the case, [390] they are condemned, and tied to the dreadful stake, one at a time.[435] The victors first strip their miserable captives quite naked, and put on their feet a pair of bear-skin maccaseenes, with the black hairy part outwards; others fasten with a grape-vine, a burning fire-brand to the pole, a little above the reach of their heads. Then they know their doom—deep black, and burning fire, are fixed seals of their death-warrant. Their punishment is always left to the women; and on account of their false standard of educa-tion, they are no way backward in their office, but perform it to the entire satisfaction of the greedy eyes of the spectators. Each of them prepares for the dreadful rejoicing, a long bundle of dry canes, or the heart of fat pitch-pine, and as the victims are led to the stake, the women and their young ones beat them with these in a most barbarous manner. Happy would it be for the miserable creatures, if their sufferings ended here, or a merciful tomo-hawk finished them at one stroke; but this shameful treatment is a prelude to future sufferings.

The death-signal being given, preparations are made for acting a more tragical part. The victims arms are fast pinioned, and a strong grape-vine is tied round his neck, to the top of the war-pole, allowing him to track around, about fifteen yards. They fix some tough clay on his head, to secure the scalp from the blazing torches. Unspeakable pleasure now fills the exulting crowd of spectators, and the circle fills with the Amazon and merciless executioners—The suffering warrior however is not dismayed; with an insulting manly voice he sings the war-song! and with gallant contempt he tramples the rattling gourd with pebbles in it to pieces, and outbraves even death itself. The women make a furious on-set with their burning torches: his pain is soon so excruciating, that he rushes out from the pole, with the fury of the most savage beast of prey, and with the vine sweeps down all before him, kicking, biting, and trampling them, with the greatest despite. The circle immediately fills again, either with the same, or fresh persons: they attack him on every side—now he runs to the pole for shelter, but the flames pursue him. Then with champing teeth, and sparkling eye-balls, he breaks through their contracted circle afresh, and acts every part, that the highest courage, most raging fury, and blackest despair can prompt him to. But he is sure to be over-power'd by numbers, and after some time the fire affects his tender parts.—Then they pour over him a quantity of cold water, and allow him a proper time of respite, [391] till his spirits recover, and he is capable of suffering new tortures. Then the like cruelties are repeated till he falls down, and happily becomes insensible of pain. Now they scalp him, in the manner before described: dismember, and carry off all the exterior branches of the body, (pudendis non exceptis) in shameful, and savage triumph.[436] This is the most favourable treatment their devoted captives receive: it would be too shocking to humanity either to give, or peruse, every particular of their conduct in such doleful tragedies—nothing can equal these scenes, but those of the merciful Romish inquisition.

Not a soul, of whatever age or sex, manifests the least pity during the prisoner's tortures: the women sing with religious joy, all the while they are torturing the devoted victim, and peals of laughter resound through the crowded theatre—especially if he fears to die. But a warrior puts on a bold austere countenance, and carries it through all his pains:—as long as he can, he whoops and out-braves the enemy, describing his own martial deeds against them, and those of his nation, who he threatens will force many of them to eat fire in revenge of his fate, as he himself had often done to some of their relations at their cost.

Though the same things operate alike upon the organs of the human body, and produce an uniformity of sensations; yet weakness, or constancy of mind derived from habit, helps in a great measure, either to heighten, or lessen the sense of pain. By this, the afflicted party has learned to stifle nature, and shew an outward unconcern, under such slow and acute tortures: and the surprising cruelty of their women, is equally owing to education and custom. Similar instances verify this, as in Lisbon, and other places, where tender-hearted ladies are transformed by their bloody priests, into so many Medeas, through deluded religious principles; and sit and see with the highest joy, the martyrs of God, drawn along in diabolical triumph to the fiery stake, and suffering death with lingering tortures.

I cannot forbear giving another instance or two here of the constancy, visible unconcern, and presence of mind, of the Indians, at the approach of death, in its most alarming dress and terrors.

[392] About four years before the Shawano Indians were forced to remove from the late Savanah town, they took a Muskohge warrior, known by the name of "Old Scrany;" they bastinadoed him in the usual manner, and condemned him to the fiery torture.[437] He underwent a great deal, without shewing any concern; his countenance and behaviour were as if he suffered not the least pain, and was formed beyond the common laws of nature. He told them, with a bold voice, that he was a very noted warrior, and gained most of his martial preferment at the expence of their nation, and was desirous of shewing them in the act of dying, that he was still as much their superior, as when he headed his gallant countrymen against them.—That although he had fallen into their hands, in forfeiting the protection of the divine power, by some impurity or other, when carrying the holy ark of war against his devoted enemies; yet he had still so much remaining virtue, as would enable him to punish himself more exquisitely than all their despicable ignorant crowd could possibly do, if they gave him liberty by untying him, and would hand to him one of the red hot gun-barrels out of the fire. The proposal, and his method of address, appeared so exceedingly bold and uncommon, that his request was granted. Then he suddenly seized one end of the red barrel, and brandishing it from side to side, he forced his way through the armed and surprised multitude, and leaped down a prodigious steep and high bank into a branch of the river, dived through it, ran over a small island, and passed the other branch, amidst a shower of bullets from the commanding ground where Fort-Moore, or New Windsor-garrison stood; and though numbers of his eager enemies were in close pursuit of him, he got to a bramble swamp, and in that naked, mangled condition, reached his own country. He proved a sharp thorn in their side afterwards to the day of his death.

The Shawano also captivated a warrior of the Anantooèah,[438] and put him to the stake, according to their usual cruel solemnities. Having unconcernedly suffered much sharp torture, he told them with scorn, they did not know how to punish a noted enemy, therefore he was willing to teach them, and would confirm the truth of his assertion, if they allowed him the opportunity. Accordingly he requested of them a pipe and some tobacco, which was given him: as soon as he lighted it, he sat down, naked as he was, on the women's burning torches, that were within his circle, and continued smoking his pipe without the least discomposure—on [393] this a head-warrior leaped up, and said, they had seen plain enough, that he was a war-rior, and not afraid of dying; nor should he have died, only that he was both spoiled by the fire, and devoted to it by their laws: however, though he was a very dangerous enemy, and his nation a treacherous people, it should ap-pear they paid a regard to bravery, even in one, who was marked over the body with war streaks, at the cost of many lives of their beloved kindred. And then by way of favour, he, with his friendly tomohawk, instantly put an end to all his pains:—though the merciful but bloody instrument was ready some minutes before it gave the blow, yet I was assured, the spectators could not perceive the sufferer to change, either his posture, or his steady erect countenance, in the least.

A party of the Senekah Indians came to war against the Katahba, bitter enemies to each other.[439] In the woods, the former discovered a sprightly warrior belonging to the latter, hunting in their usual light dress; on his perceiving them, he sprung off for a hollow rock, four or five miles distant, as they intercepted him from running homeward. He was so extremely swift, and skilful with the gun, as to kill seven of them in the running fight, before they were able to surround and take him. They carried him to their country in sad triumph: but, though he had filled them with uncommon grief and shame, for the loss of so many of their kindred, yet the love of martial virtue induced them to treat him, during their long journey, with a great deal more civility, than if he had acted the part of a coward. The women and children, when they met him at their several towns, beat and whipped him in as severe a manner as the occasion required, according to their law of justice, and at last he was formally condemned to die by the fiery tortures. It might reasonably be imagined that what he had for some time gone through, by being fed with a scanty hand, a tedious march, lying at night on the bare ground, exposed to the changes of the weather, with his arms and legs extended in a pair of rough stocks, and suffering such punishments on his entering into their hostile towns, as a prelude to those sharp torments for which he was destined, would have so impaired his health, and affected his imagination, as to have sent him to his long sleep out of the way of any more sufferings. Probably, this would have been the case with the major part of white people, under similar circumstances; but I never knew this with any [394] of the Indians: and this cool-headed brave warrior did not deviate from their rough lessons of martial virtue, but acted his part so well, as to surprise and sorely vex his numerous enemies. For, when they were taking him unpinioned, in their wild parade, to the place of torture, which lay near to a river, he suddenly dashed down those who stood in his way, sprung off, and plunged into the water, swimming under-neath like an otter, only rising to take breath till he made the opposite shore. He now ascended the steep bank: but though he had good reason to be in a hurry, as many of the enemy were in the water, and others running every way, like blood-hounds, in pursuit of him, and the bullets flying around him, from the time he took to the river, yet his heart did not allow him to leave them abruptly, without taking leave in a formal manner, in return for the extraordinary favours they had done, and intended to do him. He first turned his backside toward them, and slapped it with his hand; then moving round, be put up the shrill war whoo whoop, as his last salute, till some more convenient opportunity offered, and darted off in the manner of a beast broke loose from its torturing enemies. He continued his speed so as to run by about midnight of the same day, as far as his eager pursuers were two days in reaching. There he rested, till he happily discovered five of those Indians, who had pursued him—he lay hid a little way off their camp, till they were sound asleep. Every circumstance of his situation occurred to him, and inspired him with heroism. He was naked, torn, and hungry, and his enraged enemies were come up with him. But there was now every thing to relieve his wants, and a fair opportunity to save his life, and get great honour, and sweet revenge, by cutting them off. Resolution, a convenient spot, and sudden surprize, would effect the main object of all his wishes and hopes. He accordingly creeped towards them, took one of their tomohawks, and killed them all on the spot. He then chopped them to pieces, in as horrid a manner, as savage fury could excite, both through national and personal resentment,—he stripped off their scalps, clothed himself, took a choice gun, and as much ammunition and provisions as he could well carry in a running march. He set off afresh with a light heart, and did not sleep for several successive nights, only when he reclined as usual a little before day, with his back to a tree. As it were by instinct, when he found he was free from the pursuing enemy, he made directly to the very place where he had killed seven of his enemies, and was taken by them for the fiery torture. [395] He digged them up, scalped them, burned their bodies to ashes, and went home in safety with singular triumph. Other pursuing enemies came on the evening of the second day to the camp of their dead people, when the sight gave them a greater shock, than they had ever known before. In their chilled war council, they concluded, that, as he had done such surprising things in his defence, before he was captivated, and since that, in his naked condition, and was now well armed, if they continued the pursuit, he would spoil them all, for he surely was an enemy wizard. And therefore they returned home.

When the Chikkasah were engaged in a former war with the Muskohge, one of their young warriors set off alone against them, to revenge the blood of a near relation: his burning heart would not allow him to delay its gratification, and proceed with a company, after their usual forms of purification were observed, in order to gain success. He was replete with martial fire, and revenge prompted him to outrun his war virtue: however, he pursued as mortifying a regimen, as if he had been publicly fed like a dove, by the scanty hand of a religious waiter. But, as he would not wait a few days, and accompany the reputed holy ark, they reckoned him irreligious, by depending on the power of his own arms, instead of the powerful arm of the supreme fatherly chieftain, *Yo He Wah,* who always bestows victory on the more virtuous party. He went through the most unfrequented and thick parts of the woods, as such a dangerous enterprise required, till he arrived opposite to the great, and old beloved town of refuge, Koosah, which stands high on the eastern side of a bold river, about 250 yards broad, that runs by the late dangerous Alebahma fort, down to the black poisoning Mobille, and so into the gulph of Mexico. There he concealed himself under cover of the top of a fallen pine tree, in view of the ford of the old trading path, where the enemy now and then passed the river in their light poplar canoes. All his war store of provisions consisted in three stands of barbicued venison, till he had an opportunity to revenge blood, and return home. He waited, with watchfulness and patience almost three days, when a young man, a woman, and a girl passed a little wide of him, about an hour before sunset. The former he shot down, tomohawked the other two, and scalped each of them in a trice, in full view of the town. By way of bravado, he shaked the scalps before them, sounded the awful death whoop, and [396] set off along the trading path, trusting to his heels, while a great many of the enemy ran to their arms, and gave chace. Seven miles from thence, he entered the great blue ridge of Apalahche mountains. About an hour before day, he had ran over seventy miles of that mountainous tract;—then, after sleeping two hours in a sitting posture, leaning his back against a tree, he set off again with fresh speed. As he threw away his venison, when he found himself pursued by the enemy, he was obliged to support nature with such herbs, roots, and nuts, as his sharp eyes with a running glance, directed him to snatch up in his course. Though I often have rode that war path alone, when delay might have proved dangerous, and with as fine and strong horses as any in America, it took me five days to ride from the aforesaid Koosah, to this sprightly warrior's place in the Chikkasah country, the distance of 300 computed miles; yet he ran it, and got home safe and well, at about eleven o'clock of the third day; which was only one day and half, and two nights.

These two well known instances of the young Katahba, and this Chikkasah warrior, evince the surprising and superior abilities of the Indians in their own element. And the intrepid behaviour of the two other red stoics, their surprising contempt of, and indifference to life or death, instead of lessening, helps to confirm our belief of that supernatural power, which supported the great number of primitive martyrs, who sealed the christian faith with their blood. The Indians, as I observed in the former part, have as much belief, and expectation of a future state, as the greater part of the Israelites seem to have possessed. But the christians, of the first centuries, may justly be said to exceed even the most heroic American Indians; for they bore the bitterest persecution, with steady patience, in imitation of their divine leader, Messiah, in full confidence of divine support, and of a glorious recompence of reward; and, instead of even wishing for revenge on their cruel enemies and malicious tormentors (which is the chief principle that actuates the Indians) they not only forgave them, but in the midst of their tortures, earnestly prayed for them, with composed countenances, sincere love, and unabated fervor. And not only men of different conditions, but the delicate women and children suffered with constancy, and died praying for their tormentors: the Indian women and children, and their young men untrained to war, are incapable of displaying the like patience and magnanimity.

[397] When the Indians have finished their captive tragedies, they return to the neighbouring town in triumph, with the wild shrieking noise of destroying demons: there, they cut the scalps into several pieces, fix them on different twigs of the green leaved pine, and place them on the tops of the circular winter houses of their deceased relations—whose deaths (if by the hand of an enemy) they esteem not revenged till then, and thus their ghosts are enabled to go to their intermediate, but unknown place of rest, till, after a certain time, they return again to live for ever in that tract of land which pleased them best, when in their former state. They perform this supposed religious duty with great solemnity, attended by a long train of rejoicing women, chanting with soft voices, their grateful song of triumph to *Yo He Wah;* while the favoured warriors echo their praises of the giver of victory, with awful notes, and intermix with them the death whoo-whoop. They dance for three days and nights, rejoicing before the divine presence, for their victory; and the happiness of sending the spirits of their killed relations from the eaves of their houses which they haunted, mourning with such painful notes as *Koo-Koo-Koo,* like the suffering owls of night in pinching winter, according to their creed. In their dance, they represent all the wild cat movements they made in crawling to surprise the enemy, and their wolfish conduct in killing with safety; or the whole engagement, when they could no way attack by surprise. Now, they lift up one foot, then put it down slowly on tip-toe in a bent posture, looking sharply every way. Thus, they proceed from tree to tree, till the supposed enemy be either defeated by stratagem, or open battle. Then they strut about in parade, and the chief will tell the people he did not behave like a blind white man, who would have rushed on with his eyes shut, improvident of danger; but having wisely considered that his bare breast was not bullet proof, he cunningly covered himself from tree to tree, and by his skilful conduct vanquished the hateful

enemy, without exposing his own valuable life to danger. All people praise, or blame another's conduct, in proportion to the parity or disparity it bears to their own standard, and notion of virtue.

In the time of their rejoicings, they fix a certain day for the warriors to be crowned; for they cannot sleep sound or easy under an old title, while a new, or higher one is due. On that long-wished for day, they all appear on the field of parade, as fine and cheerful as the birds in spring. Their martial [398] drums beat, their bloody colours are displayed, and most of the young people are dancing and rejoicing, for the present success of their nation, and the safe return and preferment of their friends and relations. Every expectant warrior on that joyful day wears deer-skin maccaseenes, painted red, his body is anointed with bear's oil, a young softened otter-skin is tied on each leg, a long collar of fine swan feathers hangs round his neck, and his face is painted with the various streaks of the rain-bow. Thus they appear, when two of the old magi come forth holding as many white wands and crowns, as there are warriors to be graduated: and in a standing posture, they alternately deliver a long oration, with great vehemence of expression, chiefly commending their strict observance of the law of purity, while they accompanied the beloved ark of war, which induced the supreme chieftain to give them the victory, and they encourage the rest to continue to thirst after glory, in imitation of their brave ancestors, who died nobly in defence of their country. At the conclusion of their orations, one of the magi calls three times with a loud voice, one of the warriors by his new name, or war title, and holds up the white crown, and the scepter, or wand. He then gladly answers, and runs whooping to, and around them, three times. One of the old beloved men puts the crown on his head, and the wand into his hand; then he returns to his former place, whooping with joy. In like manner, they proceed with the rest of the graduate warriors, to the end of their triumphal ceremony, concluding with this strong caution, "Remember what you are (such a warrior, mentioning his titles) according to the old beloved speech." This is equal to the bold virtuous lessons of the honest Romans, and uncorrupted Greeks. The concluding caution of the magi to the warriors, points at the different duties of their honourable station, that they should always aspire after martial glory, and prefer their own virtue, and the welfare of their country, more than life itself. The crown is wrought round with the long feathers of a swan, at the lower end, where it surrounds his temples, and it is curiously weaved with a quantity of white down, to make it sit easy, and appear more beautiful. To this part that wreathes his brows, the skilful artist warps close together, a ringlet of the longest feathers of the swan, and turning them carefully upward, in an uniform position, he, in the exactest manner, ties them together with deer's sinews, so as the bandage will not appear to the sharpest eyes without handling it. It is a little open at the top, and about fifteen inches high. The crowns they use in constituting [399] war-leaders, are always worked with feathers of the tail of the cherubic eagle, which causes them to be three or four inches higher than the former. This latter custom bears a striking resemblance to the usage of the ancients on similar occasions, according to the constitution of their different forms of government.

They are exceedingly pointed against our methods of war, and conferring of titles. By the surprising conduct of a Georgia governor, both the Muskohge and Cheerake, who attended our army in the war before the last, against St. Augustine,[440] have entertained, and will continue to have the meanest opinion of the Carolina martial disposition, till by some notable brave actions, it wears off. The Indians concluded that there was treachery in our letting prisoners of distinction return to the fort to put the rest on their guard, and in our shutting up the batteries for four or five days successively, not having our cannon dismounted, nor annoying the enemy, but having flags of truce frequently passing and repassing. They said, that it was plain to their eyes, we only managed a sham fight with the Spaniards—and they became very uneasy, and held many conferences about our friendly intercourse with the garrison; concluding that we had decoyed them down to be slaughtered, or delivered to the Spaniard to purchase a firm peace for ourselves—and they no sooner reached their own countries, than they reported the whole affair in black colours, that we allured them to a far-distant place, where we gave them only a small quantity of bad food; and that they were obliged to drink saltish water, which, instead of allaying, inflamed their thirst, while we were carousing with various liquors, and shaking hands with the Spaniard, and sending the white beloved speech to one another, by beat of drum, although we had the assurance to affirm that we held fast the bloody tomohawk. The minutest circumstance was so strongly represented, that both nations were on the very point of commencing war against us. But the "Raven" of Euwase, a leading head warrior of the Cheerake, was confined in Augusta garrison, till he sent up runners to stop a war, that his speeches and messages had nearly fomented—his life was threatened on failure, and he had large promises given, if he complied and succeeded.[441]

The Indians are much addicted to gaming, and will often stake every thing they possess. Ball-playing is their chief and most favourite game: and is such severe exercise, as to shew it was originally calculated for a [400] hardy and expert race of people, like themselves, and the ancient Spartans. The ball is made of a piece of scraped deer-skin, moistened, and stuffed hard with deer's hair, and strongly sewed with deer's sinews.—The ball-sticks are about two feet long, the lower end somewhat resembling the palm of a hand, and which are worked with deer-skin thongs. Between these, they catch the ball, and throw it a great distance, when not prevented by some of the opposite party, who fly to intercept them. The goal is about five hundred yards in length: at each end of it, they fix two long bending poles into the ground, three yards apart below, but slanting a considerable way outwards. The party that happens to throw the ball over these, counts one; but, if it be thrown underneath, it is cast back, and played for as usual. The gamesters are equal in number on each side; and, at the beginning of every course of the ball, they throw it up high in the center of the ground, and in a direct line between the two goals. When the crowd of players prevents the one who catched the ball, from throwing it off with a long direction, he commonly sends it the right course, by an artful sharp twirl. They are so exceedingly expert in this manly exercise, that, between the goals, the ball is mostly flying the different ways, by the force of the playing sticks, without falling to the ground, for they are not allowed to catch it with their hands. It is surprising to see how swiftly they fly, when closely chased by a nimble footed pursuer; when they are intercepted by one of the opposite party, his fear of being cut by the ball sticks, commonly gives them an opportunity of throwing it perhaps a hundred yards; but the antagonist sometimes runs up behind, and by a sudden stroke dashes down the ball. It is a very unusual thing to see them act spitefully in any sort of game, not even in this severe and tempting exercise.[442]

Once, indeed, I saw some break the legs and arms of their opponents, by hurling them down, when on a descent, and running at full speed. But I afterward understood, there was a family dispute of long continuance between them: that might have raised their spleen, as much as the high bets they had then at stake, which was almost all they were worth. The Choktah are exceedingly addicted to gaming, and frequently on the slightest and most hazardous occasion, will lay their all, and as much as their credit can procure.

[401] By education, precept, and custom, as well as strong example, they have learned to shew an external acquiescence in every thing that befalls them, either as to life or death. By this means, they reckon it a scandal to the character of a steady warrior to let his temper be ruffled by any accidents,— their virtue they say, should prevent it. Their conduct is equal to their belief of the power of those principles: previous to this sharp exercise of ball playing, notwithstanding the irreligion of the Choktah in other respects, they will supplicate *Yo He Wah,* to bless them with success. To move the deity to enable them to conquer the party they are to play against, they mortify themselves in a surprising manner; and, except a small intermission, their female relations dance out of doors all the preceding night, chanting religious notes with their shrill voices, to move *Yo He Wah* to be favourable to their kindred party on the morrow. The men fast and wake from sunset, till

the ball play is over the next day, which is about one or two o'clock in the afternoon. During the whole night, they are to forbear sleeping under the penalty of reproaches and shame; which would sit very sharp upon them, if their party chanced to lose the game, as it would be ascribed to that unmanly and vicious conduct. They turn out to the ball ground, in a long row, painted white, whooping, as if Pluto's prisoners were all broke loose: when that enthusiastic emotion is over, the leader of the company begins a religious invocation, by saying *Yah,* short; then *Yo* long, which the rest of the train repeat with a short accent, and on a low key like the leader: and thus they proceed with such acclamations and invocations, as have been already noticed, on other occasions. Each party are desirous to gain the twentieth ball, which they esteem a favourite divine gift. As it is in the time of laying by the corn, in the very heat of summer, they use this severe exercise, a stranger would wonder to see them hold it so long at full speed, and under the scorching sun, hungry also, and faint with the excessive use of such sharp physic as the button snake root, the want of natural rest, and of every kind of nourishment. But their constancy, which they gain by custom, and their love of virtue, as the sure means of success, enable them to perform all their exercises, without failing in the least, be they ever so severe in the pursuit.

The warriors have another favourite game, called *Chungke;* which, with propriety of language, may be called "Running hard labour." They [402] have near their state house, a square piece of ground well cleaned, and fine sand is carefully strewed over it, when requisite, to promote a swifter motion to what they throw along the surface. Only one, or two on a side, play at this ancient game. They have a stone about two fingers broad at the edge, and two spans round: each party has a pole of about eight feet long, smooth, and tapering at each end, the points flat. They set off a-breast of each other at six yards from the end of the play ground; then one of them hurls the stone on its edge, in as direct a line as he can, a considerable distance toward the middle of the other end of the square: when they have ran a few yards, each darts his pole anointed with bear's oil, with a proper force, as near as he can guess in proportion to the motion of the stone, that the end may lie close to the stone—when this is the case, the person counts two of the game, and, in proportion to the nearness of the poles to the mark, one is counted, unless by measuring, both are found to be at an equal distance from the stone. In this manner, the players will keep running most part of the day, at half speed, under the violent heat of the sun, staking their silver ornaments, their nose, finger, and ear rings; their breast, arm, and wrist plates, and even all their wearing apparel, except that which barely covers their middle. All the American Indians are much addicted to this game, which to us appears to be a task of stupid drudgery: it seems however to be of early origin, when their fore-fathers used diversions as simple as their manners. The hurling stones they use at present, were time immemorial rubbed smooth on the rocks, and with prodigious labour; they are kept with the strictest religious care, from one generation to another, and are exempted from being buried with the dead. They belong to the town where they are used, and are carefully preserved.[443]

Their manner of rambling through the woods to kill deer, is a very laborious exercise, as they frequently walk twenty-five or thirty miles through rough and smooth grounds, and fasting, before they return back to camp, loaded. Their method of fishing may be placed among their diversions, but this is of the profitable kind. When they see large fish near the surface of the water, they fire directly upon them, sometimes only with powder, which noise and surprize however so stupifies them, that they instantly turn up their bellies and float a top, when the fisherman secures them. If they shoot at fish not deep in the water, either with an arrow or bullet, they aim [403] at the lower part of the belly, if they are near; and lower, in like manner, according to the distance, which seldom fails of killing. In a dry summer season, they gather horse chestnuts, and different sorts of roots, which having pounded pretty fine, and steeped a while in a trough, they scatter this mixture over the surface of a middle-sized pond, and stir it about with poles, till the water is sufficiently impregnated with the intoxicating bittern. The fish are soon inebriated, and make to the surface of the water, with their bellies uppermost. The fishers gather them in baskets, and barbicue the largest, covering them carefully over at night to preserve them from the supposed putrifying influence of the moon. It seems, that fish catched in this manner, are not poisoned, but only stupified; for they prove very wholesome food to us, who frequently use them. By experiments, when they are speedily moved into good water, they revive in a few minutes.[444]

The Indians have the art of catching fish in long crails [creels], made with canes and hiccory splinters, tapering to a point. They lay these at a fall of water, where stones are placed in two sloping lines from each bank, till they meet together in the middle of the rapid stream, where the intangled fish are soon drowned. Above such a place, I have known them to fasten a wreath of long grape vines together, to reach across the river, with stones fastened at proper distances to rake the bottom; they will swim a mile with it whooping, and plunging all the way, driving the fish before them into their large cane pots.[445] With this draught, which is a very heavy one, they make a town feast, or feast of love, of which every one partakes in the most social manner, and afterward they dance together, singing *Halelu-yah,* and the rest of their usual praises to the divine essence, for his bountiful gifts to the beloved people. Those Indians who are unacquainted with the use of barbed irons, are very expert in striking large fish out of their canoes, with long sharp pointed green canes, which are well bearded, and hardened in the fire. In Savanah river, I have often accompanied them in killing sturgeons with those green swamp harpoons, and which they did with much pleasure and ease; for, when we discovered the fish, we soon thrust into their bodies one of the harpoons. As the fish would immediately strike deep, and rush away to the bottom very rapidly, their strength was soon expended, by their violent struggles against the buoyant force of the green darts: as soon as the top end of them appeared again on the surface [404] of the water, we made up to them, renewed the attack, and in like manner continued it, till we secured our game.[446]

They have a surprising method of fishing under the edges of rocks, that stand over deep places of a river. There, they pull off their red breeches, or their long slip of Stroud cloth, and wrapping it round their arm, so as to reach to the lower part of the palm of their right hand, they dive under the rock where the large cat-fish lie to shelter themselves from the scorching beams of the sun, and to watch for prey: as soon as those fierce aquatic animals see that tempting bait, they immediately seize it with the greatest violence, in order to swallow it. Then is the time for the diver to improve the favourable opportunity: he accordingly opens his hand, seizes the voracious fish by his tender parts, hath a sharp struggle with it against the crevices of the rock, and at last brings it safe ashore.[447] Except the Choktah, all our Indians, both male and female, above the state of infancy, are in the watery element nearly equal to amphibious animals, by practice: and from the experiments necessity has forced them to, it seems as if few were endued with such strong natural abilities,—very few can equal them in their wild situation of life.

There is a favourite method among them of fishing with hand-nets. The nets are about three feet deep, and of the same diameter at the opening, made of hemp, and knotted after the usual manner of our nets. On each side of the mouth, they tie very securely a strong elastic green cane, to which the ends are fastened. Prepared with these, the warriors a-breast, jump in at the end of a long pond, swimming under water, with their net stretched open with both hands, and the canes in a horizontal position. In this manner, they will continue, either till their breath is expended by the want of respiration, or till the net is so ponderous as to force them to exonerate it ashore, or in a basket, fixt in a proper place for that purpose—by removing one hand, the canes instantly spring together. I have been engaged half a day at a time, with the old-friendly Chikkasah, and half drowned in the diversion—when any of us was so unfortunate as to catch water-snakes in our sweep, and emptied them ashore, we had the ranting voice of our friendly posse comitatus,[448] whooping against us, till another party was so unlucky as to meet with the like misfortune. During this exercise, the women are fishing ashore with coarse baskets, to catch the fish [405] that escape our nets. At the end of our friendly diversion, we cheerfully return home, and in an innocent and friendly manner, eat together, studiously diverting each other, on the incidents of the day, and make a cheerful night.

The Indians formerly had stone axes, which in form commonly resembled a smith's chisel. Each weighed from one to two, or three pounds weight—They were made of a flinty kind of stone: I have seen several, which chanced to escape being buried with their owners, and were carefully preserved by the old people, as respectable remains of antiquity. They twisted two or three tough hiccory slips, of about two feet long, round the notched head of the axe; and by means of this simple and obvious invention, they deadened the trees by cutting through the bark, and burned them, when they either fell by decay, or became thoroughly dry. With these trees they always kept up their annual holy fire; and they reckon it unlawful, and productive of many temporal evils, to extinguish even the culinary fire with water. In the time of a storm, when I have done it, the kindly women were in pain for me, through fear of the ill consequences attending so criminal an act. I never saw them to damp the fire, only when they hung up a brand in the appointed place, with a twisted grape-vine, as a threatening symbol of torture and death to the enemy; or when their kinsman dies. In the last case, a father or brother of the deceased, takes a fire-brand, and brandishing it two or three times round his head, with lamenting words, he with his right hand dips it into the water, and lets it sink down.

By the aforesaid difficult method of deadening the trees, and clearing the woods, the contented natives got convenient fields in process of time. And their tradition says they did not live straggling in the American woods, as do the Arabians, and rambling Tartars; for they made houses with the branches and bark of trees, for the summer-season; and warm mud-walls, mixt with soft dry grass, against the bleak winter, according to their present plan of building, which I shall presently describe. Now, in the first clearing of their plantations, they only bark the large timber, cut down the saplings and underwood, and burn them in heaps; as the suckers shoot up, they chop them off close by the stump, of which they make fires to deaden the roots, till in time they decay. Though to a stranger, this may seem to be a [406] lazy method of clearing the wood-lands; yet it is the most expeditious method they could have pitched upon, under their circumstances, as a common hoe and a small hatchet are all their implements for clearing and planting.

Every dwelling-house has a small field pretty close to it: and, as soon as the spring of the year admits, there they plant a variety of large and small beans, peas, and the smaller sort of Indian corn, which usually ripens in two months, from the time it is planted; though it is called by the English, the six weeks corn. Around this small farm, they fasten stakes in the ground, and tie a couple of long split hiccory, or white oak-sapplings, at proper distances to keep off the horses: though they cannot leap fences, yet many of the old horses will creep through these enclosures, almost as readily as swine, to the great regret of the women, who scold and give them ill names, calling them ugly mad horses, and bidding them "go along, and be sure to keep away, otherwise their hearts will hang sharp within them, and set them on to spoil them, if envy and covetousness lead them back." Thus they argue with them, and they are usually as good as their word, by striking a tomohawk into the horse, if he does not observe the friendly caution they gave him at the last parting. Their large fields lie quite open with regard to fencing, and they believe it to be agreeable to the best rules of œconomy; because, as they say, they can cultivate the best of their land here and there, as it suits their conveniency, without wasting their time in fences and childishly confining their improvements, as if the crop would eat itself. The women however tether the horses with tough young bark-ropes, and confine the swine in convenient penns, from the time the provisions are planted, till they are gathered in—the men improve this time, either in killing plenty of wild game, or coursing against the common enemy, and thereby secure the women and girls, and get their own temples surrounded with the swan-feathered cap. In this manner, the Indians have to me, excused their long-contracted habit and practice.

The chief part of the Indians begin to plant their out-fields, when the wild fruit is so ripe, as to draw off the birds from picking up the grain. This is their general rule, which is in the beginning of May, about the time the traders set off for the English settlements. Among several nations of Indians, each town usually works together. Previous thereto, an old [407] beloved man warns the inhabitants to be ready to plant on a prefixed day. At the dawn of it, one by order goes aloft, and whoops to them with shrill calls, "that the new year is far advanced,—that he who expects to eat, must work,—and that he who will not work, must expect to pay the fine according to old custom, or leave the town, as they will not sweat themselves for an healthy idle waster." At such times, may be seen many war-chieftains working in common with the people, though as great emperors, as those the Spaniards bestowed on the old simple Mexicans and Peruvians, and equal in power, (i.e. persuasive force) with the imperial and puissant Powhatan of Virginia, whom our generous writers raised to that prodigious pitch of power and grandeur, to rival the Spanish accounts. About an hour after sunrise, they enter the field agreed on by lot, and fall to work with great cheerfulness; sometimes one of their orators cheers them with jests and humorous old tales, and sings several of their most agreeable wild tunes, beating also with a stick in his right hand, on the top of an earthern pot covered with a wet and well-stretched deer-skin: thus they proceed from field to field, till their seed is sown.

Corn is their chief produce, and main dependance.[449] Of this they have three sorts; one of which hath been already mentioned. The second sort is yellow and flinty, which they call "hommony-corn." The third is the largest, of a very white and soft grain, termed "bread-corn." In July, when the chesnuts and corn are green and full grown, they half boil the former, and take off the rind; and having sliced the milky, swelled, long rows of the latter, the women pound it in a large wooden mortar, which is wide at the mouth, and gradually narrows to the bottom:[450] then they knead both together, wrap them up in green corn-blades of various sizes, about an inch-thick, and boil them well, as they do every kind of seethed food. This sort of bread is very tempting to the taste, and reckoned most delicious to their strong palates. They have another sort of boiled bread, which is mixed with beans, or potatoes; they put on the soft corn till it begins to boil, and pound it sufficiently fine;—their invention does not reach to the use of any kind of milk. When the flour is stirred, and dried by the heat of the sun or fire, they sift it with sieves of different sizes, curiously made of the coarser or finer canesplinters. The thin cakes mixt with bear's oil, were formerly baked on thin broad stones placed over a fire, or on broad earthen bottoms fit for such a use: but now they use kettles. When they intend to [408] bake great loaves, they make a strong blazing fire, with short dry split wood, on the hearth. When it is burnt down to coals, they carefully rake them off to each side, and sweep away the remaining ashes: then they put their well-kneeded broad loaf, first steeped in hot water, over the hearth, and an earthen bason above it, with the embers and coals a-top. This method of baking is as clean and efficacious as could possibly be done in any oven; when they take it off, they wash the loaf with warm water, and it soon becomes firm, and very white. It is likewise very wholesome, and well-tasted to any except the vitiated palate of an Epicure.

The French of West-Florida, and the English colonists, got from the Indians different sorts of beans and peas, with which they were before entirely unacquainted. And they plant a sort of small tobacco, which the French and English have not. All the Indian nations we have any acquaintance with, frequently use it on the most religious occasions. The women plant also pompions, and different sorts of melons, in separate fields, at a considerable distance from the town, where each owner raises an high scaffold, to overlook this favourite part of their vegetable possessions: and though the enemy sometimes kills them in this their strict watch duty, yet it is a very rare thing to pass by those fields, without seeing them there at watch. This usually is the duty of the old women, who fret at the very shadow of a crow, when he chances to pass on his wide survey of the fields; but if pinching hunger should excite him to descend, they soon frighten him away with their screeches. When the pompions are ripe, they cut them into long circling slices, which they barbacue, or dry with a slow heat. And when they have half boiled the larger sort of potatoes, they likewise dry them over a moderate fire, and chiefly use them in the spring-season, mixt with their favourite bear's oil. As soon as the larger sort of corn is full-eared, they half-boil it too, and dry it either by the sun, or over a slow fire; which might be done, as well, in a moderately hot oven, if the heat was renewed as occasion required. This they boil with venison, or any other unsalted flesh. They commonly have pretty good crops, which is owing to the richness of the soil; for they often let the weeds out-grow the corn, before they begin to be in earnest with their work, owing to their laziness and unskilfulness in planting: and this method is general through all those nations that work separately [409] in their own fields, which in a great measure checks the growth of their crops. Besides, they are so desirous of having *multum in parvo*,[451] without much sweating, that they plant the corn-hills so close, as to thereby choak up the field.—They plant their corn in straight rows, putting five or six grains into one hole, about two inches distant—They cover them with clay in the form of a small hill. Each row is a yard asunder, and in the vacant ground they plant pumpkins, water-melons, marsh-mallows, sun-flowers, and sundry sorts of beans and peas, the last two of which yield a large increase.

They have a great deal of fruit, and they dry such kinds as will bear it. At the fall of the leaf, they gather a number of hiccory-nuts, which they pound with a round stone, upon a stone, thick and hollowed for the purpose. When they are beat fine enough, they mix them with cold water, in a clay bason, where the shells subside. The other part is an oily, tough, thick, white substance, called by the traders hiccory milk, and by the Indians the flesh, or fat of hiccory-nuts, with which they eat their bread.[452] A hearty stranger would be as apt to dip into the sediments as I did, the first time this vegetable thick milk was set before me. As ranging the woods had given me a keen appetite, I was the more readily tempted to believe they only tantalized me for their diversion, when they laughed heartily at my supposed ignorance. But luckily when the bason was in danger, the bread was brought in piping hot, and the good-natured landlady being informed of my simplicity, shewed me the right way to use the vegetable liquid. It is surprising to see the great variety of dishes they make out of wild flesh, corn, beans, peas, potatoes, pompions, dried fruits, herbs and roots. They can diversify their courses, as much as the English, or perhaps the French cooks: and in either of the ways they dress their food, it is grateful to a wholesome stomach.

Their old fields abound with larger strawberries than I have seen in any part of the world; insomuch, that in the proper season, one may gather a hat-full, in the space of two or three yards square. They have a sort of wild potatoes, which grow plentifully in their rich low lands, from South-Carolina to the Missisippi, and partly serve them instead of bread, either in the woods a hunting, or at home when the foregoing summer's crop fails them.[453] They have a small vine, which twines, [410] chiefly round the watry alder; and the hogs feed often upon the grapes. Their surface is un-even, yet inclining to a round figure. They are large, of a course grain, well-tasted, and very wholesome; in the woods, they are a very agreeable repast.[454] There grows a long flag, in shallow ponds, and on the edges of running waters, with an ever-green, broad, round leaf, a little indented where it joins the stalk; it bears only one leaf, that always floats on the surface of the water, and affords plenty of cooling small nuts, which make a sweet-tasted, and favourite bread, when mixed with Indian corn flour. It is a sort of marsh-mallows, and reckoned a speedy cure for burning maladies, either outward or inward,—for the former, by an outward application of the leaf; and for the latter, by a decoction of it drank plentifully. The Choktah so highly esteem this vegetable, that they call one of their head-towns, by its name.[455]

Providence hath furnished even the uncultivated parts of America with sufficient to supply the calls of nature.—Formerly, about fifty miles to the north-east of the Chikkasah country, I saw the chief part of the main camp of the Shawano, consisting of about 450 persons, on a tedious ramble to the Muskohge country, where they settled, seventy-miles above the Alabahma-garrison: they had been straggling in the woods, for the space of four years, as they assured me, yet in general they were more corpulent than the Chik-kasah who accompanied me, notwithstanding they had lived during that time, on the wild products of the American desarts. This evinces how easily nature's wants are supplied, and that the divine goodness extends to America and its inhabitants. They are acquainted with a great many herbs and roots, of which the general part of the English have not the least knowledge. If an Indian were driven out into the extensive woods, with only a knife and tomohawk, or a small hatchet, it is not to be doubted but he would fatten, even where a wolf would starve. He could soon collect fire, by rubbing two dry pieces of wood together, make a bark hut, earthen vessels, and a bow and arrows; then kill wild game, fish, fresh water tortoises, gather a plentiful variety of vegetables, and live in affluence. Formerly, they made their knives of flint-stone, or of split canes; and sometimes they are now forced to use the like, in slaying wild animals, when in their winter hunt they have the misfortune to lose their knives.

[411] I shall mention one instance, which will confirm what I have said of their surprising skill and ability of living in desarts, inhabited only by

wild beasts. In the winter of the year 1747, one of the Chikkasah traders went from home, about ten miles, accompanied only by a negro; six of the miles was an old waste field, which the Chikkasah formerly had settled, when they were more numerous. On their return home, within two miles of the outer-houses, while riding carelesly near two steep gullies, there stood a couple of Canada Indians behind a tree, (beside two others a little way off) within a few yards of the path, with their trunk guns, watching two boys then in sight—when the trader and his servant came abreast of them, the negro's horse received a mortal shot, and after carrying him about a quarter of a mile, on leaping a difficult pass, he fell dead on the spot; the rider's heels carried him the rest of the way safe: but, unluckily, it did not fare so well with the gentleman, for as he rode a young Choktah horse, which had been used only to a rope round his neck, the reining him with a bridle, checked him, and the French savages had an opportunity to give the gentleman two mortal wounds, with brass-barbed arrows, the one in his belly, and the other a little below the heart; beside two others in his left shoulder. His horse being frightened, sprung off at full speed, and brought him home. The gentleman in his rapid course twisted the murdering arrows out of his bowels, but could not reach those that were deeply lodged in his shoulder. He lived two nights and a day after this in most exquisite tortures, but sensible to the last; when he had been forcibly kept down, a considerable time on the bed, he entreated in the most importunate manner, to be helped to lean his back against the wall, and it would give him ease. At my request it was allowed him—he immediately expired, and it is to be hoped, that, according to his desire, he immediately entered into eternal rest. While he lay a corpse, and till we the next day buried him, the Indians were silent, and almost invisible. The negro and his master, as soon as they discovered the Canadians, put up the shrill whoop, both to warn the Chikkasah, and draw them against the enemy; this made the two boys to stretch home, which they did a little before sun-set. But the lateness of the day, prevented our friends pursuing, till next morning. By the distance the enemy ran in the night, they for that time evaded their eager pursuers. Some went to the place of ambuscade, and found that the enemy being disappointed of the prey falling into their hands, had pursued till they came up with the negro's [412] horse, which they had chopped, and the saddle, with their tomohawks, all to pieces. However, about half way between the Chikkasah country and the Illinois, three old Chikkasah warriors, on their way to join the main camp, came up with those Canadians in wet bushy ground;—they closely chased them for several miles, and forced them by degrees to throw away every thing they carried, and seek their safety by leaping quite naked into a deep and broad creek, that was much frozen on the two banks; it was for some time imagined they had perished in the woods, by the severity of winter, but we were well informed afterwards, that like hardy beasts of prey, they got safe home.

None of the Indians however eat any kind of raw sallads; they reckon such food is only fit for brutes. Their taste is so very opposite to that of cannibals, that in order to destroy the blood, (which with them is an abomination to eat) they over-dress every kind of animal food they use. I have often jested them for pressing me to eat eggs, that were boiled so much as to be blue, and told them my teeth were too bad to chew bullets. They said they could not suck eggs after the manner of the white people, otherwise they would have brought them raw; but they hoped I would excuse the present, and they would take particular care not to repeat the error, the next time I favoured them with a visit. In the spring of the year, they use a great many valuable greens and herbs, which nature has peculiarly adapted to their rich, and high-situated regions: few of them have gardens, and it is but of late they have had any angelica, or belly-ach-root; this is one of their physical greens, which they call *Look-sooshe.*[456]

I shall now describe the domestic life of the Indians, and the traders among them. The Indians settle themselves in towns or villages after an easy manner; the houses are not too close to incommode one another, nor too far distant for social defence. If the nation where the English traders reside, is at war with the French, or their red confederates, which is the same, their houses are built in the middle of the town, if desired, on account of greater security. But if they are at peace with each other, both the Indians and traders chuse to settle at a very convenient distance, for the sake of their live stock, especially the latter, for the Indian youth are as destructive to the pigs and poultry, as so many young wolves or foxes. [413] Their parents now only give them ill names for such misconduct, calling them mad; but the mischievous, and thievish, were formerly sure to be dry-scratched, which punishment hath been already described.

Most of the Indians have clean, neat, dwelling houses, white-washed within and without, either with decayed oyster-shells, coarse-chalk, or white marly clay; one or other of which, each of our Indian nations abounds with, be they ever so far distant from the sea-shore: the Indians, as well as the traders, usually decorate their summer-houses with this favourite white-wash.—The former have likewise each a corn-house, fowl-house, and a hot-house, or stove for winter: and so have the traders likewise separate store-houses for their goods, as well as to contain the proper remittances received in exchange.

The traders hot-houses are appropriated to their young-rising prolific family, and their well-pleased attendants, who are always as kindly treated as brethren; and their various buildings, are like towers in cities, beyond the common size of those of the Indians. Before the Indians were corrupted by mercenary empirics, their good sense led them to esteem the traders among them as their second sun, warming their backs with the British fleeces, and keeping in their candle of life both by plentiful support, and continual protection and safety, from the fire-arms and ammunition which they annually brought to them. While the Indians were simple in manners, and uncorrupt in morals, the traders could not be reckoned unhappy; for they were kindly treated, and watchfully guarded, by a society of friendly and sagacious people, and possessed all the needful things to make a reasonable life easy. Through all the Indian countries, every person lives at his own choice, not being forced in the least degree to any thing contrary to his own inclination. Before that most impolitic step of giving general licences took place, only a sufficient number of orderly reputable traders were allowed to traffic, and reside among the Indians: by which means the last were kept under proper restraint, were easy in their minds, and peaceable, on account of the plain honest lessons daily inculcated on them. But at present, most of their countries swarm with white people, who are generally the dregs and off-scourings of our colonies. The description is so exceedingly disagreeable, that I shall only observe, the greater part of them could notably distinguish themselves, among the most profligate [414] by land or sea, no day of the week excepted, indeed the sabbath day is the worst. This is the true situation of our Indian affairs, the unavoidable result of ignorant and wicked clergy-men settled as Missionaries on the frontiers; and of that pernicious practice of general licences, by which crowds of disorderly people infest the Indian countries, corrupt their morals, and put their civilization out of the power of common means: the worst and meanest may readily get nominal security to intitle them to a trading licence; and ill uses are made of them with impunity.

Till of late years, the honest traders lived among the Indians in the greatest plenty. They abounded with hogs, which made very firm streaked bacon, and much preferable to that in the English settlements chiefly owing to the acorns and hiccory-nuts they feed on: but the Indians are now grown so proud and lazy, by having goods too cheap and plenty, that very few raise any. There are at least five times the number of trading houses in all the western Indian nations, since general licences, through the wisdom of our civil rulers, were first granted, than was formerly, while experience directed South-Carolina to pursue and enforce proper measures. Such a number of lewd, idle white savages are very hurtful to the honest part of the traders, by heightening the value of vegetables, especially in the time of light crops, to an exorbitant price; for by inebriating the Indians with their nominally prohibited, and poisoning spirits, they purchase the necessaries of life, at four or five hundred per cent cheaper, than the orderly traders; which is a great check to the few who have a love to the welfare of their country, and strictly observe the laws of trade. Besides, those men decoy the intoxicated savages to defraud the old fair dealer every winter, of many thousand pounds of drest deer-skins, by the enchanting force of liquors, which, on account of their indolence and improvident disposition, interest absolutely required him to credit them for: but when at the end of their mad career, they open their distracted eyes, and bitterly inveigh against the tempting authors of their nakedness, then there is the same necessity of trusting them a-new for the next season's hunt, and likewise the same improbability, either of better success, or any sort of redress; for family jobs must not be interrupted or retarded on any account.

[415] The industrious old traders have still a plenty of hogs, which they raise in folds, mostly on the weeds of the fields during the whole time the crops are in the ground; likewise some hundreds of fowls at once,—plenty of venison,—the dried flesh of bears and buffalos,—wild turkeys, ducks, geese, and pigeons, during the proper season of their being fat and plenty; for the former sort of fowls are lean in the summer, and the others are in these moderate climates only during the winter, for they return northward with the sun. The buffalos are now become scarce, as the thoughtless and wasteful Indians used to kill great numbers of them, only for the tongues and marrow-bones, leaving the rest of the carcases to the wild beasts.[457] The traders commonly make bacon of the bears in winter; but the Indians mostly flay off a thick tier of fat which lies over the flesh, and the latter they cut up into small pieces, and thrust them on reeds, or suckers of sweet-tasted hiccory or sassafras, which they barbecue over a slow fire. The fat they fry into clear well-tasted oil, mixing plenty of sassafras and wild cinnamon with it over the fire, which keeps sweet from one winter to another, in large earthen jars, covered in the ground. It is of a light digestion, and nutritive to hair. All who are acquainted with its qualities, prefer it to any oil, for any use whatsoever: smooth Florence is not to be compared in this respect with rough America.[458]

I have known gentlemen of the nicest taste, who on the beginning of their first trip into the Indian country, were so greatly prejudiced against eating bears-flesh, that they vehemently protested, they would as soon eat part of a barbecued rib of a wolf, or any other beast of prey, as a spare-rib of a young bear; but, by the help of a good appetite, which their exercise and change of air procured, they ventured to taste a little: and presently they fed on it more plentifully than others, to make up the loss they had sustained by their former squeamishness and neglect. In the spring of the year, bear-bacon is a favourite dish with the traders, along with herbs that the woods afford in plenty; especially with the young tops of poke, the root of which is a very strong poison. And this method they pursue year by year, as a physical regimen, in order to purge their blood.

Buffalo flesh is nothing but beef of a coarser grain, though of a sweeter taste than the tame sort: elk-flesh has the like affinity to venison. The deer [416] are very fat in winter, by reason of the great quantities of chestnuts, and various sorts of acorns, that cover the boundless woods. Though most of the traders who go to the remote Indian countries, have tame stock, as already described, and are very expert at fire-arms and ranging the woods a hunting; yet every servant that each of them fits out for the winter's hunt, brings home to his master a large heap of fat barbecued briskets, rumps, and tongues of buffalo and deer, as well as plenty of bear-ribs, which are piled on large racks: these are laid up and used not for necessity, but for the sake of variety. The traders carry up also plenty of chocolate, coffee, and sugar, which enables them with their numberless quantity of fowls-eggs, fruit, &c. to have puddings, pyes, pasties, fritters, and many other articles of the like kind, in as great plenty, as in the English settlements. Several of the Indians produce sugar out of the sweet maple-tree, by making an incision, draining the juice, and boiling it to a proper consistence.

Though in most of the Indian nations the water is good, because of their high situation, yet the traders very seldom drink any of it at home; for the women beat in mortars their flinty corn, till all husks are taken off, which having well sifted and fanned, they boil in large earthen pots; then straining off the thinnest part into a pot, they mix it with cold water, till it is sufficiently liquid for drinking: and when cold, it is both pleasant and very nourishing; and is much liked even by the genteel strangers.[459] The Indians always used mortars, instead of mills, and they had them, with almost every other convenience, when we first opened a trade with them—they cautiously burned a large log, to a proper level and length, placed fire a-top, and wet mortar round it, in order to give the utensil a proper form: and when the fire was extinguished, or occasion required, they chopped the inside with their stone-instruments, patiently continuing the slow process, till they finished the machine to the intended purpose. I have the pleasure of writing this by the side of a Chikkasah female, as great a princess as ever lived among the ancient Peruvians, or Mexicans, and she bids me be sure not to mark the paper wrong, after the manner of most of the traders; otherwise, it will spoil the making good bread, or hommony, and of course beget the ill-will of our white women.

[417] I shall now describe their method of building houses to secure themselves and their food from injury[460]—They are a very dilatory people, and noted for procrastinating every thing that admits of the least delay: but they are the readiest, and quickest of all people in going to shed blood, and returning home; whence the traders say, "that an Indian is never in haste, only when the devil is at his arse." This proverb is fully verified by their method of building; for while the memory of the bleak pinching winds

lasts, and they are covered with their winter-blackened skins, they turn out early in the spring, to strip clap-boards and cypress-bark, for the covering of their houses: but in proportion as the sun advances, they usually desist from their undertaking during that favourable season; saying, "that in the time of warm weather, they generally plant in the fields, or go to war; and that building houses in the troublesome hot summer, is a needless and foolish affair, as it occasions much sweating,"—which is the most offensive thing in life to every red warrior of manly principles. On this account, if we except the women chopping fire-wood for daily use, it is as rare to hear the sound of an ax in their countries, as if they lived under the unhospitable torrid zone; or were nearly related to the South-American animal Pigritia, that makes two or three days journey in going up a tree, and is as long in returning. When the cold weather approaches, they return to their work, and necessity forces them then to perform what a timely precaution might have executed with much more ease. When they build, the whole town, and frequently the nearest of their tribe in neighbouring towns, assist one another, well knowing that many hands make speedy work of that, which would have discouraged any of them from ever attempting by himself. In one day, they build, daub with their tough mortar mixed with dry grass, and thoroughly finish, a good commodious house.

They first trace the dimensions of the intended fabric, and every one has his task prescribed him after the exactest manner. In a few hours they get the timber ready from the stump: every piece being marked, it is readily applied to the proper place, in a great hurry, and so very secure, as if it were to screen them from an approaching hurricane. Notwithstanding they build in this hasty manner, their houses are commonly genteel and convenient. For their summer houses, they generally fix strong posts of pitch-pine deep in the ground, which will last for several ages—The trees of dried locust, and sassafras, are likewise very durable. [417] The posts are of an equal height; and the wall-plates are placed on top of these, in notches. Then they sink a large post in the center of each gable end, and another in the middle of the house where the partition is to be, in order to support the roof-tree; to these they tie the rafters with broad splinters of white oak, or hiccory, unless they make choice of such long saplings, as will reach from side to side over the ridge hole, which, with a proper notch in the middle of each of them, and bound as the other sort, lie very secure. Above those, they fix either split saplings, or three large winter canes together, at proper distances, well tied. Again, they place above the wall-plates of both sides the house, a sufficient number of strong crooks to bear up the eave-boards: and they fasten each of them, both to one of the rafters and the wall-plate, with the bandages before described. As the poplar tree is very soft, they make their eave-boards of it, with their small hatchets: having placed one on each side, upon the crooks, exceeding the length of the house, and jutting a foot beyond the wall, they cover the fabric with pine, or cypress clapboards, which they can split readily; and crown the work with the bark of the same trees, all of a proper length and breadth, which they had before provided. In order to secure this covering from the force of the high winds, they put a sufficient number of long split sapplings above the covering of each side, from end to end, and tie them fast to the end of the laths. Then they place heavy logs above, resting on the eave-boards, opposite to each crook, which overlap each other on the opposite sides, about two feet a-top, whereon they fix a convenient log, and tie them together, as well as the laths to the former, which bind it together, and thus the fabric becomes a savage philosopher's castle, the side and gables of which are bullet proof. The barrier towns cut port holes in those summer houses, daubing them over with clay, so as an enemy cannot discover them on the outside;—they draw a circle round each of them in the inside of the house, and when they are attacked, they open their port holes in a trice, and fall to work. But those, that live more at ease, indulge themselves accordingly. Herein, they teach us to secure our barrier settlements with proper places of defence, before we flatter ourselves with the uncertain hope of reaping what we plant, or grow fond of the showy parts of life. When the British empire hath a sufficient plenty of strong frontier garrisons to protect such as the weak, and valuable colony of West Florida, fine and well furnished houses will soon rise of course. The Indians always make their doors of poplar, because the timber is large, [419] and very light when seasoned, as well as easy to be hewed; they cut the tree to a proper length, and split it with a maul and hard wooden wedges, when they have indented it a little, in convenient places with their small hatchets. They often make a door of one plank in breadth, but, when it requires two planks, they fix two or three cross bars to the inner side, at a proper distance, and bore each of them with a piece of an old gun barrel, heated and battered for the purpose, and sew them together with straps of a shaved and wet buffalo hide, which tightens as it dries, and it is almost as strong as if it were done with long nails, riveted in the usual manner. Thus, they finish their summer house of pleasure, without any kind of iron, or working tools whatsoever, except a small hatchet of iron (that formerly was a long sharpened stone) and a knife; which plainly shews them to be ingenious, and capable of attaining all the liberal arts and sciences, under a proper cultivation.

The clothing of the Indians being very light, they provide themselves for the winter with hot-houses, whose properties are to retain, and reflect the heat, after the manner of the Dutch stoves. To raise these, they fix deep in the ground, a sufficient number of strong forked posts, at a proportional distance, in a circular form, all of an equal height, about five or six feet above the surface of the ground: above these, they tie very securely large pieces of the heart of white oak, which are of a tough flexible nature, interweaving this orbit, from top to bottom, with pieces of the same, or the like timber. Then, in the middle of the fabric they fix very deep in the ground, four large pine posts, in a quadrangular form, notched a-top, on which they lay a number of heavy logs, let into each other, and rounding gradually to the top. Above this huge pile, to the very top, they lay a number of long dry poles, all properly notched, to keep strong hold of the under posts and wall-plate. Then they weave them thick with their split sapplings, and daub them all over about six or seven inches thick with tough clay, well mixt with withered grass: when this cement is half dried, they thatch the house with the longest sort of dry grass, that their land produces. They first lay on one round tier, placing a split sappling a-top, well tied to different parts of the under pieces of timber, about fifteen inches below the eave: and, in this manner, they proceed circularly to the very spire, where commonly a pole is fixed, that displays on the top the figure of a large carved eagle. At a small distance [420] below which, four heavy logs are strongly tied together across, in a quadrangular form, in order to secure the roof from the power of envious blasts. The door of this winter palace, is commonly about four feet high, and so narrow as not to admit two to enter it abreast, with a winding passage for the space of six or seven feet, to secure themselves both from the power of the bleak winds, and of an invading enemy. As they usually build on rising ground, the floor is often a yard lower than the earth, which serves them as a breast work against an enemy: and a small peeping window is level with the surface of the outside ground, to enable them to rake any lurking invaders in case of an attack. As they have no metal to reflect the heat; in the fall of the year, as soon as the sun begins to lose his warming power, some of the women make a large fire of dry wood, with which they chiefly provide themselves, but only from day to day, through their thoughtlessness of to-morrow. When the fire is a little more than half burnt down, they cover it over with ashes, and, as the heat declines, they strike off some of the top embers, with a long cane, wherewith each of the couches, or broad seats, is constantly provided; and this method they pursue from time to time as need requires, till the fire is expended, which is commonly about day-light. While the new fire is burning down, the house, for want of windows and air, is full of hot smoky darkness; and all this time, a number of them lie on their broad bed places, with their heads wrapped up.

The inside of their houses is furnished with genteel couches to sit, and lie upon, raised on four forks of timber of a proper height, to give the swarming fleas some trouble in their attack, as they are not able to reach them at one spring: they tie with fine white oak splinters, a sufficient quantity of middle-sized canes of proper dimensions, to three or four bars of the same sort, which they fasten above the frame; and they put their mattresses a-top, which are made of long cane splinters. Their bedding consists of the skins of wild beasts, such as of buffalos, panthers, bears, elks, and deer, which they dress with the hair on, as soft as velvet. Their male children they chuse to raise on the skins of panthers, on account of the communicative principle, which they reckon all nature is possest of, in conveying qualities according to the regimen that is followed: and, as the panther is endued with many qualities, beyond any of his fellow animals in the American woods, as smelling, strength, cunning, [421] and a prodigious spring, they reckon such a bed is the first rudiments of war. But it is worthy of notice, they change the regimen in nurturing their young females; these they lay on the skins of fawns, or buffalo calves; because they are shy and timorous: and, if the mother be indisposed by sickness, her nearest female relation suckles the child, but only till she recovers. This practice gives a friendly lesson to such mothers, who, ostrich like, as soon as the tender infant sucks in the first breath of air, commit it to the swarthy breasts of a fotid African to graft it on her gross stock.

Their stools they cut out of poplar wood, all of one piece, and of a convenient height and shape. Their chests are made of clap-boards sewed to cross bars with scraped wet buffalo strings. Their domestic utensils consist of earthen pots, pans, jugs, mugs, jars, &c. of various antiquated sorts, which would have puzzled Adam, to have given them significant names. Their wooden dishes, and spoons made of wood and buffalo horn, shew something of a newer invention and date, being of nicer workmanship, for the sculpture of the last is plain, and represents things that are within the reach of their own ideas.

Every town has a large edifice, which with propriety may be called the mountain house, in comparison of those already described.[461] But the only difference between it, and the winter house or stove, is in its dimensions, and application. It is usually built on the top of a hill; and, in that separate and imperial state house, the old beloved men and head warriors meet on material business, or to divert themselves, and feast and dance with the rest of the people. They furnish the inside with genteel couches, either to sit or lie on, about seven feet wide, and a little more in length, with a descent towards the wall, to secure them from falling off when asleep. Every one takes his seat, according to his reputed merit; a worthless coxcomb dare not be guilty of the least intrusion—should he attempt it, he is ordered to his proper place, before the multitude, with the vilest disgrace, and bears their stinging laughter. This may not be an unprofitable lesson to some of our young red coated men, who never traversed the rough bloody fields of Flanders; they would be more respected if they were more modest, and displayed superior virtues to those whom they affect to despise. Thou, who boastest of the noble blood of the Scipios running in thy veins, [422] dost thou equal the brave actions of the Scipios? If not, thou art a disgrace to them; their virtue would renounce thee, and should make thee ashamed to own them.[462]

Formerly, the Indians made very handsome carpets. They have a wild hemp that grows about six feet high, in open, rich, level lands, and which usually ripens in July: it is plenty on our frontier settlements.[463] When it is fit for use, they pull, steep, peel, and beat it; and the old women spin it off the distaffs, with wooden machines, having some clay on the middle of them, to hasten the motion. When the coarse thread is prepared, they put it into a frame about six feet square, and instead of a shuttle, they thrust through the thread with a long cane, having a large string through the web, which they shift at every second course of the thread. When they have thus finished their arduous labour, they paint each side of the carpet with such figures, of various colours, as their fruitful imaginations devise; particularly the images of those birds and beasts they are acquainted with; and likewise of themselves, acting in their social, and martial stations. There is that due proportion, and so much wild variety in the design, that would really strike a curious eye with pleasure and admiration. J. W—t, Esq; a most skilful linguist in the Muskohge dialect,[464] assures me, that time out of mind they passed the woof with a shuttle; and they have a couple of threddles, which they move with the hand so as to enable them to make good dispatch, something, after our manner of weaving. This is sufficiently confirmed by their method of working broad garters, sashes, shot-pouches, broad belts, and the like, which are decorated all over with beautiful stripes and chequers. Probably, their method of weaving is similar to the practice of the eastern nations, when they came from thence, during the infant state of arts and sciences. People who were forced to get their daily bread in the extensive desarts with their bows and arrows, and by gathering herbs, roots, and nuts, would not be fond of making new experiments, but for the necessities of common life; and certainly they would not have chosen a more troublesome method of clothing themselves, if they knew an easier and quicker manner of effecting it—whoever knows anything of an Indian, will not accuse him of that sin.

[423] The women are the chief, if not the only manufacturers; the men judge that if they performed that office, it would exceedingly depreciate them. The weight of the oar lies on the women, as is the case with the German Americans. In the winter season, the women gather buffalo's hair, a sort of coarse brown curled wool; and having spun it as fine as they can, and properly doubled it, they put small beads of different colours upon the yarn, as they work it: the figures they work in those small webs, are generally uniform, but sometimes they diversify them on both sides. The Choktah weave shot-pouches, which have raised work inside and outside. They like-

wise make turkey feather blankets with the long feathers of the neck and breast of that large fowl—they twist the inner end of the feathers very fast into a strong double thread of hemp, or the inner bark of the mulberry tree, of the size and strength of coarse twine, as the fibres are sufficiently fine, and they work it in the manner of fine netting. As the feathers are long and glittering, this sort of blankets is not only very warm, but pleasing to the eye.

They make beautiful stone pipes; and the Cheerake the best of any of the Indians: for their mountainous country contains many different sorts and colours of soils proper for such uses. They easily form them with their tomohawks, and afterward finish them in any desired form with their knives; the pipes being of a very soft quality till they are smoked with, and used to the fire, when they become quite hard. They are often a full span long, and the bowls are about half as large again as those of our English pipes. The fore part of each commonly runs out with a sharp peak, two or three fingers broad, and a quarter of an inch thick—on both sides of the bowl, lengthwise, they cut several pictures with a great deal of skill and labour; such as a buffalo and a panther on the opposite sides of the bowl; a rabbit and a fox; and, very often, a man and a woman *puris naturalibus*.[465] Their sculpture cannot much be commended for its modesty. The savages work so slow, that one of their artists is two months at a pipe with his knife, before he finishes it: indeed, as before observed, they are great enemies to profuse sweating, and are never in a hurry about a good thing. The stems are commonly made of soft wood about two feet long, and an inch thick, cut into four squares, each scooped till they join very near the hollow of the stem; the beaus always hollow the squares, except a little at each corner to hold them together, to which they fasten a parcel of bell-buttons, different [424] sorts of fine feathers, and several small battered pieces of copper kettles hammered, round deer-skin thongs, and a red painted scalp; this is a boasting, valuable, and superlative ornament. According to their standard, such a pipe constitutes the possessor, a grand beau. They so accurately carve, or paint hieroglyphic characters on the stem, that the war-actions, and the tribe of the owner, with a great many circumstances of things, are fully delineated. This may seem strange to those who are unacquainted with the ancient skill of the Egyptians this way, and the present knowledge of the Turkish mutes. But so it is, and there is not perhaps the like number of mimic mutes on the face of the earth, nor ever were among the old Greek or Roman Pantomimi, as with the Indian Americans, for representing the great and minute things of life, by different gestures, movements of the body, and expressive countenances; and at the same time they are perfectly understood by each other.

They make the handsomest clothes baskets, I ever saw, considering their materials. They divide large swamp canes, into long, thin, narrow splinters, which they dye of several colours, and manage the workmanship so well, that both the inside and outside are covered with a beautiful variety of pleasing figures; and, though for the space of two inches below the upper edge of each basket, it is worked into one, through the other parts they are worked asunder, as if they were two joined a-top by some strong cement. A large nest consists of eight or ten baskets, contained within each other. Their dimensions are different, but they usually make the outside basket about a foot deep, a foot and a half broad, and almost a yard long.

The Indians, by reason of our supplying them so cheap with every sort of goods, have forgotten the chief part of their ancient mechanical skill, so as not to be well able now, at least for some years, to live independent of us. Formerly, those baskets which the Cheerake made, were so highly esteemed even in South Carolina, the politest of our colonies, for domestic usefulness, beauty, and skilful variety, that a large nest of them cost upwards of a moidore.[466]

They make earthen pots of very different sizes, so as to contain from two to ten gallons; large pitchers to carry water; bowls, dishes, platters, [425] basons, and a prodigious number of other vessels of such antiquated forms, as would be tedious to describe, and impossible to name. Their method of glazing them, is, they place them over a large fire of smoky pitch pine, which makes them smooth, black, and firm. Their lands abound with proper clay, for that use; and even with porcelain, as has been proved by experiment.[467]

They make perhaps the finest bows, and the smoothest barbed arrows, of all mankind. On the point of them is fixed either a scooped point of buck-horn, or turkey-cock spurs, pieces of brass, or flint stone. The latter sort our fore-fathers used, which our witty grandmothers call elf-stones, and now rub the cows with, that are so unlucky as to be shot by night fairies. One of those flint arrow-points is reckoned a very extraordinary blessing in a whole neighbourhood of old women, both for the former cure, as well as a preservative against every kind of bewitching charm.

No people are more expert than the Indians in the use of fire-arms, and the bow and quiver: they can fresh stock their guns, only with a small hatchet and a knife, and streighten the barrels, so as to shoot with proper direction. They likewise alter, and fix all the springs of the lock, with others of the sort they may have out of use; but such a job costs the red artist about two months work.

They are good sadlers, for they can finish a saddle with their usual instruments, without any kind of iron to bind the work: but the shape of it is so antiquated and mean, and so much like those of the Dutch West-Indians, that a person would be led to imagine they had formerly met, and been taught the art in the same school. The Indians provide themselves with a quantity of white oak boards, and notch them, so as to fit the saddle-trees; which consist of two pieces before, and two behind, crossing each other in notches, about three inches below the top ends of the frame. Then they take a buffalo green hide, covered with its winter curls, and having properly shaped it to the frame, they sew it with large thongs of the same skin, as tight and secure as need be; when it is thoroughly dried, it appears to have all the properties of a cuirass saddle. A trimmed bearskin serves for a pad; and formerly, their bridle was only a rope around the [426] horse's neck, with which they guided him at pleasure. Most of the Choktah use that method to this day.

It is strange that all the Indians mount a horse on the off side as we term it, especially as their horses were originally brought from Europe. In the Choktah country, when I was going to a great ball play, at a considerable distance off, in company with several of the head-warriors, we alighted at a cool stream of water, to smoke, and drink parched corn-flour and water, according to our usual custom in the woods—when we again set off, we jested each other for mounting on the wrong side. They urged it was most natural, and commodious, to put the right foot into the stirrup, and at the same time lay hold of the mane with the strongest hand, instead of using either of the farthermost or opposite ones, as they term the left. They carried it against me by a majority of voices, whooping and laughing: but, as they were boasting highly of the swiftness of their horses, and their skill in riding and guiding them, much better with a rope than with a bridle, I resolved to convince them of their mistake; for as the horse I rode was justly named Eagle, and reckoned the swiftest of any in the Chikkasah country, I invited them to a trial by way of diversion, in so merry a season, and they gladly accepted the offer. We ranged ourselves in a broad row, on each side of the wood path, which was rather narrow and crooked, as is the case in their countries—they allowed me to take the center, and at the whoop signal of the by-standers we started. My horse being used to such diversion soon left them behind, a considerable distance; presently I luckily discovered a swampy thicket, a-head on my right hand, which ran almost our direct course along-side of a creek. As the wild coursers chiefly followed one another, according to their general custom, I there flew across, and led two of them off the path, into the thicket covered with high brambles. I had little trouble in disposing of the rest; my whooping, and cracking the whip, sent each of them along with his neighbour, at full speed, and I continued them so a great way: for, as their horses were frightened, the riders had no command over them, with their boasted neck bridles. The horses, at last, brought them out into the open woods, to their great joy, when they whooped and hallooed, as despising what they had undergone; they were however in a dismal pickle. For it being their custom to carry their ornaments, and looking glasses over their shoulder, [427] on such public occasions, my companions were fully trimmed out, and did not strip themselves, as they expected no such disaster. By stooping to save themselves from being dismounted, their favourite looking glasses were shattered to pieces, the paint mostly rubbed off their faces, their skins of small hawks, and tufts of fine plumes, torn from their heads, and their other ornaments, as well as their clothing and skin, shared also in the misfortune. As soon as they could stop their horses, they alighted: and, when I had done laughing at them, they according to custom, said only, *La phene,* "O strange!" The Indians are very happy in not shewing the least emotion of anger, for any mischance that befalls them, in their sportful exercises. I jested them in commending the swiftness of their horses, even through a bramble thicket, and applauded their skill in sitting, and guiding them so well, by the help of their neck bridles. By this time, the hindmost of our company came up, who laughed heartily at the sight of our tattered horsemen, and told them, that they expected I would jockey them in some such manner. But the young ambitious heroes ascribed the whole disaster only to the viciousness of my horse, saying "he was mad."

From what hath been already said, it must be evident, that with proper cultivation, they would shine in higher spheres of life; and it is not an easy matter to seduce them from their supposed interests, to the incoherent projects, that our home-bred politicians confidently devise over their sparkling bowls and decanters. The friendly and warlike Indians have an intense affection to their country and people, and so have the British Americans: and whatever some may think of the colonists martial abilities, our wise statesmen may be soon convinced, that they will be able to maintain all the invaluable blessings of free men for themselves, and convey them to their posterity in their purity and lustre, according to the old English constitution, which is built on plain wholesome laws, and not on the sophisms of tyranny.

This leads me to speak of the Indian method of government.—In general, it consists in a fœderal union of the whole society for mutual safety. As the law of nature appoints no frail mortal to be a king, or ruler, over his brethren; and humanity forbids the taking away at pleasure, the [428] life or property of any who obey the good laws of their country, they consider that the transgressor ought to have his evil deeds retaliated upon himself in an equal manner. The Indians, therefore, have no such titles or persons, as emperors, or kings; nor an appellative for such, in any of their dialects. Their highest title, either in military or civil life, signifies only a *Chieftain:* they have no words to express despotic power, arbitrary kings, oppressed, or obedient subjects; neither can they form any other ideas of the former, than of "bad war chieftains of a numerous family, who inslaved the rest." The power of their chiefs, is an empty sound. They can only persuade or dissuade the people, either by the force of good-nature and clear reasoning, or colouring things, so as to suit their prevailing passions. It is reputed merit alone, that gives them any titles of distinction above the meanest of the people.[468] If we connect with this their opinion of a theocracy, it does not promise well to the reputed establishment of extensive and puissant Indian American empires. When any national affair is in debate, you may hear every father of a family speaking in his house on the subject, with rapid, bold language, and the utmost freedom that a people can use. Their voices, to a man, have due weight in every public affair, as it concerns their welfare alike. Every town is independent of another. Their own friendly compact continues the union. An obstinate war leader will sometimes commit acts of hostility, or make peace for his own town, contrary to the good liking of the rest of the nation. But a few individuals are very cautious of commencing war on small occasions, without the general consent of the head men: for should it prove unsuccessful, the greater part would be apt to punish them as enemies, because they abused their power, which they had only to do good to the society. They are very deliberate in their councils, and never give an immediate answer to any message sent them by strangers, but suffer some nights first to elapse. They reason in a very orderly manner, with much coolness and good-natured language, though they may differ widely in their opinions. Through respect to the silent audience, the speaker always addresses them in a standing posture. In this manner they proceed, till each of the head men hath given his opinion on the point in debate. Then they sit down together, and determine upon the affair. Not the least passionate expression is to be heard among them, and [429] they behave with the greatest civility to each other. In all their stated orations they have a beautiful modest way of expressing their dislike of ill things. They only say, "it is not good, goodly, or commendable." And their whole behaviour, on public occasions, is highly worthy of imitation by some of our British senators and lawyers.

Most of their regulations are derived from the plain law of nature. Nature's school contemns all quibbles of art, and teaches them the plain easy rule, "do to others, as you would be done by;" when they are able, without greater damage to themselves, than benefit to their creditor, they discharge their honest debts. But, though no disputes pass between them on such occasions, yet if there be some heart-burnings on particular affairs, as soon as they are publicly known, their red Archimagus, and his old beloved men, convene and decide, in a very amicable manner, when both parties become quite easy. They have no compulsive power to force the debtor to pay; yet the creditor can distrain his goods or chattels, and justly satisfy himself without the least interruption—and, by one of his relations, he sends back in a very civil manner, the overplus to the owner. These instances indeed seldom happen, for as they know each other's temper, they are very cautious of irritating, as the consequences might one day prove fatal—they never scold each other when sober—they conceal their enmity be it ever so violent, and will converse together with smooth kind language, and an obliging easy behaviour, while envy is preying on their heart. In general, they are very punctual in paying what they owe among themselves, but they are grown quite careless in discharging what they owe to the traders, since the commencement of our destructive plan of general licences. "An old debt," is a proverbial expression with them, of "nothing."

There are many petty crimes which their young people are guilty of,—to which our laws annex severe punishment, but their's only an ironical way of jesting. They commend the criminal before a large audience, for practising the virtue, opposite to the crime, that he is known to be guilty of. If it is for theft, they praise his honest principles; and they commend a warrior for having behaved valiantly against the enemy, when he acted cowardly; they introduce the minutest circumstances of the affair, with severe sarcasms which wound deeply. I have known them [430] to strike their delinquents with those sweetened darts, so good naturedly and skilfully, that they would sooner die by torture, than renew their shame by repeating the actions. In this they exceed many christians. They are capable of being shamed out of their ill habits, and their method of cure is exceedingly more proper and merciful, than what we apply. Stripes and fines only inflame the distemper; when inflicted publicly for petty crimes, the culprit loses what is most valuable to human nature, the sense of shame. He that watches for persons crimes, to benefit and enrich himself at their damage, and the ruin of their families, is an enemy to society. If it is beneath our dignity to learn from the untaught Indian, let us turn to the records of Athens, Sparta, and Rome. When their slaves were guilty of intemperance, they exposed them before their children, and thus shewed them its deformity. And, by that, they infused into them an early shame and abhorrence of vice, and a great love of virtue.

Formerly, the Indian law obliged every town to work together in one body, in sowing or planting their crops; though their fields are divided by proper marks, and their harvest is gathered separately. The Cheerake and Muskohge still observe that old custom, which is very necessary for such idle people, in their element. The delinquent is assessed more or less, according to his neglect, by proper officers appointed to collect those assessments, which they strictly fulfil, without the least interruption, or exemption of any able person. They are likewise bound to assist in raising public edifices. They have not the least trace of any other old compulsive law among them; and they did not stand in need of any other in their state. As they were neither able nor desirous to obtain any thing more than a bare support of life, they could not credit their neighbours beyond a morsel of food, and that they liberally gave, whenever they called. Most of them observe that hospitable custom to this day. Their throwing away all their old provisions, as impure food, whenever the new harvest was sanctified, helped greatly to promote a spirit of hospitality. Their wants, and daily exercise in search of needful things, kept them honest. Their ignorance of the gay part of life, helped in a great measure to preserve their virtue. In their former state of simplicity, the plain law of nature was enough; but, as they are degenerating very fast from their ancient simplicity, they, without doubt, must have new laws to terrify them from committing [431] new crimes, according to the usage of other nations, who multiply their laws, in proportion to the exigencies of time.

I shall now give their opinion of our social and military virtues; which joined with the foregoing, will set the Indians in a yet clearer light. We can trace people by their opinion of things, as well as if we saw them practise them. Most of them blame us for using a provident care in domestic life, calling it a slavish temper: they say we are covetous, because we do not give our poor relations such a share of our possessions, as would keep them from want. There are but few of themselves we can blame, on account of these crimes, for they are very kind and liberal to every one of their own tribe, even to the last morsel of food they enjoy. When we recriminate on the penurious temper of any of their people, they say, if our accusation be true, we by our ill examples tainted them on that head, for their forefathers were endued with all the virtues. They frequently tell us, that though we are possessed of a great deal of yellow and white stone, of black people, horses, cows, hogs, and every thing else our hearts delight in—yet they create us as much toil and pain, as if we had none, instead of that ease and pleasure, which flow from enjoyment; therefore we are truly poor, and deserve pity instead of envy: they wish some of their honest warriors to have these things, as they would know how to use them aright, without placing their happiness, or merit, in keeping them, which would be of great service to the poor, by diffusing them with a liberal hand. They say, they have often seen a panther in the woods, with a brace of large fat bucks at once, near a cool stream; but that they had more sense than to value the beast, on account of his large possessions: on the contrary, they hated his bad principles, because he would needlessly destroy, and covetously engross, the good things he could not use himself, nor would allow any other creature to share of, though ever so much pinched with hunger. They reckon, if we made a true estimate of things, we should consider the man without any false props, and esteem him only by the law of virtue, which ennobles men by inspiring them with good sentiments and a generous disposition; they say they are sure, from sundry observations, we sell to the highest bidder, our high titles of war, which were only due to brave men who had often fought the enemy with success in defence of their country: that they had seen, even [432] in Charles-town, several young, lazy, deformed white men, with big bellies, who seemed to require as much help to move them along, as overgrown old women; yet they understood these were paid a great deal of our beloved yellow stone for bearing the great name of warriors, which should be kept sacred from the effeminate tribe, even if they offered to purchase it with their whole possessions.—That these titles should only be conferred on those who excel in martial virtue; otherwise, it gives a false copy of imitation to the young warriors, and thereby exposes the whole body of the people to contempt and danger, by perverting the means which ought to secure their lives and properties; for, when a country has none but helpless people to guard it from hostile attempts, it is liable to become a prey to any ambitious persons, who may think proper to invade it. They allow that corpulency is compatible with marking paper black with the goose quill; and with strong-mouthed labour, or pleading at law; because old women can sit best to mark, and their mouths are always the most sharp and biting. But they reckon if our warriors had gained high titles by personal bravery, they would be at least in the shape of men, if not of active brisk warriors; for constant manly exercise keeps a due temperament of body, and a just proportion of shape. They said, some were not fit even for the service of an old woman, much less for the difficult and lively exercises which manly warriors pursue in their rough element—that they could never have gone to war, but bought their beloved, broad paper with yellow stone, or it must have passed from father to son, like the rest of their possessions; and that by their intemperate method of eating and drinking without proper exercise, they had transformed themselves into those over-grown shapes, which our weavers, taylors, and plaiters of false hair, rendered more contemptible.

The old men tell us, they remember our colonies in their infant state,—that when the inhabitants were poor and few in number, they maintained prosperous wars against the numerous combined nations of red people, who surrounded them on all sides; because in those early days, the law of reason was their only guide. In that time of simplicity, they lived after the temperate manner of the red people. They copied after honest nature, in their food, dress, and every pursuit, both in domestic and social life. That unerring guide directed them aright, as the event of things publicly declared. [433] But time is now grown perverse and childish, and has brought with it a flood of corrupting ills. Instead of observing the old beloved rule of temperance, which their honest forefathers strictly pursued, they too often besot themselves with base luxury, and thereby enervate all their manly powers, so as to reduce themselves to the state of old women, and esteem martial virtue to consist in the unmanly bulk of their bodies, and the fineness and colour of their glittering coats and jackets: whereas such forms and habits only enable the red people to sort the large buffalos, the fine-feathered par-roquets, and wood-peckers—their religious, civil, and martial titles are con-ferred on the lean, as well as the fat-bodied, without minding whether their clothes are coarse or fine, or what colour they are of. They say, their titles of war invariably bespeak the man, as they always make them the true attendants of merit, never conferring the least degree of honour on the worthless.—That corpulency, or a very genteel outward appearance, would be so far from recommending any as war-leaders, that those qualities would render them suspected, till they gave sufficient proof of their capacity of serving their country—that when any distinguished themselves by martial virtue, their fine clothes reflected new beauties on the eyes of the people, who regard a genteel appearance, only on account of the shining virtues of the gallant men who wear them.

They often ridicule us, in our gay hours, that they have observed our nominal warriors to value themselves exceedingly on those unpleasant shapes and undue covering—that like contemptible shining lizards, they swelled their breasts almost as big as their bellies, spoke very sharp to the poor people who were labouring in distress, frowned with ugly faces at them (whereas they ought to have smiled, in order to make their hearts cheerful,) and kept them off at a great distance, with their hats in hand, as if they were black people. But such conduct, always a sure token of coward-ice, testified with convincing clearness, they were unable to act the part of even an honest black man. The Indians imagine the corruption is become too general to be cured, without a thorough change of our laws of war, because when the head is sick, the feet cannot be well: and as our capi-tal towns and regular troops are much infected with that depressing and shameful malady, they reckon our country places suffer much more by our fat fine men. They fail not to flourish away as much in their own favour, as against us, [434] saying, that though they are unskilful in making the marks of our ugly lying books, which spoil people's honesty, yet they are duly taught in the honest volumes of nature, which always whisper in their ears, a strong lesson of love to all of their own family, and an utter contempt of danger in defence of their beloved country, at their own private cost; that they confer titles of honour only on those who deserve them,—that the speaking trophies of war declare the true merit of their contented warriors, without having the least recourse to any borrowed help. They say, that the virtue even of their young women does not allow them to bear the least regard to any of the young men, on account of their glittering clothes, and that none of their warriors would expect it, nor their laws allow it, if ever their country should unhappily produce so contemptible an animal. Imitation is natural, and the red people follow virtue in the old track of their honest fore-fathers, while we are bewildered by evil custom.

As their own affairs lie in a very narrow circle, it is difficult to impress

them with a favourable opinion of the wisdom and justice of our voluminous laws—They say, if our laws were honest, or wisely framed, they would
be plain and few, that the poor people might understand and remember
them, as well as the rich—That right and wrong, an honest man and a rogue,
with as many other names as our large crabbed books could contain, are
only two contraries; that simple nature enables every person to be a proper
judge of promoting good, and preventing evil, either by determinations,
rewards, or punishments; and that people cannot in justice be accused of
violating any laws, when it is out of their power to have a proper knowledge
of them. They reckon, that if our legislators were not moved by some
oblique views, instead of acting the part of mud-fish, they would imitate
the skilful bee, and extract the useful part of their unwieldy, confused, old
books, and insert it in an honest small one, that the poor people might
be able to buy, and read it, to enable them to teach their rising families to
avoid snares, and keep them from falling into the power of our cunning
speakers—who are not ashamed to scold and lie publickly when they are
well paid for it, but if interest no longer tempted them to inforce hurtful
lies for truth, would probably throw away all their dangerous quibbling
books.—That the poor people might have easy redress and justice, this
should become a public concern, and the Governor-Minggo, [435] all the
head warriors, and old beloved men, should either entirely destroy those
books, or in an artful manner send them to their enemy the French, in order to destroy their constitution: but they were of opinion, common sense
would not allow even those to receive them, under any pretence whatsoever
—therefore they ought to be burnt in the old year's accursed fire. By that
means, the honest poor could live in peace and quiet; for now they were
unable by poverty, or backward by their honesty, to buy justice, in paying
those people of cunning heads and strong mouths to speak the truth: and
the hearts of rich knaves must then become honest, as they would not needlessly give those large bribes, for painting their black actions with a white
colour.

They urge, that while litigious, expensive, and tedious suits are either
encouraged by our artful speakers, or allowed by our legislators, the honest
poor man will always be a great loser; which is a crying evil. Because he is
humble, modest, and poor, his feeble voice cannot be heard. The combined
body of the noisy rich must drown his complaints. His only satisfaction is,
that his heart is honest, though that must prove very small comfort to a wife
crying over helpless children, in a small waste house. They say, that as no
people are born rogues, truth appears plain enough; for its native dress is
always simple, and it never resides in troubled waters, but under the striking
beams of the sun. It is not therefore just, either to compel, or tempt people
to buy justice; it should be free to all, as the poor are not able to purchase it.

They affirm, that as all laws should be enacted by the joint voice of the honest part of the society for mutual good, if our great chieftain and his assistants refuse altering those that are hurtful to the people, we ought to set them aside on account of their ill principles, and for striving to support their own bad actions, by bad laws—that as wise free-men, we should with all speed chuse honest men in their room, to act the part of fathers of their country, and continue them just as long as they behaved such: for leading men are chosen only to do good to the people; and whenever they make a breach of their trust, injuring the public good, their places of course become vacant, and justly devolve to the people, who conferred them. Our law, they say, condemns little rogues, but why should it spare great ones? That we hang the former with strong ropes of hemp, [436] but we should first do so to, or shorten the heads of, the latter, with a poisoned tomohawk, as a just emblem of their mischievous poisoning conduct.

I told them, that the essential part of our laws was fixed and unalterable, and also the succession of each of our great chieftains, while they observe them faithfully, and order them to be honestly executed, but no longer. That formerly when the people's hearts became sorely aggrieved, and bitterly vexed, as pride for unlimited power, had made some of the rulers heads giddy, the enraged community had shortened some of them, and drove away others from corrupting the beloved land, without any possibility of returning in safety. May none of our present or future statesmen, by wilful misconduct, and bad principles, be ever forced to appear at the dreadful bar of an abused and enraged community! for as they mete, so it will surely be meted to them again. The Indian system seems to coincide with the grand fundamental law—"A natura lex, a virtute rex;" which the great conqueror of the east feelingly declared in his last moments to be just, by willing his crown to him who most excelled in virtue.[469]

The ill opinion they entertain of our courts of judicature, may have risen in some degree from the wrong information of our interpreters, who have occasionally accompanied them to the courts: but they generally retain a long time the first impressions they imbibe from any one they esteem. One law cause which the Chikkasah attended, proved tedious, and was carried contrary to their opinion of justice and equity: on their return to their own country, they said, that two or three of their old women would have brought in a quicker, and honester verdict. They compared our counsellors to the mercenary Choktah, who often kill people, and even one another, for the sake of a French reward, as they earnestly strove to draw suffering truth to their own side of the debate, and painted it contrary to its native form, with a deformed lying face.

They tell us, that when their head-men are deliberating on public affairs, they dispassionately examine things, and always speak the naked truth; for its honest face hates a mask, having nothing to hide from a searching eye, and its dress plain and simple; that people can as easily distinguish it from falsehood, as light from darkness, or clear and wholesome water from that which is turbid and hurtful, without giving up their reason to hired speakers, [437] who use their squint eyes and forked tongues like the chieftains of the snakes, (meaning rattle-snakes) which destroy harmless creatures for the sake of food. They say, that the quotation of dark quibbles out of their old books, should be deemed as white paint over a black man's face; or as black over one that is naturally white. They wonder that, as an honest cause is always plain, judgment is not given freely in its favour, and without the least delay; and insist, that every bad cause should meet with a suitable and severe award, in order to check vice, and promote virtue in social life.

One of the red Magi asked me, whether in our scolding houses, we did not always proportion the charges of the suit in debate, to the value of the debt, or damages. Suggesting that it was wrong to make a perplexed science of granting equity with any charges attending it, to honest poor people; that we should pity them on account of the distresses they labour under, and not in effect enslave or fine them because they are poor.

I told him and the rest of his brethren by way of excuse, that the different nature, and multiplicity of contracts in our great trading empire, with the immense difference that often happened between the eloquence and abilities of the contending parties, required a series of decisions of right and wrong to be recorded in books, as an invariable precedent to direct future public determinations, in disputes of the like nature; that most of our people were more unequal to each other in fine language than the bred lawyers; and that none were so fit to search, or could possibly understand those registers as well as they, because they spent the chief part of their time on such subjects. He granted that they might be useful members of the community, but doubted their honesty was too much exposed to the alluring temptations of our rich people's yellow stone; and that though our fore-fathers were no doubt as wise and virtuous as we, yet they were but men, and sometimes had passions to gratify, especially in favour of a worthy and unfortunate friend, or relation, who was beloved. He said, the length of stealing time must have naturally occasioned such an event; and that our wise men ought to be so far from quoting a wrong copy, as a fixed precedent, that they should erase it out of their old court books, and profit by the foibles of the old, the wise and the good.

[438] At his request, I spoke also of our skilful physicians and quack-doctors—I told him that the former commonly cured the sick, or diseased, unless the malady was of an uncommon nature, or very dangerous by not applying in time, before it took root beyond the reach of any cure; but that the empirics seldom failed of poisoning their weak patients by slow degrees; and that we had old women likewise who frequently did much good with

bare simples. He said, if our physicians used simples in due time, to assist nature, instead of burning corrosive mixtures, they would have no occasion to dismember poor people, cutting off their limbs in so horrid a manner, as several were reported to do; and that, if our law was so weak as not to condemn those to death, who took away the lives of low innocent people, yet the strong feelings of nature ought to incite the surviving relations of the murdered persons, to revenge their blood on the murderers, by beating them with long knobbed poles, while they were sensible of pain, and as soon as they recovered a little, to cut off their ears and nose with a dull knife, as in the case of adultery, in order to quench innocent blood, and teach unwary people to avoid and detest the execrated criminals. Here, the red audience highly applauded the wisdom and justice of his medical observations, because they exactly corresponded with their own standard in similar cases.

Well, said he, you have given us plainly to understand the high esteem the English bear to their people of cunning heads and strong mouths, and to the curers of ailments—If the former continue honest when they have gained deep knowledge in their old books; and the latter are successful in the killing, or healing quality of their strong medicines: We should rejoice, if you would likewise inform us, according to your written traditions, of the first rise of *Oobache*, "bringers of rain," and of *Ishtohoollo Echeto*, "high-priests, popes, or arch-bishops;" whether the supreme fatherly chieftain gave them from the beginning to the white people, or if not, how he came to give them afterward; and whether their lives give virtuous lessons to youth, to induce them to a strict observance of the divine law, as modesty and humility should always appear in the speech and behaviour of public teachers, on account of their charming influence—Inform us of their usefulness in religious and civil life, and the general opinion of the disinterested and wise part of the community concerning them; [439] as all nations of red people have lately heard a great deal of their unpeaceable, if not cruel disposition towards the British Americans, which their covetousness of heart, it is said, prompted them to, because they could not prevail upon them by their invented speeches, to give them the tenth part of the yearly produce of their honest labour—Let us know their true conduct over the broad water, whether they are covetous in demanding any part of the new harvest; and if the young people do not violate the marriage-law when the crops fail by the want of refreshing rains?

As the talk was disagreeable, I told him, had he been so particular in his enquiries concerning the two former classes, I could have much better informed him, as I had the pleasure of being long acquainted with many of them, who were learned, wise and benevolent, in a very great degree; and was convinced from my own knowledge, that several of them, not only spoke earnestly for honest poor people, and others cured them of their lingering ailments, without pay; but supplied them with needful utensils for planting provisions for their small families, till they could conveniently re-pay the value, in their own produce: but that as I neither had nor desired the least acquaintance with any of our high-placed beloved men, I was very unfit to handle such a long string of queries. He said, my denying to gratify their curiosity on so material a point, served only to raise it the higher; especially as I had given them a very favourable opinion of the gentlemen of the other two classes; and he hoped, the religious men were at least as virtuous as those, their sacred office requiring them to give an honest copy to all others, as the young people imbibed from their teachers example either good or bad principles, which must benefit or injure themselves, and the community. He so earnestly importuned me to comply with his request, that, as an Indian divine, I thus addressed the attentive red congre-gation.

In past ages, most part of all nations of people sunk into ignorance not only of the old beloved speech, (or divine law) but of the very being of the great, supreme, holy Spirit; upon which account, the glimmering image im-prest on their hearts, directed them to worship the sun, moon, and stars, because of their beneficial and powerful influence,—and the fire, light, and air, the three divine names and emblems. By [440] degrees, they chose an idol-god of such reputed qualities, as best suited with their own tempers, and the situation of their various countries, in order to receive temporal good things, and avert the opposite evils. In the length of forgetting time, they became so exceedingly stupid, as to worship vegetables, frightful and shameful images, filthy beasts, and dangerous snakes. Self-love seemed to have induced them to adore the two last through fear, and the bird also that preyed on them, became the object of their adoration. In this miserable state of darkness the world was involved, when the supreme fatherly chieftain, through tender pity to human weakness, appeared to your reputed ancestors, in the form of a blazing fire, renewed his old divine laws with one of their beloved men, and confirmed the whole, with dreadful thunders, lightnings, and other striking prodigies, to impress them with a deep awe and rever-ence of his majesty. In time, they built a most magnificent beloved house, wonderful in its form and for the great variety of beloved utensils, and em-blems it contained. The ark was one of the three most divine symbols in it. *Ishtohoollo Eloha* became their chieftain, both at home and at war. A won-derful emanation of the holy fire resided in the great divine house, while they listened to the voice of *Loache,* "the prophets," which the holy chief-tain sent to them in succession, to teach them his will as the fixt rule of all his actions. While their hearts continued honest, he enabled them to con-quer their enemies, and to gain victories over formidable armies, which like the swarms of buzzing insects in your low lands, could not be numbered, and at length settled them in as happy a state as they could reasonably wish for.

A little before that time, he called himself *A-Do-Ne-Yo, Minggo Ishtohoollo,* "the divine chief;" but then, to your enlightened (and reputed) ancestors *Yo-He-Wah* which signifies, "he lived always, and will never die." It is he, whom you invoke in your sacred songs when you are drinking your cusseena, and you derived that awful invocation, and your ark of war, from them. He is the author of life and death, and consequently, the "master of our breath," as the red people justly term him. He gave them *Loache* and *Oobache,* "Prophets and askers of rain," and prescribed to them laws that were suitable for their own government. They chiefly consisted of sacred emblems of an early divine promise to mankind, which he faithfully performed; and when the end was answered, [441] those symbols ceased. The people were enjoined a very strict purity, both in civil and religious life, especially all the priests or beloved men; and in a particular manner, the great beloved man, or high priest. He was to be equally perfect in body, and pure in heart—and was not allowed to touch the dead, as their bodies were in a corrupting state. The old beloved speech assures us, he was appointed as a representative of the people to *Ishtohoollo Aba,* and, as a lively emblem of an extraordinary divine person, who was to be sent to instruct the whole earth, and purify them from all their pollutions; which the supreme fatherly chieftain will enable us fully to inform you of, in due time. He came according to divine appointment, taught the people, as never man did before, cured them of their various ailments, even the lame and the blind, by the power of his word, and a bare touch. He had so great a command over nature, that through pity to the tender tears of the people, he awaked some who had slept a considerable time in the grave, in a warm country. They, who strove to lessen the merit of the surprising miracles he wrought, were not so weak as to deny the well known truth of them, as they had been performed at different places, and on different occasions, before a great many people, under the light of the sun, and were lasting. At last, he, as an uncommon kindly friend, gave up his innocent life to save his enemies from the burning wrath of the holy fire: and, while the anger of *Loache Ishtohoollo* lay very sharp on him, as the atoning victim, and his enemies were tormenting him with the most exquisite tortures, he earnestly spoke the beloved speech, and entreated in their favour, that he would not let his heart be cross with, nor revenge his blood upon them, as they imagined they were acting according to the divine law. As soon as that great beloved messenger died, all nature felt a prodigious shock. The graves opened, and the dead arose to see the cause of that alarming prodigy. The earth shook, the rocks burst asunder, the sun, contrary to the stated course of nature, was immediately darkened, the great beloved house rent asunder, and its guardian angels flew off to other countries: his death also exceedingly destroyed the power of *Nana Ookproo,* the evil spirits. On the third day, the master of breath awaked that great chieftain, prophet, and high priest, according to his former true speech; and when he arose, he was seen by multitudes of people, and fulfilled the old divine law, and confirmed every thing he formerly taught his humble, and kind hearted scholars.

[442] Till then, there were only twelve of them; but afterwards more were appointed in that religious station. They urged, that their sacred office, and the faithful discharge of all the duties attending it, engaged their close attention, and deserved an honest maintenance; but to check a covetous spirit among all beloved men of every rank, they freely spoke the beloved speech through every known country of the world, and maintained themselves by their own industry. As they travelled, eat, drank, and conversed daily with the great divine messenger, he perfectly taught them the divine law, which your supposed ancestors had received under very strong emblems. After his death, they spoke it with great boldness, and a most amazing power. They truly marked down on paper, most of the speeches and actions of their beloved master and themselves, without concealing their own foibles, for our instruction: and a great many true copies of them are transmitted over every quarter of the world, in different languages, which agree together, and with those early beloved books; though it is more than seventeen hundred years, since they were first drawn out by those beloved scholars. As their hearts were warmed in a very high degree, by the holy spirit of fire, the moral part of their lives were free from blemish, after the death of their master. In imitation of him, they suffered all kinds of hardships, difficulties, and dangers of life, that human beings could undergo, merely through a principle of divine love working in them, for the general good of mankind; they cured the sick and diseased, and taught every one the true beloved speech, to purify them. As they were not proud, they were not drawn with beautiful prancing horses, in costly moving houses, but walked after the manner of their divine master, and instructed the attentive people, by their humble example, and honest lessons, in the most assured hope of receiving from *Ishtohoollo Aba,* a reward equal to their virtues, after they died, knowing they were to live anew in a happy state, free from the power of death. In this manner, they, by the earnest beloved speech of the great divine messenger, were cheerfully content, and firmly trusted in the goodness of the fatherly chieftain. Indeed, soon after they entered into their sacred office, they were jealous of their master's giving preference to one, before the other of them; but he gave a strong lesson of humility and kindness for them, and all succeeding beloved men to pursue, by washing and wiping their feet with his own hands: and he assured them *Ishtohoollo* would always esteem them most, who acted best.

[443] All those beloved men, who do not join in religious communion with *Oobache Ishtohoollo,* tell us, that ancient records affirm, all of the priestly order (after the death of the divine messenger) were equal in their religious office, that deference excepted, which is always due to a virtuous seniority—and that as wisdom and virtue equally accompany either youth, middle, or old age, they continued in that brotherly state of religious simplicity, according to the true copy of the humble, all-loving, and beloved messenger, for the space of three hundred years after that period—and that, as the speech of the great divine messenger was marked in a copious language, which abounded with various words to express the same thing, the names of old men, overseers and bishops, signify one and the same rank of beloved men of the beloved house, according to the former humble conduct of their divine master; but that the words are now tortured through mercenary views, contrary to the plain simplicity of the primitive teachers. As holy things, and white emblems, are easily polluted and tarnished by people of impure hearts, and unclean hands, the divine law began then to lose its quickening influence over the beloved men of those large countries, where the sun rises out of the broad water. Their disputes ran high, and the longer they lasted, the sharper they grew. They, at last, referred them to the decision of the beloved men, toward the place where the daily sun is drowned in the great salt water, which is called Rome. As in affairs of state, so in religion, a remarkable precedent begets a custom, and this becomes a law with societies. In consequence thereof, an order of superior beloved men laid hold of this, and stretched the divine speech, so as to answer their own mercenary views.

In process of time, there sprung up a pretended great bringer of rain, who, like the hurtful spirits of corrupt darkness, by rejecting the divine speech, and despising the example of the holy messenger and his scholars, set up arrogantly for himself, against the supreme chieftain of the rain and thunder, claimed the tenth basket-full of the new harvest according to the obsolete law of your supposed ancestors, and even forgave adulterers, thieves, liars, incestuous persons, and those who accompanied with women in their lunar retreats, without any sort of purification, if they only paid him such a quantity of yellow stone, as he proportioned to the various degrees of each crime they committed. To enrich himself by their weakness, his whole tribe of black-dressed missionaries, by strict order, frightened the ignorant [444] and credulous, with the wild notion of wandering after death in the accursed place of darkness, without any possibility of avoiding that dreadful fate, unless they revealed all their crimes to them, and paid them a fixed price. Because pride and envy had spoiled some of the spirits above, and made them accursed beings; therefore, the messenger of *Ishtohoollo,* as I told you, strongly checked the like disposition in its first appearance among his scholars. But the pride of the Romish chieftain, and desire of absolute religious and civil power, became so unbounded, as to claim an unlimited authority over all the great chieftains on earth; and he boasted of being so highly actuated by the unerring divine wisdom, as to know and do every thing perfectly. He, at the same time, ordered all his scholars to involve the people in thick clouds of darkness, and impress them with a firm belief, that ignorance produces virtue. He invented a third state for the sake of his temporal interest, fixing it half way between people's favourite place of living anew, and that of the horrible darkness, which was to be a vomiting or purging state of the dead, and called it purgatory; where the dead must unavoidably call, and be detained, till surviving relations satisfied them for their enlargement. He became so highly intoxicated by pride and power, that he erected images of such dead people as most resembled himself, with various other objects for the living to invoke, instead of the great eternal *Yo He Wah,* whom you supplicate in your religious invocations: and he marked for his black scholars, a great many very evil speeches, and spoke them with a strong mouth and ill heart, and enforced them by swords and fiery faggots, contrary to the old beloved speech which was confirmed by the anointed messenger.

At length, the holy spirit of fire influenced two great beloved men in particular, according to a former prediction, to speak to the people with a strong mouth, as witnesses of the divine truth. Their ears were honest in hearing the old beloved speech, and it sunk deep into their hearts. But a great many superstitious customs still remained, for had they aimed at a perfect establishment of the divine law in their religious worship, probably the high placed religious men through a covetous spirit would have opposed the reformation with all their might; as very few of them endeavoured to teach the young people, by honest examples, to live a virtuous life, or enabled them to get refreshing showers from *Ishtohoollo Aba* to make plentiful harvests—and yet they claimed a great part of it, and even [445] of the seed corn, without the least exemption of the poor, contrary to the tender feelings even of our indigent warriors and great canoe men, who stretch out a kindly hand to their poor brethren. That part of the old beloved speech, the tenth basket-full, was calculated only for your supposed predecessors, who consisted of twelve families; one of which was devoted to the divine service. Therefore, they were allowed some part of the religious offerings, and of the yearly produce of the land, to make their own and their families hearts rejoice, and at the same time to keep them humble, and make them hospitable to the widow, the fatherless, and the stranger. They, like the humble scholars of the great beloved messenger, were always poor; they honestly minded their religious duty, and were not allowed to purchase any land, nor to expose their virtue to the temptations of heaping up yellow stone, or employing their minds on any thing, except the divine law.

The lives and manners of the early teachers of the speech of the divine messenger, as I before told you, were also strictly just and blameless. They equally taught by precept and example; and their lessons, like those of their great master, were plain, simple, and holy. They were humble in their behaviour, and moderate in their apparel, food, and drink, and faithful in the discharge of their religious office: instead of assuming the arrogant title of divine chieftains, they honestly gave themselves the lowly name of *Intooksare Ishtohoollo,* "Servants of God," in imitation of the life, precept, and example of the holy messenger, which strongly actuated their honest hearts. When they were weary after the toils of the day, by instructing the people, and working at their trade, as your beloved men do, they joyfully rested themselves in their humble cottages, and refreshed themselves with their homely fare; and there they instructed the young people to invoke *Yo-He-Wah,* and speak the divine speech. In this religious manner, they spent their time through various countries, by the direction of divine wisdom, as a strong pointed lesson to all succeeding beloved men to pursue, and they sealed the truth with their blood—such were the primitive teachers of the divine word. They lived and died in a state of equality; and were there any different degrees to be observed in the holy office of religion, learning and piety should recommend poor beloved men to the high seats of profit—but only toilsome places are now allotted them, with an allowance insufficient to support themselves, so that they cannot stretch out their kindly hand to the poor.

[446] The mouths and hearts of the superior beloved men in our day, shamefully contradict one another, to the discredit of the lively copy of the holy messenger and his beloved scholars, and the great danger of infecting those of inferior rank, by so pernicious and corrupt an example; for it is natural for the feet to follow the direction of the head. They were formerly a very insolent, covetous, and troublesome set; and being advanced by rich friends to the high sounding office of *Mingo Ishtohoollo,* "Divine chieftains," or in their own stile, "Right Reverend Fathers in God," princes and supporters of the church, great was their arrogance and power—taking advantage of the corruption of the times, they grafted themselves into the civil constitution, and to preserve their high and profitable places they became the fixed and strenuous supporters of courts, in all their measures. But they will very soon be purified. The beloved speech of *Ishotoollo* of old, has announced it, and that is always true. It has pointed to the present and approaching time, which is near to the end of measured time.

To shew you how well prepared those priestly princes are for that trying period, I shall give you the general opinion of the wise and honest people, on this and the other side of the broad water; by which you will see how far they agree with, or differ from, the original copy of the plain honest scholars of the anointed holy messenger.

They boast themselves to be the embassadors of the holy chieftain of the high church. They dwell in costly great houses, after the superb manner of our great civil chieftain; and they give them the same lofty name, Palaces, to distinguish them from the dwelling-houses of other mortals. Their dress is equally rich and singular, to strike the eye, and impress the hearts of the vulgar with a profound reverence of the divine priestly wearers. They have the revenue of princes to support their grandeur; and they are most exact in having it collected by litigious mercenaries, even to the tenth of the hive of bees, and of the unlawful and filthy young swine; and yet they act the part of *Phohe Ishto,* "Great drones, or drones of God," as soon as they obtain their rich high seat, not speaking the divine speech to the people hardly three times a year. Their food consists of a great variety of the choicest, and most delicious sorts of fish, flesh, and fowl; their drink is of the richest white, yellow, and red grape water, with other costly liquors which your language cannot express. [447] They resort to the most gay assemblies in the world, for the sake of pleasure, leaving the multitude to the divine care, or the speakings of poor religious men who are hired at low wages to do their duty, as they themselves have enough to mind and secure properly temporal concerns. In this manner, do these lamps shine, and spend their days and nights, like the great chieftains of the earth; and when they die, their bodies are laid apart from the rest of mankind, in polished and costly tombs, adorned with nice strokes of art, to perpetuate their names—the long train of virtues they so highly possessed—their great learning and eloquence— the simplicity of their lives and manners—their faithful discharge of the various duties of their religious high office—their contempt of the grandeur and vanities of this transient world—their tenderness of heart to the cries of the poor; and their singular modesty and humility, a shining copy of imitation for common priests, and other spiritual chieftains, to pursue. These fine monuments are very pleasant to the eye, but honest men say that mercenary writers and artists do not act right to belie the dead.

My red beloved friends, such is the reputed life and death of those high-seated divine chieftains of the high church; your sharp natural reason will discern the close agreement there is between the humility and simplicity of their principles and lives, with those of the early overseers of the lowly divine house. It is said that some great beloved men have an earnest desire of sending a few of their own high office, to this side of the broad water, in order to appoint young beloved men; but we strongly suspect a dangerous snake in the grass; and esteeming them dead to the true interests of religion and liberty, we think they ought to keep them at home, and even recall their present troublesome missionaries from our settlements, and allow us to enjoy our former peace and quiet—We wish them to go to some poor dark countries, and instruct the people in the honest lessons of peace, love, and charity; which they would, if they only aimed at the good of mankind, and the honour of the supreme chieftain, according to the plain copy of the great beloved messenger and his kind-hearted faithful scholars. We wish the civil powers would not tempt the religious men's virtue by such alluring delicious baits, as they propose to them, and that all ranks would become frugal and virtuous.

[448] Thus ended my LECTURE. The reverend old red pontiff immediately asked, whether they had the accursed beings on the other side of the water? I told him, I hoped not—but the religious men often spoke a strong speech of evil to those they reckoned very bad, and turned them out of the beloved house, to the evil spirits of darkness. Upon which he requested me to mention any one of the crimes that might occasion such treatment. I told him, "I have heard of a gentleman, whose heart did not allow him to love his lady sufficiently, and she having by sharp watching discovered him to give love to another, complained of it to a great beloved man; accordingly, either for the neglect, or wrong application of his love duty, he was ordered to pay her a considerable sum of money—he valuing it more than her, his heart did not allow him to give so much: whereupon a sharp speech of evil was spoke against him, and by that means he was said to become accursed." My Indian friend said, as marriage should beget joy and happiness, instead of pain and misery, if a couple married blindfold, and could not love each other afterwards, it was a crime to continue together, and a virtue to part, and make a happier choice; and as the white people did not buy their wives after the manner of the Indians, but received value along with them, in proportion to their own possessions, whatsoever the woman brought with her, she ought to be allowed to take back when they separated, that her heart might weigh even, and nothing be spoiled.—That, in his opinion, such determinations belonged to the law, and not to the great beloved men; and, if he understood me aright, the beloved man threw away the gentleman to the accursed beings of darkness, not for having acted any thing against the divine law, but for daring to oppose the words of his mouth, in imitation of the first presumptuous great beloved man, who spoiled the speech of the divine messenger. Many natural, pertinent, and humorous observations, were made by him on what he had heard.

[449]Appendix.

Advice to Statesmen;

Shewing

The advantages of mutual affection between Great Britain, and the North American colonies—A description of the Floridas, and the Mississippi lands, with their productions—The benefits of colonizing Georgiana, and civilizing the Indians—and the way to make all the colonies more valuable to the mother country.

[451]Appendix.

Advice to Statesmen.

Though Great Britain hath been many years invested with the Missisipi-possessions, and which she purchased at a very high price; little hath been done to improve them. Every friend to his country and mankind, must wish administration to pay a due regard to the inestimable value of the American colonies—which is best done in engaging the colonists, by wise and prudent conduct, to exert themselves to promote her interest in the same manner they faithfully did, till arbitrary power assailed their maritme ports, to their grief, and her own immense loss. In proportion as a mother loves, or hates her children, and strives to make them either happy or miserable, they in the same degree will exert their endeavours to make a suitable return.

Whatever scheme is unjust, it is unwise in statesmen to form, or attempt to put in execution. Instinct moves the brutal creation to defend their young ones and property at the peril of their lives. The virtue of Britons will not allow them to do less for themselves and their children. As British legislators must be convinced that honesty is the best policy, it is to be hoped they will studiously apply themselves to promote the general good of their fellow-subjects, and engage the northern colonists cheerfully to bend their force in supplying Great Britain with such staple commodities [452] as bountiful nature has given to them, but which through a strange kind of policy, she now chiefly purchases from foreigners, particularly timber and iron. The North-American trees are better in quality, than those which are brought from the Baltic, and in a far greater variety: and ships of a proper construction, might soon carry American timber to England as cheap as she has it from thence. The colonists could build either mechant-men, or men of war, of any size, much cheaper than can possibly be done in any European country, which would always insure them a ready market. French gold for their ships, would be of no disservice to Great Britain, though perhaps it might be a as disagreeable to her, as the Spanish gold and silver was from the hands of the British Americans: however, to consign their ships to some British merchants, would sufficiently silence those who might find their present account in opposing the public good.

Natural causes produce natural effects. They who sow well, reap well; and as nature has planted a great plenty of iron ore through the American high lands, we hope the time will soon come, to allow her to take in so weighty a harvest. The consequence is great, and the application ought to be proportioned to the high value of so inviting, and complicated an acquisition. Their hills not only abound with inexhaustible mines of iron ore, but lie convenient to navigable rivers; such a commodious situation would soon enable them to sell it cheaper than Britain can ever expect from the Russians, who carry it from a distance to Petersburgh, as far as from Georgiana on the Missisippi, to the city of New York. We have been assured by gentlemen of veracity, that on repeated experiments, they found the American iron to be equal in goodness to that of Russia, or Sweden. Common sense directs Britain to live independent of such supplies, within her own prodigious empire, and not lay herself at the mercy of any foreign power, lest necessity should compel her a second time, to pay as dear for her left-handed wisdom as she did in the year 1703, for Swedish tar in Swedish bottoms,—which was nearly four hundred per cent. more than she in short time paid to the American planters for the like, with her own manufactures, to the advantage of her merchants, the employment of her ships, and the increase of her seamen.[470]

[453] If Britain feels a decay of her former American trade, on account of attempting to introduce among her friendly colonies, illegal and dangerous innovations, it is high time to retract. She hath it yet in her power by a prudent and maternal conduct to enlarge her trade, to a far greater extent than it ever attained, by making it the interest of the northern planters to saw timber, and work in iron, for the British yards and merchants. She should invite the young, and unsettled families, to remove to the fertile lands of the Missisippi, and raise those valuable staple commodities she needs most. The Americans say, that, though their hearts burn with a seraphic fire, for constitutional blessings—ever sacred and inviolable; yet their tender feelings for the unhappy situation of their free-minded brethren in Great Britain and Ireland, are by sympathy, equal to their own for the sickened condition of their mourning provinces—that the fraternal tye will always incline their hearts to promote their welfare, if instead of endeavouring to oppress them, they make them such a return as brethren might justly expect on the like interesting occasion. If British legislators design to promote the true interests of their country, they will pay a steady regard to the real channel of her great wealth and power,—adopt such measures, as wisdom and honesty readily direct to, and endeavour to dispel those uneasi-

nesses from the hearts of all the American colonists, produced by the unjust and invidious representations of men, whose garb and station ought to have kept them, even from the suspicion of ever fomenting so dangerous a controversy.

Great Britain, on account of her extensive American possessions, might soon and easily repair her decayed trade, and increase it beyond conception, on a sure and permanent foundation, by upright measures. The opposite means to whatsoever caused its decay, would gradually recover it—But when once the channel of trade is stopped by violent methods, it is exceedingly difficult to make it flow again in its former cheerful course. Force can never effect it, for that she utterly contemns. No mistress is more sagacious and coy. She must first be courted, and afterward treated kindly: if folly uses any violence, or makes any material breach of good faith to her, she soon flies, and never returns, unless she is strongly invited back, and can reasonably hope for better usage. A powerful maritime state may gain new colonies by the sword, but can never settle and continue such extensive ones as the American, by force of arms,—except over people of dastardly spirits, [454] and in the enfeebling regions of the south. Even there, when the springs of the state-machine are any considerable time over-stretched, the sharp feelings of the people naturally rouse, and force them to conquer their timorous disposition, and exert their powers to break the torturing wheels, and free themselves of their pains. The voice of nature is against tyranny. It execrates the abettors, and consigns them to punishment.

As the lands in Virginia, and Maryland, are greatly exhausted by raising that impoverishing weed, tobacco,—Great Britain may expect to feel a gradual decay of that valuable branch of trade, in proportion to the increase of the people in those provinces, unless new colonies are settled on the Missisippi. Besides this tract, there is not a sufficient space of fertile land in North America, to invite planters to raise that staple commodity. Though the Ohio settlements are now numerous, and increasing fast, the settlers will only consult their own ease, as nature is there very prolific of every convenience of life; except government wisely encourages them to raise such products as would suit the mother-country, and reward them for their labour. Were proper measures adopted, the desire of gain would induce them to plant with the utmost assiduity: and smiling industry would soon beget a spirit of emulation amoung the planters, prompting each to excel his neighbour in the annual quantity and good quality of those staple commodities they were invited to fix upon. The vast tracts of fertile woods, which are now shamefully allowed to be only the haunts of wild beasts, and wolfish savages seeking for prey, might far easier be turned into valuable fine plantations by bounties, than the marshes and barren lands in Britain were, into their present flourishing condition, by the repeated encouragements of the Royal Society, and of parliament. Any thing that promotes greatly the public good, ought always to be done at the expence of the public; otherwise it will never be done, especially by labouring individuals. Charity begins at home, and every one's domestic affairs demand his close attention. To preserve the Ohio lands, cost Great Britain, and our colonies in particular, a river of blood, in consequence of the blindness and obstinacy of a haughty general. A legal constitutional form of government, ought immediately to be established there, both for the general welfare, and preventing evils that may reasonably be expected to grow up among a remote, and numerous body of people,—hardy and [455] warlike, without any public religion or civil law,—in a healthful climate, and very extensive and fertile country.

Young glittering courtiers may think their merit exceedingly depreciated, to have the offer of the Ohio government conferred on either of them—as it is now chiefly inhabited by long-legged, tawny hunters, who are clothed in winter with the shaggy skins of wild beasts, and are utterly unlearned in the polished art of smiling, when their hearts are displeased at the rash conduct of the high-headed rulers: but unless they learned the difficult lesson, "know thyself," and were endued with a frank open spirit, experience would soon convince them that they were unequal to the task of governing, or inducing the people to promote the general good of the community. The court sophistry of extending the prerogative of the crown, will never do in America—Nothing will please the inhabitants, but the old constitutional laws of Britain. Colonel Philip Skene, who gained wreaths of laurel under General Johnson, and now lives at Lake Champlain, is highly esteemed in the extensive circle of his acquiantance, and revered by all his savage neighbours, because in him is displayed the intrepid warrior, and the open friend to all.[471]—These, together with his knowledge of agriculture, render him as proper a person as any for the office—and it is to be wished that the government would appoint him to preside over the valuable district of Ohio, and he think proper to accept it. Such a measure could not fail of adding greatly to the true interests of Great-Britain and her colonies: thus, the present inhabitants would be incited to promote the public good, and multitudes of the northern people would remove to settle those fruitful lands, and cheerfully apply themselves in raising such commodities, as would prove beneficial to the community. Though the Ohio is far distant from any navigable port, yet we have full proof that every article of luxury will bear great expence for its culture, carriage by land, and freight by water: and, as the fertility of the soil by the stream and small branches of the Missisippi, is well known through North America, and the colonists cannot remove there with their live stock, through the country of the mischievous

Muskohge; doubtless numbers of industrious families would come by the Ohio, and soon enrich themselves by increasing the riches of the public.

[456] Any European state, except Great Britain, would at once improve their acquisitions, taken and purchased by an immense quantity of blood and treasure, and turn them to the public benefit. At the end of the late war, the ministry, and their adherents, held up East and West Florida before the eyes of the public, as greatly superior to those West-India islands, which Spain and France were to receive back in exchange. The islands however are rich, and annually add to the wealth and strength of those respective powers: while East Florida, is the only place of that extensive and valuable tract ceded to us, that we have any way improved; and this is little more than a negative good to our other colonies, in preventing their negroes from sheltering in that dreary country, under the protection of Fort St. Augustine. The province is a large peninsula, consisting chiefly of sandy barrens; level sour ground, abounding with tussucks; here and there is some light mixt land; but a number of low swamps, with very unwholesome water in general. In proportion as it is cleared, and a free circulation of air is produced, to dispel the noxious vapours that float over the surface of this low country, it may become more healthful; though any where out of the influence of the sea air, the inhabitants will be liable to fevers and agues. The favourable accounts our military officers gave of the pure wholesome air of St. Augustine, are very just, when they compare it with that of the sand burning Pensacola, and the low stagnated Mobille: St. Augustine stands on a pleasant hill, at the conflux of two salt water rivers, overlooking the land from three angles of the castle, and down the sound, to the ocean. Their relation of the natural advantages of this country, could extend no farther than their marches reached. I formerly went volunteer, about six hundred miles through the country, with a great body of Indians against this place; and we ranged the woods to a great extent.[472] The tracts we did not reach, we got full information of, by several of the Muskohge then with us, who had a thorough knowledge, on account of the long continued excursions they made through the country in quest of the Florida Indians; and even after they drove them into the islands of Florida, to live on fish, among clouds of musketoes. The method these Indians took to keep off those tormenting insects, as their safety would not allow them to make a fire, lest the smoke should guide their watchful enemies to surprise them, was, by anointing their bodies with rank fish oil, mixed with the juice or ashes of indigo. This perfume, and its effluvia, kept off from them every kind of [457] insect. The Indians likewise informed me, that when they went to war against the Floridians, they carried their cypress bark canoes from the head of St. John's black river, only about half a mile, when they launched them again into a

deep river, which led down to a multitude of islands to the N. W. of Cape Florida.

As this colony is incontestably much better situated for trade than West Florida, or the Missisippi lands, it is surprising that Britain does not improve the opportunity which offers, by adding to these unhealthy low grounds a sufficient quantity of waste high land to enable the settlers, and their families, to raise those staples she wants. The Muskohge who claim it, might be offered, and they would accept, what it seems to be worth in its wild state.[473] Justice to ourselves and neighbours, condemns the shortening the planter's days, by confining their industrious families to unhealthy low lands, when nature invites them to come out, to enjoy her bountiful gifts of health and wealth, where only savage beasts prey on one another, and the bloodier two-footed savages, ramble about to prey on them, or whatsoever falls in their way. Under these, and other pressing circumstances of a similar nature, does this part of America now labour. A west north-west course from the upper parts of Georgia to the Mississippi, would contain more fertile lands than are in all our colonies on the continent, eastward. As most of these colonies abound with frugal and industrious people, who are increasing very fast, and every year crowding more closely together on exhausted land, our rulers ought not to allow so mischievous and dangerous a body as the Muskohge to ingross this vast forest, mostly for wild beasts. This haughty nation is directly in the way of our valuable southern colonies, and will check them from rising to half the height of perfection, which the favourableness of the soil and climate allow, unless we give them severe correction, or drive them over the Missisippi, the first time they renew their acts of hostility against us, without sufficient retaliation. At present, West Florida is nothing but an expence to the public.—The name amuses indeed, at a distance; but were it duly extended and settled, it would become very valuable to Great Britain; and Pensacola harbour would be then serviceable also in a time of war with Spain, being in the gulph of Florida, and near to Cuba. Mobille is a black trifle. Its garrison, and that at Pensacola, cannot be properly supplied by their French neighbours though at a most exorbitant price: and, on account [458] of our own passive conduct, the Muskohge will not allow the inhabitants of Georgia to drive cattle to those places for the use of the soldiers.[474] Neither can the northern merchant-men supply them with salt and fresh provisions, but at a very unequal hazard; for the gulph stream would oblige them to sail along the Cuba shore, where they would be likely to be seized by the Spanish guarda costas, as have many fine American vessels on the false pretence of smuggling, and which, by a strange kind of policy, they have been allowed to keep as legal prizes. In brief, unless Great Britain enlarges both East and West Florida to a proper extent, and adopts other encouraging measures, for raising those staple commodities which she purchases from foreigners, the sagacious public must be convinced, that the opportunity of adding to her annual expences, by paying troops, and maintaining garrisons, to guard a narrow slip of barren sand-hills, and a tract of low grave-yards, is not an equivalent for those valuable improved islands our enemies received in exchange for them.

We will now proceed to the Missisippi, and that great extent of territory, which Great Britain also owns by exchange; and shew the quality of those lands, and how far they may really benefit her, by active and prudent management. As in Florida, so to a great distance from the shore of the gulph, the lands generally consist of burning sand, and are uninhabitable; or of wet ground, and very unhealthy. But, a little beyond this dreary desart, are many level spots very fertile, and which would suit people who are used to a low situation, and prove very valuable, both to planters, and the inhabitants of a trading town. As the river runs from north to south, the air is exceedingly pure in the high lands of this extensive tract. The soil is generally very rich; and, to the distance of six hundred miles up, from the low lands of the sea coast, it is as happy a climate as any under heaven, quite free from the extremities of heat and cold. Any product of the same clime from 31 to 45 degrees N. L. might be raised here in the greatest perfection, to the great profit of the planter and the public. Many thousands of us would heartily rejoice to see administration behave as wise men—leave their mean, or mad policy, and promote a spirit of emigration amoung the families of the crowded northern colonies. Thus the industrious poor in Britain, would find more employ in manufactures; and the public would receive from their brethren, what they now purchase chiefly from rival powers with gold and silver, with the balance of trade greatly against them.

[459] This fine country, Georgiana, invites Great Britain to smile upon it, and in return to receive its grateful tribute of tobacco, hemp, silk, flax, cotton, indigo, wine and tea, in plenty, besides many other valuable products. Hops grow wild on the Missisippi—and the tobacco raised at the Nahchee old settlement, was esteemed of superior quality to any belonging [to] France. The lands on the extensive ramifactions of the Missisippi lands are capable of producing the like. All kind of vegetables planted, or sowed in their fields, gardens, and orchards, either for profit or pleasure, would grow to greater perfection, and with less art and labour, in this tract, than any in Europe, so fruitful is the soil, and favourable the climate. As the savages live in a direct line between our northern colonies, and this, to the distance of four hundred miles above New Orleans; our northern people will be obliged to make a winding course by the Ohio, before they can reach it with their families and necessary moveables; which shews that it requires public spirit, and the support of government to settle a flourishing colony here. The two Floridas, and this, which to the great loss of the nation,

lie shamefully neglected, are the only places in the British empire, from whence she can receive a sufficient supply of those staples she wants. The prosperity, and even the welfare of Great Britain, depends on sundry accounts, in a high degree, on improving these valuable and dear bought acquisitions; and we hope her eyes will be opened soon, and her hands stretched out to do it—she will provide for the necessities of her own poor at home, by the very means that would employ a multitude of useless people in agriculture here, and bring the savages into a probable way of being civilized, and becoming christians, by contracting their circle of three thousand miles, and turning them from a lonely hunt of wild beasts, to the various good purposes of society. Should Great Britain duly exert herself as the value of this place requires, by the assistance of our old Chikkasah allies, the other Indian nations would be forced to pursue their true interest, by living peaceably with us; and be soon enticed to become very serviceable both to our planters, and the enlargement of trade.

As the Missisippi Indians are not likely to be soon corrupted by the haughty stiff Spaniards, and are mostly of a tractable dispositon, consequently they might be civilized, and their wants so greatly extended as to demand every kind of British manufactures, in imitation of their friendly, industrious, and opulent neighbours: and, as the small profits of hunting would not be sufficient to purchase a variety of such new necessaries, they might be easily [460] induced to cultivate those commodities that would best answer their demands. Raising of silk, would extremely well agree with them, on account of its easy process; mulberry trees grow spontaneously to a considerable height here, and in the low lands through all our southern colonies; which, were they topped, and transplanted near to the houses, would serve to feed the silk worms with their leaves. The easy culture of this valuable commodity, silk, would not hinder the planter from attending the inviting products of the field. Thus the Indians would be gently led out of their uncultivated state of nature, and a fair opportunity would be given to discreet, sensible and pious teachers to instruct them in the plain, and easy principles of christianity.

The prodigious number of fertile hills lying near some of the large streams, and among the numberless smaller branches of the Missisippi, from 33 to 37 degrees N. L. (and likewise in the two Floridas) are as well adapted by nature, for producing different sorts of wine, as any place whatever. The high lands naturally abound with a variety of wine grapes: if therefore these extensive lands were settled, and planters met with due encouragement, Great Britain in a few years might purchase here, with her own manufactures, a sufficient supply of as good wines as she buys from her dangerous rival France, at a great disadvantage of trade, or even from Portugal. The level lands here, as in other countries, are badly watered; which therefore would absolutely require the colony to be extended six hundred miles up the Missisippi, to answer the main design of settling it. The lands in our northern colonies are too much exhausted to raise a sufficient quantity of hemp for their own consumption: and indigo does not grow to the north of Cape Fear river, in North Carolina, on account of the coldness of the climate. And as it grows only in rich lands, it is liable to be devoured the second year by swarms of grasshoppers, and its roots are of so penetrating a nature, as not only to impoverish the ground, but requires more new fertile land than the planters can allow; so that in a short time, that product will cease of course in South Carolina, and Georgia. This favourable country will supply that growing defect. In the Carolinas, and along the sea-coast to the Missisippi, tea grows spontaneously; and doubtless, if the East-India tea was transplanted into those colonies, it would grow, as well as in the eastern regions of the same latitude. The chief point consists in curing it well: but foreigners, or experience, would soon overcome that difficulty by due encouragement. Some years ago, a gentleman of South Carolina told me he raised some [461] of the East-India tea, and it grew extremely well. He said, he had it cured in a copper kettle, well covered, and fixed in a common pot with water, which boiled three hours, was then taken out, and allowed to cool before they opened it; and that when the vessel was not filled with the leaves, they curled in the same manner as the East-India weed imported at a great loss of men and money, and better tasted.

I am well acquainted with near two thousand miles along the American continent, and have frequently been in the remote woods; but the quantity of fertile lands, in all that vast space, exclusive of what ought to be added to East and West-Florida, seems to bear only a small proportion to those between the Missisippi and Mobille-river, with its N. W. branches, which run about thirty miles north of the Chikkasah country, and intermix with pleasant branches of the great Cheerake river. In settling the two Floridas, and the Missisippi-lands, administration should not suffer them to be monopolized—nor the people to be classed and treated as slaves—Let them have a constitutional form of government, the inhabitants will be cheerful, and every thing will be prosperous. The country promises to yield as plentiful harvests of the most valuable productions, as can be wished.

There is a number of extensive and fertile Savannas, or naturally clear land, between the Missisippi and the western branches of Mobille river. They begin about two hundred and fifty miles above the low lands of the coast, and are interspersed with the woods to a great distance, probably three hundred miles. The inland parts are unknown to any but the Indians and the English traders—the warlike Chikkasah were so dreadful to the French, that even their fleet of large trading boats avoided the eastern side of the Missisippi, or near this shore under a high point of land, for the space of two hundred leagues:[475] so that, beyond what they barely saw from their boats, their accounts of the interior parts of this extensive country, are mere conjectures. The soil of the clear land, generally consists of loose rich mould to a considerable depth, and either a kind of chalk, or marl, underneath. We frequently find the grass with its seeded tops as high as our heads, when on horse-back, and very likely it would bear mowing, three or four times in one season. As the Indians gather their wild hemp, in some of these open fertile lands, both it and our hemp would grow to an admiration, with moderate tillage: as so would tobacco, indigo, cotton, and flax, in perfection. If Great-Britain exerts herself in earnest, with an helping hand [462] to this new colony; granting only for eight years, an equal bounty with that she gave to the bleak and barren settlement of Nova Scotia, she would receive at the expiration of that period, in return for her favours, an abundant variety of valuable raw materials, for employing a vast multitude of her poor at home, as well as luxurious productions, for her own consumption, and that of foreigners; greatly increase the public revenue; destroy the sale of French wines, and tobacco, the chief sinews of their state; render herself independent of foreign countries—and make millions of people easy and happy, on both sides of the broad water, by mutual industry, and reciprocal offices of friendship.

If Great Britain thus wisely improves the natural advantages of North-America, she will soon reap sufficient fruit for her expences of cultivating it: but she must certainly be a loser, in proportion to any unconstitutional attempt excited by false views, against the natural rights and chartered privileges of the colonists. We now and then see the lamentable power that illiberal prejudices and self-interest obtain over gentlemen of learning, and judgment, by transforming them from honest, wise men, into dangerous political incendiaries. Whether the colonists are large in their British imports, or are forced to more domestic frugality on account of the late severe restraints upon their trade, these sophists declare them to be rivals in trade, and devote them to destruction. The colonists however generally proportion their expences to the annual income of their possessions. If they gain but a little by trade, and labour, they spend as little in luxuries. At the very worst, they can keep the wolf of want from their doors. They are so happily situated, as to have far less real demands for gold and silver than any other civilized, increasing body of people. When they received those metals abroad by their Spanish trade, they soon remitted them to Great Britain; and they are now quite easy, if she chuses to strike her own pocket very hard, in order to hurt them. Our political physicians prescribe a strange sort of means and regimen to heal the wounds of the body politic; assuredly they will tear them open, and make them bleed fresh again, and more than ever. It is a pity, that before they thought of hunger and phlebotomy for the supposed unsound Americans, they had not duly considered the solid reasonings and un-answerable arguments of the very worthy, upright patriot, John Dickenson, Esq;[476] and other American gentlemen, and the speeches and publications of some patriots at home. Smollett's[477] observations are also very pertinent—"The natives of New-England acquired great glory [463] from the success of this enterprize against Louisbourg. Britain, which had in some instances behaved like a stepmother to her own colonies, was now convinced of their importance; and treated those as brethren whom she had too long considered as aliens and rivals. Circumstanced as the nation is, the legislature cannot too tenderly cherish the interests of the British plantations in America. They are inhabited by a brave, hardy, industrious people, animated with an active spirit of commerce, inspired with a noble zeal for liberty and independence. The trade of Great-Britain, clogged with heavy taxes and impositions, has for some time languished in many valuable branches. The French have undersold our cloths, and spoiled our markets in the Levant. Spain is no longer supplied as usual with the commodities of England: the exports to Germany must be considerably diminished by the misunderstanding between Great Britain and the house of Austria;—consequently her greatest resource must be in her communication with her own colonies, which consume her manufactures, and make immense returns in sugar, rum, tobacco, fish, timber, naval stores, iron, furs, drugs, rice, and indigo. The southern plantations likewise produce silk; and with due encouragement might furnish every thing that could be expected from the most fertile soil and the happiest climate. The continent of North America, if properly cultivated, will prove an inexhaustible fund of wealth and strength to Great Britain; and perhaps it may become the last asylum of British liberty, when the nation is enslaved by domestic despotism or foreign dominion; when her substance is wasted, her spirit broke, and the laws and consititution of England are no more: then those colonies sent off by our fathers may receive and entertain their sons as hapless exiles and ruined refugees."

Evil-minded writers depreciate those Americans most, who stand most in their way. Could their enemies subjugate them, they might then put their hands in their pockets with impunity, use scorpion-whips on their backs at pleasure, and establish the most delicious part of the Jewish law, tithes, through the whole continent.

The present Quixote scheme evidently seems to fetter the British Americans, at all events, and force them to pay for their fetters; to compel them to maintain a great body of imperious red coats to rule over them, after the manner of the miserable sons of Hibernia, without allowing them any militia, even on their barriers: otherwise our rulers think that, about twenty [464] years hence, the quick increase of the British Americans, will render the execution of their scheme impracticable. Rather than let them be free and happy, they are for reducing them, in effect, to poverty and a state of slavery. However, if they conjure right, and even allowing them that success they pine for, it cannot well be supposed that such vast multitudes of British subjects would be so inured to slavery, in the short space of twenty years, but that they would cut off their chains, and set themselves free. Some statesmen have shewn themselves to be no less strangers to the generous principles of the constitution, and feelings of humanity, than they are to the extraordinary martial abilities of the American provincials, especially in the woods, which are continued almost through all our colonies, and would prove a grave-yard to a great army of regular troops. Tame Frenchmen might submit to the yoke intended—But Britons, of revolution-principles, especially the Americans, contemn it and all its supporters, far beyond the power of language to express. Were they impoverished, and subjugated, their own bravery would soon set them free from tyranny. When sufferings become sharp, brave men always make desperate efforts, in proportion to their pain. And the annals of the world uniformly declare, that no enemies are so desperate and bitter, as despised, abused, and persecuted friends.

They who are in the lest acquainted with the principles of our colonists, can truly testify their universal attachment to the present line of Brunswick;[478] and that their hearts are faithful to the real honour and best interest of their king and country, whose interests cannot be divided. And we hope, that they who have their chief direction of public affairs, will soon cherish that disposition, so peculiar to free-minded Britons; and that condign punishment will be inflicted on those who endeavour to check it, and to foment a civil war. Thus, a profitable intercourse, a lasting peace, and perpetual friendship, will continue between the honest parent and her grateful colonies, who will not fail to be just to her, to themselves, and to their posterity. F I N I S.

Notes to Introductory Essay

Abbreviations Used

LC	Library of Congress
HAI	Adair, *History of the American Indians*
JCHA	*Journal of the Commons House of Assembly*
MPAFD	*Mississippi Provincial Archives, French Dominion*
SCDAH	South Carolina Department of Archives and History
BMP	British Microfilm Project
SCCJ	South Carolina Council Journals
DRCHNY	*Documents Relative to the Colonial History of the State of New York*
MPAED	*Mississippi Provincial Archives, English Dominion*
DAR	*Documents of the American Revolution*

Notes for Introductory Essay

1. Samuel Cole Williams, in his edition of *Adair's History of the American Indians* (National Society of Colonial Dames of America, 1930), p. viii, speculates that Adair was born in 1709 in County Antrim, Ireland, the younger son of Sir Robert Adair, a scion of the English Fitzgerald family. Williams, giving himself over entirely to speculation, mused, "as has been the case with so many scions of noble and other houses of Great Britain, facing the vice-grip of the law of primogeniture, he [James Adair] preferred the freedom and opportunities of distant climes." One Adair family history claims the same James Adair born in 1709 but assigns the father as Thomas Adair, who in 1730 migrated to Chester County, Pennsylvania. James is said to have preceded his family to South Carolina in 1735, while the rest of his family moved to the South around 1750: James Barnett Adair, *Adair History and Genealogy* (Easley, S.C.: Southern Historical Press, 1924), 269–71. The most incredible family claim, made by William Curry Harllee, is that James Adair was the alter-ego of Dr. Robert Adair of North Carolina. Despite his claims of "a perfect chain of evi-

dence" and an attempt to interweave the activities of the two men, his work fails to convince, given that Adair the author never claimed medical skills and is closely linked to the Georgia–South Carolina border rather than North Carolina. Harllee's one source of evidence that James Adair was a physician stems from Adair's description of his farcical treatment of a Natchez warrior's eye with his "materia medica" (Adair, *History of the American Indians,* 173, hereafter cited as *HAI;* all page numbers refer to the original pagination, provided in brackets in the present work). However, the possession of common medical preparations does not indicate that Adair the author was a physician. This is especially apparent in Adair's treatment of Indian medicine, which he generally praises but actually says very little about. A practicing physician would have certainly included more information on medicinal plants and practices used by the Indians. Indeed, most of Adair's contemporaries who were not physicians provided more information on such topics than he. Moreover, Adair, so far as he recorded, never administered treatment to injured Indians, as a physician might have done (see, for example, *HAI,* 357). Harllee's work did manage to convince the North Carolina Society of the Colonial Dames of America, however, and that organization dedicated a marker to "James Robert Adair M.D." in 1934 near the location of Robert Adair's home in Robeson County, North Carolina; see William Curry Harllee, *Kinfolks,* 4 vols. (New Orleans: Searcy & Pfaff, Ltd., 1935), 2: 1241, 1291). Other than common given names, to date no positive link has been established between James Adair and other Adairs in South and North Carolina, Ireland, or anywhere else. Adair was silent on his family history, and the connections made by family historians are offered without documentary evidence or support of any kind, other than family legend and hopeful speculation based on common names.

2. In his examination of Adair family history, James B. Adair relates, without providing supporting evidence, "About the time of his trip to London, or just before that time, Adair married a lady in North Carolina, and finally settled in that state. (We do not know his exact location nor the maiden name of his wife.)" Their son, James Adair, Jr., is then said to have married a "Miss Kilgore" (*Adair History and Genealogy,* 270–71). Samuel Coles Williams repeats James B. Adair's assertions, then counters with information from Emmett Starr, who found a John Adair married to a Miss Kilgore. Williams follows with a biographical sketch of a Cherokee chief who in 1833 claimed to be descended on the paternal line from James Adair the author (*Adair's History,* xviii–xix). Mariam Adair Dabbs, in *The Descendants of James Adair, Author of* The History of the American Indians (Clarksdale, Miss.: Litho-Print, Inc., 1976), wrote that it was not James but his sons by an unnamed North Carolina woman who founded the Cherokee dynasty. Given there is no evidence offered that James Adair the author married a woman in North Carolina, this weakens that argument considerably. On a more pragmatic note, given James Adair's strong connection to the Chickasaw, his acknowledged relationship with at least one Chickasaw woman, and his general disdain for the Cherokee, it seems unlikely he would have married a Cherokee woman in his later years. Considering the state of affairs

that existed in the Cherokee nation at the time of the Revolution, it is almost a certainty that he did not make his home there. Adair family genealogists may yet uncover convincing proof and connect Adair to their respective lines, but to date his family history remains foggy at best.

3. In their attempt to link their respective lines to the author James Adair, family historians often fail to realize that there was more than one individual named "James Adair" found in the Carolinas on the eve of the American Revolution. At least two men by that name appeared on lists of Protestants who had arrived from Ireland to claim South Carolina's land bounty in the 1760s. Some land claims made by men named James Adair occurred after the author had left South Carolina to pursue publication of his book. See, for example, Brent H. Holcomb, *Petitions for Land from the South Carolina Council Journals,* vol. 5, *1757–1765* (Columbia: South Carolina Magazine of Ancestral Research, 1998), 141, 144, and vol. 6, *1766–1770* (Columbia: South Carolina Magazine of Ancestral Research, 1999), 83, 155, 305. These James Adairs were most certainly not the author, and there has been no evidence uncovered to date that links them to him in any way.

4. In addition to styling himself an "English Chikkasah" (*HAI,* 276), Adair also identified himself as an "English warrior" (*HAI,* 301). Scholars have puzzled over Adair's ethnic background and speculated on its importance. For example, Raymond Fogelson has imagined in Adair at various times an "Irish sense of humor and irony" as well as "shrewd Scottish pragmatism"; see Fogelson, "On the 'Petticoat Government' of the Eighteenth-Century Cherokee," in *Personality and the Cultural Construction of Society,* edited by D. K. Jordan and M. J. Swartz (Tuscaloosa: University of Alabama Press, 1990), 164, and *The Cherokees: A Critical Bibliography* (Bloomington: Indiana University Press, 1978), 12. Malcom McGee, who came to the Chickasaw country about the time that Adair was leaving, reported to Lyman C. Draper in the 1840s that Adair was an "Irishman." He also reported, erroneously, that Adair first came to the Chickasaw towns about 1769 (notes from interview with Malcom McGee, 1841, Lyman C. Draper Manuscript Collection, Wisconsin Historical Society). One intriguing but utterly confusing clue to Adair's origin emerges from his dismissive comment regarding his political enemies during the investigation of the Choctaw revolt, whom Adair described as "a certain sett, who are known to patronize any persons if they chance to be born in the same corner of the world with themselves." Glen was Scottish and Edmond Atkin, his other nemesis, was English. Context does not reveal which "sett" Adair had in mind. Indeed, he may have simply meant those born abroad rather than in South Carolina, for it is clear that Adair's primary political allegiance was to South Carolina. The most plausible place of his origin—and one to date largely unpursued by family historians—is the Scottish Presbyterian community of Antrim, Ireland. The most noted of the Antrim Adairs, the Reverend Patrick Adair, was a politically feisty author whose manuscript history of the rise of the Presbyterian Church in Ireland is still cited by those interested in the topic; see *A True Narrative of the Rise and Progress of the Presbyterian Church in Ireland,* with an Introduction and Notes by W. D.

Killen (Belfast: C. Aitchison, 1866). James Adair, a devoutly religious man, was certainly well educated in biblical history, and a link to the Atrim Adair line is occasionally mentioned in Adair genealogies.

5. *Georgia Gazette,* October 11, 1769.

6. *South Carolina Gazette,* September 7, 1769.

7. *HAI,* preface. The *Georgia Gazette* of October 11, 1769, stated that Adair has been "intimately acquainted" with the Indians for thirty-three years.

8. *HAI,* 223. James H. Merrell, *The Indians' New World: Catawbas and their Neighbors from European Contact through the Era of Removal* (Chapel Hill: University of North Carolina Press, 1989), provides the best overview of that tribe's history.

9. See *HAI,* 344.

10. *HAI,* 240.

11. Ibid. For information on Priber, see Verner W. Crane, "A Lost Utopia on the First American Frontier," *Sewanee Review* 27 (January 1919): 48–61, and Richard Beale Davis, *Intellectual Life in the Colonial South, 1585–1763,* 3 vols. (Knoxville: University of Tennessee Press, 1978), 1: 171–72.

12. *HAI,* 243.

13. *HAI,* 65, footnote. There were two lunar eclipses in 1736, one in March, the other in early September.

14. *HAI,* 224. Adair states that he undertook the effort "a little more than twenty years ago" but does not indicate the year in which he was writing. Some of the Chickasaw returned home the following year, but others remained. See M. Eugene Sirmans, *Colonial South Carolina: A Political History, 1663–1763* (Chapel Hill: University of North Carolina Press, 1966), 198; John Pitts Corry, *Indian Affairs in Georgia, 1732–1756* (Philadelphia: G. S. Ferguson, 1936), 97. See also W. Stitt Robinson, ed., *North and South Carolina Treaties, 1654–1756,* vol. 13 of *Early American Indian Documents: Treaties and Laws, 1607–1789,* edited by Alden T. Vaughan (Frederick, Md.: University Publications of America, 2001), 13: 168. Perhaps the most important relocation of Chickasaw occurred in 1740–41, when South Carolina traders helped a sizeable number move to the Coosa town of the Upper Creeks. There, the Chickasaw established what popularly became known as the Breed Camp. See *The Journal of the Commons House of Assembly,* edited by J. H. Easterby and R. Nicholas Olsberg, 12 vols., Colonial Records of South Carolina (Columbia: Historical Commission of South Carolina and South Carolina Department of Archives, 1951–81), 3: 313–420, hereafter cited as *JCHA; Mississippi Provincial Archives, French Dominion,* 5 vols., edited by Patricia K. Galloway, vols. 4 and 5 originally collected, edited, and translated by Dunbar Rowland and A. G. Sanders (Baton Rouge: Louisiana State University Press, 1984), hereafter cited as *MPAFD,* 3: 747; and William Paape, "The Choctaw Revolt, a Chapter in the Intercolonial Rivalry in the Old Southwest" (Ph.D. diss., University of Illinois, 1946), 52.

15. Edward J. Cashin, "The Gentlemen of Augusta," in Cashin, ed., *Colonial Augusta: "Key of the Indian Countrey,"* 29–56 (Macon, Ga.: Mercer University Press, 1986), 31–32. When queried by Edmond Atkin as to when they abandoned the

South Carolina land, the Chickasaw told him at the end of King George's War (1748). See Edmond Atkin's conference with the Savannah River Chickasaw, November 14, 1758, William Henry Lyttelton Papers, William L. Clements Library, Ann Arbor, Michigan.

16. Adair gives no information on the expedition, merely reporting that he traveled "about six hundred miles through the country, with a great body of Indians" (*HAI,* 456). The first assault occurred on January 1, 1740, when Indian and regular troops attacked and burned Fort Picolata. Oglethorpe's largest Florida campaign occurred in May–July 1740. See John Tate Lanning, *The Diplomatic History of Georgia: A Study in the Epoch of Jenkins' Ear* (Chapel Hill: University of North Carolina Press, 1936), 220–29.

17. *HAI,* 456; *JCHA,* 3: 122. For information on the campaign, see Corry, *Indian Affairs,* 122–23; David H. Corkran, *The Creek Frontier, 1540–1783* (Norman: University of Oklahoma Press, 1967), 104; Phinizy Spalding, *Oglethorpe in America: The Story of Georgia's Founding Father* (Athens: University of Georgia Press, 1984), 110; and Larry E. Ivers, *British Drums on the Southern Frontier: The Military Colonization of Georgia, 1733–1749* (Chapel Hill: University of North Carolina Press, 1974). The Squirrel King led the New Windsor Chickasaw.

18. John Campbell was Red Shoe's contact. See Edmond Atkin, "Historical Account of the Revolt of the Chactaw Indians in the late War from the French to the British Alliance and of their return Since to that of the French," Lansdowne Manuscript 809, British Library, London, fo. 2.

19. "Chickasaw Chiefs to Vaudreuil," *MPAFD,* 4: 211; see also 213. Vaudreuil served as governor from his arrival in the province in May 1743 until February 1753.

20. "Vaudreuil to King Louis XV," *MPAFD,* 4: 213.

21. "Vaudreuil to Maurepas," February 12, 1744, *MPAFD,* 4: 220.

22. See copy of letter from Governor Glen to the Governor of Louisiana, enclosed in letter to Lords of Trade of May 4, 1750 (no. 2), in which Glen recounts attacks on and imprisonment of South Carolinians, including those seen in France (Great Britain, Public Record Office, Colonial Office, American and West Indies, Original Correspondence with the Secretary of State, 1744–1753, Class 5, vol. 385, microfilm copy, Library of Congress, British Microfilm Project, PRO 435, hereafter cited as BMP). There were at least four men who were sent to France during the period; see *MPAFD,* 5: 27–28.

23. Vaudreuil to King Louis XV, *MPAFD,* 4: 123.

24. *South Carolina Gazette,* June 20, 1744. For background on the early war effort in South Carolina, see Norman W. Caldwell, "The Southern Frontier during King George's War," *Journal of Southern History* 7 (February 1941): 37–40, and Paape, "The Choctaw Revolt." Alexander Wood was the man charged with the mission to the Creeks. He was later recalled when he too vociferously encouraged the Creeks to go to war against the Choctaw and French alike (Paape, "Choctaw Revolt," 87).

25. Glen was appointed governor in 1738 but did not assume office until De-

cember 1743; see W. Stitt Robinson, *James Glen: From Scottish Provost to Royal Governor of South Carolina,* Contributions in American History no. 165 (Westport, Conn.: Greenwood Press, 1996), 19.

26. *HAI,* preface.

27. James Glen manuscript, South Caroliniana Library, Columbia. In this manuscript, Glen presents his version of the Choctaw Revolt. It appears to be the document he read before the Commons and Council committee during their investigation of the Choctaw Revolt. In it he wrote that it was 1745 when Adair called on him, a fact used to discredit Glen's account by Edmond Atkin (Atkin, "Historical Account," fo. 41). Adair, who first went to the Chickasaw towns in 1744, did not return to Charleston until 1747, according to Atkin, so Glen's date appears to be in error. Regardless of exactly where, when, or how they met, the results of the meetings are agreed upon by all parties—and it is clear that they met at some point to put the entire scheme in motion.

28. Letter from Mr. Glen of South Carolina to the Board dated December . . . 1751 concerning Indian Affairs, in Great Britain, Public Record Office, Colonial Office, America and West Indies, Original South Carolina Correspondence from Governors and Others, Class 5, vol. 373, hereafter cited as CO5/373; microfilm copy, South Carolina Department of Archives and History (hereafter cited as SCDAH), British Manuscript Project, Board of Trade, Original South Carolina Correspondence from Governors and Others, vol. K, GB20, hereafter cited as James Glen to Board of Trade, December 1751, CO5/373, SCDAH, vol. K.

29. The letter was published as a "set of directions" of a "late" governor of South Carolina that had "fallen into our hands." The "Directions for obtaining a better Knowledge of Indians," according to the editor, were intended as an example of the sort of information needed by government planners and also demonstrated that the author of the directions "has studied beyond most people on this continent." The instructions, as far as internal evidence reveals, were most likely those given to John Pettycrow, who delivered the second contingent of presents from South Carolina to the Choctaw in 1749. See *American Magazine and Monthly Chronicle for the British Colonies* 1, no. 9 (June 1758): 445–52 (quotation is on 447).

30. Charles Paape believed that there was even "a fair probability" that Glen had staked Adair and his partner in his first Chickasaw trading venture ("Choctaw Revolt," 89). Adair provides scant information about this unnamed partner (*HAI,* 239, 314).

31. "Petition of James Adair," May 1750, *JCHA,* 10: 108. Adair also wrote in his history, "I was promised to be indemnified in all necessary charges attending that attempt" (*HAI,* 314). In his account of the revolt, Glen carefully denies speaking for the assembly but wrote that he "was in hopes" that the assembly would reward Adair should his mission succeed. If not, Glen offered to "write over to the Government" seeking compensation (James Glen manuscript, South Caroliniana Library, fo. 6).

32. Patricia K. Galloway, "Choctaw Factionalism and Civil War, 1746–1750," in *The Choctaw before Removal,* edited by Carolyn Keller Reeves (Jackson: University

Press of Mississippi, 1985), 131. For a concise account of Red Shoe's career, see *Colonial Wars of North America, 1512–1763: An Encyclopedia,* edited by Alan Gallay (New York: Garland, 1996), s.v. "Red Shoe."

33. McGillivray to Glen, January 14, 1745, quoted in Paape, "Choctaw Revolt," 79. McGillivray was given approval to open a dialogue with the Choctaw as well as to dispense £50 of Indian presents. In return, he was to receive a one-year monopoly for the Choctaw trade. For the situation with French commerce, see Paape, "Choctaw Revolt," 82–83. French administrators, bemoaning that the Choctaw had "been without an inch of merchandise," blamed lack of goods for the "defection" to English commerce (*MPAFD,* 4: 261). For information on McGillivray's career, see Edward J. Cashin, *Lachlan McGillivray, Indian Trader: The Shaping of the Southern Colonial Frontier* (Athens: University of Georgia Press, 1992). Enemy Chickasaw warriors followed the Choctaw into the Creek towns, where the Creeks made them relinquish their weapons. The Creeks then sought to arrange a rapprochement, and messengers moved among the Creek, Choctaw, and Chickasaw villages (*MPAFD,* 4: 260).

34. *HAI,* 314. Tatoulimataha, a Choctaw headman, confirms that Red Shoe's defection was "from the despair of seeing that the promises that had been given him in the past at Tombecbé had not been kept, together with the bad treatment that he had received, both personally and in the matter of his wives" ("Beauchamp's Journal," *MPAFD,* 4: 291). The Frenchmen accused of rape were Henri de Verbois, a cadet assigned with the distribution of trade goods at West Yazoo, and a subaltern named Chambly. De Verbois was also known as Baussière and he, along with two other traders, were the men killed. See Patricia K. Galloway, "Louisiana Post Letters: The Missing Evidence for Indian Diplomacy," *Louisiana History* 22 (1981): 35–36.

35. The French claim that Red Shoe first approached the English. Whether he sent messengers or the rumors simply reached the Chickasaw towns by chance, it is clear from several sources that the rape of Red Shoe's wife by Frenchmen played a role in his "defection" from the French interest (Galloway, "Choctaw Factionalism," 137).

36. The October date is derived from Vaudreuil's letter of October 28, 1745, in which he reported that a "blow that has just been struck at two Englishmen who were going from the Kawitas to the Chickasaw, whom a Choctaw party met and disposed of" (*MPAFD,* 4: 243). Adair is silent as to the names of the two men, only noting that in addition to his partner, "another expert brave man" was a victim in the attack. The man, an employee, was most likely a packhorseman (*HAI,* 239). In his report, Glen indicated that the other dead man was an employee; see James Glen to Board of Trade, December 1751, CO5/373, SCDAH, vol. K; Galloway, "Choctaw Factionalism," 135).

37. James Glen to Board of Trade, December 1751, CO5/373, SCDAH, vol. K. See also *JCHA,* 1: 572. Campbell had accompanied the 1738 Choctaw peace delegation to Charleston.

38. Vaudreuil indicated that Red Shoe first approached the English, presumably by sending messengers to the Chickasaw towns (*MPAFD,* 4: 298). The French iden-

tified the Chickasaw emissaries as the nephew of Imayatabe, a prominent Chickasaw chief and a Choctaw woman (ibid., 260). Adair identifies the emissaries as Pastabe, an "Archimagus," and Pahemingo-Amalahta (*HAI*, 314).

39. James Adair to Governor James Glen, February 12, 1747, quoted in Atkin, "Historical Account," fo. 36. Adair's letter was read to the South Carolina Council on March 28, 1747.

40. *HAI*, 414–15. One of the intermediaries was a Choctaw woman, presumably married to a Chickasaw Indian (*MPAFD*, 4: 260). This was in late March and early April of 1746 (Galloway, "Choctaw Factionalism," 135). Both Glen and Atkin state that John Highrider was the first to enter the Choctaw towns. Highrider was Campbell's partner (Atkin, "Historical Account", fo. 35; Glen manuscript, South Caroliniana Library, fo. 7).

41. English and French accounts differ on the number and nature of the wounded. John Campbell is usually not identified as one of those involved, since no mention of an English trader appears in French accounts of the incident. However, there is no doubt that Campbell was shot while in the Choctaw country and a woman, sometimes identified as his wife, killed. There are no other incidents, when Red Shoe was alive, when Campbell could have been injured. His involvement is described by Adair (*HAI*, 328). Adair's account is garbled by the insertion of "about a year after this period" in his description. In reality, the incident in which Campbell was wounded occurred about a year before the period under discussion. However, Adair is clearly describing the period prior to Red Shoe's death in June 1747. French reports do not mention the wounding of Campbell but indicate that one "warrior" escaped. According to French accounts, of the four under attack, "the two most famous partisans of these Chickasaws together with a woman were killed" and their scalps forwarded to Vaudreuil (*MPAFD*, 4: 298). The wording of the translated document would seem to imply that the two "partisans" were Choctaw, although following passages in the letter indicate that Red Shoe vowed vengeance for deaths of the Chickasaw (*MPAFD*, 4: 298–99). According to Adair, the emissaries sent by the Chickasaw were Pastabe and Pahemingo-Amalahta (*HAI*, 314). John Campbell, in a petition for compensation made in January 1749, claimed that he had ventured into the Choctaw towns, sold what goods he had, "settled" matters with the Choctaw, and was then shot by French-allied Choctaw, leaving his arm "shattered." He claimed that Red Shoe then escorted him back to the Chickasaw towns and made it known he would make the guilty party "pay dear." It was "about this time" that several French men were killed (Atkin, "Historical Account," fol. 35). In a later petition, presented by his creditor Isaac Barksdale, Campbell claimed he was drunk when he swore out the first petition and changed his story considerably. Historians have tended, therefore, to discount the first petition on those grounds. But his second petition was designed to distance him from Adair, who was at the center of the political controversy then brewing in Charleston. Moreover, in his second petition, Campbell did not claim to have entered the Choctaw nation prior to the arrival of the French scalps. This assertion was clearly designed to serve two political purposes:

first, that the Choctaw were responsible for their own troubles and that the civil war had not been a direct result of English interference; second, to discredit McNaire's testimony that he had been responsible for the Choctaw "revolt." Campbell's second petition pleased Edmond Atkin's Indian committee, who wished to distance South Carolina from the internecine struggle that had divided the Choctaw and driven them even more firmly into the French camp. In addition, in his second claim, Campbell denied that he took goods to the Choctaw, thereby avoiding the charge that he had been trading without a license. Given the political climate in which the second petition was delivered, the first appears to be the more trustworthy. (For the amended petition, see *JCHA*, 10: 178–79.) The first petition, which friends of the opposition "lost," was nonetheless copied and in Atkin's possession, and extracts appear in his "Historical Account." A woman also surfaced in another version of events later submitted to South Carolina by Samuel Venning. According to Venning, the woman and the Chickasaw Blind King were the emissaries and Campbell was the interpreter. Venning's account places the woman's mission prior to the murder of the three French traders and before English traders ventured into the Choctaw towns. Likewise, an affidavit by Jerome Pettycrou declared that John Campbell and the Chickasaw Blind King were the first to arrange a peace (Atkin, "Historical Account," fo. 37–38). James Glen's account of the Choctaw Revolt provides the clearest account of the attack on Campbell. According to Glen, the Chickasaw woman killed was a slave purchased from the Choctaw by Campbell (Glen manuscript, South Caroliniana Library, fo. 9). Perhaps Adair's Pahemingo-Amalahta is the Blind King, whose name is usually rendered Imayatabé in French records.

42. *HAI*, 316. French sources confirm that "white fans" were carried to the Chickasaw (Louboey to Maurepas, February 8, 1746, *MPAFD*, 4: 260).

43. *HAI*, 316–18.

44. *HAI*, 318; Galloway, "Choctaw Factionalism," 136. The three Frenchmen were murdered on August 14, 1756 (*MPAFD*, 4: 299). The dead included a subaltern from Fort Tombecbé then living as an observer in the Choctaw villages as well as two traders. See Patricia Galloway, "The Barthelemy Murders: Bienville's Establishment of the Lex Talionis as a Principle of Indian Diplomacy," *Proceedings of the French Colonial Historical Society, 1982,* edited by E. P. Fitzgerald (Lanham, Md.: University Press of America, 1985), 98. This same general account of events was repeated in a letter by James Glen to John Rattrey, later published in the "Modest Reply," and summarized by Edmond Atkin: "And in a Letter to Mr. Rattrey of Charlestown, which made its Appearance in Print about the Period of time I am now come to, the Govr said 'he was willing to pass over in Silence the Hand he himself had in bringing about the Choctaw Revolution, But that it would be unjust in him to suppress the Services done by Adair & Campbell. That they having used certain means for it, which with such of the Chactaws as coming to the Chicasaws for goods they had frequent Opportunities of conversing with, some of our Traders were invited to go into the Nation. In consequence of which one Highride by the Persuasion of Adair and Campbell ventured to go with Goods to open the Trade; at

which time not any of the Choctaws had attempted any thing against the Lives of the French. That two other Traders went afterwards, & then Campbell when everything was concluded on with the Head men. But that he being by means of the French shot at & his arm shattered, was guarded back, and that Red Shooes & his Headmen desiring that Accident might not interrupt the Trade then established, promised satisfaction both for that and for our Traders formerly killed and soon after did kill three French Officers & sent their scalps to the govr of Carolina, as well as the Little King afterwards to conclude a Treaty of Peace & commerce with that Government.'" Atkin discounted the contents of the letter ("Historical Account," fo. 35–36).

45. Proceedings of the Upper House of Assembly, 10th day of May 1750, Report on James Adair's petition, CO5/461, fo. 79.

46. Vaudreuil to Maurepas, November 20, 1746, *MPAFD*, 4: 298; see also 260. Paape, "Choctaw Revolt," 85, accepts the French version that Chickasaw emissaries were killed.

47. Atkin failed to consider the death of the two English traders in October 1745, citing the three murdered in November 1743.

48. *MPAFD*, 4: 291–92, 294; Paape, "Choctaw Revolt," 91–92. According to Vaudreuil, Red Shoe had planned additional attacks but was opposed (*MPAFD*, 4: 299).

49. *MPAFD*, 4: 292, 297n.57. See also Galloway, "Louisiana Post Letters," 37–39.

50. Charles McNaire to James Glen, November 28, 1747, in Journals of the South Carolina Council for December 14, 1747, in Great Britain, Public Record Office, Board of Trade, Journals of His Majesty's Council in South Carolina sent to England (CO5/456) (BMP D518): 1747–48, B800113, microfilm copy in South Carolina Department of Archives and History (hereafter referred to as SCCJ).

51. As ethnohistorian Patricia Galloway observed, "It seems that Adair was able to combine his own revenge with that of Red Shoe" ("Louisiana Post Letters," 39).

52. For a thorough analysis of ramifications of Red Shoe's actions and a discussion of Choctaw political organization, see Galloway, "Choctaw Factionalism."

53. Galloway, "The Barthelemy Murders," 98–99.

54. *HAI*, 318–21. Vaudreuil believed that some of the scalps were sent to the English traders among the Chickasaw and some to the Tallapoosas and Abeikas. He seemed unaware that Choctaw actually delivered the scalps to the English while the English were in the Creek nation, among the Abeika. He does corroborate Adair's account that the scalps were sent to Fort Toulouse but erroneously reports that the Abeika offered to assist the French against the Choctaw (Vaudreuil to Maurepas, November 20, 1746, *MPAFD*, 4: 299). See also ibid., 275.

55. Atkin, "Historical Account," fo. 57.

56. *HAI*, 320.

57. Ibid.

58. *HAI*, 321. Atkin, "Historical Account," fo. 36, noted that the first news of

the events in the Choctaw nation received in Charleston was read in Council on November 1, 1746. It came from letters dated September 18 from Creek traders who apparently reached some Choctaw villages by late March 1747 (Galloway, "Choctaw Factionalism," 142).

59. *JCHA*, 7: 216. Glen had earlier presented the documents to his Council (Atkin, "Historical Account," fo. 36).

60. The *South Carolina Gazette* (April 6–14, 1747) reported that forty-seven Choctaw arrived April 6. There were actually forty-seven men, seven women, and one child. Of the men, nineteen were headmen (*JCHA*, 7: 221). Edmond Atkin reported that the Choctaw arrived in Charleston on April 10 ("Historical Account," fo. 36). The Little King's proper name was Imataha Pouscouche (*MPAFD*, 4: 314, 315n., 323). He is variously described as the brother or half-brother of Red Shoe (Galloway, "Choctaw Factionalism," 135).

61. Atkin, "Historical Account," fo. 3.

62. Ibid., fo. 4. Trader character was a favorite topic with all parties. An Alabama Indian chief chided those Choctaw thinking of leaving the French by declaring that the Chickasaw traders were men of "bad character" and that one, whom he called by name, was "a robber who did not dare return home." The trader in question has been identified by one editor as John Campbell (*MPAFD*, 4: 289).

63. Atkin, "Historical Account," fo. 3, 4.

64. Ibid., fo. 4, 9. Jordan Roche was a former Chickasaw trader.

65. Ibid., fo. 5.

66. McNaire's ponderous caravan at first hoped to reach the Choctaw country by following the trade path that passed by the Tallapoosa Indian towns and made straight for Choctaw territory, entering it in the vicinity of Fort Tombecbé. But when an escort failed to show, McNaire had to backtrack and then proceed northward to Coosa and the Chickasaw path. His route, as Adair wryly observed, was "a very oblique course" (*HAI*, 323).

67. Atkin, "Historical Account," fo. 6, 7, 37; *MPAFD*, 4: 333; *HAI*, 328. According to Adair, Red Shoe was escorting Campbell "and others" from the Chickasaw towns to the Choctaw towns. Atkin, in his account, does not mention Campbell but states that Red Shoe was escorting Elsley (Paape, "Choctaw Revolt," 100).

68. *MPAFD*, 4: 312 (see also 309); Paape, "Choctaw Revolt," 100.

69. As Edmond Atkin wrote, McNaire's license was "such as is usually given to all other Indian Traders, entering into Bond to observe the Laws of the Province relating to the Indian Trade, & the Instructions given with his License; one of which was, 'That he should not presume to talk with any Indian or Indians, of Matters relating to the State or Government, without especial Directions from the Governor & Council'" (Atkin, "Historical Account," fo. 4). Paape, "Choctaw Revolt," notes that the first proclamation produced by McNaire was dated January 11, 1747, but identifies Adair's description of McNaire's "Sheep-skin, bearing the impression of a threatening lion and unicorn" as the second proclamation made by Glen some time later. Paape notes that the proclamation of January 11, 1747, which McNaire took

to London when pursuing his claim, "is unadorned." Still, it is clear that Adair is discussing the first meeting with McNaire, and it can be surmised that the seal Adair described was attached to the license.

70. *HAI,* 324. Atkin also recognized this fact in his report: "it was certainly necessary . . . that other Traders should some how or other be *discouraged* from entering into, or continuing in it [the Choctaw trade]" ("Historical Account," fo. 5).

71. Atkin, "Historical Account," fo. 6. Weoka was a small Abeika village twelve miles south-southeast of Puckantallahassee: "David Taitt's Journal to and Through the Upper Creek Nation," in *Documents of the American Revolution, 1770–1783,* edited by Kenneth G. Davies, vol. 5, *Transcripts, 1772,* 251–72 (Dublin: Irish University Press, 1974), 5: 267. Weoka was the town of Deval's Landlord, a Creek headman friendly to the English and a special friend, as the name implies, to Thomas Deval. Deval, along with Lachlan McGillivray and William Sludders, were also associated with the Charleston merchants involved in McNaire's company. These three were charged with distribution of South Carolina's presents to the Creeks in late 1747 (Atkin, "Historical Account," fo. 10). The traders dubbed their depot at Weoka "Charleston" (*MPAFD,* 4: 337).

72. *HAI,* 324, 327–28.

73. SCCJ, December 14, 1747.

74. Atkin, "Historical Account," fo. 6. According to Atkin, when McNaire first arrived among the Chickasaw, he had with him the "Public present, & some part only of his Goods" (Paape, "Choctaw Revolt," 105).

75. Atkin, "Historical Account," fo. 9. McNaire was later accused of "avarice" in pricing his goods too high, thereby suggesting that Adair's original tariff was not as unfair as he had claimed at first (Atkin, "Historical Account," fo. 32).

76. Glen manuscript, South Caroliniana Library, 17.

77. Charles McNaire to James Glen, November 28, 1747, SCCJ. In his letter, McNaire related that it was Campbell who told the Indians that all his goods were presents.

78. Ibid.; Atkin, "Historical Account," fo. 9.

79. Atkin, ibid. (italics in original).

80. Ibid., fo. 10.

81. SCCJ, December 14, 1747; Atkin, ibid.

82. *HAI,* 324; Atkin, ibid., fo. 6–7. The letter was dated April 22, 1747.

83. Atkin, ibid., fo. 6.

84. Ibid., fo. 36–37.

85. Glen later speculated that McNaire's letter was designed to have Adair excluded from the trade, "by this account of his behaviour" (Glen manuscript, South Caroliniana Library, 30).

86. *HAI,* 324–25.

87. James Glen to Board of Trade, December 1751, CO5/373, SCDAH, vol. K.

88. Atkin, "Historical Account," fo. 8. A license was apparently also issued for Campbell. This conclusion is based on the following passage from Atkin's account:

"But that when he (the Govr) afterwards shewed him by the said Commissioner's Books, that two Licences had been granted to others, he [Roche] expressed the greatest Surprize & Concern" (fo. 13). One of the names Roche expressed surprise about was Adair's, for it is known from other references that he was issued a license. The other must have been for Adair's "partner," Campbell.

89. *HAI*, 324–25. Adair's petition indicated that the first license he "ever had was on the 21st November 1747" (Proceedings of the Upper House of Assembly, 10th day of May 1750, CO5/461, fo. 79). He received the license prior to leaving Charleston.

90. *HAI*, 327.

91. Atkin, "Historical Account," fo. 12.

92. Ibid., fo. 13.

93. *HAI*, 427.

94. Statement sworn to by Charles McNaire and Matthew Roche, September 21, 1749, in McNaire's Petition to the Board of Trade, CO5/373, fo. 39.

95. *HAI*, 327.

96. *JCHA*, 10: 152–53. Adair's letter was lost. However, it seems the experienced traders were attempting to indicate that McNaire and his men, though they might have been "detained" by the friendly Choctaw, were not in danger from them. The letter is variously said to have been dated October and November 1747. It miscarried but was eventually delivered in late 1748 (*JCHA*, 10: 152–53, 161). Adair was in Charleston in November 1747 and did not know that McNaire had left the Choctaw towns until he met him on the path on his return from Charleston. Thus, the letter, whatever its date, must have been written after that time. It is possible that it could have been written at the Breed Camp and signed by the Chickasaw traders there.

97. *HAI*, 329; Paape, "Choctaw Revolt," 107; *MPAFD*, 4: 313.

98. Charles McNaire to James Glen, November 2, 28, 1747 in SCCJ, December 14, 1747; Paape, "Choctaw Revolt," 100; *MPAFD*, 4: 313.

99. *HAI*, 330. This letter was written in late December, 1747, after Adair's departure from Charleston. According to Atkin's information, McNaire delivered the letter to Adair, while the Little King stayed in the Creek Nation waiting for delivery of goods. Adair says that the Little King delivered the governor's letter. See Atkin, "Historical Account," fo. 10.

100. *HAI*, 331. In his letter to McNaire, Glen related that he had written Adair "to persuade a Number of the Chickesaws to accompany him to the Chactaw Nation & to join them in their War against the French": James Glen to Charles McNaire, December 18, 1747, CO5/373, SCDAH, vol. K. McNaire would later report that Adair's answer to the instruction to stir the Indians to war against the French had been "that if this government [South Carolina] would send an army of white men against the French Indians he would head them" (statement sworn to by Charles McNaire and Matthew Roche, September 21, 1749, in McNaire's Petition to the Board of Trade, CO5/373, fo. 39).

101. Atkin, "Historical Account," fo. 10.

102. James Glen to Charles McNaire, December 18, 1747, CO5/373, SCDAH, vol. K.

103. *HAI*, 329. McNaire admitted having to depend on Adair for goods to distribute as presents, the public goods again being unaccountably detained. See Atkin, "Historical Account," fo. 17.

104. *HAI*, 330.

105. *HAI*, 330–31. Both Adair and McNaire claim to have made a grand sweep of the Choctaw towns in an attempt to seduce the Choctaw from the French interest. It is not clear whether they traveled together or made separate journeys. McNaire indicated that John Campbell accompanied him. According to McNaire's remarks to the Council, he traveled to the Choctaw towns at the end of March 1748 and for the next four months busied himself in distributing goods and attempting to subvert French influence. Atkin, "Historical Account," fo. 14.

106. *HAI*, 331.

107. *HAI*, 3, 410. Adair gives the date as 1747. However, it clearly seems to have been in 1748. Glen reported to the Board of Trade in July of 1748 that Chartier's party (whom he calls Peter Shirtee) arrived in the Creek nation "about two months ago": copy of a letter from James Glen to the Board of Trade, July 25, 1748, CO5/385, fo. 120 (LC, BMP, PRO 435). Adair does not provide details of this mission and completely omits it in his account of the "Choctaw revolt."

108. James Glen to Board of Trade, October 10, 1748, ibid., fo. 156.

109. *MPAFD*, 4: 337.

110. James Glen to Board of Trade, February 1748, Great Britain, Public Record Office. Colonial Office, Series 5, America and West Indies, CO5/385, fo. 142; also quoted in Wilcomb E. Washburn, "James Adair's 'Noble Savages,'" in *The Colonial Legacy*, edited by L. H. Leder (New York: Harper and Row, 1973), 101.

111. *JCHA*, 8: 62, 102, 123. The entire Commons House ultimately agreed with the committee's recommendation. As Wilcomb Washburn notes, the published version of the records of the Commons House for March 7, 1748, indicates that the committee's recommendation "be now allowed." However, in the original document, the phrase is "be not allowed" (Washburn, "James Adair's Noble Savage," 101n.12). See Journal of the Commons House of Assembly from the 19th day of January in the year of our Lord 1747–8, to the 29th day of June 1748, 222, SCDAH. By comparison, the Commons House had approved payment of over £878 for various Indian expenses, including £486 to Nicholas Chinnery and John Campbell for "Indian expenses" and slightly over £97 to John Vann, "paid by the Governor's Order" (*JCHA*, 7: 369).

112. *HAI*, 331; Galloway, "Choctaw Factionalism," 144.

113. *HAI*, 357.

114. *MPAFD*, 5: 27–28.

115. Paape, "Choctaw Revolt," 114–19.

116. *MPAFD*, 5: 15–28, 30–37.

117. *HAI*, 331.

118. Atkin, "Historical Account," fo. 31; *MPAFD*, 4: 326.

119. James Glen to the Lords of Trade, October 10, 1748, fo. 156 (LC, BMP); p. 331.

120. Atkin, "Historical Account," fo. 21–22.

121. *JCHA*, 9: 271; Atkin, ibid., fo. 28.

122. *HAI*, 332, 336.

123. *HAI*, 336–38.

124. *HAI*, 339. Adair's date is confirmed by evidence he provides of meeting a Creek delegation returning from Charleston. The Creeks met with Glen and the South Carolina Council in early September 1749. The delegation included the Wolf of the Muccolossus. On his way into Charleston, Adair passed the Creeks who were returning home (*HAI*, 277).

125. *HAI*, 340.

126. Ibid.

127. *HAI*, 276–78. The Carolina leadership pondered a way to stop the party from entering Charleston for fear of spreading smallpox (*JCHA*, 9: 298, 305). The exact date of the Chickasaw delegation's arrival is unclear. However, they likely arrived after the Commons adjourned on December 14, 1749, for their meeting was with Glen and the Council only. Even though the "Modest Reply" had not been published at that time, its rumored contents were well-known (ibid., 353–54).

128. No extant copies of the pamphlet have been located to date. It was advertised in the *South Carolina Gazette* from late February through early April 1750 (see, for instance, the issue of 19–26 February 1750). According to the report of the Commons House, "the printed pamphlet" bore the date March 10, 1750. Glen's allies made two attempts to indict Timothy for printing pamphlets attacking the governor's policies, but both failed (*JCHA*, 10: 162). According to Glen, the pamphlet was "very seriously and strictly examined by the assembly." He also wrote that it was his hope to see "that the Author and Printer of such a defamatory Libel had been punished as they deserve" (extract of a letter from James Glen to Board of Trade, October 2, 1750, CO5/385, fo. 213). See also Jeffery A. Smith, "Impartiality and Revolutionary Ideology: Editorial Policies of the *South-Carolina Gazette*, 1732–1775," *Journal of Southern History* 49 (November 1983): 511–26. To his business associate Benjamin Franklin, Timothy would later report, "The wretched Management of Indian Affairs by that Gentleman [Glen] has occasioned the imposing Silence on my Press, under various Pretences"; see Peter Timothy to Benjamin Franklin, June 8, 1755, *The Papers of Benjamin Franklin*, edited by Leonard W. Labaree, vol. 6, *April 1, 1755, through September 30, 1756*, edited by Labaree (New Haven: Yale University Press, 1963), 69. Christopher Gould and Richard Parker Morgan, *South Carolina Imprints, 1731–1800: A Descriptive Bibliography* (Santa Barbara, Calif.: ABC-Clio Information Services, 1985), also failed to locate a copy; see p. 37.

129. *JCHA*, 10: 8.

130. *HAI*, 341. The Chickasaw were received by Glen and the Council. In his *History*, Adair wrote that Paya Mataha was eager to support Adair's claims regarding Choctaw matters and "was very desirous of a second public interview," thereby

implying that Paya Mataha would have appeared before the committee on Indian affairs since Adair reports that the Chickasaw "staid as late as the middle of April" (*HAI,* 341). However, Adair contradicted himself a page later when he wrote that the Chickasaw left town prior to his placing advertisements in the *South-Carolina Gazette* in February and March 1750.

131. *JCHA,* 10: 5–6. The clearest and most concise account of this aspect of the Choctaw Revolt is R. Nicholas Olsberg's introduction to vol. 10 of the published record of the Commons House Assembly, *JCHA,* 5–13.

132. Ibid., 10: 5–6.

133. Ibid., 6–7. In a letter to the Board of Trade, Glen laid McNaire's losses on "his ill management and partly by the Extravagance of those concerned with him" (extract of a Letter from James Glen to Board of Trade, October 2, 1750, CO5/385, fo. 213).

134. Atkin, "Historical Account," fo. 40.

135. Notice of Glen to the Assembly, March 17, 1750, *JCHA,* 9: 484; see also 10: 7.

136. *South-Carolina Gazette,* March 12–19, 19–26, 1750.

137. Minutes of the South Carolina Council, April 3, 1750, CO5/462 (South Carolina Archives Film GR 69).

138. *JCHA,* 10: 7–8. Quotations from the Journals of the Council, May 7, 1750, CO5/462. The attorney general's remarks were specifically aimed at Adair's "Advertizement of the 19th of March last."

139. *HAI,* 342.

140. *South-Carolina Gazette,* April 9, 1750. The advertisement for the Choctaw Treatise was unsigned, and Adair does not mention it in his *History.* He is generally regarded by scholars as the author of the advertisement (Davis, *Intellectual Life in the Colonial South,* 3: 1300–1301). Gould and Morgan, *South Carolina Imprints,* 38, note "no copy located." In fact, Adair developed his "treatise" on the Choctaw revolt into the present work.

141. *HAI,* 348.

142. Letter of James Adair, April 27, 1750, SCCJ, May 11, 1750, CO5/462 (South Carolina Archives microfilm GR 69).

143. South Carolina Council Journal, May 15, 1750, ibid.

144. *JCHA,* 10: 9; Adair to Pinckney, April 23, 1750, South Carolina Council Minutes, May 11, 15, 17, 1750, CO5/462; Paape, "Choctaw Revolt," 151.

145. *JCHA,* 10: 108.

146. *HAI,* 348.

147. *JCHA,* 10: 152–53. The first letter, written in October or November 1747, was lost and recounted from memory by Pinckney. It concerned McNaire's first trip to the Choctaw nation, his attempts to effect a monopoly, and his ineptitude in delivering the public goods. The second, written in October 1749, was more favorable and concerned the efforts of McNaire to win over the Choctaw during his tour of the Choctaw towns. The assembly was unwilling to consider the time difference or variance in circumstance and resolved that the second letter was "calculated and formed for particular purposes" (ibid., 10: 155).

148. Ibid., 10: 153; Atkin, "Historical Account," fo. 42.

149. *JCHA*, 10: 153–56. McNaire had some success in London. The Board of Trade recommended to the Earl of Holderness, the Lord of the Treasury, that he be allowed £1,000, a quarter of his stated losses, for his service. For although McNaire was unable to provide "authentick Proof of his having received a special commission in writing" from James Glen, it seemed clear from the documents that he provided, and the Board decided his mission had been undertaken "with the consent and approbation of the Governor and under assurance of reward from him" (Board of Trade to Lord of the Treasury, March 19, 1752, CO5/385, fo. 202, LC, BMP).

150. William L. McDowell, Jr., ed., *Documents Relating to Indian Affairs, May 21, 1750–August 7, 1754,* Colonial Records of South Carolina, ser. 2 (Columbia: South Carolina Archives Department, 1958), 7.

151. Atkin, "Historical Account," fo. 59; Galloway, "Choctaw Factionalism."

152. Atkin, ibid., fo. 57. James Glen attributed Adair's defection to "revenge" owing to the fact he had not been compensated for his activities among the Choctaw. He asserted that Adair "offered his service to the French" (James Glen to Board of Trade, December 1751, CO5/373, SCDAH, vol. K).

153. McDowell, *Documents Relating to Indian Affairs, 1750–1754,* 56. Adair claimed to have written an extensive account of his French encounter to the Council and Pinckney in late summer 1750. The letters have not been found. For Adair's account of his escape from Fort Toulouse, see *HAI,* 348–49.

154. Cashin, *Lachlan McGillivray,* 88.

155. "Historical Account," fo. 19–21. Atkin was particularly interested in a ship that sailed from Charleston bearing a flag of truce which was believed to have carried trade goods to Mobile.

156. "Lauglin McGilvery" [James Adair] to William H. Lyttelton, July 14, 1758, Lyttelton Papers. The letter is not in McGillivray's handwriting, and internal evidence points to James Adair as its author. See Cashin, *Lachlan McGillivray,* 171.

157. Adair noted that he was in the Lower Cherokee towns in 1750 (*HAI,* 136–37).

158. James Adair to William Pinckney, May 7, 1751, in McDowell, *Documents Relating to Indian Affairs, 1750–1754,* 56; Washburn, "James Adair's 'Noble Savages,'" 110–11.

159. McDowell, ibid., 31.

160. "Lauglin McGilvery" [James Adair] to William H. Lyttelton, July 14, 1758, Lyttelton Papers.

161. Adair's 1758 advertisement for his book specifically noted it was "Written by J. Adair, at New-Windsor" (*South-Carolina Gazette,* August 18–25, 1758).

162. *HAI,* 403.

163. The reference to a funeral at the Breed Camp, which took place in 1754, does not indicate whether he lived there or was merely passing through.

164. The names of regular traders Jerome Courtonne, John Brown, and John Highrider do appear on the list (Injunction by Edmond Atkin, September 20, 1759, Lyttelton Papers).

165. McDowell, *Documents Relating to Indian Affairs, 1754–1765,* Colonial Rec-

ords of South Carolina, ser. 2 (Columbia: SCDAH and the University of South Carolina Press, 1970), 460–61; *HAI,* 366.

166. The advertisement appeared at least twice; see *South Carolina Gazette,* August 18–25, August 25–September 1, 1758. Gould and Morgan, *South Carolina Imprints,* 46, note that this is the only advertisement for the book and that this particular edition never made it to press but eventually appeared as the present work. The advertisement identified Adair as a resident of New Windsor.

167. James Glen to William H. Lyttelton, January 23, 1758, Lyttelton Papers.

168. McDowell, ed., *Documents Relating to Indian Affairs, 1754–1765,* 373, 378, 380. Bonar's ill-fated mission is best commemorated by his "A Draught of the Creek Nation," completed in May 1757, which remains one of the best-known eighteenth-century maps of the Creek towns (British Public Record Office, CO700/Carolina 21).

169. For example, Creek agent Daniel Pepper relayed information about Mobile that he gathered from a Cherokee and Shawnee delegation who visited New Orleans and Mobile. See McDowell, *Documents Relating to Indian Affairs, 1754–1765,* 369.

170. Lachlan McGillivray to William H. Lyttelton, July 13, 1758, Lyttelton Papers.

171. Cashin, *Lachlan McGillivray,* 171. The shorter letter, written by McGillivray, carries the correct spelling of his name as well.

172. Lachlan McGillivray to William H. Lyttelton, July 13, 1758, Lyttelton Papers.

173. "Lauglin McGilvery" [James Adair] to William H. Lyttelton, July 14, 1758, Lyttelton Papers.

174. Ibid.

175. Lachlan McGillivray to William H. Lyttelton, July 13, 1758, Lyttelton Papers. Presumably, the "no connection" implied the lack of a business relationship.

176. Cashin, *Lachlan McGillivray,* 170–72.

177. For recent examinations of the cause of the war, see John Oliphant, *Peace and War on the Anglo-Cherokee Frontier, 1756–63* (Baton Rouge: Louisiana State University Press, 2001), and Robin F. A. Fabel, *Colonial Challenges: Britons, Native Americans, and Caribs, 1759–1775* (Gainesville: University Press of Florida, 2000).

178. Journal of the Commons House of Assembly, 1757–1767, Part II. Typescript, SCDAH, Columbia, 508–9.

179. The Assembly set aside £200 for each man, predicated on the notion that their active service would run for four months (ibid., 737).

180. The other two captains, Joseph Wright and Stephen Forrest, were assigned to the Creeks. See *South Carolina Gazette,* April 19–26, 1760; *Pennsylvania Gazette,* May 22, July 24, August 7, 1760; Washburn, "James Adair's 'Noble Savages,'" 112.

181. *HAI,* 251.

182. For various reports on Chickasaw participation, see *South Carolina Gazette,* July 12–19, July 26–August 2, 1760; *Pennsylvania Gazette,* April 3, June 19, July 24,

September 4, 1760. Most of the reports are reprinted from the *South Carolina Gazette*. See also *Maryland Gazette*, August 14, 1760.

183. *HAI*, 350–51.

184. *HAI*, 350. The second petition was presented April 28, 1761 (Journals of the South Carolina Commons House, March 26, 1761–December 26, 1761, CO5/ 479; microfilm copy located at SCDAH).

185. Minutes of the West Florida Council, December 12, 1764, CO5/625, fo. 15.

186. For information on the Proclamation of 1763, see Braund, *Deerskins and Duffels: Creek Indian Trade, 1685–1815* (Lincoln: University of Nebraska Press, 1993), 100–102.

187. Minutes of the West Florida Council, December 12, 1764, CO5/625, fo. 15.

188. The proceedings of the congress have been published; see Dunbar Rowland, ed., *Mississippi Provincial Archives, English Dominion, 1763–1766: Letters and Enclosures to the Secretary of State from Major Robert Farmar and Governor George Johnstone*, vol. 1 (Nashville: Brandon Printing Co., 1911), 216–55, hereafter cited as MPAED. Other than dignitaries, the proceedings fail to list those in attendance, so Adair's presence can not be definitively established.

189. *HAI*, 1, 164, 303; "List of Traders and Packhorsemen in the Chickasaw Nation," January 22, 1766, CO5/67, fo. 43. Adair was the only trader who did not list an employee. Two letters from Adair survive: "A Memorandum of some Material Heads of what was lately transacted in ye Chickasaw Nation," February 26, 1766, CO323/24, part 1, fo. 73, and James Adair to Governor Johnstone, September 16, 1766, Sir Frederick Haldimand: Unpublished Papers and Correspondence, 1758– 1784, British Museum, Additional Manuscripts, 21,671, fo. 53.

190. James Adair, "A Memorandum of some material heads of what was lately transacted in the Chickasaw Nation," February 26, 1766, CO5/67, fo. 228. Another copy of the document can be found in CO323/24, pt. 1, fo. 73.

191. *HAI*, 368.

192. Adair, "A Memorandum . . . ," February 26, 1766, CO5/67, fo. 228.

193. Ibid.; West Florida Council Minutes, CO5/632, fo. 150.

194. See *HAI*, 368–69. For more on the trouble, see J. Russell Snapp, *John Stuart and the Struggle for Empire on the Southern Frontier* (Baton Rouge: Louisiana State University Press, 1996), 84–86.

195. In another surviving letter, dated September 16, 1766, Adair wrote Johnstone from the Choctaw town of Senechasa (Haldimand Papers, 21,671, Reel 5, fo. 50).

196. "A List of Traders and Packhorsemen in the Chickasaw Nation," January 22, 1766, CO5/67, fo. 43.

197. Malcom McGee Interview Notes.

198. *HAI*, 461.

199. Atkin, "Historical Account," 8.

200. For Adair's account of the Chickasaw path, see *HAI*, 239, 144n., 349, and Edmond Atkin, *The Appalachian Indian Frontier: The Edmond Atkin Report and Plan of*

1755, edited with an introduction by Wilbur R. Jacobs (Lincoln: University of Nebraska Press, 1967), 64, hereafter cited as Atkin, *Report.*

201. *HAI,* 426.

202. *HAI,* 349, 184.

203. *HAI,* 426, 382.

204. *HAI,* 37.

205. *HAI,* 347.

206. *HAI,* 37. After one "hearty draught of punch" in 1750, Adair and his traveling companion broke into song (*HAI,* 347).

207. *HAI,* 326, 357; *MPAFD,* 1: 304 (last quotation).

208. *HAI,* 357.

209. *HAI,* 416.

210. *HAI,* 413.

211. For example, see his account of fishing with hand nets and the "friendly diversion," with his fellow Chickasaw (*HAI,* 404–5; see also 414).

212. *HAI,* 413.

213. *HAI,* 327.

214. *HAI,* 19, 87–88, 89, 92, 211, 404.

215. *HAI,* preface, 38.

216. *HAI,* 92.

217. *HAI,* 160–61, 180.

218. This was generally true of all deerskin traders. Adair's primary exposure to women and their domestic economy would have been in the households of his wife and of fellow traders. See Braund, *Deerskins and Duffels,* 86.

219. *HAI,* preface.

220. *HAI,* 32, 173n.

221. In 1768, Sir William Johnson observed that Adair's "present Circumstances are very indifferent." See *Documents Relative to the Colonial History of the State of New York: Procured in Holland, England, and France,* edited by E. B. O'Callaghan, 15 vols. (Albany: Weed, Parsons, & Co., 1856–87; Microfilm Edition: Published American Colonial Records, vol. 7, New York: Research Publications), 4: 251, hereafter referred to as *DRCHNY.*

222. The absence of evidence does not necessarily mean that Stuart was not approached or that he refused to help. However, Adair's relationship with Stuart was obviously a strained one, no doubt owing to Adair's condemnation of general licenses and Stuart's West Florida deputy. Although Stuart also opposed general licenses, many of Stuart's other policies irritated the old-line traders, including his attempt to reconcile the Creek-Choctaw War. For more on the controversy, see Snapp, *John Stuart.*

223. *DRCHNY,* 4:251–52; Milton W. Hamilton, "Sir William Johnson: Interpreter of the Iroquois," *Ethnohistory* 10 (Summer 1963): 280.

224. James Adair to Sir William Johnson, recd April 18, 1769, *DRCHNY,* 4:260. Adair asked Johnson the favor of a "recommendation" to Lord Hillsborough, the secretary of state for the colonies, reckoning that such assistance "would prove a

great advance towards obtaining satisfaction for what ye Governmt is indebted me." Adair also insinuated that Stuart made "family jobs" of various official Indian offices rather than awarding them to the most qualified and deserving men. See *HAI*, 414, as well as his various correspondence from West Florida.

225. *London Magazine,* May 1775, 252.

226. Hamilton, "Sir William Johnson," 85; James Adair Esqr to Sir Wm Johnson, May 10, 1769, *DRCHNY,* 4: 259.

227. Johnson declined the honor with the following circumlocution: "I would not disappoint your good intentions, tho' I would check the flowings of a friendly pen which unrestrained might go farther than is consistent with my inclinations" (*DRCHNY,* 4: 261). By the time the book was actually ready for press, both Johnson and Moore were dead. Moore had served two terms as governor of Jamaica prior to assuming the governorship of New York.

228. *DRCHNY,* 4: 251–52, 260. In 1773, Paya Mataha actually traveled to Mobile and told British officials he was determined to go to England. See Snapp, *John Stuart,* 85–86.

229. *HAI,* 363

230. James Adair Esqr to Sir Wm Johnson, April 30. 1769, *DRCHNY,* 4: 259–61.

231. *Georgia Gazette,* October 11, 1769. The *South Carolina Gazette* printed similar pieces; see the issue for September 7, 1769. Another "Proposal for Printing by Subscription" appeared in the *Georgia Gazette,* November 1, 1769.

232. Evidence of Adair's activities are primarily found in his letters to Sir William Johnson and various newspapers.

233. *Georgia Gazette,* November 1, 1769. An octavo volume (sometimes indicated by 8vo) is approximately 9 inches by 5½ inches—the approximate size of most modern books—and takes its name from the size of the paper, which printers folded to produce eight sheets (sixteen pages).

234. James Adair to Sir William Johnson, September 15, 1769, *DRCHNY,* 4: 262. See James Raven, *London Booksellers and American Customers: Transatlantic Literary Community and the Charleston Library Society, 1748–1811* (Columbia: University of South Carolina Press, 2002) for information on the learned community and books in South Carolina during the period.

235. Joseph Galloway to Benjamin Franklin, August 12, 1769, *The Papers of Benjamin Franklin,* vol. 16, *January 1 through December 31, 1769,* edited by William B. Willcox (New Haven: Yale University Press, 1972), 184–85.

236. *South Carolina Gazette,* September 7, 1769; James Adair to Sir William Johnson, April 30, 1769, and undated letter, *DRCHNY,* 4: 259–60.

237. James Adair to Sir William Johnson, September 15, 1769, *DRCHNY,* 4: 262.

238. Elias Boudinot, *A Star in the West, or A humble Attempt to discover the long lost ten tribes of Israel: preparatory to their return to their beloved city, Jerusalem* (Trenton, N.J.: D. Fenton, S. Hutchinson, and J. Dunham, 1816), 117, 211–12 (quotations). Livingston was governor of New Jersey after the war.

239. Ibid., 211. Boudinot states that Adair called upon him at Elizabethtown. If so, this would mean that the date was almost certainly prior to 1774 or 1775, for

after that period both Livingston and Boudinot would have been involved in activities in Philadelphia with the Continental Congress for a good part of the time. Moreover, if Boudinot's date of 1774 were correct, it would mean that Adair would have to have made the trans-Atlantic voyage twice. While not impossible, it seems highly unlikely he would have proceeded to London, returned to America for advice, and then sailed again for London.

240. Francis H. Tuckey, *The County and City of Cork Remembrancer; or, Annals of the County and City of Cork* (Cork: Savage and Son, 1837), 162–63. I am grateful to Mr. Philip Sonnichsen for providing this reference. Tuckey's book contains all manner of odd and newsworthy stories and seems to have been compiled largely from local newspapers.

241. Franklin was called to answer questions concerning the letters of Thomas Hutchinson, governor of Massachusetts, which had been published in colonial papers. He also was the most convenient target for British ire over events in Boston. For a full discussion of the episode, see W. H. Brands, *The First American: The Life and Times of Benjamin Franklin* (New York: Doubleday, 2000), 466–77.

242. *HAI,* Dedication (3).

243. Only Joseph Galloway's 1769 letter seems to have survived. But it is highly probable that he also carried a letter of introduction from Peter Timothy, Franklin's business associate and publisher of the *South Carolina Gazette.*

244. Benjamin Franklin to Charles and Edward Dilly, March 25, 1774, *Franklin Papers,* 154–55.

245. Ibid.

246. No subscriber list was published with the book, and subscriber lists have not been located. Generally, before an author could claim a profit, he had to deduct fees to the publisher as well as such production costs as ink and paper, advertising, and commission for booksellers. Regarding James Boswell's famous biography of Samuel Johnson, Alan Sisman estimated that booksellers received 33 percent of the proceeds from sales, while the publisher (Charles Dilly) received a commission of 7½ percent. When the actual printing costs and advertising costs were factored in, Boswell received a bit less than half the cover price for his two volumes—a much larger work than Adair's *History.* Yet these figures do provide some idea of the expenses and division of profit among the various interested parties. See Adam Sisman, *Boswell's Presumptuous Task: The Making of the Life of Dr. Johnson* (New York: Farrar, Straus, and Giroux, 2001), 274. Since Adair intended to take copies, which presumably he had already sold to subscribers, he would have saved the commission to booksellers.

247. L. H. Butterfield, "The American Interests of the Firm of E. and C. Dilly, with Their Letters to Benjamin Rush, 1770–1795," *Papers of the Bibliographical Society of America* 45 (1951): 293, 295. Among the many writers who lived at the Poultry was James Boswell (ibid., 284–87).

248. Benjamin Rush, *The Autobiography of Benjamin Rush; His "Travels through Life" together with his Commonplace Book for 1789–1813,* edited by George W. Corner, Memoirs of the American Philosophical Society, vol. 25 (Princeton: Princeton University Press, 1948), 63.

249. *HAI,* 288. Adair was railing against military governors with his mention of the Quebec Act, and he continued his tirade against them on 289. His remarks were meant as condemnation of not only the Quebec Act but also the governorship of General Thomas Gage, in Massachusetts, whose appointment was in response to revolutionary activities in the colony. The Quebec Act actually established a civil government for Canada. Even though not intended as part of the "Coercive Acts" designed to bring order to Massachusetts, the act was seen as punitive, particularly since it expanded the boundaries and authority of Canada southward to the Ohio River, thereby negating the claims of many of the established colonies to the region. More important, it was a major setback for those speculators and planners hoping to establish a new colony in the region.

250. Indenture between the Creek Indians and Jonathan Bryan, Jonathan Bryan Papers, no. 98, item 1, Georgia Historical Society, Savannah. The document in the Bryan Papers is a copy from the records of the Georgia Secretary's Office, dated December 24, 1794. It was copied from the Georgia Records Office Deeds, Conveyances, Book CC, fo. 729–732, having been recorded on August 22, 1776. Adair, Hugh Bryan, and Seaborn Jones, the other signers, appeared before the justice of the peace in Granville County (Beaufort District), South Carolina, on what appears to have been November 10, 1774. A copy of the deed from the Georgia Records Office has been published. See John T. Juricek, ed., *Georgia and Florida Treaties, 1763–1776,* vol. 12 of *Early American Indian Documents; Treaties and Laws, 1607–1789,* edited by Alden T. Vaughan (Bethesda, Md.: University Publications of America, 2002), 158–61.

251. See Alan Gallay, *The Formation of a Planter Elite: Jonathan Bryan and the Southern Colonial Frontier* (Athens: University of Georgia Press, 1989), for information on Bryan and the lease.

252. Bryan would soon become a member of the Georgia Council of Safety, effectively becoming the Georgia's Whig spokesman to the Creek Indians. He and George Galphin would cooperate on obtaining Creek neutrality during the conflict.

253. Ibid., 94–95.

254. For more on Bryan's plans and his relationship with the religious community at Bethesda, Georgia, as well as with England, see Cashin, *Beloved Bethesda,* 115–17.

255. William Drayton's statement in John Stuart to Lord Dartmouth, July 27, 1775, CO5/76, fo. 135.

256. See *HAI,* 457.

257. For information on Croghan's company, see Jack M. Sosin, *Whitehall and the Wilderness: The Middle West in British Colonial Policy, 1760–1775* (Lincoln: University of Nebraska Press, 1961), 140–48. For Lyman and his Company of Military Adventurers, see Robin F. A. Fabel, *The Economy of British West Florida, 1763–1783* (Tuscaloosa: University of Alabama Press, 1988), chap. 7, and "An Eighteenth Colony: Dreams for Mississippi on the Eve of the Revolution," *Journal of Southern History* 59 (November 1993): 647–72.

258. Boudinot, *Star in the West,* had to order his own copy after the war, and even

the unnamed man who served with him in Congress and who was familiar with the southern Indians seemed unaware of the publication.

259. I wish to acknowledge the courteous assistance of Catherine Sadler, librarian of the Charleston Library Society, who provided information about the book. Adair's handwritten corrections are noted in the annotations to the present work.

260. John H. Logan, *A History of the Upper Country of South Carolina, from the Earliest Periods to the Close of the War of Independence,* vol. 1 (Charleston: S. G. Courtenay & Co., 1859), 346. According to Logan and the Library Society of Charleston, the book came into the possession of John Drayton, who presented it to the library in 1802.

261. That he was not known in the Chickasaw country after 1769 is supported by notes made by Lyman Draper from a conversation with Malcolm McGee, who had entered the Chickasaw trade as a young boy. McGee said that Adair had come into the Chickasaw nation in 1769 after his own arrival and remained there only two or three years before going to the Cherokee country. His date for Adair's arrival in the Chickasaw towns is certainly incorrect, but the fact that he fails to mention Adair after the 1770s leads to the conclusion that Adair did not return to the Chickasaw nation (Malcolm McGee Interview Notes, Draper Collection). Various families, both Cherokee and non-Indian, claim connection to Adair or his brothers, but there is little evidence to connect them and no credible record published to date of Adair's presence among the Cherokee after 1775. It seems highly unlikely he would have entered the Cherokee towns during that time of turmoil and war.

262. Butterfield, "The American Interests of the Firm of E. and C. Dilly," 45: 293, 295.

263. *Adair's History of the American Indians,* edited by Samuel Cole Williams.

264. One privately printed modern version of Adair's *History* discarded much of Adair's musing on the subject and reorganized the remaining material by tribes, thereby eradicating much valuable comparative information. See *James Adair and the Indians: A New Version of the Early American Classic,* The History of the American Indians, *published in 1775,* revised and edited by Clifford Gene Snyder (North Hollywood, Calif.: JES Co, 1995). Adair is not alone in receiving such treatment. Angie Debo, who edited H. B. Cushman's nineteenth-century history of the Choctaw and Chickasaw, simply deleted most of the first sixty-one pages of the work because they dealt with "Indian race and speculations regarding its origin," including the Lost Tribes hypothesis. See H. B. Cushman, *History of the Choctaw, Chickasaw and Natchez Indians,* edited by Angie Debo, rpt. ed. (Norman: University of Oklahoma Press, 1999), 13.

265. *HAI,* 13 (quotation). For a summary of the intellectual quest prior to Adair's time, see Lee Eldridge Huddleston, *Origins of the American Indians: European Concepts, 1491–1729* (Austin: University of Texas Press, 1967).

266. Berkhofer, Introduction to Adair, *History of the American Indians,* vii. As Berkhofer notes, John Eliot, Roger Williams, Cotton Mather, and William Penn had been earlier advocates of the theory, and many others would follow, including the Mormons.

267. John H. Powell, *On the Origin of the American Indians,* address at the 131st annual meeting of the Athenæum of Philadelphia, held February 4, 1946 (Philadelphia: Athenæum, 1946), 12.

268. Basing his argument on appearance and culture and the presence of many animal and vegetable species "peculiar" to the New World, Kames wrote that "every rational conjecture leans to a separate creation." See Henry Home, Lord Kames, *Sketches of the History of Man,* 2 vols. (Edinburgh: W. Creech, W. Strahan, and T. Cadell, 1774), 2: 76.

269. *HAI,* 11.

270. *HAI,* 23.

271. See *HAI,* 363–65.

272. Charles M. Hudson, "James Adair as Anthropologist," *Ethnohistory* 24 (Fall 1977): 312.

273. Hudson (ibid.) provides the best overview of Adair as an ethnohistorical source.

274. *HAI,* dedication and 13.

275. A good example is his reference on earlobe deformation taken from the work of Antonio de Ulloa. See *HAI,* 213.

276. *HAI,* preface.

277. See *HAI,* 210. See also Le Page Du Pratz, Antoine Simon. *The history of Louisiana, or of the western parts of Virginia and Carolina: containing a description of the countries that lye on both sides of the river Missisippi: with an account of the settlements, inhabitants, soil, climate, and products. Translated from the French, (lately published) by M. Le Page du Pratz; with some notes and observations relating to our colonies* (London: T. Becket and P. A. De Hondt, 1763).

278. *HAI,* 179.

279. *London Magazine,* May 1775, 252; *Scots Magazine* 37 (June 1775): 323.

280. *The Edinburgh Magazine and Review for August 1775* 4 (August 1775): 480–85.

281. *The Monthly Review; or Literary Journal: From January to June* 59 (1776): 261–68.

282. Quotations are from ibid., 262. For Adair's reference to Jacob's cattle, see *HAI,* 4.

283. *HAI,* 10–11.

284. For example, see *HAI,* 18, 19, 31, 101–3.

285. A good example is Adair's description of the "FESTIVALS, FASTS, and RELIGIOUS RITES" of the Hebrews, *HAI,* 94–96.

286. Since De Brahm did not relate who collected his "compendium" of Cherokee words, it is not outside the realm of possibility that the work was Priber's. *De Brahm's Report of the General Survey in the Southern District of North America,* edited with an Introduction by Louis De Vorsey, Jr. (Columbia: University of South Carolina Press, 1971), 284n.42.

287. *HAI,* 37–38.

288. William Douglass, *A Summary, Historical and Political, of the First Planting, progressive Improvements, and Present State of the British Settlements in North-America;*

with some Transient Accounts of the Bordering French and Spanish Settlements, no. 11 (Boston: Rogers & Fowls, Queen Street, 1747), 179.

289. Personal communication to the editor from Professor Leon J. Weinberger, March 6, 2001.

290. Charleston's first synagogue was established in 1750, and the Charleston Jewish community prospered. See Barnett A. Elzas, *The Jews of South Carolina from the Earliest Times to the Present* (Philadelphia: J. B. Lippincott Co., 1905; reprint, Spartanburg, S.C.: Reprint Co., 1972), and Harry L. Golden, *Jewish Roots in the Carolinas: A Pattern of American Philo-Semitism* (Greensboro, N.C.: The Carolina Institute, 1955).

291. Thomas Jefferson to John Adams, June 11, 1812, in Merrill D. Peterson, ed., *Jefferson:Writings,* The Library of America (New York: Viking Press, 1984), 1261.

292. Personal communications with the editor, June 26, 2002.

293. Adair told a companion that he "did not understand the Muskohge dialect" (*HAI,* 174) but then proceeded to speak with the Creeks they had encountered.

294. Thomas Jefferson to John Adams, June 11, 1812, *Jefferson:Writings,* 1261–62.

295. Benjamin Hawkins, *Letters, Journals, and Writings of Benjamin Hawkins,* 2 vols., edited by C. L. Grant (Savannah: Beehive Press, 1980), 1: 227; Boudinot, *Star in the West,* 211–12. Boudinot relates that the friend was a member of Congress "of excellent character, who had acted as our Indian agent to the southeward, during the war." He was most likely Benjamin Hawkins, who served as a commissioner to the Creek and Cherokee Indians in 1785, then as North Carolina's senator from 1789 to 1795.

296. Edward King, Viscount Kingsborough, *Antiquities of Mexico,* 9 vols. (London, 1830–48); see Williams, *Adair's History,* xxix–xxx, for more information on Kingsborough. Jonathan Carver, *Travels through the Interior Parts of North America, in the Years 1766, 1767, and 1768* (London: For the author, 1778), proved a best-seller and went through numerous reprints. For an assessment of the work, see Edward Gaylord Bourne, "The *Travels* of Jonathan Carver," *American Historical Review* 11 (January 1906): 287–302. See also John R. Swanton, *Indians of the Southeastern United States,* Bureau of American Ethnology Bulletin no. 137 (Washington, D.C.: Government Printing Office, 1946; reprint, New York: Greenwood Press, 1969); Charles Hudson, *The Southeastern Indians* (Knoxville: University of Tennessee Press, 1976).

297. Washburn, "James Adair's 'Noble Savages,'" 111 (first quotation), 96 (second quotation), 93 (third quotation.)

298. Paape, "The Choctaw Revolt," 113.

299. Sirmans, *Colonial South Carolina,* 267–68n.29, concluded that Adair exaggerated his role in the Choctaw revolt of the 1740s in order to secure remuneration. Instead, he favored Edmond Atkin's account of events as based on documentary research rather than personal recollection. Moreover, he claimed, erroneously, that independent sources favored Atkin's interpretation. In his bibliography, Sirmans wrote that Adair was "not reliable" on the Choctaw revolt. A careful comparison with French and British documents would have disabused him of that notion.

For an answer to Sirmans's charges, see Washburn, "James Adair's 'Noble Savages,'" 108–9.

300. Atkin, *Report,* xxxiiii.

301. Washburn, "James Adair's 'Noble Savages,'" 110.

302. Gipson further noted, "The burden of proof, it would therefore seem, must rest upon those who refuse to accept his statements as being quite untrustworthy": Lawrence Henry Gipson, *Zones of International Friction: North America, South of the Great Lakes Region, 1748–1754,* vol. 4 of *The British Empire Before the American Revolution* (New York: Alfred A. Knopf, 1939), 91n.18. On the other hand, Francis Jennings dismissed Adair's book as "unreliable as history," joining historian Richard White as another of those misled by Atkin's denunciations of Adair (Francis Jennings, "Adair, James," *American National Biography,* 60).

303. The advertisement for the proposed "Treatise of the Choctaw Affair" promised to be supported by "Records, original letters, and living witnesses."

304. *HAI,* 315, for quotations.

305. Fogelson, *The Cherokees: A Critical Biography,* 12. Gary Nash held the same view, writing that Adair's work was "the most complete statement of the integrity of Indian culture"; see Nash, "The Image of the Indian in the Southern Colonial Mind," *William and Mary Quarterly* 3d ser. 29 (1972); 224. Clara Sue Kidwell and Charles Roberts, *The Choctaws: A Critical Biography* (Bloomington: Indiana University Press, 1980), 16, agree with Fogelson's assessment. On the other hand, Verner Crane found the book "a curious medley of frontier history and pseudo-ethnology" (Crane, "A Lost Utopia," 49).

306. Theda Perdue, *Cherokee Women: Gender and Culture Change, 1700–1835* (Lincoln: University of Nebraska Press, 1998), 4.

307. Patricia Galloway, "Henri de Tonti du village des Chacta, 1702: The Beginning of the French Alliance," in *La Salle and His Legacy: Frenchmen and Indians in the Lower Mississippi Valley,* edited by Galloway (Jackson: University of Mississippi Press, 1982), 165.

308. Hudson, "James Adair," 317–18.

309. Ibid., 320.

310. For example, see Mary C. Churchill, "The Oppositional Paradigm of Purity versus Pollution in Charles Hudson's *The Southeastern Indians,*" *American Indian Quarterly* 20 (Fall 1996): 563–93, and Charles Hudson, "Reply to Mary Churchill," *American Indian Quarterly* 24 (Summer 2000): 494–502.

Annotations to Adair's Text

1. Actually George Croghan, Sir William Johnson's deputy, one of the most respected traders in the Ohio region. George Galphin and Lachlan McGillivray were Adair's colleagues and respected traders of long experience among the Creek and Cherokee Indians.

2. To err is human (Seneca, *Naturales Quaestiones* 4.2).

3. For an examination of the importance of the skin color of American Indians in the development of European attitudes toward them, see Alden T. Vaughan, "From White Man to Redskin: Changing Anglo-American Perceptions of the American Indian," *American Historical Review* 87 (October 1982): 917–53.

4. The Shawnee Indians, of Algonquian linguistic stock, were known to the English of Adair's day by a variety of names, including Savannahs and Chaouanons. Beginning in the 1670s, Iroquois raiders dislodged this confederation of tribes from the Ohio Valley. One group removed to the Cumberland Valley. Eventually, they migrated again and, in the early 1730s, settled north of the Ohio River at the mouth of the Scioto River, a site that came to be known as the Old Shawnee Town. A second group settled at the headwaters of the Savannah River, a location to which they gave their name. At this Savannah Town, South Carolina established Fort Moore in 1715, following the Yamasee War, to protect the traders there. These Shawnee soon left South Carolina, settling in Pennsylvania among the Delaware Indians. It was not until the mid-eighteenth century that the groups reunited in the Ohio Valley. Some of the early Shawnee migrants settled among the Creek Indians. See *The Colonial Wars of North America, 1512–1763: An Encyclopedia,* edited by Alan Gallay (New York: Garland, 1996), s.v. "Shawnee"; *Encyclopedia of North American Indians: Native American History, Culture, and Life from Paleo-Indians to the Present,* edited by Frederick E. Hoxie (Boston: Houghton Mifflin Co., 1996), s.v. "Shawnee"; Edmond Atkin, *The Appalachian Indian Frontier: The Edmond Atkin Report and Plan of 1755,* edited with an Introduction by Wilbur R. Jacobs (Lincoln: University of Nebraska Press, 1967), 66, hereafter cited as Atkin, *Report.*

5. Henry Home, Lord Kames, published his *Sketches of the History of Man* in

Edinburgh in 1774. In his writing, he addressed the origin of the American Indians and concluded they were the result of "local creation," a polygenist view that argued for separate creations of races, with the conclusion that the races were actually different species. For a brief examination of Kames's work, see George W. Stocking, Jr., "Scotland as the Model of Mankind: Lord Kames' Philosophical View of Civilization," in *Toward a Science of Man: Essays in the History of Anthropology,* edited by Timothy H. H. Thoresen (The Hague: Mouton, 1975), 67–89. For a modern examination into the question of race and color within the context of early contact, see Nancy Shoemaker, "How Indians Got to Be Red," *American Historical Review* 102 (June 1997): 625–44.

6. Adair uses the term *orientalist* on several occasions, thereby indicating his belief Indians are from the East, meaning of Jewish origin.

7. Careful readers will note that Adair's rule concerning the lack of "plurality" with proper Indian tribal names does not extend to the Creek Indians, whom Adair frequently refers to as Creeks. They are the exception to the rule because "Creeks" is an appellation given to the tribe by the English, and therefore it is not considered their proper "national" name. Adair employs the rule when referring to that tribe by their "proper" name: the Muskohge. Adair's explanation for the reason the Muskohge are called Creeks differs from the explanation devised by Verner W. Crane. See Adair, *History of the American Indians,* 257, hereafter cited as *HAI.* All page numbers refer to the original pagination, provided in brackets in the present work. For Crane's view, see "The Origin of the Name of the Creek Indians," *Mississippi Valley Historical Review* 5 (December 1918): 339–42.

8. The idea that environmental and cultural factors were responsible for the darker hue of Indians had been espoused by the earliest English settlers. See Karen Ordahl Kupperman, *Indians and English: Facing Off in Early America* (Ithaca: Cornell University Press, 2000), 58–59. Moreover, the transforming properties of Indian cultural traditions such as the use of paint and "grease" were obvious as white captives of Indians, by most accounts, soon took on a "tawny" Indian appearance. See James Axtell, *Natives and Newcomers: The Cultural Origins of North America* (Oxford: Oxford University Press, 2001), 195. Adair's contemporaries agreed with his general observations: "The infants of the natives are white when born, but they soon turn brown, as they are rubbed with bear's oil and exposed to the sun"; see Antoine Simon Le Page Du Pratz, *The history of Louisiana, or of the western parts of Virginia and Carolina: containing a description of the countries that lye on both sides of the river Missisippi: with an account of the settlements, inhabitants, soil, climate, and products. Translated from the French, (lately published) by M. Le Page du Pratz; with some notes and observations relating to our colonies* (London: T. Becket, 1774), 324. John Lawson, writing in 1709, made a similar observation concerning the Indians of North Carolina: "Their Colour is of a tawny, which would not be so dark, did they not dawb themselves with Bears Oil, and a Colour like burnt Cork. This is begun in their Infancy, and continued for a long time, which fills the Pores, and enables them better to endure the Extremity of the Weather." See Lawson, *A New Voyage to Carolina; Containing the Exact Description and Natural History of the Country: Together with the Present*

State thereof; and a Journal of a Thousand Miles, Travel'd thro' several Nations of Indians, Giving a particular Account of their Customs, Manners, Etc., edited and with an Introduction by Hugh Talmage Lefler (Chapel Hill: University of North Carolina Press, 1967), 174.

One American physician who tackled the problem of color was John Mitchell. See "An Essay upon the Causes of the Different Colours of People in Different Climates; By John Mitchell, M.D. Communicated to the Royal Society by Mr. Peter Collinson, F.R.S.," *Philosophical Transactions of the Royal Society* 43 (1744–45): 102–50. His thesis had less to do with any substance under the epidermis than with the manner in which skin types of different thickness reflected light.

9. The Shawano main camp, as Adair later states, was "about fifty miles to the north-east of the Chikkasah country" (*HAI,* 410). Although Adair dates the trip to 1747, it seems to have occurred in 1748. The exact date is unknown, but by November of 1748 the French had been apprised of the mission. It could be that the journey occurred in the first three months of that year. See *Mississippi Provincial Archives, French Dominion,* 5 vols., edited by Patricia K. Galloway, vols. 4 and 5 originally collected, edited, and translated by Dunbar Rowland and A. G. Sanders (Baton Rouge: Louisiana State University Press, 1984), 4: 337, hereafter cited as *MPAFD.* Under the Julian calendar, the year would have been 1747 until March 25.

10. Adair's Spanish lady is likely the celebrated example of maternal impression discussed in the highly popular guide to childbirth, *Aristotle's Masterpiece,* which appeared in 1684 and was reprinted numerous times in the eighteenth century. It also mentions Jacob's cattle. See *Aristotle's Masterpiece Compleated in Two Parts* (London: Printed by B. H., 1698), part I, 38, for the examples of maternal impression discussed by Adair. For more on maternal impression and "monstrous conceptions," see Mary E. Fissell, "Hairy Women and Naked Truths: Gender and the Politics of Knowledge in *Aristotle's Masterpiece,*" *William and Mary Quarterly,* 3d ser. 60 (January 2003): 43–74. The white children produced by black parents were most likely albinos. "White" or "spotted" Africans and Indians were curiosities to eighteenth-century natural historians, who examined them hoping to discern the cause of the color variations in humankind. Adair's contemporary Jean-Bernard Bossu also mentioned maternal impression in his account of the Southeast, citing the French writer Joseph-François Lafitau. See Bossu, *Travels in the Interior of North America, 1751–1762,* translated and edited by Seymour Feiler (Norman: University of Oklahoma Press, 1962), 208–9.

11. Peter Chartier was the son of Martin Chartier, a French trader, and a Shawnee woman. A licensed Pennsylvania trader, he was the leader of a group of Shawnees who settled among the Creeks in 1748. He later urged the Cherokee to oppose the establishment of Fort Loudoun and was openly antagonistic to English traders. The name appears variously in eighteenth-century English documents as Shirtee, Sartee, Shirtier, and Chertee; see Atkin, *Report,* 65–66, and David H. Corkran, *The Creek Frontier, 1540–1783* (Norman: University of Oklahoma Press, 1967), 181, 186. Daniel Pepper, one of Adair's contemporaries who was the agent of South Carolina to the Creeks, described Chartier as the "dangerous Ringleader [of the French fac-

tion], our inveterate Enemy." See William L. McDowell, Jr., ed., *Documents Relating to Indian Affairs, 1754–1765,* Colonial Records of South Carolina, Series 2 (Columbia: South Carolina Department of Archives and History, 1970), 298. Chartier was also called Savannah Tom: John R. Alden, *John Stuart and the Southern Colonial Frontier: A Study of Indian Relations, War, Trade and Land Problems in the Southern Wilderness, 1754–1775,* University of Michigan Publications in History and Political Science, no. 15 (Ann Arbor: University of Michigan Press, 1944; reprint, New York: Gordian, 1966), 53.

12. The lack of physical deformities among southeastern Indians was noted by many observers, but perhaps the notion was overstated. Adair later notes that he met a "hair-lipped warrior" (*HAI,* 277).

13. Adair is using the literal meaning of these Latin terms: beardless and without pubic hair. *Imbuberes* is a Latin legal term, specifying a minor between the ages of seven and twelve years (fourteen for females). William Gerard De Brahm reported that Cherokee men removed the eyebrows as well as beards. See *De Brahm's Report of the General Survey in the Southern District of North America,* edited with an Introduction by Louis De Vorsey, Jr. (Columbia: University of South Carolina Press, 1971), 109–10.

14. Adair's description of the "former" clothing is instructive and one of the few extant descriptions of Indian fashion in the pre-European trade era. While the material changed with the arrival of European textiles, styles, including men's hunting shirts and women's skirts, were retained, as were deerskin shoes. The reference to the color red in regard to the scalps carried on war pipes is his first reference to this symbolic color of war. Various kinds of brass and silver bells were common trade items and generally sold under the generic term *Hawk's bells.* For a concise examination of the types of bells traded in the Southeast, see Ian W. Brown, "Bells," in *Tunica Treasure,* edited by Jeffrey P. Brain, Papers of the Peabody Museum of Archaeology and Ethnology, Harvard University, vol. 71 (Cambridge, Mass.: Peabody Museum of Archaeology and Ethnology, 1979), 195–205. Most bells were used, as Adair indicates, on ceremonial items and clothing.

15. The members of what Adair termed "fashionable society" were wearing an astounding variety of trade cloth, ready-to-wear shirts and coats, and other goods that had largely replaced clothing manufactured from hides and furs, which he described above. For another contemporary account of southeastern Indian clothing styles, which takes into account trade cloth and other items, see *William Bartram on the Southeastern Indians,* edited by Gregory A. Waselkov and Kathryn E. Holland Braund (Lincoln: University of Nebraska Press, 1995), 120–23, hereafter cited as *Bartram on the Southeastern Indians.* For a comprehensive list of trade items carried by English traders, see Gregory A. Waselkov, "The Eighteenth-Century Anglo-Indian Trade in Southeastern North America," in *New Faces of the Fur Trade: Selected Papers of the Seventh North American Fur Trade Conference, Halifax, Nova Scotia, 1995,* edited by Jo-Anne Fiske, Susan Sleeper-Smith, and William Wicken (East Lansing: Michigan State University Press, 1998), 193–222. Kathryn E. Holland Braund, *Deerskins and Duffels: Creek Indian Trade with Anglo-America, 1685–1815* (Lincoln: Univer-

sity of Nebraska Press, 1993), examines the impact of the deerskin trade on the Creek people.

16. Adair uses the term *synhedria* here to refer to winter council houses of the southeastern Indians. Commonly, these were referred to by traders as "hot houses." Adair's term is derived from the Greek word *synedrion,* or council. More specifically, the term *Sanhedrin* is used for the religious and civil council of the Jewish people during the Roman occupation. See R. J. Zwi Werblowsky and Geoffrey Wigoden, eds., *Oxford Dictionary of the Jewish Religion* (Oxford: Oxford University Press, 1997), s.v. "Sanhedrin." Adair's choice of words is designed to highlight what he perceives to be the similarities of Jewish and Indian custom. It was not a term commonly used for Indian council houses.

17. Stroud cloth was manufactured in Stroud, England, specifically for sale to the American Indians. Usually of blue or red color, this all-season wool cloth was the most popular of all the woolen fabrics (Braund, *Deerskins and Duffels,* 122–23). The breechcloth described by Adair was commonly known as a "flap." Adair was not the only writer to observe that southeastern Indian men squatted to urinate. See Bernard Romans, *A Concise Natural History of East and West Florida* [1775], edited and with an Introduction by Kathryn E. Holland Braund (Tuscaloosa: University of Alabama Press, 1999), 112. Extant portrayals of Indian women's skirts confirm that they reached to the "hams" [knees].

18. Cranial deformation earned the Choctaw Indians the epithet "flat heads" (*Bartram on the Southeastern Indians,* 129). As Adair notes, the practice was widespread across the Southeast but was in decline by the end of the eighteenth century.

19. Red Shoe of Couëchitto. For his career, see Patricia K. Galloway, "Choctaw Factionalism and Civil War, 1746–1750," in *The Choctaw before Removal,* edited by Carolyn Keller Reeves (Jackson: University Press of Mississippi, 1985), 120–56. Also called Red Shoe I by a recent scholar in order to distinguish this leader from the Red Shoe (Red Shoe II) who was prominent during the British period. See James Taylor Carson, *Searching for the Bright Path: The Choctaws from Prehistory to Removal* (Lincoln: University of Nebraska Press, 1999). See also Richard White, "Red Shoes: Warrior and Diplomat," in *Struggle and Survival in Colonial America,* edited by David G. Sweet and Gary B. Nash (Berkeley: University of California Press, 1981), 49–68.

20. The pre-Adamite theory held that Adam was not the first man but that other human beings had existed before the biblical creation. The theory, which raised comment in the early Christian world as Christians and Jews attempted to explain those ancient societies outside their faiths, was given new consideration in the age of discovery as philosophers and churchmen sought to explain the Indians. For a discussion of the topic, see Richard H. Popkin, "The Pre-Adamite Theory in the Renaissance," in *Philosophy and Humanism: Renaissance Essays in Honor of Paul Oskar Kristeller,* edited by Edward P. Mahoney (New York: Columbia University Press, 1976), 50–69. William G. McLoughlin and Walter H. Conser, Jr., explore Adair's theory, as well as the Pre-Adamite, Chinese, Tartar, Scythian, and other theories of the period, in "'The First Man was Red': Cherokee Responses to the Debate over Indian Origins, 1760–1860," *American Quarterly* 41 (June 1989): 243–64. Adair's

contemporary Bernard Romans included fuller discussions of these theories in his *Concise Natural History,* 113–21, as did Bossu, *Travels,* 207–16.

21. This is Adair's clearest statement on his belief on the origins of the Indians, and there is ample room for confusion on a number of issues. Israel can refer to two distinct polities. The first Israel, ruled by Saul, David, and Solomon, existed until 922 B.C., when Israel split into two divisions with the death of Solomon. The northern Kingdom of Israel incorporated ten of the twelve Hebrew tribes. The Kingdom of Israel was conquered by Shalmaneser V of Assyria in 721 B.C. and the Israelites were dispersed; they disappeared forever from history and are now known as the Ten Lost Tribes. The southern Kingdom of Judah (comprised of the tribes of Judah and Benjamin) was later carried into captivity by Nebuchadrezzar II of Babylon. The destruction of the Temple at Jerusalem, the sacred site for the Kingdom of Judah, was completed in 604 B.C. Adair, who counts only nine and a half missing tribes (*HAI,* 27), also refers to their conquest and dispersal as "captivity." Thus, Adair's American Israelites are presumed to have been the long-lost tribes of Israel. However, by making references to the First Temple, the seventy years of captivity (*HAI,* 76) (presumably the Babylonian Captivity), and other matters, Adair does not dogmatically trace the Indians from the Ten Lost Tribes but from Hebrews in general, whom he refers to variously as Jews, Hebrews, and Israelites. For a discussion of the Hebrew theory as opposed to the Lost Tribes theory, see Lee Eldridge Huddleston, *Origins of the American Indians: European Concepts, 1491–1729* (Austin: University of Texas Press, 1967), 34–40, 132–35. Modern scholarship uses the term *Hebrew* to denote the ancestors of the Jews, and Adair also uses the term in this fashion. In modern writing, these people are known as Israelites through the Babylonian Captivity of exile. After that time, they are generally referred to as Jews. As to when the migration to America occurred, Adair reckoned it to be "above twenty centuries" (*HAI,* 16) and felt that it must have been early in their history, before the rise of sects. He specifically placed their removal from their homeland "before the destruction of the first temple" (*HAI,* 27), the temple of the Kingdom of Judah at Jerusalem. Two of Adair's main sources, Humphrey Prideaux and Thomas Thorowgood, discussed these events in Jewish history in great detail. Thorowgood, in particular, traced the descent of Americans from the Lost Tribes. For a concise discussion of many of the works cited by Adair, see Don Cameron Allen, *The Legend of Noah: Renaissance Rationalism in Art, Science, and Letters,* vol. 33, nos. 3–4, Illinois Studies in Language and Literature (Urbana: University of Illinois, 1949; reprint, 1963), 119–32.

22. No attempt has been made to identify every classical or biblical reference in Adair's text or to provide extensive annotation for every person, place, or concept relating to Jewish and Christian history and theology or classical literature. Readers seeking basic information on such matters will find the following general reference works useful: Bruce M. Metzger and Michael D. Coogan, eds., *Oxford Guide to People and Places of the Bible* (Oxford: Oxford University Press, 2001); Werblowsky and Wigoden, eds., *Oxford Dictionary of the Jewish Religion;* and *The Catholic Encyclopedia: An International Work of Reference on the Constitution, Doctrine, Discipline, and History*

of the Catholic Church, 15 vols., edited by Charles G. Herbermann, Edward A. Pace, et al. (New York: Appleton, 1907–12).

23. Adair's "families" are the matrilineal clans of the southeastern tribes. Here, Adair makes an attempt to link the totemic clan names used by Indians to cherubimic emblems of the Jews, as well as to the various mythical winged beings of southeastern Indian cosmology. Cherubim are winged heavenly beings having characteristics of both human and nonhuman animals. They serve as both chariot and throne for God and appear in numerous places in the Jewish temple and in visions. See Werblowsky and Wigoden, eds., *Oxford Dictionary of the Jewish Religion,* s.v. "Cherubim." Unfortunately, Adair's obsession with his theory led him to omit discussion of matrilineal kinship and tribal social structure. Moreover, although he certainly understood the difference between "tribe" and clan, he refers to clans as tribes in his discussion here. His argument is that the "tribes" of Israel are the forebearers of Indian clans ("primo-genial tribes"). He wrote that in the "various revolutions . . . through a long-forgotten measure of time," the various distinctive "nations" of Indians developed that contain the descendants of these Israelite tribes, better known in modern literature as clans. Each clan had a totemic symbol, some of which Adair identifies with the "four principal standards of Israel." Quotations from *HAI,* 16–17.

24. Most likely from Richard Cumberland's *Sanchoniatho's Phoenician History* (London: R. Wilkin, 1720).

25. Note that Adair makes a distinction between clan or family member and "others." William Bartram went further and declared that the Creek Indians would receive "a Traveler or Sojourner of whatever Nation, Colour or Language, (without distinction of rank, or any other exception of person) and here treat him as a Brother or his own Child, as long as he pleases to Stay . . . he would divide with you the last grain of corn, or piece of flesh" (*Bartram on the Southeastern Indians,* 160–61).

26. Tlanuwa, the famous bird of prey in Cherokee legend. See Charles M. Hudson, *The Southeastern Indians* (Knoxville: University of Tennessee Press, 1976), 136–39.

27. For William Bartram's account of his experience at the "state house" in Autossee, a Creek town, see *Bartram on the Southeastern Indians,* 102–4.

28. Here again, Adair uses the term *tribe* for clan in keeping with his Hebrew theory. Adair's view is completely at odds with reality, for southeastern Indians reckoned descent through the matrilineal line. Adair's confusion on the issue was not unusual, and most Europeans, whether traders or diplomats, overlooked the importance of the matrilineal organization in their dealings with southeastern Indians. For a recent examination of matrilineality and the role of clans among the Cherokee, see Theda Perdue, *Cherokee Women: Gender and Culture Change, 1700–1835* (Lincoln: University of Nebraska Press, 1998), 41–59.

29. In his discussion of the various names given to "the true and living God" by Jews and Christians, Adair introduces his assertion that the ritual notes of southeastern Indian ceremonies, which he renders "Yohewah," was a corruption of Jeho-

vah. Adair continues this theme throughout his work. Elsewhere, he also introduces additional names for the deity from Hebrew tradition, including Elohim. For a discussion of the various names of God, see Werblowsky and Wigoden, eds., *Oxford Dictionary of the Jewish Religion,* s.v. "God, Names of."

30. Alan Kilpatrick provides an introductory analysis to Cherokee conceptions of the Creator in "A Note on Cherokee Theological Concepts," *American Indian Quarterly* 19 (Summer 1995): 389–406. Jason Baird Jackson explores the nature of the Creator in Yuchi belief and provides a good entry point for an examination of southeastern Indian ritual and belief in *Yuchi Ceremonial Life: Performance, Meaning, and Tradition in a Contemporary American Indian Community* (Lincoln: University of Nebraska Press, 2003), 69–73.

31. This is the first of many references to a magus (priest), arch-magus (high-priest) or magi (priests) by Adair. He is referring to either religious leaders or, in some cases, peace officials or, as on *HAI,* 31, old beloved men. He derives the term *magus* from the hereditary class of priests among the ancient Persians and, by his reckoning, the ancient Hebrews. The term was not used by others to refer to Indian religious leaders.

32. In general, southeastern Indians viewed the Sun as a celestial representative of the Creator, while the sacred fire maintained in their towns was the Sun's earthly representative. The best sources for understanding the Indian view of the Sun, Moon, and Heavens are the sacred stories of the various tribes. A number of compilations are available, including George E. Lankford, ed., *Native American Legends, Southeastern Legends: Tales from the Natchez, Caddo, Biloxi, Chickasaw, and Other Nations* (Little Rock, Ark.: August House Publishers, 1987), and John R. Swanton, *Myths and Tales of the Southeastern Indians,* Bureau of American Ethnology Bulletin 88 (Washington, D.C.: Smithsonian Institution, 1929); reprint, with an introduction by George E. Lankford (Norman: University of Oklahoma Press, 1995). See also Charles Hudson, *Conversations with the High Priest of Coosa* (Chapel Hill: University of North Carolina Press, 2003) for an imaginative attempt to reconstruct the world view of the Mississippian-era ancestors of Adair's historic tribes, and Bill Grantham, *Creation Myths and Legends of the Creek Indians* (Gainesville: University Press of Florida, 2002).

33. Priapus was the Greek god of fertility, often portrayed with an enlarged penis. References to statuary in the Creek country are rare. Bartram reported that the cabins at the town square in Otasse had sculptures, as well as what he termed "hieroglyphic paintings." His imprecise description of these "paintings and sculptures" suggests totemic figures. Unlike Adair, Bartram did find some of the paintings to be "very ludicrous & even obscene, & [showing] even the privates of men" (*Bartram on the Southeastern Indians,* 105, 144). Vernon James Knight, Jr., has suggested that a statue such as described by Adair might be linked to earlier Mississippian cult institutions. See "The Institutional Organization of Mississippian Religion," *American Antiquity* 51 (1986): 683–84. Adair again mentions statuary on p. 30. As for the location of the statue mentioned here, perhaps Adair is referring to Hoithlewaule as the "head war town of the Creeks." Benjamin Hawkins reported that Hoithlewaule

had, at one time, possessed the right to declare war for the Creeks; see *Letters, Journals, and Writings of Benjamin Hawkins,* edited by C. L. Grant, 2 vols. (Savannah: Beehive Press, 1980), 1: 293, hereafter cited as *Writings.* George Stiggins likewise indicated that Hoithlewaule was an important war town, roughly translating the name of the town as "Division of War." See Theron A. Nuñez, Jr., "Creek Nativism and the Creek War of 1813–1814 (George Stiggins Manuscript)," *Ethnohistory* 5 (Winter 1958): 25. Knight identified the town as Tuckabatchee ("The Institutional Organization of Mississippian Religion," 684). However, in the eighteenth and early nineteenth centuries, Tuckabatchee was a white or peace town (Hawkins, *Writings,* 1: 306–7).

34. This drunken lark speaks to more than mere curiosity, for Europeans were very curious about the self-presentation, gender, and sexuality of native peoples, particularly when they spotted those who appeared to be biologically male or female dressed in clothing of the opposite sex or assuming the opposite gender role. See Kupperman, *Indians and English,* 54–55.

35. References to dreams are not uncommon in extant literature. Writing in the nineteenth century, H. B. Cushman observed that the "Choctaws regarded dreams as the direct avenues to the invisible world, the divine revelations of the Great Spirit." See *History of the Choctaw, Chickasaw and Natchez Indians,* edited by Angie Debo (reprint, Norman: University of Oklahoma Press, 1999), 173. Bartram reported that Indians of Apalachia abandoned their ancient town site for another, "having been repeatedly warned by apparitions and dreams to leave it" (*Bartram on the Southeastern Indians,* 92; see also 150). Dii Penates and Dii Lares are household gods or local gods or deities. Teraphim are household gods or idols, frequently mentioned in the Old Testament. See Genesis 31:19 or Judges 17:5ff.

36. Jewish tradition puts this sentiment in the mouth of Abraham, who is trying to convince his father, Terach, of the folly of idol worship. See the Jewish Midrash (Genesis Rabbah 38:13). The story also appears in the Koran (6:74). However, neither source used the exact wording, which most likely comes from Hereclitus, *Fragments.*

37. Messengers of the gods.

38. Romans provided similar information, in regard to the Choctaw Indians: "There is also a species of *Motacilla* (which I often endeavoured to catch, in vain) whose chirping near their camp, will occasion their immediate return" (*Concise Natural History,* 132). For more information on birds as omens, see Hudson, *Southeastern Indians,* 128–31.

39. Shalmaneser V, king of Assyria, who conquered the Kingdom of Israel in 721 B.C. The Kingdom of Israel had been formed by ten of the original twelve Hebrew tribes. The other two tribes (Judah and Benjamin) had established the kingdom of Judah to the south.

40. Here Adair uses another name for the supreme being. See *HAI,* 18–19.

41. By "the latter," Adair means Indians; another reference to the "master of breath."

42. Bartram variously described the eagle tail as the "national," "royal," or "im-

perial" standard of the Creeks, and there is ample evidence for use of white eagle tail feathers in ceremonials among the southeastern Indians (*Bartram on the Southeastern Indians,* 47, 49, 105, 173). In addition to use as "standards" on display in villages, eagles' tails were used as presentation peace offerings. The Cherokee Indians repeatedly presented eagles' tails to the British at the end of the Anglo-Cherokee War in 1761. See David H. Corkran, *The Cherokee Frontier: Conflict and Survival, 1740–1762* (Norman: University of Oklahoma Press, 1962), 269–70.

The correct identification of the bird from which the feathers were taken on such occasions is virtually impossible because of conflicting or incomplete descriptions of the tail feathers, compounded by Adair's assertion that "the bald eagle they do not esteem." Generally, the southern Bald Eagle (*Haliaeetus leucocephalus*) is regarded as the source of eagle tail feathers in southeastern ceremonials (Hudson, *Southeastern Indians,* 163–64). However, it is possible that various tribes used the feathers of different species and that even among the same tribes, different eagle feathers were used in different ceremonies. Bartram noted that the eagle feathers used by the Creek Indians were tipped with brown or black and were not completely white. His description calls to mind the tail feathers of the immature Golden Eagle (*Aquila chrysaëtos canadensis*) and would somewhat support Adair's assertion concerning the Bald Eagle.

43. Among the southeastern Indians, red and white were the two essential divisions, indicating war and peace. The "war seats" were designated for warriors and the "white seats" for civil or peace officials. Here, Adair uses "Synhedria" to designate winter council houses. It is not clear if he is writing here of winter council houses or the cabins in square grounds. When Bartram visited the Tallapoosa villages, he noted that the cabins of the square grounds there were decorated with paintings and sculptures. At Otasse, he specifically noted that "pillars supporting the front or piazza of the council-house of the square, were ingeniously formed in the likeness of vast speckled serpents, ascending upward; the Otasses being of the snake family or tribe" (*Bartram on the Southeastern Indians,* 105). Although such descriptions of sculptures as provided by Bartram and Adair are rare, it is clear that wood carving and statuary were important components of public art in the early South. See Hudson, *Southeastern Indians,* 308–4, for a brief introduction to the topic.

44. See Romans, *Concise Natural History,* 143, for his sketch of a Creek war chief wearing a headdress with bison horns such as described by Adair. Adair's reference to the cherubimical figures is from the Ezekiel's dream or vision of a four-headed cherubim on the chariot of God (Ezekial 1:10).

45. Beloved men were elders. Benjamin Hawkins described the Creek "beloved men" as "great men who have been war leaders, and who altho of various ranks, have become estimable in the long course of public service" (*Writings,* 1: 319). See Fred Gearing, "Priests and Warriors: Social Structures for Cherokee Politics in the Eighteenth Century," American Anthropological Association *Memoir 93,* vol. 64, no. 5, pt. 2 (October 1962): 23, 39, 48.

46. Compare with Bartram's description of Creek paintings (*Bartram on the Southeastern Indians,* 143–45).

47. The first quotation can be translated as "it seemed otherwise to the gods" or "the gods judged otherwise" (*Aeneid* 2.428). The passage that follows is taken from ibid., 8.396, 398, 399, and describes Venus's lament over the fate of Troy: "Had such a thing [prayer is implied here] been given, I could have armed the Teucrians. Neither Jove nor Destiny had grudged ten added years of life to Troy and Priam." The second quotation, as given by Adair, is incomplete.

48. In the third heaven, in an earthly paradise, or in the fiery element (in the region where the stars exist). Here, Adair alludes to the fact that Indians considered smoke a link between the earthly fire and the heavens, noting that they believed God resides both "above the clouds" and in the smoke. For a discussion of the importance of fire in southeastern ritual, see James H. Howard, *The Southeastern Ceremonial Complex and Its Interpretation,* Memoir No. 6, Missouri Archaeological Society (Columbia: Missouri Archaeological Society, 1968), 19–24.

49. For an investigation of supernaturalism among the Cherokee, see Alan Kilpatrick, *The Night Has a Naked Soul: Witchcraft and Sorcery among the Western Cherokee* (Syracuse, N.Y.: Syracuse University Press, 1997).

50. Ocmulgee was originally a Lower Creek town on the Chattahoochee River. Like many of the Lower Creeks, the people from Ocmulgee removed to Ochese Creek, as the Ocmulgee River was then known, sometime prior to 1696. The move was precipitated by Spanish hostility and a desire to be nearer their new South Carolina trade partners and allies. The settlement was abandoned during the Yamasee War. The site is preserved today as the Ocmulgee National Monument, near Macon, Georgia. For the most comprehensive collection of essays on the site, see David J. Hally, ed., *Ocmulgee Archaeology, 1936–1986* (Athens: University of Georgia Press, 1994).

51. Samuel Bochart, 1599–1667, a linguist and a biblical scholar. His *Hierozoicon, sive, bipertitum opus De animalibus Sacr Scripturae,* 2 vols. (London, 1663), dealt with animals mentioned in the Scripture. Another of his Latin works, *Hoc est Phaleg, Cannan, et Hierozoicon . . .* (Lugduni Batavorum, 1692), was cited frequently by the author of *An Enquiry into the Origin of the Cherokees: A Letter to a Member of Parliament* (Oxford: James Fletcher, 1762). It seems likely that much of Adair's Hebrew derives from the works of Bochart or derivatives of his works.

52. Adair's chimerical effort to draw links between Hebrew and American Indian languages is not without value, for careful readers and serious scholars can deduce much about trader knowledge of Indian dialects as well as commonly used words and idiomatic expressions of the eighteenth-century tribes. Although Adair sometimes indicates the language that the words discussed below derive from, frequently he does not. For those seeking more information on the meaning of Indian words, a number of excellent dictionaries are available: Jack B. Martin and Margaret McKane Mauldin, *A Dictionary of Creek/Muskogee with Notes on the Florida and Oklahoma Seminole Dialects of Creek* (Lincoln: University of Nebraska Press, 2000); Robert M. Loughridge and David M. Hodge, *English and Muskokee Dictionary, Collected from Various Sources and Revised,* reprint (Okmulgee, Okla.: B. Frank Belvin, 1964); Cyrus Byington, *A Dictionary of the Choctaw Language,* edited by John R.

Swanton and Henry S. Halbert, Smithsonian Institution Bureau of American Ethnology, Bulletin 46 (Washington, D.C.: GPO, 1915); Pamela Munro and Catherine Willmond, *Chickasaw: An Analytical Dictionary* (Norman: University of Oklahoma Press, 1994); and Durbin Feeling, *Cherokee-English Dictionary,* edited by William Pulte, in collaboration with Agnes Cowen and the Dictionary Committee (Talequah: Cherokee Nation of Oklahoma, 1975).

53. Podex signifies the fundament or anus. *Meus, teus,* and *illius* are pronouns signifying *my* or *mine, your,* and *his, hers,* or *its.*

54. The four Hebrew letters that are used to symbolize the proper name of the deity, variously transcribed as YHWH or JHWH and rendered Yahweh, are known as the tetragrammaton. Adair equates the long musical note sung by the black drink server with the name of the diety. This note, usually written "Yahola," is also part of the title of the Creek official who served the drink. Caleb Swan provided a description on the black drink ceremony among the Creeks: "Position and State of Manners and Arts in the Creek, or Muscogee Nation in 1791," in *Information Respecting the History, Condition, and Prospects of the Indian Tribes of the United States,* edited by Henry Rowe Schoolcraft (Philadelphia: J. B. Lippincott Co., 1852–57), vol. 5, 266–67.

55. Yaupon holly (*Ilex vomitoria* Ait.) is used in the preparation of cassina or black drink. For a comprehensive look at the shrub and its use, including contemporary descriptions of the practice, see Charles M. Hudson, ed., *Black Drink: A Native American Tea* (Athens: University of Georgia Press, 1979).

56. Literally, "altars and hearths," meaning for the sake of religion and home or country.

57. Adair is describing "dry scratching." Other sources mention the use of gar teeth. Adair provides a fuller description of the practice on p. 120.

58. See Jerald T. Milanich, "Origins and Prehistoric Distributions of Black Drink and Ceremonial Shell Drinking Cup," in Hudson, ed., *Black Drink,* 83–119, for particulars on the shells used. In later periods, gourds were also used to serve black drink.

59. In the Charleston Library Society copy of Adair's *History,* a "Y" is added prior to "O." The corrected line phrase reads: "the awful monosyllable, YO."

60. In the Charleston Library Society copy of Adair's *History,* the words "commonly termed" are inserted before the word JEHOVAH.

61. Adair was not the only deerskin trader to reach this conclusion. Abram Mordecai, a Jewish trader among the Creeks, was reported to have "confidently believed that the Indians were originally of his people, and he asserted that in their Green Corn Dances he heard them often utter in graceful tunes, the word Yavoyaha! Yavoyaha! He was always informed by the Indians that this meant Jehovah, or the Great Spirit, and that they were returning thanks for the abundant harvest with which they were blessed." See H. B. Cushman, *History of the Choctaw, Chickasaw and Natchez Indians* (Greenville, Texas: Headlight Printing House, 1899), 20. For his part, Bartram recollected the sound as "two long notes are very solemn, and at once

strike the imagination with a religious awe or homage to the Supreme, sounding somewhat like a-hoo—ojah and a-lu—yah" (*Bartram on the Southeastern Indians*, 104).

62. In the Charleston Library Society copy of Adair's *History*, "Wah Wah" are inserted after He He. The corrected phrase reads: "they sing Yo Yo, He He, Wah Wah, and repeat those sacred notes, on every religion occasion."

63. The practice of disgorging black drink was duly noted by European observers, most of whom failed to record whether they also spat out the liquid. Here, Adair provides not only the reason for the practice but also valuable information about European participation in the ritual. *Ilex vomitoria*, from the practices of regurgitation by Indians, acquired a reputation as an emetic, but the reaction was purely voluntary. Caleb Swan reported that Creek men, after drinking a large quantity of liquid, "by hugging his arms across his stomach, and leaning forward, disgorges the liquor in a large stream from his mouth, to the distance of six or eight feet" ("Position and State of Manners," 267).

64. In the Charleston Library Society copy of Adair's *History*, the spelling of the word *synhedrion* is corrected.

65. In the Charleston Library Society copy of Adair's *History*, an "a" is inserted after the word *Ansa*. The corrected word reads *Ansaa*.

66. In the Charleston Library Society copy of Adair's *History*, the word *unspeakable* is crossed out and the phrase "which we are allowed to mention" is added to the end of the sentence. The corrected sentence reads, "and I likewise attest it, by his other beloved, sacred, essential name, which we are allowed to mention."

67. Sir Alexander Cuming visited the Cherokee in 1730. By unabashed boldness and what must have been overwhelming personal charm, he recruited a delegation of seven Cherokee headmen who traveled with him to England, where they met King George II. Part of Cuming's bizarre plans included a settlement of Jews among the Cherokee; see "Journal of Sir Alexander Cuming (1730)," in *Early Travels in the Tennessee Country, 1540–1800*, edited by Samuel Cole Williams (Johnson City, Tenn.: Watauga Press, 1928), 115–43. For information on Cuming, his expedition to the Cherokee towns, and the Cherokee expedition to London, see Carolyn Thomas Foreman, *Indians Abroad, 1493–1938* (Norman: University of Oklahoma Press, 1943); Richard Beale Davis, *Intellectual Life in the Colonial South, 1585–1763*, 3 vols. (Knoxville: University of Tennessee Press, 1978), 1: 170–71; Tom Hatley, *The Dividing Paths: Cherokees and South Carolinians through the Era of the Revolution* (New York: Oxford University Press, 1993), 67–68; and Stanley W. Hoig, *The Cherokees and Their Chiefs: In the Wake of Empire* (Fayetteville: University of Arkansas Press, 1998), 19–22.

68. In the Charleston Library Society copy of Adair's *History*, an "h" is inserted in the word *To e u ah*, so that the corrected word is meant to read *To eu hah*.

69. The treaty between Georgia and the Creek Indians was actually negotiated in 1733. Adair is correct regarding the fixing of the boundary with the tidal line. For information on Georgia's early boundary, see John T. Juricek, ed., *Georgia*

Treaties, 1733–1763, vol. 11 of *Early American Indian Documents; Treaties and Laws, 1607–1789,* edited by Alden T. Vaughan (Bethesda, Md.: University Publications of America, 1989), 1–6.

70. Adair is referring to Cadwallader Colden, whose history of the Five Nations went through several editions in the early and mid-eighteenth century; see *The History of the Five Indian Nations depending on the Province of New-York in America* (Ithaca, New York: Great Seal Books, 1958). Adair met the Reverend John Ogilvie when he visited Sir William Johnson. Ogilvie was a missionary to the Mohawk tribe and a professor at King's College, New York. Adair's account of Colden's error cannot be confirmed. In his second edition, Colden notes the use of the term "*Yo-hah,*" by Six Nations tribesmen participating in a conference with New York. On 95n., he reports that "The *Yo-hah* denotes Approbation, being a loud Shourt or Cry, consisting of a few Notes pronounced by all the *Indians* in a very musical manner in the Nature of our Huzza's."

71. This town was generally referred to as the Breed Camp by the English and appears on William Bonar's 1757 map by that name ("Draught of the Creek Nation," British Public Record Office, CO700/Carolina 21). The Breed Camp was established in 1740–41 and served as the transshipment point for merchandise going to the Chickasaw nation. The Chickasaw who moved there served as escorts for traders' pack trains bound for their towns. Part of the motivation for the settlement was security for the Chickasaw traders. Equally important in the original settlement of the town was that the Chickasaw would be provided with goods at the same rates as those of the Creek trade at that location, since trade goods were generally sold at a greater price in the Chickasaw towns themselves because of the higher cost of transportation and greater expectation of losses. See W. L. McDowell, ed., *Journals of the Commissioners of the Indian Trade, September 20, 1710–August 29, 1718,* Colonial Records of South Carolina (Columbia: South Carolina Archives Department, 1955), 238, 249. See also *The Journal of the Commons House of Assembly,* edited by J. H. Easterby and R. Nicholas Olsberg, 12 vols., Colonial Records of South Carolina (Columbia: Historical Commission of South Carolina and South Carolina Department of Archives, 1951–81), 3: 313–420, hereafter cited as *JCHA,* and *MPAFD,* 3: 747. Edmond Atkin listed the population of the settlement at 80 gunmen in 1755 (Atkin, *Report,* 42). (A gunman is a man capable of bearing arms. Europeans recorded Indians in this manner rather than estimating total population.) On page 319 of the present work, Adair states that Ooe-Asah was peopled by both Chickasaw and Natchez Indians. The Natchez soon settled their own town. A 1765 census assigned 33 gunmen to the Breed Camp and 20 to the nearby settlement of Natchez Indians, simply known as Natchees. Their town among the Creeks provided relative safety, and for their abandonment of their native land, John Stuart reported that the residents of the Breed Camp were "despised by their brave Countrymen who remain at home, as Dastards, who basely deserted their Country" (John Stuart to Board of Trade, March 9, 1764, in Great Britain, Public Record Office, Colonial Office, Series 323, America and West Indies, vol. 17, fo. 254, hereafter cited as John

Stuart's 1764 report. Hereafter, Colonial Office material will be cited as CO series/ volume, first folio page number). See "A List of Towns and Number of Gun Men in the Creek Nation," in William Ogilvie to Thomas Gage, July 8, 1768, Papers of General Thomas Gage Relating to His Command in North America, 1762–76, William L. Clements Library, Ann Arbor, Michigan.

72. In the Charleston Library Society copy of Adair's *History*, the plural "s" is struck from the word names and the word "a" is inserted so that the corrected phrase is intended to read "name of a monkey."

73. In the Charleston Library Society copy of Adair's *History*, the words *malum malorum* are crossed out and the following phrase inserted: "יוען; Wo Wo, *malum malorum.*"

74. Adair's account of weeping is confirmed by numerous others, including the trader who passed through the town of a great Choctaw war chief not long after his death and found "every one in Tears": Charles Stuart to Haldimand, 29 October 1767, Sir Frederick Haldimand Papers, Unpublished Papers and Correspondence, 1758–84 (microfilm copies, London: Microfilm World Publications, 1977). Bernard Romans noted that among the Chickasaw "they bury their dead almost the moment the breath is out of the body, in the very spot under the couch on which the deceased died, and the nearest relations mourn over it with woeful lamentations; the women are very vociferous in it, but the men do it in silence." He reported that the mourning lasted "about a year" and that "they are every morning and evening, and at first throughout the day at different times, employed in the exercise of this last duty" (*Concise Natural History*, 129). He likewise commented on the "loud howlings" of the Choctaw for deceased relations (140–41).

75. Swan wings are usually mentioned in eighteenth-century documents in relation to peace ceremonies. For example, in 1765, the Mortar of Okchai presented each British dignitary with a "white Wing, as an Emblem of Peace" when the Creeks met with them at Pensacola to ratify a peace treaty. The British were then "Saluted with and fanned by Eagles Tails." See "Congress of Pensacola," in Dunbar Rowland, ed., *Mississippi Provincial Archives, English Dominion, 1763–1766: Letters and Enclosures to the Secretary of State from Major Robert Farmar and Governor George Johnstone* (Nashville: Brandon Printing Co., 1911), 1: 189, hereafter cited as *MPAED*. In 1776, John Stuart reported that when the Choctaw and Creek Indians met to end the Creek-Choctaw war, the parties "halted about three hundred yards distance from each other their principal chiefs singing the Peace song and waving Eagles Tails and Swans wings over their heads" (John Stuart to Lord Germaine, October 26, 1776, in CO5/78, fo. 15). The wings were likely from the whistling swan (*Cygnus columbianus*). Of all the large swimming birds, only swans have solid white wings devoid of black wing-tips; see Roger Tory Peterson, *A Field Guide to the Birds: Giving Field Marks of All Species Found East of the Rockies* (Boston: Houghton Mifflin Company, 1947), 20–21. Thomas Nairne recorded that swan "feathers are great ornaments among the Chicasaws. They are taken out of ponds, with lights at night"; see *Nairne's Muskhogean Journals: The 1708 Expedition to the Mississippi River*, edited by

Alexander Moore (Jackson: University Press of Mississippi, 1988), 48. Caleb Swan, appropriately enough, mentioned swans' wings among the Creeks ("Position and State of Manners," 265).

76. The Saponi Indians, a remnant tribe usually treated as part of the Catawba by the eighteenth century. See James H. Merrell, *The Indians' New World: Catawbas and Their Neighbors from European Contact through the Era of Removal* (Chapel Hill: University of North Carolina Press, 1989, 23–26, for information on their migrations. On Powhatan, see Helen C. Rountree, *Pocahontas's People: The Powhatan Indians of Virginia through Four Centuries* (Norman: University of Oklahoma Press, 1990).

77. A reference to what Adair perceived as gross mismanagement of Indian affairs by Governor James Glen. See introductory essay, this volume.

78. There were two lunar eclipses in 1736. The first occurred on March 26 early in the evening, with the moon already in full eclipse. It was complete by 8:51 P.M. EST. Since the sky was not totally dark during this period and the eclipse was over quickly, a better possibility for Adair's observance was the eclipse of September 19. It began later in the evening, starting at approximately 6:51 EST with a full eclipse occurring at 9:01 P.M. The totality began to end at 10:45 and the eclipse ended, with the moon fully visible again, at 11:48. It was still reddish in color until 12:58 A.M. This would have been a spectacular eclipse and would have been very prominent in the night sky with good weather conditions likely, given the time of year. (Special thanks to Dr. John Hall and Dr. Gene Byrd of the Alabama Museum of Natural History for providing the information on this historical eclipse.) H. B. Cushman recorded that the Choctaw believed that black squirrels were eating up the sun during eclipses, and they behaved in much the same way as the Cherokee to frighten away the squirrel: "Some would throw sticks towards the declining sun, whooping and yelling, at the same time shooting arrows toward the supposed black squirrels"; see *History of the Choctaw, Chickasaw and Natchez Indians,* ed. Debo (1999), 229–31, 308 (quotation). He reported that the Chickasaw had no such "superstitious views" but did have special terms for various eclipses (410).

79. The Chakchiuma of the Upper Yazoo River valley. For an examination of origin stories and their significance, see Patricia Galloway, *Choctaw Genesis, 1500– 1700* (Lincoln: University of Nebraska Press, 1995), 330 ff.

80. This town was apparently abandoned after 1723. It was located on the south side of Chiwapa Creek in modern southeastern Pontotoc County. See James R. Atkinson, "Historic Chickasaw Cultural Material: A More Comprehensive Identification," *Mississippi Archaeology* 22 (1985): 34.

81. To break camp.

82. Southeastern Indians generally reckoned the passage of time by the seasonal changes in weather and vegetation. For a fuller discussion of the manner in which Choctaw reckoned time, see John R. Swanton, *Source Material for the Social and Ceremonial Life of the Choctaw Indians,* Bureau of American Ethnology Bulletin no. 103 (Washington, D.C.: Government Printing Office, 1931); reprint with foreword by Kenneth H. Carleton (Tuscaloosa: University of Alabama Press, 2001), 44–46. For the Creeks, see John R. Swanton, *Social Organization and Social Usages of the Indians*

of the Creek Confederacy, Bureau of American Ethnology Bulletin no. 42 (Washington, D.C.: Government Printing Office, 1928; reprint, New York: Johnson Reprint Corp., 1970), 398–405.

83. "Without food (Ceres) and wine (Bacchus), love (Venus) grows cold" (Terence, *Eunuchus* 732).

84. Cushman also described the "bundle of twigs . . . called fuli (sticks) kauah (broken) broken sticks" among the Choctaw (*History of the Choctaw, Chickasaw and Natchez Indians,* ed. Debo [1999], 194). David Taitt encountered cane sticks on two occasions among the Creeks, as they called meetings to hear his talks from Superintendent John Stuart. Among the Creeks, the sticks were discarded each day to mark the passage of time. "David Taitt's Journal," in *Documents of the American Revolution, 1770–1783,* 21 vols., edited by Kenneth G. Davies (Dublin: Irish University Press, 1974), 5: 258, 268, hereafter referred to as *DAR.* The knotted strings Adair mentions are the quipus used by the Inca. These mnemonic devices consisted of colored and specially knotted cords and were used for calculating commercial transactions.

85. Humphrey Prideaux (1648–1724), the author *The Old and New Testaments Connected in the history of the Jews and Neighbouring Nations from the declensions of the Kingdoms of Israel and Judah to the time of Christ,* 4 vols. (London: R. Knaplock and J. Tonson 1718), a standard historical work that appeared in repeated editions throughout the eighteenth century.

86. The green corn ceremony or Busk is described more fully beginning on page 96 of the original work. Caleb Swan confirmed Adair's observations for the Creek year: "Position and State of Manners," 5: 276–77. For an overview of the annual cycle of various southeastern tribes, see John R. Swanton, *Indians of the Southeastern United States,* Bureau of American Ethnology Bulletin no. 137 (Washington, D.C.: Government Printing Office, 1946; reprint, New York: Greenwood Press, 1969), 255–65. For a more nuanced look at the ceremony in the context of the modern Yuchi tribe, see Jackson, *Yuchi Ceremonial Life,* 206–40.

87. Tugaloo. In early 1716, a Creek peace delegation to the Cherokee were killed at the Tugaloo council house, touching off intermittent conflict that lasted until 1752, when Tugaloo, along with most of the other Lower Towns, was destroyed by the Creeks. By the year 1764, the town population was listed as a mere twenty gunmen. For population of the Cherokee towns in 1760, see John Stuart's 1764 report, CO323/17, fo. 243; John Phillip Reid, *A Better Kind of Hatchet: Law, Trade, and Diplomacy in the Cherokee Nation during the Early Years of European Contact* (University Park: Pennsylvania State University Press, 1976), 61–73; Corkran, *Cherokee Frontier,* 35–36.

88. *Sanctum Sanctorum* is literally "holy of holies" and is the term given to the most interior sacred chamber of a Jewish temple. Here, Adair applies the term to the inner chamber of the Creek mico's cabin, also described by William Bartram, who wrote that the central part of the principal cabin in a Creek square ground contained a "Back apartment . . . quite close and dark, except three very low arched *Holes* or *Doors* for admittance of the Priests. In this place are deposited all the most

valuable Publick Things, (as the *Eagle Tail,* or National Standard) *Calumet & War Pipe, Drums* & all the *Sacred Things or Apparatus of the Priests* &c." (*Bartram on the Southeastern Indians,* 172–73).

89. In the Charleston Library Society copy of Adair's *History,* the word *Muskohge* is crossed out and the word *Chickasah* inserted.

90. The Venerable Bede (d. 735) is best remembered for his *Historia Ecclesiastica Gentis Anglorum (Ecclesiastical History of the English People)* which traced the development of the English church to Bede's own time, Here, Adair makes reference to his *De temporum ratione (The Reckoning of Time)* which dealt with the calendar and, ultimately, the "ages" of the world. Adair's secondary source for this reference is unclear. For more information on Bede, see George Hardin Brown, *Bede, the Venerable* (Boston: Twayne, 1987). *De temporum ratione* remains in print some twelve centuries after Bede's death. See Bede, *The reckoning of time,* translated, with introduction, notes, and commentary by Faith Wallis (Liverpool: Liverpool University Press, 1999).

91. Adair uses the term *Loáche* in the sense of a prophet or priest, including those like rainmakers whose ceremonies can influence nature.

92. Connecorte (Old Hop) acquired his English appellation from a leg wound he received when a young man that left him with a limp. From early 1752 until his death in 1760, Old Hop was acknowledged the Emperor of the Cherokee and their leading spokesman. His career is covered in Corkran, *Cherokee Frontier.*

93. Chota, on the Little Tennessee River, was the leading Overhill Town and was considered the founding town of the Cherokee people (Corkran, *Cherokee Frontier,* 3–4). Colin G. Calloway examines the town in the late eighteenth century. See *The American Revolution in the Indian Country: Crisis and Diversity in Native American Communities* (Cambridge: Cambridge University Press, 1995), chap. 7.

94. Attakullakulla or the Little Carpenter was probably the best known Cherokee of the eighteenth century and a lifelong ally of the British. He was among the Cherokee delegation to London in 1730 and was a major force in winning acceptance of the 1755 land cession to South Carolina. During the Anglo-Cherokee war, he personally protected John Stuart and played a leading role in the reestablishment of peace. See James C. Kelly, "Notable Persons in Cherokee History: Attakullakulla," *Journal of Cherokee Studies* 3 (Winter 1978): 2–34; *Colonial Wars of North America,* s.v. "Attakullakulla (also known as Little Carpenter, c. 1710–1780"; and Hoig, *The Cherokees and their Chiefs,* 22. See also *HAI,* 326.

95. "Where barefoot kings observe festal sabbaths, and a long-established clemency grants long life to pigs" (Juvenal, *Satires* 6.159–60).

96. Given Adair's lack of skill at botanical identification and nomenclature, it is almost impossible to say with certainty what this root was. Most likely, it was pucoon (*Sanguinaria canadensis* L.), commonly known as bloodroot. Although it was dried and reduced to powder and used as a coloring and dye, its primary use was as an emetic. See Virgil J. Vogel, *American Indian Medicine* (Norman: University of Oklahoma Press, 1970), 354, and Steven Foster and James A. Duke, *A Field Guide*

to *Medicinal Plants of Eastern and Central North America,* 2d ed., Peterson Field Guide Series (Boston: Houghton Mifflin, 2000), 54–55. Romans, a much better botanist than Adair, also noted that the Choctaw "have a root by means of which they dye most substances of a bright lasting scarlet, but hitherto I have not been able to discover what it was" (*Concise Natural History,* 138). It is important to note that Adair is making a distinction between the use of this dye for a "holy" or peace ceremony and using it for a war ceremony. For a discussion of the significance of the "white maccasenes," see Patricia Galloway, "'So Many Little Republics': British Negotiations with the Choctaw Confederacy, 1765," *Ethnohistory* 41 (Fall 1994): 534n.37 De Brahm reported that at the "installation" ceremony, the Cherokee "King of Estatowee" began with his two attendants "putting on his Feet a pair of Socks (Mokasins) made of white dressed Deer Skin" (*De Brahm's Report,* 111–12). He notes that the "installation" took place during the Green Corn Ceremony.

97. Anthropologist Charles Hudson, *Southeastern Indians,* 370–75, provides an account of the ceremony derived from Adair. For a brief discussion of the iconographic symbols and designs on shell gorgets, see ibid., 386–88.

98. Adair's impression that the rainmaker blamed drought and floods on various breaches of social and ceremonial laws is confirmed by others. For example, see an oration of a Creek "conjuror" reported by John Pope, *A Tour of through the Southern and Western Territories of the United States of North-America,* facsimile reproduction of the 1792 edition with introduction by J. Barton Starr, Bicentennial Floridiana Facsimile Series (Gainesville: University Presses of Florida, 1979), 60–62. Cushman discusses Choctaw and Chickasaw rainmakers in *History of the Choctaw, Chickasaw and Natchez Indians,* ed. Debo (1999), 201–3, 405. See Hudson, *Southeastern Indians,* 337–38, for a brief primer on weather control techniques.

99. Rendered variously as Tomassee or Tenassee.

100. Cherokee Indians believed that such divining crystals (quartz) came from the Uktena, a winged snake. See Charles Hudson, "Uktena: A Cherokee Anomalous Monster," *Journal of Cherokee Studies* 3 (Spring 1978): 62–75, and Hudson, *Southeastern Indians,* 131–33, 356–58. Henry Timberlake also mentioned stones used by the Cherokee in "conjuring ceremonies"; see *Lieut. Henry Timberlake's Memoirs,* edited by Samuel Cole Williams (Johnson City, Tenn.: Watauga Press, 1927), 73–75. See also Nathaniel J. Sheidley, "Unruly Men: Indians, Settlers, and the Ethos of Frontier Patriarchy in the Upper Tennessee Watershed, 1763–1815," Ph.D. diss., Princeton University, 1999, 42–43, for a discussion of the Uktena as "a crosser of spatial boundaries." Adair refers to "chrystaline stones" (*HAI,* 237).

101. Adair refers to Button Snake Root (*Eryngium aquaticum* L. or *Eryngium yuccafolium* Michx.) a number of times in his work. His assessment of the root as a purgative and in busk and other ceremonial uses is confirmed by other sources, although the vomiting may have been culturally conditioned. See Vogel, *American Indian Medicine,* 103, 371; John R. Swanton, "Religious Beliefs and Medical Practices of the Creek Indians," in *Forty-second Annual Report of the Bureau of American Ethnology* (Washington, D.C.: Government Printing Office, 1928), 655–56. In this

passage, the rainmakers are Choctaw. Romans also commented on Choctaw rainmakers, who called the plant *Esta Hoola*. He wrote that he saw two species of the plant but could not identify it (*Concise Natural History,* 138–39).

102. Also known as pack or burden baskets, these large baskets, holding approximately three bushels, were carried on women's backs, supported by a tumpline that encompassed the neck of the basket and crossed the wearer's forehead or chest. For information on basketry, see Sarah H. Hill, *Weaving New Worlds: Southeastern Cherokee Women and Their Basketry* (Chapel Hill: University of North Carolina Press, 1997), 49, 228 (photograph).

103. Charles Hudson analyses this dialogue in "James Adair as Anthropologist," *Ethnohistory* 24 (Fall 1977): 318–19. He speculates that the "loache" might have been Pastabe, The Jockey.

104. For an interesting approach to the questions on why Indians are designated as "red folks," see Nancy Shoemaker, "How Indians Got to Be Red."

105. There are a growing number of studies on both the historic and modern ceremonial lives of southeastern Indians. See, for example, Amelia R. Bell, "Creek Ritual: The Path to Peace," Ph.d. diss., University of Chicago, 1984; David Lewis, Jr., and Ann T. Jordan, *Creek Indian Medicine Ways: The Enduring Power of Mvskoke Religion* (Albuquerque: University of New Mexico Press, 2002); and Jackson, *Yuchi Ceremonial Life.* For an overview of southeastern ceremonials, see Howard, *The Southeastern Ceremonial Complex.* Older but still essential are James Mooney's classic works on the Cherokee, including "Myths of the Cherokee," in *Nineteenth Annual Report of the Bureau of American Ethnology,* 11–576 (Washington, D.C.: GPO, 1900), and "Sacred Formulas of the Cherokees," in *Seventh Annual Report of the Bureau of Ethnology* (Washington, D.C.: GPO, 1891).

106. Here, Adair gives what appears to be a composite account of the annual ceremonial variously known as the Busk (from the Muskogee word *Posketa*) or Green Corn Dance of the southeastern Indians. It is generally taken to be his account of the Chickasaw ceremony, but he clearly intends to indicate that the ceremony is universal. See p. 102, on which he refers to traders' observations about "these numerous nations of Indians." He is certainly referring to the Chickasaw when he states on p. 100 that "if the whole nation lies in a narrow compass, they make but one annual offering." But there were clearly differences in the tribal ceremonies. Thomas Nairne recorded that the Chickasaw did not "keep the busks as the Ochesees [Creeks], but only make a great generall Dance, when they Eat the first green corn" (*Muskhogean Journals,* 48). Likewise, Malcolm McGee, a deerskin trader among the Chickasaw after the Revolutionary War, reported that "they had no green-corn dances as had the Creeks" (see Malcom McGee Interview Notes, Draper's Notes and Correspondence, 1854–1886, Lyman Draper Collection, Wisconsin Historical Society). By all accounts, the Creek ceremony was the most elaborate in the Southeast, or at least the best described. Perhaps the best account of the Creek Busk is provided by John Howard Payne in the nineteenth century. See John R. Swanton, "The Green Corn Dance," *Chronicles of Oklahoma* 10 (June 1932):

170–95. For other accounts of the Creek Busk, see Hawkins, *Writings,* 1: 322–24, and Theron A. Nunez, Jr., "Creek Nativism and the Creek War of 1813–1814," *Ethnohistory* 5 (Winter 1958): 40–41, 131–32. Hudson, *Southeastern Indians,* 365–75, relies almost exclusively on Adair for his discussion of the ceremony.

107. Adair mentions "a certain red root" used with bear's oil to color the skin (*HAI,* 3), "a certain red root . . . which is their fixed red symbol of holy things" (*HAI,* 83), and this "emblematical red root" used to paint the war cabin. He fails to provide enough information to identify them botanically or to say with assurance if he is discussing two or three different roots, although he is clearly making a distinction between the root that symbolized "holy things" and was used for peace purposes and the "emblematical red root of war" used to paint the war cabin.

108. Here Adair inserts an aside, comparing war dances with the annual harvest ceremony. He might be referring here to the Choctaw, deeming those under discussion "warlike savages," an epithet he rarely uses for the Chickasaw. Moreover, the Choctaw were at war with the Creeks more often than with the Chickasaw. Perhaps this incident occurred during the Creek-Choctaw war of the 1760s.

109. The four sides of the square represent the four cardinal directions and encompass a sacred space. Central to the space was the sacred fire. For a discussion of the symbolism in a Creek square ground, see Howard, *Southeastern Ceremonial Complex,* 124–38.

110. In this description of the Green Corn Ceremony, Adair notes two uses of Button Snake Root: as part of the offering to the fire (*HAI,* 100) and as an emetic drink (*HAI,* 102). Benjamin Hawkins also noted the use of the root, a powerful emetic, at the Busk. He termed the concoction *possau* (*Writings,* 1: 322–24). Major Caleb Swan reported that "button snake-root, or senneca" was taken on the second day of the Busk and was used "in such quantities as often to injure their health by producing spasms, &c." ("Position and State of Manners," 268).

111. Watermelons (*Citrullus lanatus* [Thunberg] Matsumara & Nakai) are native to Africa but were brought to Florida by the Spanish. They were widely cultivated by Florida Indians and spread rapidly throughout the Southeast. For instance, during the Cherokee War, in July 1760, a Chickasaw war party surprised three Cherokee warriors eating watermelons near the town of Toxaway (*Pennsylvania Gazette,* September 4, 1760). For more on this topic, see Leonard W. Blake, "Early Acceptance of Watermelon by Indians of the United States," *Journal of Ethnobiology* 1 (1981): 193–99.

112. Although Adair identifies fire as "the breath master," more generally the Creek Indians identified the sacred fire as the earthly representative of the supreme deity, who is generally identified as "Master of Breath" by interpreters and appears repeatedly in speeches of the period. According to Bartram, "They have no notion or conception of any other God but the Great Spirit on High, the Giver & Taker Away of the Breath of Life—which is as much as to say that Eternal Supreme being who created & governs the Universe. They worship none else" (*Bartram on the Southeastern Indians,* 145 for quotation, 148–50).

113. Two containers associated with the fire ritual are described in Brett H. Riggs, "Archaeological Evidence of Fire Ceremonialism in the Late Prehistoric Southeast," *McClung Museum Research Notes Number 11* (September 1992).

114. Amid music and dancing.

115. "Every table abstains from animals that have wool. It is a crime there to kill a kid" (Juvenal, *Satires* 15.11–12).

116. For a clearer picture of the standard seating arrangement in a Creek square ground, see Hawkins, *Writings,* 1:318–19. Bartram is the best source for the architecture and arrangement of the cabins in the Creek square ground (*Bartram on the Southeastern Indians,* 168–76).

117. The "Mississippi Floridians" were usually called the "Nations on the Mississippi" or the "Small Tribes on the Mississippi." They included the remnants of the Biloxi, Houma, Tunica, and others. These towns were on the eastern side of the Mississippi River in territory that became part of British West Florida after the Seven Years' War. For more on the small tribes see Daniel H. Usner, Jr., *American Indians in the Lower Mississippi Valley: Social and Economic Histories* (Lincoln: University of Nebraska Press, 1998), 33–55. On their tenure under British rule, see Robin F. A. Fabel, *Colonial Challenges: Britons, Native Americans, and Caribs, 1759–1775* (Gainesville: University Press of Florida, 2000), 88 ff.

118. Ethnologist Jason Baird Jackson suggests that Adair's "feast of love" represents a community-oriented as opposed to a martial ceremony. Such feasts are usually held in the spring and involve not only gendered food exchange and ball play but also contain references to the cycle of natural rebirth and social relations (pers. comm. with the editor, March 19, 2003). Although the Yuchi are not those to whom Adair refers, Jackson's analysis of the Yuchi ceremonial cycle provides an excellent starting point for those seeking information on southeastern Indian ceremonialism (see *Yuchi Ceremonial Life*). Elsewhere (*HAI,* 403) Adair defines "feast of love" as a town feast. In the example he provides, the town feast celebrates a successful fishing expedition.

119. By the early 1770s, Coosa Old Town had been virtually deserted. Taitt wrote in 1772 that it was "mostly grown over with small oaks, people from Tallassiehatchie are now building houses and making plantations where the old town formerly stood" ("David Taitt's Journal," *DAR,* 5: 266). The town was on the east bank of the Coosa River, approximately 100 miles from Tuckabatchee, and appeared on Taitt's map of the Creek country. See "A Map of West Florida, part of East Florida, Georgia and part of South Carolina" [Stuart-Gage map], William L. Clements Library, Ann Arbor, Michigan. See also Marvin T. Smith, *Coosa: The Rise and Fall of a Southeastern Mississippian Chiefdom,* Ripley P. Bullen Series of the Florida Museum of Natural History (Gainesville: University Press of Florida, 2000).

120. Creek and Seminole Indians used gourd masks in their Old People's Dance. See James H. Howard, *Oklahoma Seminoles: Medicines, Magic, and Religion,* Willie Lena, collaborator (Norman: University of Oklahoma Press, 1984), 177–78. See also Frank G. Speck, *Gourds of the Southeastern Indians: A Prolegomenon on the Lagenaria*

Gourd in the Culture of the Southeastern Indians (Boston: New England Gourd Society, 1941). This ceremonial dance is very different from the better-known "booger dance" of the Cherokee, which usually took place in the fall. See Raymond D. Fogelson and Amelia R. Bell, "Cherokee Booger Mask Tradition," in *The Power of Symbols: Masks and Masquerade in the Americas,* edited by N. Ross Crumrine and Marjorie Halpin, 48–69 (Vancouver: University of British Columbia Press, 1983).

121. As Charles Hudson has noted, Adair clearly observed women—likely those in his own household—making this "daily sacrifice," but in the case of Indian men his prose reveals that he had to rely on white traders who had fully adopted the Indian "religious system" for information about the practices of Indian men. Since Adair was not a "proselyte," some behavior was closed to his observation because Indians did not practice their rituals freely in the presence of those with "contrary principles" (Hudson, "James Adair as Anthropologist," 319–20). The passage is also instructive for it reveals the degree to which some white traders converted to Indian beliefs and customs. For another example, see *HAI,* 238–39.

122. Romans likewise observed that the Creeks "make a caustick salt out of a kind of moss found at the bottom of creeks and rivers, which although a vegetable salt, does not deliquiate on exposing to the air" (*Concise Natural History,* 145). See also William W. Winn, *The Old Beloved Path: Daily Life among the Indians of the Chattahoochee River Valley* (Eufaula, Ala.: Historic Chattahoochee Commission, 1992), 66.

123. John Pope confirms Adair's observations on the practice among the Creek Indians: "The *Creeks* regularly make a Burnt Offering of what they conceive to be the most delicious Parts of every Animal taken in Hunting, before they presume to taste a Mouthful. The Parts they commit to the Flames are proportioned to the Size of the Animal, probably about 2 or 3 lb. from a *Buffalo,* and still less in a regular gradation down to the smallest Quadrupede, Fish or Bird" (*A Tour through the Southern and Western Territories,* 59).

124. Adair mentions "religious ablutions and purifications in any deep clean water" (*HAI,* 25) throughout his work. For an examination on the significance of the ritual among the Cherokee, see Alan Kilpatrick, "Going to the Water: A Structural Analysis of Cherokee Purification Rituals," *American Indian Culture and Research Journal* 15 (1991): 49–58.

125. As Adair notes, bleeding a person by dry scratching could provide a corrective to unacceptable behavior. Wet scratching was used to cure illness or to restore proper balance. For an interesting attempted use of dry scratching to "remedy" Bartram's transgression against the snake world, see *Bartram on the Southeastern Indians,* 70–71. Charles Hudson suggests that the humiliation of being dry scratched was more painful than the actual scarification (*Southeastern Indians,* 232–33).

126. "Whence now so many perfumes? Flying hither through the breezes, you breathe them out and rain them down," a Neo-Latin translation of Anacreon's fifteenth ode (originally Greek).

127. Hair "curled with hot iron, and wet with myrrh" (Virgil, *Aeneid* 12.100).

128. The importance of bear oil in southeastern Indian culture cannot be overstated. It was prized as a cooking oil and a condiment and also served as a hair

dressing and skin conditioner. Not only was it prized for its emollient properties, but reportedly it had the additional benefit of repelling bugs and mosquitoes. It was also used to dress wounds. By the middle of the eighteenth century, it had also become a valuable trade item. See *Bartram on the Southeastern Indians,* 60, 63, 120, and Romans, *Concise Natural History,* 145. See *HAI,* 415, for Adair's discussion of bear oil and fat as food.

129. Scholars have relied heavily on James Adair's conceptualization of southeastern Indian ritual in terms of "purity" and "pollution" or "uncleanness." For a discussion on the topic, see Mary C. Churchill, "The Oppositional Paradigm of Purity versus Pollution in Charles Hudson's *The Southeastern Indians*," *American Indian Quarterly* 20 (Fall 1996): 563–93, and Charles Hudson, "Reply to Mary Churchill," *American Indian Quarterly* 24 (Summer 2000): 494–502.

130. Adair is referring to menstrual separation. The best study of the topic to date is Patricia Galloway, "Where Have All the Menstrual Huts Gone? The Invisibility of Menstrual Seclusion in the Late Prehistoric Southeast," in *Women and Prehistory: North America and Mesoamerica,* edited by Cheryl Claassen and Rosemary A. Joyce (Philadelphia: University of Pennsylvania Press, 1997), 47–62. See also J. Michelle Schohn, "A Lodge of Their Own: A Look at Vessel Function at a Possible Cofitachequi Women's Lodge" (Master's thesis, University of South Carolina, 2001). For the Cherokee view on menstruating women, see Perdue, *Cherokee Women,* 30–31. For an account of the Choctaw male view of food prepared by women during their "retreat," see John R. Swanton, "An Early Account of the Choctaw Indians," *Memoirs of the American Anthropological Association,* vol. 5, no. 2 (April–June 1918): 60.

131. Adair's account of Dark-lanthorn's conversion inspired Cherokee scholar Raymond D. Fogelson to examine the status of women in Cherokee society in "On the 'Petticoat Government' of the Eighteenth-Century Cherokee," in *Personality and the Cultural Construction of Society,* edited by D. K. Jordan and M. J. Swartz (Tuscaloosa: University of Alabama Press, 1990), 161–81.

132. Literally, a rare bird, used in the sense of a prodigy.

133. Romans also reported euthanasia among the Choctaw: "if a disorder is obstinate or incurable, the relations of the patient assemble in his house, bewail his misfortune, cry bitterly, take their leave of him, and he tells them how tired he is of life, that his misfortunes are unsufferable, and that it is good he should die; upon this an universal howl is raised, the nearest male relation jumps on him, and violently in a moment breaks the neck of the patient, and then they rejoice that his misery is over, but lamentations for his departure soon succeed" (*Concise Natural History,* 140). Regarding the Creeks, Bartram made it a point to inquire on reports he had heard that the old and infirm were routinely killed by family members. Indian traders told him that mercy killings, to their knowledge, were performed only at the request of the victim (*Bartram on the Southeastern Indians,* 119). Choctaw mortuary practices are mentioned more fully on p. 183 of the original text.

134. The common chicken. As indicated by Adair's conversation with the woman (most likely a Chickasaw), southeastern Indians found both domestic poultry and swine abhorrent at first due to the fact that both feed on garbage and in refuse

heaps, but they eventually overcame their distaste. This seems to have been particularly true in the case of Indian women whose European husbands brought up the animals and had their wives or "domestics" learn to cook European-style foods. See *HAI,* 143–45, and Swanton, "An Early Account of the Choctaw Indians," 67.

135. This is most likely rabies. Most southeastern Indians, including the Creek, Chickasaw, and Cherokee Indians, generally attributed many illnesses and diseases to animal origin, usually as a result of some offense or insult to the animal spirit. Many diseases were known by the name of the species thought responsible for the disease. On the other hand, plants were seen as curative. For more on the disease theory of southeastern Indians, see Howard, *Oklahoma Seminoles,* 20–21. For a list of diseases associated with various animal species by the Chickasaw, see Swanton, "Social and Religious Beliefs and Usages of the Chickasaw Indians," 266–68. See also Swanton, "Religious Beliefs and Medical Practices of the Creek Indians," 636–47; James Mooney, "Cherokee Theory and Practice of Medicine," *Journal of American Folklore* 3 (1890): 44–50; Robert F. Greenlee, "Medicine and Curing Practices of the Modern Florida Seminole," *American Anthropologist* 46 (1944): 317–28; T. N. Campbell, "Medicinal Plants used by Choctaw, Chickasaw, and Creek Indians in the Early Nineteenth Century," *Journal of the Washington Academy of Sciences* 41 (September 1951): 285–90; and Waselkov and Braund, eds., *William Bartram on the Southeastern Indians,* 276–77.

136. Adair's description suggests mumps. The most obvious sign of mumps is swelling of the cheeks and jaw, caused by inflammation in the salivary glands, and usually accompanied by fever and headache. Swelling of the testicles occurs in 15 to 25 percent of infected males.

137. The Cape or Florida Indians was the name given to several remnant groups, including the Calusa, whom the Creek Indians preyed upon from the 1740s through the 1760s. Other tribes settled in mission villages around St. Augustine as protection from Creek raiders included Tocobaga, Jororo, and Pohoy Indians. When Spain withdrew from St. Augustine, their mission Indians evacuated with them. See Jerald T. Milanich, *Florida's Indians from Ancient Times to the Present* (Gainesville: University Press of Florida, 1998), 175–76. Romans reported that "about eighty families" removed with the Spanish (*Concise Natural History,* 260).

138. One might render Adair's Latin phrase "Eunuch with foreskin uncovered or removed"—a circumcised eunuch. See Charlton T. Lewis and Charles Short, *A Latin Dictionary. Founded on Andrews' edition of Freund's Latin dictionary. revised, enlarged, and in great part rewritten by. Charlton T. Lewis, Ph.D. and. Charles Short, LL.D* (1879; reprint, Oxford: Clarendon Press, 1975). Charles Hudson translated the phrase as "Eunuch, your foreskin is uncovered" ("James Adair as Anthropologist," 24: 316). Whatever Adair meant to imply, what the Indians actually meant is another matter entirely. The insult seems to have been directed at the size of the penis or lack of testicles (castration) rather than a reference to circumcision. On the following page, Adair reports that the Catawba insulted the Cherokee by calling them "short-tailed eunuchs." See also *HAI,* 190, for a reference to *"pene brevi"* or short penis and 137 for castration. In effect, the insult robbed a warrior of his male identity.

The fact that Indians did employ circumcision was the fatal flaw in the Jewish theory, as noted by Romans (*Concise Natural History,* 114). Even earlier, Hamon L'Estrande in *Americans no Jewes, or Improbabilities that the Americans are of that race* (London: Henry Seile, 1652), 46, had denounced the Hebrew theory on this ground. Here, Adair makes an obvious attempt to satisfy this argument. What American Indians thought of circumcised men, they clearly considered the epithet "eunuch" as inflammatory. At the 1765 Congress of Mobile, Tomatly Mingo of Ceneacha, a Great Medal Chief from the Six Villages division, complained to the governor of West Florida and the assembled British representatives that the traders "often Treat our Warriours with Indecent Language they often call them Eunuchs (Ubacktubac) which is the most opprobrious Term that can be used in our Language" (*MPAED,* 238).

139. This was actually in 1751. See Adair's letter to William Pinckney, May 7, 1751, in William L. McDowell, Jr., ed., *Documents Relating to Indian Affairs, May 21, 1750–August 7, 1754,* Colonial Records of South Carolina, ser. 2 (Columbia: South Carolina Archives Department, 1958), 56.

140. Adair is referring to the fact that the Jews did not perform circumcision on those born during the time in the wilderness. As he notes, Joshua reimposed the practice (Joshua 5:2–9). See Werblowsky and Wigoden, eds., *Oxford Dictionary of the Jewish Religion,* s.v. "Circumcision." One of Adair's primary sources, Thomas Thorowgood, discussed the "fact" that Americans (Indians) did perform circumcision and implies the use of stone knives, pointing out the biblical references to their use by Jews as well as American Indians (*Jewes in America,* 9). Here, Adair is obviously attempting to explain why uncircumcised Americans would have forgone the use of such instruments.

141. A *sponsalia de futuro* is a betrothal of the future, in which the vows taken are done in a future tense. Under Catholic Church law, this betrothal could be broken so long as no consummation had taken place. A *sponsalia de presenti* is the actual wedding, which was valid from that point forward.

142. *Usucapio* is a legal term indicating the acquisition of ownership by virtue of long possession or long use—in this case, a common law marriage or wife.

143. By purchase.

144. For an examination of the problems European men encountered in understanding and describing Indian women and issues of sexuality, see Theda Perdue, "Native Women in the Early Republic: Old World Perceptions, New World Realities," in *Native Americans in the Early Republic,* edited by Frederick E. Hoxie and Ronald Hoffman (Charlottesville: University Press of Virginia, 1998), 85–122. See also Perdue, *Cherokee Women,* 44–45, 56–59.

145. Bartram provided details on how one injured Creek husband took his revenge on an adulterous trader by gathering a party of warriors, who "armed themselves with knotty cudgels of green Hickory, which they concealed under their mantles" and then paid the trader a visit. When they had the trader alone and outside, he was stripped and beaten. On this occasion, he managed to escape before he lost his ears (*Bartram on the Southeastern Indians,* 101). The identity of the men mentioned

by Adair has not been ascertained to date. The "disciple of Black Beard, the pirate," must have been a hardy soul indeed. Black Beard (Edward Teach) was executed for piracy in 1718.

146. The practice of scalping was an ancient one, predating the arrival of Europeans. For a discussion of scalping and its importance to the Creeks, see Le Clerc Milfort, *Memoirs or A Quick Glance at my various Travels and my Sojourn in the Creek Nation,* translated and edited by Ben C. McCary (Kennesaw, Ga.: Continental Book Company, 1959), 154–56. For a broader historical perspective on the practice, see James Axtell, "The Moral Dilemmas of Scalping," in Axtell, *Natives and Newcomers,* 259–79.

147. For an examination of the concept of retaliation, see Patricia Galloway, "The Barthelemy Murders: Bienville's Establishment of the *Lex Talionis* as a Principle of Indian Diplomacy," *Proceedings of the Eighth Annual Meeting of the French Colonial Historical Society, 1982,* edited by E. P. Fitzgerald (Lanham, Md.: University Press of America, 1985), 91–103. John Phillip Reid has explored Cherokee law in two volumes: *A Law of Blood: The Primitive Law of the Cherokee Nation* (New York: New York University Press, 1970) and *A Better Kind of Hatchet.*

148. The law of retribution: "an eye for an eye, a tooth for a tooth."

149. By the 1760s, the Creek Indians had virtually destroyed the indigenous tribes of Florida with war and slave raids. The most famous expeditions, against Apalachee, were undertaken in conjunction with Carolinians. After the destruction of the Apalachee missions, the Creeks continued their raids of the Calusa and other "cape" tribes. See Allan Gallay, *The Indian Slave Trade: The Rise of the English Empire in the American South, 1670–1717* (New Haven: Yale University Press, 2002).

150. Here Adair refers to the unsuccessful French expeditions against the Chickasaw in 1736, led by Jean-Baptiste Le Moyne de Bienville and Major Pierre d'Artaguette, and another in 1740. Adair provides a more detailed account of the Franco-Chickasaw wars beginning on p. 354 of the original edition.

151. Okchai was an Upper Creek town.

152. Malatchi, the headman of Coweta, informed Glen of the murder of these two men "near the Coosaws" and later mentioned the incident at a conference held in Charleston in May 1753. According to him, their fear of reprisals owing to the murders kept the Cherokee headmen from attending the conference. See McDowell, ed., *Documents Relating to Indian Affairs, 1750–1754,* 394 (quotation), 400.

153. Two Shawnee towns can be identified among the Creeks. The first to be settled appears on maps and in documentary sources as Savannuca, Sawanogi, or Swaglaws. According to Edmond Atkin, this town of about 45 gunmen was first settled in early 1744, and he indicates that they settled seven miles below Fort Toulouse because of their regard for the French. Contacts between the Creeks and the Shawnees can be documented much earlier, for by 1730 Creeks had admitted Shawnees into their confederacy. Peter Chartier's group of 140 gunmen also hoped to settle near Fort Toulouse, but the Creeks required them to settle away from the fort, on the northern edge of Creek town settlements on the Coosa River, near the town of Coosa. This Shawnee town, Chillachcaggees (or Shalachcaggie), appears on

the William Bonar map of 1757, as does Oswagloes. Atkin says the Shawnee settled in two towns, but other sources do not confirm it. All the Shawnees, with the exception of Cartier's band, declared their allegiance for the British during the Seven Years' War. Other Shawnees moved into Muccolossus and Tuckabatchee, two leading Tallapoosa towns that were also pro-British (Atkin, *Report,* 65; Kathryn H. Braund, "Classification of Creek Towns," paper presented at the sixty-second annual meeting of the Society for American Archaeology. Nashville, Tennessee, April 5, 1997; McDowell, ed., *Documents Relating to Indian Affairs, 1750–1754,* 215). A French census of the early 1760s likewise lists two Shawnee (Chaouanon) towns: Chalakagay with a population of 50 gunmen and Petilchaouanons (Oswegglees), also with a population of 50 gunmen (*MPAED,* 94–96). See also *MPAFD,* 4: 28, 5: 48.

154. Southeastern Indians frequently used such titles for various civil and war offices, although their exact status and official functions are not clear.

155. For a discussion of white or "holy" towns, see Hudson, *Southeastern Indians,* 238–39. As Adair mentions on p. 195, these towns were generally the oldest or "mother" towns.

156. Adair's organizing principles of purity and pollution have been exceedingly influential in modern interpretations of southeastern Indians. See Churchill, "The Oppositional Paradigm of Purity versus Pollution in Charles' Hudson's *The Southeastern Indians,*" and Hudson, "Reply to Mary Churchill."

157. Benjamin Hawkins reported the use of possau (Button Snake Root) as part of the "war physic" (*Writings,* 1: 324). For the use of the root by the Creeks and Seminole, see Charles H. Fairbanks, "The Function of Black Drink among the Creeks," in *Black Drink: A Native American Tea,* edited by Charles M. Hudson (Athens: University of Georgia Press, 1979), 120–49.

158. The "Indian ark" described by Adair is a medicine bundle. The contents varied by tribe, but the usual contents were sacred herbs and minerals and, among the Cherokee, vessels containing coals from a sacred fire (Hudson, *Southeastern Indians,* 244). Vernon James Knight, Jr., links the Chickasaw ark described by Adair to earlier Mississippian cult institutions in "Institutional Organization of Mississippian Religion," *American Antiquity* 51 (1986): 682.

159. Osteneco, or Judd's Friend, the Second Warrior of the Overhills, led Cherokee warriors against the Shawnee town of Scioto on the Ohio in 1756. See E. Raymond Evans, "Notable Persons in Cherokee History: Ostenaco," *Journal of Cherokee Studies* 2 (Summer 1976): 41–56. For information on the failed Big Sandy expedition, a combination of Cherokee and provincial Virginia troops, see Corkran, *Cherokee Frontier,* 66–67. Ostenaco was among the three Cherokee who traveled with Lieutenant Henry Timberlake to England in 1762. See Carolyn Thomas Foreman, *Indians Abroad, 1493–1938* (Norman: University of Oklahoma Press, 1943), 65–81.

160. Adair is relating a version of Chickasaw and Choctaw migration history. For an overview of the topic, see Galloway, *Choctaw Genesis,* 331–37. For an analysis of the famous Creek migrations legend, including a discussion of the meaning of the "rod" or warpole, see Amelia Bell Walker, "The Kasihta Myth," *Anthropology Tomorrow* 12 (1979): 46–63. An older but still useful study of the Creek migration

myth is Albert S. Gatschet, *A Migration Legend of the Creek Indians,* vol. 1, Brinton's Library of Aboriginal American Literature, number IV (1884; reprint, New York: AMS Press, 1969).

161. Temporarily.

162. Captain Jacob was the leading warrior of the Delaware. In the early stages of the Seven Years' War, after being refused aid by the English, the Delaware Indians joined the French. Captain Jacob terrorized the back settlements of Pennsylvania and Virginia until he was killed in a raid on the town of Upper Kittanning in 1756. See Fred Anderson, *Crucible of War: The Seven Years' War and the Fate of Empire in British North America, 1754–1766* (New York: Alfred A. Knopf, 2000), 109–10, 162–64. For an examination of captivity narratives, see June Namias, *White Captives: Gender and Ethnicity on the American Frontier* (Chapel Hill: University of North Carolina Press, 1993). Adair's comments regarding sexual violation of female captives is generally true. Regarding Captain Jacob's comments, Adair was citing *A Narrative of the Sufferings and Surprizing Deliverance of William and Elizabeth Fleming, Who were taken captive by Capt. Jacob . . . ,* an account published in Philadelphia in 1756: "They [Captain Jacob and his warriors] then told me not to be afraid that they should abuse my Wife, for they would not do it for Fear of affronting their God (and pointed their Hands toward Heaven) for the Man that affronts his God, will surely be kill'd when he goes out to War; this, continued they, is what makes the English have such bad Luck" (16). The Flemings' narrative is available in reprint in the Garland Library of Narratives of North American Indian Captivities, vol. 8 (New York: Garland, 1968).

163. For a brief discussion of sexual taboo surrounding captive women, see Axtell, *Natives and Newcomers,* 197–98.

164. If Adair's date of 1765 is correct, he is referring to the expedition of Major Robert Farmar up the Mississippi to take possession of several French forts, including Fort Rosalie and Fort Chartres. The Chickasaw assisted the expedition by providing fresh meat and protecting them from potentially hostile tribes. For an account of the expedition, see Robert R. Rea, *Major Robert Farmar of Mobile* (Tuscaloosa: University of Alabama Press, 1990). In a 1766 report to the British government in West Florida, Adair mentioned the expedition to "the Illinois" (A Memorandum of some Material Heads of what was lately transacted in the Chickasaw Nation, February 26, 1766, CO323/21, pt. 1, fo. 73).

165. Adair's comments are true of Indian-European conferences as well. For a discussion of Creek ceremony at one such conference, see Kathryn E. Holland Braund, "'The Congress Held in a Pavilion': John Bartram and the Creek Indian Congress at Picolata, 1765," in *America's Curious Botanist,* edited by Nancy E. Hoffman and John C. Van Horn, Memoirs of the American Philosophical Society, No. 249 (Philadelphia: APS, 2004), 79–96.

166. Adair's trip to the Cherokee Lower Towns dates to 1751. See his letter to Pinckney in McDowell, ed., *Documents Relating to Indian Affairs, 1750–1754,* 56.

167. For Augusta's history, see Edward J. Cashin, ed., *Colonial Augusta: "Key of the Indian Countrey"* (Macon, Ga.: Mercer University Press, 1986).

168. Here, Adair extends the name Mobile River to its eastern tributary, the Alabama River. Adair's Kooasahte was Coosada, a town on the Alabama River three to four miles below the junction of the Tallapoosa and Alabama rivers (Braund, "Classification of Creek Towns"). "Cusatees" is shown on William Bonar's 1757 map.

169. Although Adair mentions the famous use of wampum by the Narragansett Indians, such belts are not so well known in the South. However, southeastern Indians did exchange beaded belts in the historic period, although by that time, the shells had been replaced by beads of European manufacture. Southeastern Indians used beads primarily as ornaments and on clothing (Braund, *Deerskins and Duffels,* 123–24). For an examination of the importance of beads, both symbolic and economic, in North American Indian culture, see Christopher L. Miller and George R. Hamell, "A New Perspective on Indian-White Contact: Cultural Symbols and Colonial Trade," *Journal of American History* 73 (1986): 311–28. See also George R. Hamell, "The Iroquois and the World's Rim: Speculations on Color, Culture, and Contact," *American Indian Quarterly* 16 (Fall 1992): 451–69. For an analysis of the variety of beads found at one West Florida location, see Gregory A. Waselkov and Bonnie L. Gums, *Plantation Archaeology at Rivière aux Chiens, ca. 1725–1848* (Mobile: University of South Alabama Center for Archaeological Studies, 2000), 164–66, 185–89, 195–200.

170. Bartram also described the process. See *Bartram on the Southeastern Indians,* 120–21. Romans's portrait, "Characteristic Head of a Creek War Chief" (*Concise Natural History,* 143), ably illustrates the result of the ear deformation.

171. For information on gourds, see Speck, *Gourds of the Southeastern Indians.*

172. This incident, in addition to exposing Adair's mischievous side, provides clues as to the common curatives used in the eighteenth century. His Roman vitriol was probably sulphate of copper. Alum is potassium aluminum sulfate, generally used as an astringent and a styptic. For a look at the contents of an eighteenth-century medical kit, see *Medicine in Colonial Massachusetts, 1620–1820,* Publications of the Colonial Society of Massachusetts, vol. 57 (Boston: Colonial Society of Massachusetts by the University Press of Virginia, 1980). *Sheela na Guira* is an Irish folk melody.

173. The "Negroe-Banger" is a banjo, the earliest of which were made from gourds specifically cut and fitted with leather and usually strung with four strings. For information on the banjo's early history, see Dena J. Epstein, "The Folk Banjo: A Documentary History," *Ethnomusicology* 19 (Summer 1975): 347–71.

174. Asafetida, *Ferula foetida* (Regel.), is also known as devil's dung because of its odor. A resin obtained from the root is used as a carminative and a laxative. Jesuit's bark is Cinchona, which contains quinine and is used for malarial and typhoid fevers. The usual substitute for this medicinal plant in the Southeast was the bark of the Cucumber magnolia (*Magnolia acuminata* L.) (Foster and Duke, *A Field Guide to Medicinal Plants of Eastern and Central North America,* 318).

175. Samuel 18:10 reads, "The next day an evil spirit from God came forcefully upon Saul." In Latin: *post diem autem alteram invasit spiritus Dei malus Saul.* The verb should be *carpo,* as in to seize, thus, seized by madness.

176. Lactantius was a fourth-century scholar whose *Divinae Institutiones* was the first comprehensive survey of Christian theology compared to pagan beliefs.

177. Alan Kilpatrick mistakenly identifies this individual as a Cherokee medicine man in his work on Cherokee witchcraft, in spite of the fact that Adair was known to be in the Chickasaw towns in 1765 and specifically attributes "old Chikkasah virtues" to his visitor. See *The Night Has a Naked Soul,* 63. For a discussion of witches, see Raymond D. Fogelson, "An Analysis of Cherokee Sorcery and Witchcraft," in *Four Centuries of Southern Indians,* edited by Charles M. Hudson (Athens: University of Georgia Press, 1975), 113–31, and Hudson, *Southeastern Indians,* 174–83.

178. For a detailed description of the personal effects recovered at one Creek burial, see Smith, *Coosa,* 110–12. Interestingly, this burial included a copper plate, much as described by Adair.

179. Malatchi of Coweta (Opiya Mico) was recognized by Georgia as the leading spokesman for Coweta following the death of Brims. Georgia documentary records list Brims as his father. Malatchi is probably best known for his role in the land title controversies with Georgia and his relative, Mary Musgrove. He died in 1756. On his career, see Corkran, *Creek Frontier,* 119 ff.; Juricek, ed., *Georgia Treaties, 1733–1763,* 179, and McDowell, ed., *Documents Relating to Indian Affairs, 1754–1765,* 103. Speculation on the Brims-Malatchi "dynasty" has given rise to a number of interpretations regarding the relationship of kinship and authority among the Creeks; see William S. Willis, Jr., "Patrilineal Institutions in Southeastern North America," *Ethnohistory* 10 (Winter 1963): 250–69. More recently, Vernon J. Knight, Jr., has attempted to reconcile matrilineal kinship, agnatic inheritance of political offices, and Mississippian aristocratic organization; see "Social Organization and the Evolution of Hierarchy in Southeastern Chiefdoms," *Journal of Anthropological Research* 46 (Spring 1990): 16–17. The determination of Oglethorpe to secure a single spokesman for the Lower Creeks, the lack of comprehension of matrilineal kinship by the English and their insistence on patrilineal succession, and their desire to wring land from the Creeks continue to mire our understanding of the true power structure at Coweta.

180. The practice Adair describes—the collection and reinterment of disarticulated bones—is called bundle burials by modern archaeologists. For an examination of types and meaning of Chickasaw burials, see Jay K. Johnson, "Ethnohistory, Archaeology, and Chickasaw Burial Mode during the Eighteenth Century," *Ethnohistory* 41 (Summer 1994): 431–46.

181. Old Bracket, also variously spelled Brisket or Brekit, was the venerable head warrior of Tuckabatchee; his official title was Ispokogi Mico. He was, according to South Carolina agent Daniel Pepper, "a firm and true Friend to the English." When the Shawnee and Cherokee tried to turn the Creeks against the British during the Seven Years' War, Old Bracket, "although one hundred and forty Years old . . . stuck his Head full of Turkey Buzzard Feathers, painted himself in a warlike Manner, and . . . gave them such a strong Talk that seemed to strike Terror in the stoutest of them" (McDowell, ed., *Documents Relating to Indian Affairs, 1754–1765,* 253; Juricek, ed., *Georgia Treaties, 1733–1763,* 220).

182. Many other visitors described the plates, including Caleb Swan at the end of the eighteenth century and George Stiggins in the early nineteenth. The plates (or celts) were ceremonially transported west during the forced removal of the Tuckabatchee from their homeland. For the best summary of sources concerning the plates, including an analysis of the ceremonial significance of copper plates and spatulate axes, see Howard, *The Southeastern Ceremonial Complex,* 64–74. See also Marvin T. Smith, "Early Historic Period Vestiges of the Southern Cult," in *The Southeastern Ceremonial Complex: Artifacts and Analysis, The Cottonlandia Conference,* edited by Patricia Galloway, 142–46 (Lincoln: University of Nebraska Press, 1989). See E. S. Greer, Jr., "A Tukabahchee Plate from the Coosa River," *Journal of Alabama Archaeology* 12 (1996): 156–58, for a description of a copper plate recovered from a burial at the Whorton's Bend site in Alabama. Vernon James Knight, Jr., attempts to reconcile the plates with the ethnic affiliation of the town ("Tukatatchee: Archaeological Investigations at an Historic Creek Town, Elmore County, Alabama, 1984," Report of Investigations 45, Office of Archaeological Research, Alabama State Museum of Natural History, University of Alabama, 1985). For a discussion of aboriginal sheet brass ornaments (gorgets), see Gregory A. Waselkov, "Seventeenth-Century Trade in the Colonial South," *Southeastern Archaeology* 8 (Winter 1989): 121–27.

183. Adair's description of burial traditions is marred by the fact he witnessed only one burial firsthand. For the best general analysis of eighteenth-century mortuary practices, including an assessment of Adair's evidence, see Galloway, *Choctaw Genesis,* 289–304. The Chickasaw burial described by Adair is almost certainly that of "the old Jockey," described elsewhere in Adair's work as Pastabe (*HAI,* 314). The Jockey died at the Breed Camp (Ooeasa) in January 1754, "much lamented by both white and red. . . . He was always a Friend to all white People" (McDowell, ed., *Documents Relating to Indian Affairs, 1750–1754,* 510). Adair also mentions the death of Pahemingo-Amalahta, a warrior who died of consumption at Augusta (*HAI,* 314–15). The description given here—"a great favourite of the English, and chieftain of Ooeasa"—more closely matches the description of the Jockey. Moreover, Adair's description suggests interment in a house, noting clay was used to cap the tomb "on a level with the rest of the floor" (*HAI,* 182). Presumably this fits the circumstances of a burial in the village of Ooeasa better than in Augusta.

184. Adair describes a Chickasaw burial. Compare with Romans's account of the manner in which the Creek Indians interred their dead: "The dead are buried in a sitting posture, and they are furnished with a musket, powder and ball, a hatchet, pipe, some tobacco, a club, a bow and arrows, a looking glass, some vermilion and other trinkets, in order to come well provided in the world of spirits" (*Concise Natural History,* 148). Archaeological evidence confirms Romans's observations; see Diane S. Mueller, "Intrasite Settlement at the Historic Creek Town of Hickory Ground (1EE8), Elmore County, Alabama (1990–1991)," *Journal of Alabama Archaeology* 41 (December 1995): 107–34. According to archaeologist Gregory Waselkov, "most historic Creek burials are on their backs with the arms flexed at the elbows, hands to one side or on the chest, and legs flexed and drawn up to one side." A few

Creek burials have been found with the body actually sitting upright (pers. comm. with the editor, March 13, 2003). It seems likely that when contemporary observers noted that bodies were buried in "sitting posture," they actually meant a flexed burial.

185. "Do not touch me, heretics, neither in life nor in death."

186. Romans also provided an account of Choctaw mortuary practices, as well as a drawing of a Choctaw burial (*Concise Natural History,* 140–42). See also Bartram's short report in *Bartram on the Southeastern Indians,* 129. For an analysis of Choctaw practices in relation to other tribes, see Patricia Galloway, "Confederacy as a Solution to Chiefdom Dissolution," in *The Forgotten Centuries: Indians and Europeans in the American South, 1521–1704,* edited by Charles Hudson and Carmen Chaves Tesser (Athens: University of Georgia Press, 1994), 410–12, and Galloway, *Choctaw Genesis,* 276–304. For an early French account of Choctaw burial practices, see Swanton, "An Early Account of the Choctaw Indians," 5: 64–65.

187. John Lawson likewise noted the "heaps of Stones" left as monuments to dead warriors (*New Voyage to Carolina,* 50).

188. Crossroads gods.

189. This partial quote is from Arnobius, *Adversus Gentes,* Book 1. The translation for the full quotation would read: "When I have met with a smooth stone, smeared with oil, supposing a spiritual power to be connected with it, I worshiped it, paid my addresses to it, and requested blessings."

190. Thomas Nairne, who briefly visited the Chickasaw in 1708, reported that Chickasaw widows mourned for one year, after which time they could be remarried to a "nigh kinsman" (i.e., brother or other close clan member of the deceased) (*Nairne's Muskhogean Journals,* 48–49). Romans likewise noted that the mourning continued "for about a year" (*Concise Natural History,* 129). Here, Adair seems to distinguish between the period of mourning ("the first year of her widowhood") in which the widow is required to perform daily lamentations and the length of time required before she could remarry (three years for Chickasaw women and four for Creek women). Taitt reported Creek women were required to "remain a widow four years" ("David Taitt's Journal," *DAR,* 5: 269).

191. A reference to the battle involving Colonel Archibald Montgomery's forces, near War Woman's Creek in June of 1760 (Corkran, *Cherokee Frontier,* 210–15).

192. The general thrust of these insulting remarks calls to question the individual's male attributes. By denouncing a man as having no testicles (eunuch) and a short penis (*pene brevi*), the widows are, in effect, denouncing the men who spurn them as being not truly men. Adair's fixation on the Hebrew theory and his attempt to link "short tail" or "short penis" to circumcision merely cloud the issue, for circumcision was not an issue among southeastern Indians until Europeans arrived, and the practice surely raised comment among Indian women married to European men. It is entirely possible that the use of the Indian words to indicate "short tail" was applied to circumcised men—European men—a fact that, if true, Adair failed to appreciate, and it may explain why it was such an insult to Indian men. Although Adair does not indicate this in translation, the Chickasaw word for a sterile or in-

fertile person is *hobak* (*Hoobuk*). It is also likely that the women were accusing the men of impotence as well.

193. Penis with foreskin uncovered.

194. Cyrus Byington, a missionary and highly respected Choctaw linguist, confirms much of Adair's translation of the *Shulashummashtabe,* which was not merely the name of an individual but the title of the war leader of the Choctaw: *shulush* is a moccasin and *humma* is red. *Imastabi* is perhaps better translated as "he who took and killed." Patricia Galloway believes that *shulush* was "a loanword from the French *soulier.*" See Byington, *A Dictionary of the Choctaw Language,* 335, 534, and Galloway, "'So Many Little Republics,'" 533n.27. Generally, the moccasins of the war leader were all red. See *HAI,* 83, for a description of the ceremonial moccasins of the man clearly in charge of a peace ceremony whose toes only were dyed red. It should be noted that Adair's "Archi-magus" was probably a Chickasaw peace chief. Unfortunately, he makes no tribal distinctions regarding the shoes used only at the annual "yearly atonement of sin," or Green Corn Ceremony, and those of the war leader.

195. The Raven of Hiwassee was the head warrior of the Valley Towns and a leading player in the Great Tellico-Hiwassee coalition that sought to counter Chota as the center of Cherokee power. He served as the guardian of Ammonscossittee, the teenage son of the Emperor Moytoy, following Moytoy's death in 1741. Ammonscossittee was eventually disavowed and the title of emperor assumed by Old Hop of Chota. Until his death in 1756, he remained a steady ally of the British (Corkran, *Cherokee Frontier,* 16, 19, 32, 88).

According to De Brahm, Cherokee war titles were awarded on the basis of the number of scalps acquired. The ranks were, in ascending order, slave-catcher, raven, man-killer, warrior (*De Brahm's Report,* 109).

196. Adair relied heavily on Thomas Thorowgood, *Jewes in America, or Probabilities That the Americans are of that Race. With the Removall of some contrary reasonings, and earnest desires for effectuall endeavours to make them Christian* (London: Tho. Slater, 1650), as an authority on Spanish, French, and other early sources, including Laët, Emanuel de Moraes, Acosta, Lerius (de Lery), Peter Martyr, and others. However, a close comparison of the two works reveals that while Adair, according to accepted practice of the times, liberally quotes Thorowgood without attribution, he is not merely repeating Thorowgood's narrative but rather creatively combining sources and information gained from the work, which he then cites. It is also likely that some of his information was derived from other, more contemporary compilations of translated writings, such as Edward Cavendish Drake, *A New Universal Collection of Authentic and Entertaining Voyages and Travels, from the earliest accounts to the present time* (London: J. Cooke, 1768).

197. Such stories, purporting to explain the origin of races, were developed by Native Americans after their encounters with Europeans and Africans. For a thoughtful examination of the development of racial concepts among the Indians, see Kathleen Brown, "Native Americans and Early Modern Concepts of Race," in *Empire and Others: British Encounters with Indigenous Peoples, 1600–1850,* edited by

Martin Daunton and Rick Halpern, 79–100 (Philadelphia: University of Pennsylvania Press, 1999). See also Joyce E. Chaplin, "Natural Philosophy and an Early Racial Idiom in North America: Comparing English and Indian Bodies," *William and Mary Quarterly* 3d ser., 54 (January 1997): 229–52.

198. The Quapaw Indians, allies of the French. For a brief summary of Quapaw history, see George Sabo III, "The Quapaw Indians of Arkansas, 1673–1803," in *Indians of the Greater Southeast: Historical Archaeology and Ethnohistory,* edited by Bonnie G. McEwan, 178–203 (Gainesville: University Press of Florida, 2000).

199. LeClerc Milfort also wrote that during their journey eastward, the Muskoghee lived in caves in "Yazau lands" for a time (*Memoirs,* 145, 160). By "Mississippi-Nachee," Adair is implying the original towns of the Natchez and not those of the refugees settled among the Chickasaw and Creek Indians.

200. Literally, "a son of the earth," meaning a man of unknown origin.

201. For more information on the Chickasaw towns, see *HAI,* 352 ff. Bartram relayed the same information about the migration and horses in his "Observations" (*Bartram on the Southeastern Indians,* 121). A barb is a breed of light horse from North Africa (the Barbary Coast) famous for their speed and endurance and frequently used as pack animals. The story related here seems to be a garbled account of the migration legend as well as accounts of later raids against the Spanish settlements.

202. Peter Martyr d'Anghera (Peter Martyr), charged by the State Council of the Indies with collecting and chronicling Spain's New World activities, had access to explorers and their writers. His *De Orbe Novo,* published in 1520, is considered the earliest and best account of Spain's early history in the New World.

203. José de Acosta's influential two-volume history of the Indies, *Historia natural y moral de las Indias,* first appeared in 1590 and was subsequently reprinted in English, French, Dutch and Italian. For a modern English edition, see *The Natural and Moral History of the Indies by Father Joseph de Acosta reprinted from the English Translated Edition of Edward Grimston, 1604,* edited by Clements R. Markham, 2 vols. (London: Hakluyt Society, 1880). As to the origin of the American Indians, Acosta held that they had traveled overland to America from Tartary and Siberia. See Joan-Pau Rubies, "Hugo Grotius's Dissertation on the Origin of the American Peoples and the Use of Comparative Methods," *Journal of the History of Ideas* 52 (April–June 1991): 224–25. Adair's statement, attributed to Acosta, that the Indians have no proper name for God is likely taken from Thorowgood, *Jewes in America,* 15. For the passage in Acosta's work, see *Natural and Moral History of the Indies,* 2: 301–2. Nahuatl was the language of the Aztec empire.

204. Francisco López de Gómara was the chaplain of Hernándo Cortés after his return from the New World. He had not been a member of the American expedition but composed an account of it based on information from members of the expedition. His *Hispania Victrix; First and Second Parts of the General History of the Indies, with the whole discovery and notable things that have happened since they were acquired until the year 1551, with the conquest of Mexico and New Spain* appeared in 1552. His work was found to be seriously flawed and was banned in 1553 but later appeared in a collection of early historical accounts of the New World by Spanish

writers. His account was reprinted in Pietro Martire d'Anghiera's *The History of Travayle in the West and East Indies . . . ,* translated by Richard Eden and Richard Willes (London, 1577). See Vaughan, "From White Man to Redskin," 923.

205. Gian Battista Ramusio was the foremost editor and translator of sixteenth-century travel literature and published numerous editions of his *Delle Navigazioni e Viaggi.* His version of Álvar Núñez de Cabeza de Vaca's journey appeared in the third volume, published in Venice in 1556. For a fuller account of his writings, see J. H. Parry, *The Age of Reconnaissance: Discovery, Exploration and Settlement 1450–1650* (Berkeley: University of California Press, 1981), 342n.4.

206. Jacques Le Moyne De Morgues, Nicolas Le Challeux, and René Laudonnière were French writers, not Spanish, who all left accounts of the French settlement at Fort Caroline on the St. Johns River, beginning in 1564. In addition to his written account of the failed Florida venture, Le Moyne also left a series of highly detailed drawings. His work was first published in 1591 by Theodore de Bry. See Charles E. Bennett, trans., *Three Voyages: René Laudonnière* (Gainesville: University Presses of Florida, 1975), pp. xvi–xix, and *The New World: The First Pictures of America made by John White and Jacques Le Moyne and engraved by Theodore de Bry, with contemporary narratives of the French settlements in Florida, 1562–1565, and the English colonies in Virginia, 1585–1590,* edited and annotated by Stefan Lorant (New York: Duell, Sloan and Pearce, 1965). For an overview of the French explorations and settlement in Florida, see Carl O. Sauer, *Sixteenth Century North America: The Land and the People as Seen by the Europeans* (Berkeley: University of California Press, 1971), 196–212.

207. Thus passes away the glory of the world.

208. Nicolas Le Challeux's account went through a number of French and English editions and appeared in Girolamo Benzoni, *Histoire nouvelle du Nouveau Monde* (Geneva, 1579). For a modern version, see Lorant, ed., *The New World.*

209. Juan Ortiz, the survivor of the Narváez expedition, was found living among the Florida Indians by De Soto's army and served as their translator until the winter of 1541–42. For his experiences, see Charles M. Hudson, *Knights of Spain, Warriors of the Sun: Hernando de Soto and the South's Ancient Chiefdoms* (Athens: University of Georgia Press, 1997), 80–84, 334.

210. Adair is referring to Girolamo Benzoni, who published a number of works on America. His *Historia del Mondo Nuovo* was first published in Venice in 1565, and his work was later translated into Latin and other languages. His illustrations were published by Theodore De Bry. Generally unfavorable to the Spanish, he also included a Latin translation of Nicolas Le Challeux's account of the destruction of France's colony in his *Novae Novi Orbis Historiae* (Geneva, 1578). Thorowgood frequently cited Benzoni's work as Hieronimus Benzo, *Nova noi orbis Historia* (*Jewes in America,* 1). For an English version of Benzoni's work, see *History of the New World, by Girolamo Benzoni, shewing his travels in America, from A.D. 1541 to 1556, with some particulars of the island of Canary,* translated and edited by W. H. Smyth, Works Issued by the Hakluyt Society, ser. 1, no. 21, 1970 (New York: B. Franklin, 1970).

211. David Ingram was an English sailor who claimed to have landed on the

Florida Gulf coast in late 1567 and then walked to Maine over the course of the next year. He was eventually picked up by a French vessel and made his way back to England. His fantastic accounts of the native peoples and animals were—as others soon found—exaggerated but were highly popular in English pubs, and his account was eventually published. See David B. Quinn, *New American World: A Documentary History of North America to 1612* and with a commentary by David B. Quinn, with the assistance of Alison M. Quinn and Susan Hillier (New York: Arno Press, 1979), 3: 212–13. See also Samuel Eliot Morison, *The European Discovery of America: The Northern Voyages, A.D. 500–1600* (New York: Oxford University Press, 1974), 467–68.

212. Johan Lerius (Jean de Léry) published an account of his journey to Brazil in 1565. See *History of a Voyage to the Land of Brazil, otherwise called America,* edited and translated by Janet Whatley (Berkeley: University of California Press, 1990), 141, for the passage referenced by Adair.

213. Sir Francis Drake sought refuge to repair his leaking ship, the *Golden Hind,* in a harbor on the coast of North America that he dubbed New Albion in June of 1579. The exact location of the harbor is argued by various scholars and locales all the way along the Pacific coast from California to the state of Washington. For information on Drake's voyage, see Harry Kelsey, *Sir Francis Drake: The Queen's Pirate* (New Haven: Yale University Press, 1998).

214. Don Antonio de Ulloa, a scientist and naval officer, was sent on a scientific mission by the king of Spain and published an account of his findings in 1748. A French edition followed, and the English edition, *A voyage to South-America,* was originally published in London in 1758, with a number of reprinted editions. He became governor of Spanish Louisiana in 1766, but open revolt by the citizenry forced him to flee in 1768. He published a natural history of Spanish America, *Noticias Americanas,* in Madrid in 1772, which was translated into French and German and was abstracted in various English publications. Adair was not alone in his praise for Ulloa's work, and he was widely acclaimed as a scholar in Europe for his astronomical and natural history observations. For more on his life, see John J. TePaske's introduction to Antonio de Ulloa, *Discourse and Political Reflections on the Kingdoms of Peru* (Norman: University of Oklahoma Press, 1978).

215. Jerónimo Román y Zamora was an Augustinian friar who wrote his *Repúblicas de Indias, idolatrías y govierno en México y Perú antes de la conquista* (Salamanca, Spain, 1575) from his experiences in the New World. See Huddleston, *Origins of the American Indians,* 30–31, for a discussion of his work.

216. Adair is referring to René Laudonnière, whose name has been Anglicized as Laudon here. Laudonnière established Fort Caroline near the St. Johns River in Florida in 1564. His accounts of his experiences can be found in Bennett, *Three Voyages: René Laudonnière.* Laudonnière was preceded by Jean Ribault, who attempted to establish a French colony on Parris Island, South Carolina, in 1562. For Ribaut's 1563 account, see *The whole & true discouerye of Terra Florida,* facsimile reproduction with introduction by David L. Dowd (Gainesville: University of Florida

Press, 1964). Ribaut's name is also spelled Ribault. Adair seems to have fused the names, possibly from his unidentified published source which seems to embellished the accounts of these men.

217. Petrus Galatinus, a sixteenth-century scholar, is credited by some as the originator of the word *Jehovah* for the sacred name rather than Yahweh, although the use of Jehovah by Christians apparently predates his work. See Werblowsky and Wigoden, eds., *Oxford Dictionary of the Jewish Religion,* s.v. "God, Names of."

218. Diodorus Siculus (c. 90–21 B.C.) was a widely read Greek historian of the ancient world. Strabo was a Greek geographer and historian of the reign of Augustus.

219. Garcilaso de la Vega, el Inca, was the son of a Spanish conquistador and the granddaughter of an Inca emperor. He wrote several works, including a history of Peru and an account of De Soto's expedition. For an examination of his life and work, see Frances G. Crowley, "Garcilaso de la Vega, the Inca," in *The De Soto Chronicles: The Expedition of Hernando de Soto to North America in 1539–1543,* 2 vols., edited by Lawrence A. Clayton, Vernon James Knight, Jr., and Edward C. Moore (Tuscaloosa: University of Alabama Press, 1993), 2: 1–24. The wild sheep referred to by Adair were actually llama.

220. Antoine Simon Le Page Du Pratz's *Histoire de la Louisiane,* 3 vols. (Paris: De Bure, Delaguette, Lambert, 1758), appeared as a two-volume English edition in 1763 under the title *The history of Louisiana, or of the western parts of Virginia and Carolina: containing a description of the countries that lye on both sides of the river Missisippi: with an account of the settlements, inhabitants, soil, climate, and products. Translated from the French, (lately published) by M. Le Page du Pratz; with some notes and observations relating to our colonies.* The Nachee are the Natchez Indians.

221. Adair erroneously believed that the Chickasaw language did have an *r* sound; at least his ear seemed to detect the sound, as when he placed the letter *r* in a number of words, including the names of their towns. Others seemed to detect the sound as well. Cushman reported that he had "often heard the Choctaws, when engaged in their ancient dances . . . utter in concert and in solemn tone of voice Yar-vo-hah, Yar-vo-yar-hah!" (*History of the Choctaw, Chickasaw and Natchez Indians,* 1899, 20).

222. Thomas Malvenda, *De Antichristo libri undecim* (Rome, 1604) was cited by Thorowgood in his *Jewes in America.* However, this reference to Montezuma's oration upon the arrival of the Spaniards, discussed by Thorowgood and paraphrased here by Adair, is attributed to Peter Martyr by Thorowgood in the text. Malvenda's work is noted in the margin opposite the passage in question (*Jewes in America,* 3–4). This error, and several other like mistakes, indicate that Adair's access to Thorowgood was likely brief and his comments based upon hastily made notes.

223. Adair's information on the deformation of earlobes by weights is found in Antonio de Ulloa's *A voyage to South America; describing at large the Spanish cities, towns, provinces, &c. on that extensive continent: undertaken, by command of the king of Spain, by Don George Juan, and Don Antonio de Ulloa . . . translated from the original Spanish,* 2 vols. (London: L. Davis and C. Reymers, 1758), 1: 395.

224. Emanuel de Moraës, a Brazilian, was also cited by Romans in *Concise Natural History,* 115. Although frequently mentioned by those speculating on the origins of American Indians, his work seems not to have survived. Emanuel de Moraës held that the natives of America were "derived from the Carthaginians and Jewes" (Thorowgood, *Jewes in America,* 3). Adair's source on Emanuel de Moraës is Thorowgood (3, 5), who cites De Laet as his authority.

Johannes de Laet was the author of *L'histoire du Nouveau Monde: ou, description des Indes Occidentales* (Leiden, 1640). De Laet and Hugo Grotius engaged in printed debate on the origin of the Indians. See Rubies, "Hugo Grotius's Dissertation on the Origin of the American Peoples," 221–44. Compare Adair's text to Thorowgood, 5. John de Laët published his works on the new world in the seventeenth century. See also John H. Powell, *On the Origin of the American Indians: An Address Presented at the 131st Annual Meeting of the Anthenæum of Philadelphia, February 4, 1946* (Philadelphia, 1946), 15–16.

225. Here Adair again relies on Thorowgood for information. Thorowgood cites Laet as his source (*Jewes in America,* 15). Thorowgood's work was quickly answered by Hamon L'Estrange, *Americans no Jewes, or Improbabilities that the American are of that race* (London: Henry Seile, 1652).

226. Adair copied the material in this paragraph, virtually verbatim, from Thorowgood, including the rather incomplete footnote citation he provides. Adair expands on him by inserting information about the burial of personal effects with the deceased. See Thorowgood, *Jewes in America,* 13.

227. Jean de Biencourt, Sieur de Poutrincourt, Baron de Saint-Just, was instrumental in the founding of Port Royal, Nova Scotia. The London edition of his exploits, *Noua Francia: or the Description of that part of New France, which is one continent with Virginia,* appeared in 1609.

228. Peter Martyr d'Anghera (Peter Martyr), a high-ranking church and government official in the Spanish bureaucracy, was the author of numerous accounts of Spain's New World conquests and knew many of the early explorers, including Christopher Columbus.

229. This is Roger Williams, who founded Providence, Rhode Island, in 1636. Adair is referring to his *Key into the Languages of America or, An help to the language of the natives in that part of America called New-England: together with briefe observations of the customes, manners and worships, &c. of the aforesaid natives, in peace and warre, in life and death : on all which are added spirituall observations, generall and particular, by the authour* (London: Printed by Gregory Dexter, 1643). Adair derived this secondarily from Thorowgood, *Jewes in America.* Compare Adair's sentence to Thorowgood's paragraph, on p. 10, complete with a reference to Williams's work: "The Americans have in some parts an exact form of King, Priest, (*q*) and Prophet, as was aforetime in *Cannan.*" The notation (*q*) refers to a marginal notation: "Mr Will. Key. p. 100." Earlier in this work (3), Thorowgood refers to Mr. Williams and cites his *Key of the Language of Amer.*

230. Lahontan arrived in New France in 1683 and participated in expeditions against the Iroquois as well as other activities around the Great Lakes. His *Nouveaux*

Voyages de Mr. le Baron de Lahontan dans l'Amérique Septentrionale was published in Paris in 1703. The first English edition, *New Voyages to North-America,* appeared also in 1703.

231. "The History of North-America, from the first Discovery thereof; Vol. I," by Samuel Nevill (pseudonym Sylvanus Americanus), appeared in serial form in the *New American Magazine* between January 1758 and March 1760.

232. Ophir was an overseas kingdom from which Solomon procured gold, precious wood, and exotic animals. It is generally believed to be India. For the part that Ophir played in various origin theories, see Huddleston, *Origins of the American Indians,* 4, 7, 23. Adair's likely source here was Humphrey Prideaux, *The Old and New Testaments.* See 1: 3–5.

233. For a examination of the Catawbas, see Merrell, *The Indians' New World,* and Charles M. Hudson, *The Catawba Nation* (Athens: University of Georgia Press, 1970).

234. New Windsor Township was the settlement that developed around Fort Moore. Primarily inhabited by Indian traders, it was the trailhead for the great series of Indian trading paths into the interior. It was soon eclipsed by Augusta, Georgia, which was more conveniently located on the west side of the Savannah River; see *Colonial Wars of America,* s.v. "Fort Moore (South Carolina)," and Braund, *Deerskins and Duffels,* 35, 41. In 1738, the colony deeded a tract of 21,774 acres to the Chickasaw as an inducement to remain in South Carolina rather than to move across the river to "New Savannah," a settlement just below Augusta. Edmond Atkin reported that the settlers (primarily those involved in the Indian trade) frequently attempted to acquire title to portions of it by trading "Punch and Rum" to the Indians, who, he noted, were "much Debauched." For Atkin's discussion of the Chickasaw Indians on the Savannah River, see Atkin, *Report,* 45–46, and Edward J. Cashin, *Lachlan McGillivray, Indian Trader: The Shaping of the Southern Colonial Frontier* (Athens: University of Georgia Press, 1992), 179–83. McGillivray was among those who acquired the Chickasaw land. See McDowell, *Documents, 1754–1765,* 371; W. Stitt Robinson, ed., *North and South Carolina Treaties, 1654–1756,* vol. 13 of *Early American Indian Documents: Treaties and Laws, 1607–1789,* edited by Alden T. Vaughan (Frederick, Md.: University Publications of America, 2001), 168.

235. Adair neglects to mention the Yamasee War, which occurred before his day but was responsible for the inclusion of the Yamasee in the Katawba nation. For more on the war and early South Carolina contact with these remnant tribes, see Gallay, *The Indian Slave Trade.* The early classic on the period remains Verner W. Crane, *The Southern Frontier, 1670–1732* (Durham, N.C.: Duke University Press, 1928; reprint, New York: Norton, 1981).

236. For a fuller discussion of the origin and meaning of the term *Cherokee,* see Russell Thornton, *The Cherokees: A Population History* (Lincoln: University of Nebraska Press, 1990), 7–8.

237. There were four major Cherokee divisions or settlement areas, geographically based, but they also exhibited both linguistic and cultural differences. The

Lower Towns were located at the headwaters of the Chattahoochee and Savannah rivers. The Overhill Towns, Adair's "mountainous" division, lay in the area now occupied by eastern Tennessee and northwestern North Carolina at the foot of the Unaka Mountains. As their name suggests, the Middle Towns were located roughly between the Lower and Overhill Towns along the Little Tennessee and Tuckasegee rivers. The northern barrier towns, often called the Out Towns in the eighteenth century, were part of this division. The fourth, the Valley Towns, were situated in the floodplains of the Valley and Hiwassee rivers. For example, see John Stuart's 1764 report, CO323/17, fo. 242. For concise descriptions of the Cherokee towns, see Thornton, *The Cherokees: A Population History,* 23–28. For an attempt to locate Cherokee towns, see Betty Anderson Smith, "Distribution of Eighteenth-Century Cherokee Settlements," in *The Cherokee Nation: A Troubled History,* edited by Duane King (Knoxville: University of Tennessee Press, 1979), 46–60. For the best description of the Cherokee territory and the way of life in a Cherokee town, see Hill, *Weaving New Worlds,* 1–7, 67–74. A dated but still useful examination of Cherokee village life is Gearing, "Priests and Warriors."

238. Echoi and Estatoe were destroyed by the Creeks in 1750. Estatoe was also burned during the Anglo-Cherokee war in 1760. All the Lower Cherokee towns, including Toogaloo, suffered from repeated blows (Corkran, *Cherokee Frontier,* 23, 209). M. Thomas Hatley examines the repeated trials of one Cherokee village in "The Three Lives of Keowee: Loss and Recovery in Eighteenth-Century Cherokee Villages," in *Powhatan's Mantle: Indians in the Colonial Southeast,* edited by Peter H. Wood, Gregory A. Waselkov, and M. Thomas Hatley (Lincoln: University of Nebraska Press, 1989), 223–48.

239. John Stuart's comprehensive report of 1764 on the tribes in his district placed Cherokee population at 2,750 gunmen. CO323/17, fo. 242. For the best examination of Cherokee population trends, see Thornton, *The Cherokees: A Population History.*

240. Adair is referring to Montgomery's encounter with the Cherokee at Tessuntee old town, in the vicinity of Etchoe and Nequassee, in late July 1760. See Corkran, *Cherokee Frontier,* 212–13.

241. For more information on canebrakes, see Steven G. Platt and Christopher G. Brantley, "Canebreakes: An Ecological and Historical Perspective," *Castanea* 62 (March 1997): 8–21.

242. A reference to the general licenses legalized under the Proclamation of 1763. See Braund, *Deerskins and Duffels,* 110–11, for an account of trade reform after 1763.

243. The spring was near Estatoe Old Fields. Herbert's Spring is shown on Thomas Mante's map, near "Old Steco," or Old Estatoe, a town near Etchoe. Grant's forces camped at Herbert's Spring. In his account of Grant's progress, Christopher Gadsden stated that the spring was near "Estatowih Old Town" and, on the next line, indicates that the army reached Etchowih ("A Particular Scheme of the Transactions of each Day . . . from the 7th June, when the Army marched from Kee-

howee, to the 4th July, when they are supposed to return to the Dividings," in Hatley, *The Dividing Paths,* fig. 8). The modern spellings are Estatoe Old Fields and Etchoe. Colonel John Herbert, the commissioner of Indian Affairs for South Carolina from 1727 to 1733, toured the area in 1727–1728. See *Journal of Colonel John Herbert, Commissioner of Indian Affairs for the Province of South Carolina, October 17, 1727, to March 19, 1727/8,* edited by A. S. Salley (Columbia: Historical Commission of South Carolina, 1936).

244. The 1738 epidemic affected approximately one-half the population of Charleston and killed more than 300. For a discussion of the impact of the epidemic on the Cherokee, see Russell Thornton, *The Cherokees: A Population History,* 28–30. See also Peter H. Wood, "The Impact of Smallpox on the Native Population of the 18th Century South," in *Early American Medicine: A Symposium,* edited by Robert I. Goler and Pascal James Imperato (New York City: Fraunces Tavern Museum, 1987), 22–28.

245. Sweating and bathing were common purification rituals among the southeastern Indians. For references to the practice, see Lawson, *A New Voyage,* 48, 55. Bartram noted that "the Indian Physicians, injoin the patient strictly to regimen during the attendance on them and the Stove or Sweat house are in constant practice" (*Bartram on the Southeastern Indians,* 276n.63).

246. Tanase, an Overhill town. Adair is in error on the distance from Fort Prince George. See p. 348, where he correctly notes that one could reach Tanase only after getting "over the mountain." Perhaps he meant to indicate the town's proximity to Fort Loudoun.

247. Cheoah, a Lower Cherokee town.

248. Alum root (*Heuchera americana* L.) was widely used as an antiseptic on wounds. See Vogel, *American Indian Medicine,* 271. Samuel Cole Williams, ed., *Adair's History,* 247, identified mountain alum as cranesbill or wild geranium (*Geranium maculatum*), but it seems to have been used primarily for internal complaints rather than as a wound dressing (Vogel, 390–91). Bartram provided a more detailed report on Native American pharmacopoeia (*Bartram on the Southeastern Indians,* 161–64).

249. The term *snakeroot* was applied to a variety of roots. By "Seneeka," Adair meant to indicate Seneca snakeroot (*Polygala senega* L.) or milkwort. For a discussion of snakebite cures, see Vogel, *American Indian Medicine,* 20–24, 368–74.

250. In 1743, upon receiving information that a silver mine had been discovered and was being worked in the Cherokee country, William Bull, governor of South Carolina, issued a proclamation prohibiting anyone without a license from seeking and operating mines on Indian lands (*South Carolina Gazette,* November 21, 1743).

251. The reputed power of rattlesnakes to "fascinate" or hypnotize prey and "draw it to them" was widely discussed by eighteenth-century natural historians. Bartram made inquiries on the subject but did not believe that the Indians were convinced that snakes held the power to fascinate (*Bartram on the Southeastern Indians,* 70–71, 250n.78). However, they did consider the snakes he discussed here as powerful and dangerous creatures associated with the underworld. The creatures

Adair describes—with a "large carbuncle" on the head—were uktena, the powerful mythical snake-beings revered by the Cherokee. Hudson has identified the uktena lair described by Adair as somewhere along the "upper reaches of the Cowee Mountains to the north and east of Franklin, N.C." ("Uktena," 74n.18).

252. In October 1745, French reports noted that two Englishmen had been killed on their way from Coweta to the Chickasaw towns (*MPAFD*, 4: 243). They were not the first. In late 1743 or in very early 1744, a party of thirty-five Choctaw Indians attacked an English trade convoy on the way to the Chickasaw nation, killing three Englishmen and two Chickasaw Indians (*MPAFD*, 4: 220).

253. Christian Gottlieb Priber was described by one historian as "perhaps the most interesting and enigmatic figure in the history of Anglo-French Cherokee relations." He was a German who first went to England and then migrated to America. By 1736, he had settled among the Cherokee, where he adopted their customs and language and began working to establish a separatist community founded on communal property. He soon began seeking French assistance for his bizarre plan. He was captured by the Creeks when passing through their territory on his way to Mobile and turned over to Georgia authorities. For more on Priber, see Verner W. Crane, "A Lost Utopia on the First American Frontier," *Sewanee Review* 27 (January 1919): 48–61; Davis, *Intellectual Life in the Colonial South*, 1: 171–72; and Knox Mellon, Jr., "Christian Priber's Cherokee 'Kingdom of Paradise,'" *Georgia Historical Quarterly* 57 (1973): 319–31.

254. Colonel Fox is listed as "Col. Jos. Fox" in the expense report for the expedition (*JCHA*, 6: 662). Crane identifies Priber's captor as Colonel Joseph Fox ("Lost Utopia," 57).

255. Louis De Vorsey, Jr., has suggested that Priber's dictionary might have been the inspiration for the one used by De Brahm in his essay on the southeast (*De Brahm's Report*, 284n.42).

256. Great Tellico, an Overhill Cherokee town.

257. A reference to Governor James Glen and his successor, William Henry Lyttelton. Glen's "parade" to Ninety-Six took place in 1756.

258. The settlement lay on the Congaree route to the Cherokee. In his edition of Adair's book (p. 259), Samuel Cole Williams erroneously wrote that Ninety-Six was so named because it was ninety-six miles from Charleston. It was approximately two hundred miles from Charleston. Early traders reckoned that area, where a number of trails converged, to be ninety-six miles from Keowee, the closest Cherokee town. See De Brahm's notation to that effect on his 1757 "A Map of South Carolina and a Part of Georgia," map 310 in William P. Cumming and Louis De Vorsey, Jr., *The Southeast in Early Maps*, 3d ed. (Chapel Hill: University of North Carolina Press, 1986). One branch of the trail led to Fort Moore. The settlement appeared on a 1730 map by George Hunter and was located in present Laurens County, South Carolina. See Robert L. Meriwether, *The Expansion of South Carolina, 1729–1765* (Kingsport, Tenn.: Southern Publishers, 1940), 118.

259. For recent examinations of the Cherokee war, its causes and consequences,

see John Oliphant, *Peace and War on the Anglo-Cherokee Frontier, 1756–63* (Baton Rouge: Louisiana State University Press, 2001); Fabel, *Colonial Challenges,* 1–87; and Hatley, *Dividing Paths,* 105–75.

260. In 1758, a number of Cherokee warriors led by the Mankiller of Estatoe assisted George Croghan on an expedition to relieve Colonel John Stanwix in Pennsylvania. See Corkran, *Cherokee Frontier,* 125–27; Nicholas B. Wainwright, *George Croghan: Wilderness Diplomat* (Chapel Hill: University of North Carolina Press, 1959), 127.

261. Adair is correct in the report that various parties of Cherokee warriors were attacked and even scalped by settlers and quasi-military patrols, although his figure of forty fatalities seems high. For details on these incidents, see Corkran, *Cherokee Frontier,* 157–60, and Hatley, *Dividing Paths,* 99–101.

262. Adair's accusations concerning the rape of Cherokee women are confirmed by extant contemporary letters. See Oliphant, *Peace and War,* 84–86.

263. William Henry Lyttelton replaced James Glen as governor of South Carolina, serving in that capacity from 1756 until April 1760. Lyttelton's visit took place in June 1758. See Cashin, *Lachlan McGillivray,* 169, and *Colonial Wars of North America,* s.v. "Lyttelton, William Henry (1724–1808)."

264. Most likely, this is George Pawley, a surveyor and colonel in the Craven County militia (Meriwether, *Expansion of South Carolina,* 194).

265. Round O of Stecoe, who stood with the peace faction during the Anglo-Cherokee war. He died of smallpox while serving as voluntary hostage at Fort Prince George in 1760 (Corkran, *Cherokee Frontier,* 164, 182, 189–90).

266. Adair refers to the murder of twenty-two Cherokee warriors held hostage at Fort Prince George after a Cherokee lured an English officer into the open and then killed him. See Corkran, *Cherokee Frontier,* 178–95. Official reports are at variance with Adair's description of how the Cherokee hostages were killed. Oliphant, *Peace and War,* wrote, "The truth is probably much nearer to the version provided by Adair" (p. 111). For a contemporary published version of events surrounding the murder of the Cherokee hostages, see *Pennsylvania Gazette,* April 3, 1760.

267. Perhaps John Brown, who, with Adair, led a company of Chickasaw Indians and whites dressed as Indians to scavenge the Lower Towns in the wake of the Montgomery expedition (*South Carolina Gazette,* April 19–26, 1760). See Corkran, *Cherokee Frontier,* 216–17.

268. Colonel Archibald Montgomery, who, under orders from General Jeffrey Amherst, led an expedition of approximately 1,600 men against the Lower Cherokee towns in order to relieve Fort Prince George. He burned most of the Lower Cherokee towns. For more details on Montgomery's campaign, see Corkran, *Cherokee Frontier,* 207–15, and Richard C. Cole, "Montgomerie's Cherokee Campaign, 1760: Two Contemporary Views," *North Carolina Historical Review* 74 (January 1997): 19–36.

269. James Grant (1720–1806) was the governor of East Florida from 1764 until 1771. Adair is referring to Grant's activity during the Anglo-Cherokee War, when he destroyed fifteen Middle Cherokee towns. For a survey of his career, see Paul

David Nelson, *General James Grant: Scottish Soldier and Royal Governor of East Florida* (Gainesville: University Press of Florida, 1993). For details of his Cherokee campaign, see Corkran, *Cherokee Frontier,* 243 ff.

270. Edmond Atkin served as the first superintendent of Indian affairs for the Southern Department from 1758 until his death in 1761; see *Colonial Wars of North America,* s.v. "Atkin, Edmond (1697–1761)." In assessing Atkin, Wilbur Jacobs noted his "arrogance and obvious ineptitude" in performing his duties (Atkin, *Report,* xxix).

271. Captain Montault de Monberaut served as commander at Fort Toulouse from 1755 to 1759. He was succeeded by Captain Jean Baptiste Benoist Aubert. See Daniel H. Thomas, *Fort Toulouse: The French Outpost at the Alabamas on the Coosa,* introduction by Gregory A. Waselkov (Tuscaloosa: University of Alabama Press, 1989), xxxii, n. 32.

272. The Mortar was the principal warrior of the Upper Creek town of Okchai. His war name was Yahatastanage, which loosely translates as Wolf Warrior. Regarded as the leader of the "French party" among the Creeks, his activities were often not so much pro-French or anti-British as pro-Creek. The British were ultimately forced to recognize his importance in the Creek polity, and he accepted the position of Great Medal Chief in 1765. He was killed in December 1774 in a skirmish during the Creek-Choctaw War; see *Colonial Wars of North America,* s.v. "Mortar of the Okchai (?–1774)."

273. For an account of Atkin's encounter with the Totscadeter, the Tobacco Eater, see Corkran, *Creek Frontier,* 206 ff.

274. In all, eleven men were murdered: five traders, five of their employees, and one black slave. Although popular opinion linked the murders to the Mortar, he was not in the Creek country at the time, and it is likely there were more complex reasons for the episode. Corkran (*Creek Frontier,* 216–17) agrees with Adair and links the murders to a broader French-inspired conspiracy against the British. For the most recent examination of the murders, see Joshua Aaron Piker, " 'Peculiarly Connected': The Creek Town of Oakfuskee and the Study of Colonial American Communities, 1708–1785," Ph.D. diss., Cornell University, 1998, 118–22.

275. The Congress at Augusta was held in October 1763 to reestablish peaceful relations and negotiate boundary lines with the southern tribes at the conclusion of the Seven Years' War. In addition to John Stuart, Governor James Wright of Georgia, Governor Arthur Dobbs of North Carolina, Governor Thomas Boone of South Carolina, and Lieutenant Governor Francis Fauquier of Virginia represented the British side. See Alden, *John Stuart,* 176 ff., for the best overall discussion of the proceedings. See also Louis DeVorsey, Jr., *The Indian Boundary in the Southern Colonies, 1763–1775* (Chapel Hill: University of North Carolina Press, 1966), 149–51.

276. The Creek leadership unanimously disavowed the actions of the Long Canes murders, and the incident had little long-term effect on British-Creek relations. The murderers were all Lower Creeks and, seemingly, were not associated with the Mortar's faction. For an account of diplomatic activity in the wake of the Long Canes murders, see Alden, *John Stuart,* 186–91.

277. Henry Ellis, the second royal governor of Georgia, served in that capacity from 1757 until 1760. For a look at his career, see Edward J. Cashin, "Governor Henry Ellis and the American Colonial Frontier," *Gulf Coast Historical Review* 7 (Spring 1992): 17–30, and *Governor Henry Ellis and the Transformation of British North America* (Athens: University of Georgia Press, 1994). The two great trading houses are those of George Galphin and Lachlin McGillivray. For an examination of the efforts of these men to preserve the Anglo-Creek alliance, see Cashin, *Lachlan McGillivray,* 193–98. As Adair suggests, they were instrumental in securing the assistance of the Chickasaw and Creek Indians as Cherokee war parties descended on the Savannah River in late December 1759 and early 1760. Lieutenant-governor William Bull was the acting governor of South Carolina.

278. Adair's short list of the most powerful Creek towns includes two Abeika towns (Okfuskee and Okchai), two Tallapoosa towns (Tuckabatchee and Tallassee), and two Lower Creek towns (Coweta and Chehaw). Depending on the era, census makers generally listed from fifty to sixty major towns. Population estimates varied but generally agreed with Adair's count of gunmen. For a complete list of Creek towns, see Corkran, *Creek Frontier,* 6–7.

279. These towns comprised the Alabama component of the Creek confederacy of towns, although not all the towns were of the Alabama tribe. The collective population of these diverse tribes was roughly 18 percent of the Creek total, and the number and location of the major Alabama towns remained relatively stable throughout the eighteenth century. They were, following Adair's order, Tamaytas, Tuskegee, Little Okchai, Puckna, and Wetumky. Tamaytas was a small town and is usually listed as being near or incorporated with Wetumky, although a 1761 Georgia trade list associated it with Conchatys. The French spelling for these two towns was Tamaytas and Tamaupas. Adair's Shawnee town is variously identified as Savannuca, Sawanogi, Oswegglees or Swaglaws, and the Natchez town is usually given as Natchee or Nauchee. Adair's two Koasati towns are Conchatys and Canachaquay, which one early French census listed as being amalgamated into the same village. In the nineteenth century, Conchatys was frequently spelled Ecunchate and was known as the Red Ground. One town, Coosada, variously known as Conchas or Little Cassauties, is missing from Adair's list. This town was near Tuskegee, approximately one-quarter mile from Fort Toulouse. It is sometimes confused with Coosa, an Abeika town on the Coosa River. See Braund, "Classification of Creek Towns."

280. In addition to remnant towns of Oconee and Uchee Indians, the Lower Creek towns were also peopled by Hitchiti, Sawokli, and other remnant tribes. The two largest and most powerful towns, Coweta and Cussita, were of Muskogean stock. For information on these affiliated tribes, see John R. Swanton, *Early History of the Creek Indians and Their Neighbors,* Bureau of American Ethnology Bulletin 73 (Washington, D.C.: Government Printing Office, 1946; reprint, New York: Greenwood Press, 1969).

281. The Creek and Cherokee Indians were involved in a long series of wars and border conflicts from 1716 until 1754. Here, Adair is referring to the brutal and successful attacks on Lower Cherokee towns by the Lower Creeks in the early

1750s. See *Colonial Wars of North America, 1512–1763,* s.v. "Creek-Cherokee Wars (c. 1716–1754)."

282. Adair is referring to Fort Toulouse, established in 1717 at the confluence of the Coosa and Tallapoosa rivers. For information on the fort, which was located near modern Wetumpka, Alabama, see Thomas, *Fort Toulouse.*

283. Taffy or tafia is a spirit made from molasses or brown sugar. In contrast, rum is produced from sugarcane. Some writers use the words tafia and rum interchangeably. Bossu provides a description of its manufacture (*Travels,* 195–96).

284. The three were killed at the town of Socuspoga. In the Charleston Library Society copy of Adair's *History,* several identifications are provided for those murdered. The corrections are not in the same handwriting as that attributed to Adair by the editor of the present edition. The "negroe" is identified as Tom, the "trader" as John Ross, and after "other two," the name William Mitchell is written. These identifications are correct. William Mitchell was a packhorseman employed by Ross, and Tom was his slave (*South Carolina Gazette,* June 14–21, 1760). Traders were prohibited from employing slaves in the Indian trade, but there were many violators, including John Ross, who was listed as having one slave in the Creek nation in 1757. See McDowell, *Documents Relating to Indian Affairs, 1754–1765,* 357.

285. In the Charleston Library Society copy of Adair's *History,* "Wm Rae" [William Rae] is inserted prior to "the youth" and "John Rae" is added after J. R. The identifications are correct. See *South Carolina Gazette,* June 14–21, 1760. In all, eleven people were killed in the incident, which took place on May 16, 1760. For various interpretations of the cause and meaning of the affair, see Braund, *Deerskins and Duffels,* 108; Corkran, *Creek Frontier,* 215–18; and Piker, "Peculiarly Connected," 118–22.

286. The Wolf or Wolf King of the Muccolossus (Tustanah Imothla) was one of the leading pro-British Creek headmen of the eighteenth century and was made a Great Medal Chief by the British in 1765. His rise to prominence began in 1740, when he boldly defended his town's English trader against an attack by the pro-French faction. In 1760, he again protected traders following the murder of eleven others by the Upper Creeks (Corkran, *Creek Frontier,* 107, 216–17; Juricek, ed., *Georgia Treaties, 1733–1763,* 220).

287. These Apalachee Indians resettled in the Pensacola and Mobile Bay area after the Creek Indians forced them from their traditional village sites in the early eighteenth century. For information on the Apalachee, see John H. Hann and Bonnie G. McEwan, *The Apalachee Indians and Mission San Luis* (Gainesville: University Press of Florida, 1998), and Waselkov and Gums, *Plantation Archaeology at Rivière aux Chiens,* 92.

288. Another reference to the growing divisions between the colonists and Great Britain in the 1770s.

289. The Koo-a-sah-te Indians, who had established towns among the Alabama Indians, left their towns to settle on the Tombigbee River when the French abandoned Fort Tombecbé after the cession of French territory in West Florida to Great Britain following the Seven Years' War. When war erupted between the Creek and

Choctaw Indians in early 1766, they found themselves caught between two very hostile powers. They wished to remain neutral but were harassed by both sides. Ultimately, they abandoned their new settlements, and for a time a group of about two hundred Coosada settled near the relative safety of Mobile and Pensacola. But, as Adair notes (298), even their proximity to the British settlements did not render them immune from attack. Their tribal name is spelled various ways, the most common being Coosada and Coushatta. As Adair indicates, most of the Coosada ultimately returned to their former location among the Creeks, although a small party did relocate, with the blessing of the British, to the area west of the Mississippi. See John Stuart to Board of Trade, December 2, 1766, CO5/67, fo. 199; Charles Stuart to John Stuart, December 2, 1772, in *DAR,* 5: 228–29; Talk of Topoye, alias the Fighter, to Deputy Superintendent, June 23, 1766, CO5/67, fo. 236; *Pennsylvania Gazette,* December 11, 1766; Thomas Gage to Lord Shelburne, April 29, 1767, in Clarence E. Carter, ed., *The Correspondence of General Thomas Gage with the Secretaries of State, and with the War office and Treasury, 1763–1775,* 2 vols. (New Haven: Yale University Press, 1931–33), 1:138; Romans, *Concise Natural History,* 280, 283–84.

290. The Tombecbé post was built by the French in 1736 as a staging point for Bienville's campaign against the Chickasaw. It was near modern Epes, Alabama. For its history, see *Colonial Wars of North America,* s.v. "Fort Tombecbé (Alabama)," and Joe Wilkins, "Outpost of Empire: The Founding of Fort Tombecbe and de Bienville's Chickasaw Expedition of 1736," in *Proceedings of the Twelfth Meeting of the French Colonial Historical Society, Ste. Geneviève, May 1986,* edited by Philip P. Boucher and Serge Courville, 133–53 (Lanham, Md.: University Press of America, 1988). The "Alabahma French garrison" is Fort Toulouse, at the junction of the Coosa and Tallapoosa rivers.

291. For further information on the mulberry feast, see Swanton, "Religious Beliefs and Medical Practices of the Creek Indians," 550–51.

292. These non-Muskoghean-speaking Creeks were often termed "Stinkards" or, as British Superintendent Edmond Atkin called them, "Stinking Lingua Indians" (Injunction by Edmond Atkin, September 7, 1759, William Henry Lyttelton Papers, Clements Library). They included not only the Shawnee but also remnant tribes from the Gulf coastal area who had joined with the Alabama component of the Creek confederacy.

293. The mediation by Stuart was avidly sought by both Choctaw and Creek leaders (John Stuart to Hillsborough, December 2, 1770, CO5/72, fo. 81). The peace effort failed, though, and by early 1771 the war was raging again. It did not end until 1776 when, under Stuart's auspices, hostilities were officially closed by ceremonies in Pensacola. For a brief summary of the war, see *Colonial Wars of North America,* s.v. "Creek-Choctaw Wars (c. 1702–1776").

294. There was limited contact between a small number of Creek headmen and the Spanish in early 1767, and some of the Creeks visited Havana. However, there was never any real possibility of a serious alliance or real danger from the contact, although the activity did alarm the British establishment (Corkran, *Creek Frontier,* 267).

295. A Cherokee delegation traveled to New Orleans in late 1756. The French lavished presents on their guests and encouraged them to join the Shawnee, Choctaw, and pro-French Creeks in waging war against the Chickasaw and the English settlements and destroying the English forts; Governor Kerlerec also promised trade, but his promises never materialized (ibid., 100–101). In early 1759, Governor Lyttelton reported that the French were planning an expedition to Fort Loudoun (Fabel, *Colonial Challenges,* 43). Samuel Cole Williams identified the "deep and dangerous cataract" as the Boiling Pot or Suck near Hale's Bar on the Tennessee River, near Chattanooga (*Adair's History,* 287n).

296. Emisteseguo of Little Tallassee, one of the most prominent headmen of the Creek towns from 1763 until his death in 1782, was John Stuart's most solid ally among the Creeks. The meeting referred to by Adair actually took place in Pensacola; see *Colonial Wars of North America,* s.v. "Emisteseguo," and Richard L. Blanco, ed., *The American Revolution, 1775–1783: An Encyclopedia* (New York City: Garland Publishing, 1993), s.v. "Emisteseguo of Little Tallassee."

297. George Galphin and Lachlan McGillivray, friends and business associates of Adair. McGillivray's career is covered by Cashin, *Lachlan McGillivray.* Information on Galphin can be found in Fritz Hamer, "Indian Traders and Power: A Comparative Study of George Galphin on the Southern Frontier and Three Northern Traders," Master's thesis, University of South Carolina, 1982, and "George Galphin," *Dictionary of Georgia Biography,* edited by Kenneth Coleman and Charles Stephen Gurr, 2 vols. (Athens: University of Georgia Press, 1983), 1: 335–37. See also Braund, *Deerskins and Duffels,* 40–58.

298. The pamphlet was titled "A Modest Reply to his Excellency the Governor's Written Answer to the Affidavit of Charles McNair & Mathew Roche, concerning the Late Revolt of the Chactaw nation of Indians from the French to the British Interest." It was submitted to the Commons House of Assembly by Matthew Roche in conjunction with a petition concerning compensation for services in attempting to sway the Choctaw Indians. To date, an extant copy of the essay has not been located.

299. John Stuart's mediation attempt followed on the heels of unsuccessful Creek attempts to patch up the war with the Choctaw Indians, which the Chickasaw had joined. Stuart believed that it was best for the British to mediate the peace, fearing that if the Creeks managed to mend the breach on their own, an unsettling Indian coalition against white expansion might emerge. The attempt failed, and by the winter of 1770–71 the Mortar of Okchai was seeking Chickasaw mediation to help end the Choctaw conflict. Adair's assertion that peace tokens had been sent by the Creeks to the Chickasaw Indians in early 1768 is confirmed by other sources, and it was reported that the Creeks had stopped war parties, although Adair's detailed account indicates otherwise. See George Galphin to John Stuart, June 2, 1768, in John Stuart to Thomas Gage, July 2, 1768, Gage Papers. Chickasaw Indians, undoubtedly inspired by English traders, also murdered two of the Mortar's brothers, whom they mistook for the Mortar himself, in early 1764 (Stuart to Gage, May 22, 1764, ibid.). In his edition of Adair's book, Williams erroneously identified "the

superintendent's deputy" as Capt. John Stuart (*Adair's History*, 290n.157). Charles Stuart was appointed deputy superintendent of Indian affairs in January 1766 (Alden, *John Stuart*, 212). The person referred to here is likely Stuart's commissary, Roderick McIntosh, who was sent to the Creek towns in February 1768 with talks from John Stuart. See Kathryn E. Holland [Braund], "The Path Between the Wars: Creek Relations with the British Colonies, 1763–1774" (Master's thesis, Auburn University, 1980), 72. On page 275, Adair refers back to "the superintendant's deputy before mentioned," and in this case he is clearly referring to McIntosh.

300. For a discussion of crossing rivers along the trade path, see Braund, *Deerskins and Duffels*, 92–95.

301. Adair is referring to the boundary expedition of 1768, which began work in June under the direction of Creek Commissary Roderick McIntosh (De Vorsey, *Indian Boundary*, 156). Adair's account of McIntosh's difficulties is not directly corroborated by other sources, but the official records do note many difficulties and squabbles as well as McIntosh's temper, and he was soon replaced by Lachlan McGillivray as the head of the boundary expedition. Given his relationship with McGillivray, Adair's account seems plausible. For an account of the boundary expedition, see Cashin, *Lachlan McGillivray*, 238–44. See also Holland [Braund], "The Path Between the Wars," 107–8.

302. George Galphin assisted Georgia in persuading the Creeks that the boundary should be run to Williams Creek, not Uptons Creek. This was, as Adair suggests, an important victory for Galphin and Georgia, as the colony had already granted land in the disputed area. See De Vorsey, *Indian Boundary*, 153–56.

303. George Galphin and Lachlan McGillivray.

304. In the Charleston Library Society copy of Adair's *History*, the following words are crossed out: "their leader who stood foremost came and." The word "I" is substituted. The corrected sentence thus reads: "While I held my gun ready in my right hand, about five yards distant from them, I struck my breast with the but-end of one of my pistols, which I had in my left hand."

305. A Middle Cherokee town. Tuckaseigee's population was listed at seventy gunmen in John Stuart's 1764 report, CO323/17, fo. 243.

306. In the Charleston Library Society copy of Adair's *History*, the words "as I" are inserted between the words "soon out." The resultant correction seems to be incomplete, and the phrase thus reads "as soon as I out of their view." Perhaps Adair intended "as soon as I was out of their view."

307. The Wolf King of the Muccolossus (Tustanah Imothla) and the others were carrying presents not only for themselves but also goods for their townspeople—although in this case, the saddle was clearly intended as personal property. The Wolf King was long remembered for his tenacious support of the English trade and the bounty the trade brought to his people. Lord Adam Gordon, who met the Wolf King in 1765, wrote that he "seemed a Sensible Old Man, said he might be a hundred years old, and that the fatigues he had undergone in going down to the Colonies in Georgia and Carolina, had effected him and made him look as old as he did"; see his "Journal of an Officer who Travelled in America and the West Indies in 1764

and 1765," in *Travels in the American Colonies,* edited by Newton D. Mereness (New York: Macmillan Co., 1916), 385, and Corkran, *Creek Frontier,* 107, 121, 187, 216–17. During his stay at Muccolossus in 1775, Bartram met the Wolf King and "was struck with awe and veneration at the appearance of a very aged man: his hair, what little he had, was as white as snow . . . he looked as smiling and cheerful as youth, yet stone-blind by extreme old age; he was the most ancient chief of the town, and they all seemed to reverence him." The Wolf King told Bartram that he was the first man who had brought goods into his town, "which he did on his back from Charleston, five hundred miles on foot, for they had no horses then amongst them" (*Bartram on the Southeastern Indians,* 119–20). The Creek headmen had met with Glen in early September 1749. See Corkran, *Creek Frontier,* 129–30, for a brief summary of the meeting. The records of the conference can be found in Journals of His Majesty's Council in South Carolina sent to England, Great Britain, Public Records Office, Board of Trade, CO5/456 (microfilm BMP D518), September 4–11, 1749. His name appears on the list of Creek Indians in attendance as "Tusskenia, a Noted Man." His town is not given, but he is listed as one of eight Tallapoosa Indians in attendance. Adair's declaration that he intended to "give them leg-bail" prior to recognizing the Creek party is a colloquial phrase, implying a speedy and surreptitious retreat. According to the *Oxford English Dictionary,* which cites Adair on usage for the term, it is derived from sporting language and means "(jocular): to be beholden to one's own legs for escape, to run away."

308. The official report to the South Carolina General Assembly on March 15, 1750, merely noted that the culprits were "French Indians" (*JCHA,* 9:467). Later reports identified them as Nottawagoes (ibid., 10:171). Corkran identified the murderers as Senecas (*Creek Frontier,* 146). Adair's description of the Indians as Savannah or Shawnee is probably the correct one. Nottawagoes is used variably to indicate Shawanees, to the Six Nations in general and particularly to the Conostogas. See Lawrence Henry Gipson, *Zones of International Friction: North America, South of the Great Lakes Region, 1748–1754,* vol. 4 of *The British Empire Before the American Revolution* (New York: Alfred A. Knopf, 1939), 66n.43.

309. A reference to Governor James Glen and his efforts to mediate the Creek-Cherokee conflict. The reasons for Glen's intervention were more complex than Adair suggests. See Corkran, *Cherokee Frontier,* 22–23, 35–41.

310. Included in this number were Cornelius Dougherty and Anthony Dean (ibid., 22).

311. Lachlan McGillivray.

312. See McDowell, ed., *Documents Relating to Indian Affairs, 1750–1754,* 387–414, for an account of Governor James Glen's conference with the Creek Indians in May 1753.

313. Strength in unity.

314. For Ellis's efforts to involve the Creeks in the Carolina-Cherokee war, see Corkran, *Creek Frontier,* 211 ff. Though divided, most Creeks, as Adair indicates, refused to join the English in their war against the Cherokee.

315. The Choctaw confederacy was actually composed of four divisions whose

villages were located in what is now east-central Mississippi. The Western Towns were primarily near the head of the Pearl River, near Nanih Waiya. The Eastern Towns were on the western tributaries of the Tombigbee River. The Six Towns were located south of the Western Towns on tributaries of the Chickasawhay River, and the Chickasawhay Towns were on the Chickasawhay River. See Galloway, *Choctaw Genesis,* 2, 198–99, and Romans, *Concise Natural History,* 130–31.

316. For a recent analysis of Choctaw settlement patterns based on archaeological techniques, see John H. Blitz, "Choctaw Archaeology in Mississippi," *Journal of Alabama Archaeology* 41 (December 1995): 135–61.

317. Romans reported that "the Choctaws are said to be thieves, but I can assure the reader that the Chicasaws are a thousand times more so" (*Concise Natural History,* 124). Moreover, he reported encounters with a gang of Choctaw bandits during his expedition to the Choctaw towns (ibid., 281). American Indian notions of sharing and hospitality often clashed with the new mercantile exchange economy, frequently leading to charges of theft. In less complicated times, Indians would not have had to ask a host for what they needed.

318. Although some scholars have been skeptical of reports that Choctaw Indians were poor swimmers, both Adair and Romans mentioned the fact, and even colonial newspapers reported it during the eighteenth century. For Romans's thoughts on the subject, see ibid., 130, 139, 387n.75.

319. Romans noted Coosa on his journey through the Choctaw towns in 1771–72. For a reconstruction of his portion of the famous Stuart-Gage map, see ibid. H. S. Halbert commented on Romans's map in "Bernard Romans' Map of 1772," *Mississippi Historical Society Publications,* 6: 415–39 (Jackson: Mississippi Historical Society, 1902). Halbert called the town Coosha. It is usually rendered Concha or Coucha by modern scholars. Concha was the leading town in the Eastern Division (Galloway, *Choctaw Genesis,* 199).

320. See *Colonial Wars of North America,* s.v. "Fort Tombecbé (Alabama)," for more details on the garrison.

321. For the diplomatic turmoil that accompanied the transfer of West Florida from French to British control, see *The Mémoire Justificatif of the Chevalier Montault de Monberaut,* translated and edited by Milo B. Howard, Jr., and Robert R. Rea, Southern Historical Publications no. 3 (Tuscaloosa: University of Alabama Press, 1965).

322. Adair was referring to events during the tenure of the first acting governor of West Florida, Major Robert Farmar. He provided a rather muddled picture of two early events in Farmar's administration that turned the trader community, including Adair, against the major. In the first, Farmar ordered the whipping of a trader for insulting the daughter of a prominent French settler. In the second, concerning the kettle, Farmar required the British merchant to refund payment for what an Indian claimed was a damaged kettle. The repercussions mentioned by Adair followed when the trader, Daniel Ward, refused to comply with Farmar's order. Contrary to Adair's opinion, the desertion of the French from the new British colony had less to do with Farmar's regime than with the loyalty oath they would have been required

to take. For a more balanced examination of the Farmar regime, see Rea, *Major Robert Farmar,* 40–43. In his edition of *Adair's History,* Samuel Cole Williams incorrectly identified the military governor as William Johnstone (307n.166). Farmar held the position until the arrival of George Johnstone. On the latter's career, see Robin F. A. Fabel, *Bombast and Broadsides: The Lives of George Johnstone* (Tuscaloosa: University of Alabama Press, 1987).

323. The Quebec Act was signed into law on June 22, 1774.

324. The French evacuated Fort Toulouse, "the Alebahma garrison," between November 1763 and January 1764 (Thomas, *Fort Toulouse,* 66). It was not occupied by the British at the insistence of the Alabama towns.

325. Adair is referring to the cutbacks in the Indian Department after 1768. See Braund, *Deerskins and Duffels,* 115–18. As a result of budget cuts, the commissary was recalled as was the gunsmith promised at the 1765 Congress of Mobile. Paya Mataha, the Great Medal Chief of the Chickasaw, aired his complaints about the removal of the commissary and gunsmith and the general breakdown of trading regulations at a congress held at Mobile, December 21, 1771 through January 6, 1772 (CO5/73, fo. 67).

326. The Torrepine Chieftain was Opaya Mingo Luxi, sometimes written Paya Mingo Eluxy or Belixy. The Chickasaw term for turtle (terrapin) is rendered *loksi* in modern Chickasaw (Munro and Willmond, *Chickasaw*). He was Paya Mataha's chief rival and allied with a number of traders who opposed new trade regulations. See J. Russell Snapp, *John Stuart and the Struggle for Empire on the Southern Frontier* (Baton Rouge: Louisiana State University Press, 1996), 97–98. For speculation on the Mortar's mission, see John T. Juricek, ed., *Georgia and Florida Treaties, 1763–1776,* vol. 12 of *Early American Indian Documents: Treaties and Laws, 1607–1789,* edited by Alden T. Vaughan (Bethesda, Md.: University Publications of America, 2002), 283–84. Adair envisioned a dastardly conspiracy brewing against the British. Given the fact that the Creek and Choctaw people had just taken up arms against each other, it may have been less sinister than Adair imagined and may have been aimed primarily at seeking Chickasaw mediation in the war. There is no doubt, however, that the Mortar and other Indian leaders were increasingly concerned with encroachments on their land by whites, particularly by traders who established plantations. See *HAI,* 369, for a renewed discussion of this topic by Adair. Wendy St. Jean has discerned division between the peace and war chiefs throughout the eighteenth century. For an examination of factionalism in relation to peace and war towns and chiefs, see "Chickasaws: Firm Friends of the English?" *Journal of Mississippi History* 58 (Winter 1996): 345–58.

327. Adair is referring to the Congress of Pensacola (May 1765) that addressed areas of concern between British West Florida and the Creek Indians. Governor Johnstone and John Stuart, superintendent of Indian affairs, distributed presents to leading men after the proceedings. See *MPAED,* 188–215.

328. As John Juricek notes, Adair provides the only account for Johnstone's proposed hostage-taking, presumably prior to the Congress of Pensacola in 1765. Juricek deems Adair's account "credible" for two reasons: Adair's regard for John-

stone and the fact Adair criticized Governor Lyttelton for taking Cherokee hostages previously. He dates the incident May 10 or 11, 1765. See Juricek, ed., *Georgia and Florida Treaties, 1763–1776,* 282, 544n.4.

329. John Stuart's appointee as Choctaw commissary was Elias Legardere. The best biographical sketch available can be found in Alden, *John Stuart,* 212–13n.90. Adair is correct in that the garrison had been withdrawn during this period.

330. Kapteny Humma Echeto is more properly a title than a name, but Choctaw leaders, to the confusion of Adair, his contemporaries, and modern scholars alike, are generally known by their proper titles. The title translates Great (*chito*) Red (*ouma*) Captain (*kapitani*). Adair calls him both Red Captain and Red Chief during his discussion. According to Adair, Kapteny Humma Echeto's house "lay in one of their northern barrier towns" (p. 293 of the original edition). Perhaps this is Captain Houma, whose village was listed as Chickatalya and who was made a Great Medal Chief of the Choctaw by the British in 1765. Chickatalya is a northern barrier town of the western division and appears on Romans's map as Kaffittalaya (*Concise Natural History,* inset map). Juricek notes that the town of the Great Medal Chief Captain Houma varies in a number of official British documents (*Georgia and Florida Treaties, 1763–1776,* 533n.36). In most every village, the war chief was usually known as *soulouche oumastabe* (red shoe killer) or as *mingo ouma* (red chief), and there are also war captains. In the case of certain individuals, these war titles become the popular name of prominent individuals. See Galloway, "Factionalism and Civil War," 123, for a discussion of war titles.

331. According to the inventory of cession of the Tombecbé, the fort consisted of "four Bastions, with their Curtains Constructed with Stakes and Earth, with their Banquets, all in good condition except the South side and Banquets" (*MPAED,* 98).

332. Edmond Atkin.

333. Many speculators, politicians, and hopeful settlers were promoting the establishment of colonies west of the Proclamation Line of 1763. Adair dubbed the colony Georgiana or New Georgiana and encouraged the establishment of such a colony a number of times. The proposed colony would have occupied the fertile Mississippi River valley north of West Florida up to the Ohio River. A small publication, published anonymously in 1773 but attributed to Bayly Anselm, titled *The Advantages of a Settlement upon the Ohio in North America,* specifically refers to the proposed colony. For a brief discussion of the colony, see Clarence W. Alvord, *The Mississippi Valley in British Politics; A Study of the Trade, Land Speculation, and Experiments in Imperialism Culminating in the American Revolution,* 2 vols. (Cleveland: A. H. Clark, 1917; reprint, New York: Russell and Russell, 1959), 2: 174–75.

334. Montfort Browne served as lieutenant governor of West Florida during George Johnstone's administration and succeeded him as acting governor upon his departure until the arrival of John Eliot in 1769.

335. According to the official report, the man executed (John Plumb) was a soldier who killed the Choctaw in a "Drunken Fray." A number of Choctaw Indians were present for the trial and execution (John Stuart to General Thomas Gage, January 21, 1766, Gage Papers). See also Juricek, ed., *Georgia and Florida Treaties, 1763–1776,* 544n.3.

336. For an examination of the difficulty in rendering justice in the context of intercultural relationships, see Galloway, "The Barthelemy Murders." To date, no evidence from French records has been recovered to confirm Adair's information on the 1740 execution at Fort Toulouse. Patricia Galloway accepts Adair's evidence on the matter (102n.39).

337. Elias Legardere was the commissary to the Choctaw stationed at Fort Tombecbé. Lieutenant John Ritchey was in command at the fort. The white man was murdered by a party of eight Choctaw warriors led by a Chocolacta, a small medal chief. The Choctaw claimed they mistook the man for a Creek. Following the murder, a delegation of leading Choctaw men visited Lagardere at Fort Tombecbé to discuss the matter. Official correspondence does not confirm Adair's account of Legardere's conduct but does indicate that Lieutenant Ritchey's actions were less than diplomatic. See Elias Legardere to Charles Stuart, March 4, 1767, Deposition of John Farrell, Frederick Haldimand to General Gage, March 23, 1767, and Charles Stuart to Montfort Browne, March 14, 1767, both in Haldimand Papers. According to Legardere, the leader who came to report the murder was "Capt. Houma great Medal of Askennepe" (Elias Lagardere to Charles Stuart, March 4, 1767, ibid.). This was almost certainly the Red Captain of Chickatalya. Skunnepaw, the northernmost Choctaw town on the Chickasaw path, was deserted during the Creek war, and it appears that the Red Captain was living in Chickatalya. See Romans, *Concise Natural History,* map insert. See also Juricek, ed., *Georgia and Florida Treaties, 1763–1776,* 555n.33, for a discussion of the matter.

338. Seemingly a reference to Lieutenant James Henderson, who replaced Legardere as commissary to the East and West Choctaw villages in 1768. Lieutenant Charles Tayler replaced Legardere among the Six Village Choctaw (Alden, *John Stuart,* 254).

339. This town, called Couëchitto by the French, was destroyed in the Choctaw civil war and is shown on the Stuart-Gage map as East Congeeto. Here, Adair refers to the Red Shoe prominent in the Choctaw civil war, 1746–50, who sought assistance from the English.

340. Adair is correct concerning the town of "the present Red Shoes." He is identified as "Sulashummastabe of Yassoo" by John Stuart in 1764. See Juricek, ed., *Georgia and Florida Treaties, 1763–1776,* 209.

341. Yowani was in the Chickasawhay division of the Choctaw polity (Galloway, *Choctaw Genesis,* 2, 198–99). The spelling of Yowani varies widely, most often appearing as Youanny, Yoani, Eouané, or Ewany in contemporary literature. It was the southernmost Choctaw village in the late eighteenth century. See Romans, *Concise Natural History,* map inset.

342. The traders killed were John Goodwin and Andrew Davies (Charles Stuart to John Stuart, 1 October 1766, CO5/67, fo. 205; Mr. Robert Hannah's Declaration, August 30, 1766, Haldimand Papers). Since Adair asserts that the town of "Minggo Humma Echeto" is "Yowanne," this is likely Captain Ouma of Eouané, who appears on a 1765 list of Choctaw headmen as a "Gorget Chief." In 1765, Governor George Johnstone of West Florida sent a message to "Captain Houma of the Youane." Other leaders specifically addressed in the message were the Red

Captain (of Chisatalaya) and "Mingo Houma of Mungalahsa of the East" (East Imongoulasha). See Juricek, ed., *Georgia and Florida Treaties,* 279, 292.

343. Charles Stuart.

344. The Stuart-Gage Map, Clements Library, provides the most accurate location of Choctaw villages during Adair's time, as well as the many trade paths that linked the Chickasaw and Choctaw villages. The seven towns "that lie close together" are the Oocoloo-Hanale or Six Villages.

345. The attack on the Cussada town was in October 1766 (*Pennsylvania Gazette,* December 11, 1766). See also Juricek, ed., *Georgia and Florida Treaties, 1763–1776,* 312, 547n.31.

346. According to another report, the Creeks seem to have executed only one man for the murder of the two traders while another escaped (*Pennsylvania Gazette,* December 11, 1766). Governor Johnstone's hard line met with disapproval from General Thomas Gage. For more details on this episode, see Corkran, *Creek Frontier,* 254–57.

347. See the introductory essay for an account of Adair's "public business."

348. Adair's observations concerning alcohol were repeated by many others (Braund, *Deerskins and Duffels,* 125–27). Young men (warriors) were particularly noted for their tendency to overindulge. For a brief examination of this topic, see Carson, *Searching for the Bright Path,* 62–63.

349. This was most likely a pit that had been created by digging to obtain clay to be used as daub for buildings or pottery making. See *Bartram on the Southeastern Indians,* 260n.139.

350. Kanootare or Conutory was one of the Cherokee "Out Towns" along the Tuckaseigee River. Conutory and neighboring towns Stecoe, Tuckareetchee, and Kithuwa were destroyed by James Grant in 1761. For references to the town, see McDowell, ed., *Documents Relating to Indian Affairs, 1750–1754,* 68, 87, 72, 79, and Corkran, *Cherokee Frontier,* 26, 251–53.

351. Abraham Wood led an exploring party from Virginia west toward the Mississippi Valley in 1650 but did not reach the Mississippi River. See Helen Delpar, ed., *The Discoverers: An Encyclopedia of Explorers and Exploration* (New York: McGraw-Hill, 1980), 425. Doctor Cox of New Jersey is Dr. Daniel Coxe, author of *Description of the English Province of Carolina* (London, 1722.) For an early discussion of the importance of Wood's explorations, see Clarence W. Alvord and Lee Bidgood, *The First Explorations of the Trans-Allegheny Region by the Virginians, 1650–1674* (Cleveland: Arthur H. Clark Co., 1912). A reprint of Coxe's work is available as *A Description of the English Province of Carolana, By the Spaniards call'd Florida, And by the French La Louisiane,* edited by William S. Coker, Floridiana Facsimile and Reprint Series (Gainesville: University Presses of Florida, 1976).

352. "Savage bears are at peace among themselves" (Juvenal, *Satires* 15.164).

353. The post was abandoned in 1768 because the garrison was expensive and impossible to support adequately in the event of war with the Indians. See Lord Hillsborough to Thomas Gage, in *Correspondence of Thomas Gage,* 2: 62.

354. The battle described here actually occurred on October 8, 1767. The Red Captain and his warriors were surprised near the Cahaba River. Contrary to Adair's

account, official reports state that fifteen escaped, while the rest were killed or captured. The Red Captain was reportedly flayed alive and his Great Medal returned to the British. Adair is correct in that one of those captured, although wounded in the head, managed to escape. John Ritchey listed the number of the Red Captain's party at forty-one, while Bernard Romans recorded forty and Creek commissary Roderick McIntosh counted forty-five. McIntosh reported that one hundred and fifty Creek warriors took part. See John Ritchey to Sir Frederick Haldimand, November 16, 1767, Haldimand Papers, BM21,671. Reel 5, fo. 263; Romans, *Concise Natural History,* 130, 384–85n.58; Roderick McIntosh to John Stuart, November 16, 1767, Gage Papers; John Stuart to Hillsborough, December 28, 1768, CO5/70; and *Pennsylvania Gazette,* December 17, 1767.

In this passage, Adair relates that "Minggo Humma Echeto" was the war chief killed in the great battle of 1767. In the Choctaw language, *mingo ouma* signifies red chief; *chito* denotes great. Earlier in his narrative, he names the war chief of Yowani "Minggo Humma Echeto" (Great Red Chief). It would seem Adair has transposed the name of the leader of Yowani with the celebrated Red Captain, whom he correctly identifies as "Kapteny Humma Echeto" (Great Red Captain) elsewhere. See *HAI,* p. 292. The Choctaw designation for captain is *kapitani.* This was the Great Medal Chief of Chistalaya who died in 1767. In this passage, Adair does not give the chief's town, merely referring to him as "their distinguished war-leader, before spoken of." Both the Yowani and Chistalaya war chiefs were mentioned previously. For a discussion of the difficulty in identifying various Choctaw chiefs, see Juricek, ed., *Georgia and Florida Treaties, 1763–1776,* 533n.36. To confuse matters further, another prominent chief was Mingo Houma Chito of Imongoulasha. It appears that Adair, like many of his contemporaries, had difficulty with Choctaw titles, given the number of "red captains" and "red chiefs."

355. James Glen. What follows is Adair's account of the Choctaw civil war, the role of the English (particularly James Adair) in fomenting hostilities against the French, and the serious consequences of the devastating war. See introductory essay, this volume. For an account of the war, see Charles William Paape, "The Choctaw Revolt, a Chapter in the Intercolonial Rivalry in the Old Southwest" (Ph.D. diss., University of Illinois, 1946). For an examination of the civil war from the Choctaw perspective, see Galloway, "Choctaw Factionalism and Civil War." W. Stitt Robinson details events from the South Carolina perspective and explores the complexities of the aftermath in *James Glen: From Scottish Provost to Royal Governor of South Carolina,* Contributions in American History no. 165 (Westport, Conn.: Greenwood Press, 1996), chap. 3. The most concise account of Adair's role can be found in Wilcomb E. Washburn, "James Adair's 'Noble Savages,'" in *The Colonial Legacy, III & IV,* edited by L. H. Leder, 91–120 (New York: Harper and Row, 1973); see esp. 96–110.

356. Tatoulimataha, a Choctaw chief, also assigned Red Shoe's defection to the bad treatment he had received from the French, "both personally and in the matter of his wives" (*MPAFD,* 4: 291).

357. The Chakchiuma, who lived south of Chickasaw territory, between the Chickasaw and Choctaw towns, were allies of the Chickasaw Indians.

358. See *HAI,* 180, for a description of The Jockey's burial. According to both

French documents and Atkin's report, it was the Blind King who sent his nephew and a Choctaw woman as emissaries to Red Shoes. The Blind King, Imayatabé, was a Great Chief among the Chickasaw. The French appended Leborgne (*le borgne* or "the one-eyed man") to his name. See *MPAFD,* 4: 61–62, 260, and Edmond Atkin, "Historical Account of the Revolt of the Chactaw Indians in the late War from the French to the British Alliance and of their return Since to that of the French" (Lansdowne Ms. 809, British Library, London), hereafter "Historical Account," fo. 37–38.

359. The three Frenchmen were murdered on August 14, 1756 (*MPAFD,* 4: 299). For a discussion of the event, see introductory essay, this edition.

360. For Adair's explanation of "broken days" using "sticks hieroglyphically painted," see *HAI,* 75.

361. The Breed Camp.

362. It is significant the Creek Indians sent the scalps of the French wrapped in a white deerskin, for it represented peace. French sources confirm the treatment of the scalps and relate that "the Abihkas, Talapoosas, and Alabamas detested with all their hearts the despicable action of the Choctaws" (*MPAFD,* 4: 275). Thus, the Upper Creeks were, at least from the French perspective, declaring neutrality and peaceful intentions.

363. The actual date was May 1747 (*MPAFD,* 5: 33; Paape, "Choctaw Revolt," 129). The Aquahpah Indians are the Quapaw.

364. Adair's name for Charles McNaire and Company. McNaire had no experience in the Indian trade but, according to Edmond Atkin, was "a more Sober decent sort of Man than commonly goes to trade"; see Atkin, "Historical Account," fo. 4. Though he lacked experience, he did have important contacts. McNaire's venture was funded by his relations Mathew and Jordan Roche and James Maxwell, all prominent Charleston merchants. Joining McNaire as working partners were Arthur Harvey, Thomas Maxwell, and John Vann, an experienced trader. Dr. Thomas Glen, the governor's brother, was allowed into the venture when the governor promised to obtain a monopoly for the company. Adair's name for the company is doubtless related to the opposition's portrayal of Glen as a Pharaoh whose pride brought plagues on Egypt. See the caustic poem in *South Carolina Gazette,* April 29–May 6, 1751.

365. Atkin reported that McNaire fitted out "no less than about 200 Horses" ("Historical Account," 6).

366. Atkin related that McNaire had taken "more than double the Time upon his Journey, in which it is usually performed at the same Season of the Year by other Traders" (ibid., 6–7).

367. What Adair appears to be describing is a duly issued trading license from South Carolina, as indicated by his description of the seal of the Carolina colony, which bears a lion and a unicorn. Paape ("Choctaw Revolt," 110n.34) notes that the document, dated January 11, 1747, which McNaire eventually produced in London to buttress his claim, did not have the seal. Paape thus reads Adair's description given here as a reference to a later proclamation by the governor. However, it is clear

that Adair is describing McNaire's first meeting with the Chickasaw traders, in which he produced an issued license as well as a proclamation from Glen banning unlicensed trade and prohibiting unauthorized "talks" to the Choctaw.

368. Glen's letter of April 22, 1747, was cited by Atkin in his account of the revolt. Doubtless, the "things of the measures of government" (*HAI*, 324) that Adair was reluctant to divulge was the instruction from Glen to "stir up the Chactaws against the French, & to take Tambekbe Fort" ("Historical Account," 7).

369. George Galphin.

370. Alexander Wood was one of the best-known South Carolina traders to the Creek Indians, and he occasionally acted as an official envoy for the colony. He directed the building of an English "fort" at Okfuskee in the 1740s. See Piker, "Peculiarly Connected," 94–95.

371. Paya Mataha was the leading spokesman for the Chickasaw towns in the 1760s and 1770s and was a Great Medal Chief. Romans reported that he had killed "upwards of forty times," making him one of the region's most respected warriors (*Concise Natural History,* 125). Imataha Pouscouche, or Minko Puskus, was better known to the English as Little King (Robinson, *James Glen,* 46). The "Sphynx-company" beau was Charles McNaire. The trio arrived in Charleston on December 29, 1747, and they stayed a fortnight. Atkin and others thought the appearance of the lone Choctaw chief "extraordinary." There were no public ceremonies, only private meetings with the governor ("Historical Account," fo. 12).

372. John Campbell. Adair is describing the period in late 1747, prior to setting out on his visit to South Carolina.

373. John Campbell, noting the wound that Adair describes here, wrote to Governor James Glen that he was "lamed by a Shot in my Arm" while serving the "Public." Adair writes that this was "about a year after" the period under discussion. Actually, it was about a year before, in 1746. Campbell was killed in November 1750. See McDowell, ed., *Documents Relating to Indian Affairs, 1750–1754,* 6 (quotation), 7, 36.

374. Charles McNaire stated that Red Shoes was escorting Chickasaw trader Henry Elsley when he was killed but did not list others in the caravan. Elsley was a well-known Chickasaw trader (Paape, "Choctaw Revolt," 100; Atkin, *Report,* 6). Perhaps Elsley was one of the "others" mentioned by Adair.

375. According to Atkin's account, taken from Charles McNaire's letters, it was McNaire who delivered the governor's letter to Adair. Atkin wrote that McNaire arrived in the Chickasaw towns near the end of March.

376. This appears to be a reference to Nanih Waiya, a mound known as the hill of origin in Choctaw tradition. Adair's reference to "subterranean brethren" alludes to the fact that the Choctaw believed that they emerged from the interior of the mound. Romans also noted that the Choctaw told him of their emergence from a "hole" (*Concise Natural History,* 121, 129). For a discussion on the concept of mounds as a "naval" or "womb" of emergence, see Vernon J. Knight, "Symbolism of Mississippian Mounds," in *Powhatan's Mantle: Indians in the Colonial Southeast,* edited by Peter H. Wood, Gregory A. Waselkov, and M. Thomas Hatley (Lincoln: University

of Nebraska Press, 1989), 279–91. The mound is located northeast of Philadelphia, Mississippi. For a succinct summary and analysis of the Choctaw origin stories, see Galloway, *Choctaw Genesis,* 330–37.

377. See Wood, "The Impact of Smallpox," 27.

378. This dangerous part of the trail was known as *Book'pharaoh,* the Long Swamp (*HAI,* 349). Adair seems to indicate on 271–72 that this swamp was along the Sipsey River.

379. Escochabey, or the Young Lieutenant of the Coweta, was the head warrior of Coweta and ultimately exhibited pro-French proclivities during Seven Years' War (Corkran, *Creek Frontier,* 200).

380. For more details on the French-Natchez war, and the Natchez relationship to the Chickasaw, see *HAI,* 354.

381. Adair's contemporary Bossu provided a good discussion of the use the Indians of Louisiana made of buffalo (bison): "the meat is salted or smoked, and blankets are made of hide. The bull is covered with fine wool from which good mattresses are made, the suet is used for candles, and the sinews supply the Indians with strings for their bows. The horns are worked into spoons, with which the natives eat their corn meal mush, or into containers for their powder. The buffalo has a hump on its back like a camel, long hair on its head like a goat, and wool covering its body like a sheep. The Indian women spin this wool into yarn" (Bossu, *Travels,* 196–97). For information on bison, see Robert W. Neuman, "The Buffalo in Southeastern United States Post-Pleistocene Prehistory," in *Southeastern Natives and Their Pasts,* edited by D. G. Wyckoff and J. L. Hofman, 261–80, Oklahoma Archaeological Survey, Studies in Oklahoma's Past, no. 11 (Norman: OAS, 1983), and Erhard Rostland, "The Geographic Range of the Historic Bison in the Southeast," *Annals of the Association of American Geographers* 50 (1960): 395–407.

382. Romans showed two Yazoo towns on his map: East and West Yazoo. For a discussion of these villages, see Halbert, "Bernard Romans' Map of 1772," 422–23, 427.

383. The return of three prisoners to the French, devoid of detail, was reported by John Highrider when he visited the Choctaw nation in early 1750 (McDowell, ed., *Documents Relating to Indian Affairs, 1750–1754,* 40). French intelligence at first reported that four prisoners had been sold to the English (*MPAFD,* 4: 25).

384. Adair was at the Breed Camp by October 1749 (*JCHA,* 9: 305). He stayed in Charleston until April 1750. For his controversial letter, inserted in the "Modest Reply," see the introduction to this edition.

385. Adair's notice to that effect appeared in the *South Carolina Gazette,* March 12–19, 1750.

386. For a discussion of these "settlement Indians," see Merrell, *Indians' New World,* 99–106.

387. The Indian commissioner was George Pawley, who was sent to the Cherokee in 1746 to purchase land. G. H. is George Haig, a surveyor and trader to the Catawba Indian. Haig was a partner of Thomas Brown, an early Catawba trader

who had a store at the Congarees. He died in 1747. See Corkran, *Cherokee Frontier*, 19–21; Meriwether, *Expansion of South Carolina*, 53, 58–59.

388. Most likely Colonel Henry Fox, who had served on missions to the Catawba Indians for South Carolina.

389. George Haig and the son of Thomas Brown were captured in 1748. As Adair reported, Brown's son was eventually freed (Meriwether, *Expansion of South Carolina*, 58–59; Merrell, *Indians' New World*, 137–38).

390. Perhaps Captain John Postell, later in charge of a provincial company at Fort Loudoun. See McDowell, ed., *Documents Relating to Indian Affairs, 1754–1765*, for various manuscripts concerning his career.

391. George Galphin's residence and store were located at Silver Bluff, South Carolina. The Yuchi or Uchee settlement was approximately seventy miles upriver from Savannah.

392. Harry Forster (or Foster), variously identified as the stepson or son-in-law of James Francis of Ninety-Six. The date was actually May 1751 (McDowell, ed., *Documents Relating to Indian Affairs, 1750–1754*, 113–14; Meriwether, *Expansion of South Carolina*, 120; *JCHA*, 9: 444–45). Keowee was the leading Lower Cherokee town, described by historian Corkran as the "gateway to the Carolina trade" (*Cherokee Frontier*, 3).

393. In the Charleston Library Society copy of Adair's *History*, the word "an" is inserted before "many," which is marked out, as is the "es" at the end of expresses, making the word singular. The corrected phrase reads: "an express with intelligence I sent."

394. A reference to Governor Glen's changing attitude toward Adair in regard to the Choctaw Revolt.

395. In the Charleston Library Society copy of Adair's *History*, the word "poor" is marked out.

396. The Tallapoosa River was frequently called the Okwhuske (Okfuskee) River by eighteenth-century traders, after the largest Upper Creek town of Okfuskee, located some miles upstream from the junction of the Tallapoosa and Coosa rivers.

397. Adair's motive for going to the fort remains a subject of speculation. His only extant account of his visit, other than the one provided here, appeared in a letter to William Pinckney, in which he refers to earlier letters sent to both Pinckney and the South Carolina Council "shewing the Force I lay under of going to the French; the Contents were very large and the why as uncommon." See James Adair to William Pinckney, May 7, 1751, in McDowell, ed., *Documents relating to Indian Affairs, 1750–1754*, 56.

398. Here, Adair refers to Governor James Glen and his successor, William Henry Lyttelton.

399. Adair's memorial was presented to the South Carolina Commons House of Assembly on April 28, 1761.

400. Fort Loudoun was built in 1756 by South Carolina at the request of the

Overhill Cherokee. During the Anglo-Cherokee war, 1759–60, the fort was besieged and ultimately surrendered. The retreating South Carolina troops were attacked and many were killed. Some, notably John Stuart, were spared. The fort was later burned and never reoccupied. The area is now a state historic area, near modern Vonore, Tennessee. Adair's computation of miles is largely accurate, although the distance by land from Fort Loudoun to the "Chickasaw landing place" would seem to be in error. See *Colonial Wars of North America,* s.v. "Fort Loudoun (Tennessee)." The "Chickasaw landing place," or Chickasaw Bluffs, near modern Memphis, Tennessee, was approximately 170 miles overland from the Chickasaw towns (*HAI,* 355).

401. The Chickasaw towns on the upper tributaries of the western fork of the Tombigbee River are in Lee County, Mississippi, in the vicinity of modern Tupelo. For a fuller evaluation of the location, see Atkinson, "Historic Chickasaw Cultural Material: A More Comprehensive Identification," and Jay K. Johnson, Patricia K. Galloway, and Walter Belokon, "Historic Chickasaw Settlement Patterns in Lee County, Mississippi: A First Approximation," *Mississippi Archaeology* 24 (1989): 45–52. The Chickasaw Old Fields were located in northeastern Mississippi, near the Tombigbee River in the vicinity of modern Tupelo. See Swanton, "Social and Religious Beliefs and Usages of the Chickasaw Indians," 175–77, regarding migration legends in relation to the Old Fields.

402. For an assessment of Adair's Chickasaw migration legend, see Galloway, *Choctaw Genesis,* 330–31, 336.

403. Adair's list of surviving Chickasaw towns is one of the few from the late colonial period. Romans, who visited the towns and mapped them for John Stuart, listed them as follows: "*Melattaw* (i.e.) hat and feather, *Chatelaw* (i.e.), copper town, *Chukafalaya* (i.e.) long town, *Hikihaw* (i.e.) stand still, *Chucalissa* (i.e.) great town, *Tuckahaw* (i.e.) a certain weed, and *Ashuck hooma* (i.e.) red grass" (*Concise Natural History,* 124). In his report of 1755, Atkin also noted they lived in seven towns, closely allied and fortified for protection (Atkin, *Report,* 67). Earlier, in 1708, Nairne reported eight villages (*Muskhogean Journals,* 36). A list compiled by Frenchman Claude Delisle in 1702 contained eighteen villages, some of which contained only a few "huts." For this list, see Daniel H. Usner, Jr. *Indians, Settlers and Slaves in a Frontier Exchange Economy* (Chapel Hill: University of North Carolina Press, for the Institute of Early American History and Culture, Williamsburg, Virginia, 1992), 21. Swanton provides a discussion and chart depicting five lists of Chickasaw towns (*Social and Religious Beliefs and Usages of the Chickasaw Indian,* 212–13). For an examination of Tchoukafala (Adair's *Chookka Phaŕaah*) during the post-1763 era, see Calloway, *The American Revolution in the Indian Country,* chap. 8.

404. The Natchez war against the French began in late 1729 when they attacked Fort Rosalie and surrounding settlements and killed an estimated 238 settlers and soldiers. Adair's explanation of the cause of the tensions is incomplete. His assessment of the result is not, for, in the end, the French forced the Natchez to abandon their villages. Survivors sought refuge among the Chickasaw and Creek towns. See *Colonial Wars of America,* s.v. "Natchez War (1729–1733)." For more information on the Natchez, see Karl G. Lorenz, "The Natchez of Southwest Mississippi," in

Indians of the Greater Southeast: Historical Archaeology and Ethnohistory, edited by
Bonnie G. McEwan, 142–77 (Gainesville: University Press of Florida, 2000). The
major Natchez village has been examined archaeologically; see Robert S. Neitzel,
*The Grand Village of the Natchez Revisited: Excavations at the Fatherland Site, Adams
County, Mississippi, 1972,* Archaeological Report no. 12 (Jackson: Mississippi De-
partment of Archives and History, 1983).

405. The two great battles of the 1736 French-Chickasaw war, in which the
French were routed, took place on March 25, 1736, at Ogoula Tchetoka (Chuckalisa
or Big Town to the English) and on May 26, 1736, at Ackia (Hikihaw to the English). Another expedition was mounted in 1739–40, and hostilities continued inter-
mittently until the withdrawal of the French from North America following their
defeat in the Seven Years' War. See *Colonial Wars of North America,* s.v. "Ackia, Battle
of (1736) and Ogoula Tchetoka, Battle of (1736)"; James R. Atkinson, "The Ackia
and Ogoula Tchetoka Chickasaw Village Locations in 1736 during the French-
Chickasaw War," *Mississippi Archaeology* 20 (1985): 53–72; Joseph Peyser, "The
Chickasaw Wars of 1736 and 1740: French Military Drawings and Plans Document
the Struggle for the Lower Mississippi," *Journal of Mississippi History* 44 (February
1982): 1–25. See also Michael James Foret, "On the Marchlands of Empire: Trade,
Diplomacy and War on the Southeastern Frontier, 1733–1763," Ph.D. diss., College
of William and Mary, 1990, and "War or Peace? Louisiana, the Choctaws, and the
Chickasaws, 1733–1735," *Louisiana History* 31 (Summer 1990): 272–93. The excla-
mation uttered by the defeated French reported here by Adair as "Oh morblieu!"
seems to be *Mort de Dieu,* death of God.

406. Just when the engagement described by Adair took place is unclear—it was
likely the 1736 invasion. Both French and English sources note the use of grenades
in the French campaigns against the Chickasaw as well as the fact that the Chickasaw understood how to thwart their use. See Juricek, ed., *Georgia Treaties, 1733–1763,*
11: 77, and *MPAFD,* 1: 308, 4: 150. The use of "wool-pack" vests was well remembered by the Chickasaw, who in 1752 reported that an army of three hundred
Frenchmen were advancing toward their towns "and that each of them had a small
Bagg of Wool fixed before their Brest." Only three Frenchmen arrived with a party
of Choctaw warriors on that occasion. See McDowell, ed., *Documents Relating to Indian Affairs, 1750–1754,* 382–83 (quotations), 364–65. The battles against the French
and their Choctaw allies, including the use of grenades and "legging" (purposefully
firing at the legs of the French opponents whose chests were protected by wool
bags), would be remembered fondly by English traders and passed along as oral tradition well into the nineteenth century. See Malcom McGee Interview Notes,
Draper's Notes and Correspondence, 1854–86, Lyman Draper Collection, Wisconsin
Historical Society. There are no reports that grenades were used in 1752, so Adair's
souvenir grenades must have dated from the 1736 campaign.

407. This is likely a reference to the explorations by the Company of Military
Adventurers, a group of veterans led by General Phineas Lyman who attempted to
establish a settlement in West Florida. See Robin F. A. Fabel, *The Economy of British
West Florida, 1763–1783* (Tuscaloosa: University of Alabama Press, 1988), 153 ff.

408. "Bacchus loves mountains," a saying found in various forms (Martial 4.44.3; Vergil, *Georgics,* 2.112).

409. Bartram also reported seeing the "Chicasaw plumb," which he named "Prunus Chicasaw." He wrote that the plant was "certainly a native of America, yet I never saw it wild in the forests, but always in old deserted Indian plantations: I suppose it to have been brought from the S.W. beyond the Mississippi, by the Chicasaws" (*Bartram on the Southeastern Indians,* 39). However, Thomas Campbell, who traveled from Pensacola to the Creek towns in 1765, did spot plum trees as he traveled through the woods; see Robin F. A. Fabel and Robert R. Rea, "Lieutenant Thomas Campbell's Sojourn among the Creeks, November, 1764–May, 1765," *Alabama Historical Quarterly* 36 (Summer 1974): 104, 107.

410. Bartram reported that some Indians used the pods of the honey locust (*Gleditisia triacanthos* L.) to produce "beer" (*Bartram on the Southeastern Indians,* 238). See also Kristian Hvidt, ed. *Von Reck's Voyage: Drawings and Journal of Philip George Friedrich Von Reck* (Savannah: Beehive Press, 1980), 98–99.

411. The "East-India insipid and costly tea" is a reference to the troubles in America caused by the Tea Act and the hated tax on imported East Indian tea. Romans, who published his study of the southeast in 1775 as well, also denounced British tea as "a despicable weed, and of late attempted to be made a dirty conduit, to lead a stream of oppressions into these happy regions" (*Concise Natural History,* 189–90). Adair added this material after his visit to Sir William Johnson at his "Mohawk Castle." For information on the botanical characteristics and species of "casseena" or yaupon holly (*Ilex vomitoria* Ait.) and its range, see Hudson, *Black Drink.*

412. Ginseng (*Panax quinquefolius* L.) continues to be a valuable medicinal root (Vogel, *American Indian Medicine,* 307–10).

413. The Quebec Act established a civil government in the new British colony of Canada following the Seven Years' War. Among its other provisions, the act granted religious toleration to the French Catholic population.

414. A reference to the Treaty of Paris, 1763, by which France transferred title to lands east of the Mississippi to the victorious British. Due to problems with maps used by the diplomatic delegation, there was confusion over the exact boundary. One immediate problem was the isle of New Orleans, which remained in French hands. For a discussion of the boundary issues, see Zenab Esmat Rashed, *The Peace of Paris, 1763* (Liverpool: University Press, 1951). By "monopolies," Adair means the extraordinarily large grants of land to favored individuals. In the views of many Americans, these grants stifled settlement by those Adair terms "industrious inhabitants" and left the colonies of East and West Florida vulnerable because of low population density. The real problem, of course, was that most of the "unsettled" land in the colonies was acknowledged as Indian territory.

415. Both Adair and John Brown were awarded captain's commissions and led a contingent of over forty Chickasaw warriors during the Cherokee war. The Chickasaw acted as scouts and provided intelligence. See, for example, *South Carolina Gazette,* July 2–July 19, 1760; *Pennsylvania Gazette,* May 22, 1760; and *Maryland Gazette,* August 14, 1768.

416. The prices of trade goods, which the Creeks repeatedly claimed were too high, were a major issue in the years following the Seven Years' War. Creeks wanted their trade lowered to the Cherokee standard; the Chickasaw and Choctaw demanded the Creek standard. For a discussion of the issue, see Braund, *Deerskins and Duffels,* 89–90, 112, 127.

417. The Congress of Mobile with the Choctaw and Chickasaw Indians took place in late March 1765. The proceedings can be found in *MPAED,* 216–55.

418. Lieutenant Colonel David Wedderburn, who alone among the West Florida military establishment supported Governor Johnstone (Fabel, *Bombast and Broadsides,* 35).

419. James Adair, A Memorandum of some Material Heads of what was lately Transacted in ye Chickasaw Nation, February 26, 1766, CO 323/24, fo. 73. A copy of the sworn memorandum can also be found in CO5/67, fo. 228.

420. The meeting described here by Adair must have taken place before the Congress of Mobile in 1765. By the Proclamation of October 7, 1763, the British government prohibited surveys and the issuance of land grants beyond the Appalachian divide or on "any lands whatever" that had not been ceded to the Crown or legally purchased from the Indians. Citing the action as "just and reasonable, and essential to our interest and the security of our colonies," the proclamation further prohibited individual purchases of land directly from the Indians, reserving that right to crown officials. Moreover, it ordered any who had "either wilfully or inadvertently" settled on unceded land to remove immediately. The Proclamation also directed the establishment of civil governments for the new British colonies in the Floridas and Canada. The portion of the document relating to Indian lands can be found in Charles J. Kappler, ed., *Indian Affairs: Laws and Treaties,* 7 vols. (1929; reprint, Washington, D.C.: Government Printing Office, 1975–79), 4: 1172–73. Traders continued to violate the proclamation, and by the 1770s there were numerous trader settlements in the Chickasaw towns. The "deputy" who obtained the land mentioned here by Adair was the commissary, John McIntosh. His "plantation," established contrary to the 1763 prohibition, was plotted by Romans in the 1770s. The Stuart-Gage map also indicates the plantations of "McGillivray and Struthers," "Colbert," and "the late John Highrider," as well as two "hog crawls" owned by whites. See "A map of West Florida part of E^t: Florida, Georgia part of So: Carolina" [Stuart-Gage map], William L. Clements Library. I gratefully acknowledge Dr. Louis De Vorsey, Jr., who allowed me to view his copy of this map.

421. This phrase does not appear in the two extant copies of Adair's memorandum of February 26, 1766. It is possible that the extant copies are partial versions of Adair's original statement, or there may have been an additional statement. The West Florida council heard complaints about the traders mentioned specifically by Adair on February 25, 1766. His statement was probably written to support the charges and was dated the next day with the location given as" Chickasaws." So it is unlikely that Adair made an appearance before the council in February. Both copies of Adair's "Memorandum" indicate his statement was attested to on May 17, 1766, thus providing a clue for the date of the conference with the traders. The

record of the West Florida conference has not been located. Adair is correct in his assertion that the government was unable to enforce the trade laws.

422. Captain James Colbert was a highly respected and long-time trader among the Chickasaw. Like Adair, he led Chickasaw to assist South Carolina against the Cherokee in the Anglo-Cherokee war. He was frequently used by John Stuart as an emissary to both the Upper Creeks and Chickasaw (Alden, *John Stuart*, 128, 129, 172, 200). Colbert established a plantation among the Chickasaw and raised a family that ultimately became important in Chickasaw politics (Charles Stuart to John Stuart, December 16, 1770, CO5/72, fo. 179).

423. George Croghan. His career is covered in Wainwright, *George Croghan*.

424. Here Adair refers to the Indian congress at Kaskaskia in 1766, where Croghan was able to negotiate differences between the Shawnee and Illinois Indians (ibid., 235).

425. Georgia sent two agents among the Creeks to ascertain if the Carolina-based traders there had also obtained licenses from Georgia, Patrick McKay in 1735 and John Tanner in 1736. For a quick summary of the controversy, see Corkran, *Creek Frontier*, 91–93; John Pitts Corry, *Indian Affairs in Georgia, 1732–1756* (Philadelphia: G. S. Ferguson, 1936), 55–56. More detailed depositions from the traders involved are reprinted in *JCHA*, 1: 85 ff. Mr. J. G–r is John Gardiner, a Cherokee trader whose goods were seized by Roger Lacey, the Georgia agent among the Cherokee. For Gardiner's story, see *JCHA*, 1: 134–38.

426. Here Adair again appears to refer to Nanih Waiya, although his translation of the name is incorrect. In Choctaw, "nanih" is a hill or mound, and Nanih Waiya is usually translated as leaning mound. Cushman, based on a testimony of Israel Folsom, also recorded that there were fortifications at the site, which he identified as the terminal point of the Choctaw migration point from the west (*History of the Choctaw, Chickasaw and Natchez Indians*, ed. Debo [1999], 299–300). Although Adair identifies the mounds and entrenchments as defensive structures, that is not necessarily the case. This description does match that of the Nanih Waiya site, which, in addition to the large rectangular-shaped platform mound, also contained a smaller burial mound, all encompassed by a ditch and embankment. The best compilation of source material on the mound is found in Swanton, *Source Material for the Social and Ceremonial Life of the Choctaw Indians*, 5–37. For information on fortifications, see Louis H. Larson, "Functional Considerations of Warfare in the Southeast during the Mississippi Period," *American Antiquity* 37 (1972): 383–92.

427. George Augustus, Lord Howe, who was killed at the Battle of Ticonderoga (1758) during the Seven Years' War; James Wolfe, famous for his victory (and death) at Quebec in 1759 during that war; and Peter Warren, famous for his role in the Anglo-Spanish War (1739–40) and the Louisbourg expedition during King George's War. Warren died in 1752. For a general survey of the war, see Anderson, *Crucible of War*.

428. Le Clerc Milfort, a Frenchman who married into the family of Alexander McGillivray, the famous Creek leader, lived among the Creeks and left an account of his experiences. He claimed to have been made a war chief of the Creeks. His

account of war parties, including the manner of marching as described here by Adair, is a worthwhile supplement to Adair's account, although Milfort certainly embellishes his role among the Creeks and did not possess the understanding of the ceremonies and symbols that Adair evidences. See *Memoirs,* 135 ff.

429. Romans reported that if Choctaw warriors heard "a species of *Motacilla* (which I often endeavoured to catch, in vain) . . . chirping near the [war] camp," they would abandon their expedition (*Concise Natural History,* 132).

430. This town has numerous spellings in eighteenth-century documents, including Estanaree and Oustanalle. In a 1751 proposal for the regulation of the Cherokee trade, Oustanalle and Keowee were considered a "district" of two hundred gunmen (McDowell, ed., *Documents Relating to Indian Affairs, 1750–1754,* 86–87).

431. In the Charleston Library Society copy of Adair's *History,* the word "minutes" is marked out and the word "seconds" is substituted.

432. Bartram described the scalps fluttering from the tops of torture posts in Creek towns in the 1770s: "the scalp, with the hair on them, are stretched or strained on a little hoop, usually 5 or 6 inches in width, which are suspended by a string six or seven inches in length; round about the top of the pole where they remain as along as they last. I have seen some that have been there so long as to lose all the hair, and the skin remaining as white as paper or parchment. . . . In some of their towns, I have counted 6 or 8 scalps fluttering on one pole in these yards." The scalps he noted were almost certainly Choctaw (*Bartram on the Southeastern Indians,* 154).

433. A dated but still useful overview of torture methods employed by Indians east of the Mississippi River is Nathaniel Knowles, "The Torture of Captives by the Indians of Eastern North America," *Proceedings of the American Philosophical Society* 82 (March 1940): 151–225. For Choctaw practices, see Swanton, "An Early Account of the Choctaw Indians," 5: 66–67.

434. The word *tattoo* is of Tahitian derivation, and until its introduction into the English language at the end of the eighteenth century early writers struggled to describe the permanent marks produced by the introduction of pigment under the skin. Like Adair, others frequently called the marks hieroglyphics. Bartram saw warriors whose "breast, and muscular parts of the body, [were] very curiously inscribed, or adorned with hieroglyphick scroles, flowers, figures of animals, stars, crescents, and the sun in the centre of the breast. This painting of the flesh, I understand, is performed in their youth, by picking the skin with a needle, until the blood starts, and rubbing in a blueish tinct, which is as permanent as their life" (*Bartram on the Southeastern Indians,* 122). These designs were often more than mere ornament and, as Adair indicates, were frequently marks of distinction or rank, especially among warriors (Hudson, *Southeastern Indians,* 30). However, both men and women practiced body tattooing. For example, see the "Characteristic Choctaw Busts" in Romans, *Concise Natural History,* 136. De Brahm reported that among the Cherokee the marks were made "with Scratchings of a Pin and Gun Powder or Coal dust" (*De Brahm's Report,* 109).

435. Bartram described these stakes among the Creeks, or "slave posts" as he termed them, as being approximately twelve feet in height and "usually decorated

with the scalps of their slain enemies" in the Creek towns he visited (*Bartram on the Southeastern Indians,* 154).

436. Adair's Latin phrase indicates that the sexual organs were also "carried off." Lawson also reported that once a captive was tortured to death, "every one strives to get a Bone or some Relick" (*New Voyage to Carolina,* 207).

437. Here, Adair refers to the settlement of Shawnee Indians on the Savannah River (Savannah Town), where Fort Moore was established. The Shawnee abandoned the area in the aftermath of the Yamasee War, in 1715. See Crane, *The Southern Frontier, 1670–1731,* 187–88; Atkin, *Report,* 66. In the May 1775 *London Magazine* excerpt of *HAI,* Old Scrany is listed as a "Katahba" Indian.

438. Seneca Indians are called *Ho-non-ne-hó-ont* (*Encyclopedia of North American Indians,* s.v. "Seneca"). In his dissertation, Henry Broadus Jones noted that Adair's account of this condemned warrior's stoic smoking was "strikingly like an incident" described in *Oroonoko: or, the Royal Slave,* a novel by Aphra Behn that first appeared in 1698 and was reprinted numerous times in the eighteenth century. Jones noted that Adair's testimony was "easily believable, so far as the traditional Indian stoicism is concerned," but was of the opinion that "one may well suspect that Adair included in his extensive reading this popular novel," implying that the incident was ficticious rather than factual. In Behn's novel, Oroonoka, an African prince enslaved in Surinam, West Indies, smoked tobacco stoically as he was ritually dismembered, losing first his "members," then ears and nose. He continued to smoke even after losing his first arm but dropped the pipe from his mouth when his second arm was removed. A close comparison reveals that smoking is the only similarity in the accounts since, as far as Adair relates, the Seneca warrior was not dismembered. It is equally probable that Ms. Behn was inspired by reading tales of American Indian warriors when she wrote her fictitious description of smoking and torture. See Jones, "The Death Song of the 'Noble Savage': A Study in the Idealization of the American Indian" (Ph.D. diss., University of Chicago, 1924), 58–60. I am indebted to Professor Raymond Fogelson for this reference.

439. See Merrell, *The Indians' New World,* 41 ff., for details on the Catawba troubles with invading tribes.

440. Adair is referring to the action against Spanish Florida during the War of Jenkins' Ear. See John Tate Lanning, ed., *The St. Augustine Expedition of 1740: A Report to the South Carolina General Assembly* (Columbia: South Carolina Department of Archives and History, 1954). Adair must have written this part of his account after King George's War (prior to the Seven Years' War).

441. Perhaps the Raven of Hiwassee. If so, perhaps this is a mangled account of his role in securing calm after an incident in the Cherokee town of Stecoe in 1751. See Corkran, *Cherokee Frontier,* 26.

442. The importance of the ball game among southeastern Indians cannot be overstated. For an introduction to the topic on a regional basis, see Hudson, *Southeastern Indians,* 408–21. For a more detailed discussion of the game among the Oklahoma Creeks, see Mary Haas, "Creek Inter-Town Relations," *American Anthropolo-*

gist 42 (1940): 479–89. Kendall Blanchard, in *The Mississippi Choctaws at Play: The Serious Side of Leisure* (Chicago: University of Chicago Press, 1981), examines the historical background of modern Choctaw sport.

443. Chunkey was popular throughout the Southeast, and "chunkey yards" were prominent features in southeastern Indian towns. For a discussion of the game, see Hudson, *Southeastern Indians,* 421–25. For an examination of the larger issues inherent in the game, see Warren R. De Boer, "Like a Rolling Stone: The Chunkey Game and Political Organization in Eastern North America," *Southeastern Archaeology* 12 (Winter 1993): 83–92. Adair's contemporary, Bernard Romans, also left an exacting description of the game (*Concise Natural History,* 134–35).

444. For the use of stupefying toxins, see Swanton, *Indians of the Southeastern United States,* 332–44.

445. Page 403. See Timberlake, *Memoirs,* 69, for another description of weirs.

446. Both shortnose (*Acipenser brevirostrum*) and Atlantic sturgeon (*Acipenser oxyrinchus*) are found in the Savannah River in modern times.

447. This technique was most likely used on sturgeon and catfish. This manner of catching fish is still practiced by sports fisherman in modern times and is known as noodling or tickling.

448. Literally, "power of the country," used here in the sense of a company of people.

449. For general information on corn varieties and method of cultivation and preparation, see Hudson, *Southeastern Indians,* 292–99, 302–7. See also Muriel Wright, "American Indian Corn Dishes," *Chronicles of Oklahoma* 36 (1958): 155–66.

450. An early French account described Choctaw foods as well as their mortars, "which they make out of the trunk of a tree, hollowed by means of burning embers. The pestle belonging to it is sometimes ten feet long and as small around as the arm. The upper end is an unshaped mass which serves to weigh it down and to give force to this pestle in falling back, in order to crush the corn more easily" (Swanton, "An Early Account," 57–58).

451. Much in little.

452. Bartram wrote that "Hiccory milk . . . is as sweet and rich as fresh cream, and is an ingredient in most of their cookery, especially homony and corn cakes" (*Bartram on the Southeastern Indians,* 39). Romans reported that Chickasaw enjoyed sweet potatoes with hickory nut milk (*Concise Natural History,* 127). See Herbert G. Battle, "The Domestic Use of Oil Among the Southern Aborigines," *American Anthropologist* 24 (1922): 171–82, for information on the production and use of nut oil.

453. Romans mentioned that the Creeks made use of a wild plant "found in the low woods . . . called potatoes" (*Concise Natural History,* 145). The similarity to Adair's description is striking. Swanton identified the plant mentioned by Romans as the wild sweet potato (*Ipomoea pandurata* L.) (*Indians of the Southeastern United States,* 286). This is the wild morning glory, whose tap root can weigh up to thirty pounds. However, *Ipomoea pandurata* prefers light, dry alluvial soils. Elsewhere, I have suggested that the food plant mentioned by both Romans and Adair was the swamp

potato, the root of the arrowhead (*Sagittifolia* L.). See Merritt L. Fernald and Alfred C. Kinsey, *Edible Wild Plants of Eastern North America* (New York: Harper Brothers, 1958), 86–89, 326. It seems a likely candidate for Adair's wild potato as well.

454. It is difficult to determine which of the numerous species of domestic grape (*V. vinifera* L.) is described here. Bartram described low-growing grapes in the trees and shrubs along the Alabama River, worthy of comparison with those mentioned by Adair, and reported the juice of the "very large" grapes was "sweet and rich. The Indians gather great quantities of them, which they prepare for keeping, by first sweating them on hurdles over a gentle fire, and afterwards dry them on their branches in the sun and air, and store them up for provisions: these Grape vines do not climb into high trees, but creep along from one low shrub to another, extending their branches to a great distance horizontally round about . . . almost touching the earth, indeed some of them lie upon the ground." See *The Travels of William Bartram, Naturalist Edition*, edited by Francis Harper (New Haven: Yale University Press, 1958), 254. Harper suggested these were fox grapes (*Vitis labrusca* L.) (521). Another possibility for the grapes described by both Bartram and Adair is the wild muscadine grape (*Vitis rotundifolia* Michx.).

455. Possibly the American Lotus (*Nelumbo lutea*) whose seeds are edible. Adair's assertion that one of the Choctaw towns is named for the plant could not be ascertained.

456. Bartram also reported the virtues of "White Root" or "belly-ache root," which he identified as "perhaps Angelica Lucida" (*Bartram on the Southeastern Indians*, 74, 164, quotation). However, he did not mention the use of the leaves as a green vegetable. This plant has been variously identified as *Angelica atropurpurea* L. (purplesteam angelica) by Vogel (*American Indian Medicine*, 272–73) or *Angelica lucida* L. (seacoast angelica). Francis Harper identified Bartram's *Angelica lucida* as *Ligusticum canadense* [L.] Britt. (Canadian licorice-root) (*Travels of William Bartram*, 438). For information on angelica and Canadian licorice-root, see USDA, NRCS 1999, PLANTS database (http://plants.usda.gov/plants), National Plant Data Center, Baton Rouge, Louisiana.

457. Buffalo tongue was favored not only by the Indians but by white southerners as well. Romans decried the decimation of the bison herds for the tongue only when he believed that the meat and wool would prove viable exports for the southern colonies (*Concise Natural History*, 193).

458. Florence refers to olive oil.

459. Bartram reported that the Creek Indians at one town he visited were fasting for seven or eight days, taking only "a meagre gruel, made of a little corn-flour and water" (*Bartram on the Southeastern Indians*, 106). On other occasions, he was served a cool drink made from corn flour and water mixed with hickory nut oil (77, 238).

460. Adair's description of the building methods and materials of both public and private habitations is among the best available for the eighteenth century. While he asserts that the methods described are universal, there were many important variations in technique among various tribes; Adair's description rests largely on his

observations of Chickasaw habitations. For example, some details mentioned by Adair differ from those employed by the Creeks. For an analysis of Creek architecture, see Gregory A. Waselkov, "Historic Creek Architectural Adaptations to the Deerskin Trade," in Gregory A. Waselkov, John W. Cottier, and Craig T. Sheldon, Jr., *Archaeological Excavations at the Early Historic Creek Indian Town of Fusihatchee (Phase I, 1988–1989),* Report to the Nation Science Foundation, Grant No. BNS-8718934, May 1990, 39–44, and Craig T. Sheldon, Jr., "Upper Creek Architecture at Fusihatchee," ibid., 45–76. For other contemporary descriptions of building techniques among various tribes, see Timberlake, *Memoirs,* 59 (Cherokee town house); *De Brahm's Report,* 100 (Cherokee); Waselkov and Braund, eds., *William Bartram on the Southeastern Indians,* 154–60, 168–86 (Creek and Cherokee); Swanton, *Social Material for the Social and Ceremonial Life of the Choctaw Indians,* 37–40 (Choctaw); Swanton, "An Early Account of the Choctaw Indians," 5: 56–57 (Choctaw). Peter Nabokov and Robert Easton provide an excellent synthesis on southeastern Indian architecture in *Native American Architecture* (New York: Oxford University Press, 1989), 93–120.

461. Here Adair is referring to the winter council house, usually called a "hot house" by the English. Among the better descriptions of hot houses are those of the Creek Indians. David Taitt provided a detailed description of one at Tuckabatchee ("David Taitt's Journal," in *DAR,* 5: 254), also quoted in Braund, *Deerskins and Duffels,* 16–17. Bartram also provided expansive descriptions of winter council houses, which he called a "counsel-house or rotunda" (*Bartram on the Southeastern Indians,* 102–4, 168 ff.). See *De Brahm's Report,* 110, for a description of a Cherokee "hot-house."

462. Adair refers to the family of Scipio Africanus, the Roman general who defeated Hannibal and destroyed Carthage.

463. Most likely Indian hemp (*Apocynum cannabinum* L.).

464. Undoubtedly Joseph Wright, who came to Georgia in the early 1740s and was licensed to trade at Tuckabatchee and other Tallapoosa towns. He was an official interpreter to the Creeks for Georgia on several occasions. See Allen D. Candler, Kenneth Coleman, and Milton Ready, eds., *Colonial Records of the State of Georgia,* 28 vols. (Atlanta: C. P. Byrd, 1904–16; reprint, Athens: University of Georgia Press, 1974–76), 7: 643; Corkran, *Creek Frontier,* 188, 220; McDowell, ed., *Documents Relating to Indian Affairs, 1750–1754,* 129.

465. In a state of nature—stark naked.

466. See Hill, *Weaving New Worlds,* for an intriguing look at native baskets and their relationship to history and culture. A moidore was a Portuguese gold coin often used in eighteenth-century English colonies. It had a value of twenty-seven shillings, and by the later part of the century a moidore was used in reference to that sum (*OED*).

467. The pottery produced by John Bartlam using South Carolina clay would seem to support Adair's assertion about the quality of American clay. For information on this early southern potter, see Stanley South, *The Search for John Bartlam at Cain Hoy: America's First Creamware Potter,* Research Manuscript Series 219, South

Carolina Institute of Archaeology and Anthropology (Columbia: University of South Carolina, 1993).

468. Adair's observations on the power of chiefs is confirmed by other contemporary observers. For example, see *Nairne's Muskhogean Journals,* 32–33, 38, and *Bartram on the Southeastern Indians,* 145–48. An old but still valuable examination of Cherokee government is Gearing, "Priests and Warriors: Social Structures for Cherokee Politics in the Eighteenth Century."

469. Law by nature, king by virtue. Alexander the Great, when asked who he wished to succeed him, is supposed to have replied, "the strongest."

470. Adair is referring to the naval stores act of 1705, which placed a bounty on American products, including tar, pitch, and other naval stores. It was designed to ensure self-sufficiency in these essential products, whose prices, as Adair notes, climbed to exorbitant heights during several wars of the late seventeenth and early eighteenth century, notably the Great Northern War between Sweden and Russia. For details, see Justin Williams, "English Mercantilism and Carolina Naval Stores, 1705–1776," *Journal of Southern History* 1 (May 1935): 169–85, and John J. McCusker and Russell R. Menard, *The Economy of British America, 1607–1789* (Chapel Hill: University of North Carolina Press, 1985), 179–80.

471. Philip Skene, a British army officer, served at Crown Point and Ticonderoga during the Seven Years' War. He left the army in late 1759 and, together with a group of investors, successfully petitioned for a grant of 25,000 acres in the Lake Champlain region (*American Revolution,* s.v. "Skene, Philip (1725–1780)." Col. William Johnson is Sir William Johnson, superintendent of Indian affairs for the Northern Department, who led the Crown Point expedition (*Colonial Wars of North American,* s.v. "Johnson, Sir William (1715–1774)."

472. Indian war parties ventured against St. Augustine on a number of occasions during the 1740s. Adair's lack of details makes it impossible to ascertain when he participated. Oglethorpe's assault against the Spanish in 1740 included a sizeable number of Indians, primarily Creek and Cherokee Indians but also a party of Chickasaw Indians led by the Squirrel King. Perhaps Adair took part in this expedition. See Corkran, *Creek Frontier,* 104, and *JCHA,* 3: 122, for information on the Squirrel King. The South Carolinians were highly critical of Oglethorpe's actions during the expedition. For details on the expedition and controversy, see John Tate Lanning, *The Diplomatic History of Georgia: A Study in the Epoch of Jenkins' Ear* (Chapel Hill: University of North Carolina Press, 1936), 220–29, and Lanning, ed., *The St. Augustine Expedition of 1740.*

473. Adair is referring to East Florida. Contrary to his view, the leading Lower Creeks did not seem willing to part with large tracts there. See Braund, "'The Congress Held in a Pavilion': John Bartram and the Creek Indian Congress at Picolata, 1765." However, he was aware that certain Creeks could be persuaded to discuss ceding or leasing significant areas owing to involvement with Jonathan Bryan, who managed to obtain, without official sanction, a lease to parts of the Apalachee region. Adair signed the second Bryan lease (see introductory essay, this

volume). On Bryan, see Alan Gallay, *The Formation of a Planter Elite: Jonathan Bryan and the Southern Colonial Frontier* (Athens: University of Georgia Press, 1989).

474. A reference to a controversial cattle drive from Georgia to West Florida undertaken by George Galphin in 1764–65. See Braund, *Deerskins and Duffels,* 50–51.

475. The Chickasaw Bluffs, a long line of headlands on the eastern bank of the Mississippi River, at modern Memphis, Tennessee.

476. John Dickinson, whose best-known work was his *Letters from a Farmer in Pennsylvania to the inhabitants of the British colonies* (Boston: Edes and Gill, 1768).

477. Tobias Smollett's observations on the reduction of the French fortress of Louisbourg in 1745, during King George's War, by New England forces. The quotation is taken from *The History of England, from the Revolution in 1688, to the Death of George the Second* (reprint, Philadelphia: Thomas Davis, 1844), 472–73.

478. A reference to George III of the House of Hanover (or Brunswick).

Bibliography

Manuscripts

British Library. London, England.

    Atkin, Edmond. Historical Account of the Revolt of the Chactaw Indians in the late War from the French to the British Alliance and of their return Since to that of the French. Lansdowne Manuscript 809.

    Sir Frederick Haldimand, Unpublished Papers and Correspondence, 1758–1784. Microfilm copies of manuscripts by Microfilm World Publications.

Georgia Historical Society. Savannah, Georgia.

    Jonathan Bryan Papers, No. 98, Item 1.

Great Britain, Public Record Office. Kew, England.

    Colonial Office, Series 5, America and West Indies.

South Carolina Department of Archives and History, Columbia.

    Journal of the Commons House of Assembly, 1757–1767, Part II. Typescript.

    Journals of His Majesty's Council in South Carolina sent to England, Great Britain, Public Records Office, Board of Trade, CO5/456 (microfilm, BMP D518).

South Caroliniana Library. Columbia.

    James Glen Manuscripts.

William L. Clements Library, Ann Arbor, Michigan.

    Papers of General Thomas Gage Relating to His Command in North America, 1762–1776.

    William Henry Lyttelton Papers.

Wisconsin Historical Society.

    Notes from interview with Malcom McGee, 1841, Draper's Notes and Correspondence, 1854–1856. Lyman C. Draper Manuscript Collection.

Maps

Bonar, William. "Draught of the Creek Nation." British Public Record Office, CO700/Carolina 21.

"A Map of West Florida, part of East Florida, Georgia and part of South Carolina" [Stuart-Gage map]. William L. Clements Library, Ann Arbor, Michigan.

Newspapers

American Magazine and Monthly Chronicle for the British Colonies, 1758.
The Edinburgh Magazine and Review for August 1775.
Georgia Gazette, 1769–70.
Gentleman's Magazine, 1763.
London Magazine, 1775.
Maryland Gazette, 1760.
Monthly Review; or Literary Journal, 1776.
Pennsylvania Gazette, 1760–66.
Scots Magazine, 1775.
South Carolina Gazette, 1740–75.

Primary Sources

Acosta, José de. *The Natural and Moral History of the Indies by Father Joseph de Acosta reprinted from the English Translated Edition of Edward Grimston, 1604.* Edited by Clements R. Markham. 2 vols. London: Hakluyt Society, 1880.

Adair, James. *Adair's History of the American Indians.* Edited by Samuel Cole Williams under the auspices of the National Society of Colonial Dames of America, in Tennessee. Johnson City, Tenn.: Watauga Press, 1930; reprint, New York: Argonaut Press, 1966.

———. *Geschichte der amerikanischen Indianer besonders der am Missisippi [sic], an Ost- und Westflorida, Georgien, Sud-und Nord-Karolina und Virginien angrenzenden Nationen : nebst einem Anhange.* Translated from English by Schack Hermann Ewald. Bresslau, Germany: Verlegts Johann Ernest Meyer, 1782.

———. *The History of the American Indians; Particularly those Nations adjoining to the Mississippi, East and West Florida, Georgia, South and North Carolina, and Virginia: Containing an Account of their Origins, Language, Manners, Religious and Civil Customs, Laws, Form of Government, Punishments, Conduct in War and Domestic Life, their Habits, Diet, Agriculture, Manufactures, Diseases and Method of Cure, and other Particulars, sufficient to render it A Complete Indian System.* London: Edward and Charles Dilly, 1775.

———. *The History of the American Indians.* Facsimile reprint edition with an Introduction by Robert K. Berkhofer, Jr. New York: Johnson Reprint Company, 1968.

———. *James Adair and the Indians: A New Version of the Early American Classic,* The History of the American Indians, *published in 1775.* Revised and edited by Clifford Gene Snyder. North Hollywood, Calif.: JES Co., 1995.

"A Conjectural Essay Concerning the First Peopling of America." *South Carolina Gazette,* Monday, October 2–Friday, October 6, 1758.

An Enquiry into the Origin of the Cherokees: A Letter to a Member of Parliament. Oxford: James Fletcher, 1762.

Anselm, Bayly. *The Advantages of a Settlement upon the Ohio in North America.* London, 1763 [1773].

Aristotle's Masterpiece Compleated in Two Parts. London: Printed by B. H., 1698.

Atkin, Edmond. *The Appalachian Indian Frontier: The Edmond Atkin Report and Plan of 1755.* Edited and with an introduction by Wilbur R. Jacobs. Lincoln: University of Nebraska Press, 1967.

Bartram, William. *Travels of William Bartram: Naturalist's Edition.* Edited by Francis Harper. New Haven: Yale University Press, 1958.

———. *William Bartram on the Southeastern Indians.* Edited by Gregory A. Waselkov and Kathryn E. Holland Braund. Lincoln: University of Nebraska Press, 1995.

Bennett, Charles E. *Three Voyages: René Laudonnière.* Gainesville: University Presses of Florida, 1975.

Benzoni, Girolamo. *History of the New World, by Girolamo Benzoni, shewing his travels in America, from A.D. 1541 to 1556, with some particulars of the island of Canary.* Translated and edited by W. H. Smyth. Works issued by the Hakluyt Society, ser. 1, no. 21, 1970. New York: B. Franklin, 1970.

Biencourt, Jean de, Sieur de Poutrincourt. *Noua Francia: or the Description of that part of New France, which is one continent with Virginia.* London, 1609.

Bossu, Jean-Bernard. *Travels in the Interior of North America, 1751–1762.* Translated and edited by Seymour Feiler. Norman: University of Oklahoma Press, 1962.

Boudinot, Elias. *A Star in the West, or A humble Attempt to discover the long lost ten tribes of Israel: preparatory to their return to their beloved city, Jerusalem.* Trenton, N.J.: D. Fenton, S. Hutchinson, and J. Dunham, 1816.

Butterfield, L. H. "The American Interests of the Firm of E. and C. Dilly, with their Letters to Benjamin Rush, 1770–1795." *Papers of the Bibliographical Society of America* 45 (1951): 283–332.

Candler, Allen D., Kenneth Coleman, and Milton Ready, eds. *Colonial Records of the State of Georgia.* 28 vols. Atlanta: C. P. Byrd, 1904–16; Athens: University of Georgia Press, 1974–76.

Carter, Clarence E., ed. *The Correspondence of General Thomas Gage with the Secretaries of State, and with the War office and Treasury, 1763–1775.* 2 vols. Yale Historical Publications, Manuscripts and Edited Texts, vol. 12. New Haven: Yale University Press, 1931–33.

Carver, Jonathan. *Travels through the Interior Parts of North America, in the Years 1766, 1767, and 1768.* London, 1778.

Clayton, Lawrence A., Vernon James Knight, Jr., and Edward C. Moore, eds. *The De Soto Chronicles: The Expedition of Hernando de Soto to North America in 1539–1543.* 2 vols. Tuscaloosa: University of Alabama Press, 1993.

Colden, Cadwallader. *The History of the Five Indian Nations depending on the Province of New-York in America.* Ithaca, N.Y.: Great Seal Books, 1958.

Coxe, Daniel. *A Description of the English Province of Carolana, By the Spaniards call'd Florida, And by the French La Louisiane.* Edited with an Introduction by William S.

Coker. Floridiana Facsimile and Reprint Series. Gainesville: University Presses of Florida, 1976.

Cumberland, Richard. *Sanchoniatho's Phoenician History.* London: R. Wilkin, 1720.

Cuming, Sir Alexander. "Journal of Sir Alexander Cuming (1730)." In *Early Travels in the Tennessee Country, 1540–1800,* edited by Samuel Cole Williams, 115–43. Johnson City, Tenn.: Watauga Press, 1928.

Cushman, H. B. *History of the Choctaw, Chickasaw and Natchez Indians.* Greenville, Tex.: Headlight Printing House, 1899.

———. *History of the Choctaw, Chickasaw and Natchez Indians.* Edited by Angie Debo. Reprint, Norman: University of Oklahoma Press, 1999.

d'Anghiera, Pietro Martire. *The History of Travayle in the West and East Indies . . . .* Translated by Richard Eden and Richard Willes. London, 1577.

De Brahm, William Gerard. *De Brahm's Report of the General Survey in the Southern District of North America.* Edited with an Introduction by Louis De Vorsey, Jr. Columbia: University of South Carolina Press, 1971.

de Laet, Johannes. *L'histoire du Nouveau Monde: ou, description des Indes Occidentales.* Leiden, 1640.

Dickinson, John. *Letters from a Farmer in Pennsylvania to the inhabitants of the British colonies.* Boston: Edes and Gill, 1768.

Documents of the American Revolution, 1770–1783. Edited by Kenneth G. Davies. 20 vols. Dublin: Irish University Press, 1972–79.

Documents Relative to the Colonial History of the State of New York: Procured in Holland, England, and France. Edited by E. B. O'Callaghan. 15 vols. Albany: Weed, Parsons, & Co., 1856–87. Microfilm edition: Published American Colonial Records, vol. 7. New York: Research Publications.

Douglass, William. *A Summary, Historical and Political, of the First Planting, progressive Improvements, and Present State of the British Settlements in North-America; with some Transient Accounts of the Bordering French and Spanish Settlements.* No. 11. Boston: Rogers & Fowls, Queen Street, 1747.

Drake, Edward Cavendish. *A New Universal Collection of Authentic and Entertaining Voyages and Travels, from the earliest accounts to the present time.* London: J. Cooke, 1768.

Fabel, Robin F. A., and Robert R. Rea. "Lieutenant Thomas Campbell's Sojourn among the Creeks, November, 1764–May, 1765." *Alabama Historical Quarterly* 36 (Summer 1974): 97–111.

Fleming, William, and Elizabeth Fleming. *A Narrative of the Sufferings and Surprizing Deliverance of William and Elizabeth Fleming, Who were taken captive by Capt. Jacob. . . .* Reprint, The Garland Library of Narratives of North American Indian Captivities, vol. 8. New York: Garland, 1978.

Franklin, Benjamin. *The Papers of Benjamin Franklin.* Edited by Leonard W. Labaree et al. 36 vols. New Haven: Yale University Press, 1959–2002.

Gordon, Lord Adam. "Journal of an Officer who Travelled in America and the West Indies in 1764 and 1765." In *Travels in the American Colonies,* edited by Newton D. Mereness, 367–456. New York: Macmillan Co., 1916.

Hawkins, Benjamin. *Letters, Journals, and Writings of Benjamin Hawkins.* 2 vols. Edited by C. L. Grant. Savannah: Beehive Press, 1980.

Henry Home, Lord Kames. *Sketches of the History of Man.* 2 vols. Edinburgh: W. Creech, W. Strahan, and T. Cadell, 1774.

Herbert, John. *Journal of Colonel John Herbert, Commissioner of Indian Affairs for the Province of South Carolina, October 17, 1727, to March 19, 1727/8.* Edited by A. S. Salley. Columbia: Historical Commission of South Carolina, 1936.

Hvidt, Kristian, ed. *Von Reck's Voyage: Drawings and Journal of Philip George Friedrich Von Reck.* Savannah: Beehive Press, 1980.

The Journal of the Commons House of Assembly. Edited by J. H. Easterby and R. Nicholas Olsberg. 12 vols. Colonial Records of South Carolina. Columbia: Historical Commission of South Carolina and South Carolina Department of Archives, 1951–81.

Juricek, John T., ed. *Georgia Treaties, 1733–1763.* Vol. 11 of *Early American Indian Documents: Treaties and Laws, 1607–1789,* edited by Alden T. Vaughan. Frederick, Md.: University Publications of America, 1989.

———. *Georgia and Florida Treaties, 1763–1776.* Vol. 12 of *Early American Indian Documents; Treaties and Laws, 1607–1789,* edited by Alden T. Vaughan. Bethesda, Md.: University Publications of America, 2002.

Kappler, Charles J., ed. *Indian Affairs: Laws and Treaties.* 7 vols. 1929; reprint, Washington, D.C.: Government Printing Office, 1975–79.

Lahontan, Lom D'Arce, Louis-Armand de, baron de Lahontan. *New Voyages to North-America.* London, 1703.

Lankford, George E., ed. *Native American Legends, Southeastern Legends: Tales from the Natchez, Caddo, Biloxi, Chickasaw, and Other Nations.* Little Rock, Ark.: August House Publishers, 1987.

Lanning, John Tate, ed. *The St. Augustine Expedition of 1740: A Report to the South Carolina General Assembly.* Columbia: South Carolina Department of Archives and History, 1954.

Lawson, John. *A New Voyage to Carolina; Containing the Exact Description and Natural History of the Country: Together with the Present State thereof; and a Journal of a Thousand Miles, Travel'd thro' several Nations of Indians, Giving a particular Account of their Customs, Manners, Etc.* Edited and with an Introduction by Hugh Talmage Lefler. Chapel Hill: University of North Carolina Press, 1967.

Le Page Du Pratz, Antoine Simon. *The history of Louisiana, or of the western parts of Virginia and Carolina: containing a description of the countries that lye on both sides of the river Missisippi: with an account of the settlements, inhabitants, soil, climate, and products. Translated from the French, (lately published) by M. Le Page du Pratz; with some notes and observations relating to our colonies.* London: T. Becket and P. A. De Hondt, 1763.

Lerius, Johan (Jean de Léry). *History of a Voyage to the Land of Brazil, otherwise called America.* Translated and edited by Janet Whatley. Berkeley: University of California Press, 1990.

L'Estrange, Hamon. *Americans no Jewes, or Improbabilities that the Americans are of that race.* London: Henry Seile, 1652.

Lorant, Stefan, ed. *The New World: the First Pictures of America made by John White and Jacques Le Moyne and engraved by Theodore de Bry, with contemporary narratives of the French settlements in Florida, 1562–1565, and the English colonies in Virginia, 1585–1590.* New York: Duell, Sloan and Pearce, 1965.

McDowell, William L., Jr., ed. *Documents Relating to Indian Affairs, May 21, 1750–August 7, 1754,* The Colonial Records of South Carolina, ser. 2. Columbia: South Carolina Archives Department, 1958.

——. *Documents Relating to Indian Affairs, 1754–1765.* The Colonial Records of South Carolina, ser. 2. Columbia: South Carolina Department of Archives and History and the University of South Carolina Press, 1970.

——. *Journals of the Commissioners of the Indian Trade, September 20, 1710–August 29, 1718.* The Colonial Records of South Carolina, ser. 2. Columbia: South Carolina Archives Department, 1955.

The Mémoire Justificatif of the Chevalier Montault de Monberaut. Translated and edited by Milo B. Howard, Jr., and Robert R. Rea. Southern Historical Publications no. 3. Tuscaloosa: University of Alabama Press, 1965.

Milfort, Le Clerc. *Memoirs or A Quick Glance at my various Travels and my Sojourn in the Creek Nation.* Translated and edited by Ben C. McCary. Kennesaw, Ga.: Continental Book Company, 1959.

Milligan, Jacob. *A Short Description of the Province of South-Carolina, with an Account of the Air, Weather, and Diseases, at Charles-Town, Written in the Year 1763.* London: John Henton, 1770.

Mississippi Provincial Archives, French Dominion. 5 vols. Edited by Patricia K. Galloway. Vols. 4 and 5 originally collected, edited, and translated by Dunbar Rowland and A. G. Sanders. Baton Rouge: Louisiana State University Press, 1984.

Mitchell, John. "An Essay upon the Causes of the Different Colours of People in Different Climates; By John Mitchell, M.D. Communicated to the Royal Society by Mr. Peter Collinson, F.R.S." *Philosophical Transactions of the Royal Society* 43 (1744–45): 102–50.

Nairne, Thomas. *Nairne's Muskhogean Journals: The 1708 Expedition to the Mississippi River.* Edited by Alexander Moore. Jackson: University Press of Mississippi, 1988.

Nevill, Samuel [Sylvanus Americanus]. "The History of North-America, from the first Discovery thereof; Vol. I." *New American Magazine,* 1758–60.

Nuñez, Theron A., Jr. "Creek Nativism and the Creek War of 1813–1814 (George Stiggins Manuscript)." *Ethnohistory* 5 (Winter 1958): 1–47, 131–75, 292–301.

Peterson, Merrill D., ed. *Jefferson: Writings.* The Library of America. New York: Viking Press, 1984.

Pope, John. *A Tour through the Southern and Western Territories of the United States of North-America.* Facsimile reproduction of the 1792 edition with introduction by J. Barton Starr. Bicentennial Floridiana Facsimile Series. Gainesville: University Presses of Florida, 1979.

Prideaux, Humphrey. *The Old and New Testaments Connected in the history of the Jews and Neighbouring Nations from the declensions of the Kingdoms of Israel and Judah to the time of Christ,* 4 vols. London: R. Knaplock and J. Tonson 1718.

Quinn, David B. *New American World: A Documentary History of North America to 1612.* Edited, with a commentary by David B. Quinn, with the assistance of Alison M. Quinn and Susan Hillier. 5 vols. New York: Arno Press, Hector Bye, 1979.

Ribault, Jean. *The whole & true discouerye of Terra Florida.* Facsimile reproduction with introduction by David L. Dowd. Gainesville: University of Florida Press, 1964.

Robinson, W. Stitt, ed. *North and South Carolina Treaties, 1654–1756.* Vol. 13 of *Early American Indian Documents: Treaties and Laws, 1607–1789,* edited by Alden T. Vaughan. Frederick, Md.: University Publications of America, 2001.

Román y Zamora, Jerónimo. *Repúblicas de Indias, idolatrías y govierno en México y Perú antes de la conquista.* Salamanca, Spain, 1575.

Romans, Bernard. *A Concise Natural History of East and West Florida* [1775]. Edited and with an Introduction by Kathryn E. Holland Braund. Tuscaloosa: University of Alabama Press, 1999.

Rowland, Dunbar, ed. *Mississippi Provincial Archives, English Dominion, 1763–1766: Letters and Enclosures to the Secretary of State from Major Robert Farmar and Governor George Johnstone.* Vol. 1. Nashville: Brandon Printing Co., 1911.

Rush, Benjamin. *The Autobiography of Benjamin Rush; His "Travels through Life" together with his Commonplace Book for 1789–1813.* Edited by George W. Corner. Memoirs of the American Philosophical Society, vol. 25. Princeton: Princeton University Press, 1948.

Sauer, Carl O. *Sixteenth Century North America: The Land and the People as Seen by the Europeans.* Berkeley: University of California Press, 1971.

Swan, Caleb. "Position and State of Manners and Arts in the Creek, or Muscogee Nation in 1791." In *Information Respecting the History, Condition, and Prospects of the Indian Tribes of the United States,* 6 vols., edited by Henry Rowe Schoolcraft, vol. 5, 251–83. Philadelphia: J. B. Lippincott Co., 1852–57.

Swanton, John R. "An Early Account of the Choctaw Indians." *Memoirs of the American Anthropological Association* 5, no. 2 (April–June 1918): 53–72.

———. *Myths and Tales of the Southeastern Indians.* Bureau of American Ethnology Bulletin 88. Washington, D.C.: Smithsonian Institution, 1929. Reprint with an Introduction by George E. Lankford, Norman: University of Oklahoma Press, 1995.

Taitt, David. "David Taitt's Journal to and Through the Upper Creek Nation." In *Documents of the American Revolution, 1770–1783,* edited by Kenneth G. Davies. Vol. 5, *Transcripts, 1772,* 251–72. Dublin: Irish University Press, 1974.

Thorowgood, Thomas. *Jewes in America, or Probabilities That the Americans are of that Race. With the Removall of some contrary reasonings, and earnest desires for effectuall endeavours to make them Christian.* London: Tho. Slater, 1650.

Timberlake, Henry. *Lieut. Henry Timberlake's Memoirs.* Edited by Samuel Cole Williams. Johnson City, Tenn.: Watauga Press, 1927.

Tuckey, Francis H. *The County and City of Cork Remembrancer; or, Annals of the County and City of Cork.* Cork: Osborne Savage and Son, 1837.

Ulloa, Antonio de. *A voyage to South America; describing at large the Spanish cities, towns, provinces, &c. on that extensive continent: undertaken, by command of the king of Spain, by Don George Juan, and Don Antonio de Ulloa . . . translated from the original Spanish.* 2 vols. London: L. Davis and C. Reymers, 1758.

———. *Discourse and Political Reflections on the Kingdoms of Peru.* Edited by John J. TePaske. Norman: University of Oklahoma Press, 1978.

Williams, Roger. *Key into the Languages of America or, An help to the language of the natives in that part of America called New-England: together with briefe observations of the customes, manners and worships, &c. of the aforesaid natives, in peace and warre, in life and death: on all which are added spirituall observations, generall and particular, by the authour.* London: Printed by Gregory Dexter, 1643.

Secondary Sources

Adair, James Barnett. *Adair History and Genealogy.* Easley, S.C.: Southern Historical Press, 1924.

Adair, Patrick. *A True Narrative of the Rise and Progress of the Presbyterian Church in Ireland.* With an Introduction and Notes by W. D. Killen. Belfast: C. Aitchison, 1866.

Alden, John R. *John Stuart and the Southern Colonial Frontier: A Study of Indian Relations, War, Trade and Land Problems in the Southern Wilderness, 1754–1775.* University of Michigan Publications in History and Political Science, no. 15. Ann Arbor: University of Michigan Press, 1944; reprint, New York: Gordian, 1966.

Allen, Don Cameron. *The Legend of Noah: Renaissance Rationalism in Art, Science, and Letters.* Illinois Studies in Language and Literature, vol. 33, nos. 3–4. Urbana: University of Illinois, 1949; reprint, 1963.

Alvord, Clarence W. *The Mississippi Valley in British Politics: A Study of the Trade, Land Speculation, and Experiments in Imperialism Culminating in the American Revolution.* 2 vols. Cleveland: A. H. Clark, 1917; reprint, New York: Russell & Russell, 1959.

Alvord, Clarence W., and Lee Bidgood. *The First Explorations of the Trans-Allegheny Region by the Virginians, 1650–1674.* Cleveland: Arthur H. Clark Co., 1912.

The American Revolution, 1775–1783: An Encyclopedia. Edited by Richard L. Blanco. 2 vols. New York City: Garland Publishing, 1993.

Anderson, Fred. *Crucible of War: The Seven Years' War and the Fate of Empire in British North America, 1754–1766.* New York: Alfred A. Knopf, 2000.

Atkinson, James R. "Historic Chickasaw Cultural Material: A More Comprehensive Identification." *Mississippi Archaeology* 22 (1985): 32–62.

———. "The Ackia and Ogoula Tchetoka Chickasaw Village Locations in 1736 during the French-Chickasaw War." *Mississippi Archaeology* 20 (1985): 53–72.

Axtell, James. *Natives and Newcomers: The Cultural Origins of North America.* Oxford: Oxford University Press, 2001.

Battle, Herbert G. "The Domestic Use of Oil Among the Southern Aborigines." *American Anthropologist* 24 (1922): 171–82.

Bell, Amelia R. "Creek Ritual: The Path to Peace." Ph.D. diss., University of Chicago, 1984.

Blake, Leonard W. "Early Acceptance of Watermelon by Indians of the United States." *Journal of Ethnobiology* 1 (1981): 193–99.

Blanchard, Kendall. *The Mississippi Choctaws at Play: The Serious Side of Leisure.* Chicago: University of Chicago Press, 1981.

Blitz, John H. "Choctaw Archaeology in Mississippi." *Journal of Alabama Archaeology* 41 (December 1995): 135–61.

Bourne, Edward Gaylord. "The Travels of Johnathan Carver." *American Historical Review* 11 (January 1906): 287–302.

Brands, W. H. *The First American: The Life and Times of Benjamin Franklin.* New York: Doubleday, 2000.

Braund, Kathryn E. Holland. "Classification of Creek Towns." Paper at Annual Meeting of the Society for American Archaeology, Nashville, April 5, 1997.

———. *Deerskins and Duffels: Creek Indian Trade with Anglo-America, 1685–1815.* Lincoln: University of Nebraska Press, 1993.

———. "'The Congress Held in a Pavilion': John Bartram and the Creek Indian Congress at Picolata, 1765." In *America's Curious Botanist.* Edited by Nancy E. Hoffman and John C. Van Horn, 79–96. Memoirs of the American Philosophical Society, No. 249. Philadelphia: APS, 2004.

Brown, Ian W. "Bells." In *Tunica Treasure,* edited by Jeffrey P. Brain. Papers of the Peabody Museum of Archaeology and Ethnology, Harvard University, 71: 195–205. Cambridge, Mass.: Peabody Museum of Archaeology and Ethnology, 1979.

Brown, Kathleen. "Native Americans and Early Modern Concepts of Race." In *Empire and Others: British Encounters with Indigenous Peoples, 1600–1850,* edited by Martin Daunton and Rick Halpern, 79–100. Philadelphia: University of Pennsylvania Press, 1990.

Byington, Cyrus. *A Dictionary of the Choctaw Language.* Edited by John R. Swanton and Henry S. Halbert. Smithsonian Institution Bureau of American Ethnology Bulletin 46. Washington, D.C.: Government Printing Office, 1915.

Caldwell, Norman W. "The Southern Frontier during King George's War." *Journal of Southern History* 7 (February 1941): 37–54.

Calloway, Colin G. *The American Revolution in the Indian Country: Crisis and Diversity in Native American Communities.* Cambridge: Cambridge University Press, 1995.

Campbell, T. N. "Medicinal Plants used by Choctaw, Chickasaw, and Creek Indians in the Early Nineteenth Century." *Journal of the Washington Academy of Sciences* 41 (September 1951): 285–90.

Carson, James Taylor. *Searching for the Bright Path: The Choctaws from Prehistory to Removal.* Lincoln: University of Nebraska Press, 1999.

Cashin, Edward J. *Beloved Bethesda: A History of George Whitefield's Home for Boys, 1740–2000.* Macon, Ga.: Mercer University Press, 2001.

———. "Governor Henry Ellis and the American Colonial Frontier." *Gulf Coast Historical Review* 7 (Spring 1992): 17–30.

———. *Governor Henry Ellis and the Transformation of British North America*. Athens: University of Georgia Press, 1994.

———. *Lachlan McGillivray, Indian Trader: The Shaping of the Southern Colonial Frontier*. Athens: University of Georgia Press, 1992.

———, ed. *Colonial Augusta: "Key of the Indian Countrey."* Macon: Mercer University Press, 1986.

The Catholic Encyclopedia; An International Work of Reference on the Constitution, Doctrine, Discipline, and History of the Catholic Church. 15 vols. Edited by Charles G. Herbermann, Edward A. Pace, et al. New York: Appleton, 1907–12.

Chaplin, Joyce E. "Natural Philosophy and an Early Racial Idiom in North America: Comparing English and Indian Bodies." *William and Mary Quarterly* 3d ser., 54 (January 1997): 229–52.

Churchill, Mary C. "The Oppositional Paradigm of Purity versus Pollution in Charles Hudson's *The Southeastern Indians.*" *American Indian Quarterly* 20 (Fall 1996): 563–93.

Cole, Richard C. "Montgomerie's Cherokee Campaign, 1760: Two Contemporary Views." *North Carolina Historical Review* 74 (January 1997): 19–36.

Colonial Wars of North America, 1512–1763: An Encyclopedia. Edited by Alan Gallay. New York: Garland, 1996.

Corkran, David H. *The Cherokee Frontier: Conflict and Survival, 1740–1762*. Norman: University of Oklahoma Press, 1962.

———. *The Creek Frontier, 1540–1783*. Norman: University of Oklahoma Press, 1967.

Corry, John Pitts. *Indian Affairs in Georgia, 1732–1756*. Philadelphia: G. S. Ferguson, 1936.

Crane, Verner W. "A Lost Utopia on the First American Frontier." *Sewanee Review* 27 (January 1919): 48–61.

———. "The Origin of the Name of the Creek Indians." *Mississippi Valley Historical Review* 5 (December 1918): 339–42.

———. *The Southern Frontier, 1670–1732*. Durham, N.C.: Duke University Press, 1928; reprint, New York: W. W. Norton, 1981.

Cumming, William P., and Louis De Vorsey, Jr. *The Southeast in Early Maps*. 3d ed. Chapel Hill: University of North Carolina Press, 1986.

Dabbs, Mariam Adair. *The Descendants of James Adair, Author of* The History of the American Indians. Clarksdale, Miss.: Litho-Print, Inc., 1976.

Davis, Richard Beale. *Intellectual Life in the Colonial South, 1585–1763*. 3 vols. Knoxville: University of Tennessee Press, 1978.

De Boer, Warren R. "Like a Rolling Stone: The Chunkey Game and Political Organization in Eastern North America." *Southeastern Archaeology* 12 (Winter 1993): 83–92.

De Vorsey, Louis, Jr. *The Indian Boundary in the Southern Colonies, 1763–1775*. Chapel Hill: University of North Carolina Press, 1966.

Dictionary of Georgia Biography. Edited by Kenneth Coleman and Charles Stephen Gurr. 2 vols. Athens: University of Georgia Press, 1983.

The Discoverers: An Encyclopedia of Explorers and Exploration. Edited by Helen Delpar. New York: McGraw-Hill, 1980.

Elzas, Barnett A. *The Jews of South Carolina from the Earliest Times to the Present.* Philadelphia: J. B. Lippincott Co., 1905; reprint, Spartanburg, S.C.: Reprint Co., 1972.

Encyclopedia of North American Indians: Native American History, Culture, and Life from Paleo-Indians to the Present. Edited by Frederick E. Hoxie. Boston: Houghton Mifflin Co., 1996.

Epstein, Dena J. "The Folk Banjo: A Documentary History." *Ethnomusicology* 19 (Summer 1975): 347–71.

Evans, E. Raymond. "Notable Persons in Cherokee History: Ostenaco." *Journal of Cherokee Studies* 2 (Summer 1976): 41–56.

Fabel, Robin F. A. "An Eighteenth Colony: Dreams for Mississippi on the Eve of the Revolution." *Journal of Southern History* 59 (November 1993): 647–72.

——. *Bombast and Broadsides: The Lives of George Johnstone.* Tuscaloosa: University of Alabama Press, 1987.

——. *Colonial Challenges: Britons, Native Americans, and Caribs, 1759–1775.* Gainesville: University Press of Florida, 2000.

——. *The Economy of British West Florida, 1763–1783.* Tuscaloosa: University of Alabama Press, 1988.

Fairbanks, Charles H. "The Function of Black Drink among the Creeks." In *Black Drink: A Native American Tea,* edited by Charles M. Hudson, 120–49. Athens: University of Georgia Press, 1979.

Feeling, Durbin. *Cherokee-English Dictionary.* Edited by William Pulte, in collaboration with Agnes Cowen and the Dictionary Committee. Talequah: Cherokee Nation of Oklahoma, 1975.

Fernald, Merritt L., and Alfred C. Kinsey. *Edible Wild Plants of Eastern North America.* New York: Harper Brothers, 1958.

Fissell, Mary E. "Hairy Women and Naked Truths: Gender and the Politics of Knowledge in *Aristotle's Masterpiece.*" *William and Mary Quarterly* 3d ser., 60 (January 2003): 43–74.

Fogelson, Raymond D. "An Analysis of Cherokee Sorcery and Witchcraft." In *Four Centuries of Southern Indians,* edited by Charles M. Hudson, 113–31. Athens: University of Georgia Press, 1975.

——. "Cherokee Notions of Power." In *The Anthropology of Power: Ethnographic Studies from Asia, Oceania and the New World,* edited by Raymond D. Fogelson and Richard N. Adams, 185–94. New York: Academic Press, 1977.

——. *The Cherokees: A Critical Bibliography.* Bloomington: Indiana University Press, 1978.

——. "On the 'Petticoat Government' of the Eighteenth-Century Cherokee." In *Personality and the Cultural Construction of Society,* edited by D. K. Jordan and M. J. Swartz, 161–81. Tuscaloosa: University of Alabama Press, 1990.

Fogelson, Raymond D., and Amelia R. Bell. "Cherokee Booger Mask Tradition." In *The Power of Symbols: Masks and Masquerade in the Americas,* edited by N. Ross

Crumrine and Marjorie Halpin, 48–69. Vancouver: University of British Columbia Press, 1983.

Foreman, Carolyn Thomas. *Indians Abroad, 1493–1938.* Norman: University of Oklahoma Press, 1943.

Foret, Michael James. "On the Marchlands of Empire: Trade, Diplomacy and War on the Southeastern Frontier, 1733–1763." Ph.D. diss., College of William and Mary, 1990.

———. "War or Peace? Louisiana, the Choctaws, and the Chickasaws, 1733–1735." *Louisiana History* 31 (Summer 1990): 272–93.

Foster, Steven, and James A. Duke. *A Field Guide to Medicinal Plants of Eastern and Central North America.* 2d ed. Peterson Field Guide Series. Boston: Houghton Mifflin, 2000.

Gallay, Alan. *The Formation of a Planter Elite: Jonathan Bryan and the Southern Colonial Frontier.* Athens: University of Georgia Press, 1989.

———. *The Indian Slave Trade: The Rise of the English Empire in the American South, 1670–1717.* New Haven: Yale University Press, 2002.

Galloway, Patricia K. "The Barthelemy Murders: Bienville's Establishment of the *Lex Talionis* as a Principle of Indian Diplomacy." In *Proceedings of the Eighth Annual Meeting of the French Colonial Historical Society, 1982,* edited by E. P. Fitzgerald, 91–103. Lanham, Md.: University Press of America, 1985.

———. "'The Chief Who Is Your Father': Choctaw and French Views of the Diplomatic Relation." In *Powhatan's Mantle: Indians in the Colonial South,* edited by Peter H. Wood, Gregory A. Waselkov, and M. Thomas Hatley, 254–78. Lincoln: University of Nebraska Press, 1989.

———. "Choctaw Factionalism and Civil War, 1746–1750." In *The Choctaw before Removal,* edited by Carolyn Keller Reeves, 120–56. Jackson: University Press of Mississippi, 1985.

———. *Choctaw Genesis, 1500–1700.* Lincoln: University of Nebraska Press, 1995.

———. "Confederacy as a Solution to Chiefdom Dissolution." In *The Forgotten Centuries: Indians and Europeans in the American South, 1521–1704,* edited by Charles Hudson and Carmen Chaves Tesser, 393–420. Athens: University of Georgia Press, 1994.

———. "Louisiana Post Letters: The Missing Evidence for Indian Diplomacy." *Louisiana History* 22 (1981): 31–44.

———. "'So Many Little Republics': British Negotiations with the Choctaw Confederacy, 1765." *Ethnohistory* 41 (Fall 1994): 513–37.

———. "Where Have All the Menstrual Huts Gone? The Invisibility of Menstrual Seclusion in the Late Prehistoric Southeast." In *Women and Prehistory: North America and Mesoamerica,* edited by Cheryl Claassen and Rosemary A. Joyce, 47–62. Philadelphia: University of Pennsylvania Press, 1997.

———, ed. *La Salle and His Legacy: Frenchmen and Indians in the Lower Mississippi Valley.* Jackson: University Press of Mississippi, 1982.

Gatschet, Albert S. *A Migration Legend of the Creek Indians.* Vol. 1. Brinton's Library of Aboriginal American Literature, Number 4. Reprint, New York: AMS Press, 1969.

Gearing, Fred. *Priests and Warriors: Social Structures for Cherokee Politics in the Eighteenth Century.* American Anthropological Association Memoir 93, vol. 64, no. 5, pt. 2 (October 1962).

Gipson, Lawrence Henry. *Zones of International Friction: North America, South of the Great Lakes Region, 1748–1754.* Vol. 4 of *The British Empire Before the American Revolution.* New York: Alfred A. Knopf, 1939.

Golden, Harry L. *Jewish Roots in the Carolinas: A Pattern of American Philo-Semitism.* Greensboro, N.C.: The Carolina Institute, 1955.

Gould, Christopher, and Richard Parker Morgan. *South Carolina Imprints, 1731–1800: A Descriptive Bibliography.* Santa Barbara, Calif.: ABC-Clio Information Services, 1985.

Grantham, Bill. *Creation Myths and Legends of the Creek Indians.* Gainesville: University Press of Florida, 2002.

Greenlee, Robert F. "Medicine and Curing Practices of the Modern Florida Seminole." *American Anthropologist* 46 (1944): 317–28.

Greer, E. S., Jr. "A Tukabahchee Plate from the Coosa River." *Journal of Alabama Archaeology* 12 (1996): 156–58.

Haas, Mary. "Creek Inter-Town Relations." *American Anthropologist* 42 (1940): 479–89.

Halbert, H. S. "Bernard Romans' Map of 1772." *Mississippi Historical Society Publications* vol. 6, 415–39. Jackson: Mississippi Historical Society, 1902.

Hally, David J., ed. *Ocmulgee Archaeology, 1936–1986.* Athens: University of Georgia Press, 1994.

Hamilton, Milton W. "Sir William Johnson: Interpreter of the Iroquois." *Ethnohistory* 10 (Summer 1963): 270–86.

Hamell, George R. "The Iroquois and the World's Rim: Speculations on Color, Culture, and Contact." *American Indian Quarterly* 16 (Fall 1992): 451–69.

Hamer, Fritz. "Indian Traders and Power: A Comparative Study of George Galphin on the Southern Frontier and Three Northern Traders." Master's thesis, University of South Carolina, 1982.

Hann, John H., and Bonnie G. McEwan. *The Apalachee Indians and Mission San Luis.* Gainesville: University Press of Florida, 1998.

Harllee, William Curry. *Kinfolks.* 4 vols. New Orleans: Searcy & Pfaff, Ltd., 1935.

Harper, Francis. "*Vultur sacra* of William Bartram." *Auk* 53 (1936): 381–92.

Hatley, M. Thomas. *The Dividing Paths: Cherokees and South Carolinians through the Era of the Revolution.* New York: Oxford University Press, 1993.

———. "The Three Lives of Keowee: Loss and Recovery in Eighteenth-Century Cherokee Villages." In *Powhatan's Mantle: Indians in the Colonial Southeast,* edited by Peter H. Wood, Gregory A. Waselkov, and M. Thomas Hatley, 223–48. Lincoln: University of Nebraska Press, 1989.

Hill, Sarah H. *Weaving New Worlds: Southeastern Cherokee Women and Their Basketry.* Chapel Hill: University of North Carolina Press, 1997.

Hoig, Stanley W. *The Cherokees and Their Chiefs: In the Wake of Empire.* Fayetteville: University of Arkansas Press, 1998.

Holcomb, Brent H., ed. *Petitions for Land from the South Carolina Council Journals,* vol. 5, *1757–1765.* Columbia: South Carolina Magazine of Ancestral Research, 1998.

———. *Petitions for Land from the South Carolina Council Journals,* vol. 6, *1766–1770.* Columbia: South Carolina Magazine of Ancestral Research, 1999.

Holland [Braund], Kathryn E. "The Path Between the Wars: Creek Relations with the British Colonies, 1763–1774." Master's thesis, Auburn University, 1980.

Howard, James H. *Oklahoma Seminoles: Medicines, Magic, and Religion.* Willie Lena, collaborator. Norman: University of Oklahoma Press, 1984.

———. *The Southeastern Ceremonial Complex and Its Interpretation.* Memoir no. 6. Columbia: Missouri Archaeological Society, 1968.

Huddleston, Lee Eldridge. *Origins of the American Indians: European Concepts, 1491–1729.* Austin: University of Texas Press, 1967.

Hudson, Charles. *The Catawba Nation.* Athens: University of Georgia Press, 1970.

———. *Conversations with the High Priest of Coosa.* Chapel Hill: University of North Carolina Press, 2003.

———. "James Adair as Anthropologist." *Ethnohistory* 24 (Fall 1977): 311–28.

———. *Knights of Spain, Warriors of the Sun: Hernando de Soto and the South's Ancient Chiefdoms.* Athens: University of Georgia Press, 1997.

———. "Reply to Mary Churchill." *American Indian Quarterly* 24 (Summer 2000): 494–502.

———. *The Southeastern Indians.* Knoxville: University of Tennessee Press, 1976.

———. "Uktena: A Cherokee Anomalous Monster." *Journal of Cherokee Studies* 3 (Spring 1978): 62–75.

———, ed. *Black Drink: A Native American Tea.* Athens: University of Georgia Press, 1979.

Ivers, Larry E. *British Drums on the Southern Frontier: The Military Colonization of Georgia, 1733–1749.* Chapel Hill: University of North Carolina Press, 1974.

Jackson, Jason Baird. *Yuchi Ceremonial Life: Performance, Meaning, and Tradition in a Contemporary American Indian Community.* Studies in the Anthropology of North American Indians Series. Lincoln: University of Nebraska Press, 2003.

Jennings, Francis. "Adair, James." In *American National Biography,* John A. Garraty and Mark C. Carnes, general editors, 60–61. New York: Oxford University Press, 1999.

Johnson, Jay K. "Ethnohistory, Archaeology, and Chickasaw Burial Mode during the Eighteenth Century." *Ethnohistory* 41 (Summer 1994): 431–46.

Johnson, Jay K., Patricia K. Galloway, and Walter Belokon. "Historic Chickasaw Settlement Patterns in Lee County, Mississippi: A First Approximation." *Mississippi Archaeology* 24 (1989): 45–52.

Jones, Henry Broadus. "The Death Song of the 'Noble Savage': A Study in the Idealization of the American Indian." Ph.D. diss., University of Chicago, 1924.

Kelly, James C. "Notable Persons in Cherokee History: Attakullakulla." *Journal of Cherokee Studies* 3 (Winter 1978): 2–34.

Kelsey, Harry. *Sir Francis Drake: The Queen's Pirate.* New Haven: Yale University Press, 1998.

Kidwell, Clara Sue, and Charles Roberts. *The Choctaws: A Critical Biography.* Bloomington: Indiana University Press, 1980.

Kilpatrick, Alan. "A Note on Cherokee Theological Concepts." *American Indian Quarterly* 19 (Summer 1995): 389–406.

———. "Going to the Water: A Structural Analysis of Cherokee Purification Rituals." *American Indian Culture and Research Journal* 15 (1991): 49–58.

———. *The Night Has a Naked Soul: Witchcraft and Sorcery among the Western Cherokee.* Syracuse, N.Y.: Syracuse University Press, 1997.

Kingsborough, Edward King, viscount. *Antiquities of Mexico; comprising facsimiles of Ancient Mexican Paintings and Hieroglyphics . . . with Monuments of New Spain.* 9 vols. London: R. Havell, H. G. Bohn, 1830–48.

Knight, Vernon James, Jr. "The Institutional Organization of Mississippian Religion." *American Antiquity* 51 (1986): 675–87.

———. "Social Organization and the Evolution of Hierarchy in Southeastern Chiefdoms." *Journal of Anthropological Research* 46 (Spring 1990): 1–23.

———. "Symbolism of Mississippian Mounds." In *Powhatan's Mantle: Indians in the Colonial Southeast,* edited by Peter H. Wood, Gregory A. Waselkov, and M. Thomas Hatley, 279–91. Lincoln: University of Nebraska Press, 1989.

———. "Tukabatchee: Archaeological Investigations at an Historic Creek Town, Elmore County, Alabama, 1984." Report of Investigations 45, Office of Archaeological Research, Alabama State Museum of Natural History, University of Alabama, 1985.

Knowles, Nathaniel. "The Torture of Captives by the Indians of Eastern North America." *Proceedings of the American Philosophical Society* 82 (March 1940): 151–225.

Kupperman, Karen Ordahl. *Indians and English: Facing Off in Early America.* Ithaca: Cornell University Press, 2000.

Lanning, John Tate. *The Diplomatic History of Georgia: A Study in the Epoch of Jenkins' Ear.* Chapel Hill: University of North Carolina Press, 1936.

Larson, Lewis H., Jr. "Functional Considerations of Warfare in the Southeast During the Mississippi Period." *American Antiquity* 37 (1972): 383–92.

Lee, John Thomas. "James Adair's *History of the American Indians.*" *The Nation* 99 (August 27, 1914): 250–51.

Lewis, Charlton T., and Charles Short. *A Latin Dictionary. Founded on Andrews' edition of Freund's Latin dictionary. revised, enlarged, and in great part rewritten by. Charlton T. Lewis, Ph.D. and. Charles Short, LL.D.* 1879; reprint, Oxford: Clarendon Press, 1975.

Lewis, David, Jr., and Ann T. Jordan. *Creek Indian Medicine Ways: The Enduring Power of Mvskoke Religion.* Albuquerque: University of New Mexico Press, 2002.

Logan, John H. *A History of the Upper Country of South Carolina, from the Earliest Periods to the Close of the War of Independence.* Vol. 1. Charleston: S. G. Courtenay & Co., 1859.

Lorenz, Karl G. "The Natchez of Southwest Mississippi." In *Indians of the Greater Southeast: Historical Archaeology and Ethnohistory,* edited by Bonnie G. McEwan, 142–77. Gainesville: University Press of Florida, 2000.

Loughridge, Robert M., and David M. Hodge. *English and Muskokee Dictionary, Collected from Various Sources and Revised.* St. Louis: House of J. T. Smith, 1890; reprint, Okmulgee, Okla.: B. Frank Belvin, 1964.

McConnell, Michael N. *A Country Between: The Upper Ohio Valley and Its Peoples, 1724–1774.* Lincoln: University of Nebraska Press, 1992.

McCusker, John J., and Russell R. Menard. *The Economy of British America, 1607–1789.* Chapel Hill: University of North Carolina Press, 1985.

McEwan, Bonnie G., ed. *Indians of the Greater Southeast: Historical Archaeology and Ethnohistory.* Gainesville: University Press of Florida, 2000.

McLoughlin, William G., and Walter H. Conser, Jr. "'The First Man was Red': Cherokee Responses to the Debate over Indian Origins, 1760–1860." *American Quarterly* 41 (June 1989): 243–64.

Maness, Harold S. *Forgotten Outpost: Fort Moore & Savannah Town, 1685–1765.* Beech Island, S.C.: Harold S. Maness Family & Beech Island Historical Society, 1986.

Martin, Jack B., and Margaret McKane Mauldin. *A Dictionary of Creek/Muskogee with Notes on the Florida and Oklahoma Seminole Dialects of Creek.* Lincoln: University of Nebraska Press, 2000.

Medicine in Colonial Massachusetts, 1620–1820. Publications of the Colonial Society of Massachusetts, vol. 57. Boston: Colonial Society of Massachusetts by the University Press of Virginia, 1980.

Mellon, Knox, Jr. "Christian Priber's Cherokee 'Kingdom of Paradise.'" *Georgia Historical Quarterly* 57 (1973): 319–31.

Meriwether, Robert L. *The Expansion of South Carolina, 1729–1765.* Kingsport, Tenn.: Southern Publishers, 1940.

Merrell, James H. *The Indians' New World: Catawbas and Their Neighbors from European Contact through the Era of Removal.* Chapel Hill: University of North Carolina Press, 1989.

Metzger, Bruce M., and Michael D. Coogan. *Oxford Guide to People and Places of the Bible.* Oxford: Oxford University Press, 2001.

Milanich, Jerald T. *Florida's Indians from Ancient Times to the Present.* Gainesville: University Press of Florida, 1998.

———. "Origins and Prehistoric Distributions of Black Drink and Ceremonial Shell Drinking Cup." In *Black Drink: A Native American Tea,* edited by Charles Hudson, 83–119. Athens: University of Georgia Press, 1979.

Miller, Christopher L., and George R. Hamell. "A New Perspective on Indian-White Contact: Cultural Symbols and Colonial Trade." *Journal of American History* 73 (1986): 311–28.

Mooney, James. "Cherokee Theory and Practice of Medicine." *Journal of American Folklore* 3 (1890): 44–50.

———. "Myths of the Cherokee." In *Nineteenth Annual Report of the Bureau of*

American Ethnology, 11–576. Washington, D.C.: Government Printing Office, 1900.

——. "Sacred Formulas of the Cherokees." In *Seventh Annual Report of the Bureau of Ethnology.* Washington, D.C.: Government Printing Office, 1891.

——. *The Swimmer Manuscript: Cherokee Sacred Formulas and Medicinal Prescriptions.* Revised, completed, and edited by Frans M. Olbrechts. Bureau of American Ethnology Bulletin 99. Washington, D.C.: Government Printing Office, 1932.

Morison, Samuel Eliot. *The European Discovery of America: The Northern Voyages, A.D. 500–1600.* New York: Oxford University Press, 1974.

Moses, L. G. *The Indian Man: A Biography of James Mooney.* Lincoln: University of Nebraska Press, 1984.

Mueller, Diane S. "Intrasite Settlement at the Historic Creek Town of Hickory Ground (1EE8), Elmore County, Alabama (1990–1991)." *Journal of Alabama Archaeology* 41 (December 1995): 107–34.

Munro, Pamela, and Catherine Willmond. *Chickasaw: An Analytical Dictionary.* Norman: University of Oklahoma Press, 1994.

Nabokov, Peter, and Robert Easton. *Native American Architecture.* New York: Oxford University Press, 1989.

Namias, June. *White Captives: Gender and Ethnicity on the American Frontier.* Chapel Hill: University of North Carolina Press, 1993.

Nash, Gary B. "The Image of the Indian in the Southern Colonial Mind." *William and Mary Quarterly* 3d ser., 29 (1972): 197–230.

Neitzel, Robert S. *The Grand Village of the Natchez Revisited: Excavations at the Fatherland Site, Adams County, Mississippi, 1972.* Archaeological Report No. 12. Jackson: Mississippi Department of Archives and History, 1983.

Nelson, Paul David. *General James Grant: Scottish Soldier and Royal Governor of East Florida.* Gainesville: University Press of Florida, 1993.

Neuman, Robert W. "The Buffalo in Southeastern United States Post-Pleistocene Prehistory." In *Southeastern Natives and Their Pasts,* edited by D. G. Wyckoff and J. L Hofman, 261–80. Oklahoma Archaeological Survey, Studies in Oklahoma's Past, no. 11. Norman: OAS, 1983.

Oliphant, John. *Peace and War on the Anglo-Cherokee Frontier, 1756–63.* Baton Rouge: Louisiana State University Press, 2001.

Paape, Charles William. "The Choctaw Revolt, a Chapter in the Intercolonial Rivalry in the Old Southwest." Ph.D. diss., University of Illinois, 1946.

Parry, J. H. *The Age of Reconnaissance: Discovery, Exploration and Settlement, 1450–1650.* Berkeley: University of California Press, 1981.

Perdue, Theda. *Cherokee Women: Gender and Culture Change, 1700–1835.* Lincoln: University of Nebraska Press, 1998.

——. "Native Women in the Early Republic: Old World Perceptions, New World Realities." In *Native Americans in the Early Republic,* edited by Frederick E. Hoxie and Ronald Hoffman, 85–122. Charlottesville: University Press of Virginia, 1998.

Peterson, Roger Tory. *A Field Guide to the Birds: Giving Field Marks of All Species Found East of the Rockies.* Boston: Houghton Mifflin Company, 1947.

Peyser, Joseph. "The Chickasaw Wars of 1736 and 1740: French Military Drawings and Plans Document the Struggle for the Lower Mississippi." *Journal of Mississippi History* 44 (February 1982): 1–25.

Phelps, Dawson A. "The Vaudreuil Expedition, 1752." *William and Mary Quarterly* 3d ser., 15 (October 1958): 483–93.

Piker, Joshua Aaron. "'Peculiarly Connected': The Creek Town of Oakfuskee and the Study of Colonial American Communities, 1708–1785." Ph.D. diss., Cornell University, 1998.

Platt, Steven G., and Christopher G. Brantley. "Canebreakes: An Ecological and Historical Perspective." *Castanea* 62 (March 1997): 8–21.

Popkin, Richard H. "The Pre-Adamite Theory in the Renaissance." In *Philosophy and Humanism: Renaissance Essays in Honor of Paul Oskar Kristeller,* edited by Edward P. Mahoney, 50–69. New York: Columbia University Press, 1976.

Powell, John H. "On the Origin of the American Indians." Paper presented at the 131st Annual Meeting of the Anthenæum of Philadelphia, February 4, 1946. Philadelphia: Athenæum, 1946.

Rashed, Zenab Esmat. *The Peace of Paris, 1763.* Liverpool: University Press, 1951.

Raven, James. *London Booksellers and American Customers: Transatlantic Literary Community and the Charleston Library Society, 1748–1811.* Columbia: University of South Carolina Press, 2002.

Rea, Robert R. *Major Robert Farmar of Mobile.* Tuscaloosa: University of Alabama Press, 1990.

Reid, John Phillip. *A Better Kind of Hatchet: Law, Trade, and Diplomacy in the Cherokee Nation during the Early Years of European Contact.* University Park: Pennsylvania State University Press, 1976.

———. *A Law of Blood: The Primitive Law of the Cherokee Nation.* New York: New York University Press, 1970.

Riggs, Brett H. "Archaeological Evidence of Fire Ceremonialism in the Late Prehistoric Southeast." *McClung Museum Research Notes Number 11* (September 1992). See http://mcclungmuseum.utk.edu/research/renotes/rn-11txt.htm.

Robinson, W. Stitt. *James Glen: From Scottish Provost to Royal Governor of South Carolina.* Contributions in American History, no. 165. Westport, Conn.: Greenwood Press, 1996.

Rostland, Erhard. "The Geographic Range of the Historic Bison in the Southeast." *Annals of the Association of American Geographers* 50 (1960): 395–407.

Rountree, Helen C. *Pocahontas's People: The Powhatan Indians of Virginia through Four Centuries.* Norman: University of Oklahoma Press, 1990.

Rubies, Joan-Pau. "Hugo Grotius's Dissertation on the Origin of the American Peoples and the Use of Comparative Methods." *Journal of the History of Ideas* 52 (April–June 1991): 221–44.

Russell Thornton, *The Cherokees: A Population History.* Lincoln: University of Nebraska Press, 1990.

Sabo, George, III. "The Quapaw Indians of Arkansas, 1673–1803." In *Indians of the Greater Southeast: Historical Archaeology and Ethnohistory,* edited by Bonnie McEwan, 178–203. Gainesville: University Press of Florida, 2000.

St. Jean, Wendy. "Chickasaws: Firm Friends of the English?" *Journal of Mississippi History* 58 (Winter 1995): 345–58.

Schohn, J. Michelle. "A Lodge of Their Own: A Look at Vessel Function at a Possible Cofitachequi Women's Lodge." Master's thesis, University of South Carolina, 2001.

Sheidley, Nathaniel J. "Unruly Men: Indians, Settlers, and the Ethos of Frontier Patriarchy in the Upper Tennessee Watershed, 1763–1815." Ph.D. diss., Princeton University, 1999.

Sheldon, Craig T., Jr. "Upper Creek Architecture at Fusihatchee." In Gregory A. Waselkov, John W. Cottier, and Craig T. Sheldon, Jr., *Archaeological Excavations at the Early Historic Creek Indian Town of Fusihatchee (Phase I, 1988–1989).* Report to the National Science Foundation, Grant No. BNS-8718934. May 1990.

Shoemaker, Nancy. "How Indians Got to Be Red." *American Historical Review* 102 (June 1997): 625–44.

Sirmans, M. Eugene. *Colonial South Carolina: A Political History, 1663–1763.* Chapel Hill: University of North Carolina Press, 1966.

Sisman, Adam. *Boswell's Presumptuous Task: The Making of the Life of Dr. Johnson.* New York: Farrar, Straus, and Giroux, 2001.

Smith, Betty Anderson. "Distribution of Eighteenth-Century Cherokee Settlements." In *The Cherokee Nation: A Troubled History,* edited by Duane King, 46–60. Knoxville: University of Tennessee Press, 1979.

Smith, Jeffery A. "Impartiality and Revolutionary Ideology: Editorial Policies of the *South-Carolina Gazette,* 1732–1775." *Journal of Southern History* 49 (November 1983): 511–26.

Smith, Marvin T. *Coosa: The Rise and Fall of a Southeastern Mississippian Chiefdom.* Ripley P. Bullen Series of the Florida Museum of Natural History. Gainesville: University Press of Florida, 2000.

———. "Early Historic Period Vestiges of the Southern Cult." In *The Southeastern Ceremonial Complex: Artifacts and Analysis, The Cottonlandia Conference,* edited by Patricia Galloway with a foreword by James B. Griffin, 142–46. Lincoln: University of Nebraska Press, 1989.

Smollett, Tobias. *The History of England, from the Revolution in 1688, to the Death of George the Second.* Reprint, Philadelphia: Thomas Davis, 1844.

Snapp, J. Russell. *John Stuart and the Struggle for Empire on the Southern Frontier.* Baton Rouge: Louisiana State University Press, 1996.

Sosin, Jack M. *Whitehall and the Wilderness: The Middle West in British Colonial Policy, 1760–1775.* Lincoln: University of Nebraska Press, 1961.

South, Stanley. *The Search for John Bartlam at Cain Hoy: America's First Creamware Potter.* Research Manuscript ser. 219, South Carolina Institute of Archaeology and Anthropology. Columbia: University of South Carolina, 1993.

Spalding, Phinizy. *Oglethorpe in America: The Story of Georgia's Founding Father.* Athens: University of Georgia Press, 1984.

Speck, Frank G. *Gourds of the Southeastern Indians: A Prolegomenon on the Lagenaria Gourd in the Culture of the Southeastern Indians.* Boston: New England Gourd Society, 1941.

Stocking, George W., Jr. "Scotland as a Model of Mankind: Lord Kames' Philosophical View of Civilization." In *Toward a Science of Man: Essays in the History of Anthropology,* edited by Timothy H. H. Thoresen, 67–89. The Hague: Mouton, 1975.

Swanton, John R. *Early History of the Creek Indians and Their Neighbors.* Bureau of American Ethnology Bulletin 73. Washington, D.C.: Government Printing Office, 1946; reprint, New York: Greenwood Press, 1969.

———. "The Green Corn Dance." *Chronicles of Oklahoma* 10 (June 1932): 170–95.

———. *Indians of the Southeastern United States.* Bureau of American Ethnology Bulletin 137. Washington, D.C.: Government Printing Office, 1946; reprint, New York: Greenwood Press, 1969.

———. "Religious Beliefs and Medical Practices of the Creek Indians." In *Forty-Second Annual Report of the Bureau of American Ethnology.* Washington, D.C.: Government Printing Office, 1928.

———. "Social and Religious Beliefs and Usages of the Chickasaw Indians." In *Forty-Fourth Annual Report of the Bureau of American Ethnology.* Washington, D.C.: Government Printing Office, 1928.

———. *Social Organization and Social Usages of the Indians of the Creek Confederacy.* Bureau of American Ethnology Bulletin no. 42. Washington, D.C.: Government Printing Office, 1928; reprint, New York: Johnson Reprint Corp., 1970.

———. *Source Material for the Social and Ceremonial Life of the Choctaw Indians.* Bureau of American Ethnology Bulletin no. 103. Washington, D.C.: Government Printing Office, 1931; reprint, with Foreword by Kenneth H. Carleton, Tuscaloosa: University of Alabama Press, 2001.

Thomas, Daniel H. *Fort Toulouse: The French Outpost at the Alabamas on the Coosa.* Introduction by Gregory A. Waselkov. Tuscaloosa: University of Alabama Press, 1989.

Thornton, Russell. *The Cherokees: A Population History.* Lincoln: University of Nebraska Press, 1990.

Usner, Daniel H., Jr. *American Indians in the Lower Mississippi Valley: Social and Economic Histories.* Lincoln: University of Nebraska Press, 1998.

———. *Indians, Settlers and Slaves in a Frontier Exchange Economy.* Chapel Hill: University of North Carolina Press, for the Institute of Early American History and Culture, Williamsburg, Virginia, 1992.

Vaughan, Alden T. "From White Man to Redskin: Changing Anglo-American Perceptions of the American Indian." *American Historical Review* 87 (October 1982): 917–53.

Vogel, Virgil J. *American Indian Medicine.* Norman: University of Oklahoma Press, 1970.

Wainwright, Nicholas B. *George Croghan: Wilderness Diplomat.* Chapel Hill: Institute of Early American History and Culture and University of North Carolina Press, 1959.

Walker, Amelia Bell. "The Kasihta Myth." *Anthropology Tomorrow* 12 (1979): 46–63.

Waselkov, Gregory A. "The Eighteenth-Century Anglo-Indian Trade in Southeastern North America." In *New Faces of the Fur Trade: Selected Papers of the Seventh North American Fur Trade Conference, Halifax, Nova Scotia, 1995,* edited by Jo-Anne Fiske, Susan Sleeper-Smith, and William Wicken, 193–222. East Lansing: Michigan State University Press, 1998.

——. "Historic Creek Architectural Adaptations to the Deerskin Trade." In Gregory A. Waselkov, John W. Cottier, and Craig T. Sheldon, Jr., *Archaeological Excavations at the Early Historic Creek Indian Town of Fusihatchee (Phase I, 1988–1989).* Report to the Nation Science Foundation, Grant No. BNS-8718934. May 1990.

——. "Seventeenth-Century Trade in the Colonial South." *Southeastern Archaeology* 8 (Winter 1989): 117–33.

Waselkov, Gregory A., and Bonnie L. Gums. *Plantation Archaeology at Rivière aux Chiens, ca. 1725–1848.* Mobile: University of South Alabama Center for Archaeological Studies, 2000.

Washburn, Wilcomb E. "Adair, James." In *History of Indian-White Relations,* edited by Wilbur E. Washburn, 617–18. Vol. 4 of *Handbook of North American Indians.* Washington, D.C.: Smithsonian Institution, 1988.

——. "James Adair's 'Noble Savages.'" In *The Colonial Legacy,* edited by L. H. Leder, vol. 3, 91–120. New York: Harper and Row, 1973.

Werblowsky, R. J. Zwi, and Geoffrey Wigoden, eds. *Oxford Dictionary of the Jewish Religion.* Oxford: Oxford University Press, 1997.

White, Richard. "Red Shoes: Warrior and Diplomat." In *Struggle and Survival in Colonial America,* edited by David G. Sweet and Gary B. Nash, 49–68. Berkeley: University of California Press, 1981.

Wilkins, Joe. "Outpost of Empire: The Founding of Fort Tombecbe and de Bienville's Chickasaw Expedition of 1736." In *Proceedings of the Twelfth Meeting of the French Colonial Historical Society, Ste. Geneviève, May 1986,* edited by Philip P. Boucher and Serge Courville, 133–53. Lanham, Md.: University Press of America, 1988.

Williams, Justin. "English Mercantilism and Carolina Naval Stores, 1705–1776." *Journal of Southern History* 1 (May 1935): 169–85.

Willis, William S., Jr., "Patrilineal Institutions in Southeastern North America." *Ethnohistory* 10 (Winter 1963): 250–69.

Winn, William W. *The Old Beloved Path: Daily Life Among the Indians of the Chattahoochee River Valley.* Eufaula, Ala.: Historic Chattahoochee Commission, 1992.

Wood, Peter H. "The Impact of Smallpox on the Native Population of the 18th Century South." In *Early American Medicine: A Symposium,* edited by Robert I. Goler and Pascal James Imperato, 22–28. New York: Fraunces Tavern Museum, 1987.

Wright, Muriel. "American Indian Corn Dishes." *Chronicles of Oklahoma* 36 (1958): 155–66.

Index

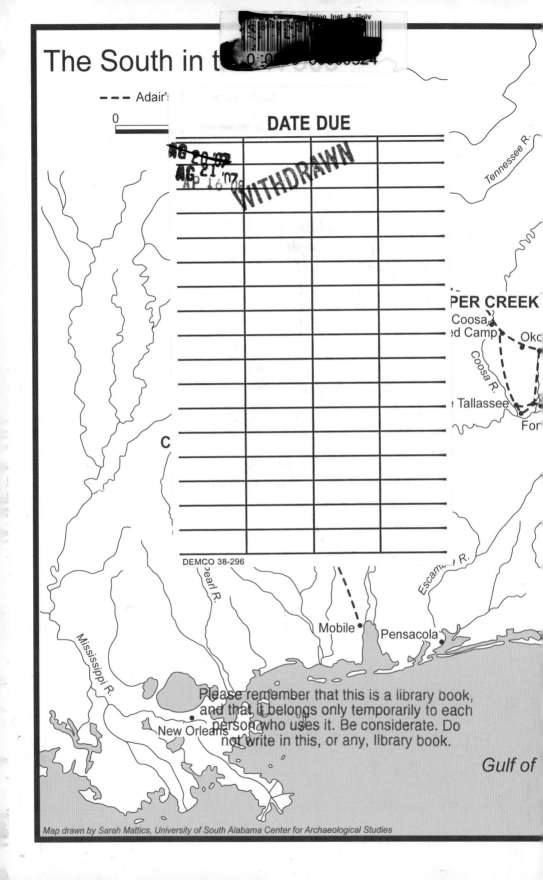

The South in t̶ ...

--- Adair'...

0

DATE DUE

AG 20 '0?			
AG 21 '07			
AP 16 '08			

WITHDRAWN

DEMCO 38-296

Tennessee R.

PER CREEK

Coosa
ed Camp   Okc

Coosa R.

Tallassee

For

C

Escam... R.

Pearl R.

Mobile • Pensacola

Mississippi R.

Please remember that this is a library book,
and that it belongs only temporarily to each
person who uses it. Be considerate. Do
not write in this, or any, library book.

New Orleans

Gulf of

Map drawn by Sarah Mattics, University of South Alabama Center for Archaeological Studies